P.J.D. Wiles

Economic Institutions Compared

BASIL BLACKWELL
OXFORD

British Library Cataloguing in Publication Data

Wiles, Peter John de la Fosse
Economic institutions compared.
Index.
ISBN 0-631-16990-3
1. Title
330.12 HB 171
Economics

PRINTED IN GREAT BRITAIN
BY WESTERN PRINTING SERVICES LTD,
BRISTOL
BOUND BY THE KEMP HALL BINDERY, OXFORD

Contents

Instead of an Acknowledgement

The pavement artists in Trafalgar Square write beneath their chalk pictures 'All My Own Work'. How arrogant! – I reject sole responsibility even for the mistakes. There are many detailed acknowledgements in footnotes, but for the rest I do not know whose work this is, except it be my wife's, who worked with me at all stages of preparation. It is also my publisher's, who made me cut it considerably – a health-giving process that took a year (he was forced to accept back a text with equally long additions, but far better). For the rest let me simply quote St. Bernard of Chartres: 'We are like dwarfs seated on the shoulders of giants. We see more things than the Ancients and things more distant, but it is due neither to the sharpness of our sight not to the greatness of our stature; it is simply because they have lent us their own.'

Instead of an Acknowledgement

[illegible]

Abbreviations

and Special Terms Used in this Book

ACE	Advanced Capitalist Economy
ACES	Association for Comparative Economic Studies
Adscriptio glebae	The binding to the soil (in a residential sense) of the feudal serf
AER	American Economic Review
Atlantis	Formalized version of an ACE, q.v.
Aufsichtsrat	The supervisory board of a German limited company
AVA	Average value added
Banco Ejidal	State bank designed to finance ejidos, q.v.
Commune	A group of families or individuals having production and consumption in common
Community	A village with traditional, mildly collectivist arrangements
Control	The strong English word that does not correspond to French controle, German Kontroll, Russian kontrol'. These all mean 'audit'.
CRE	Co-efficient of relative effectiveness, the Communist shadow rate of interest, used by planners to distinguish between basically similar projects with different fixed and variable costs. It is a number of years' purchase, and basically $= \frac{I_1 - I_2}{C_2 - C_1}$, where I is initial cost and C current cost including amortization
DDR	German Democratic Republic
E.b.f.	Equity bearing factor, e.g. capital receiving a variable dividend, labour receiving a bonus
EDCC	Economic Development and Cultural Change
EEC	European Economic Community
Ejidatario	A member of an ejido, q.v.
Ejido	A Mexican 'community' q.v.
Ejido colectivo	A Mexican kolkhoz, q.v.
FPR	Factor productivity residual
FRG	Federal Republic of Germany
Gosplan	The Soviet (or Soviet-type) State Planning Commission

Gossnab	Generic term for the Soviet (or Soviet-type) inter-enterprise supply organizations
Helvetia	Formalized version of an economy dominated by petty competitive capitalism
IBRD	International Bank for Reconstruction and Development
Idiorrhythmy	A community of quasi-independent workers who share and maintain a common infrastructure
Illyria	Formalized version of an economy with producers' co-operatives
IMF	International Monetary Fund
KGB	(Soviet) Committee of State Security
Khozraschet	Russian abbreviation for economic accountability; normally associated with passive money, q.v.
Kibbutz	Israeli agricultural, or agro-industrial, commune, q.v.
Kolkhoz (pl. Kolkhozy)	Russian abbreviation for collective farm, i.e. an agricultural producers' co-operative
Kolkhoz market	Free market for sale of surplus products of kolkhoz, their members and indeed all citizens
Komuna	Lowest organ of Yugoslav local government
Kontraktatsia	The legally compulsory conclusion of a detailed contract between two subordinate Soviet-type authorities, in accordance with a general plan that obliges them both
Mir	The council of the obshchina, q.v.
Mitbestimmung	(Workers) co-determination in the FRG
Monobank	A single nation-wide bank performing, through its headquarters and its branches, the functions of a central bank and of deposit banks simultaneously
Moshav ovdim	Israeli non-traditional village community, loosely resembling a traditional community, q.v.
MTS	Machine-tractor station: a now obsolete Soviet-type state organ providing tractor services to kolkhozy, q.v.
MVA	Marginal value added
MVD	Soviet Ministry of Internal Affairs
NEM	New Economic Mechanism (in Hungary, since Jan. 1968)
NEP	(Soviet) New Economic Policy, 1921–9
Obshchina	Pre-Revolutionary Russian community, q.v.
OECD	Organization for Economic Co-operation and Development
Optimality	An allocation of scarce resources such that marginal cost equals price, in the absence of externalities. Here only applied to the short run and a given technique
Pannonia	Formalized version of a state socialist market economy

Pantouflage	French for the practice whereby civil servants join the private enterprises they used to administer
Passive money	Soviet-type inter-enterprise money, which must be paid but does not affect decision-making since it is an epiphenomenon on the physical plan
Possession	The relation of a lawful tenant to the property he occupies
QJE	Quarterly Journal of Economics
Rationality	An arrangement of the means that achieves the ends, whatever they may be. It is therefore a broader concept than optimality, q.v.
Sovkhoz (pl. Sovkhozy)	A Soviet state farm
Sovkhozizatsia	The conversion of kolkhozy into sovkhozy
STE	Soviet-type economy
TCOI	Tolerated-cost-overrun inflation
Trudoden' (pl. Trudodni)	Labour-day, the old accounting unit in the kolkhoz for the payment of labour
UDC	Underdeveloped country
X-efficiency	The quick application of the appropriate technique; in contrast with optimality, q.v.

References to sources: op. cit., loc. cit., etc., refer back only to a source given in a footnote in the same chapter. Every topic receives a select bibliography in some appropriate footnote.

Exceptions: Wiles 1961 – *Price, Cost and Output*, 2nd edn., Blackwell 1961;
Wiles 1962 – *The Political Economy of Communism*, Blackwell 1962;
Wiles 1969 – *Communist International Economics*, Blackwell and Praeger 1969.

I

Introduction

I

1. This chapter is mostly about how difficult the book has been to write. Perhaps then it deserves some more modest title, like 'preface'. It contains no solid information, but it is after all of methodological importance, in a branch of economics where methodology is quite unsettled, and at a time when the *Methodenstreit* has flared up again.[1]

First, should such books be written at all? Is there really such a subject as 'economic institutions'? In my own opinion only barely. My approach may be interesting and even promise fertility in the future. But while I hope the book is itself a contribution to learning I am not confident that this promise will be fulfilled. The contribution of economic analysis is greater than once was thought: modern books are very different from those of the 1920s that discredited the subject. But analysis only gets us so far: when we get down to fundamentals human beings in all their variety raise their heads and we have to proceed further by other means. At best we can say that 'institutions compared' will be as fertile as most other branches of economics!

What are the chapter headings when we compare economic systems? What role has orthodox economic analysis? How far may, nay must, we step into other social sciences and history? What subjects should we cover? For all the steady trickle of textbooks with similar titles, these questions remain quite unsettled; especially if, as here, the book has pretensions to suit also the graduate student and the intelligent layman who once read economics.

First as to orthodox analysis, I have long lost any passionate interest in it. But from time to time particular issues seemed tractable by it, and doubtless a good deal more underlies the reasoning. Though extremely suspicious, not of the truth, but of the value of abstract economics, I still have enough respect for it to hope that this background knowledge has kept me out of some errors. It is a good thing to have learned and forgotten, like anatomy for students of drawing. I am also grateful to the many colleagues whose knowledge of this or that branch of theory is less obsolete than mine, and who have had the patience to explain it.

The incidence of serious economic analysis is thus very patchy. It is brought in only where it has a quick, valid and interesting contribution to make, as, notably, in the passages on self-management. Of these three restricting adjectives, 'quick' will doubtless seem the most shocking. But the longer the chain of reasoning the greater the certainty of a weak link: probably a special premise smuggled in to enable things to go forward at all. Those who respect such methods more will resent the *ad hoc* way in which, for instance, algebra is 'plugged in' for brief periods and then discarded again. But I have no general algebraical theory to present, and am above all unwilling to wander off into the particular abstract questions such methods can answer, while much bigger questions wait. I have selected what seemed important, not what seemed soluble; but within those limits have tried to solve rigorously when opportunity arose.

This is, to repeat, no general theory of economic institutions, not even a literary one. It is an attempt to get the subject together and bring it forward a little. Nor is that a modest claim, since it deals with all human economic history and much else besides. It is not a strictly economic claim either, for economic institutions are like economic development: far too important to be left to economists. There is much politics and sociology here, and in the agricultural passages even a little technology. The principle of inclusion has been shamelessly simple: how can this economic institution best be understood? If this principle be sincerely accepted, it follows at once that long passages of political history are a *necessary* part of any work with this title. The comparison of economic institutions is political economy – by definition. Comparisons that leave out non-economic types of information and reasoning are a fraud.

2. And yet for all the array of models and motives the range of this book is exceedingly narrow. For first, it only covers economic, not whole social, systems; yet many different societies can grow out of one economic substratum, or at least out of capitalism. We occasionally draw attention to this fact, e.g. in chapters 8, 11, 18, 19. A further sharp limitation is that we only cover the economies of literate and technically quite advanced societies, in which some deliberate thought has been given to the system. That is to say, I have selected 'modern' systems, which have achieved, or can probably achieve, high levels of production and technology, or at least of culture. This is not to say that the societies of our principal concern are rich, for intellectual interest also counts high: China rates many more mentions than Sweden. But China, as her war industry shows, can use the most modern techniques.

In other words I have neglected anthropological economics. To each tribe or group of tribes its separate system; this means, then, the omission of many hundreds of interesting systems, each viable *at least* at a low level of subsistence, each as different from the other as it is from, say, Yugoslavia, or as Yugoslavia is from USA. The main reason for this neglect is the tolerable limits to book sizes and prices; the second of course is my ignorance. But thirdly these systems are not, alas, likely to last very much further into history. It is almost irrelevant for a quasi-scientific analysis how old an institution is, or how many people practise it; but not how long it will survive.

On much the same grounds I have neglected underdeveloped countries, unless Communist. For despite the interest of their many experiments, we can again not be sure how long they will last. Indeed there are, as I see it, mercifully only a certain number of 'classical countries', whose economic institutions are stable and different and worth comparing: China, USSR, Yugoslavia, Hungary, Israel, Mexico, Cuba, France. We need of course some normal ACE as well, and I have suited my own convenience with UK or USA. The future is more likely to add Communist than non-Communist countries to this brief list. But in a general way Communism is far more inclined to experiments.[2] This then, and not my background as a Sovietologist, accounts for the preponderance of Communism in these pages.

There is another deficiency, by subject rather than by system. Certain central economic questions have been omitted, also for lack of space: notably location, foreign trade and development policy. Much could have been said about the relation of these to institutions, but the book is already too large.

As to the chapter headings, a work of social science is almost compelled to arrange things by problems or sectors, not by periods or countries. But however the subject is arranged, someone will say it is wrong. The important thing, then, is a mass of cross-references and a good index. But the passages of historical explanation are in the main continuous, and occur at the first serious reference to any country or institution, even at the cost of immediate imbalance and irrelevance. These admirable qualities must only be sought in the book as a whole. Thus at some point or other I have set down 'what every gentleman ought to know' about the Yugoslav ideology and the industrial system to which it gave rise. There is a historical introduction in chapter 3, which also deals with property, and the relevant sections of other chapters, all clearly headed 'Yugoslavia' or 'Illyria', assume this knowledge.

3. Next a few words about prejudice and passion. A flat-footed approach to this exciting subject is a supreme virtue. By contrast, extremists to the right and the left who discuss, for instance, resource allocation, juxtapose the perfect (and non-existent) form of what they like with the imperfect (and maybe the only attainable) form of what they do not like. But in fact just as competition can be perfect or imperfect, so can computation. Again we praise the relative equality of wages in Lenin's writings, without enquiring what the equality is in the actual USSR before our eyes. We praise the ending of alienation by self-management, without asking why Yugoslavs strike, now that it has been reluctantly permitted. We justly point out political freedom only flourishes under capitalism, and forget that many capitalist countries are dictatorships. If we belong to the Soviet underground we complain about the militarization of the Soviet not the US economy – and ludicrously allege that defence takes up 40 per cent of the national income. Living under capitalism, we write on ecology as if socialism had in fact coped with these externalities any better.

Our subject arouses unsually strong passions, from which no author is

TABLE 1/I

The Valuation and Performance of Certain Economic Systems

Chapter references	Goals	Weights: Economists: PW rich countries	PW poor countries	Chicago	Governments[a]: Soviet-type	China	Capitalist	Yugoslav	Rank Orders in Performance[g] (inverted): poor countries STE	China	Cap.	Yu.	rich countries STE	Cap.	Yu.[i]	all agriculture (except very poor) STE	Cap.	Yu.
10, 11	Micro-optimality[f]	10	5	100	1	5	25	15	1	3	4	2	1	3	2	1	3	2
15	Growth	10	30	*[b]	36	17	25	33	3·5	3·5	1	2	1[c]	3[c]	2[c]	1	3	2
14	Full employment[h]	20	20	*[b]	18	15	30	10	3·5	3·5	1·5	1·5[j]	3	1·5	1·5	3	1·5	1·5
16	Equality	20	20	?[d]	18	30	8	14	3	4	1	2	3	1	2	3		2
14	Price stability	15	10	*[b]	13	13	7	1	3·5	3·5	2	1	3	2	1	3	2	1
2, 21	Altruistic motivation	0	0	0	14	20	0	3	3	4	1	2	3	1	2	3	1	2
21	Low degree of alienation	25	15	0	*[k]	*[k]	5	24	1	4	2	3	1	2	3	1	3	
	(Total)	100	100	100	100	100	100	100										
	Acceptability to the people								1·5	1·5[l]	3	4	1	2	3	1	3[e]	2
17	Compatibility with political freedom								1·5	1·5	4	3	1	3	2	1	3[e]	2

immune. My personal passions are indicated in Table 1/I, though I rank political freedom above all the economic items listed, at least for rich countries. Our ecological crisis has recently weaned me from an attachment to economic growth in rich countries, and I never cared much for optimal resource allocation – but cannot see why it should be actually neglected or its theory denied. I would therefore naturally prefer most kinds of socialism to most kinds of capitalism – were it not for my fear of the intolerance and contempt for the incompetence of actual socialists. But prejudices can be kept down if not out, and if a science free of the observer's values cannot be attained it can most certainly be approached. I claim to be looking at the various economic systems, with a dry eye, and at arm's length. For a discussion of 'false consciousness', however, see chapter 17, sec. 12.

We try then, to keep out our own ideas, but what of other people's? Ideas about systems should interest us mainly for the actual effects they have. This book is flatly about what does happen, not what should happen. Nevertheless ideologies are immensely influential; even when they are violated they strongly constrain the manner and the degree of the violation. To dismiss, say, Marxism as something to which Russians pay only lip service is not scepticism, which is always serious about facts, but cynicism, i.e. a form of ignorance. We deal, then, mainly with 'revealed governmental preference', and note that ideas are of great but seldom decisive practical importance.

4. Which system, then, is best? The highly tentative results of this book are summed up in Table 1/I. This table is of course very naïf and monstrously ambitious. But the avoidance of naïveté and ambition is most

---

Notes to Table 1/I

a. These weights are what I observe these governments to choose, and not necessarily what their ideologists and speech-writers profess.
b. Held to be a direct consequence of micro-optimality: see text.
c. I invert the rank order because I consider that self-management in an advanced society would be very resistant to the adoption of technical progress, and STEs have shown themselves bad at generating it. The reference here is not to 'rich' but to 'very rich' countries.
d. Either zero or as in (b).
e. The reference is to family farms, not latifundia.
f. Meaning consumers' sovereignty, consumers' convenience, economy in production and investment, due care for externalities including ecology.
g. By my judgement. The best performance scores 4 or 3, in order that the reader may conveniently apply his own weights to obtain a total that scores highest for the best performance.
h. Considered to be in many cases contrary to growth, and an end in itself.
i. There is no 'rich Yugoslavia'. This column has had to be imagined.
j. Correctly viewed, and given here most favourable circumstances, Yugoslavia has a fairly successful employment policy (chapter 14, sec. 12).
k. Held to be a direct concomitant of altruistic motivation.
l. China's economic system rests upon overwhelming totalitarian controls. So I judge it to have low acceptability despite high success.

unscientific. It is precisely the business of this book to provide tentative answers to such large questions, because these are the questions that people ask, and very rightly. All systems, then, must do the same things, and these are set out under 'Goals'. But governments and people attach different weights to these goals, and performance may or may not be in accordance with any of these weights. The reader may amuse himself by inserting his own weights, or those of kibbutzniks, hippies, the Cuban government, Mahatma Gandhi, etc.; and by revising and refining the rank orders.

Let us state the major qualifications.

(i) All the weighting columns except that labelled 'Chicago' imply acceptance of the idea that the desired goals must be traded off against each other. Thus whatever the ideology says, STEs certainly show awareness that rapid growth raises prices. They also hold, perhaps wrongly, that growth requires inequality. My understanding of basic Chicago doctrine, on the other hand, is that most economic goals are complementary, indeed complementary with the one outstanding one among them: micro-optimality. This goal then becomes a virtual panacea.

(ii) We have only considered the most ultimate goals. We might have listed, and we do discuss later, balance of payments equilibrium; but it is only a constraint under which all systems operate. The avoidance of output fluctuations, again, is implicit in micro-optimality and in full employment. This latter, on the other hand, has been accepted as a goal separate from, and competing with, growth, in all UDCs and dual economies.

(iii) The governmental weights are based on governmental preferences as perceived by me. The government may well be struggling very hard against the natural pathology of the system it operates: e.g. capitalist governments put a lot of effort into cost-benefit analysis and monopoly control, yet are far from achieving micro-optimality in the face of oligopoly and the extension of the sphere of public goods. Or the government may go with the grain of its system, and tolerate its natural pathology: e.g. Soviet-type governments do not give a fig for micro-optimality, which their systems in any case altogether exclude.

(iv) Rank order is not enough: a more refined analysis would clearly allow for cardinal rates of growth, unemployment, inflation, etc. But it would also require us to quantify micro-optimality (sec. 7 here), alienation (chapter 21) and equality (chapter 16).

For the rest, one example suffices to show how quantification might alter the picture. The high Chicago weighting for micro-optimality puts capitalism easily in the top place, with a weighted rank order of 300. But this really refers to a perfectly competitive system, in which an irreducible minimum of public goods is also issued on the most cost-beneficial lines possible. This, and not the actual allocation under actual capitalism, is the panacea. It is open to any such true believer to hold that minor increases in market perfection, as between an STE and an ACE, would have little effect on, say, growth; and that in such circumstances capitalism might well not come out best. This is a straight application of the doctrine of the second best.

5. What economic laws do systems share, and which characterize only this or that system? Man's capacity to discover and apply new knowledge, social and technological, does differ from system to system, but old knowledge tends to be everywhere the same. It only 'tends' because of the problem of X-efficiency (chapter 15). Inertia, passion, prejudice and self-interest slow the spread of technology between countries, and within countries between enterprises. Social inventions like cost-benefit are even more strongly retarded by the same factors.

Yet at least the 'laws of production' are evidently everywhere the same. Can we explain this by saying they are themselves laws of nature? It seems, no. The commonly accepted laws of production are not on the whole technological, but a philosophically very mixed bag. Some depend on limitations of human capacity and psychology that no economic system has hitherto affected, and only some are laws of nature. Three, even, are only useful tautologies:

(i) Returns always diminish to a single factor, if other factors are held constant; but this is a concealed definition, since otherwise the factors held constant would have no effect on production – so that they could not be called factors of production.

(ii) Good land yields a rent, if the product price is the same. This too is tautologous, defining 'good'.

(iii) Material balances are inexorable. This is an accounting identity, so also a tautology. Money balances notoriously behave in the same way, with ex post identities reducing ex ante inequalities to order.

Of these Marxists are inclined to reject (i) and (ii). Marx hated Malthus, and so himself condemned (i), which had in his day no other application. (ii) is alleged to be a law of markets only, and so inapplicable to socialism. Stalin even showed much impatience with (iii).

Returns also increase with scale under all systems: costs of production fall as producing units grow until they become too big to run in the old centralistic way. Thereafter the cost curve flattens out, and would indeed rise again if we did not decentralize, thereby laying open to question what is meant by a 'producing unit' (Wiles 1961, chapter 12). Now on the side of the *diseconomies of large-scale management* this is only to say that human beings are of limited capacity. The manager's span of control is only so big, so that if he tries to keep the same centralized grip over a large enterprise as previously over a small one he becomes a bottleneck, a fixed factor of production which causes returns to diminish to the varied factors. He merely instantiates the law of diminishing returns. As in other cases, technical progress in the arts of management enables him only to put off the evil day.

But the *economies of large-scale production* are indeed mainly technological. The cost of making a pipe of any length increases in proportion to its radius but its capacity in proportion to the square of its radius; long runs reduce the cost of resetting machinery, etc., etc. Such economies of scale need never yield to diseconomies, since a technical process or unit can always be reduplicated. They can also continue to be reaped even after the diseconomies of large-scale management set in, and offset them; so that the average total curve of an enterprise is usually L, not U, shaped (Wiles, loc. cit.).

It is this side of the matter that makes large-scale catnip to Marxists: they cannot resist the spectacle of new relations of production emerging from new forces of production, independently of human will. But they neglect the equally valid human law that large-scale management is inefficient, as their own centralized planning amply shows. They also, like most technocrats, lay much weight on the 'humanly technological' fact that specialization increases skill. But they forget that even humble kinds of human labour will 'act up', offsetting in an irregular but catastrophic way the economies of large scale. Alienation increases with specialization and the scale of the enterprise, no matter what the efficiency of its production or the inefficiency of its management. This is a social or psychological phenomenon occurring also in all systems (chapter 21, sec. 16). But a sufficiently totalitarian system can suppress the overt symptoms (strikes, sabotage).

6. Some of the functions of money are cut away by the STE, where inter-enterprise money is 'passive', i.e. does not normally affect anyone's decisions (chapter 11). The commune abolishes money outright, except for external relations.

The nature of the enterprise varies from system to system, particularly its maximand (chapter 4). Therefore enterprises' demand and supply curves and their elasticities depend on economic systems (chapter 10, sec. 13). The self-managed enterprise has a peculiar maximand, and an inelastic supply curve. The Soviet-type enterprise has no maximand, and the whole notion of its supply curve must be rethought in view of the passivity of money (chapter 11, sec. 3).

Individuals are more constant. The negative supply curve of individual labour is a law of individual psychology, and applies everywhere with respect to monetary incentives. But moral incentives may affect its elasticity and position. The quantity of these depends of course on the system (chapter 2, sec. 11) and it may be possible, by education and propaganda, to make any given quantity more effective.

Demand curves for products by consumers are even less amenable. They seem to be quite insensitive to systems. Of course the abolition of money in a commune makes demand difficult to analyse, but it still slopes downwards and there is no reason to suppose it has a different elasticity. All this is now recognized (it used not to be) by Communists, who conduct very orthodox market research. In kibbutzim however there is still resistance to this knowledge, let alone to the use of it. Consumers' sovereignty as a normative proposition does not follow in any case, and is only very partially recognized even in STEs.

Aspiration levels however are another matter. The whole object of most communes (notably kibbutzim) and of quasi-communes like the Cuban economy, is to reduce them, while under capitalism the whole object of advertising is to increase them. Specifically, new goods have this effect, and certainly communes are hostile to new goods. For the marginal utility of old goods falls rapidly, and aspirations in terms of them alone can perhaps be fully satisfied (chapter 21).

The Keynesian economics has no application where money is passive or non-existent and production is carried on by command (chapter 14). In such cases inflation affects only the black market. But Malthusian, technological and seasonal unemployment depend on techniques, factor endowment, etc.; so they occur under all systems. However, cures for them differ.

Income distribution between individuals depends very greatly on systems (chapter 16).

Summing up, systems do not alter human nature, but they can suppress some of its symptoms. An exception is communes, which might or not affect the level of aspiration and the position and elasticity but not the negativity of the supply curve of labour. Systems do not change technology or other knowledge – truth is truth everywhere; but they do change our ability to discover it and adapt ourselves. What systems mainly influence is that of which they consist: human organizations. But that is another tautology! In this book the differences, naturally, are stressed far more than the similarities.

7. When we consider other systems, must we take a different view of resource allocation? As a life-long depreciator of Western welfare economics, holding it unimportant for both students and administrators, I must assert a tepid conviction that it is logically unassailable. The neo-classical account is entirely correct and system-free, and the Marxist refusal to accept it entirely inexcusable. This refusal, based on the false labour theory of value, is now everywhere weakening. The nationalization of the means of production, the substitution of command and plan for markets, the evolution of the STE into Full Communism – none of this makes any difference at all. Greater equality and more rapid growth make no difference. The actual allocation optimal to these new conditions is of course different, but what it is can only be established in the old way. There is no planning, or socialist, principle different from a market, or

capitalist, principle. The very procedures adopted by computers and planners consciously simulate a perfectly competitive market. If they do not, they are wrong.

Production, then, should be carried on until marginal social cost equals marginal social utility. If there are money and prices this implies that an excellent approximation is where marginal private cost = price = marginal private utility. But if we must be completely rigid about the principles of optimal allocation we must not fall into the trap of thinking them overwhelmingly important. Many questions of efficiency (chapter 15) and income distribution (chapter 16) have little or nothing to do with them. It is a secure part of the Keynesian revolution that unemployment has little or nothing to do with them. An economy can grow and produce happy citizens while disregarding them. While it is impossible to be a good economist without understanding them (note the circularity of this assertion), it is possible to run an economy well, for management and understanding are distinct. Sub-optimality loses us surprisingly little welfare (chapter 10, sec. 3). It may even, by this or that set of institutions, be tied in one way or another to economic advance.

I hold it undesirable that the 'welfare' rules should be relaxed in the particular case of investment policy.[3] The relaxation at this point may be a necessary by-product of something else, but it is never an end in itself. The rules do not point a developing economy in the wrong direction. The fact that STEs can more easily break, and have more often broken, them is unlikely to explain their superior performance. Rather to the contrary, it is a negative item that makes the other elements of superiority all the more impressive. But this book shuns, for reasons of space, all or nearly all development issues. As to externalities, the neo-classical economics has always provided just the right theoretical framework for treating them (chapters 11, 15). Not even the world-wide ecological crisis affects that proposition. The principal externalities that plague capitalism tend to turn up in force under other systems; i.e. if the market cannot internalize them neither can subordinate units in planning hierarchies.

Notes

1. Notably, it would appear, in Britain, where economists are becoming more and more impatient with the practical sterility of mainstream methods. Cf. E. H. Phelps Brown and G. D. N. Worswick in *E.J.*, March 1972; N. Kaldor in *E.J.*, December 1972. It is no accident that I have myself joined that company, in *E.J.*, June 1973. For similar foreign misgivings compare Benjamin Ward, *What's Wrong with Economists?*, London 1972; Janos Kornai, *Anti-Equilibrium*, Amsterdam 1971.

2. Other countries I have found it expedient to know something about: Japan, Bulgaria, Algeria, Poland, Nazi Germany, Fascist Italy.

3. Cf. Wiles 1962, chapters 15, 16; Wiles 1969, chapter 8.

2

Incentives to Work

'. . . That reason, passion, answers one great aim
That true self-love and social are the same.'

Pope

1. 'Benthamite' incentives
2. The shocking discovery of their efficacy
3. Force and the origins of socialism
4. Non-Benthamite incentives
5. Some misunderstandings
6. Work as pleasure
7. Institutions and incentives
8. The STE
9. Soviet-type and capitalistic managers
10. Titles and medals
11. Cuba and 'War' Communism
12. Labour has a negative supply curve

2

1. The social sciences are inextricably moral. We can, and indeed for the most part should, talk of them in neutral tones, i.e. amorally, but the scientist is himself a moral being and he often fails. And since his object in studying them is to derive principles of conduct, his fundamental aim is in any case moral. Moreover, and above all, he is usually studying other people's morality. He can only purify his logic and his observations, never his subject-matter. The besetting sin of Western economists is to try to purify their subject-matter; and this is nowhere more obvious than in their narrow-minded and unimaginative attitude to that quintessentially moralistic part of their subject, the motivation of economic activity. This motivation is not uniform among men, even as a first approximation. Institutions are changed, and blood is shed, in order that this or that doctrine of economic motivation be fulfilled. Beside this subject, property, equality, growth and full employment take second place.

This discussion of incentives pretends to no psychological sophistication, and rests on no clear-cut theory. The psychologist will find it innocently eclectic. Our aim is only to distinguish these incentives in a manner useful to our subject.

The incentives to economic activity are not themselves all 'economic', or 'materialistic', or 'selfish' or 'pecuniary' – each adjective betrays us somehow. But we shall begin with this kind, since it is in fact the most important, and call it 'Benthamite', where the inverted commas are very important.

(A) By a 'Benthamite' incentive, then, we mean one that rationally confronts a free individual, in exchange for work, with the promise of some specific good or service, or with general command over such things; but always outside working hours. Work is pure means, a pain and not a pleasure, and the promised reward pure end. Such incentives are: profit, plan-fulfilment bonus, piece-rates, a straight rise in pay, increased fringe benefits, promotion, demotion,[1] firing,[1] a fine.[1] An unchanged wage or salary is not, strictly speaking, an incentive to work (sec. 5). It is the threat of its cessation, or the promise of its increase, that makes us do things.

(B) Then there is the *unfree individual.* We define here 'free' as 'not subject to physical restraint by another human being'. The unfree, then, respond to the incentives of physical punishment and torture, the threat of imprisonment and the prospect of liberation.

Now these too are direct appeals to the reason of the individual and are external to his feelings about work. They are therefore *sensu stricto*

Benthamite. Indeed Jeremy Bentham was nothing if not a penologist, and included this type of incentive quite inextricably along with list (A). But here we have confined the adjective to list (A) alone, hence the inverted commas. List (A) incentives are very often offered to prisoners and slaves, in order to extract marginal supplies of effort and skill over and above what mere force can grind out (chapter 8).

2. Western economics largely assumes that the items (A) are the only incentives. Indeed the foundation of this kind of economics dates from the assertion that such incentives not only could but also did and should fuel the economic system; that 'private vice is public virtue' in that luxury spending creates employment (Mandeville); that competition plus selfishness are a 'hidden hand' directing us to work for the common weal (Smith); that 'it is not from the benevolence of the butcher, the brewer or the baker, that we expect our dinner, but from their regard to their own interest' (Smith). These statements were shocking and cynical in their day. They destroyed the medieval outlook on the economy, which was that incentives – or should we say motives? – such as those in C, sec. 4 below, not only should but could and did fuel the system.

Thus the moralistic Christian attitude to incentives, already much shaken, was explicitly overthrown in the eighteenth century. This was an event of the first importance in mankind's intellectual history. Not only did it put self-interest in command, it also invited men to study rationally and objectively the social results of self-interest, especially under competition, monopoly and absentee management. The discovery that competition plus direct owner-management makes self-interest a very tolerable motive is the first great discovery in modern economics. Outside the pages of Machiavelli, it is perhaps the first great discovery of the social sciences. Our whole modern notion of a maximand, for individuals or enterprises (chapter 4), stems from this. The maximand is a morally loaded concept.

But the discovery seemed and seems too cynical to most people. The reformed churches resisted it feebly for a while. The Roman Catholic church was never reconciled, and continues to propound a large body of doctrine based explicitly upon its partial rejection. This is the doctrine of the just wage and the just price. We shall see in chapter 16 good reason to reject attempts to redistribute income through the price mechanism. It is enough to note here that such attempts depend either on taxes and subsidies, or on the free choice of men not to maximize their profits. The just wage and the just price were, until recently, conceived in the latter way, i.e. morally. They were to be the product of self-restraint, not government.

By 1820 a full tide of more radical reaction to self-interest had set in, this time irreligious. Its first manifestation was co-operation, and its slogan 'co-operation not competition'. There was to be a 'New *Moral* Order' – the words are Robert Owen's but the italics are mine. *Voluntarily* emerging from the intellectual prison of capitalism, humanity, including the capitalist class, was to gain (regain?) its altruism. Moreover this could all be done on a decentralized basis. The British co-operative shop is the direct but degenerate descendant of this movement (chapter 6). Co-operation, moreover, is almost co-terminous with populism, which rests squarely on the proposition that the common people are good, while evil motives characterize the corrupt and artificial establishment (chapter 5).

3. Hard on the heels of co-operation (*c.* 1830), and for long not adequately distinguished from it, came a less optimistic doctrine: socialism. This too is primarily a moral doctrine of economic incentives. But man – certainly the capitalist class and probably also the proletarian class – is too unregenerate. Revolution, force and centralization will long be necessary before altruism assumes its sway.

Whenever a particular kind of socialism makes its peace with Jeremy Bentham, others arise to the left of it, urging that the direct love of society be substituted for mere objective service to society, mediated by a system of incentives based on self-love. It is this above all that distinguishes China, Cuba and Albania from other Communist countries, in the West and Yugoslavia the New Left from the Old Left, and in India the Gandhi/Bhave tradition[2] from the government.

This revolution of thought in the eighteenth century was not wholly cynical. The new stress on self-interest and automatism also led to the rejection of force. Perhaps prematurely and without too much evidence, it was decided that the list (B) incentives (sec. 1) were not merely immoral but also expensive to administer and inefficient in eliciting effort. The notion gained ground that even unskilled and boring labour would be better performed freely and for money. If cotton was picked under direct compulsion until 1864, British navvies, with spade, wheelbarrow and freely agreed wages, were already the wonder of Europe in 1830.

Yet Stalin's experience in these matters (chapter 8) should make us chary of easy and optimistic generalizations. In sensible climatic conditions, some of his skilled prisoners even designed good aircraft. In USA, for that matter, the ante-bellum South had many good slave craftsmen. The Romans, relying on the promise of manumission, even had efficient and honest slave administrators. Much, in fact, depends upon the admixture of list (A) incentives. It is more certain that force is immoral and degrading than that it does not work.

Self-interest, then, was in its day a liberating and moralizing influence. It broke the remnants of feudalism, and put an end to slavery. Indeed even now, whenever 'Benthamite' incentives do not work, the authorities may talk about altruism (D) or work as its own reward (C), but they actually resort to force.

4. What then are these 'non-Benthamite' incentives? In some cases (C)

work is its own reward. This is Thorstein Veblen's Instinct of Workmanship. We do it because we have an intellectual interest in it, we enjoy practising our skill, we get a physical kick out of it, or we are proud of the product. Perhaps some kinds of prestige come within this rubric. Thus the admiration of our fellow-workmen, or the customer, may in certain circumstances be neither of economic benefit nor of public record, and may be pursued for its own sake. But this is a marginal case at best. A stronger case is the mere avoidance of boredom: we are plagued by animal spirits and excess of energy, and those of us who do not take them out in crime take them out in work.

This very strong incentive to work has been most adequately discussed elsewhere. We are all familiar with the designer, the teacher, the researcher, the musician, the doctor carrying on regardless. In fact they carry on under all systems. Mere changes in pay and ownership do not affect them, but certain other rather unexpected things do. They resent the technical interference of superiors, and they resent above all bad tools. So they strongly tend to migrate to rich market economies, where superiors, always too numerous, are at least not part of the government and not monopsonists; and where co-operant factors are plentiful and of good quality. Very much of the brain drain is due, not to 'Benthamite' motives, but to the desire to perform one's work freely and well. The command economy as such, and poverty as such, are bad for the 'instinct of workmanship'. This 'instinct' (a word with doubtless false biological implications) is not, of course, altruistic (chapter 15, sec. 16).

(D) In other cases *work is altruism or duty*. Thus the medieval Christian church told believers to 'work and pray' (*ora et labora*), in tones that implied work was prayer, and therefore a form of honour to God. Many people work for other human beings, with or without the urging of religion; and this is especially true in families and communes. In a country at war, or in the grip of a recent socialist revolution, many are motivated by altruism to put in voluntary overtime or change their residence and/or careers (cf. sec. 11 here, chapter 10, sec. 11).

Altruism is often confused with 'group Benthamism'. If for instance a man works hard, introduces innovations, etc., in a very small kibbutz, may it not be that he expects 2 per cent of it back to himself anyway? Is this very different from the father of a large family, who might expect 15 per cent of it back? Group Benthamism clearly shades off into altruism as numbers increase. An even stronger case is a strike. The trade union uses the rhetoric of altruism to maintain morale, but each striker stands to gain money for himself, and normally he thinks mostly of that. Many of the early Soviet experiments in new motivation amounted only to a swap of material benefits for work on a group basis. Of course the material inducements offered to groups went to individuals. 'Collective consumption', that very misleading phrase, is only collectively financed individual consumption. But collective enjoyment *sensu stricto* excludes 'group Benthamism'. It is our altruistic enjoyment of others' consumption.

(E) Then come prestige, medals, other public honours and publicity. It is a matter of definition whether we call these 'Benthamism', since the desire for recognition is selfish, but in an immaterial way (sec. 10). We assimilate the case rather to (D), and call them both together 'moral incentives', since that is the Cuban usage (sec. 11).

(F) But commoner by far are those who work by *habit, convention or mere compliance*, not thinking much about why they do it or requiring any special stimulus. In particular once a man has taken up a particular job it is usually enough to tell him exactly what the job requires at a given time and place; and easy or difficult, pleasant or unpleasant, he will do just that without further ado. Moreover he will do it more readily a second time. Mere routine, eked out with direct commands that do not greatly offend against it, and by rational *ad hoc* persuasion, is the mightiest force of all. As March and Simon put it:

> 'In one respect an employee's relation to the organization is quite different from that of the other participants. In joining the organization he accepts an authority relation: i.e. he agrees that within some limits (defined both explicitly and implicitly by the terms of the employment contract) he will accept as the premises of his behaviour orders and instructions supplied to him by the organization . . . An employee will be willing to enter into an employment *contract* only if it does not matter to him "very much" what activities (within the area of acceptance agreed on in the contract) the organization will instruct him to perform, or if he is compensated in some way for the possibility that the organization will impose unpleasant activities on him.'[3]

This 'zone of compliance' is always partly, often entirely, informal and implicit. We discover where it is when we (employer or employee) violate it, and bring into play some of the other motives for work. All systems operate day by day within the zone of compliance.

5. Before proceeding we must examine some *common misapprehensions* about 'Benthamite' incentives.

(i) The first of these is 'vulgar Benthamism': we do what we like, and that is our incentive. This is so vague and all-inclusive as to be irrefutable; it tells us virtually nothing more than that we do what we do. Threatened with a beating, the slave picks cotton: he prefers it to a beating. Promised a bonus, the Soviet manager overfulfils his plan: he wants rubles. Appealed to by his leader, the Cuban revolutionary cuts cane: his personal aim is to improve his country's balance of payments. Offered a golden handshake, the founder of the upstart firm retires when it is taken over: he had rather not play second fiddle, and with all that money he can start again. All these people are doing what they like – it is hard to think of someone who doesn't.

(ii) Secondly the search for material reward is not necessarily materialist. The command over scarce resources that incentives of list (A) offer may be sought for all kinds of reasons. For John Wesley the reasons were charitable: 'Gain all you can, give all you can.' The pious save for a pilgrimage to Mecca or Lourdes. Others again want wealth in order to buy power: you need an unearned income before you stand for Parliament, or you may wish to give to the revolutionary movement of your choice. Bentham himself would doubtless have recognized as much.

(iii) Indeed, thirdly, pure materialism, the desire to maximize command over goods and services, is self-contradictory unless leisure is recognized as a good both complementary, in that other goods and services cannot be truly had without it, and competitive, in that having it gets in the way of acquiring the others. Leisure has been very adequately dealt with by others.[4] It is enough here to point out that leisure to consume is purely 'Benthamite': it has opportunity costs and money costs and in general behaves like other goods and services. The promise of such leisure in the future is an excellent incentive to work in the present. 'Leisure' to work in other ways has been accounted for above (C, sec. 4). It follows that the negative supply curve of labour is entirely 'Benthamite', provided only that our rising incomes raise our desire for leisure to consume in (sec. 12).

(iv) Profit is of course not the only 'Benthamite' incentive. Any form of piece-work, any overtime, any *ad hoc* fee, or in larger matters the promise of promotion or the offer of a fixed but higher wage or salary, functions almost exactly like profit. So, above all, does the Soviet-type plan-fulfilment bonus. There is no truth at all in the common notion that the Soviet manager faces no Benthamite incentives. On the contrary he faces far more of them than any capitalist executive, not to mention the executive of a Western public corporation. The plan-fulfilment bonus (sec. 9) is a sort of piece-work for managers. It presents a far more constant and immediate incentive to effort than any increase in annual salary (since it can also diminish), or than the rare bonuses a capitalist executive may expect. Nor need it have any connexion at all with profits: for it is administratively as easy to pay it out of the wage-fund as out of profits, and if the former the bonus may quite easily be paid although the enterprise has made a loss. The plan, of course, is in physical units, and its fulfilment has no clear relation to the financial outturn. Indeed the bonus for fulfilling the physical plan can be an incentive to increase the financial loss![5] And such was, precisely, the situation in the USSR before 1965, and in most other STEs until about that date. Thereafter bonus from profit has tended to replace plan-fulfilment bonus out of wage-fund, and the manager has indeed acquired 'the profit motive', *sensu stricto*.

(v) 'The profit motive,' in sum, and fifthly, is a very loose and misleading phrase. It is much too narrow to stand for all Benthamite incentives, and by insisting on profit rather than income it appears to exclude wages and salaries, and wholly obscures the Soviet-type plan-fulfilment bonus. What there is, is an *income motive*, and this does fairly describe all 'Benthamite' behaviour. We tend to maximize our life-time incomes (duly discounted for futurity and risk), from whatever sources they come. We are not, as 'Benthamites', interested in the profit or any other performance indicator of our enterprise, even under capitalism, except in so far as it contributes to our own life-time income. Indeed enterprises are not people, and so cannot be stimulated by any incentive – that is a logical impossibility (chapter 4). All language implying the contrary is metaphysical. Enterprise profit can be a 'criterion' for socialist planners or capitalist managers; it can also be an 'indicator' for socialist managers or junior executives generally.[6] And it can also be none of these things, but simply something irrelevant, generated ex post by the accounting process. What it cannot be is an incentive: only a personal share of profit can be that. The interaction between the constant propensity of 'Benthamite' individuals to maximize their life-time income and the varying structures of the enterprise leads to exceedingly various behaviour by the enterprise. This is the subject of chapter 4. Here we confine ourselves to individuals.

(vi) Good treatment and high pay are not in themselves 'Benthamite' incentives or indeed any sort of incentive. For our current absolute level of welfare is a secondary matter: it is our ability to change it by working that constitutes the incentive. But our current level affects these changes in two ways. On the one hand – and this is an economist's commonplace – the marginal utility of income diminishes as income rises, and for even the most dedicated craftsman the *marginal* utility of work is usually negative and increasingly so as work is prolonged. Consequently a high initial level of pay *dis*courages further work, and diminishes the effect of a given incentive scheme (sec. 12).

(vii) But on the other hand – and economists are far too slow to recognize this – our physical ability to provide work is enhanced by greater income, at least up to a point. For the richer we are the better we eat, the better our medical care, the more books we read, the more enriching experiences we have, the better our morale and attitude to others, etc., etc. This is the phenomenon of 'productive consumption', and its principal application is to concentration camps.[7] Starving men *cannot* work. To get more effort from them we must offer, indeed we must have already applied, a better food/effort ratio. And yet again, overeating and alcoholism make one work less well; after too many elegant and illuminating experiences one will refuse to go down a mine, and so on. It is at least evident that only prospective changes in income constitute 'Benthamite' incentives, and that the present level of income has treacherous and uncertain consequences for the effect of these incentives. Indeed, so long as it is enough to keep us alive and in rather moderate health, quite likely the lower it is the more effective will any given incentive be.

(viii) In reaction to Benthamism many point to participation, self-management, the ending of alienation, etc. But these are not incentives or motives to work. First, they can be abused; they give the idle the power to do less work than ever. Secondly they take up time and distract one from the labour for which one is paid. Indeed, thirdly, they are rather like a high real income already being earned. They increase our level of satisfaction and reduce sabotage and grumbling; but they have little effect on hard work, and that little effect is probably negative. They have other virtues.

6. Our next misapprehension is the rigid Benthamite distinction between work and pleasure, where pleasure is leisure and all work is a disutility. For an astoundingly large minority of human beings, the hedonistic balance of work as such, quite apart from pay, seems to be positive, whether through altruism or craftsmanship or sheer joy in work. They might be 44 per cent of the population of working age in USA.[8] Such people – the author is among them – are singularly blessed. It should be one of the first tasks of humanity, not to abolish work – for 'the Devil' does indeed 'find work for idle hands to do' – but to render it a positive pleasure for the rest of us. This will not normally be possible at the marginal hour, of course, since everyone gets bored with everything in the end. But above all the extreme subdivision of labour, repetitive work on moving belts, is for most but not all workers highly unpleasant. Often labour costs are actually decreased by the removal of moving belts, simply because of the improvement in labour morale; in other words extreme Benthamism is self-defeating in its own terms.[9]

For many not only is work pleasurable but the distinction between it and leisure hard to maintain. Finally, soul-destroying work is not the same as, i.e. does not exhaust the concept of, Marxian *alienation*. For in addition to the alienation that we feel, which is taken up in the supply curve of labour and does not in any way threaten economic theory, there is, or may be, unfelt alienation. For all these matters, and for the apparent contemporary changes in human attitudes to labour, see chapter 21.

An incentive system is required to make a worker: take up work, change jobs, perfect and exercise his skills, seek promotion, do overtime, work conscientiously, be content with the social system. We must judge each incentive system separately by its effectiveness in these many respects, which need not have the same results. Thus we are particularly open to moral appeals in the choice of job and the conscientiousness with which we work. We take a craftsman's pride in our skills, many of which are therefore 'under'-rewarded. We are socially content when the result of the system is fairly egalitarian; which makes it hard for 'Benthamite' systems, but not impossible. Overtime on the other hand is best elicited by more money.

7. There is always a loose connexion between the predominant type of incentive and the institutional set-up, but some set-ups and some incentives are precisely designed for each other.

The 'Benthamite' motives operate all the time. They are *part* of human nature, I am inclined to say a strictly genetical part that can be overlaid by much training but will always return, if only in the next generation. From the kibbutz to the Soviet-type factory manager, one of the important and exciting things in economics is the survival of these motives in hostile or odd environments, and the havoc they wreak if denied. Societies pretending to do without them are like societies that prohibit alcohol.

The kibbutz, as we see in chapter 6, is designed for the altruistic incentives of list (D). But it is being bankrupted by its members' excessive pressure for more consumption. They still have equality of consumption and moneylessness within the commune; i.e. they are by no means fully 'Benthamite'. But they do not accept poverty and self-restraint, so may be said to hover between altruism and 'group Benthamism'. The competition of urban living standards is bringing the movement down, for while inequality within the kibbutz could be used to dissuade those most likely to leave, at far lower cost to the collective (chapter 6, sec. 13), it is unthinkable. Equality and migration are for ever at loggerheads, as is shown by any brain drain between two countries.

Altruism is far from unnatural; on the contrary, in the form of mere benevolence it is present in nearly all of us. But it is simply not strong enough to guide our everyday actions, unless reinforced by an unusual emotional and ideological commitment. Small religious sects and orders, the nuclear family and war have hitherto alone been strong enough to fuel an economy with altruism. Revolutionary movements have failed, even in Cuba, which has tried harder and longer (sec. 10).

The situation in other STEs is only quantitatively different from that in an ACE, where the young often engage, by long tradition, in voluntary service for low pay, and the priest corresponds to the Party member. Communist altruism has failed because 'Benthamism' was far too deeply rooted among the people, who anyway were compelled, without the least consultation, to be the objects of this experiment. At least the kibbutznik is a volunteer, and undergoes a thorough preparation. In other words, the authorities, like those of a well-run monastic order, know that they are making very unusual demands on human nature, and impose a novitiate.

Religious sects have a much stronger and more permanent hold; notably the Hutterites[10] have run an altruistic economy for centuries. But they are a very small minority movement, like the kibbutzim. They are not an all-embracing national church, like a ruling Communist Party. They permit the discontented freely to leave, and they indoctrinate from birth with far greater thoroughness than any Communist state.

The exclusive appeal to altruism seems to be invariably accompanied by the imposition of a commune, even if only on a nationwide scale ('War' Communism). No one, that is, supposes that families operating outside a tight community will give each other their labour. The most altruism of which such families are capable is the small amounts they set aside for charity, the extra efforts they make in wartime, and whatever they do for the extended family, usually under the strong pressure of some 'anthropological' arrangement. But if general altruism between citizens is the order of the day the nuclear family, which interferes with it, must go.

War is another good case of altruism. When the combative passions of men run high enough they need no 'Benthamite' incentives. Moreover they are intolerant of others, less passionate, who still do, and governments are unwilling to spend money, now required for the war, on such frivolities. For of course the incentives not out of list (i) are cheaper in the short run, and so we turn to them above all in temporary crises. Thus commonly in war, but also often in communes, force not money is the accepted alternative to failures of altruism. It appeals simultaneously to the intolerance and to the thrift of the dominant group in the society concerned.

Even so, however, in war economies there is always differentiated pay, and the post-war possibility of enjoying one's savings. The nuclear family is not attacked, far from it. There is general recognition among ordinary men that altruism and force are like an orgy: they cannot last and they leave a hangover. The notion, associated with Mandeville and Smith, that appeals to selfishness are cheaper in the long run, has never been disproved.

8. As to the STE, with its plan-fulfilment bonuses, its piece-work and its differentiated wages and salaries, is it at all less 'Benthamite' than capitalism? The answer is that is certainly wishes to be less, it has not forgotten or wholly rejected 'War' Communism (sec. 11), its self-image is that of a genuinely socialist society. In practice some items are more and some less 'Benthamite' than under capitalism. On balance, however, there is both more altruism and more force in the STE, and thus the cheerless lesson is reinforced, that selfishness leaves us most free.

Let us particularize. The worker in the nationalized sector faces almost identical incentives, except that they are rather stronger. There is more piece-work, and punishments and fines are common. Social services bulk larger in total income, but are themselves differentiated. The marginal rate of income-tax is about 13 per cent at the top. The manager faces much more directly 'Benthamite' incentives than under capitalism, as we have seen. The same goes for the collective farm chairman and the rest of the agricultural élite, while the ordinary collective farmer either faces a highly differentiated system of labour-day payments (chapter 6) or (lately) a differentiated tariff of piece-work and bonuses. Not all these incentives work very well, to be sure, especially in agriculture, but the individual is undeniably exposed to them.

Yet all our theories seem powerless to explain one overwhelming fact: labour in STEs does not work hard. One source for this statement is common observation, unbacked by statistics.[11] Taking it to be true, what reasons can we suggest?

(i) national character. Russians, Poles and Hungarians, like the English, dislike work under all economic systems.

(ii) hatred of the system as such. This is specially marked among Poles, and even more so among the traditionally hard-working Czechs since 1968.

(iii) the irritating lack of small tools and regular supplies, so offensive to the Instinct of Workmanship (sec. 4).

(iv) the improbability of being fired (chapter 7, sec. 9).

(v) the low purchasing power of marginal earnings. For truly the command economy and the collective farm create extraordinary incentives to moonlight, scrimshank and steal. Who will do overtime in a factory at double pay if his family is living in one room, if there is no proper housing list, if he knows where he can 'acquire' lumber, and if it is legal to build huts in towns? Such a man will devote all his efforts at work to stealing nails and tools, once he is sure of his basic wage. Again, what housewife will work overtime when it takes two hours to queue for cheap groceries, the cost of which is already covered by the family income? And what collective farmer can resist his private plot, even in the changed price situation of today (chapter 6)?

But altruism is also very important; and force, its ever-present shadow, goes with it. Young people, above all, are asked to do more than they are paid for. The youth leagues 'persuade' them into this, that and the other campaign of underpaid labour, often in cold and distant parts of the country; fresh graduates are assigned to jobs, more or less in their speciality but unpopular, for the first three years on graduation; schooling is often interrupted for special local drives that require unskilled labour. Military conscription is never removed at the height of peace, and conscientious objection to it is not permitted. Demobilized conscripts are particularly liable to be 'persuaded' to 'volunteer' for some unpopular civilian job. Indeed in all societies youth may be forced, or is expected to act altruistically, or both. This is but a milder continuation of the compulsions to which children are habitually submitted (chapter 8).

Then again on special occasions the proletariat is supposed to work overtime, or whole shifts, or special Saturdays and Sundays (*subbotniki*), perhaps on different jobs, all without pay, out of revolutionary enthusiasm, for its own government, which cannot by definition exploit it. Party members, a special priesthood, are often directed to jobs and places by the Party. Prison labour and the control of migration deserve a whole chapter to themselves (8); in these cases of course altruism does not apply at all, and force is basic. But in the short-run, day-to-day affairs of prison labour the 'Benthamite' incentives are also freely used, as explained above.

9. Capitalism is surprisingly similar. The main difference is that far less – though similar – appeal is made to altruism or resort had to force. This is obvious and we need not expand upon it. A minor difference, however, demands more space: top management is rather differently motivated. First, in actual capitalist corporations salaries are much more invariant than in an STE.[12] Bonuses are paid only in some years and to some managers. But – and it is a very big but and of the essence of capitalism – the stock exchange is immensely important. The equity share makes possible occasional stock option bonuses, golden handshakes and the corrupt use of inside information that would make a Soviet director green with envy. Thirdly, however, both income tax and death duties are far heavier, even in practice and allowing for evasion.

On the other hand, and by a paradoxical contrast, it is often forgotten how much of top management under capitalism works for the state: whether as civil servants or as economic administrators or as teachers, scientists, etc. The capitalist state is no great believer in 'Benthamism'. It pays no bonuses or managerial piece-work at all. If its economic enterprises make a profit the management gets no part of it. There is even a whole theory of the 'disinterested management' of alcoholic drink (chapter 4).

Mostly, in supposing the STE to be less 'Benthamite', we succumb to ignorance, or to the official propaganda of either side; or we confuse the profit motive with the totality of economic self-interest; or we attribute the more equal distribution of income to the incentive system instead of the suppression of capitalism (chapter 16). But when all qualifications are made, force and altruism do play a larger part, and as the slow movement to Full Communism goes on they will play a yet larger one (chapter 21).

Yugoslavia is intermediate here, indeed very nearly indistinguishable from capitalism in these respects (chapters 4, 6).

10. Then too the state issues titles and medals, quite as freely as under Communism. The Légion d'Honneur is a pallid affair compared with the British honours system, and a capitalist country needs a monarch to make this kind of thing work at all. We have no idea, let alone any computation, of its effectiveness.

Now medals and titles have the peculiarity that they cost the giver nothing while yet offering the recipient something. No wonder public sectors, characteristically mean the world over, like to issue them. It is true that Communist countries are much keener on these incentives, and for obvious ideological reasons. But they are also 100 per cent public sectors and monopsonists of labour. It goes with this peculiarity that we compete for such awards, yet the winner does the losers no economic damage.[13] The Cubans, for whom all this is of the greatest importance, distinguish between (capitalist) *competencia* and (socialist) *emulación*. If 'emulation' really worked, a system of prestige awards would be excellent. But it leads to rather more corner-cutting and quality-worsening, in the context of an STE, than does 'competition' in a market. For consumers are not all fools, and their sovereignty sets a limit to the damage done by competition. Moreover the fact that competition damages the losers is on balance good: it eliminates the inefficient, i.e. it also works against corner-cutting. Emulation probably has its best effects when it is superimposed on a market and competition. Competition, *per contra*, is impossible in an STE.

In the early Soviet period ('War' Communism and the first FYP) medals and titles were issued only to groups, so strong was the collectivism. Today they are mostly individual, though group awards continue on a far greater scale than under capitalism.

11. The STE, if we may call it that, which has taken 'moral incentives' (altruism + prestige) most seriously is Cuba,[14] and this merits longer discussion. By comparison China has been a fitful experimenter; with two short tries she hardly outdoes the Soviet record.

The best moment for altruism is of course immediately after seizing power. But the post-revolutionary 'high' does not last very long, as was demonstrated by 'War' Communism in USSR (July 1918–April 1921). This was an utter failure. Still less can the 'high' be brought back at will many years later – as Mao tried to do in 1958 (the Chinese People's Communes) and 1967–9 (the Cultural Revolution). At present China expects altruism only of the young and of Party members, if even that.[15]

But Che Guevara imposed a seemingly indelible stamp on Cuban Communism. He did not exploit the post-revolutionary high but on the contrary had to battle against an imported Soviet orthodoxy on income distribution and incentives for three years (1959–62). In 1963–5 he made of Cuba a mild version of USSR's 'War' Communism (1918–21): moneyless transfers of goods between enterprises, all enterprise money transactions pass through the budget not the bank,[16] managers have little autonomy of physical decision either, many small consumer services provided free, much else rationed at low prices. He saw extreme centralization as part and parcel of moral incentives. But this is not necessarily so, since managers on moral incentives can act very independently: indeed not otherwise can we decentralize while avoiding the profit motive, as China shows (chapter 10, sec. 11). Moreover it is easy to establish a dichotomy between the criteria the manager must use (e.g. profit) and the *incentives* to which both he and his work force should respond. But fine distinctions of that kind do not appeal to Communists.

Guevara lost part of his battle, and resigned in 1965. But hardly a year passed before Guevarism came back,[17] this time with greater emphasis on efficiency but little organizational change. Cuba's planning system and her incentive system are best described as half-way over to 'War' Communism until 1970. This was the year of the great sugar harvest failure, after a deluge of propaganda for moral incentives. From 1970 Soviet-type normality has set in.

Turning from the general background, we must distinguish the weight of moral incentives (the number of medals, the prominence and frequency of propaganda, the length and passion of the rhetoric) from their effectiveness. Moral incentives are subject to a law of diminishing returns, just as the marginal utility of money diminishes. At the lowest and most intimate level moral incentives are used by everyone in subordinate authority in all systems; a man needs the foreman's constant encouragement, a secretary must be flirted with once a day, just as we need hourly reassurance from our loved ones. We tire of all this no more easily than of money. But praise from a central source, meted out impersonally, is quite another matter. It is quite possible that the British honours system, so sanctified by tradition, may be more effective than the Cuban. But it is far too small to fuel the economy, and it is possible that the much larger Cuban system is as effective as it can be.

Besides, we can easily exaggerate the extent to which moral incentives are really offered. Many Cuban workers have exchanged a promise of gratis overtime against a promise of larger social security benefits: the sceptic wonders how much overtime they actually perform, and are expected to perform. Many volunteer to change careers and residence – at their present rate of pay (e.g. men abandon white-collar jobs to women and go into agriculture): the sceptic wonders whether they seriously expected to keep their old jobs otherwise. Very many volunteer to cut sugar a while – at their current rate of pay: but this is entered in the *carnet laboral* (the extensive work record that each Cuban must have), and the sceptic wonders how many volunteer as a general long-term political investment, or in hope of promotion, or in fear of demotion, back at the office. A specialized part of the army is a labour army (shades of Trotsky!), which includes conscripted hooligans and layabouts: the sceptic wonders how the knowledge of this affects others who volunteer. Moreover the government retains in any case, and uses, the power to direct labour; but the writer himself volunteered to join the British army while conscription was on.

On the other hand the wage-spread is genuinely very low, and rationing and economic stagnation[18] have sharply reduced the uses of marginal money. So it must also be said that the government has deprived itself of non-moral incentives, and since people do change jobs, seek promotion and work overtime they must be responding to moral ones! Moreover there is also a large number of the young and the convinced, to whom no scepticism applies. If education increases their number, clearly the system will work as it is meant to and be more successful.

Cuban economic performance, however, is very poor. There are many reasons for this, and I have not courage enough to assign the incentive system its part in the (doubtless negative) factor productivity residual. Cuban statistics are very bad, whereas they would have to be preternaturally good to make so fine a distinction.

12. In conclusion, is the supply curve of labour negatively sloped in every kind of society, and is this 'Benthamite'? The professor who says that the slope is negative among primitive people, and that industrialization and modernity make it positive, himself probably works less, *ceteris paribus*, as his hourly remuneration rises. When once we realize that the income-elasticity of demand for leisure is positive, we are bound to admit that most rises in average hourly remuneration reduce, *ceteris paribus*, the offer of work. There is no clear difference between advanced and primitive people here, nor between one set of institutions and another (communes excepted). In UDCs and ACEs alike there is plentiful evidence for a negative slope: simply the naïf untreated data of economic history show a negative correlation between *total* hours of work and real income, and sophisticated re-working does nothing to destroy it.[19] We have no reason to suppose that people are different in STEs, where the government decides on hours of work, and has a strong ideological bias towards making them much shorter (chapter 21, sec. 3). For in a free market their subjects would doubtless choose to make them somewhat shorter anyhow.

The *whole* supply curve is negatively sloped, except perhaps right on the subsistence margin: starving men cannot work at all, so the more they are fed the more they work, up to a point (sec. 5/vii). For the rest the main apparent exception is dynamic: as development proceeds we earn and consume more, new opportunities for year-round work present themselves, our horizons widen and many more types of consumer goods appear. So the marginal utility of money rises and we work more. No doubt this extremely common dynamic sequence is the main reason why economically unsophisticated people think the supply curve of individual labour has a positive slope. But it only applies in limited historical phases to people at a low stage of development, and not to the 'informed poor' of advanced countries.

A rather similar effect can be imagined at a higher level of development: leisure becomes highly complementary with very expensive 'leisure goods', so less attractive unless we have more money. This effect has not been shown to be strong enough to diminish leisure, but it may be acting to slow down its growth (chapter 21, sec. 12).

But in any case it is not pedantry, and it does not at all lack practical importance in all societies, to point out that the supply curve is by definition a static concept. For static situations are exceedingly common and important. Negative supply, then, is wholly rational under nearly all conditions, and planners or employers who act on any other assumption are in for trouble.

In so far as people have 'non-Benthamite' motivations they – again however primitive or sophisticated they may be – have no supply curves at all. *Ex hypothesi* the price of labour does not influence them. Driven by fear or altruism or the instinct of workmanship they do, *ceteris paribus*, produce more when asked. But prestige is a reward rather like money: so it has diminishing marginal utility. Therefore labour that seeks it may well be negatively supplied if it is handed out too generously.

Notes

1. Negative incentives are as good as positive ones, of course; and this applies right through the analysis. This is not an unfair account of Bentham's position. Though he admits elsewhere, *en passant*, that labour can be its own reward, he directly denies it in the 'Table of the Springs of Action', where his mind is on the subject. Cf. John Bowring's edition of the works, N.Y. 1962, vol. VII p. 568, vol. I, pp. 204, 214.

2. Strictly speaking this tradition is populist, not socialist. Accordingly it demands self-restraint of the rich and the élite, but accepts the unregenerate nature of the poor. The Russian populists, from whom Gandhi in part derived his doctrine, also partially rejected self-interest as a motive. Cf. James A. Rogers in *Slavic Review*, 3, 1963. This moderate rejection was similar to that of the Roman Catholic church, though the Russian populists would not have liked the comparison.

3. James G. March and Herbert A. Simon, *Organizations*, N.Y. 1958, pp. 90–1.

4. For a brief recent summary cf. Elizabeth W. Gilboy, *The Economics of Consumption*, N.Y. 1968, chapter 4. More original is John Owen, *The Price of Leisure*, Rotterdam 1969. Cf. also chapter 4 here.

5. The Soviet-type bank is virtually compelled to make up unplanned losses, and these are very often due to excessive payments of personal incomes. Planned losses are the responsibility of the Treasury, and it should come as no surprise at all that plan-fulfilment bonuses are compatible with them. Whether the enterprise's loss is planned or unplanned, then, personal incomes attached to the wage-fund are guaranteed by the state (chapter 14).

6. For criteria and indicators cf. chapter 9.

7. Chapter 8, sec. 1. But forced productive consumption is also a Communist device for controlling excessive leisure among the well paid (chapter 21, sec. 3).

8. Not each hour of labour will be pleasurable, because the marginal disutility

of labour for such people is still negative, as we saw. Again the labour market does not reduce one's pay in such jobs enough to compensate altogether for the greater enjoyment; since that process only applies to the marginal worker. What I am saying is that the psychological rents of intra-marginal workers are far, far greater in certain occupations than others. The figure in the text is a guesstimate based on answers to the question, 'Would you continue in the same type of work if you inherited a fortune?' (Nancy C. Morse and Robert S. Weiss in *American Sociological Review*, 1955). Other questions produce more favourable answers. I have included guesses for housewives and other groups not covered by the survey. Cf. Robert Blauner, *Alienation and Freedom*, Chicago 1964, pp. 196, 201, 207, 208, idem. in ed. Walter A. Galenson and Seymour M. Lipset, *Labour and Trade Unionism*, N.Y. 1960, pp. 340–3. Workings available on request. A British survey produces even more remarkable, indeed flatly incredible, results (Mark Abrams in *Social Trends*, HMSO 1973, pp. 40, 46). I extract the following replies from many others:

Satisfaction, self-rated (7 high)		don't know	1	2	3	4	5	6	7	mean
		percentage giving each rating								
(100%=182) Job:	Housewives	0	4	3	4	8	13	26	42	5·7
(100%=303)	Employed	0	1	1	2	5	18	32	41	6·0
(100%=593) Standard of living		2	3	3	7	15	27	25	18	5·1

Social class Assent (=7), dissent (=1) to these questions:	AB	C1	C2	DE	
	average of ratings given				
(100%=303) 'The work is interesting'	6·5	6·0	6·0	5·8	6·0
,, ,, 'The pay is good'	5·6	5·3	5·1	4·4	5·3

These results, and especially the last two rows, are extremely 'upbeat'. The average manual labourer cannot seriously rate the interest of his job 5·8 on a 7 point scale, especially when this question is one of 16 about his job, and he shows a fair capacity to differentiate his answers. But each panel at least demonstrates that felt alienation is less than simple economic discontent. A much more left-wing scholar admits, however, to very similar results: Charles Musgrove, *Ecstasy and Holiness*, London 1974, chapter 9.

9. Cf. R. H. Guest in ed. Gene Lyons, *America, Purpose and Power*, New Hampshire 1965; Henri Douard in *Preuves*, Paris, I/1973.

10. The Hutterites are a German, agricultural, Anabaptist sect in North America. They hold nearly all goods in common. Cf. chapter 6, sec. 12.

11. Probably such refined data are only available in multi-national companies. Cf. my attempt to place the English will to work in an international scale: *Oxford Economic Papers*, January 1951.

12. In USSR managerial bonuses used to be paid on the basis of monthly performance. In 1959 the basis became quarterly. The amount is around 20–30 per cent of basic salary (Barry Richman, *Soviet Management*, N.J. 1965, chapter 7). The capitalist bonus is never more frequent than annual, and often much less so. It is more in the nature of a loyalty premium, or a general judgement of a man's efficiency. It is very seldom closely related to current output. Not all managers can expect it every year.

13. Except that his enhanced reputation may get him more orders in future – if we are in a market economy.

14. Cf. Carmelo Mesa-Lago, *The Labour Sector and Socialist Distribution in*

Cuba, N.Y. 1968; Roberto Bernardo, *The Theory of Moral Incentives in Cuba*, Alabama 1971.

15. The university-educated youths who go into the countryside to work and live are all forced ('sent down').

16. This is the opposite of Khozraschet (chapter 11, sec. 13), which Guevara specifically condemned as a big step towards inter-enterprise market relations.

17. Though not every detail of his policy. Notably more sugar was to be planted, in order to finance the Soviet debt. On this later period cf. Carmelo Mesa-Lago, *Cuba in the 1970s*, New Mexico 1974, chapter 2.

18. Not, as is often alleged, sheer general poverty. Many countries much poorer than Cuba (about $400 per head in 1972, at 1972 prices) have unequal incomes, and so can offer material incentives even if they do not grow. General growth makes it easy for a socialist government to offer material incentives, since no-one need lose.

19. Positive supply will of course hold for *parts* of our labour effort, e.g. for a cash crop, a freelance professional activity, or above all the market labour of housewives. Five supply curves of poor married US males are given by Robert E. Hall in ed. Glen G. Cain and Harold W. Watts, *Income Maintenance and Labour Supply*, Chicago 1973, p. 155. Three have a slight negative slope throughout, while the two that include non-participants in the labour force are positive in the lower reaches. But a male non-participant is clearly either like a housewife (doing something useful with his time which the statistics do not record), or sick or a hippie. In the first case we do not know how much he is really working or at what 'real wage'. In the second case he is of no interest. In the third we must estimate his *potential* wage from his other social characteristics (Hall, pp. 111–17) – a most dangerous procedure. Cf. Cain and Watts, ibid., pp. 349 and 352. Further on USA cf. Owen, op cit., pp. 17–18, 151; chapter 21, sec. 12 here. For UDCs cf. Edwin Dean, *The Supply Response of African Farmers*, Amsterdam 1966, pp. 1–10, 81–2; criticized in my *Distribution of Income East and West*, Amsterdam 1974, Lecture IV.

3

Property and Ideology

3

1. Our first duty is to avoid the Victorian and Marxist oversimplification that ownership is an unambiguous, all-embracing, absolute power to dispose of something. The *Idealtypus* here is the owner-manager of a small capitalist enterprise – or the Soviet state under Stalin. Both images are quite obsolete, neither was really illuminating even in its heyday. On the contrary, ownership is a bundle of particular rights. If *enough* of these are united, even temporarily, in one person or organization, we call him or it the owner. There is no question of anyone ever, in any legal, economic or social system, being able to 'do what he likes with his own', if only because he may not commit a crime with it. Only Robinson Crusoe had that power – because he did not live in a society.

The ownership bundle must include at least the following rights:

(i) to found, extend, contract and wind up the business, or in the case of a consumer good to acquire it, consume it or destroy it;
(ii) to take the residual profit of the business or enjoy the residual use of the thing. I say 'residual' because profit is always taxed, and may also be shared out in part, whether under a voluntary or a compulsory scheme, to workers; also land and housing are subject to rights of way, etc.;
(iii) to sell the business, or the right to receive profits from it, in whole or in part;
(iv) to appoint the manager or tenant, if any;
(v) to do whatever is not specified as someone else's prerogative; i.e. to possess the residual power;
(vi) to deal with major crises of all sorts, if there is time;
(vii) to sue and be sued on behalf of the business;
(viii) to be liable, subject to statutory limitations, if any, for the enterprise's debts if it goes bankrupt.

Current decisions as to price, output and employment, and the use of depreciation funds, are often and easily divorced from ownership. Matters of new investment, technique, location and managerial appointment are more often reserved. So are 'important' matters, which is not quite the same thing. But of all these points perhaps (v) is *primus inter pares:* If we were silly enough to want a simple, single distinction between public and private ownership, we should be least silly in enquiring, who has the residual power?

Often the owner delegates the current powers of use, control and enjoyment. The possibilities of such delegation are literally endless, as innumerable as the forms of political organization of which they are a part. But there are two main types: the owner can hand over *possession* or merely *management.*

A characteristic possessor is the tenant of an unfurnished house. Unlike the manager he pays for this privilege. He has the present enjoyment, and is not held to account for any normal thing he does, even if he repaints, so long as he pays the rent. He has a defined security of *tenure* – and for once etymological resemblances are not misleading. The owner even needs permission to enter the building, except in crises affecting the external structure (vi above). The tenant is very hard – increasingly hard – to evict even when he does default. Not for nothing do we say 'possession is nine points of the law'. The owner, in such cases, verges upon a mere creditor, mortgage holder or financier of hire purchase. The owner is or can be distant, the possessor is always close. Husbands own, lovers possess.

Possession is also a business form in the case of small operators vis-à-vis their landlords: tenant farmers, concessionaires. Occasionally the word 'concession' covers a very large business indeed, like an oil company in a UDC, or any capitalist corporation during the Soviet NEP. In Yugoslav ideology the workers' council is a little more than a possessor, and the government, vaguely representing society as a whole (sec. 5 below), is something less than an owner. In Hungary the official position of the director is something between that of a capitalist manager and that of a tenant, since he not only is free to decide current operations but also receives a share of profit; but he has no security of tenure. Market socialism, we may generalize, is a system of private profit and public ownership. It is very much a question whether any system of private profit can be properly called socialist.

2. The contrast between management or control[1] and ownership is better known. No powers are legally transferred. The manager is the mere creature of the owner. Rather than pay for his privileges, he is paid for his services. He has only minimal security of tenure. His practical independence may be very great indeed, and his advice may be invariably accepted in the largest matters, but he is still an employee. Even if he gets a bonus from profit (chapter 2, sec. 9), he does so by the owner's order, not as a right. The people called managers in the various forms of socialism and capitalism have all these traits.

The managerial revolution (chapter 20) is when the manager, as the man on the spot and with the knowledge, informally usurps the owner's power without much changing the legal position, or perhaps even the distribution of income. But the change can be formalized, and indeed opposed, by appointing a committee that frankly represents the owners and examines from time to time the manager's conduct from that point of view. Such in German capitalism is the *Aufsichtsrat*, which has been legally compulsory in a corporation since at least 1870. It originated as a way of countering the managerial revolution, but it has hardly succeeded! Even so it is much better than the absence of any such provision, and its relation to management has often been compared with that of the Yugoslav workers' council to the enterprise director. For the workers' council, as we saw, is almost a complete owner, and it certainly does not manage. Indeed its position is being steadily eroded by the technocracy, just like that of capitalist shareholders.

The managerial revolution has a different aspect in an STE. For strictly there is now only one enterprise, of which the omnipotent single state is both owner and possessor, exercising all the functions enumerated above. But the state is not an actual person or persons, converting the profits, capital gains, etc. of his ownership into consumer goods or political power. There is no such person: political power has already been captured by the Communist Party anyway, surplus profits just go into the general budget and consumer goods are distributed on other principles. The state is conducted by the Party for the sake of ideological satisfactions, and ownership is fundamentally ideological. The power of the Communist Party, then, is what corresponds to that of the shareholders under capitalism; and it is this that the technocracy erodes, introducing rational, non-ideological considerations both at the centre and at the periphery. When, on the other hand, 'enterprise' directors – perhaps we should better call them branch managers – gain freedom from central planners, we call that decentralization. Mere decentralization is, as someone said of the Reformation, *une querelle des moines*; it is within the profession, and need not affect the fundamental order of things. Its relation to the managerial revolution in an STE is very complicated, and must be deferred to chapter 20.

There could be, and indeed sometimes there has been, a similar 'tenants' revolution', in which the possessor has informally eroded the owner's power. Such a thing is the increasing reluctance to raise rents or to evict in the modern world. But mostly changes in the possessor–owner relation are formalized in law, since that is the essence of the relation anyhow: e.g. rent control. Moreover the tenant is no technocrat. It is not expertise that increases his power, but superior political pull.

The classical enterprise owns all its factors of production, and disposes of them by sale or technical transformation exactly as it pleases. In the real world it is often merely the possessor of one factor or another, and this is as important as the question, who owns or possesses the enterprise itself? Indeed in economic and social history, and particularly in theories of capitalist development or of class struggle, the ownership of particular factors of production holds pride of place. In the past social change has been mainly, in the present it is still largely, a matter of shifts of factor-ownership. When we describe feudalism, or the rise of the gentry, or the guild system or the industrial revolution it is the first consideration. Thus the feudal lord owned the demesne farm but had merely certain rights over other land and over labour. The sharecropper, alone among entrepreneurs, owns the labour. The Russian peasant used to say to his master 'you own us but we own the land'. The Yorkshire woollen trade in the eighteenth century was distinguished in that the weaver himself (not the putter-out) owned the yarn; while the Nottinghamshire hosiers did not even own their frames. The Soviet collective farm owns the land but the State owns the growing crops, etc. The typical modern capitalist firm is not very classical either. In theory it owns the product and all factors but the labour and possibly the land. But there are important exceptions: distribution is undertaken by commission agents, runners and brokers who do not own their wares; boots are manufactured with machinery hired from a monopoly; wool is combed and woollen cloth finished on commission; labour is subject in places to indenture or to more severe compulsion; in other places it owns the machinery, and so on.

3. Ownership is a highly ideological matter also outside STEs. By ideology I mean any part normative, part factual, systematic, supposedly rational, emotionally charged and strongly believed social doctrine.[2] It may be taken as a good rule that *serious economic ideologies are about ownership*, for ownership is connected with political power. There do exist economic ideologies with other bases, such as that of the hippies which is really about motivation, or that of the Chicago School of economics, which is really about decentralization. But these strictly entail attitudes to ownership, and therefore political power is never far from the centre of their attention. In each case the definition of ownership is vague and/or wrong, but men are not rational beings and these foolishnesses have shown great power to move them. Economic institutions would not be what they are without these definitions.

The essence of an ownership ideology is a figurehead or Madison Avenue-type image or Weberian *Idealtypus*: 'the' owner, whose position the doctrine exists to *justify*. Ideology is, of course, about justice. In theory this owner holds at least the eight powers and duties enumerated in sec. 1. In practice he may have more, displacing all 'tenants' and 'managers', or less. But if he has less we must speak of a divergence between ideology and fact. In such a case the economy is being conducted in his name, or under his auspices – whatever those words may mean – but not by him nor even, perhaps, in his interest. Believers in the ideology become uneasy and resort to rationalization or – it is much the same – obscurantism. For to them the subject has, as we have seen by our definition of the word, a strong emotional charge. They love their preferred type of owner, and are liable to kill, lie and/or put their heads in the sand to protect him or their image of him.

Ideologies tend to avoid definition and the specification of detail. Indeed they had better, for only by being vague can they survive the buffetings of rational enquiry and actual events. But there is an exception to that rule: Soviet ideology. The Russians are an extremely religious people with a positively Orthodox insistence on static, formal creeds, not subject to reformulation, indeed only to be reinterpreted by the central power itself. Their brand of Communism differs notably in this even from that obtaining in their East European satellites, let alone Yugoslavia, China or Cuba. It is this intellectual virtuosity in defence of a false but rigid system that gives Soviet thought its fascination to certain perverted minds.

4. We begin with two extremes. Early capitalism and Soviet Communism share the great virtue of clarity: ownership means absolute power, unobstructed by subordinates, visibly located. Indeed the two ideologies are in some respects identical. Both apply the same owner-manager-of-the-small-business image to the modern capitalistic world. Both dislike the doctrine of the managerial revolution, and especially deny that it is happening to them. The differences are that the Soviet ideology sees no virtue at all, but only chaos, in competition on a market; and that it simply extends the ownership image to the socialist state, so that the whole STE is supposed to be an enterprise. So a view of property that gives rise to pure *laissez-faire*, and makes state intervention an undesirable impossibility, becomes, simply by concentrating all property in one hand and overlooking the administrative problem, the basis for the myth of perfect central command socialism.

This single enterprise is identified with the state. Its Board of Directors is the Cabinet (or maybe the Politburo). Its treasurer is the Minister of Finance. The profits of its branches, rather misleadingly called enterprises, go automatically to this Minister; they are decentrally retained by grace and favour only. In periods of maximum centralization not merely their profits but their revenues and expenses pass through the state budget (chapter 2, sec. 11). The very word *khozraschet* (commercial accountancy) means the exclusion from the state budget of these ordinary revenues and expenses, and the restriction of the budget-enterprise link to profits, subsidies and investment grants (sec. 12 here). There is not even any distinction between managers and civil servants. There is just one career structure, with total transferability of pension rights, seniority, etc.

In both these cases the view downwards from the enterprise to the worker is very similar. He owns nothing, he is a mere employee, socialist rhetoric notwithstanding. It is no coincidence that in neither system has he even a union to defend him (chapter 7).

In the USSR the simplistic view of capitalist property carries over into the regulation of the domestic non-socialist sector. *Individual* work is permitted, under pretty stringent safeguards, but it is not permitted to employ others or to own enough of the means of production to make that necessary (private work). For that is capitalism and therefore exploitation,[3] the prevention of which is what the October Revolution was about. For instance one kolkhoznik may not offer another a commission to take his produce to the town free market and sell it. For that is employing another, and so exploiting him, even though it is perfectly legal to sell one's own produce this way. Once permitted, individual work is hardly controlled at all; there is essentially *laissez-faire.*

5. We turn to co-operative property. For the moribund ideology of consumers' co-operation see chapter 6, sec. 3. We deal here with the much more vigorous producers' form. Looking downwards, first, from the point of view of the state, what is 'co-operative property' supposed to mean? Populism[4] and Titoism have basically vague, but nonetheless strong attitudes to the subject. Ownership is or ought to be in the hands of the people, not the state; the means of production must be neither private nor nationalized but 'socialized'. The small groups that manage these means, and enjoy their usufruct, are not owners but tenants or possessors. It is important that in many European languages (not the Romance ones) there are two words for 'social'. One has the Latin root (sozial, sotsial'ny, socjalni) and refers to social services, social cost, social considerations; there is always a hint of externalities and of the summation of individual interests. The other word has no common root (gesellschaftlich, obshchestvenny, spoleczni) and means of or pertaining to the community. It is this, the populist, sense of social we are now using.

The community is not, of course, the state. It is not even the public – a bourgeois legal term (öffentlich, publichny, publiczni). It is simply one of those indefinable words for which people like to die. The transition from the impossible to the meaningless does not diminish the importance of ideology, but it does require us to spend more time in its elucidation. When people are muddled, we know what they 'really mean' only when we see what they do. And each of these groups does something different.

The Russian populists stood on the left of populism considered internationally. In their imagination, not the individual peasant but the co-operative village was so to speak a strong tenant, and the community a weak owner, of the land. Their 'ideological owner' was, essentially, this tenant. If pressed for an interpretation of the word 'community' they would have had to come down, with infinite misgivings and for want of anything else, in favour of the state. The state could, naturally, fix tariffs and taxes – they were not anarchists – but what exactly it could do as landowner, after the initial distribution of capitalist and noble estates, is not revealed. Moreover only the land was thus distinguished. Other agricultural property, such as livestock, was and should be private; non-agricultural property could be private or nationalized for all the Russian populists cared.

Lenin's original land expropriation decree – the wording of which he took from a Russian populist newspaper – also gave this idea practical expression. Later the Communists captured the populist rhetoric for their own concept: property under Full Communism, when the state has withered away, will become *obshchestvenny* – as if 'the community' could be a single central planning authority.

Now looking downwards from the village community to the peasant, what does 'co-operative' mean? All livestock, crops and tools belonged to private peasants. Believing in that, the populists would hardly have been allowed today to assume the name 'Socialist-Revolutionary', as they did. Indeed we would call the village's (actual[5] or proposed) manner of owning the land itself co-operative, meaning something less than socialist. Each family is a weak sub-tenant of the strong tenant-in-chief, who can redistribute land according to social need, and decree cropping techniques and timing. No family may sell or mortgage 'its' land. The basic notion is of upper and lower limitations on the amount of land per head, and of independently operating individuals who however enjoy only the usufruct.

The Mexican ejido has a similar system[6] and philosophy. Only instead of periodic redistribution each family is subjected to an upper limit of land-ownership, and severe restrictions on sale. This, then, is even less socialistic, although it too has succeeded in exciting very left-wing emotions in urban intellectuals. Just as anthropologists, so do students of the peasantry see socialism where none is. Even the English open-field village, that nest of petty capitalist vipers, has been enveloped in a socialistic haze by anti-capitalist historians (chapter 5, sec. 4). There is, then, a whole large category of traditional co-operative villages that treat the land (but not other factors of production) as a resource open to all qualified by birth or formal settlement. They therefore restrict its sale so that no family shall impoverish its heirs by improvidence; and restrict its accumulation in few hands so that there shall always be some available for everyone; and even deliberately redistribute it as particular families increase and diminish. They even intervene, therefore, in the relations of paterfamilias with his children, making him into a willy-nilly trustee.[7] Land ownership, then, is in such cases the whole body of laws and customs pertaining: but when is ownership anything else?

6. Modern *Yugoslav* ideology resembles Russian populism in its vague use of the word 'social' to describe the relation between the government and the co-operative. At the beginning of a long but necessary historical digression, one wonders whether too much attention is not paid to Yugoslavia. Twenty million people (only 3½ million engaged in self-management) keep cropping up, chapter by chapter, and not always in a very creditable light, nor in one that is really 'classical', i.e. divorced from an overwhelming mass of historical particularity. Yet if they had not existed it would have been necessary to invent them. They do, after all, tell us *something* about a co-operative society, though in all probability were there many such, Yugoslavia would be a very peculiar case. For, first, this used to be an exceptionally Stalinist country, the nearest to a complete STE of all the new Communist states in Eastern Europe. The Second

World War and the Axis occupation had been hardly more than concomitants of a civil war between the nationalities, with the Communists as the only representatives of Yugoslavia as a whole. All this had left a legacy of great bitterness, and the police practised out-and-out terrorism. Yugoslav foreign policy was exceptionally aggressive towards the West, in ways very embarrassing to the USSR.

Yet in retrospect we can see that the Yugoslav Communists had something the others did not. They had gained power themselves, they were *Stalinists by choice*. They were therefore not infiltrated by Soviet agents: the crucial element in their subsequent self-liberation. They were Protean and rather subtle, hiding themselves behind various front organizations though already in power. They lacked Stalin's mistrust of ordinary people, they held the post-revolutionary progress to socialism to be a spontaneous mass movement. 'Spontaneity' was something Stalin had specifically denounced. They were bound to quarrel with Stalin.

The quarrel began in 1948; its immediate causes do not concern us. Until 1950 the Yugoslav Communists tried very hard to prove themselves even better Stalinists; for instance they ran an agricultural collectivization campaign of great brutality. But the old man wanted submission, not orthodoxy; so they abandoned orthodoxy.

There were two main strands of thought: that of the economic planner Kidrič and that of the more politically minded leaders Djilas and Kardelj. Kidrič wanted to use the market in order to alleviate the rigidities of central planning – which none knew better than he. He never came out publicly for self-management,[8] a reticence which is extremely marked in its context, and strongly implies that he disapproved of it. It was rather the energies of trained managers that he wished to liberate. His own slogan was 'socialist commodity production', which is virtually the translation into Marxian of 'market socialism'. Slightly later Tito adopted and publicized the Djilas/Kardelj slogan of 'workers' councils'. The basic idea here had still less to do with economic rationality. It was precisely that spontaneity mentioned above: Stalinist planning was a straitjacket for the energies of the people as a whole, and workers' councils would set these free.

Growth statistics for this early period are bad, and we cannot say whether Yugoslavia's subsequent rapid but irregular growth was greater than in the Stalinist years, or would have been smaller under continued Stalinism. A glance at Bulgaria next door tells us that there is nothing much in it: that the release of people's energies was countervailed by inflation and the other drawbacks the new system revealed (chapters 6, 14).

Parallel lines point in the same direction: Tito was not possible without Kidrič, since workers' councils, unlike state-appointed directors, must have something to direct. The new system rapidly reduced the banks' 'control by the dinar', the planners' operative annual plan and the administrative allocation of raw materials to nothing.[9] But Kidrič's own dry nostrum could not have stirred the world in the way Tito's did, when he said in parliament, 'the factories to the workers'.

Both leaders concurred, however, in two further ideas. First, the value added in production[10] must be disposed of by those who generated it, and not the central treasury. So rules are promulgated, not dissimilar from the reformed Soviet rules except that they include labour incomes, to regulate this disposal. The federal, and indeed the republican, share of the total surplus is supposed to be small, whereas that of local government can remain as big as that of the enterprise itself. In fact this idea has failed. Workers cannot be trusted with their own added value, since they allocate it all to their own current consumption. They do not hesitate to exploit monopolies and windfalls to this end. The demands of society as a whole are insatiable, and conflict with that of the workers. The percentage of value added taken by tax and persuasion remains much greater than was hoped for in 1950. Innumerable sets of taxes and appropriation rules have been enunciated, and they are a main economic preoccupation of the federal government. It would be very tedious to enumerate these changes, but none of them has been satisfactory.

Secondly, both leaders held that the mistake of USSR had been that the state was not even beginning to wither away. Its vast bureaucracy constituted state capitalism (secs. 12, 13), and Yugoslavia must do better. So in conditions of extreme internal and external danger, when the coercive organs of the state must clearly be retained, a beginning must be made with the planning bureaucracy. This view had innumerable virtues, but one quality it did not have: an orthodox, or even a scholarly and truthful, relation to Marx' own ideas on the withering away of the state (Wiles 1962, chapter 18). It seems on balance more likely that Tito got the workers' council idea from Mussolini (chapter 7, sec. 7). But of course it is in any case an old one.

It is tempting to think of the decentralization of 1948–50 as a concession to regionalism, but it was not so. This is the most regional of all countries in the world, with six republics and (now) two autonomous areas. The richest of these politically defined areas has consistently since 1948 had four times the income per head of the poorest. They differ by language, religion, script and history. However, 'economic concessions to regionalism' means:

(i) a decentralization of the banking system;
(ii) a reduction in the flow of federal tax funds to poor areas;
(iii) greater republican retention of foreign exchange earnings.

Of these, (i) began in 1953, (ii) in 1965, (iii) in 1972. Only the earliest of these concessions to regionalism even appears to be connected with the original reforms. We refer in this case to the increased influence of local councils, not regional governments, over the bank's lending to enterprises on their territories (chapter 6, sec. 2).

The initial Yugoslav reforms, then, reached past regional power centres right down to individuals, enterprises and townships. The nationalities problem came to bedevil this early effort only later, when native influences partly replaced Marxism (or what passed as such). From the middle 'fifties we can speak of a new populist–Marxist–Yugoslav ideology which has driven out anything that could be called orthodox Marxism. The régime's fundamental legitimation is no longer the historically necessary dictatorship of the proletariat but a self-managed society. Both a market economy and a federal state follow at once.

All this affected doctrines of property. State property was good enough for USSR, but it must now be succeeded by 'general-social' (opšte-društveni). And this is what erstwhile nationalized property is now called, and certainly a change of name was appropriate to the very great change of status that occurred in 1950. But what does 'general-social' really mean? Is the workers' council the real 'ideological owner'? If not, how does society make its ownership felt? The answer is, through the remaining, genuinely much weaker, state planning machine, through the special status of the director and through the League[11] of Communists. And this answer in turn can only be specified by describing Yugoslav planning[12] and the relation between director and workers' councils (chapter 20).

Looking now downwards from the Yugoslav co-operative enterprise towards the worker, we meet again a historical prerequisite, much as in Mexico or Tsarist Russia. Only this time it is not slow-growing, deeply-rooted tradition[13] but revolution. Yugoslavia used, as we have seen, to be an unusually Stalinist country. She neither can nor wishes to deny utterly that tradition. First the capitalists were driven out without compensation (and that is a considerable understatement); then an STE was set up; then the enterprises were converted into producers' co-operatives and set free on a market. In the only country that ever seriously imitated her, Algeria, at least the first and third stages were reproduced (chapter 7, sec. 11). This history shifts the nature of the co-operative to the left: since that which is now co-operatized was previously nationalized, there are no relics of private property about it. No ex-peasants keep private plots and cows in a Yugoslav enterprise, or remember with nostalgia how their fathers tilled these very fields in private; these are ex-workers who, by a revolution from above, have been *compelled* to administer *industrial* property, erstwhile wholly nationalized. Producers' co-operation is bound to differ according to whether the general society is capitalist or socialist.

The workers administer but do not own their enterprise. 'Samo-upravljanje' means self-administration, not self-government. The basic idea is of a spontaneous, grass-roots movement of the whole people, liberated by the revolution, towards a more perfect socialism. The people are good and getting better; so they can be trusted with the decentralized current operation of a system whose general movement is predetermined. As to the line between socialist self-administration and petty capitalist exploitation, there remain laws, especially about income distribution. The director, although decentrally elected, is responsible to the government for the observance of these laws. (For recent trends towards mixed and private ownership in Yugoslavia, cf. chapter 20.) Her Algerian imitator, meanwhile, has returned to state ownership.

7. Co-operative property has dogged also Soviet history. This is partly the heritage of Russia, but much more that of the ageing Engels (chapter 5, sec. 7). In USSR co-operation, like so much else, is actually compulsory (where it is not prohibited). The very notion of compulsory co-operation is of course anathema to true believers in the co-operative ideal. This was the basic issue in the allegedly voluntary but in fact bloodily coercive collectivization of agriculture in 1929–30. In other STEs except Poland, but including China, the situation is not widely different. However many millions of peasants are involved, the collectivization of Soviet-type agriculture remains a purely historical phenomenon, defying generalization, logic and – I hope – imitation. It is accordingly postponed to chapter 5, the 'unprincipled' chapter.

But these co-operative farms must eventually be nationalized. Now what is the exact nature of proletarian property? Just how does the victorious proletariat own the means of production? The answer until Tito came along was of course by centralized state ownership, an ownership so centralized that it is not even exercised through independent public corporations but through civil servants, subordinate to ministers who sit in the cabinet. Titoism flatly substituted co-operative for state property as the highest form. And the matter might have rested there, with the Yugoslavs insisting on a formulation that put their industrial set-up nearer full Communism, and the Russians on one that did the same for theirs. But there was the condition of agricultural property to consider also. Now Titoism is essentially a doctrine of 'socialism', and there is no developed Yugoslav view of Full Communism (chapter 21, sec. 4). So Titoists are not unduly worried that since 1953 (when collectivization was declared voluntary) their agriculture shows only the primitive peasant form of private property. It is indeed nothing for a Communist Party to boast about, but it certainly does not affect the standpoint that *co-operative* property is better than *state*. Indeed quite the contrary: for Yugoslav agriculture is still scheduled for ultimate co-operativization. In USSR on the other hand there was a difficulty: if state property is best kolkhozy must be nationalized.

This proposal has a long history. To my knowledge it was never proposed directly to nationalize peasant property before collectivizing it: indeed in USSR, Poland, Hungary, and above all the DDR, large capitalist farms suitable for direct conversion into state farms have actually been broken up among private peasants, with the ultimate intention of collectivizing them, and nationalizing them only after that. The only exception proves the rule: Cuba (chapter 5, sec. 7). In USSR in 1932, that is to say after the 'success' of collectivization, a few proposals were seriously made to change kolkhozy into sovkhozy, a policy later known as 'sovkhozizatsia'. But they were condemned as premature.[14]

Indeed Stalin became hostile to sovkhozy themselves: they cost too much and he thought they should be liquidated.[15] How then could he favour sovkhozizatsia? Yet he had to do something about the ideologically backward form of co-operative property. Before the war he, like Mao in 1958, had thought the kolkhozy should become separate communes, and this remained orthodox until at least 1946. But later he for some reason abandoned this idea. What was he to put in its place? First he allowed his ambitious young minion, Khrushchev, to amalgamate the kolkhozy in the ratio of $2\frac{1}{2}$ to 1 (1950: chapter 5, sec. 6). This was still compatible with the idea of separate communes, though no one said so any more. Then in his last work[16] Stalin did not mention sovkhozy at all. He rejected 'natsionalizatsia', which is of course a periphrasis for sovkhozizatsia, and again took flight forward into Full Communism, but this time on a nation-wide scale. Nationalization is socialization when there is a government; what he now wanted to do was to socialize kolkhoz property along with all other into 'general-people's' property when the state withered away.

When Stalin died the proponents of 'sovkhozizatsia' had a few initial successes, in the strengthening of the planning and audit power of the MTS over kolkhozy, the actual sovkhozizatsia of certain kolkhozy, and the colonization of the virgin lands mainly by new sovkhozy. But in 1958 the main issue was decided against 'sovkhozizatsia': the MTS were abolished and 'we shall take the kolkhozy with us into Full Communism'. Now since the tractors had to be sold to the kolkhozy this was ideologically a step backwards: state property had become co-operative property. So the nature of property under Full Communism had to be re-defined. As this is written, it is orthodox to say that both state and co-operative property will develop into 'general-people's property' – a phrase clearly intended to take the sting out of changes that must remain tantamount to the nationalization of the kolkhozy. It has not yet been revealed what – if any – changes will be made in industry, etc., to convert 'state' into 'general-people's' property. Thus for reasons entirely un-Yugoslav,[17] Khrushchev also demoted 'state' property from first place.

Nevertheless, very many kolkhozy were turned into sovkhozy under Khrushchev, for various reasons: because they were hopelessly inefficient, because they were very intensive and had little labour, or in order to specialize them in suburban horticulture. Khrushchev was certainly not dogmatic on this point.[18]

Khrushchev's successors (1965) stopped even this slow process. For sovkhozizatsia is very expensive to the state, since it is absolutely bound to guarantee the farmer a wage (the kolkhoznik's labour day is just the kolkhoz 'dividend' on the year's unsubsidized working). Moreover a sovkhoz 'must' have better equipment and current supplies – which as a socialist enterprise it gets free of charge. Instead Brezhnev has emphasized another, pre-existing, trend: slow internal changes of the kolkhoz. Already Khrushchev had declared the 'indivisible funds' (i.e. the collective property other than land) of the remaining kolkhozy to 'belong to the whole people'. The phrase is largely meaningless but had at least two practical consequences: kolkhozniki get no compensation when their collective property is sovkhozized,[19] and kolkhoz managements can be ordered to perform such state tasks as school-building out of their own money. He also made it financially possible for kolkhozy to pay monthly advances on the annual labour dividend. These have now become a virtually guaranteed wage at the levels prevailing in sovkhozy, and we cannot speak of the labour-day system any more. Again Khrushchev brought both kinds of farm under one planning, procurement and administrative hierarchy – his successors have changed the hierarchy but not this feature. The looser treatment of state enterprises by the planning reforms of 1965 has helped. For when eventually these were applied to agriculture the sovkhozy received many of the financial liberties (so-called 'full' Khozraschet) that kolkhozy had enjoyed all along. All in all, this is an astounding tale of moderation and pragmatism, and a practical recognition that 'property' is a metaphysical term.

Even so, no one has sanctified the present type of co-operative property. Essentially a kolkhoz, 'democratically' owning and managing an independent bundle of means of production, resembles a Yugoslav state farm with self-management. There are very important historical differences, as we have seen, but they are after all only historical. Whatever 'general-people's property' may mean, it certainly does not mean anything as decentralized as that. And the rejection of such a view led official spokesmen to reject also, even before it was ever formulated, the late 1958 Chinese claim that communes are a step towards Full Communism. For no matter how many of the classical items of Full Communism are realized within a commune, the commune remains an individual group differing in productivity and income levels from other communes, and less than perfectly subject to national central planning. Full Communism is, if not world-wide, certainly at least nation-wide.

This, then, is another, more Marxist, way of 'socializing' state property. The Soviet state has been forced into a 'withering-away' competition by the weight of Marxist tradition and the superior attractiveness of the Yugoslav model. In USSR too property will one day become 'general-people's', but Marxian tradition is better observed in not confusing, as do the Yugoslavs, the obsolescence of the coercive organs of the state with the decentralization of economic planning. For such planning is in Marx central and unitary, and moreover freely entered into by rational men. It will outlast the end of coercion, nay will go on for ever.

8. Many milder doctrines of property, hardly meriting the dread name of ideology, have nevertheless influenced men's behaviour. In some, private property is accepted as good, or at least expedient, but its indefinite accumulation in few hands is bad. 'Wealth', in Francis Bacon's words, 'is like muck; it is not good but if it be spread'. The sharp, but alas avoidable, British death duty and the annual Swedish capital tax are redistributive devices wholly compatible with capitalism. The functioning of the system, in particular the supply of individual thrift, is scarcely at all prejudiced by such taxes – particularly when there are so many alternative sources of public and corporate thrift (chapter 13).

Rather sharper was the practice of the ancient Hebrews: total debt forgiveness within the tribe every seventh year.[20] This must indeed have been a great sacrifice of accumulation upon the altar of equality. But in nomadic conditions, when the principal capital is public land, which is there anyway, irrespective of all thrift, and private livestock, whose numbers vary more with weather and epidemics, the debt amnesty is not so very serious. It is a common practice, however, at the beginning of a new king's reign, even in crop-tilling societies. Indeed, kolkhoz debts were forgiven at the beginning of Brezhnev's 'reign' – a clear harkback to an older tradition. Of course, kolkhoz thrift is enforceable by central decree, so acts of debt forgiveness have no very serious effect on it. I have no record of regular industrial debt-forgiveness in any advanced capitalist society.

Schemes that do not prescribe upper limits, or limit inheritance, or periodically cancel debt are quite ineffective. Into this class falls the West German '*people's capitalism*'; equities in public corporations are sold off to employees and poor people only. But there are no restrictions on resale or inheritance, so the shares eventually find their way into the portfolios of the rich, while the original poor holders merely pocket the mark-up that the favourable terms of issue presented to them. This, then, is the reprivatization of public property coupled with an arbitrary subsidy to the particular poor people who first buy it.

9. *Co-ownership* has larger aims. This is the regular, and perhaps legally compulsory, sale of equity shares in a private enterprise to its own work force. The sale may be at special prices, or even an actual give-away; in this case the share comes as part of a bonus distribution out of profit, and the money bonus that would have been given is deemed to have been paid by the employee for the share. But either way the object is peacefully to make the employees of existing capitalist firms into voting shareholders. The scheme has long been advocated and practised, not without minor success,[21] but seems not to have caught on. We may be brief about the reasons, since many of them also cause difficulties in Yugoslavia (chapters 4, 13).

First – and here co-ownership differs from the revolutionary Yugoslav way – the sums that can be set aside out of dividend for the distribution of employee shares are far too small to affect the structure of ownership within measurable time. Even if the shares are genuinely sold, the sale is inhibited by the normal restraints on a company making new issues: capital gearing, trouble with existing shareholders. It meets also the unwillingness and incapacity of employees to buy. Indeed many employees take a straightforwardly capitalist attitude: why should they risk their savings in the same business that pays their wages? Common sense tells them to put their money into other equities, or insurance, or the special, tax-exempt, fixed interest small savings that abound in welfare states. Above all, resale, death and retirement impose very special problems, since the employee's shares ought always somehow to revert to the labour force. For if they pass by inheritance they pass into the population at large, and eventually into the hands of rich men; and so co-ownership, like people's capitalism, shades off into capitalism. If the shares are sold while the original purchaser is still an employee this process is only quickened; but why should a man not resell a security he has freely bought – indeed if he may not do so why should he buy it? There are many crises in one's life that rationally demand the realization of savings – and one of them is retirement, the precise moment when one ceases to have a moral right to the vote.

The company, then, or some trust fund, must stand ready to re-buy employee shares at all times, and this raises the further problem of who shall vote such shares while they are in limbo. It will be readily seen that these problems are all soluble. But co-ownership begs a very basic question: since it cannot *ex hypothesi* apply to public corporations, and since nationalization as such gives employees no voice, but some other scheme must be imposed on it, why not impose the same scheme on private companies too? If we are British at least, we shall not shrink from asymmetry, but must we substitute a slow and imperfect scheme for a quick and definite one? Such schemes, involving no share transfers, come under the general heading of co-determination (chapter 7).

10. Post-war *British nationalization*, at one time an internationally influential way of dealing with property, has been written off by the author as 'muddled but moderate Stalinism' (Wiles 1962, chapter 1). Whole large branches of production were cut off the capitalist tree, and tied together into single state monopolies under almost unlimited direct state control. We deal with this under state capitalism (sec. 12), of which it forms an undoubted part. But the pre-war public corporation was of rather less muddled lineage: the trusteeship concept.

A trustee, in strict legal parlance, is a sort of disinterested tenant, administering the property for a fee on behalf of the real owner, who enjoys the usufruct. The owner is a minor, a lunatic or someone similar. The British pre-war public corporation was a trust in this sense, the owner being not the state but the public – whatever that meant. This vague phrase enables us to say there is 'general-people's property' already under capitalism! The 'trustees' were not even appointed by the government but by *ad hoc* boards, and they were very free of day-to-day state control. The corporation's charter, which corresponds to the private trust deed, was reviewed by Parliament on renewal, and that was the main control.

It was an honourable concept, and surely also a better one than the state underling to which the Labour government reduced the public corporation after the war. It included a mistrust not only of the state but also of monopoly: the absurd notion that a public corporation should cover a whole sector was rejected. But not enough people were emotionally committed to it, nor was there any real body of doctrine as to how the trustees should behave. 'Disinterested management' (chapter 4, sec. 5, chapter 10, sec. 8) is a highly imprecise idea: one would not die for it. Trusteeship was not a popular ideology but a membrane over a power vacuum. We have already pointed out the connexion between ownership and political power: in this case the state effortlessly occupied the vacuum when it wished to.

Syndicalism, though a strong ideology, had not been able to pre-empt it. Britain had only one syndicalist union, that of the post-office workers, who had naturally become very cynical about state management and wished to run things themselves. But the trouble with syndicalism is that it is fundamentally Marxist: it denies the existence of management. The *present* union leaders will take charge, and their personalities will not change along with their duties. Other British unions were intelligent enough to see that management by unions splits them irrevocably. Consequently they supported the post-war (Labour) concept of nationalization after the General Strike (1926), while tolerating 'trusteeship'.[22] It seems that French and Italian unions have still not learned this.

Syndicalism is completely different from self-management, which requires that trade unions be virtually abolished (chapter 7). This elementary proposition is still considered a paradox in Britain, so both pre- and the post-war ideas on public ownership confused them and condemned them both. To this day the only proletarian supporters of self-management in Britain are syndicalist![23]

11. From mild ideology to none. Many economic systems are fuelled by no religious passion at all, no great view of how society ought to be, or even where political power ought to rest. As a result ownership forms are variegated, experimental and undogmatic. The principal economic system – if we can call it that – without an ideology is developed capitalism. Basically what has happened is extremely simple: the enterprise has become much larger, and this trivial little circumstance has knocked the props out from under the ideology of early capitalism. Thus:

(i) ownership is divorced from management, and the owner-manager is dead;

(ii) limited liability has taken away from the small shareholder the feeling of responsibility;

(iii) technical improvements on the stock exchange affect him similarly: his dividend is not something he decides but a mere investment income like interest; he sells and buys equities as easily as bonds;

(iv) still more important, as a geographically scattered and unenthusiastic absentee he is utterly powerless vis-à-vis block votes of genuinely concerned shareholders: e.g. the founding family, a take-over syndicate or even the existing management (directors *must* own shares);[24]

(v) saving is by managerial fiat, not personal abstinence.

Moreover when we look aside from ownership to other aspects of this non-ideology we find that competition is highly imperfect. This is more due to the diversification of products that affluence and technology bring about than to any monopoly movement, and it is even doubtful whether early capitalism, with its narrow markets, poor communications and unstandardized products, was in fact more perfectly competitive. What is sure is that developed capitalism *seems* to be less so.

Nothing can *justify* such a situation. For it leaves the shareholder, the heir to the proud owner-manager, a fainéant relic, *unequally* enjoying the fruits of an industry he cannot control. Also the whole thing just grew. It is unwilled and unplanned, and most people are so naïf as to suppose justice a product of collective human volition. Then there is a lack of intellectual tidiness; many people are so obsessive that they prefer logical syntheses – which are invariably bogus – to unco-ordinated bits and pieces each of which is internally consistent. Moreover nobody pretends to justify late capitalism in philosophical terms. Under the various types of Communism reality lags behind the ideal, under capitalism it leads.

However the system is expedient, it feeds us, it is the devil we know, we would only kill each other if we tried to change it. Above all, it is highly *tolerant*. It is the only soil on which political freedom can grow (chapter 17), and it makes room for many experiments, even very socialistic ones. Communes, nationalized monopolies, traditional villages – the great corporate forest will accommodate any undergrowth.

12. Nevertheless the state flourishes, and no ACE is free of it. So there occurs that symbiosis of state and corporations we shall call, following Lenin and others, *state capitalism*. The decline of early capitalist ideology has liberated society from inhibitions against the state, and it intervenes in ownership by nationalizing, setting up in business on its own, participating in share capital, and lending at short or long term. It also intervenes as regulator, customer and supplier. Yet little of this worries the capitalists: at the worst they are duly compensated and can start another business (for

the late capitalist economy is a growing one); at the best they make a great deal of money corruptly. For state capitalism as a functioning system, especially in France, cf. chapters 9, 17, 18.

There are three types of state capitalist ownership. (i) The state itself owns very little, and devolves most public ownership on to independent public corporations. These, however closely controlled, derive from the pre-war British trustee system described above. (ii) In a manner characteristically French, the state participates as an equity holder in a business that formally operates under private capitalist law (*compagnies mixtes*), There are lamentably few British examples of this, and those mainly connected with some imperialist venture (British Petroleum, the old Anglo-Iranian Oil and Suez Canal Companies). (iii) Capitalism confines direct government ownership and management, i.e. the Soviet form, to its arsenals and post offices, which used to be royal property and pre-date the state. The British, in a rare burst of logic, actually nationalized (de-statified) the Post Office in 1970 (and the Americans in 1971). The French retain more of this type, under the name *régie* (sometimes now misused): ideally it is confined to simple manufacturing and service operations thought to require little managerial competence, like the tobacco monopoly.

A particularly important case is the state capitalism of Tsarist Russia, which has bequeathed so very much to the USSR, and so to STEs generally. This was in a general way very French, nay actually St. Simonian (chapter 12), with enormous reliance on state-owned or -influenced banks. Both the *companie mixte* and the *régie* were known, and the latter gave to the Communists the name and the idea of *Khozraschet*. For if the *régie*'s gross revenues and expenses pass through the budget, it is a budgetary or non-*Khozraschet* unit, very closely managed by the government. But if only the appropriation account, or possibly the profit and loss account, figure on both sides of the budget, the unit is said to be on *Khozraschet*, i.e. extra-budgetary or a *régie autonome*.[25]

There is precious little ideology in state capitalism – except when the term is abusively applied to USSR by dissident Marxists. But the notion that the Central Committee are a new 'class' of owners, exploiting the proletariat and living off the surplus value yielded by their property, seems to me to darken counsel. The Soviet Union is a state, and as such it has a government, the members of which of course live well, as elsewhere. Foreign policy and internal security are of course twisted to serve these people's own interests, as elsewhere. If it happens that this particular state is a socialist state, so what? If it is a corrupt and tyrannical betrayal of socialist ideals, that is only to be expected, and only a madman will call it capitalist just because it is bad. In any case it certainly has an ideology, which sets it quite apart from real state capitalism.

For in the genuine article there is more or less indifference about property; so how could there be a proper ideology? It might seem that no more need be said, but the End of Ideology is hard to accept. We postpone the argument about False Consciousness and state capitalism to chapter 17, sec. 12.

13. In theory any market system can harbour all the diverse forms of ownership, and this brings us to the question of *institutional laissez-faire*.[26] *Laissez-faire* is normally understood as freedom of production and location decisions: a purely market concept concerned only with business details. But we ask now whether government, law and public opinion are indifferent between the models themselves. Are enterprises of each model permitted to develop freely under the judgement of, say, the market and the willingness of people to work in them? Is there institutional competition or institutional monopoly? Are taxation and licensing indifferent between models?

Astonishingly little attention has been paid to these questions. Yet they seem to the writer absolutely crucial. For obviously institutional *laissez-faire* is a good thing in itself: it subjects dogma to the test of experience. Nor is the market (or planning) test to which the competing models submit one of profit at standard rates of pay: a model which people like to work in for lower reward may beat a more 'efficient' but less happy model. Thus small shops survive, paying their owners profits lower than the average wage of an assistant in a supermarket; Hutterite communities survive, despite a tremendous renunciation of modern ways and living standards, etc., etc. And of course not all people like the same thing, so that if the test of competition shows that most small shops succumb to supermarkets the fact of institutional *laissez-faire* nevertheless permits the eccentric to open another small shop – if he really likes that life let him have it. Thus at least some square pegs find square holes, or at the very least the boring of square holes is not forbidden. On the other hand where the model is compulsory we may be working neither in the most efficient nor in the happiest way, unless by some chance we all resemble each other and the chosen model is also the 'best' one for us. Moreover, since men and techniques change, the best model of today may be tomorrow's second best, and that is yet another argument for institutional *laissez-faire*.

Freedom does not mean that the state must never intervene to protect a particular model; for every kind of circumstance may militate against fair and equal opportunity, and a sort of Federal Trade Commission may be necessary here too to protect 'peaceful co-existence'. For instance in many countries capitalist traders have conspired to strangle consumers' co-operation.

Even the STE can co-exist with, or contain within its national boundaries, other models. Most simply, it can leave a capitalist or co-operative sector on a market and deal with it as if it were a foreign country. Or again, while preserving differences of ownership, the kolkhoz and the private peasant can be given the same kind of enterprise plan as the sovkhoz. In this case the three types can be judged on their 'competitive' ability to deliver the goods under a system of central command, instead of in a market. And in fact Poland until 1971 imposed compulsory deliveries on its peasants, much as if they were collective farms.[27]

The STE commonly operates the same mixture of ownership in handicrafts, but less often in transport, trade, building and light industry. It is quite unknown in heavy industry and banking, the 'commanding heights'. The greatest case is the East German mixed industrial enterprises.[28] These were kept semi-nationalized by Ulbricht in pious hope of the reunification of all Germany. But they were fully integrated into the industrial planning system, and distinguished only by the large profit the 'owners' drew. Honecker brought this to an end in 1971–2, when the success of Bonn's new *Ostpolitik* stabilized all German frontiers and reduced reunification prospects to nil. But all along these enterprises were bogus, for since the 'owner's' profits depended on extremely detailed state action they had no social function as criterion, incentive or indicator. The issue here is the degree of detail in the enterprise plan. In Communist agriculture there is plenty left over for an entrepreneur to decide once he has made his compulsory deliveries; in industry scarcely anything. But we have it on good authority that PAX, the fellow-travelling Catholic organization in Poland, ran its publishing and light industrial enterprises more efficiently than the state, although they were fully planned. Here again, since we are dealing directly with the consumer, there must have been some decentralization.[29]

Where the STE's relations to these peripheral bodies are not those of plan-and-command but of market, their existence is a very great technical advantage to the planners, since it provides a cushion for all their miscalculations. If their plans cause the demand for any product or factor of production to exceed or fall short of supply, there is the free market to absorb or disgorge the differences. True, there are political difficulties: the free enterprises may work either too well or not at all. For instance, they are told to keep off certain raw materials or markets required in the planned sector, so they cease to make profits. They must then somehow be included in the plan, perhaps even subsidized; so why not nationalize them and be done? Or at the other extreme they successfully exploit the bottlenecks and the black markets that central planning invariably creates, and become irrationally profitable. Then either the plan should be changed so as to put them out of business or again they should be nationalized. But none of that lies in the technical necessities of the Soviet-type model; rather in the likely political reaction of the sort of state that establishes it.

All other models are, so far as their mere machinery goes, as compatible with democracy as with totalitarianism. Political totalitarianism, moreover (if not Marxist), may well permit institutional *laissez-faire* (below). Or if its theology is basically economic it may enforce a model other than the Soviet one, as in Yugoslavia (co-operative and municipal socialism, and woe betide you if you express doubts about them), or in many capitalist countries (where at certain periods it has been dangerous to support co-operative or socialist models). In Yugoslavia the slogan 'our own road to socialism' has meant not institutional *laissez-faire* at all, but the right of the local Communist Party to settle its own model: *cujus regio ejus religio*.

To *enforce* a model other than the STE, then, is even more totalitarian than freely to choose an STE. It implies that the ruling group know what people 'really' want, and is going to give it them at any cost. The classic case of this is the Communist refusal to let collective farms freely and fairly compete with peasant farms. But one cannot exempt many British socialists from the same condemnation, since unlike the socialists of Western Europe they evidently intended[30] monopolistic nationalization to be a universal pattern, not subject to empirical tests. The electoral pendulum, however, brought about a co-existence of their own model and that of advanced capitalism before the latter could be altogether destroyed. To all scholarly attempts to see which is better these socialists turned a deaf ear.

Finally it is not sufficiently realized that institutional *laissez-faire* has already given rise to countless experiments. In free countries every model except that of the STE has very often been tried out–and the capitalist war economy reproduces many features of that, too. Even where advocates of capitalism have a disproportionate influence on law, opinion and government, other models are seldom interfered with. Indeed they often obtain subsidies and legislative favours. We are, then, entirely justified in pointing to the empirical results in the markets of capitalist countries as an *indication* of the relative efficiency of the models. Mexican and Israeli agriculture are the classic cases.

But there are two big qualifications. First different people have different traditions – it is not a question of 'own ways to socialism' but of 'own ways to economic organization of any kind'. Who can doubt, for instance, that the genius of the American people is not best expressed by public enterprise?

Secondly, a model needs elbow room. To function properly it requires a large group of ideologically committed, or at least tolerant, employees and practitioners. There must be a specialized press and trade schools. It is not enough that laws and taxes be neutral: the government must be willing to help with new laws, to modify particularly burdensome taxes, etc. All this, co-operative forms have achieved in ACEs, especially Israel. But neither Yugoslavia nor China nor any STE provides as much for models other than the one preferred: far from it indeed. Even in China and the DDR capitalists were politically and fiscally hounded even during the periods, now over, when they were officially permitted. Elbow room is a matter of political will. All the countries named here are run by Communist Parties, and this is the reason for their common intolerance. But there is an additional, more technical, factor: the STE differs from all the other models in that it includes the state by definition. It does not require state favour, it *is* the state; and to grant state favour to other models would be to undermine itself.

On these grounds, then, there is a very great deal to be said for developed capitalism, but only because it is tolerant. We are really arguing against ideologies, and not the economic systems to which they have given rise. We may even go further and admit that these systems could only have been brought into being by fanatics: that there is an initial resistance to change which no merely tolerant person can overcome.

Note also that a non-economic ideology, believed in by a racist or religious fanatic, can make use of virtually any system. Indeed such fanatics are often very empirical and open-minded in these peripheral matters. The Nazis come to mind. They supported agricultural prices, prohibited the parcellation of small farms, introduced people's capitalism, liquidated collective bargaining, controlled wages and prices, invented exchange control, nationalized nothing directly, set up state enterprises when thev felt it necessary, and also sold them off.[31]

14. The formal incidence of the income and/or profits tax in a country is a beautiful example of economic ideology at work. In individualist theory there is no such thing as public income, only the incomes of persons. Therefore the private corporation is only a group of individuals, who must be taxed as such, and to tax a corporation as such is to imply it has a moral identity, over and above its necessary minimum of legal identity, that it does not deserve. Indirect taxes are of course levied on goods, and it is no sin if corporations, as the sellers of these goods, have to pay the taxes. But direct taxes, whether on income or on capital, fall on persons alone. This doctrine was carried forward in Britain until 1937. The corporation paid the standard rate of income tax on whatever it ploughed back, simply because it would have been administratively impossible to attribute the ploughback to each shareholder and tax him on his aliquot part at the rate appropriate to him. But on dividends paid out each shareholder did pay at the latter rate. If the corporation here too was forced to deduct the standard rate and pay it directly to the treasury this was merely to facilitate collection; the shareholder reported this deduction, and then paid or received the difference so as to make up his appropriate personal rate. There was no profit tax or other tax on corporate incomes as such: it would have been double taxation.

In 1937–65 this inhibition disappeared. All profits of incorporated businesses, whether distributed or not, were subjected to a special extra tax. According to the old philosophy this was to tax the profits of a group of people who had incorporated their business more heavily than if they had been a partnership or a number of separate owner-managers, or indeed bondholders of the same business. In other words it was simply and solely to penalize incorporation, though the legal act itself had already been subjected to special fees and charges, and incorporated enterprises were already far more strictly controlled; and to impose the necessity of higher profit margins on goods produced by them.

The case against such discrimination seems to me now, as it did to the primitive capitalists who made it then, irrefutable. But left-wing Britain actually reverted to more or less the old system in 1965, in contrast to such reactionary places as Germany, Switzerland and USA.[32] Not to double-tax corporate profits is to be deaf to the music of the times: nobody argues about it any more. Whatever its origins in local jealousy, fiscal greed or sheer unreason – nay, very likely in the envy and malice of small businessmen – this discrimination now rests securely on the separate legal identity of the corporation in a developed capitalist society. The needs of the law stringently demand this identity – but how, when taxes take 40 per cent of the national income, could a legal entity avoid being a fiscal one?!

Western textbooks on the national income often neglect or mistreat the item, incomes of state enterprises. For even double-taxed corporate incomes have the decency to accrue in the end to persons, whatever the philosophy of the tax-collector or the lawyer. Even when undistributed they can be set down, in a perhaps self-contradictory phrase, as private but not personal savings. But state profits are by the maxims of early capitalism an ontological absurdity: income not accruing to a person. Being very small under capitalism they can be hidden away as budgetary revenue. But this they are not; they are not transfers through taxation but income generated by production, a normal yield on capital which just happens to be publicly held. It is true that in capitalist countries state enterprises are not allowed to raise their prices, and their yields are unnaturally low, and it is true that the opposite holds in STEs. But this does not alter the logical status of these profits, it is merely one more doubtful facet of the actual quantities recorded in national income accounts.

There exist, then, both private and public undistributed profits. The former, under capitalism, are usually attributed to shareholders in general and taxed at an average rate of income tax, plus the corporation tax on all profits. The latter are usually taxed at the same rate – which tells us volumes about the 'ideology' of advanced capitalism. The STE knows nothing of private corporate profits but does generate very large public profits. For these it has a very special régime. For the state cannot tax what it already directly owns: to tax is to transfer into the ownership of the state. The profits accrue in principle to the treasury, and are retained lower down as a privilege, just as they would be by the branch establishment of a capitalist corporation. Some are even distributed, in various forms of controlled bonus. But the largest part, especially in the classical STE, is paid to the treasury under the name 'deduction' (*ischislenie*), not 'tax', and under two headings: first, such and such a percentage of planned profit, secondly a lower rate on above-plan profit, thirdly, the 'free remainder' at 100 per cent.

The free remainder is a highly significant item, clearly betraying the ownership theory that prevails. Whatever may not be retained for this or that specific purpose goes straight to the boss. It is, to repeat, not a tax but an administrative clawback, just such as operates for government departments (including *régies*) under capitalism.

In Yugoslavia the personal income tax and the profits tax are amalgamated into one tax on the enterprise's value added or income (*dochodak*). There is no other tax on personal income from work in the socialist sector, since there are no wages but only 'personal receipts' (*lična primanja*), which are a particular way in which value added is appropriated. Since there is no profit either but again only value added there is no profit tax. So in this case there really is no double taxation, and the dominance of ideology is demonstrated once more. Note the impossibility of a progressive personal income tax under these rules – a fateful restriction upon a market economy dedicated to social justice. The tax on enterprise income is formally paid of course by the enterprise, not the worker.

Notes

1. Foreign readers, to whom some other European language is native, should remember that 'control' is a very strong word in English. It means much more than merely 'audit' or 'check'.

2. In the young Marx ideology is neither systematic nor supposedly rational, but unconscious and only revealed to the outside observer, who should preferably be the young Marx. Modern Communists use the word more or less as I do, but without pejorative overtones: since they include Marxism as an ideology, but while not denying its emotional charge endeavour to erect a theory of knowledge that makes an epistemological virtue of it.

3. But one may engage in private medical practice as a single person, and even exercise a craft. Maidservants are also allowed, since the labour theory of value only applies to goods, not services! For the definition of exploitation, cf. my article 'Ausbeutung' in *Sowjetsystem und Demokratische Gesellschaft, eine Vergleichende Enzyklopädie*, Freiburg 1966; and Wiles 1969, chapter 1. We do not further discuss exploitation in this book.

4. For the non-economic aspects of Populism cf. chapter 5, sec. 16. For the semantic distinctions that follow I am indebted to Wlodzimierz Brus.

5. I.e. actual in many regions until Stolypin's reforms of 1906; and never wholly abolished until collectivization in 1929.

6. Except the collective ejidos founded in the 1930s: cf. chapter 6.

7. This branch of law and custom continues even in the kolkhoz. Cf. chapter 16, sec. 6.

8. Cf. Wiles 1962, pp. 36–41. But if Kidrič wanted more 'rationality', he understood the term quite vaguely, since he knew no Western welfare economics: cf. I. Maksimović in *Essays in Honour of Oskar Lange*, Warsaw 1964, pp. 349–50. Milovan Djilas' memory must be at fault here, but for the rest I adopt his version of these events. Cf. his *The Unperfect Society*. N.Y. 1969, pp. 219–222.

9. In a general way if a Communist country has not these three institutions it is not an STE. Hungary and China are the other notable examples.

10. Kidrič said 'surplus value' – cf. my loc. cit. But it is clear he meant also the incomes of the labour force.

11. No longer Party, for it too is withering away! As this is written, after the purge of Serbian liberals, in late 1972, the League is regaining importance in the economy.

12. I do not attempt this virtually impossible feat. For the general flavour cf. Wiles 1962, p. 75; chapter 12, sec. 20 here; Deborah Milenkovitch, *Plan and Market in Yugoslav Economic Thought*, New Haven 1971; George Macesich, *Yugoslavia*, Virginia 1964.

13. In Mexico it is disputable, and in Russia it was more than disputable, whether the co-operative village had such roots or was a recent creation.

14. Compare the references in V. Gsovsky, *Soviet Civil Law*, Ann Arbor 1948, Vol. I, p. 708.

15 As was revealed by Khrushchev later in *Pravda*, 7 March 1964.

16. *Economic Problems of Socialism in U.S.S.R.*, Moscow 1952, 'Concerning Yaroshenko'.

17. 'General-social' (*opšte-društveni*) is a normal Yugoslav word for property in the socialist sector of that country, since workers' control was introduced. The Russian is *obshche-narodni.* The distinction between 'social' and 'people's' is probably without ideological significance.

18. Allan Ballard in *Problems of Communism*, July 1961; Karl-Eugen Wädekin, *Die Sowjetischen Staatsgüter*, Harassowitz, Wiesbaden 1969.

19. This is not unfair since they continue to benefit from the productivity of these assets.

20. *Deuteronomy*, 15/1–6. This is clearly allied to the prohibition of usury within the tribe: *Deuteronomy*, 23/19–20. Cf. Benjamin Nelson, *The Idea of Usury*, Princeton 1949.

21. French law now supports it: cf. Pierre Sudreau (chairman of working group), *La Réforme de l'Entreprise*, Documentation Française, Paris 1975. For UK cf. Acton Society Trust, *Wider Shareholding*, London 1959; A. B. Atkinson in *Economica*, August 1972; George Goyder, *The Future of Private Enterprise*, Oxford 1951.

22. On early British public corporations cf. Herbert Morrison, *Socialization and Transport*, London 1933; Lincoln Gordon, *The Public Corporation in Great Britain*, Oxford 1938. For the post-war period cf. D. N. Chester, *The Nationalised Industries*, 2nd edn., London 1951.

23. Cf. ed. Ken Coates and Tony Topham, *Workers' Control*, revised edn., London 1970.

24. Banks and insurance companies often have block votes, but prefer to lie low, except in West Germany.

25. Cf. R. W. Davies, *The Development of the Soviet Budgetary System*, Cambridge 1958. For the Cuban controversy on this matter chapter 2 here. For *Khozraschet* cf. chapter 12, sec. 15.

26. Here I paraphrase my op. cit. 1962, pp. 12–15.

27. The Soviet kolkhoznik's private plot also suffered in this way until 1957.

28. China had more of them for a long time, but is and was not an STE. Today Yugoslavia leads in the tolerance of petty capitalism.

29. G. Pisarski, 'PAX', in *Zycie Gospodarcze*, 7 July 1957.

30. I use the past tense because the Party Congress of October 1957 makes it probable that this tendency has been finally defeated.

31. C. W. Guillebaud, *The Economic Recovery of Germany*, 1933–8, London 1939, esp. pp. 104, 218–22. Maxine Y. Woolston, *The Structure of the Nazi Economy*, N.Y. 1941; also chapter 7, sec. 7 here.

32. Note that all three were federal countries in the nineteenth century. The lead in taxing corporations was taken by state governments, unable otherwise to strike at out-of-state recipients of incomes generated in their territories. The federal governments merely followed in their wake. On this whole question cf. Edwin R. A. Seligman, *Essays in Taxation*, N.Y. 1897, pp. 243–54; Harrison B. Spaulding, *The Income Tax in Great Britain and the United States*, London 1927, chapter 7; Cesare Cosciani, *The Effects of Differential Tax Treatment of Corporate and Non-Corporate Enterprises*, OEEC, Paris 1959. Note too the less ideologically offensive discrimination between ploughback and dividend. We tax the former more heavily in order to force funds back out onto the stock exchange and so increase the perfection of the capital market; or the latter more heavily in order to increase investment volume. Cf. A. R. Prest, *Public Finance*, 5th edn. London 1975, pp. 175–6, 362–72.

4
Enterprise Types and their Maximands

4

1. An enterprise is a congeries of people. It is not a mere congeries, since it has more solidarity than an 'agency', like a trade union (chapter 7), but it has less than a commune or a family (chapter 6; sec. 9 here). An enterprise has, strictly speaking, no interests of its own, or as I have said elsewhere: 'Having, as the lawyers say, neither body to be imprisoned nor soul to be damned, the firm has no leisure to be preferred either' (Wiles 1961, p. 176). It cannot even respond to incentives, since it has no appetite. It cannot discount the future since it has no impatience. Everything we say about enterprises is a dangerous generalization about group behaviour. All language to the contrary, treating the enterprise as an individual is metaphysical. Thus lawyers, in order to sue it, openly resort to legal fictions.

This simple fact has implications for the theory of the firm that should be described as revolutionary. Just as once Mrs. Robinson[1] said of monopoly:

> 'Now no sooner has Mr. Sraffa released the analysis of monopoly from its uncomfortable pen in a chapter in the middle of the book than it immediately swallowed up the competitive analysis without the smallest difficulty',

so now we must say of the 'Illyrian', or labour-controlled, enterprise that it is swallowing up the whole theory of the firm without the smallest difficulty, and subsuming it under the theory of the individual.

Indeed we must go further still: neo-classical economics has no theory of the firm, but a theory of markets, i.e. of the firm's 'foreign policy'. I feel great piety towards the theory of markets and do not wish to denigrate it. But it presupposes owner-managed capitalist enterprises, and that is not enough. Its firm is a 'black box', or at best a total-profit-maximizer with a production function.[2] It is administration theorists, not economists, who have opened up this black box. And this situation is unobjectionable so long as we recognize our limitations. But there are questions about the internal behaviour of firms that only economists put, whoever answers them. It is the *Illyrian revolution* in the theory of the firm that begins to throw light in this area.

For why has 'imperfect competition' been such a poor guide to economic realities? Why have economists so little of value to say about take-over bids; the internal structure of large firms; the influence on farm investment of the farmer's age; the low-dividend-high-capital-gain corporation? Why, above all, is there no positive theory of private investment decisions? The answer is, because we have all implicitly assumed that the firm is the appropriate thing to have theories about. It is not. The actors in the economy, even in a centralized command economy, are individuals; they coagulate, rather transitorily, into the entities we call firms, which have but limited claims on their loyalties.

Yet at the same time every enterprise is a small command economy. The very best definition of an enterprise is any group of people among whom methods of command or administration are used, and who are not expected to respond in the short run to market stimuli.[3] When the foreman of the morning shift reaches the steelworks he does not say to the roller: 'Joe, I notice in my *Financial Times* (or it says here on the ticker tape from company HQ) that there's going to be a good market for sheet $\frac{1}{8}$ inch thick: why don't you run some of that off for a change and see how it affects your bonus?' The foreman says, 'Joe, $\frac{1}{8}$ inch this morning.' He gives an order, and the market does not directly play any role. If it did, Joe would be earning a fee not a wage; he would be an independent contractor.

There is no contradiction here. The firm remains a congeries of individuals, but it has bought their time. Within limits, known as his zone of compliance (chapter 2, sec. 4), Joe will do as he is commanded. What that zone is, has been settled more or less in some previous wage bargain. Market relations only act when the zone is transgressed or renegotiated.

An individual *might* choose to maximize his profits: though it would mean he wanted money more than any other thing at all, and that, as we saw in chapter 2, is a most unlikely state of affairs. But if he did, he would be maximizing, not some organization's profit, but his own discounted life-stream of income.[4] Our problem is the extent of the *consilience of individual life-time income with enterprise profit*. In what follows we consider the top or middle-level manager, the capitalist shareholder and the member of the Yugoslav workers' council – anyone able to influence the enterprise's actions by non-market means. A striking worker, be it noted, is using market means, at least under capitalism. His strike is a cost to the enterprise like any other, and determines the conditions under which profits can be made.

Now one way in which our manager can increase his income-stream is promotion within his department; but this may depend on some other indicator than the firm's profit, e.g. sales or number of employees. Secondly, he can seek promotion by leaving the enterprise, in which case any damage to it is acceptable to him. Thirdly, he can buy equity shares in competitors or customers. He may also combine these two moves; especially if he carries with him trade secrets, his marginal 'productivity' will far exceed his skill. Fifthly, he must eventually retire, and will therefore shorten his time horizon while the others concerned do not. Sixthly, he has to rest and amuse himself. The interest of the enterprise is that he should have no more leisure than the minimum required for his efficiency.

But his own life-time plans include a private life and a large element of psychic income from leisure. Last but not least he may engage in every possible form of corruption.

Broadly speaking, the Chicago school treats men as enterprises, while the present writer treats enterprises as (composed of) men. That is, the 'human capital' analysis subsumes all, or at any rate much, of individual behaviour under the theory of the firm. It further carries over the notion of a maximand: for 'profit' read 'life-time income'. The 'Illyrian' analysis, as we have seen, flatly breaks up the firm into a democracy, or an oligarchy, or at any rate a polity, of individuals. It may or may not insist on the non-economic, i.e. non-maximizing, behaviour of these individuals, both as the firm and as themselves.

2. If we look at the firm in this way, we ask, *to whom* does the profit accrue? At least the following beneficiaries can be distinguished:

(a) the equity shareholder, as in sec. 6 below (Atlantis);
(b) the worker, as in Yugoslavia (Illyria);
(c) the landowner, as in share-cropping (sec. 21);
(d) an owner providing both capital and labour, as in sec. 3 (Helvetia);
(e) the state, as provider of capital. Cf. sec. 4 (Pannonia, the 'Hungarian' market socialism), sec. 5 (disinterested management), sec. 14 (the STE);
(f) the consumer or other purchaser, as in a retail co-operative shop.

The state of course is also a group of people, and a particularly complicated one.

Following Benjamin Ward, we shall often prefer, for analytical purposes, *Idealtypen* to actual countries. We build upon his inspired choice of the appropriate classical place-name, Illyria. Each such place-name denotes a mythically pure country using only the beneficiary listed, who is further supposed to maximize his benefit. Other types of purity, notably perfect competition, are not assumed.

We see that any factor of production may be the *equity-bearing factor* (*e.b.f.*). It will receive the residual income and take the ultimate decisions.[5] The e.b.f. therefore seeks to maximize its life-time income, i.e. the rate of income or profit per unit of e.b.f., and not the absolute sum of the enterprise's profit. But given units of the factor may not bear the equity. Thus loan capital is simply hired at fixed interest, and has no control at all; even in bankruptcy it is merely one of the classes of debtor and assumes neither more nor less control than other debtors. Yet loan capital 'works' alongside equity capital. Again there can be hired labour in a co-operative or commune, working under the conditions of a fixed contract and sharing no power, no *membership*, in the enterprise. Strictly, however, and in sharp contrast to loan capital under capitalism, hired labour is forbidden in Yugoslav co-ops, though outside the law it is common enough.

Kibbutz ideology is no less opposed to hired labour. But the Israeli government does not share this ideology, and faces an unemployment problem among unskilled immigrants. It forces all enterprises, including kibbutzim, to employ them, but kibbutzim are properly choosy about admission to membership, and confine this labour to the industrial enterprises on the periphery of the kibbutz (which however now yield one half of their gross). In Britain the many producers' co-operatives of the nineteenth century took one of two paths: extinction through labour indiscipline and failure to plough back, or 'bourgeoisification'. The latter path meant the expansion of hired, unskilled labour while the nucleus of co-operators degenerated into shareholders who happened to work in the enterprise. The best non-ideologically charged example of hired labour working alongside members is the lawyers' and stockbrokers' partnerships of capitalism.

These distinctions matter less so long as the quantity of the e.b.f. is constant. For then whatever increases the profit of the firm increases also the life-time income of each unit of the factor, i.e. the firm continues in principle to maximize the *rate* per unit of e.b.f., but does succeed *en passant* in maximizing an absolute sum. It follows that it equates marginal cost with revenue in the textbook manner. For that is of course only possible if total profit, and no rate of return on anything, is maximized. Where capital is the e.b.f., we think, loosely[6] but not misleadingly, that only investment decisions increase its quantity, so only investment raises the question of divergences between the absolute sum and the rate, and then only when it is financed by a new equity issue. So for the most part capital is quite fairly treated like any other hired input as simply a cost.

It might seem that this whole analysis applied to the labour-controlled or the mixed enterprise (d above): we simply substitute the appropriate e.b.f. But the trouble arises when labour is the e.b.f. in that it is a so much more variable input than capital. Not only investment but also current output decisions throw up divergences between the life-time income of the unit on the factor and the profit of the enterprise, as we have seen. A further objection to the doctrine of symmetry[7] between Illyria and Atlantis is that equity capital is mobile and self-confident. No sane person is forced to invest his capital, like his labour, all in one place. So capital does not have to behave like a dog in the manger, resisting all expansions and lay-offs. Nevertheless for perfection we should be in 'Pannonia', where there is no e.b.f. at all. For an e.b.f. always interferes with optimality (sec. 7 here, and chapter 10, sec. 13).

To maximize the profit of the enterprise, without asking how it affects the ultimate beneficiaries, is to reify it. Our 'congeries of people' becomes a person, and we have followed the lawyers into making fictions about corporations. The very phrase, 'the theory of the firm', is philosophically dangerous. A firm might be too complicated an entity to generate any theories at all.

3. *Could*, then, an enterprise maximize its profit? What intra-group conditions would have to hold for that? Let us confine ourselves to enterprise forms that at least might behave accordingly.

The first and in many ways the best case is where the enterprise is only a person (or nuclear family), and so is almost a stranger to intra-group conflict. Such are peasant farms and single pedlars or craftsmen. Small, rebarbative and vigorously independent, we call them, of course, 'Helvetian'. Here the whole labour force is 'managerial' in the most thoroughgoing way, devoting itself to the business. If they want to maximize their profits they will, subject only to leisure preference, which interferes with their supply of equity-bearing labour, and to futurity discount, which similarly restricts their supply of equity-bearing capital. Conceptually these are quite difficult. Presumably we want to say that the peasant's backward-sloping supply curve of products is identical to the worker's backward-sloping supply curve of labour (chapter 2, sec. 12). Then we must say that there is a psychic cost of specifically entrepreneurial labour, which the peasant enterprise treats as external, and 'buys in'. So the profit that is maximized is net of this cost, and includes any quasi-rents connected with it. And this holds even though entrepreneurial labour 'demands itself', i.e. determines the number of firms that exist; and though it is divisible into hours, and so is in no way fixed, the peasant can increase his supply of it, perhaps hiring manual labour to make up the difference.[7a] The shape of the supply curve remains upsetting, but the causes for it are quintessentially Benthamite. In the same way the enterprise may not plough back very much because of 'its' (i.e. the owner's) low futurity discount, and much will depend on the age of the present head of the family. A more real exception to the profit maximand in this enterprise is that, employing only family members, it pays them the average not the marginal product of labour. For all are equal, and the supply of labour is demographically determined (sec. 9).

A less good case is the small one-man-owner-managed capitalist enterprise. Here again no intra-group problems arise. Hired labour there now is but it is unskilled and without influence on the firm's policy. Its supply curve is simply a part of the objective cost conditions. But there remain conflicts of interest within the manager's breast. For he too can acquire an equity in a competitor or customer, and sacrifice the interests of his enterprise to his own. And his approach to retirement remains a very serious distorting factor – he may with entire ease run down the firm's capital to buy an annuity, and he may even liquidate it for lack of a suitable heir, although a stranger could have carried it on. One conflict of interest at least is excluded: corruption. To bribe the owner-manager or peasant is in no way different from offering them a higher price. They are the only incorruptible manager; because they are so by definition. Where corruption is logically possible, it occurs.

4. Another very likely case for profit maximization is 'Pannonia'. In what used to be an STE detailed planning of inputs, outputs and technology is abolished, and the order is given to the (single) director to maximize enterprise profit on a market. Also, bonuses to him and senior employees are made proportional to profit. So *he is not allowed to choose another maximand*, and even just before retirement his interpretations of this policy should not change. Further, the absence of capitalism means that conflicts of interest are minimized. These, we have seen, are the great stumbling block in the movement from the individual to the enterprise. Salesmen still want products that sell well regardless of cost, because that way lies promotion for them, and engineers still want to use the latest technique regardless of cost, for the same reason. But at least no one has equity shares in customers or competing enterprises. It is evident that the consilience of employee's life-time income and enterprise's profit is far from complete even in principle. But a better case will hardly be found among large enterprises.

5. An at least simple case is what we may call 'disinterested management'. This phrase arose in the nineteenth century in connexion with the trade in alcoholic beverages: in Sweden and certain other places pubs were nationalized and the managers were instructed not to push or advertise, but simply to serve the customer within the limitations laid down by law. They were paid a salary; profit or loss went to the government, or possibly some trustee.[8] British readers will recognize, *mutatis mutandis*, their own nationalized industry boards. To a capitalist or Soviet-type[9] Communist this is a queer arrangement: for how can a manager who does not personally benefit from the results, however defined, of the enterprise, be efficient? The senior capitalist manager is compelled by the articles of association to possess equity shares, and that interests him in the profit; the Soviet manager gets a bonus for plan-fulfilment.

Certainly the probability of mere idleness is rather great; and although this is a rational, 'Benthamite' solution of the manager's personal energy-leisure-income equation it is very bad for national efficiency and growth. Now in one-man enterprises such a system, setting no limits on leisure-preference, would be a disaster, but in a large business the manager's own labour input is not all in all. Nay more, enterprises under disinterested management often form large linked systems, offering *promotion*. Indeed a civil servant is a disinterested manager, albeit without an enterprise, and the hope of promotion keeps him working adequately. Moreover, why in any case should such a manager *not* maximize his enterprise's profits, or 'go Pannonian'? What other outlet have his energies than to make profit, since it is not forbidden? Only perhaps, this, that in corrupt societies (i.e. nearly all societies) he can develop side-interests which he can further by misusing the enterprise committed to his charge.

Most important of all, the middle-level manager in a capitalist corporation is 'disinterested', unless on a bonus system. It is, then, no idle question how such people conduct themselves.

By a curious inversion, it is the highest and not the middle levels of Soviet management that are disinterested. Plan-fulfilment bonuses form about 20 per cent of the enterprise director's income (below). They have been proposed for workers above the association or trust: in *glavki*, ministries and the Gosplan. But how could they be fairly and convincingly estimated? Such workers can do infinite good and infinite harm by the stroke of a pen: is the cost of a dry canal or a ten-year subsidy to a steel mill to be stopped out of the Minister's pay? If workers in a distant enterprise cease their covert sabotage does he deserve a bonus? Indeed why do capitalist managers at his level get one? – for at least some stock options are allocated according to the firm's profit. It is clear that the marginal productivity and direct responsibility of very senior men cannot be measured.

6. It was with the large capitalist corporation that this whole subject began: with its specialized department heads and its split between ownership and management who was really running it, and with what aim? It would appear that there are too many clashes here, and that the resultant of so many forces is unpredictable. The corporation is so very different from the small Helvetian *Idealtypus*, and so particularly different with regard to its maximand, that it deserves a name of its own: something ill-defined and ill-fated like 'Atlantis'. There is now no equity-bearing labour at all, and the factor enterprise must be separately distinguished as a kind of paid labour. The e.b.f. is that part of the capital that is not hired. Since it has almost altogether lost control it can seldom ensure that the dividend is maximized. So nothing is maximized (cf. secs. 13, 14).

Yet it is not unlikely that the corporation will maximize profits at least in the short run; nay, more broadly, at least under partial adaptation, i.e. where no fixed investment is contemplated, even in the long run. For the corporation is a society of men, and no such society can operate from day to day unless in fundamental agreement, unless there is a code we can follow without thinking about it. The few crucial (fixed investment) decisions can be mulled over at length, and subjected to the interplay of important interests: we return to them below. But the many day-to-day decisions require one simple rule, which offends fewest interests, and that rule is clearly to maximize the absolute sum of the enterprise's profit.

There are other reasons, too, for giving the textbook simplicities a brief reprieve in the study of the corporation:

(a) *losses*, even among corporations, are very common. They threaten the very survival of the enterprise and so are contrary to nearly everyone's interest. Only certain kinds of tax dodgers and certain kinds of corrupt employee like losses. Therefore firms in the red maximize profits;

(b) there is a low-key ideology of trusteeship on behalf of the shareholders. Men like to be guided by a vision, and follow this one in default of one more inspiring;

(c) all kinds of exceptions to the rule turn out to be merely apparent. 'Even the full cost principle is not necessarily an instance: it is possible to equate true m.c. with m.r. while merely doing lip-service to full cost. Nor is the sacrifice of some immediate gain to liquidity and stability. In fact short- and long-term profits very often diverge, and many apparent exceptions boil down merely to this . . . The habit of following precedent is not necessarily an instance, for if the situation is doubtful to the point of incalculability, and a profitable precedent exists, it is most profitable to follow it.'[10]

7. This exhausts the list of enterprise types for which maximum profit is an even plausible criterion. The Yugoslav labour-controlled enterprise does not belong to this list, and deserves longer attention. The trouble in this case is that the decision-makers' own search for life-time income impinges too directly and too constantly on their management of the enterprise. Another generally agreed day-to-day criterion is required, and that must be to maximize the enterprise income per head of existing labour force. So while the individual continues to maximize an absolute amount the enterprise maximizes only a rate. For it has no interest apart from its members, not even in the short run or by some agreed fiction.

Applying the usual geometry, the theoretical Yugoslav, or 'Illyrian', enterprise behaves like this:

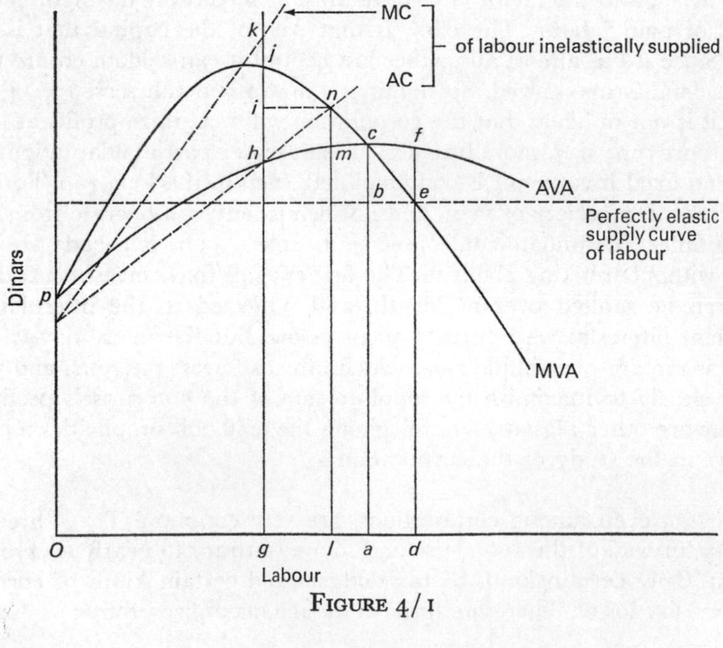

FIGURE 4/1

The basic proposition is that the Illyrian enterprise stops short at *Oa* workers, producing *ac* each, even if supply is perfectly elastic and marginal product still exceeds it. A capitalist firm in these conditions would go to *Od*. Illyria is restrictive, even in perfect competition, owing to its maximand.[11] An Illyrian monopoly would be doubly restrictive. Since the maximand is the income of labour, the 'demand' curve for labour is *phca*.

8. We postpone many details, especially those concerning the relations of Illyria to Yugoslavia,[12] the supply curve of the product,[13] imperfect competition (chapter 10, sec. 13), and capital-intensity (sec. 18 here). We confine ourselves here to the demand of such an enterprise for labour. We assume:

(i) that the relative rewards of labour qualities are fixed by custom, and all qualities are iso-elastically supplied; so that although different qualities are paid less and more we can talk in terms of 'labour';

(ii) that the co-operative is not a disguised community: it has difficulty in getting rid of labour since labourers are members, but has total control over admission (sec. 9 here; chapter 6, sec. 7);

(iii) that all other factor prices and quantities are constant, and that our concept of value added (VA) excludes them all, including interest on borrowed capital;

(iv) perfect competition in the product market.

Then if the supply of labour is perfectly elastic it can be brought in, i.e. members co-opted, by promising an income of $ab < ac$. The latter is the maximum value added per head, attained by a labour force of *Oa*. But it is illegal to discriminate, i.e. to pay less than AVA, so the law-abiding will not expand further than *Oa*.

Now if the workers *ad* could be paid less they would come for *ab*, and the enterprise could pocket *cbe*, paying it out to the nuclear labour force *Oa*, over and above their average of *ac*. Hence a number of dodges to get round the law:

(a) permanent workers are disguised as temporary fee-takers, who acquire no membership;

(b) work is sub-contracted out to a low-income enterprise, i.e. the rich enterprise, instead of having to co-opt workers at *ac*, buys in their product at – *mutatis mutandis* – *ab*.

(c) skilled workers are taken on in unskilled grades, i.e. the relevant AVA for payment is lower than the actual AVA for productivity, but no law is broken, and yet the marginal worker's supply price is met.

These dodges failing, the labour *ad* is simply not taken on. Expansion stops at *Oa*.

Suppose the supply curve slopes upwards, and cuts AVA before the point *c*? Then we are tempted to say that the firm is a monopsonist of labour, so that the marginal cost of labour to it rises more rapidly than the average payment, which is the supply curve from the point of view of the workers. But this is no longer true. The payment to those already employed rises with AVA not average cost (AC), and these people *are* the firm. It is rising AVA that prompts them to take on more labour. The offer of *hg* brings in the marginal man, and the AC curve remains of course the supply curve from the point of view of outside labour; but it does not represent what it gets. It gets, of course, the appropriate AVA, which exceeds its opportunity cost to the firm up to the point *h*. The fact that this marginal man causes more than *hg* to be paid out in toto is precisely the motive for employing him. Moreover, the extra total payout is not *k*, the amount inferable from the marginal cost (MC) curve of labour, for labour has no marginal cost any more. We have constructed the MC curve according to the ordinary geometrical rules, but these rules have no longer any empirical referent, since to the left of *g* labour was being paid more than the average cost of acquiring it. On the contrary the extra total payment is *gj*, or the MVA at that point: it is in other words whatever there is to be paid out to the equity-bearing factor.

However, if the firm can discriminate *in favour* of marginal labour, it will now do so. For it can now acquire *gl* at the fixed wage *ln*, which exceeds any potential AVA of the existing *Og*, but these latter will benefit to the tune of *inj*. This smaller area is their *profit from discrimination*, just like *cbe* in the former case. All such discrimination is illegal in Illyria, but it is still highly probable. Thus in Yugoslavia the admission of experts to full membership is avoided. They are paid high consultants' fees instead.

Strictly the above case only occurs if there are several firms in perfect competition for, and prepared to make illegal concessions to, extra labour. If the firm is a discriminating monopsonist we must draw a new, and for once meaningful, MC curve of labour, which runs out of *h* as shown in Fig. 4/2; and it is where this curve cuts MVA that hiring ceases, for this section of the MC curve has genuine meaning to such a firm. Extra hiring is now $gt < gl$, at a series of increasing wages that average *tr*. The profit from discrimination is $jqh = jqri$.

Thus if labour supply is elastic, or while inelastic still passes south-east of point *c*, it pays to discriminate in favour of the existing members and against the newcomers, and vice versa.

This analysis may be applied, *mutatis mutandis*, to a star footballer, hired at far above the rate for the rest of the team. The gate goes up, and so does their bonus – if they can swallow their jealousy.

But footballers are mere employees, so strictly irrelevant. In Illyria on the other hand the choice between types of labour input is extremely tricky. We now drop the assumption of homogeneous labour, but retain those of perfectly elastic supply and one-man-one-vote among the existing members. If, further, each grade gets an income bearing an absolutely fixed relation to the average, everyone will vote to hire such numbers in each grade as would maximize average income. Then provided wastage also gets rid of members quickly enough, the marginal productivity ratio of any two grades will tend to equal the ratio of their incomes, and the Illyrian gap between m.p. and pay will be everywhere the same (in absolute, not percentage, terms).

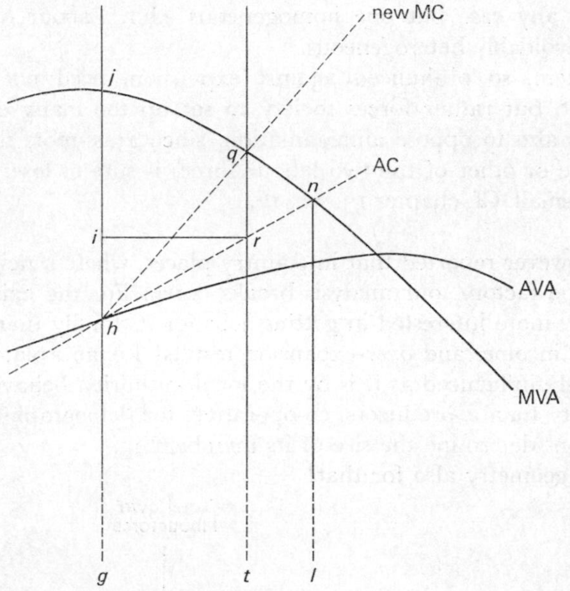

Figure 4/2

But if the income ratios are adjustable the rational individualist member will vote to keep his own grade scarce so as to enhance his relation to the average, subject to two constraints. The first is political: he may, or may not, need many colleagues of his own grade so that he can have a block of votes on this question (if they were in any case in a minority this might be considered dirty pool and so counter-productive). But certainly in a general way politics requires that he have more people in his grade, as surely as economics requires that he have less. The second constraint is that his grade not be so scarce or plentiful as to reduce, through the inefficiency of the whole enterprise, the average income of his workmates so much that he also suffers. Thus let the average income of all members be X and the individual get aX. Let some measure of 'political' expansion or 'economic' restriction raise a by b but diminish X by Y. Then it is profitable if $(a+b)(X-Y)>aX$, or (omitting bY as negligible) $bx>aY$.

The mind boggles at the complications here implied, so we shall leave this question to more specialized works; also the awkwardness that labour supply can be inelastic, indeed differently inelastic, grade by grade. But the reason for all these difficulties at least is clear: the Illyrian hiring decision is like the 'Atlantic' investment decision (sec. 6). All additions to the e.b.f. threaten to dilute the equity and change the power structure; therefore they are political. But in addition capital is nearly homogeneous. We are compelled to divide it into no more than three categories, short- and long-term risk avoiding (bills and bonds) and risk-taking (shares). It gives us in any case but one homogeneous e.b.f. Labour on the other hand is unavoidably heterogeneous.

This system, so prejudiced against expansion, need not create unemployment, but rather forces society to set up too many enterprises.[14] Its effect is also to oppose amalgamation, since grass-roots democracy is lost and one or other of the two labour forces is sure to lose. So the firm tends to be small. Cf. chapter 13, sec. 16.

9. It is however reported that in country places, where a neighbourhood has only one factory, our analysis breaks down. For the existing labour force is now more interested in getting jobs for its family than in increasing its own income, and *over*-expansion results! I.e. an isolated Yugoslav firm, strongly influenced as it is by the local authority, behaves more like a community than a producers' co-operative, for demography and not its own decisions determine the size of its membership.

There is geometry also for that!

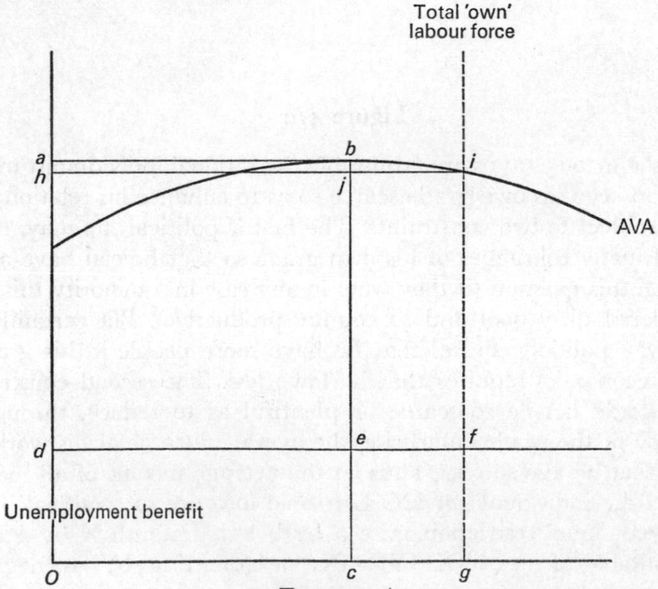

FIGURE 4/3

If we impose a dole *Od* on an Illyrian firm in respect of 'its' labour force, however that be defined, it will expand employment to *Og* where the dole $efgc \leqslant abjh$, where *abjh* is what an absolutely selfish existing membership stands to lose. A trade union under capitalism, responsible under its own private scheme for unemployment benefit, will act similarly (cf. chapter 7). An Illyrian enterprise having human feelings, or where the unemployed are felt to be part of the community, will expand more – so long as $igcj > abjh$. This leads to 'over'-employment. Indeed in Yugoslavia men are sometimes paid not to come to work, i.e. MVA$<$O, and we have recreated the Malthusian peasant family in quasi-modern conditions.

The Malthusian peasants and Yugoslav mountain villages are cases of something not Illyrian at all: *communities with demographically fixed labour supply*. Every kolkhoz and commune (chapter 6) is like this. They must all employ the labour that there is, and they therefore produce the biggest output that this labour can. They do not maximize employment at all, and they maximize output only in respect of technology (X-efficiency) or the appropriateness of the mix (allocative efficiency). A country is a large and decentralized version of such a community; in this case *Oc* is the optimum population.

The problem for these communities, to which orthodox theory can contribute most, is the decision on hours of labour. Where Y is income or product and H is hours, Fig. 4/4 shows the basic alternatives for, say, a kolkhoz. The members wish to supply H according to their marginal disutility of labour (*md*). This is, alas, a curve of inter-personally comparable disutilities. Each hour of each member is separately ranged according to this comparison on the single community supply curve. The members can generate income *internally* according to their average and marginal productivity curves within the kolkhoz (*ap* and *mp*). Further they may have opportunities for outside work, and they are all of equal skill. I.e. the community is by definition bound to care for the person and may not, as in Illyria, press him to 'migrate'. Assume first no outside opportunities. Then the community might as well be a tight commune, with a prejudice against outside work or a prohibition on inequality, and the following maximands suggest themselves:

(i) Y/H, or internal employment OA. This would be great silliness, since it would waste a great deal of fairly painless labour: AF or AP as the case may be. This labour would add to net utility. Accordingly we dismiss Y/H. Note the extreme difference from Illyria.

(ii) Y, subject to $dY/dH \geqslant md$. This leads to employment OF, and a dichotomy between general and individual interest. For at OF the going dividend is FJ and extra hours in excess of OF will be offered to the administration. The latter either will or will not be able to convince the suppliers (who are part of their electorate) that it is not in the general interest to employ labour at $md<mp$. For what member can understand the concept of group mp?

(iii) Y, subject to $Y/H \geqslant md$. This would employ OP while PT would refuse the offer. The individuals supplying most of FP would be very happy with this arrangement, since $PQ \geqslant$ their md; while those who had mostly supplied OF, and were not well represented among the 'overtime' hours FP, would suffer a rather small decline in hourly return from FJ to PQ on a constant disutility of labour. They could no doubt be conned into attributing this to the bad harvest or a statistical illusion or what not;

Figure 4/4

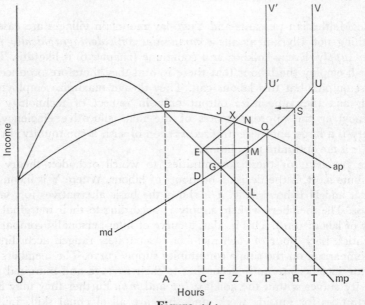

and the few who stood to gain much would surely have their way over the many who stood to lose little. (iii) is therefore a more likely outcome than (ii), unless each person is rather equally represented in OF and FP. But even then the individual, perceiving only his short-run interest, is likely to insist on (iii), and to fail to understand the arguments for (ii).

(iv) Y, i.e. employ OT. This is subject to the natural constraint that PT will not offer their labour. It therefore amounts in practice to (iii).

Now imagine an outside opportunity in a perfect, wage-paying, labour market. If this wage is $RS>AB$ the community should close down. If it is KM, and principle (iii) is in force, no one takes any notice. But it would certainly pay everyone to do so. The community should discriminate, flatly extruding the labour CK and allowing it to keep its outside earnings CEMK. The md curve of internally employable labour now becomes DEX, where EX//MU. Keeping to principle (iii), the community now employs OC+CZ internally. Total employment rises, since CZ$>$KP (because EX$>$MQ). The exported hours CK can be brought up to the average emolument by a tax on everyone else, and yet everyone gains, since there is more to distribute: the exported labour produces (or at any rate receives) EML extra, the CZ produce more per head than the corresponding KP, and the intra-marginal OC produce as much as before.[15] Moreover these hours used to be rewarded at the rate PQ, but now receive ZX.

To inject a little realism, CZ might be healthy grandmothers on a kolkhoz, who will work in the collective fields if the price is right. They are, of course, transferred from their initial position at K and further out. The exported labour CK is younger and more mobile.

The community may also be underpopulated: *md* may cut *ap* to the left of B. In that case all these problems disappear. The demand curve for labour is the *ap* curve up to B, as in Illyria. An external wage $<$*ap* is of no interest at all. One greater than *ap*, however, abolishes the community, as before. Up to B the community may even encourage 'immigration', by reasoning similar to that for an optimum population. After B it will revert to a restrictive attitude in this matter exactly like that of Illyria. The difference is only that Illyrian firms are not bound to accept members' children.

10. Before leaving the current operations of the Illyrian – let alone the Yugoslav – enterprise we must ward off some misinterpretations.

The slope and height of AVA depend of course on the demand for the product and the enterprise's degree of monopoly. Even in Illyria there is monopoly, and enterprises seek and exploit it. Our figures make no assumption about the elasticity of demand for the product, and this makes no difference at all to our present analysis; but see chapter 10, sec. 13.

Secondly, there are innumerable decisions under any system that do not affect employment or output directly: technology, quality of product, even price may all be changed without a predictable reaction on employment. In all these cases the old rule holds that where the e.b.f. is constant it itself wishes the absolute sum of profit maximized. All the other factors of production have perfectly ordinary supply curves, giving rise to m.c. – to – enterprise curves, to which the enterprise reacts in a capitalist manner, equating the marginal cost of each factor to its marginal revenue product.

Thirdly, we have already explained the dangers of the doctrine of symmetry between Illyria and Atlantis, with equity capital playing a restrictive role in the latter. But danger is instructive. Thus the parallel drawn by Dubravčić is very strong in the *rights issue*. To be a member of any club is by definition to have privileges, and this one is that of making a small input for a big yield, open only to members. Under capitalism, equity shareholders get part or all of any new issue at a price below that on the Stock Exchange; indeed this is compensation for their loss of power. In Yugoslavia worker-members similarly seek privileges: overtime, the co-optation of their relatives, etc. Again when a senior post falls empty there is the question, shall we submit this to outside competitors, or shall its emolument be treated as a sort of rights issue for existing members? – even the losers will move up one, and so benefit too.[16]

Fourthly, firing is always more difficult than hiring: how much more so when it is 'expulsion' versus 'admission'. Contrasting the two main e.b.f.s we note that

(i) Equity capital simply remains and accepts a lower dividend. No social services, no 'minimum dividend' buoy it up. It can also sell up and leave without pain. Its feeling of membership is minimal and ordinarily any one saver has a whole portfolio of small holdings.

(ii) But equity workers cannot sell their places unless many people conspire to break the law. Yet, with AVA > the going income elsewhere, the place may be very valuable. Moreover if they merely leave they relinquish their aliquot yield on the ploughback made during their membership. Neither point matters much, of course, if the enterprise is failing, but expulsion for bad behaviour, and even mere retirement, make the issue a serious one.

(iii) So the labour-managed enterprise gets round these problems by short time and by farming people out, i.e. giving them leave to take temporary outside work (cf. sec. 9).

(iv) But labour-management does have one solid advantage: there is no, or only a low, fixed wage. Downward flexibility of income is built into the system, and this relieves much of the pressure to get rid of people.

Lastly, there is the mixed case of the professional *partnership*. The partners bring in both capital and skilled labour, treating both hired capital and hired labour as non-e.b.f.s. By definition a partner is a man sharing the equity of an enterprise but having a veto on the admission of new partners; i.e. the equity capital cannot be freely sold since it goes with equity labour, and this must in all systems go through a formal admissions procedure. There is not to my knowledge any theory yet of what exactly 'Benthamite' partners, each bringing in two e.b.f.s., would maximize. If they could agree on a transformation ratio their problem would of course be solved; but the theory would have to explain precisely this ratio. For instance old partners with a life-time of accumulation behind them, and *a fortiori* sleeping partners, will want a ratio favouring capital; young, poor or particularly skilled partners one favouring labour, etc. Professional partnerships tend strongly to 'idiorrhythmy' (sec. 23).

11. The co-operative retail enterprise is run, in 'pure' theory, for the

benefit of its customer-shareholders (chapter 6, sec. 3). Their shareholding is kept minimal, and exists to entitle them to a dividend on their recorded purchases. Non-shareholders are encouraged to buy but get no dividend. This dividend is substantial, and this is what co-ops are 'about'. But a set of 'Benthamite' customers will maximize neither the rate nor the amount of it. Not the rate, because the dividend is only a discount off the retail price, and the customer is equally well off whether it is high on a high price or low on a low price. And not the amount, because this would require him to purchase as much as possible; i.e. not merely to buy from no other shop, but also not to save anything, and to maximize his money income. The 'Benthamite' co-op minimizes its retail prices net of dividend; so it must buy as cheaply as possible and be as efficient as possible. In perfect parallelism to Illyria, the members *minimize 'value subtracted'* per commodity acquired. Whether their policy is for high prices and dividends or for low is a question of the elasticity of demand by non-shareholding purchasers: for the profit on their custom swells the dividend. These people are the formal equivalent of hired labour in Illyria. As to the members' micro-choices, these should be settled by the usual criterion that marginal cost ratios equal net price ratios. Note how different, and how much more simple, this is than the parallel Illyrian case of choice between types of labour (above). The reason is of course that not consumer goods but consumers are the equity bearing 'factor'. The consumers pay for what they get and do not interfere with each other.

What formally most distinguishes this enterprise from Illyria, and indeed Yugoslavia, is that it cannot control members' input, and so its own output. The members buy as much as they want; the co-op does the best it can for them under the circumstances. Only perhaps has it discretion in insisting that some marginal cost – say the storage of slow-moving items – is prohibitive. In other words it is an *agency not an enterprise*: they command it, not it them, even in the short run. Whereas the management of a producers' co-op commands in the short run and is commanded only in the long.

But the policy of retail co-ops is in reality culturally determined – and as we see in chapter 6 practice at no point diverges further from pure theory. For the really important thing about the traditional retail co-op was that it maximized nothing at all: it was a 'voluntary public enterprise' (chapter 10, sec. 8).

The farmers' co-op is more likely to be a pure maximizer. It too is an 'agency', and treats both purchases from and sales to members (e.g. crops and fertilizers) as does the retail co-op. Indeed the whole doctrine of Illyria began with this type of organization, and not the Yugoslav industrial enterprise.[17] Probably too the doctrine is most realistic in this field.

12. So far we have considered only 'Benthamite' motivations, and the

clash of individual and enterprise has belonged merely to the pathology of *homo economicus*. What of non-income, non-profit motivations? Why be *homo economicus* at all?

There is of course no reason. Quite especially strong is the motive of *technological display*, regardless of cost, even if charitably and 'dynamically' interpreted (chapter 15). At the opposite end of the spectrum comes technological conservatism. Both are aspects of the instinct of workmanship (chapter 2). It is remarkable how emotional are human attitudes to technology. So it should not surprise us that irrational resistance is as common as irrational acceptance.

Another common managerial motivation is to gain power over one's fellow man. This can be achieved, first, by expanding the company's production volume and its equity holdings in other companies. This process often looks like profit maximization; a company with a growing plant is surely profitable, and so surely is one that has a finger in many pies and can dictate to many quasi-independent firms. But not always: a smaller company enjoying its monopoly might bring in more to the shareholders. Indeed the maximization of the directors' power only coincides with the maximization of the firm's profit when the industry is competitive. If the firm is a monopoly its power-loving managers have a choice before them. They may feel that economic power is best embodied in great profit, and proceed to maximize profits as in a textbook by output restriction. Or they may prefer mere size. In this case they will not restrict output but push it ever upwards so long as there is no overall loss. Now we may suspect that where ownership is divorced from control, profits are less popular as a symbol of success and power than mere size: for the shareholders may get wind of profits, insist on high dividends and spoil the managers' schemes – nor will the tax-gatherer be far behind. Better then not to earn them, or at least to conceal them and plough them back as soon as possible; and as ownership is usually divorced from control it follows that large monopolies whose managers desire power do not restrict output in a textbook way.[18]

Secondly, the manager may fail to equate his power with the firm's. He may aim simply at expanding the clerical labour force or the department subordinate to him personally. This is an easier and less glorious process, employed more often by subordinate members of the management. Often really such people are maximizing their life-time incomes, as we have seen. But in any case their interests diverge from the company's. For a large subordinate staff is the quickest way to promotion, including promotion outside the firm.

In the same view, specialized department heads pursue incompatible professionalisms, some of them bordering on altruism (chapter 2) and some on technological display (above).

The engineer requires the very latest gadget regardless of cost, or possibly the very oldest techniques because he learned them as a boy (above), while the personnel department would prefer to raise wages and the sales department demand that the product be radically revised. Decisions on how to allocate money between these three uses may eventually be taken on a rational basis, but in the short and often the medium run quite contradictory policies may be pursued by the three departments. For the professional employed by the firm is still a professional, and his education has drummed into him a whole series of criteria incompatible both with those of other professions and with the maximization of profit.

The independent professional or professional partnership deviates still further in the same direction. Nay more we all expect it to, and so does the professional school that sets the tone. The visitor to North America encounters its profit-maximizing doctors and dentists with a sense of betrayal, of moral outrage, and certainly they are an unusual exception. But it is not logic that forbids such behaviour in a professional, and it might well be an improvement, hastening the adoption of new techniques, lowering costs, spreading information and the like. If we observe the situation more coolly we see that the North American medico sins by maximizing profits while retaining his traditional professional monopoly. Moreover, we may well be objecting because we are accustomed to state subsidies, not full fees.

Note that we cannot speak of non-Benthamite maximands, only criteria. For most of these enterprise goals leave even in theory a wide tolerance; they are nothing like specific enough to be called maximands, rather are they mere constraints on behaviour. If within these margins they leave action undetermined, there is nothing wrong with that. Human behaviour might perfectly well be indeterminate; there is nothing in the social sciences that says otherwise except our vanity,[19] and there is no *a priori* case for having maximands at all (see sec. 15).

13. In free societies with decentralized economies individuals and enterprises mostly choose their own maximands, and those differ. In any capitalist market there are old and young[20] peasants, corporations pursuing a certain *a priori* market share, new small firms seeking short-run profit, old big ones seeking long-term profits, co-operatives maximizing members' average revenue, non-profit-making trusts and heaven knows what besides.

All this variety is an aspect of imperfect competition. It has never been shown that this kind of imperfection is more serious than those variations in the elasticity of demand and the number of enterprises, on which the textbooks concentrate. Funny maximands are evidently quite workable; the market is a tolerant matrix.

There is also a dictated maximand – a whole new reason for variety. A large corporation can easily enforce 'abnormal' behaviour on its middle management, just as that management imposes piece-work, time-work, etc., on the labour force. Moreover, Parliament or the Minister can vary the maximand(s) for a nationalized enterprise, and state schools and hospitals traditionally have all sorts of input-output ratios (size of class, bed turnover, etc.) as goals. Quartermasters and other military 'entrepreneurs' are yet another case – so similar to the Soviet that they may be postponed. Occasionally, too, the church may get after us to work harder, or the trade union to work less hard. Or the monopolies commission may press the manager to produce beyond the point of greatest profit; or again the church may press him to pay wages above, or charge prices below, the market rate. But they have rather little effect.

But Pannonia is the purest case of a dictated maximand – and we should be very clear that Hungary is a different place. The Hungarian Communist Party allows, but does not demand, profit maximization, and it imposes many unprofitable duties such as price restraint or 'social' investment projects. In Pannonia, however, where there is no e.b.f., the clockwork must somehow be wound up. The government by tying bonus to profit tells the manager what to do. Indeed the very existence of an e.b.f. makes dictation difficult; the factor will simply not supply itself if it dislikes the maximand.

14. We can now cope with the Soviet-type enterprise. In the classical STE the enterprise had so little independence that it could not be called a firm, only an 'establishment', in the derogatory wording of the British censuses of production. Strictly this entity falls, unlike the Cuban or the Chinese, within the Benthamite category, since the main influence on the manager is his plan-fulfilment bonus out of the wage-fund, or, latterly, his cut of the profit. Now if the latter existed in pure form USSR would be Hungary, and present no problem. But in fact after the 1965 reforms, a detailed output-input-technology plan must be fulfilled before any bonus is payable out of profit, and all prices are still centralized. So the director is only free to seek profit in respect of above-plan output, and since plans are still taut (chapter 11, sec. 14) this leaves him mostly where he was before 1965, only with the bonus for plan-fulfilment coming out of a different fund.

The detailed plan presents the director with *many maximands*: each separate line of output, each separate input (minimands), profit, sales; with non-quantifiable criteria such as the introduction of new technology. These latter strictly cannot be called maximands, any more than the non-Benthamite criteria above. Now since maximands compete and conflict,[21] *many maximands are no maximand*: you can't have as much profit as possible if you simultaneously make as much of the product as possible, or introduce the latest technique as quickly as possible. So you perform a balancing act, guided by common sense, or your private values, or what you think the latest *Pravda* leader is really hinting at.[22]

15. So a person or enterprise with many maximands falls as quickly into

indeterminacy, that dread turnip-ghost of all good economists, as one with none. Seemingly worse in the eyes of economic 'science' than to have an unusual maximand is to have many or none. Illyria and Pannonia can be forgiven (indeed they generate a lot of geometry and publications), but the STE and the capitalist public enterprise are cast into the outer darkness of mere Administration (chapter 11).

Does indeterminacy matter? The fact that theorists take it to be an affront is neither here nor there. The determinacy of perfect competition is purely of the 'blackboard' variety: we can say that we would be able to predict everything if we had all the requisite data, which are of a simple kind but very numerous. But of course we haven't the data, and we can hardly predict anything (we'd be exceedingly rich if we could), and it doesn't matter anyway. Even oligopolistic indeterminacy does not matter, since the behaviour of an oligopolistic market as a whole is as easy to predict as that of a perfect market.[23]

Theory apart, indeterminacy is no great practical threat in a market since only other minor units of the system have to cope with it. So long as the system is 'viscous', i.e. slow to change, it does not matter much that planners don't know how it will change. They can adapt themselves, or with a modicum of intervention can correct things *ex post facto*.

On the other hand a central physical command system that really tried to arrange everything down to the last detail could not tolerate indeterminacy either. The classical solution, based on Marxist delusions of omnipotence, was to plan everything exactly right and omit nothing. Thus locked into step, the enterprise would do nothing except everything it had been told, and the whole notion of a maximand implied more freedom than this robot possessed.

But this is in practice quite impossible, and the enterprise has *de facto* autonomy to make all sorts of minor adjustment within the plan, and to commit innumerable violations of it too. The indeterminacy of its actions becomes tolerable, since other enterprises have an equivalent freedom to adjust themselves to it. It remains true that all these peripheral movements can be controlled and given some theoretical determinacy (if that is a good thing to have) by setting a single maximand. To 'set' is to attach the bonus exclusively to: it is of course the bonus that determines managerial behaviour and expresses objective state priorities.

Now the maximand usually chosen is a mix of physical outputs, or latterly the money value of all output. But any other, such as profit or input minimization, would have done as well, and the choice of this particular one is not due even mainly to the desire for determinacy. It results rather from the Bolshevik temperament, for which statistically measurable increases in production are the supreme value. A sophisticated modern Polish alternative is to attach the bonus to a weighted function of sub-maximands: so much for cost reduction, so much for output, so much for profit.

16. More than the capitalist, even more than the Yugoslav, enterprise the Soviet-type one is a congeries of individuals, an agency. However it is an agency not of those individuals but of the government. The detailed command plan reaches, in pure Communist theory, down to the individual worker: the Dictatorship of the Proletariat is planning the economic part of the general historical conduct of the Proletarians. Hence the unusual language applied to labour: never 'labour market' but 'labour placement' (*trudoustroistvo*); and though piece-work (*akkord*) is extremely frequent it is after all a price offered to the worker to which he may adjust himself – we think rather of labour norms (*trudoviye normy*), which are targets he must meet, whether on piece or on time, just as if he were a director. Hence too the fantastic and exuberant complication of Soviet labour law – which is all about punishment for lateness and for wasting materials, and of course never once mentions strikes or collective bargaining, but does deal at length with dismissals.[24] Another consequence is the extreme plasticity of the enterprise: for ever being merged and reconstituted, subordinated to trusts and liberated from trusts, just as if it were one of the superior intermediate organs in the planning hierarchy.

This attitude has consequences for Soviet-type full-employment policy: the government orders the enterprises to take on workers it cannot afford and does not need (chapter 14, sec. 11). It also affects the attitude of managers to enterprises. They are employees of the single state headquarters, so liable to transfer at any moment. They are in fact often transferred. So they do not identify with the enterprise: they are not, in particular, anxious to risk their current bonus by introducing new technology (chapter 15).

The notion dies hard, then, that the government in organizing each individual directly. So the enterprise is its agency, and the theory of the firm must again be subsumed under that of the individual.

17. Investment, we can now see, has always been so difficult to predict and so impervious to theory because it engages people's ultimate interests too directly. They no longer accept the short-term rule of thumb (sec. 6), that their interests coincide with the enterprise's absolute profit. They at no point think less in terms of enterprises or more in terms of their own life-time income. In what follows we discuss first saving and borrowing, then the exact criteria for spending the money available. These criteria include non-investment items in the appropriation account, an important but forgotten category. But we do not deal with planners' criteria or with normative questions. We can therefore omit, as usual, Soviet investment policy and general development theory, as subjects too far removed from the comparison of institutions.

To begin then, with saving and borrowing, we have already met the simplest examples: the ageing or heirless peasant's or owner-manager's disinterest in his enterprise, and tendency to disinvest. Here at any rate is a really reliable economic law of investment, obscured only by our misguided obsession with the theory of the firm.

18. The Yugoslav enterprise is similar. Ploughback is a voluntary decision of the workers, but 'they can't take it with them'. They have no rights to sell on retirement, on leaving or in an emergency. The enterprise's absolute profit never concerned them. But the future average income of workers doesn't necessarily concern them either. They only benefit from ploughback during their period of membership. If they expect this to be short they will require staggering rates of interest to compensate them.[25] Members are therefore tempted to vote as follows. The young man, who has not yet done his stint as a migratory worker in Munich, has no attachment to the given enterprise, and votes for larger payments and smaller ploughback. The old man about to retire votes the same way: he too will not be around to enjoy the benefits of investment. His pension is not affected by the future fate of the enterprise, provided it is solvent. Even a middle-aged and settled worker of low rank will feel psychologically unidentified with the expansion of his enterprise. Since he has other savings outlets, under his own control, he will choose them; and so indeed he does, as Yugoslav sociologists have shown. Only the enterprise Establishment will be really enthusiastic; to them it means promotion and the 'Veblenian' satisfactions of achievement. So there would be very little ploughback were it not for the League of Communists (heavily represented on the executive committee of the workers' council and in other places of power), the local authority (which formally appoints the director and has other official influence) and the fiscal restraints on actually distributing revenue to members.

Borrowing is quite a different matter. And here we revert, for speed and simplicity, to algebra and Illyria. Like anyone else, the Illyrian worker is happy to use someone else's savings if the price is right: for the profit after debt service accrues quickly and one does not initially place one's own money beyond one's control. Indeed he will more readily borrow than a capitalist, and tend to more capital-intensive solutions. Thus let a capitalist firm face two possibilities of expansion, equally profitable:

I is capital-intensive. There is no more labour ($\Delta L = O$) only loan capital is added ($\Delta K > O$), and the addition to *net* profit is ΔP_1, which goes of course to equity.

II is labour intensive. More labour is hired ($\Delta L > O$) but no more capital ($\Delta K = O$), and $\Delta P_2 = \Delta P_1$.

The capitalist, then, is indifferent, but not so the Illyrian enterprise faced with the same choice of technology and the same market situation; in particular with the same rate of interest on external loan capital. Its maximand is not P but $\frac{wL+P}{L}$, where w is the wage the capitalist would have paid:

$$\text{In case I}\quad \Delta\frac{(wL+P)}{L}=\frac{\Delta P+wL+P}{L}-\frac{wL+P}{L}=\frac{\Delta P}{L}.$$

$$\text{In case II}\quad \Delta\frac{(wL+P)}{L}=\frac{w\Delta L+\Delta P+wL+P}{L+\Delta L}-\frac{wL+P}{L}=\frac{L\Delta P-P\Delta L}{L(L+\Delta L)}.$$

Illyria, therefore, will prefer more capital-intensive solutions so long as she can borrow, though the incentive to do so is not very great. For the difference between I and II verges on the second order of smalls:

$$\text{I}-\text{II}=\frac{(P+\Delta P)\Delta L}{L(L+\Delta L)}.$$

Note that if the capitalist firm finds both courses of action unprofitable ($P<O$), but still equally unprofitable, Illyria will prefer the labour-intensive variant. Again if she must plough back she may prefer more labour-intensive solutions, for she requires very high internal rates of return, out of all proportion to the rates on loan capital. Let r be the excess of this rate over the (common) price of loan capital. Then in case I we must subtract $r\Delta K/L$ from the r.h.s., and this magnitude also enters into I–II, which becomes approximately

$$\frac{P\Delta L-rL\Delta K}{L(L+\Delta L)}.$$

But P is of the same order of magnitude as ΔK, and ΔL as rL. This then is a very small quantity indeed, whether positive or negative.

It seems highly probable that this argument also describes Yugoslavia. For Yugoslav proposals as to bonds and equity shares, cf. chapter 13, sec. 11.

19. The commune is in all respects but one like Illyria: it is not averse from ploughback. For here the individual is indeed unlikely to leave, and his psychological commitment is great even if he is young, unskilled or old. Indeed as a pensioner he continues to live in and depend on the commune. Some much looser communities have the same obligation towards the old, and the same tradition of labour immobility. It follows that even the kolkhoznik, as his years advance, has a certain interest in ploughback.

When we come to developed capitalism and to the STE there is much less to be said. In the Soviet-type case saving and investment are at central government whim (the non-policy side is dealt with in chapter 13). They are not properly speaking functions of the Soviet-type enterprise; and this fits very well with our statement, above, that it is not properly speaking a firm but an 'establishment'.

20. The muddle in the capitalist corporation, however, is less easy to shrug off. The 'members' of this body, i.e. those able to affect investment from the inside, are more heterogeneous even than in Yugoslavia. They include:

(a) shareholders from the founding family, with a psychological commitment to the survival, but perhaps not to the growth, of the firm, and to the continuance of certain products, technologies and locations;

(b) shareholders with preponderant interests in customer or competing firms;

(c) banks and insurance companies with large shareholdings, anxious if at all possible not to draw attention to themselves, but aware of their decisive power and wanting to maximize capital gain or maintainable dividend;

(d) pirate shareholders contemplating take-over bids;

(e) trade union shareholders, especially those managing pension funds (chapter 7, sec. 6);

(f) fainéant shareholders, mainly small;

(g) very senior managers, who have already made investments and want them justified by future measures;

(h) newly appointed 'whizz kids', who want to show (g) to be in the wrong and have their own pet schemes;

(i) specialized department heads, grinding their professional axes as in sec. 1 above, and contemplating promotion outside the firm;

and so on: this is not a treatise on capitalist investment policies, so why prolong the agony?

Moreover, without formality of shareholding, voting or threatening take-over certain groups can still insert themselves into the policy-making process merely by market power. These are the trade union, which is a permanent monopolist of the main input; in cases of threatened bankruptcy the bank or bondholders, who exercise a similar power; and in the case of munitions the defence department, which is a permanent monopsonist of the whole output (chapters 7, 8, 9).

It is unlikely that all the rogues in this gallery will agree to maximize the enterprise's long-run profit, or any of the less reputable indicators like market share or sales. Moreover – an important point often forgotten – no one knows precisely whether a given policy will maximize any particular indicator, but everyone must interpret inaccurate and irrelevant data according to his best *judgement*. But mere judgement is invariably clouded by interest, habit and emotion. So even agreement on what to do implies no agreement on how to do it. Rather will those who really want to do something else interpret the data accordingly.

I therefore do not share the usual distress at economics' failure to provide a positive theory of investment by large capitalist firms.[26] There is nothing disgraceful about indeterminacy and ignorance. The disgrace is to pretend they are not there.

21. In pure theory *share-cropping*[27] is a consortium of three e.b.f.s.: land in the person of the landowner, and labour and circulating capital in the person of the tenant (who therefore receives a mixed income). Fixed capital is supplied by negotiation between the two entrepreneurs: which mirrors the 'political' element in large investment projects when there is more than one person, let alone one e.b.f. involved (cf. sec. 20).

The common objection to share-cropping, dating from Arthur Young's *Travels in France* (1787–9), is that the landlord's fixed proportion of the net crop is an income tax on the peasant, and a gross disincentive to labour; therefore the land should not be an e.b.f. at all but a 'hired' factor at a fixed rent.

The modern theory of labour supply under an income tax cannot quite confirm this. Let a flat rent and a proportionate rent be so arranged that a tenant can earn £30 per week with 40 hours' work (point x) either paying £20 flat rent or splitting 60 per cent–40 per cent with the landlord. Let the marginal physical product of labour be, for simplicity, constant. Then the tenant's earnings from labour are either £1.25 or £0.75 per hour:

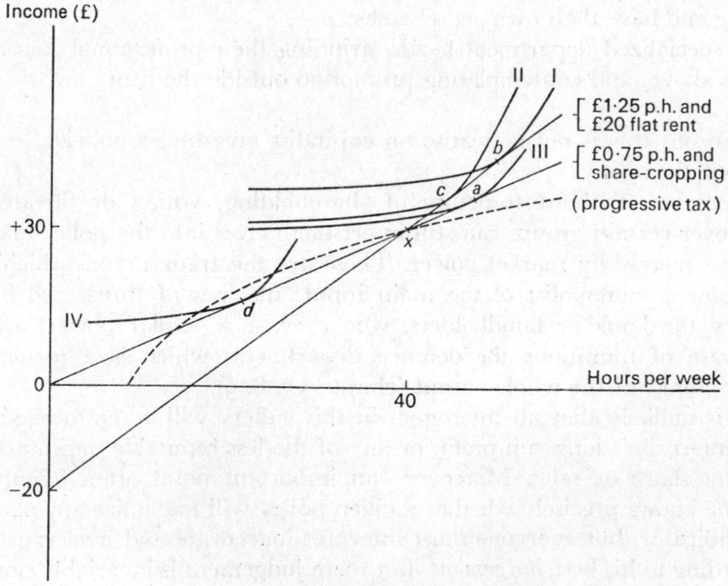

Figure 4/5

We are tempted to say that no matter what shape or general position the tenant's indifference curves between work and income may have, he will work longer as the sole e.b.f., and so *a fortiori* earn more income ($b > a$). But this is not necessarily so, since curves of the general shape II/III (bunched to the south-west and fanned out to the north-east) could in fact be drawn so as to bring c hours $< a$ hours, and even £$1.25c$ – £20 $<$ £$0.75a$ (the share-cropper gets more income). It seems unnatural to draw such curves, but this geometrical intuition is not information about human beings. I.e. curves of the general shape I/III (either 'normal' or bunched to the north-east and fanned out to the south-west), which make the share-cropper do less work ($b > a$), are not an *a priori* necessity. The paradox is largely explained by the fact that the share-cropper does not face any more change in earnings per hour than the flat rent payer: both are on a proportional 'income tax' (the latter at a zero rate). It is the progressive 'tax' that most discourages work – and even that is not a certain proposition.[28] What is true is that the share-cropping tenant can, if lazy, settle for a lower rent than £20 (point d, indifference curve IV).

Besides, indifference curves conceal much from us, even much that is straight economics:

(i) share-croppers are usually near to starvation and bankruptcy. A flat rent is too *risky* in a bad harvest or a price depression. But our figure pre-supposes certainty.

(ii) the system favours cheating more than a flat rent, since it pays the tenant to conceal his output, whereas he cannot conceal non-payment of a fixed rent.

(iii) in innumerable decisions the work input is constant, and the shared equity unites the interests of tenant and landlord, like any profit-sharing scheme with few participants. This facilitates, notably, fixed investment.

(iv) whatever the nature of the rent contract, it may pay the landlord to keep his tenant unproductive enough to remain in debt to him. The share-cropper then approximates a fixed rent payer. This may be the situation in West Bengal.[29]

(v) granted the land is subdivisible and the contracts enforceable, share-cropping does not lead to an irrational allocation of land, whatever its effect on labour (Cheung, op cit., chapter 2).

It would be hard to balance the good and the evil, the efficiency and the inefficiency, in all this. Share-cropping has close resemblances not only to income-taxation but to profit-sharing for managers and piece-work for workers. Cheung also points with justice to its success in petrol stations and snack-counter concessions. The evils attributed to it may perfectly well have other causes. What is basically lacking in the ordinary share-cropping situation is social equality between the co-entrepreneurs or any felt community of interest. Fixed rents would not alter that.

22. Some writers treat landlord and share-cropper as one enterprise, but not landlord and tenant at fixed rent. Well they may: the share-cropper is like an employee on an incentive scheme. The more 'transparent' or 'jellified' notion of the enterprise here put forward marries very well with the *systems approach*: system boundaries are not watertight, individuals move from one system to another, individuals in one system react differently upon individuals in another or in none, without passing through 'channels'. The sociology of the enterprise has expanded from Weber's strict authoritarian hierarchy to take account of the fact of looser forms.

But extremism is out of place. Hierarchy is still there and authority is still exercised, especially in immediate emergencies and medium-term issues of moderate importance. In short-term routine issues however they are replaced by complicated informal routines and by general spontaneous agreement. But these cannot be such as to destroy hierarchy and authority; they co-exist with them, work for them and are tolerated by them. On the other hand great issues that present no emergency are settled, not by but through the hierarchy – by individuals in their own interest. Some of these individuals, especially but not only at the top of the hierarchy, will use an ideology of reification of the enterprise (or the state or the Communist Party), and brandish the dread word 'loyalty'; but they do this mainly because that is *their* interest. Society consists of individuals; organizations are a convenience, they have no rights. And precisely convenience is a day-to-day, short-term concept, rights a long-term one.

Again 'jellification' is not a proper theory, a coherent body of interesting propositions. It is merely Max Weber's comeuppance,[30] a refutation of a proper theory that substitutes nothing positive. There is no systems theory, only the systems approach.

Enterprises can also lose their clear definition by semi-absorption into larger units: the capitalist holding company and the Soviet-type association. If property is only a bundle of rights, sovereignty is a bundle of powers, and can be divided too. We do not discuss the holding company, but the association figures among the intermediate planning organs in chapter 9.

23. But there is another way in which hard lines of definition can be lost. It is less obvious and more amusing, but equally important for our understanding. For we misunderstand fundamentally the partnership, the kolkhoz and the university if we assimilate them to a Yugoslav, or even to an Illyrian, labour-managed enterprise. For such an enterprise is like any other in that there is a technically necessary work discipline. The worker sells or gives or what-not his whole working time, and from then on he is under command, even if of his own representatives. If he did not, the machinery would break down. Such a state of affairs is certainly as compatible with labour-management as with capitalism or state socialism.

But between the firm and the, say, loose traditional village community (which, for instance, merely enforces limits on private land holdings – chapter 6) there lies another, quite distinguishable unit which we might or might not want to call an enterprise: the *idiorrhythmic organization.* In this it is possible for individuals to dispose of their own time at work, profitably to themselves and yet without disrupting the shared infrastructure of the unit. Since their work is difficult to supervise they are permitted more or less freely to make individual profit, provided that they pay adequately for, and give some of their own time to, the common services. These services might not be administered democratically: indeed some seniority system is likely to decide access to them. But some approach to democracy in this centralized part is likely, since the rest of the economic activity is unavoidably individualistic.

Now the word idiorrhythmic is derived from a current within Orthodox monasticism, exemplified by nine out of the twenty monasteries on Mount Athos.[31] So first a word on the history of Christian monasticism – the reader will readily grasp its very strict relevance if he has patience. We start in the second century with perfectly independent hermits in the Egyptian desert, seeking each his own communion with God (*eremitic*). Their reputation for holiness attracts food supplies and disciples (the suppliers seek merit, the disciples holiness, and these two things are at all times the 'saleable output' of the monk; though Western monks also produce actual goods for the market). But the hermits grow peculiar and indeed mad in their isolation, and about A.D. 380 St. Basil sets up places where they can live in common (*coenobitic*), for mutual support and correction, and according to sensible and regular customs. From this develops the Roman monastery in the West, under St. Benedict (*c.* 500). This, *more Romano*, has a strict and detailed rule, laid down centrally. In later centuries there is subdivision into different but still centralized Orders, much like the federations of kibbutzim (chapter 6). But Orthodoxy knows no orders, only individual monasteries, and these each continue in the slightly looser Basilian way. This is very definitely coenobitic, but the eremitic tradition never dies, and the form of monastic governance never really settles down.

Mount Athos in particular, the Holy Mountain of all Orthodoxy on the Chalcidican Peninsula, attracts many hermits, some of whom by A.D. 900 have come together in a looser than Basilian way, into communities called *lavras*. By today's standards these are idiorrhythmic, but the word lavra has lost most of this connotation, and now means any large walled monastery. In 959 St. Athanasios forms the first great coenobitic lavra, that survives today as the Great Lavra (though it has in the meantime gone back to idiorrhythmy). There follows a strongly coenobitic period – though an eremitic periphery continues. Idiorrhythmy proper raises its head about 1400, and one of the last Byzantine emperors tries to regulate and restrain both it and eremitism. For obvious reasons both bishop and emperor have always disliked idiorrhythmy, since it is *inter alia* democratic. Incidentally Mt. Athos as a whole has been at all times a sort of theocratic democracy, i.e. a formally constituted quasi-sovereign federation of monasteries.

In 1452 Constantinople falls. The Turks are tolerant but abolish all the Christian princes who have hitherto provided the money. Freed of external control, and facing a grave financial crisis, Mt. Athos does a *sauve qui peut* into idiorrhythmy. For each monk is an economic burden on the coenobitic establishment, so since this must be reduced why not put the monks on *Khozraschet*? The trouble is of course that idiorrhythmy has acquired an economic as well as a spiritual base. It is no longer just a matter of spiritual freedom and ecclesiastical democracy, which Greeks have to their credit always prized more than, say, Italians or Russians.[32] It is a question of who has relatives that will stump up. Idiorrhythmy is a half-way house no longer only towards eremitism, but also towards capitalism. The monk is allowed to own, enjoy and administer an outside fortune, provided that he bequeaths it to the monastery. The principal divine services are the only compulsory communal element: the monks live in 'flats' and for the most part feed themselves off plots of land allocated by the monastery. The buildings and common services are maintained out of the endowment.

By the eighteenth century all twenty monasteries were idiorrhythmic, but by today eleven have reverted to coenobiosis. In the remaining nine class distinctions are rampant. Government is not by the abbot (*hegoumenos*) characteristic of coenobiosis, but by an oligarchy of the rich (*proistamenoi*), who literally employ the propertyless and illiterate poor (*paramikroi*), in their 'flats' (much better than the average) or on their plots of land. But the former are very democratic *inter se*, and their elected executive committee exercises its authority collegially. *All* members enjoy greater spiritual and intellectual freedom.

Idiorrhythmy is thus quite inferior in its asceticism: so it is suspect also to the eremites, who might find it a tolerable system of government. On the other hand all sources are unanimous that learning and art flourish more in such monasteries; and it is they that have received the distinguished refugees from the outside world, and been the nurseries of primates and patriarchs. The contrast between idiorrhythmy and ceonobiosis is the monastic paradigm of that between capitalism and socialism. Capitalist market conditions also flourish between monasteries, and between the monasteries and their dependent annexes. The vow of poverty, though still taken, is incompatible with idiorrhythmism. There is even more use of machinery, and acceptance of technical progress, in idiorrhythmic monasteries.

Now all this has close parallels in other, more strictly economic, fields. Notably it is clear that *universities*, although they began in the Roman West, were yet from the start idiorrhythmic. The wandering scholars *were* eremites, and they *were* persuaded to settle down together in particular places. They were, too, clerks in holy orders: like Orthodox monks, often in minor orders, so not priests. In British and German universities, to name but two cases, these traditions never died. All over the world they have now strongly revived, only this time without religion.

Thus consider the summing up of yet another French expert on Orthodox monasticism as a whole.[33] His words throw up many comical but perfectly genuine parallels to the situation in universities. I put the most obvious in brackets:

> 'Byzantinized monasticism retains, in spite of all, an inner resolution to be faithful to its origins (Conservative as to teaching techniques), whether we speak of its individualism or of the primacy it accords to salvation (Publish or perish).'
>
> 'It has no notion of religious orders . . . There is no rule, only customs claiming their origin in Sabas, Basil or Theodoros the Studite. There is a uniform tendency to bar the interference of the bishop: the monk is master in his own house (He has academic freedom). Prayer (Research), communal or private, is his essential occupation. He is not a missionary; he declines organized intellectual or manual labour (He won't take the classes ancillary to others' lectures, he dislikes drawing up booklists. He doesn't want his department to be a service department) . . . The monk is only a monk. Priesthood is for him a dangerous ambition (He doesn't want to be Chairman or Dean). His director, his "spiritual father", the sole arbiter of his conscience after God or in the place of God, may not be a priest (He is a member of the Chicago School; but the leader of that School holds no administrative position, even at Chicago): his spiritual investiture does not proceed, in the last analysis, from ordination (The administration does not sit on the tenure committee) . . .'
>
> 'This situation is automatically propitious to initiative, a sense of responsibility, freedom of inspiration. It can excite suspect and peripheral movements . . .'

We may add further parallels. The idiorrhythmic monk may keep his personal fortune, while the professor keeps the royalties from what he has written on university premises and time. Both again have formal tenure, preceded by periods of formal probation. This is because both are in origin eremites, who insist on their own freedom above all else. True co-operatives on the other hand bear down much more heavily on the individual, since their whole means of production are common, and not a mere shared infrastructure. But formal tenure has spread, alas, across the face of the earth.

Moreover, the word 'universitas' means guild, and a guild is a loose *partnership* (sec. 10), and working partners (as opposed to sleeping partners) are almost invariably idiorrhythmic. They can, and often do, function 'eremitically': doctors, lawyers, architects. Such partnerships, then, are not ordinary producers' co-ops. So history and logic combine to impose upon us the recognition of this as a separate form of economic organization. It is, to repeat, too loose to be Illyrian, and above all its technological conditions are wholly different. An economic model of the university must be based on the idiorrhythmy, not the enterprise, which we have already defined as a small command economy (sec. 1), even in Illyria. An intellectual, functioning as such, *cannot* be an employee, since he cannot be fulfilling another's detailed command.

The parallels in agricultural communities (open-field village, moshav, obshchina, ejido) are less exact, and certainly owe little to history. But wherever there is a substantial private plot, or plenty of opportunity for outside work, and permission to retain these private earnings, but some form of commonly owned infrastructure, we must call the unit idiorrhythmic. The kolkhoz, the moshav shitufi and the ejido colectivo are in the penumbra between Mt. Athos and Illyria. The perfect marginal case is the modern decentralized kolkhoz or even sovkhoz, whose internal 'links' have separate accountancy (chapter 6, sec. 9).

Similar moreover is that very traditional figure, the salesman on commission. Recently waiters in a capitalist restaurant, where tips bulk large, have been assimilated to them. Each waiter keeps a separate account with the management of the food he has sold; he is debited with it and must pay for it out of the customer's bill, which is his own gross revenue.

A special case is of interest: when the hours of work for the collective can be settled separately by each member, or, say, traded off privately between those who find collective duties more or less burdensome.[34] This is not only true of the kolkhoz but even of capitalist industrial enterprises. When industrialism was young a factory was often only a roof over the head of many craftsmen working independently. A typing pool is like that still, and shop assistants, counter clerks, etc., work in the same conditions. The idiorrhythmy, then, is the precursor of that ultra-modern device of advanced personnel management, *flexitime*. In these cases the price, place and nature of the work are still determined by what we must still call an enterprise, but time and the identity of the performer are no longer under its control. This is profitable because it reduces alienation and raises productivity.

Notes

1. *Economics of Imperfect Competition*, London 1933, p. 4.
2. I am greatly indebted here to my colleague and student Stefan Markowski.
3. Cf. R. H. Coase in *Economica*, November 1937; and sec. 22 here.
4. Income, not consumption, to allow for legacies. Cf. chapter 16.

5. Except in the kolkhoz, where labour receives the residual but the state takes the decisions. This is an unstable and hypocritical form.

6. Strictly each addition to current output entails a prior addition to labour and raw materials, and we must borrow or plough back to finance this. If we plough back we are increasing 'owners' capital employed', i.e. the e.b.f.

7. Cf. Dinko Dubravčić in *Economica*, 1970.

7a. The authorities on this question seem to me to be making too heavy weather of it. Cf. Tibor Scitovsky in *The Review of Economic Studies*, 1943; Milton Friedman, *Price Theory, a Provisional Text*, 2nd edn, Chicago 1967; Stefan Markowski, *The Micro-Economics of Illyria*, London Ph.D. Thesis 1974, ch. 3. 3.

8. Cf. Arthur Shadwell, *Drink, Temperance and Legislation*, London 1902; idem, *A Study of Disinterested Management*, True Temperance Association, London 1926. Cf. Sidney and Beatrice Webb, The History of Liquor Licensing in England, in their *English Local Government*, vol. 11, London 1963.

9. Also, in a different way, to a Chinese or Cuban Communist. For in these two countries there is also only salary, and no bonus; but the word 'disinterested' is counter-revolutionary. The manager must do his very best to expand production, but only for honour's sake.

10. Wiles 1961, pp. 200–1. The long term in this passage does not necessarily mean a change in fixed assets but simply a long time.

11. Basic literature on Illyria: Benjamin Ward in *AER*, May 1965 Evsey Domar in AER, 4/1966; Benjamin Ward, *The Socialist Economy*, N.Y. 1967; Jaroslav Vanek, *General Theory of Labor-Managed Market Economies*, Ithaca 1970; Deborah Milenkovitch, *Plan and Market in Yugoslav Economic Thought*, New Haven 1971; James E. Meade in *E.J.*, March 1972 (supplement); Egon Neuberger and Estelle James, *The Yugoslav Self-Managed Enterprise*, Indiana University, May 1971. Orthodox Yugoslavs, e.g. Branko Horvat, *An Essay on Yugoslav Society*, N.Y. 1969, reject the Illyrian analysis in favour of absolute profit maximization; cf. Milenkovitch, op. cit., chapter 8.

12. Chapter 6, sec. 7; Jan Vanek, *The Economics of Workers' Management*, London 1972.

13. Those who are familiar with Illyria should however note already that the supply curve of a single-product enterprise in perfect competition is very inelastic, since no product price change can move the maximum of AVA far away from *Oa*. Those who say this supply curve *must* be negative are in error (chapter 10, sec. 13).

14. For the actual unemployment in the actual Yugoslavia cf. chapter 14, sec. 12. For the foundation of new enterprises cf. chapter 13, sec. 16 and chapter 10, sec. 12.

15. Strictly this subsidy to the extruded labour lowers the average dividend on internal labour below ZX, and therefore reduces the offer of labour CZ a little.

16. This also happens in very many capitalist and Soviet-type organizations. Cf. Peter B. Doeringer and Michael J. Piore, *Internal Labor Markets*... Mass. 1971.

17. J. R. Wilson in *Economic Record*, May 1952; Job K. Savage in *Journal of Farm Economics*, August 1954; Peter G. Helmberger and Sidney Hoos, ibid., May 1962; Helmberger, ibid., August 1964. For a realistic treatment cf. Eldon C. Smith in ed. Kurt R. Anschel *et al.*, *Agricultural Co-operatives and Markets in Developing Countries*, N.Y. 1969.

18. I lift this and certain following passages directly from my op. cit. 1961, pp. 188 sqq.

19. Cf. my op. cit. 1961, pp. 94–100. Note that even a maximizable function may be multi-modal, with nothing but chance to guide us to the *maximum maximorum.*

20. I had originally written 'lazy and energetic', but that, to repeat, is a difference in taste not maximand. Everyone is interested in both leisure and other forms of real income. Laziness can most certainly be 'profit-maximizing' (i.e. 'Benthamite') behaviour.

21. In theory they could be monotonically related, but in practice this is never so over the whole range.

22. Note how exactly like the Chinese system this last criterion is (chapter 10).

23. Cf. Wiles 1961, s.v. 'indeterminacy'.

24. And in fact puts very many reasonable legal obstacles in its way: chapter 7, sec. 9.

25. If the real rate of interest in the savings bank is 5 per cent p.a. a rational Illyrian who expects to leave in twelve months will require a yield of 105 per cent. p.a.: Milenkovitch, op. cit., p. 220. However this is close to the Chicagoan assumption that bequest is irrational (chapter 16, sec. 9); we may be sure that Yugoslavs are not so selfish.

26. According to econometricians at present the most reliable rule is that the more money the firm has in the appropriation account the more it will invest. This rule has very many exceptions, however, and is of macro-economic interest only, since it does not say in what or with what purpose we invest.

27. This system is still very common in Asia. Cf. N. S. Cheung, *The Theory of Share Tenancy*, Chicago 1969 (but despite its originality this book is obscure and ill reasoned; the assumption that the share-cropping landlord can make his tenant do a certain amount of work by legally enforceable contract is crucial to his argument, but surely untenable. The first two chapters are the most valuable); J. S. Mill, *Principles of Political Economy*, Ashley's edn., Book II, chapters 1–7.

28. A progressive tax with the same probable yield as a proportional tax would yield the broken-line earnings curve. It is clear that the indifference curves could be fiddled so as to produce a man who worked longer even under this system.

29. Cf. Amit Bhaduri in *E.J.*, March 1973. But Mr. Bhaduri presents no actual figures, and neglects the possibilities that landlords had rather raise the crop-share, or invest in more share-cropping agreements with other peasants, than keep on making consumption loans.

30. Cf. chapter 11, secs. 10–11. It is not asserted that Weber's theory *was* untrue; quite likely the systems approach is a reaction to a change in bureaucratic style.

31. Cf. E. Amand de Mendieta, *La Presqu'ile des Caloyers*, Paris 1955, pp. 11–12, 41–7, 83, 85–92; Jean Decarreaux, 'Du Monachisme Primitif au Monachisme Athonite', in *Le Millénaire du Mont Athos, Etudes et Mélanges*, Chevetogne 1963, pp. 46–52; Michael Choukas, *Black Angels of Athos*, Vermont 1934, pp. 14–48, 119–57, 243–61. All have extensive bibliographies.

32. Russian Orthodoxy condemns idiorrhythmy. All its monasteries are coenobitic.

33. *Encyclopaedia Universalis*, Paris 1968, art. 'Monachisme'.

34. Cf. sec. 9 above; Joan Robinson in *AER*, March 1967, Dipak Mazumdar, privately circulated, 1973.

5

Peasants, Agriculture, Populism

5

1. Agriculture is a highly special case. With rare exceptions – Australasia, Northern Kazakhstan, the Argentine pampas, the middle and west of North America – it is the *industrie-mère* from which humanity has come. It embodies our past while other sectors (but precisely which ones?!) pre-figure our future. It is highly anthropological. Dominated by historical chance, tradition and localism, its organization is extremely diverse. Yet over and above all that it is dominated by topography and the micro-climate, so its techniques are extremely diverse. It presents, then, methods and enterprise forms all far more intimately bound up with the culture than in nearly any other activity. The priest blesses the farmer's harvest, and the nursery rhymes confirm his sense of his worth. And these things are slow to die. Thus the Hindu farmer worships his oxen; but sell him a tractor and he does *puja* to that instead, with a garland over the radiator.

Above all the farmer lives over his shop: his wife helps him with the harvest, he pushes aside his dinner plate to do the accounts. Heads of state, ambassadors, prime ministers, artists, writers, heads of Oxbridge colleges – the list is not long of those who preserve the medieval unity of life and work. So the farmer is in enviable company here (chapter 21, sec. 16), and is himself rightly envied on this account. He is not an alienated man, in perhaps the most important sense of that Protean word (chapter 21, sec. 16). Yet how small a benefit it is not to be alienated – the general miseries of the agricultural life show the great costs of such a state of affairs. Indeed the farmer reminds us of his still more unfortunate sister the housewife, who also 'preserves the medieval unity of life and work' – and would give her eye-teeth for a little more alienation.

The following anecdote sums up the peculiarities of agriculture, and the reasons why this separate chapter is necessary. A Russian émigré of right-wing views, high intelligence and Tsarist culture returned after 40 years to his native country as a member of a British delegation. It was an emotional and ambivalent occasion: he saw, for instance, the house of his childhood converted into an institute, and was warmly welcomed by its director, who apologized for all the changes. One Sunday the party drove out in several cars to the untouched old town of Vladimir to see the Kremlin; he rode with a Party member of rigid views and some forty summers. It was harvest time, and a sunny day after rain. Suddenly they turned off the macadam surface on to the dried mud verge, and as the dust rose through the floorboards they saw that the peasants had spread the grain all along the road to dry (there were no grain-driers in Vladimir). Ducks and chickens, doubtless privately owned, were helping themselves to the co-operative grain; no one stopped them. In Vladimir it was the local saint's name-day and very many people were drunk. A priest in full vestments stood in the street (not illegal in USSR, but rare and highly disapproved), blessing something. They saw over the Kremlin and drove back to Moscow. The dust, the peasants, the grain and the chickens were still at it. The Party member's face resembled a black cloud and at length he said to the émigré: 'Well, now you have seen it all. But you come to the virgin lands; that's different, that's real agriculture. A man gets on his plough in the morning and drives a single furrow until mid-day. Then he turns round his tractor, has lunch, and drives a single furrow back home. That's how it ought to be, and as for these people, let them rot.'

2. What exactly is agriculture, anyway? Basically it is tilling the soil or herding stock from a fixed abode.[1] But the more primitive the society the wider the concept, until whoever mainly does these things is said to be engaged in agriculture, even when he is building, trading or transporting.[2] This is just laziness: we classify people according to their main occupation, a habit tolerable in our simple civilized societies where people specialize, but grossly misleading in the more complicated polities from which these sprang. Truly to classify primitive man according to our modern categories, we need a seasonal and an hourly breakdown of what he does.

Before the Revolution the Russians had the right view of this matter. They confined modern census categories to the towns, and all else was 'village economy' (*sel'skoye khozyaistvo*). Russia had a classically dual economy, in the primitive sector of which the average worker was agriculturist, builder, small-scale manufacturer, trader and transporter according to season or to need. There was no Russian for 'agriculture', since the word was interpreted, according to its Latin roots, as meaning the tilling of the soil (*zemledeliye*); livestock care (*zhivotnovodstvo*) was a separate concept and the sum of the two had no appellation. Today the agriculturist is not supposed to engage in craft manufacture, trade or transport[3] (though of course he does), and the Russian language has acquired a phrase for agriculture: *sel'skoye khozyaistvo*! Yet even today the agriculturist, notably the kolkhoznik, officially performs innumerable tasks no longer considered agricultural in advanced countries. Not only must he build pig-sties (which we capitalists call 'construction' because it is mostly done by builders); he performs artificial insemination (which we call a medical service because it is mostly done by vets); he makes farm and indeed extra-farm roads, he drives loads down to the railway siding, he mends tractors . . . To a very large extent, then, the shrinkage of the agricultural sector in ACEs is an optical illusion, due to reclassification.

'Agriculture' and 'farm' cover the same concept, but are not 'countryside'. The countryside contains schools, mines, cement factories, railway signal boxes . . ., even apart from the 'specialization out of agriculture' referred to in the previous paragraph. Moreover, 'countryside' is an administrative, not an economic, concept. There are farms within town boundaries, though not many. But the official demographic concept of *rural non-farm* embraces about five times as many people as 'agriculture' or 'farm' in USA, and about one half as many in USSR.[4]

In this book 'peasant' is a technical term. It means a very small capitalist, employing his own family and, seasonally, a few hired hands, in 'village economy' as defined above for Tsarist Russia. A peasant, then, is *mainly* an agriculturist. He is very probably head over heels in debt. He is not above working for wages, perhaps to help out a neighbour during the harvest peak, perhaps in winter in a factory. He is probably a Populist (sec. 16). If he becomes richer without changing his life-style or techniques he is a 'kulak' or rich peasant. If he becomes still richer, puts on airs, does less manual work, gets a little education and buys some machines he is a 'capitalist farmer' – we avoid 'farmer' *tout court* as ambiguous. As to workers, i.e. proletarians, those in agriculture or the countryside do not differ from those in towns or other occupations, except that they may be a little poorer. Agricultural capitalism and socialism, then, are in little need of special treatment. It is mainly peasants and co-operative farms that interest us.

3. Why does the agriculturist live over his shop? The reason is very obvious, but like many obvious things it is not often enough analysed. Almost alone among enterprises,[5] the farm has great *internal distances* to be covered and must not be in a built-up area. Therefore while it is technically possible to commute to a farm it is rare. So his house is in it – who ever saw a factory with a house in the middle of the shop floor? – or very near it. On a big farm he may even have a camp to sleep in, when night catches him out. The only commuting is seasonal, and is done by seasonal workers (sec. 11). And they too use camps in or near the farm when they are working on it.

These internal distances affect the economies of scale. Ordinarily we measure scale by output, and it is a gross intellectual error to measure it by acreage in agriculture. Similarly economies are a matter of average total cost, so efficiency must not be measured by yield per acre. But the fact of acreage remains crucial. Time between jobs goes up, and labour supervision becomes very difficult, so the economies of scale cease at an earlier point than in most businesses. But this is all. As elsewhere there are no violent diseconomies that send costs soaring as the optimum size is passed, for they can be put off by decentralizing farm management:[6] the gang leader takes control, and the gang camps out overnight, or the milking operation is permanently entrusted to a responsible foreman. Such decentralization above all characterizes the vast Communist farm of today (kolkhoz or sovkhoz), but ideological and incentive matters gravely complicate that issue (chapter 6).

It is internal distance, again, that renders agricultural labour so unsupervisable. Duck behind the hill, stand upright behind the tree, and who knows where you are? The tasks, too, tend to be unique: you can plough the same field to the same depth year by year, but the soil is always differently heavy, and it is too expensive for the foreman to find out and make allowances. This unsupervisability also most powerfully limits the economies of scale. Few activities depend more on unsupervised labour morale; in few is the form of institution, its acceptability to the worker, more directly an input.

So each act of ploughing is unique. Uniqueness, as we see in more than one place, makes costing very difficult. It affects not only market forms but also institutions. After R and D and construction,[7] the principal case of unique products is certain sectors of agriculture. Hence the distinction between 'left- and right-wing crops'. The former are those where operations are most standardized, like grain. The latter are such crops as wine grapes, which require much individual attention by skilled labour. Most livestock (the exception is sheep) are a 'right-wing crop'. Communist methods are as unsuited to these latter as to R and D, construction and personal services. It is not only that these methods depend on large scale – there are very large milking machines and vineyards under capitalism. It is not only the Communist preference for capital-intensity – vineyards are always heavily capitalized. It is the element of personal attention and good labour morale. Communism seldom provides this, and particularly not in agriculture where it is so unpopular. So it relies on crude incentive schemes, and these, where labour is unsupervisable, lead to the cutting of corners. This is the basic reason for the shortage of livestock products that plagues most Communist countries: their workers will not get up in the middle of the night to help their favourite cow in labour, because they have no favourite cow.[8]

4. The problem of intra-enterprise distance further affects the lay-out of the village (if any) and the fields. Indeed these are one lay-out, not two. Town-planning is beyond the scope of this book, since it is so very loosely related to property, ideology and the market, and is almost totally unrelated to the internal technology of factories. But village-planning is of the essence of our subject. Patterns of residence and cultivation strongly influence each other, mostly with the latter leading.

It would need many volumes to treat this subject adequately, so indefinitely various are the possible solutions, so few and treacherous the generalizations, and so high from time to time the political passions.[9] Let us begin our small sample with the North European medieval open-field village, known from England to Russia. Basically a group has cleared a piece of forest, and bands together at night for protection. Further they know no better than a three-year rotation, with every third year fallow; and fencing is expensive but they have a good deal of livestock. These things put together make the open-field village almost a necessity. The houses must be together and defensible, so there has to be a village. It must be in the centre of the cultivated area, to save walking time. The fields must be large, so that fencing is spared and stock grazes freely.[10] There must be three fields. Yet we are not socialists or even kolkhozniks, so we shall each cultivate his own land, just as we own our own stock. Therefore each family must own a strip or strips in each field. Moreover such scattering is good insurance against hailstorms, cattle let out at the wrong time, noblemen's hunting parties, and other highly localized disasters.

Let us skip several centuries. Feudalism has come and gone: it imposed many extra burdens on us and was most exploitative, but it was an upper-class phenomenon, so it never touched us basically, i.e. in our village community. We are now at 1750–1800 in England (peak period of enclosures), or 1906 in Russia (Stolypin). Techniques have improved: a three-course rotation is no longer necessary – but it is impossible to get agreement on the delimitation of, say, four fields; livestock-breeding is now a fine art, but I cannot fence my good cow away from your scrub bull. In Marx's immortal words[11] the relations of production 'have become a fetter on the technique of production which has grown up with and under them' – what a pity he applied this to capitalism, where it is not true! Also why did he neglect revolution from above?

Things have become intolerable and the government intervenes, to bring again the relations of production into harmony with the technique of production. In England parliamentary commissioners actually divide up and consolidate the land, with an act of parliament for each village. They include the common, which is uncultivated land belonging to the village but outside its three basic fields. The lion's share of this is taken by the ex-feudal lord, whose rights in the common are one of the really important results of feudalism. Consequently, he is the initiator and beneficiary of enclosure. In Russia the ex-feudal lord has been selling off land, he does not want to be a farmer; so the Stolypin reforms have little effect on him. The government is supporting kulaks. In villages where periodical repartition has already ceased private ownership is made compulsory at a stroke. Elsewhere the peasants are encouraged to vote for it in the council of the village community, while there are provisions whereby an individual may consolidate himself out.

But the result for residence-and-cultivation patterns is the same. The English capitalist farmer sets up a house inside his newly consolidated farm; but the village is a too deeply rooted institution and has continued to house the agricultural proletariat and the 'rural non-farm' elements. Approximately this compromise has been exported to the overseas lands of Anglo-Saxon settlement. The system is ideal for pure capitalism, and passes almost without notice in textbooks. Similarly a Russian could still live in a central village and farm a large consolidated area granted to him by the village council in exchange for his strips (the *otrub* of the early twentieth century). Only in fact this was inconvenient, and he tended, like the English kulak 100–200 years earlier, to move out and build on his own property (the *khutor* of the same period).[12] In 1929 these small *khutors* were not so distant from the village as to be impossible to collectivize.

5. This gradual enclosure went on through the NEP, but was not complete by 1929. Historical chance willed it that compulsory collectivization should first take place in a country where settlement was still mainly of the three-big-open-fields pattern; it was the easiest of all patterns to collectivize. Indeed since it automatically consolidated the strips collectivization conferred at least the advantages of enclosure – a point much too little stressed in Western accounts.

It is not obvious how to collectivize other patterns of settlement. First, suppose the *khutor* is extremely large and well established, as in modern England or indeed in USA. How does one approach a Texan *khutor* of 100,000 acres? It is not entirely chance that collectivization has never been tried in England or Texas; for very large *khutors* go with ACEs, and so do not have Communist governments.

But East Germany did go Communist, and presented another problem: the latifundium, or large capitalist farm run by a manager and employing a large non-seasonal proletariat (the North American farm is as large, but labour productivity is so high that its proletariat is only seasonal – sec. 11). So the latifundium, while such an obvious type, is not common. It survives in Southern Spain and Latin America. The obvious thing to do with it, being itself a 'superior' capitalist form, is to make it into a 'superior' socialist form, the sovkhoz; but for reasons shown in sec. 7 a very wrongheaded imitation of USSR was pursued instead. The large and efficient latifundium was first split among its employees, who thereby went 'backwards', becoming peasants; and later collectivized! History, it seems, may only run one course.

Then, finally, there are mini-villages no bigger than an extended family. Both the Celtic run-rig (well known in Scotland and North Wales) and the Serbian zadruga belong to this class. Related nuclear families lived cheek by jowl or in one large house and co-operated on certain tasks but not others, according to tradition, and under the direction of the patriarch. A respectable collective farm would have to contain several of these units, but how to co-ordinate them? We have no experience, because the Serbian zadruga had long been replaced by a *khutor* pattern when in 1949 Yugoslavia had her collectivization drive.[13]

The problem of how to collectivize inconvenient village-and-farm systems diminishes with progress in the arts of communication. Telephones, walky-talkies, even a good compact dirt road and some bicycles make a lot of difference. But at present it remains a very hard problem, and one quite additional to that of mere size.

6. Villages, then, are necessitated by small and scattered holdings. If holdings are large and compact, the actual farmers leave the village to live on them. But all sorts of other people live in villages, and they have other functions. Among these is the security function. Originally formed by the people to protect themselves from wolves, nomads, guerrillas, border raiders, etc., etc., villages are now encouraged by the security police so as to facilitate their tasks of control and repression. Moreover the village is a step towards the town, and therefore towards 'civilization', at least as understood by the government that pays the security police. And all this reacts back on the patterns and sizes of holdings.

'Villagization' by governments, then, has become quite common. Sometimes, as in Malaya against the Communists, or in Kikuyuland against the Mau-Mau, it is the compulsory act of colonial governments. In these cases it is not economic, but serves its primary purpose: control and repression. In this context, note the origin of 'concentration camps'. They were open prisons in which the British army forced Boer families to live together during the South African War (1899–1902). Egress for work by day was permitted. The idea was to abolish independent farmsteads (*khutors* again!), which could feed and shelter Boer guerrillas. This, then, as the phrase literally implies, was a super-compulsory villagization.

In Tanzania, on the other hand, it was the government of a newly liberated people that villagized the countryside, gratuitously and with disastrous results. Tanganyika[14] gained her independence from Britain in December 1961. She had unusual political unity under the TANU Party, which was undisturbed by tribal jealousies inside or outside the Party. The normal pattern of settlement was by *khutor*: there were often no villages. Somehow this fact was perceived as an economic and social problem requiring urgent solution. Certainly on the macro-scale there was a similar problem: the vast territory of the country is very thinly populated by very poor people, and most of them live around the periphery, without good communication to the capital. So the natural preoccupation of the new régime with long-distance communications ('centralization') seems to have slopped over into an obsession with villagization, without however collectivization of the fields. From January 1963 to April 1966 an extremely expensive campaign was conducted. It was of course voluntary but it brought, and could have brought, no economic benefits at all. It was eventually judged that the gains in direct contact with the people did not outweigh the discontent, upheaval and expense. But after a villagization has set in again, with collectivization added! – the celebrated *ujamaa* villages. There has been a good deal of violence, especially to peasant property, with officials accused, à la Staline, of exceeding their mandate. But for reasons unknown to the writer the world has averted its eyes this time. Tunisia has been through a similar experience.

To the 'civilization' and security arguments for the village succeed those for the small town. The Soviet kolkhozy, as we saw, were formed one-to-one out of existing villages. But villages too present a security problem: in large wooded tracts whole villages used to exist in Tsarist Russia (and later, it is rumoured) unknown to the authorities. In one-storey houses, too, the neighbours cannot spy on you. But the main point is that villagization does not abolish the difference between town and country: the village *is* the country, so not 'civilized'. Hence arose in 1950 the notion of the *agrogorod* or agro-town, which, rejected at the time after virtually public debate, has persisted to this day with many vicissitudes. Two-storey houses, paved and lighted streets, a cinema – the thing is a Marxist's dream and the peasants have got to like it.

Yet again the pattern of cultivation and farm management must be changed to suit the new residence pattern: the ideal *agrogorod* lies in the middle of an amalgamated kolkhoz (say three old ones), or at the corner where several sovkhozy meet, in the virgin lands. In the former case the peasants from the two abandoned villages are now separated from their private plots by a substantial walking distance – an ideological step forward. The collective fields, too, can be bigger than ever before. The economies of scale from amalgamation itself are quite genuine: the kolkhoz is an unpopular and inefficient kind of farm at all times, but the bigger it is the lower the administrative overheads, etc.[15] The economies of 'agrogorodization', however, are quite another matter, since the whole concept neglects the problem of internal space.[16]

7. Is there any regularity in all this? Yes, something positive can be said, but it is not very consoling. It is that field boundaries and rural roads are, along with place-names, among the most ancient and immovable of human monuments. Agriculture is dreadfully intractable and particular. Whoever first settles an area determines its residence-and-cultivation pattern until some major catastrophe: invasion followed by genocide, enclosure, collectivization. Mere revolutions in towns have no effect. The Russian village community was as strong in 1925 as in 1910. Even genocide may be unavailing: the Anglo-Saxon invasion pushed back run-rig to the Celtic fringes, substituting the open-field village, but not in Kent, where the field boundaries survive since Roman times.[17] No wonder, then, that Marxist experts on agriculture prefer virgin land: they like to deny a role to historical chance.

Indeed since Marxism, or ideologies claiming that name, covers one third of humanity, it is important to see how its attitudes to agriculture developed historically. Indeed they will not otherwise be understood. Note, amid all the follies and crimes, the grandeur of the whole movement and the tenacity with which a rather unchanging ultimate goal has been pursued. In contrast capitalist agriculture has 'just growed', in a random process occasionally interrupted by populist interventions. The governments of ACEs scarcely dare even to touch farm boundaries and strip consolidation. It is ironical indeed that where Communism is most different from capitalism it has also proved to be most inferior.

Marx and Engels began, in the *Communist Manifesto* (1848), with sovkhozy alone. The notion that the concentration of capital will lag in agriculture, and that there will still be peasants after the revolution, is missing. Armies of labourers will work voluntarily on factory farms. Town and country will be assimilated. Agriculture will present no special difficulty.

Marx never really returned to agriculture, nor did Engels until Marx's death (1883). The *Grundrisse*, *Anti-Dühring*, *Kapital*, the *Critique of the Gotha Programme* – none has anything specific. It is true that in 1876 Marx wrote his celebrated letter to Vera Zasulich, the Russian populist, that the Bolsheviks were to suppress until 1924. He was flattered by enquiries from such a quarter. Yes, the village community could carry Russia directly into socialism, without an intervening stage of capitalism. The course of events in *Kapital* had no reference to Russia, provided the community was not shortly destroyed. But the letter to Zasulich presented agriculture (or village economy) rather as a leading than as a lagging sector. However, it may possibly have given Engels (did he ever see it?) the idea for the kolkhoz.

For the German Social Democrats were gaining electoral experience. The Communist Manifesto was poison in rural constituencies. To promise sovkhozy was bad enough, when peasants wanted their own land. To promise them only after capitalist concentration and increasing misery had done their long work was crazy. Besides, the Revisionists kept pointing out that on the continent of Europe (and they might have added Ireland) capital was not in fact concentrating or misery increasing in agriculture. On the contrary medical progress had outstripped industrial progress, and, the farm population growing, peasants were continuing to subdivide their properties as of yore; but technical progress was such that the peasant was getting a better living than ever out of his smaller area.

So in 1894, in the journal *Neue Zeit*,[18] the old Engels rendered himself more important than the young Marx was ever to be. Following the Danish socialists he recommended to the German party the voluntary co-operatization of the poor peasants after the revolution. In this way their sentiment of ownership would not be offended, since they would still get rent on the land they contributed, while the economies of scale which every Marxist discerns in agriculture would also be obtained. Larger peasants, employing a little wage-labour, would of course be a greater problem; it was not easy to define in the village the battle-lines of the class-war.

Thus was the kolkhoz born into the world. The idea was accepted by the Bolsheviks, who did indeed give tax incentives for the formation of kolkhozy of one sort or another from the moment of their seizure of power. They formed very few sovkhozy, even from the various model farms and latifundia that they took over. Rather was their first step an anarchic, populist land reform: the unsteady, town-based régime encouraged the peasants to seize the (little remaining) land of the nobles, the church and the Tsar, and divide it up amongst themselves. Their sincere assumption was that the Russian peasantry would really be won over to voluntary collectivization, and would really be put off by nationalization.[19]

So with their infinite capacity for self-deception, the Bolsheviks plunged in 1929 into all-out forcible collectivization, calling it voluntary. The new kolkhoz was mixed up with many extraneous matters: tractorization, the expulsion and death of the kulaks and the use of their property as a bribe, compulsory procurement,[20] illicit livestock slaughter ('the Soviets won't have my property, I'll eat it'). There was even famine later, but *not* due to a fall in harvests. Rather was it due to over-zealous procurement, which in a way shows how efficient the new institution was. The Fairy Carabosse was indeed present at this birth: the Soviet kolkhoz is too historically special for us to judge from it the efficiency of the institution *per se.*

No Communist country has repeated the story in its full horror, but each has repeated it more or less. This is a remarkable tribute to the notion of Soviet Infallibility: like the Papal kind, it condemns the movement not merely to speak but to act as if every previous action, particularly in USSR, had been right. The mere empirical acts of stumbling and panicky men today become sacred parts of the canon tomorrow. So collectivization becomes right for all times and places, for if once we allow that circumstances alter cases we not only set ourselves free of the holy precedents, but also encourage enquiry into what were the circumstances of the original case, and how it itself was justified. So satellite ontogeny recapitulates Soviet phylogeny, as the biologists might say.

The most striking example, we saw, is that Ulbricht did not turn the Junkers' estates into sovkhozy on the spot; but split them up into peasant holdings and then with much sweat collectivized them years later! Yet he had the Red Army at his back, and he knew as well as any man that forced collectivization is not a whit more popular than nationalization.

Nevertheless, by tax concessions, threats and gradualism, and above all by not deporting kulaks but allowing them into the new kolkhoz, all subsequent STEs have made less of a mess of the process.[21] Yet in all cases production fell and livestock was slaughtered.[22]

8. Clearly kolkhozy are not socialism. So what is to be the next step? For the property and ideology aspects compare chapter 3, sec. 7. That passage necessarily also explains one of the most plausible next steps, *sovkhozizatsia*, and the extent of its victory. We may pass over the creation (1932) and liquidation (1958) of the machine and tractor station (MTS) as a mere episode in our long view (chapter 6, sec. 10). The amalgamation of kolkhozy in 1950 was explained in sec. 6. The idea of making them

into separate communes was dropped, we saw, by Stalin himself (chapter 3).

Of these measures most other STEs have imitated kolkhoz amalgamation. For most of them too were lucky enough to have backward villages without *khutors*, and so formed small one-village kolkhozy in the first place. Most, too, have set up and subsequently liquidated MTS. None has gone so far in *sovkhozizatsia*.

But it is hard to generalize any more, and there is by now great variety.[23] In particular Bulgaria has *vertically integrated* her (amalgamated) collective and state farms with state processing, transporting and even exporting enterprises. These are the 'agro-industrial complexes', within which however the old kolkhozy retain a sufficient formal identity for their members still to be called peasants ('co-operators' in the polite Bulgarian phrase), not workers. This is surely the most promising of all paths to agricultural socialism, and has been widely copied.[24] Such vertical integration has long been progressing under capitalism; it corresponds to system-free technological trends.

Hungary has gone to the other extreme, decentralizing her kolkhozy internally without amalgamating them (chapter 6, sec. 9). Her kolkhozy also invest 'downstream' in shops, transport, construction enterprises, brickworks, etc. Thus small *co-operative* agro-industrial complexes are formed – an ideologically most retrograde tendency which it has required state power to repress.

China cut herself out of the Soviet tradition in 1958, at the point equivalent to kolkhoz amalgamation. This she brought forward to only three years after collectivization, but in a very new form. For the sad fate of the monstrous People's Communes, see chapter 6, sec. 9.

Note in all these, and in the following, cases the sympathy of agricultural forms with the general political and economic movement of the country. Bulgaria has become extremely centralized (chapter 9, sec. 11); Hungary decentralized and ideologically cool (chapter 10, sec. 10); China decentralized and ideologically quite rabid (chapter 10, sec. 11).

Only one Communist state rejected absolutely from the start the doctrine of Soviet Infallibility: Cuba. This is because Fidel Castro had never been, and still is not, under Party discipline. Consequently Cuban ontogeny does not recapitulate Soviet phylogeny, not even, as in Poland, Yugoslavia or China, a part of it. The Cuban 'land reform' was quite informal and extra-legal, since in that first year (1959) Cuba was not Communist, but certain of her provincial bosses were. Quite large peasant holdings were left intact, but the confiscated latifundia were not divided up. So the question arose, how do we manage them? The situation was much like that in Algeria in 1962, when the French landowners ran away. The Algerians, who never did go Communist, turned all the farms over to workers' councils, but in Cuba this only happened to sugar cane plantations, while the great livestock ranches were directly nationalized.

I.e. where much pre-revolutionary capital had been accumulated the state took it over and directly founded sovkhozy. But the labour-intensive farms, which could not profit by running down capital, were allowed self-management. This was more nearly on the pattern of the Yugoslav factory or state farm than of the kolkhoz.[25]

This distinction would appear to be quite essential for an undogmatic Communist government dedicated, as is the Cuban, to equality. Quite apart, too, from historically created capital, why should any group of farmers enjoy the rent of confiscated land? The kolkhoz system allows them to keep any rent that the chances and vagaries of procurement and multiple pricing leave – and that is not a little. Nay more, even after the revolution luck and good management pile up capital in one place more than another. There is thus yet again no doubt that sovkhozy are more egalitarian, for the state takes both profit and rent (cf. chapter 16).

Subsequently both Cuba and Algeria have sovkhozized their self-managed farms, but mainly because they were mismanaged.

9. But two Communist countries, having experimented with the kolkhoz, went back to individual peasants: Yugoslavia (1953) and Poland (1956). In Poland a few collective farms remain, living proof that poor peasants offered sufficient tax incentives and supply privileges will do the thing voluntarily. There is also a sovkhoz sector about as big and inefficient as in other East European countries. The Polish peasants, like the Polish church, are tolerated deviations within the strictly Soviet bloc. But Yugoslavia is a genuinely independent country, whose non-farm sector is also quite different. She too has what began as state farms, only since 1950 they have been self-managed on a market. So they look very like kolkhozy with genuine democracy, but in view of their historical origins we call them 'Yugoslav state farms' (strictly 'combines, estates and farms'); the real kolkhozy (strictly 'co-operatives' or *zadruge*) were mostly liquidated in 1953.

The third case of a peasant agriculture under Communism is the Soviet NEP. The *locus classicus* of Sovietology, and the *pons asinorum* for all students of historical inevitability, is: *did Stalin have to end the NEP*? – at all, when he did, in that manner, at that speed?[26] Now Yugoslavia and Poland show national income growth not smaller than during the first Soviet Five-Year Plan, their farm sectors do as well as any contemporary Soviet-type agriculture, and their régimes are not threatened by peasant subversion; and each of these propositions is also true of the Soviet NEP. So *prima facie* Stalin must be condemned altogether: there was no need to end NEP ever. Could a more detailed analysis justify him?

In 'lower-middle-class economies', just after industrial take-off, town-country[27] relations partake of the nature of international trade. The prices of the products exchanged yield terms of trade; the balance of this trade leads to money flows; some of this money is hot; productivity levels differ greatly; migration should be controlled, etc., etc. The economy is dual, and the line of duality runs precisely here. All this was standard analysis in Moscow until 1929. The conclusion should have been drawn that if the Soviet state can profit from co-existence and trade with capitalist countries (and this was in fact enthusiastically believed) it can do the same with its own countryside. Now in the NEP and in modern Yugoslavia the non-farm sectors, though socialist, constitute a market economy. But if a command economy is for some reason desirable, and if, as is evident, it too can co-exist and trade with the capitalist world market, it too can leave free peasants and a rural market – and this is what Poland has demonstrated. The opposite conclusion, that our countryside is part of the world market and therefore part of the world capitalist conspiracy is inside our borders, is mystical Marxist paranoia. Treat a peasant halfway decently and he is no security problem.

Does not the concentration of capital threaten the régime with actual large capitalists? But the process is extremely slow and can be completely stopped by taxation and the law. Moreover a few large capitalists are more easily controlled than many small, and pose less of a threat. It is interesting that there are no formal upper limits to holdings in Poland, or in the USSR under NEP, though there are in Yugoslavia. The reason seems to be that if the state intervenes legally to regulate private land ownership, and sets a maximum, it grants ideological recognition to that maximum. But high and progressive taxes are and were levied on non-socialist income. No Communist government need allow the concentration of private capital. Of course this does pose problems for the overall volume of investment, to which we shall come.

Perhaps, then, the supply of the staple food to the towns is somehow endangered – and certainly the kolkhoz performs its function of grain pump magnificently, especially in 1932–3 when the townsman was better fed than the countryman, and the latter starved to death although the harvest was good. But *speculation* against the towns is a minor matter, and a sane government can counter it within the market system, e.g. by a very few well-publicized imports. After all it is better to have a system that actually *produces* food. This is particularly true of small countries which cannot rely on a good harvest in any region, so must often import their staple: for them the export and general production capability of agriculture is much more important than the security of a particular staple.

Can a peasant village economy extrude labour quickly enough for employment in industry? The historical answer is simply yes: idle unskilled labour is a great feature of Soviet-type industry, so the rate of absorption could be lower. Poland today has hundreds of thousands of underemployed, as well in the factories as on the farm, plus a considerable economic emigration; USSR under the NEP, with a rate of industrial growth not inferior to most later Communist rates, was unable to absorb the surplus labour its peasantry created. There were 1.6 million unemployed in 1929, or 13 per cent of the non-peasant labour force. Thereafter Stalin abolished rural crafts and set the surplus peasantry to idle in factory and prison, but not in statistics. Besides, he still suffered in his own opinion from a labour surplus in 1932, or otherwise he would surely not have reintroduced the Tsarist internal passport system, which had the main purpose of keeping the peasant out of the towns. For other citizens have a permanently valid passport, while the kolkhoznik only gets an *ad hoc* travel document. Other citizens, then, are legally far more mobile: as 'paid-up' members of the socialist sector, they are already 'in', and can move with some freedom except into major towns. But if the distinction was still drawn until January 1975, how can there have been a shortage of unskilled labour in the socialist sector? (The supply of skilled labour of course depends on education, not migration.)

Nor is it clear that anything so inefficient as a kolkhoz does require less labour than individual farms. The kolkhozniks clearly will not work so hard, or so long. They will probably slaughter their draft animals, and (it was certainly so in USSR until 1940) the supply of tractors will probably be insufficient to replace them. Post-war statistics lead to the same conclusion: with much more capital and land than individual peasants, kolkhozy need only somewhat less labour to produce as much, many years after the upheaval that introduced them. The factor productivity residual was negative for many years.[28]

Does collectivization somehow generate more saving and taxes? Here is a more serious argument. Clearly it does: the kolkhoz is as good a finance pump as a grain pump. In so far as this surplus is ploughed back into the farm, capital is being substituted for efficiency. The production figures tell us it would be better to have no kolkhoz and a smaller surplus. But certainly the kolkhoz can also be exploited in this way for state or non-farm purposes. Mostly free peasants will save only for ploughback, they evade direct taxes with great ease. As to indirect taxes, exactly which ones will hit peasants harder than townsmen? We see in sec. 14 but one out of many false allegations that this is so. But if certain ones do, they will turn the terms of trade against the peasant, who will simply produce less – or eat more. The kolkhoz on the other hand is subject to command planning and procurement; its elasticity of supply is lower, so indirect taxes on it yield more.[29]

But the most serious argument for collectivization is that peasants are not socialist, which Yugoslavia and Poland aim to be. Moreover agricultural productivity must rise, so capital must be accumulated; but by whom? Both countries have the same general answer: co-operatize, even nationalize, additional modern farm capital in 'Danish-type' co-ops or Soviet-type MTS, but leave livestock, land and buildings in private hands for many decades. In the long run new fixed capital will be concentrated in state hands and peasants will become not only dependent on it but fond of it: machines lighten labour. The agricultural population will diminish owing to development elsewhere, and this too will help to abate land-fetishism. Moreover (as in Poland today) older peasants without direct heirs can be encouraged to sell their farms to the state, in exchange for an annuity. So only after a long period of erosion will it be time for the kolkhoz, or more probably the sovkhoz.

Poland and Yugoslavia have undoubtedly an attractive policy, and Soviet impatience and cruelty did much damage. But the most recent tendencies in both countries leave us wondering how far they will succeed (chapter 6, sec. 4).

Alternatively one could forget about socialism in agriculture.

10. So the state of affairs bequeathed by history is of extreme importance, but radical reorganization is always tempting. Agriculture is the classic sector where organization is an input, and change in organization a potentially productive investment. But the cost of this input is invariably underestimated. We are asked to spend money, not on tangible objects nor even on 'productive work', but on propaganda, political effort or legal actions; and all this, like a construction project, always takes more time and money than one supposes. So we take the shortcut of blanket legislation and force, which ought to save money or at least time. But the outturn is likely to be just the contrary: counter-revolution, flight from the land, livestock slaughter, wholesale slackness and sabotage, etc. And when we say 'likely' we mean no statistically measurable probability, since there is no exactly comparable experience on which to base such a thing.

Besides, the benefits are apt to be smaller than what we promise; for the technical efficiency of the existing system is always higher than the reformer supposes, since the peasant is never quite the fool he supposes, and he has good rational reasons to prefer stability. If latifundia can co-exist with small holdings, if in efficient and modern Germany ruthless and self-seeking peasants can prefer strips, we should think twice and humbly before interfering. Agricultural reorganization is not a matter for simple-minded dogmatists. Indeed the pattern of settlement and cultivation probably matters much less than technical education and capital-intensity. Moreover there exists a whole spectrum of techniques, adapted to farms of every size. No wonder STEs do not manufacture small tractors! For what would happen to the economies of scale, if each kolkhoznik could use his private rotavator on his private plot? The rotavators would be better maintained than the tractors, and the argument for encroaching on the collective fields would be irresistible.

All in all, land reform is a very risky investment. Of course it is much more than an investment, with its overt socio-political aims. But that does not make it any less risky, far from it; since those aims are never exactly obtained either. It is a striking fact that the FPR of Soviet agriculture was negative or zero in 1928–53 (above). In this period land area was not much increased, so returns cannot have diminished; clearly the kolkhoz was less efficient than the peasant farm. In periods when agriculture takes in more land, as e.g. in USSR under Khrushchev, a negative residual is only to be expected. In other periods it is a very striking phenomenon indeed.

11. Let us turn to some technically economic considerations. Agriculture (in the strict sense of tillage and livestock care) is highly seasonal. There is a small peak demand for labour in spring and a very big one in autumn. In snowy climates labour in winter, except on livestock, so far from being demanded, is impossible. The more livestock there are, and the warmer the winter, the less true this is. This seasonality has two enormous institutional effects: winter crafts and migrant gangs.

If after the industrial revolution and the improvement of communications small crafts and 'village economy' survive, it is because of the winter surplus of farm labour. For it is not worth while to organize anything capital-intensive, or even merely large-scale, with such temporary labour. There is even an intermediate stage: home crafts yield to seasonal, medium-scale but light, industry in nearby towns. In either case the specialization and sophistication of these products is often very great, and they attain the great accolade of being exported. Whole villages develop specialized skills. Besides, the life of such a worker is healthy and varied. It seems, indeed, in a rich country that can afford it, the kind of inefficiency that should be promoted.[30]

The STE's hostility to crafts and, in a lesser way, to seasonal movement is a most peculiar example of blind dogmatism. Although we may certainly infer from the works of Marx a general hostility to small scale and to economic freedom, Marx showed every possible understanding of periods of transition. Until the climate is so far mastered, or tillage techniques so far changed, as to abolish the seasonal labour peaks, unemployment is the only alternative to winter crafts. But this is for the very far future, and meanwhile either the kolkhoz or the sovkhoz could easily accommodate such activity. It need not even be private, it could itself be co-operatized, à la Chinoise. The fact that China is more rational in this respect is one of the main reasons for not calling her an STE.

In North America and a few other rich places an alternative solution has been built up. The farmer is rare and skilled. There are so few of him that he is busy all year, and knows nothing of winter crafts. The seasonal peak is met by migrant gangs who, following it from place to place across a continent, get many months of employment. Socially speaking this is a lamentable alternative. The migrant is a despised nomad in a settled society. Being virtually without a home he cannot educate his children or defend himself in a court of law. Contrary to received opinion, the migrant gets a good hourly wage. But he has little power to enforce honest accountancy or safety measures.[31] The Russian or German type of migration, from one farm to one factory by a solid citizen with roots, is infinitely preferable. This is a classic demonstration that one should not always take advantage of the division of labour.

12. Then again agriculture is perfectly competitive for the most part. That it has many firms is obvious, and that its prices are set in centralized professional markets. That it produces homogeneous products is sometimes denied. But the products are homogeneous in the required sense: the price difference between one grade and another is determined on the open market, by equal bargaining (chapter 10, secs. 2, 5). Moreover entry is easy: the farmer can easily sow one crop rather than another, and entry into farming itself is not what is meant. It is a myth that perfect competition is a myth. The real myth is that there could be perfect competition throughout the economy – even the inputs into agriculture are sold and bought on imperfect markets.

The consequence of this market perfection is that when the government intervenes it does so in a highly special way, quite different from those mainly discussed in chapter 10. Above all, where the seller does not normally set the price himself, as in all kinds of imperfect competition, it is hardly possible for the government to do so. The tradition of an independently higgled bargain is too strong and the number of bargainers too great. We deal first with the situation where the government's object is to raise the price. Simply to exclude imports may suffice, as for any product. But if this will not work we face controls of a new type, institutionally different from those in use where prices are administered: subsidies and cropping quotas.

Only rich governments can afford subsidies, and even they must (if democratic) have some reason other than the technical difficulties of price control to offer the taxpayer. The three main ones are: Keynesian pump-priming, the protection of poor food consumers and the protection of poor marginal farmers. But the last two items raise another 'technical difficulty': that of confining a benefit conferred by price manipulation, e.g. subsidy, to poor people on either side of the market. No serious attempt is ever made, and large farmers in particular make enormous gains. But large farmers are seldom corporations. It is of course distributively neutral if corporations make more money, since they employ and are owned by a random sample of the population. But owing to the persistence of the family farm large farmers are rich men. Indeed the choice of price manipulation entails virtual indifference to income distribution. Only if agricultural prices were very depressed, say as under Stalin or during the world slump, could one defend the raising of agricultural prices as a redistribution of income from rich (town) to poor (country).

The government that subsidizes a crop engages in an open market operation, just as surely as if it were buying bills in Lombard Street. It increases the supply of money equally in both cases, unless (in either case) its funds come from a current budget surplus; in the agricultural case only the new money does not directly become a liquidity base in a system of fractional reserves. In both cases the open market is a perfect market; in both cases price control is almost impossible – though in the money market it has often enough been tried.[32] In both cases the appeal is to the profit motive: the government is immensely powerful in the market, and it pays no one to deal at a different price. In neither case could a private agency do the same thing.

If in subsidizing prices the government is unique, in imposing cropping quotas it only follows the lead of private cartels. For the cartel in this sector also has difficulty in imposing its will, and must also renounce the control of prices. Output restriction (or more precisely sowing restriction, for who can control the harvest?) is comparatively easy because an official of the cartel or a civil servant with a good detailed map just drives round to see what area is sown with the crop in question. Often the government limits its liabilities through price support by imposing quotas as well. Otherwise it will probably generate a burdensome surplus that must be exported – with a yet greater subsidy.

13. To lower prices is quite another matter. If politics and the balance of payments permit, one can import. But often imports are impossible, and yet we still want to lower prices to the consumer while keeping up or even increasing domestic supply. It is worse than useless in this very common case simply to decree a lower price, or to establish a government monopoly at a lower price, as the Bolsheviks did in 1926.[33] We have somehow to increase or maintain off-farm sales at this new price.

This is the situation well known to military commanders and Communist governments as the procurement crisis. For procurement in general, a cross between 'purchase' and 'confiscation', see chapter 9, sec. 14. Only very strong governments, with plenty of loyal native-speaking troops on the ground, can actually confiscate the peasants' crops, so they bully them to deliver at low prices. The very same causes that make agriculture perfectly competitive make it 'non-confiscable'.

'War' Communism, then, did not really work. Stalin's celebrated answer, in 1929, was a compulsory increase in enterprise size beyond the threshold of 'confiscability', and this was the essence of collectivization at that time. For its later development, cf. chapter 6. Note the parallel, though less sanguinary, interest of the French government in larger enterprises (chapter 9 sec. 6).[34]

In the Soviet annual plan only the sowing plan and the procurements figure, since it is a command document. The whole of agricultural production figures in the FYP which we saw is only a perspective plan from which the annual commands are supposed to be inferred.

It is also possible to increase agricultural supply cheaply by forcing labour to stay on the farm. One form of this is the feudal *adscriptio glebae*, which was rather for the profit of the landlord than of the townsman; the adscripted villein had to perform labour service on the demesne farm. The modern form of this is the Soviet refusal to give the kolkhoznik an internal passport.[35]

14. Agriculture is favoured by the government in rich countries, and perhaps given less than its due in poor ones. Why is this so? Take the poor country first:

(i) The agriculturist is poor and ignorant. The country probably has no democratic institutions, and he would in any case not know how to use them.

(ii) In poor countries towns and industry enjoy the mystique. The ruling ideology is likely to be anti-agricultural. Populism (sec. 15) is sure to be virulently present; but it will normally be a minority creed.

(iii) Planning is nowadays the rule, and planners are educated townsmen. They share the popular mystique. They also want to create jobs for people like themselves – and such people hate the countryside. Again they prefer to put capital into things that can be easily planned.

(iv) Non-farm occupations are unionized, and cost inflation is rampant. Unless manufactured imports[36] are permitted, agriculture's terms of trade decline.

(v) Rich landowners, if any survive, live in towns, and put their money into trade, construction and industry (in that order), rather than plough it back into their land.

(vi) The government is too poor to help so many people.

Nevertheless we should beware of taking expressions of intention for fiscal actuality. Consumer taxes surely fall more heavily on non-farmers simply because they consume more.[37] Non-farmers are richer because they are more skilled. Over-population in agriculture is a very difficult problem, and the government that fails to solve it is not necessarily exploitative.

But in ACEs the boot is undoubtedly on the other foot:

(a) The government is rich and farmers are few.

(b) There is probably parliamentary democracy. If so constituencies are on a territorial basis. Then agriculture and mining are uniquely privileged in possessing pocket MPs to do their log-rolling – another effect of the peculiar spatial properties of agriculture.

(c) The farmers are rich and educated and their trade union is particularly effective (sec. 15).

(d) The dominant socio-economic mystique is one of nostalgia. The farmer is not quite the repository of all virtue that populists make out (sec. 15); for populism is an unsophisticated creed of early opposition to towns and industrialism. But the people are sick of pollution and suburbia; they want to preserve the countryside and the denizens thereof.

(e) The fact of perfect competition makes it difficult for the government to intervene except by subsidy.

(f) Rich landowners, if there are any left, are interested in agriculture.

(g) A 'tail' of genuinely poor marginal farmers remains. But rich states are welfare states, so these farmers must be helped. Yet the ordinary social services for the non-farm poor do not fit their case, so the government manipulates prices. But such measures partake of the nature of farm subsidies – and help much richer farmers too.

Under Communism we observe something like the same evolution. Communist countries used to be very poor; they inherited anti-agricultural attitudes; they had the tremendous Marxist prejudices explained above; agricultural subsidies would have meant subsidies to peasants, i.e. to capitalists. Even so the sovkhozy, treated according to the ordinary rules of the socialist sector, received enormous subsidies from the very beginning. For they were almost as inefficient as kolkhozy, they tended to be on marginal land, and yet they had to pay a guaranteed wage. With hindsight, one can perceive that the sovkhoz's regular 'unprofitability' was the germ of the general Communist agricultural subsidy. The later steps on this Calvary have been: the desire for autarky in food, the recognition that after a decade or two of collectivization the kolkhoznik is not a capitalist but himself needs a living wage, the increasing wealth of the country, the shrinking number of kolkhozniks, the extreme inefficiency of livestock raising. Today we find that USSR now pays as high agricultural subsidies as any country in the world.[38]

15. In STEs, as usual, trade unions worthy of the name may not be formed on sovkhozy (chapter 7). *A fortiori* the discontented kolkhoznik is not allowed even a semblance of a union. Is he not a free co-operator?! Did he not elect his chairman?! But in all agricultures the important thing is the farmers' or peasants' union, an entirely different thing. These unions often split: by region, by crop, and by size of farm, so by income and temperament. We can only generalize about the latter kind of split.

The large capitalist farmers' union, say the American Farm Bureau Federation, interpenetrates the Establishment and hobnobs on equal social terms. Its members prefer the classic measures that leave them most free to be capitalistic: tariffs, export subsidies, tax relief. They suspect price supports, as leading to quotas; but naturally are far better able to turn such things to their advantage if they are nevertheless imposed. There is really very little to say about the rich farmers' union – *mutatis mutandis* it is like any federation of employers in industry. A basic reason for this is that large capital is mobile: it scarcely recognizes a distinction between farm and non-farm. But small capital is usually auxiliary to the capitalist's own labour, and so tied down to its present occupation. Hence its greater vigour in defending that occupation as such.

The peasants' or small farmers' union (notably the Poujadistes in France and the US National Farmers' Union) is a quite different animal. It has an ideology, namely populism, as already briefly described in chapter 3. Peasant co-operative ownership is left-wing populism, and small, private, non-corporate farms are right-wing populism. Such a movement is very seldom revolutionary, as we shall see, but often spasmodically violent, and without economic or political sophistication. Its leaders have no entrée into the establishment, and they would not last as leaders if they had. The union advocates every kind of state support, including the most socialistic, since the freedom of the market never did its members any good. It may even advocate the outright nationalization of such activities ancillary to agriculture as railways, grain elevators and mills, banks. But it fiercely defends – no less fiercely than the rich farmers' union – private or at least co-operative property in farms themselves.

The members are as poor as poor industrial workers, but they cannot strike since they employ themselves. Nay more, they are capitalists as well as workers; indebted as they may be, they still supply equity capital, and certainly enterprise. Also they like it that way. So instead of withdrawing their labour they withdraw their produce. As Mary Elizabeth Lease said to her followers in USA in about 1890, 'Raise less corn and more hell'. Hence the burning of crops, the symbolic pouring away of milk in public places, etc. But what if non-members continue to 'raise corn'? Why, then they are blacklegs and must be picketed. But the countryside is large and many roads lead to market: it is not like picketing a factory. To be effective, we must be violent. Hence the burning of other people's crops, the blocking of roads to farm lorries, etc. We note again the influence upon agriculture of mere space. It follows from the simple facts of topography that the poor farmers' union cannot have the discipline of even a purely unskilled workers' union, and must be less law-abiding.

16. There is of course much more to populism than certain behaviour traits. From these oppressed and indebted worker-entrepreneurs has emerged a whole life-style and complex of attitudes, neither socialist nor capitalist, yet reasonably uniform across the world in the last 100 years, and not unscientifically to be called by one name. Populism has thrown up its own great leaders like W. J. Bryan and Mahatma Gandhi (who also define the 'right'- and 'left'-wing extremes within which the word may be applied) – both great and good men, unlike Hitler and Mao Tse-tung who stood upon its periphery and owed much to it. The various forms of socialism are not the only ideologies.

Let us end with a few additional elements of populist ideology, not mentioned above or in chapter 3: hostility to technology and high finance. The latter is easily enough understood: farmers are always in debt. Moreover deflation is a further injury to the debtor, and in the nineteenth century high (as opposed to the low, or local) finance stood for stable money.

The simple populist scratches his head when modern central banks support inflation. His ideal inflation is something he can understand and legislate once for all, like bimetallism or unbacked Treasury notes; not fiduciary issues or open-market operations, which confer executive power on technocrats he mistrusts.

There is then a general populist affinity for rising prices, which sets it aside from socialism. Your true socialist will tolerate any monetary disaster, including gross deflation, that weakens capitalism, but takes toward money under socialism a straightforward, old-fashioned and commonsensical attitude: it must behave itself until it withers away. But the populist, while he may be a socialist towards other sectors of the economy, is a capitalist or co-operator towards his own. For that, as we have seen, is where his capital is tied down, and he wants monetary policies that will increase it.

The undoubted hostility to technology and science is less defensible, since it seems to arise out of jealousy and anti-intellectualism. But it is actually a reasonable losers' reaction to the competition of corporate farms, and their large-scale operations. Since the ecological crisis and the failure of scientific nerve these attitudes have become more attractive, and the academic boom in the Narodniki[39] is highly typical of today's intelligentsia. When W. J. Bryan attacked Darwinism at the Scopes Trial he was only carrying the Narodniki's anti-industrialism to its logical conclusion.[40]

Above all populism represents a class: the small farmers or peasants. It wages class-war, and speaks that kind of paranoid language about the Establishment, the financiers, etc. It only happens that the war-aims are limited. Naturally, then, the basic premise holds: our class is morally good, yours (even the proletariat) is corrupted. The trouble with these fundamentally moderate people is that their passion is unaccompanied by a stable belief system at all relevant to the modern world: their ideology simply will not 'stand up'.

Notes

1. Fishing, hunting, logging and food-gathering are never called agriculture. Nor is nomadic herdsmanship.

2. Transport within the farm boundaries is in all cases agriculture, just as a forklift truck in a factory warehouse is manufacture.

3. But private rural building is the norm, and even private urban building is very common.

4. USA: 25 per cent and 5 per cent in 1960; USSR: 17 per cent and 27 per cent in 1970. But the definitions are tricky.

5. Other cases: mines (but mines are not livable, and have very few entrances) and transport organizations (but these do not own livable space, indeed may own very little space at all; moreover the vehicle is programmed to be ready for the worker when and where he comes to work).

6. Cf. Wiles 1961, chapter 12; A. H. Maunder, *Size and Efficiency in Farming*, Oxford 1952.

7. Cf. chapter 15, esp. sec. 6.

8. Draft animals are particularly 'right-wing'. Cf. chapter 6, sec. 10.

9. The uninitiated can get a good general idea from Harold J. E. Peake, 'Village Community' in *Encyclopedia of the Social Sciences*, N.Y. 1935.

10. On the fallow field at all times; on the other two when, after harvest, only stubble remains. Beyond the cultivated area all usable land is common and so permanently open to everyone's livestock.

11. Adapted from *Capital*, vol. I, chapter 24.

12. The South German peasant, however, whose village has been through a similar history, actually avoids the consolidation of all his strips into one farm. They are now his permanent property and he certainly may sell or swap them so as to arrive at the English Nirvana, but he often prefers largish scattered holdings to balance his soils and crops, insure against localized hailstorms, etc. Nor are all the economies of large-scale cultivation lost, for he can still arrange for machinery to run straight across his holding and his neighbour's, say on a particular hillside. In Southern Germany today, then, there must still be a central village.

13. Ed. Alfred Stead, *Servia by the Servians*, London 1909, pp. 172–4, 236–239.

14. Strictly, Tanzania is Tanganyika plus Zanzibar, which were nominally united in 1964. We refer only to Tanganyika.

15. Cf. N. S. Khrushchev in *Pravda*, 25 April 1950.

16. And the cost of moving the houses. In fact the agrogorod was to have been obligatory, and the peasants were to receive no pay for moving their houses (in mid-winter). Nor were they to be given any tools to do it with. The houses would all have collapsed in the spring when the snow melted.

17. Howard L. Gray, *English Field Systems*, London 1915.

18. 13th Jahrgang, no. 10; reprinted in Marx-Engels *Gesamtausgabe*, Dietz Verlag, 1963, vol. 22. On all this compare David Mitrany, *Marx against the Peasant*, London 1951.

19. Hence the deprecatory abbreviation *sov*khoz (Soviet farm), instead of the more natural goskhoz (state farm). This threadbare pretence has not been maintained in translation, even into German or Polish.

20. For this important concept cf. sec. 13 below.

21. The Chinese were infinitely more brutal against landlords, and defined the term so broadly as to include many kulaks. But that was in the first, or 'land reform', stage (1950). The reason is that Chinese landlords were not noblemen, and did not have large estates. Rather were they moderately rich officials and capitalists, genuinely hard to distinguish from kulaks. All the more reason, therefore, for severity, lest they merge with the peasantry who were compelled to murder them. Collectivization (1955) was almost bloodless.

22. The Soviet government even found it necessary to issue a special decree against livestock slaughter during kolkhoz amalgamation in 1950!

23. Cf. Everett Jacobs in ed. Peter Wiles, *The Prediction of Communist Economic Performance*, Cambridge 1971.

24. Not least by USSR. Cf. Karl-Eugen Wädekin in *Ost-Europa*, 8/1974; Henri Chambre in *Economies et Sociétés* (Geneva), January 1971.

25. Cf. René Dumont, *Cuba est-il Socialiste?*, Paris 1970, pp. 23–31; Ian Clegg, *Workers' Self-Management in Algeria*, London 1971. One third of the

land in Cuba is still in private farms, though these are as closely planned and commanded as East German private industry used to be.

26. Cf. Alec Nove, the title essay in *Was Stalin Really Necessary?*, London 1964; idem, *Economic History of USSR*, London 1969, chapters 6, 7; Peter Wiles, in *Problems of Communism*, April 1963; Moshe Lewin, *Russian Peasants and Soviet Power*, London 1968; Jerzy Karcz, Robert Davies and Jerzy Karcz in *Soviet Studies*, April 1967, January 1970, October 1970.

27. To repeat, 'country' means 'village economy', not merely agriculture.

28. Cf. Wiles in ed. Wiles, *The Prediction of Communist Economic Performance*, Cambridge 1971, pp. 332–4.

29. On the fiscal and other effects of collectivization once it had settled down cf. James Millar and Alec Nove in *Soviet Studies*, July 1970, January 1971, October 1971; James Millar in *Slavic Review*, December 1974.

30. In the late nineteenth century the sociologist M. F. Le Play greatly admired the 'Russian system' of seasonal migration. Cf. his *Les Ouvriers Européens*, Paris 1855, pp. 61–71.

31. The case is better with migrant combine-operators, who are highly skilled and capitalized. I refer mainly to the 'stoop labour' that picks fruit, lifts potatoes, etc. Usually this labour compounds its misery by belonging to some cultural or racial minority.

32. The usury laws indeed remain in many countries, but at very high rates, to limit the activities of loan sharks. The general failure of the usury laws is a classic demonstration of how not to control prices under perfect competition.

33. For this amazing action, specifically called 'the lowering of prices of goods in short supply', cf. Alec Nove, op. cit., 1969, pp. 139–42.

34. Communist governments other than Yugoslavia also procure from private peasants and kolkhozniks' private plots. The Polish government indeed has had a more rigid procurement system than any other (but the profits went into the coffers of 'Danish-type' co-ops, not the budget). This system was abolished in 1971.

35. Cf. sec. 9 here; chapter 8, sec. 10; chapter 10, sec. 16.

36. The 'Prebisch doctrine' that agricultural countries are poor and suffer ever worsening terms of trade with industrial countries, which are rich, is false. Cf. Wiles 1969, pp. 182–4.

37. Thus the story that the Tsars taxed agriculture to finance Russian state industry is surely false. Cf. Olga Crisp, 'The Pattern of Russia's Industrialization up to 1914' in *L'Industrialisation en Europe au XIX Siècle*, Colloques Internationaux du Centre National de la Recherche Scientifique, no. 540, pp. 452, 455, 456 (1971). It is scarcely likely that the quasi-populist Tsars would have consciously done such a thing. It is even very doubtful if Stalin, who wished to do it, succeeded: Millar, op. cit.

38. Equivalent to 4 per cent of the national income in 1970 on meat alone (Alec Nove, privately circulated). Thus we can still say that USSR never directly subsidized its collective farms. But Czechoslovakia has paid income subsidies in order to render collective farming attractive in comparison with a large surviving peasant sector. And every STE 'subsidizes' the collective farm in the sense that private peasants are more heavily taxed.

39. These were the precursors of the Russian Socialist Revolutionaries: isolated urban intellectuals who, debarred by Tsarism from overt political opposition, thought up history's only revolutionary populist ideology. It was ascetic, opposing both industry and affluence; it was atheistic, attributing many

of Russia's evils to the church – an attitude that did not survive the beginnings of parliamentary democracy and the foundation of a populist political party with voters; above all it laid great stress on the village community as highly traditional, expressive of the true Russian soul, and the source of all good things. For all their eccentricities the Narodniki were undeniably populist in the general sense.

40. However as good atheists – and so bad populists – the Narodniki themselves supported Darwin. Mr. Scopes was a teacher in Tennessee who in 1925 was fined for teaching Darwinism in violation of state law.

6

Co-operatives, Communities and Communes

1. Definitions
2. Local government
3. Retail co-ops
4. Farmers' co-ops, including Poland and Yugoslavia
5. Producers' co-operation under capitalism
6. Co-ops versus trade unions
7. Producers' co-operation in Yugoslavia
8. The village community, especially the ejido
9. The kolkhoz: basic internal workings
10. The kolkhoz: MTS, outside income, social services
11. The collective ejido
12. The commune, especially the kibbutz
13. The commune's social side
14. The STE cannot digest co-ops
15. The market corrupts them
16. They are evasive devices
17. A political conclusion

6

'To my surprise, I found there [Carlisle] six or seven Co-operative Societies in different parts of the town, doing well as they think, that is, making some profit by joint stock retail trading. It is, however, high time to put an end to the notion very prevalent in the public mind that this is the system which we contemplate, or that it will form any part of the arrangements in the New Moral World.'

Robert Owen, 1836

1. We use the following definitions, which more or less follow common usage:

a *community* is defined residentially. Everybody born there has a virtually automatic right to adult membership, and extrusion is psychologically painful and legally difficult. The community has, therefore, certain obligations for child care, education, general health and old-age pensions; it is a separate welfare state. It also enforces a degree of property and income equality on the active members; but in respect of their activities within the community – external inequality is frowned on but permitted. These provide land, labour, capital and enterprise together; but these factors can also be hired. Current economic activity may or may not be socialized.

a *commune* is a left-wing community, in which not only all production but also much of consumption is socialized, and economic equality is virtually complete. Usually no outside labour or capital is allowed but alas, outside capital is rendered necessary by deficits.

a *co-operative* is not necessarily residential. Current economic activity is carried on in the name of the members as a unit, but since these do not necessarily provide land, labour, capital and enterprise all together we cannot always say that production is socialized. Thus in a co-operative shop the members are the shoppers, and the only factor they provide is capital. No one has, by birth or status or any other thing, an automatic claim to membership in a co-operative, but extrusion from membership once acquired remains painful. The organization enforces a degree of property, income and work equality on its members, but only in their relations with itself.

Equality and mutual aid instead of unlimited accumulation and competition, voluntarism and decentralization instead of compulsion and hierarchy, independent growth by the poor instead of confiscation from the rich; such concepts embrace all these forms, and give them their peculiar moral attraction. It is, too, with them and not with socialism that the revulsion against industrial capitalism began (chapter 2). The socialist-capitalist dichotomy has done very great harm: many attractive alternative ways of living have disappeared down an ontological hole.

These definitions have certain corollaries.

A commune must be a community. Economic activity in a non-communal community must be co-operative, but a co-operative does not have to be a community, since it permits outside ties. A commune is by definition socialist, as well as co-operative, so it may be arrived at by two roads: the Soviet road through ordinary socialism, which however leads us to a single nation-wide commune (Full Communism, chapter 21), and the co-operative or populist road of directly and peacefully founding many small communes, never to be amalgamated into one. Thus the kibbutz is basically the creation of very left-wing Russian-Jewish populists. A co-operative is not socialist (though it was in the looser nineteenth-century usage); neither is a co-operative a community.

In all three *members* are *co-opted*, not *employees hired*. This cannot be often enough repeated. In the language of chapter 4, labour is the e.b.f. The capital used is borrowed at fixed interest or accumulated by the labour, or was originally contributed by the founder-labourers (usually free of charge). Labour is the boss. This status of labour makes it particularly difficult to get rid of. In communes and other communities, members even have the hereditary right to join. The virtually sole exception is the co-operative shop (sec. 3).

2. In France and Yugoslavia 'commune' or 'komuna' has always meant the lowest unit of local government. Unfortunately for us, but seemingly quite by coincidence, in both cases this unit has played its part in and stamped its name on the history of socialism. The Paris Commune of 1871 was a populist-and-socialist revolt by most of the population of Paris against the Prussian peace terms and the French government that accepted them. Precious little was done that we would today call socialist,[1] but passions were deeply stirred by the radical welfare measures taken, and the government suppressed the revolt with characteristic brutality. The incident is deeply graven on the Marxist-Leninist psyche, but the name commune meant and means the lowest organ of French local government. The Yugoslav komuna fulfils large managerial and financial functions vis-à-vis the co-operative enterprises on its territory, in addition to the ordinary things local government does everywhere. Notably, it runs a bank (or greatly influences an inter-communal consortium bank), and can veto the workers' council's choice of a director.

But, just to confuse us further, all communities fulfil these same functions. So if a state takes seriously the existence of communities in our sense it must constitute them organs of local government. This is what Tsar Alexander II did to the Russian village community in 1861 (chapter 8, sec. 10) and Mao Tse-tung to the Chinese People's Communes in 1958 (chapter 5, sec. 8); the former issued internal passports, chose conscript recruits and apportioned the land redemption payments, the latter organized even the militia. The Israeli state has constituted the kibbutzim and moshavim a part of its local government structure; but they, particularly the kibbutzim, often contract out of certain services.

We can infer from these definitions that communal and co-operative communities tend strongly to be rural, and to practise 'village economy' (chapter 5, sec. 2). For in towns residence fluctuates too much, and is seldom near one's workplace. The logic of space, so much insisted upon in the previous chapter, militates strongly against the urban commune. The only government to try them seriously has been the Chinese (1959). But the organizational difficulties were too great and the alleged benefits too small: *why* should one factory's employees all live in the same street, and *why* should just their wives form a sewing circle? What happens when someone changes his job? It is said that the urban communes were the issue that finally lost Mao his support, and brought the Great Leap Forward to an end.

The pure co-operative however can be located anywhere. It can practise heavy industry, banking, shipping – what you will.

3. We shall now go through the various types of co-operative. The co-operative retail shop is the most capitalistic of them all. It seems to be a British invention (early nineteenth century; perfected at Rochdale in 1844). Known all over the capitalist world, it functions best today in Sweden (below). The nominal owner is an equity shareholder, characteristically limited to one inexpensive share (always on tap at par value to new members) which gives him one vote at meetings. The rest of the capital is ploughed back or borrowed at fixed interest. The employees have no vote unless they are shareholders. If they hold shares and vote more often than under pure capitalism, and have more power at meetings, this is by no means because labour is the e.b.f., but only because there is much more democratic sentiment in the co-operative movement, and the mere proportion of other shares is smaller.

At the beginning of the British movement the factories attached to it were producers' co-operatives (sec. 5). But this system, wherein labour is the e.b.f., died out of the English movement in 1875.[2] The capital extracted from retail co-ops was to finance the setting up of socialist factories and housing, and so to spread socialism peacefully across the whole economy. So the bonus to labour in the attached factories was ideologically crucial, and it had a hard death, for it seemed a betrayal of the original intention to move on from mere consumers' co-operation to a democratic, decentralized socialism. Indeed, why 'seemed'? What was left was certainly neither socialism nor the promise of it. Pure consumers' co-operation makes the consumer into a limited capitalist, not a limited worker. When we say that the consumer is the e.b.f., we mean that a queer sort of capital is the e.b.f.

For in the system as it now is, the shareholder is supposed to buy as much as possible at his shop, and give his share number to the assistant. In this way profit (but not voting power) accrues to him in proportion to his purchases, he provides capital to the enterprise and he receives a dividend: the celebrated co-op 'divi', which is the movement's principal gimmick. The original idea was that the surplus value taken by the capitalist would in this way accrue to the shopper, or to the altruistic purposes of the co-op itself. For the Rochdale pioneers thought that capitalist shopkeepers were taking a lot of unnecessary money out of the working man. They were wrong: their system only substituted dividends for interest. For if there is less equity capital there must, in the absence of a new technique, be more loan capital at long term. And the remaining equity shares do receive, after all, a low dividend. As to short-term capital, the customer is willing to pay higher prices in order *later* to receive higher dividends. I.e. the equity-bearing customer provides mainly *short*-term capital for a variable dividend. Deducting administrative costs, there is a trivial saving on the rate of this dividend and that, it would appear, is all.

But it is not quite all. There are two further sources of co-operative finance: the lower salary of the manager and the greater loyalty of the customers, in the ordinary sense of goodwill under imperfect competition. These factors used to be a real source of accumulation, and the twentieth-century history of the movement is the history of their decline – and so of the *economic* decline *within* capitalism of a movement which was already irretrievably non-socialist in 1875. From 11 per cent of UK retail trade turnover in 1932–5[3] and again in 1961 the co-ops have declined to 7 per cent in 1971.

High prices, high dividends, low managerial salaries, small shops and general loyalty characterize the co-ops in Northern England, where an independent working-class culture survives. One leaves one's dividend to accumulate. By custom these savings belong to the housewife,[4] so the Northern working-class wife is the backbone of the system. In the South the consumer goes comparison-shopping in capitalist shops, uses other means of small saving than her co-op account, and expects to pay the market rate for the best managers he can find. The dividend on purchases is consequently low, and has even suffered the ultimate degradation of becoming a stamp with a fixed redemption power, like any capitalist trading stamp. Besides which, the co-ops in the South sell alcohol and allow hire-purchase, thus violating the temperance and cash-only taboos. In a word, the South is bourgeois.

For the essence of British retail co-operation is the *recognition of limits*:

one maximizes nothing, but rubs along. The fact that it is more capitalist than socialist is of course irrelevant; it is really a kind of urban populism, with an ideology of class solidarity. The proletariat was to pool its savings and buy its freedom. The shops were the leading link and the factories would follow. But there is nothing more conservative than a purely proletarian, as opposed to a strictly socialist, movement. It has retained its identity by resisting not only the unequal accumulation of private capital, but the whole modern world: wine, hire purchase, high salaries, large scale, even – for a time – self-service. In each case the adoption of almost any maximand – profit, volume of sales – would have breached the barrier. This even applies to the appropriate Benthamite maximand laid down in chapter 4: minimum price net of dividend. Clearly that too would have introduced alcohol and self-service, and excluded altruistic appropriations of surplus. For these co-ops also appropriate unusually much money, in comparison with capitalism, for altruistic purposes. They are, or were, one of the best examples of how to avoid the pathology of the market by not maximizing anything at all (chapter 10, sec. 8).

In Sweden, the country *par excellence* of the public enterprise, the co-op has attracted far better entrepreneurial ability, and has taken more seriously the theoretical minimand of net prices. In pursuit of lower prices the retail co-op organization has set up many factories in the British manner, but with a twist: it has gone into aggressive competition with one monopolistic capitalist producer after another. In pursuit of efficiency and the theoretical minimand, virtually all trace of the Rochdale ideology has been jettisoned. Relations with labour are as unclouded by left-wing cant as those of any Swedish employer. There is no pretence that the co-ops are part of a proletarian movement: they are run by able and idealistic bourgeois, or bourgeoisified proletarians. They eschew politics.

It is difficult not to be sarcastic about consumers' co-operation. It is so square and decent and Victorian beside the headier ideologies of the modern world. Yet it is most strongly to be hoped that it will survive and recover its élan. It never killed anyone. It has made millions happier. It has been an outlet for wasted managerial talents. It has fought monopoly and beaten it. It has made the thriftless save. It has educated and re-housed. Therefore it is surely the most virtuous of all economic systems. Therefore it will never hold the attention of students.

The Soviet 'village co-operative shop' (*sel'po*) is only formally and historically a co-op at all. Its status and functioning today are hardly distinguishable, except by greater inefficiency, from the nationalized urban shops. Cf. sec. 14 below.

4. From the consumer to the farmer (capitalist or peasant). Resenting, as we saw in chapter 5, interference with his own farm, he nevertheless likes to control ancillary enterprises: buying, selling, processing before sale, machine rental, credit, insurance, a prize bull, etc. Populists in North

Dakota and Saskatchewan have installed 'socialist' state or provincial governments in order to achieve these ends,[5] but mostly it happens on a smaller scale, via 'Danish-type' or 'farmers'' co-operation. In this the individual farmer is the voting member, on the basis of having contributed equity capital. There is as usual a limitation on who may contribute, and how much. The farmer provides no labour, which then is all hired and not an e.b.f. at all. He probably has the further right to force the co-op to buy, sell, or process as much as he requires regardless of its profitability. The main dividend is likely to be on these transactions, not capital. The co-op is his agent, and maximizes his revenue or minimizes his expenditure (chapter 4, sec. 11).

Farmers' co-ops are not more efficient than capitalist ancillary enterprises. They compete with them, as in the case of the retail shop, by such marginal means as customer loyalty. They save no capital costs, contrary to simple appearances, and they suffer diseconomies of small scale. What they do is satisfy in part those desires for security and personal power that are at least as natural as the desire for wealth.

Yugoslavia and Poland have tried to build the farmers' co-op into a new way of socializing agriculture. Disgusted with the kolkhoz, that takes away land, livestock and the will to work, they have established farmers' co-ops that are nearly compulsory (Yugoslavia) and monopolists of nearly all new industrial inputs (both countries). In this way it is hoped that most farm capital will come to be socialist, the farmer will become accustomed to handling socialist capital (and often be compelled to do so only on a collective basis), land and livestock will lose their psychological significance and in the end be easily socialized themselves.

What objections are there to this more humane and efficient programme for a Communist agriculture?

(i) While it is clearly in every possible way superior to forced collectivization there is nothing at all to show that it is better than leaving capitalism alone.

(ii) After all it is still a Communist government, and the peasants do not trust the co-op.

(iii) Some immovable machinery (e.g. milking machines), most current inputs (e.g. mineral fertilizers), and nearly all buildings simply must be private. There are not all that many assets divorcible from the land and the livestock. So a good deal of capital can only be accumulated by private peasants, if there is to be more output.

(iv) Time is of the essence. So slow a socialization will, on the one hand, leave the Party firebrands discontented, and on the other expose us meanwhile to the accidents of history. Suppose, notably, that in a few years there is a harvest failure or a balance-of-payments crisis (even a non-agricultural one) or a riot (even an urban one). It is then necessary to make concessions to the peasantry, to keep them quiet or get more output.

(v) These concessions will include a weakening of the co-ops themselves, and the personal possession of small tractors (sec. 10). The small personal tractor is the absolute antithesis of the whole scheme.

(vi) Another concession may be government help in consolidating strips, or the sale of public land not in use. These measures also are good for agriculture but bad for socialism, since they render the existing system too efficient.

The full road through the farmers' co-op to socialism has not yet been trodden. There is (1972) not even any advance along it – in Poland capitalism is gaining, in the form of concessions since Gomułka's fall.[6] The same must be said of Yugoslavia, which now actually produces its own small tractors – an ideological concession of some importance, however much the reader may smile. The constant pressure for immediate output makes this a very long road to socialism. If peasants must be helped in each successive short run, how can they be abolished in the long?

The form, but hardly the content, of the farmers' co-op has been imitated by the US Federal Reserve Board – a national central bank nominally owned by other banks – and the Port of London Authority – a docks and harbour board rather more genuinely owned by the shipping lines. In each case government control (and ownership in the case of the P.L.A.) has supervened. But both these examples show how capitalistic the 'farmers' co-op' can be, since it shades over into an *ad hoc* consortium of capitalist corporations. All that is required for a consortium is that the equity be closely held by defined organizations, with a limit on the voting power of each. The social and psychological differences are enormous, but the institutional concept is precisely that of a farmers' co-op.

5. There has been much co-operative production also in capitalist states. Nor should this surprise us: the market is tolerant, and any institution can survive on it that pays its way. But co-operative production is more or less impossible in an STE (sec. 14). However it has not distinguished itself in markets, competing with capitalist enterprises.

In ACEs co-operative production was extremely common in the nineteenth century, and it has survived here and there until today.[7] We distinguish it from the 'labour-influenced enterprise' of chapter 7, which is growing and flourishing; we mean here the pure case where labour provides the management openly and bears the equity. Such enterprises were started in UK by the retail co-op movement (which provided for them a stable, closed market), by the Christian Socialists and by individual enterprising workmen. By the end of the century the movement was pretty much over, for the following reasons:

(i) lack of labour discipline: the worker who is also the boss comes in late, leaves early and breaks the rules;

(ii) lack of initial capital: all three kinds of founder, mentioned above, had too little, and spread it too thin;

(iii) refusal to plough back: the worker who is also the boss prefers to distribute gross revenue to himself;

(iv) egalitarianism: pay, though differentiated, was still too low to attract the best managers from outside;

(v) suspicion of technical progress, as requiring more capital, stricter discipline and higher-paid managers;

(vi) bourgeoisification: the nucleus of genuine members hires ancillary employees, and so converts itself into a kind of capitalist employer.

There were few legal or social handicaps, merely the neutral and unsympathetic market. This catalogue of weaknesses applies well enough to the fate of co-operative production in other ACEs. In some, however, the state has offered tax advantages and protected markets. By reason of these, for instance, Italian roadworkers are still today often organized in this way.

6. Trade unions, too, have mostly been sympathetic in principle but obstructive in practice. For unions and producers' co-ops, see chapter 7, sec. 10. As to consumers' co-ops, they are not specially good employers. How could they be? The managers of a consumers' co-op are themselves working men, only more resourceful than the average. This alone makes them intolerant, but in addition they have an ideology that gives them a moral superiority capitalist employers do not feel. In Britain the struggle to unionize co-operative shops was quite bitter, and for a long time employees were forbidden to hold shares. The objection was that co-operative democracy, like other grass-roots democracy, suffers from apathy and ill-attended meetings, which a minority of employee shareholders could dominate. Such resistance is paradoxical in a movement that supported producers' co-operation in factories, but the fear was justified and the clash of principles a genuine one. For the employee shareholder is likely to be a trade-unionist, and to 'march to the beat of a different drummer'.[8]

The producers' co-op too is tempted to hire ancillary labour, or *ad hoc* labour, at a fixed wage: a matter we explored geometrically in chapter 4. When it does so, the poor but complacent Establishment of the co-op is as unsympathetic as in the consumer case.

7. It seems that co-operative production is too inefficient to survive where capitalist firms compete and business unions press. It needs monopoly, tax advantages, or a whole co-operative society, to flourish. Such a society is Yugoslavia. Here alone the whole socialist sector consists of producers' co-operatives, and large capitalist enterprises are forbidden.[9] Here alone the trade unions cannot destroy the system – for they are of Stalinist type and do what the government tells them. Here alone the

hiring of ancillary employees is forbidden by law – all workers must be members. Perhaps there are some macro-benefits in having a whole system of this kind, with no foreign bodies in it?

As a way of reducing alienation on a national scale Yugoslav self-administration is second to none. The workers' council *does* mean something to its electors, the manager *does* pay attention to it, the notion that this is 'our' enterprise is *not* absurd. Of course this is only in comparison with all other systems, and of course small size under capitalism is as good a way of avoiding alienation as formal democracy. But it is still a remarkable achievement. Yet in the late 'sixties, as the twentieth anniversary of the workers' councils approached, more and more criticisms were heard. Let us first enumerate them:

(i) Inflation is rampant and permanent. While certainly the workers' reluctance to plough back is important, there are also other causes of inflation in Yugoslavia (chapter 14).

(ii) The councils refuse to expand employment, which leads to too many small firms (chapter 4).

(iii) This refusal, i.e. the 'funny' maximand, leads to sub-optimal allocations, not only in Illyria but in real life (chapter 10).

(iv) The enterprise uses too much borrowed capital (chapter 4). But since ploughback is unpopular and the country is poor, it does not use too much capital overall. Besides, there is another bias in that direction due to Marxism in high places, not to self-management.

(v) Enterprises refuse to amalgamate, when optimum size increases (here).

(vi) Foreign equity capital is ideologically unacceptable, but very necessary (chapter 13, section 11).

(vii) There is prejudice against the young and technically well educated (here).

(viii) The enterprise has a negative elasticity of supply – this is untrue (chapter 10, sec. 14).

(ix) All the ordinary pathology of a capitalist market is present in addition: oligopoly, excessive advertising, price discrimination,[10] cartels[11] – this is obvious, whatever Yugoslav theorists may say, and requires no further discussion. It simply means that, whatever their precise maximand, the enterprises are behaving selfishly.

(x) The system perpetuates personal inequality: not merely between skills and grades, which is tolerable in a poor country needing growth, but also between whole enterprises, since it does not attack rents or quasi-rents (chapter 16).

(xi) It is also blamed for things arising out of the Yugoslav historical situation, which it allegedly should have cured: underdevelopment, over-population, economic emigration, unemployment, gross regional inequality – but why should it have cured these things? As far as the first two go, the rate of growth has been very respectable, and no more need be said. Economic emigration, again, is an excellent thing. For unemployment at home, where the record is indeed spotty, cf. chapter 14, sec. 12. Finally regional equality is something for which we have little space. Certainly the Yugoslav record is very unimpressive. We suggest in chapter 19, sec. 17, that the main blame lies with the weak economic powers of the central government, rather than the existence of a market or of workers' councils.

This is a substantial list of faults, but only (v–vii) fall to be discussed here. These are all resistances to technical progress. Thus enterprises refuse to amalgamate because self-administration works best on a small scale, because workers' councils are jealous, because there is no undemocratic mechanism like the capitalist take-over bid or the Soviet-type administrative order; but above all because the members of the richer enterprise stand necessarily to lose, which is not the case where regular wages are paid.

The prejudice against young technicians is probably a unique and temporary state of affairs. It is true that petty egalitarianism and jealousy are given full rein by self-management, but after all the country is very achievement-oriented and there is a competitive external market as well. The trouble is, or was, more a concentration of old and incompetent revolutionary war-horses in the top economic positions – a trouble widespread in Eastern Europe in the 'sixties.

So every one of these complaints is correct except (viii) and (xi). Let us, then, dare to make a judgement: probably genuine capitalist competition within Yugoslavia would bankrupt its self-managed enterprises. For where labour is less alienated it is mostly, and in the short run, less efficient. Yugoslavia has done nothing to meet the objections to producers' co-operation voiced by Beatrice Webb 70 years ago (op. cit.), nor any of the more sophisticated ones added by those who have studied her directly. But she has also proved that such a society is viable given a strong government. The experience of her Algerian imitator, where the state was neutral, has been disastrous (chapter 7, sec. 10, chapter 20, sec. 6); but the *ejidos colectivos* (sec. 8) have on the whole been backed by the Mexican state, and survived. These systems are capable of growth and they make people happy. Compromises, introducing worker consultation, self-management within defined bounds and a generally looser style of administration, are the order of the day in ACEs and even in STEs.

8. From the co-operative to the non-communal community. The loosest forms of this are the various traditional villages, already described (chapter 5, sec. 4). It is unnecessary to say more on the details of daily operation. But note that if the traditional village is of a good size its council, reeve or headman is a part of the country's official structure of authority. For he

or it claims so much power over individuals that the conflict with the state machine would otherwise be too frequent and intolerable. This is almost a part of our definition of a community.

Similar communities continue to be founded; they are not just historical survivals. Tsar Alexander II strengthened and refurbished his village communities when he emancipated the serfs (1861). The most successful form of Israeli agriculture today, outstripping the kibbutz in growth and equalling it in efficiency, is the *moshav ovdim*. This rests on individual landholdings subject to an upper limit, alienable only with permission of the moshav. Many services but only a few cultivation tasks are communal. Each member pays for his seed and gets credit for his harvest (if indeed normally through the moshav's co-operative trading unit), and owns his own livestock. There can of course be no question of tradition here, since very few Jews had been peasants.[12]

Perhaps the great modern case is Mexico. The Mexican Revolution (1910–17) virtually refounded the rather similar ejido,[13] the history of which requires here a word. The Aztecs had a traditional community (the *calpullí*), with inalienable and limited ownership of strips. Many of the usual problems between great landlord and peasant community arose, and the *calpullí* was in decline by the time of the Conquest. But the Spaniards brought in very similar traditions – indeed medieval Spain was quite peculiarly co-operative;[14] so the *calpullí* carried on as the ejido. But imperialism, as opposed to colonization proper, is not co-operative. Spanish capitalism developed, and could not be stopped; it took the form of latifundia on which the Indians worked as labourers. In 1890–4 the ejidos were formally dissolved: being replaced by ownership in severalty – a thing very much to the advantage of white (including US) capitalists, who could now buy. The ejido was revived by the revolutionary land reform of 1917 (Art. 27 of the constitution of that year), mainly the work of Emiliano Zapata. It now held all the land of its members in common, not merely pasturage and woodland as in 1894. But cultivation and usufruct were still in severalty. The new ejido grew by the return of alienated land, but this was both prior to and different from the Bolshevik revolution: there was compensation (by the state, not the ejido), and the transfer of land was very gradual, being subject to local decision.

Now Zapata was a backward-looking populist. He had no idea of economic progress, so his ejidos were in fact limbos for the Indian population, still unincorporated into the capitalist mainstream of modern Mexico. They were not seriously meant to contain that population for ever, and no socialist future lay in store for them. Capitalist agriculture, in particular, continued to develop, even with latifundia, alongside a half-hearted application of the 1917 reform. This seemed tolerable to the Mexican presidents up to Lázaro Cárdenas (1934–40). It was now that the remarkable system of pluralistic one-party rule, with rigid six-year presidential terms and no self-succession, finally established itself. Cárdenas, if one were to be forced to pin down his essence in a few words, was a cross between a left-wing, pro-Indian,[15] populist, and what we should now call a Titoist. That is, he liked workers' control, and indeed installed it in the (nationalized) railways (1938). And of course the collective farm, nay even the kolkhoz, is a Titoist enterprise, if you take its formal democracy seriously – which Cárdenas did.

In 1936 there was a particularly bitter strike on some irrigated cotton-growing latifundia in the Laguna region. One cause of the bitterness was the 20 years' failure to implement the land reform at all in this region; it was rightly objected that the parcellation of the land within standard ejidos would destroy the irrigation system. So Cárdenas gave the reform a new twist. As elsewhere the ejidos were to take over much of the latifundia's land, but this time it was to be operated collectively – a very radical change indeed. In so far as there was a foreign model at all, it was the kolkhoz, to which we must first turn. But there were in fact fleeting domestic precedents from before Stalin.[16]

9. The origins of the kolkhoz, as we saw in chapter 5, sec. 7, were in no traditional community, but in the cerebrations of an elderly Marxist. But they were not foolish cerebrations. They could have been presented as being in continuity with the traditional community, but they were not. They could have been favoured, not enforced. They would have justified a less collectivist specific model, already present and functioning in USSR in 1929.

This model was the *TOZ* (*tovarishchestvo obrabatyvayushchee zemlyu*, co-operative for cultivating the soil). Livestock was privately held, but the co-operative performed all major cultivation and sold the crop. Payment was partly according to work done, partly rent on land contributed. More collective than the (still surviving) traditional community, the TOZ was still a very popular form of co-operative, not least because it enjoyed many tax advantages. Indeed it was the majority form in 1928. Had Stalin chosen it, no livestock would have been slaughtered, and about 4 per cent of the capital of the Soviet people would not have been eaten in two years.

The *commune* also existed in USSR in fair numbers in 1928. But it had intellectual, nay even Trotskyite, possibly Zionist, associations (cf. sec. 14). In other words the communes (some of them were urban) sheltered a left-wing opposition to Stalin, and were the product of that dread anti-Soviet phenomenon, spontaneity.[17] So the chosen model was another pre-existent form, intermediate between TOZ and commune: the *artel*. Artel is the ordinary Russian word for a craftsmen's (not peasants') producers' co-operative. Favoured and officially regulated before the revolution, the craftsmen's artel survived and flourished until 1929, and then until 1960 as a part of socialist industry distinguished in legal form, but in very little else, from the ordinary enterprise.[18] But in agriculture the artel, hardly known before the Revolution, became the only permitted form of kolkhoz, and was and is genuinely different from the state farm.

In its finished pre-Khrushchevian form the agricultural artel permitted a private house, and a limited private plot and livestock herd. All else was collective, and all collective labour was credited with 'labour-days'. The labour-day (*trudoden'*) is an accounting unit, allocated at rates varying mostly between one half and two to a clock day of labour according to the type of work. These rates were centrally fixed, and a minimum of clock days of work per annum was also (more or less) fixed. But the actual amount of work done is very much subject to argument, since no one can be sacked, there is no legal compulsion to work on any specific day, and alternative work is plentiful and attractive. The value of the trudoden' is fixed annually after the farm's accounts, and the members then get this value multiplied by the number credited to them.

There is thus a dividend to labour, but no wage, in the true logic of the co-operative enterprise. After the compulsory delivery (chapter 5, sec. 13) this was the most important feature of the kolkhoz to the Soviet régime: in case of a bad harvest it did not have to pay a guaranteed wage. Nay more, as the 1932–3 famine showed, one could combine the 'advantages' of strict procurement and dividend to labour by legally confiscating the grain and legally leaving people to starve. During this famine, and again in 1946–7, the towns ate better than the countryside. We have already seen (chapter 5, sec. 8) how expensive it is to give up this advantage by nationalizing the kolkhoz. However, the trudoden' is now gradually yielding to a guaranteed monthly wage (see sec. 11/xiv here).

The kolkhoz is so big (say 800 families in a modern Soviet or Bulgarian kolkhoz) that its internal organization is a matter of public policy. How decentralized should it be, and into how big units? Sufficient decentralization into small enough units virtually abolishes it, and this was the fate of the Chinese People's Communes (founded 1958, during the Great Leap Forward). These were a most ambitious scheme: actual communes averaging 50,000 people – 150 times as big as a kibbutz, but compulsory and without the least preparatory novitiate for members! They failed totally within one year, and deserve no serious discussion here.[19] Formally they survive as local authorities with planning power and power over investment finance. The basic decision-making and income-distributing unit in the Chinese countryside is now again the Agricultural Producers' Co-operative, of about 20 families. The commune is now a sort of estate office and local authority: the mere shell of its former self. There is no more perfect example of the conundrum, when is a decentralized enterprise no longer an enterprise?

The Soviet kolkhoz has swung between large and small internal units: brigade and link. A link might be ten or fewer people responsible for a piggery. They are quasi-permanent and may well be related to each other. If they have a separate accountancy, say a trudoden' value decided on the outturn of the piggery alone, they are like the insecure tenants of a share-cropping landlord; i.e. they are practically capitalists. For this reason the link works very well and is ideologically most suspect. No responsible authority, whose proceedings are public, has ever discussed this hot potato. Separate accountancy is normally denied it. The brigade on the other hand is suited to 'left-wing' crops and simple cultivating operations. It might have 100 people and during its brief existence its composition would vary daily. It is clearly very socialist, though in no good sense of that word. A migrant North American gang has more cohesion, and is more specialized.[20]

Hungary, however, has publicly proclaimed its own version of the link, the Nádudvar system, now in use on more than 80 per cent of kolkhozy. A piece of land is assigned to a small work unit to cultivate for specialized row crops or a vineyard, or for livestock care. The peasants receive a guaranteed percentage of total output plus a labour-day payment based on separate accountancy.[21] Exactly the same applies to the small factories, shops and transport organizations that the kolkhozy set up, so that they outbid the socialist sector in the urban labour market!

Note that both these link systems amount to share-cropping; indeed Nádudvar *is* share-cropping. On the rationality of such a system of tenure, cf. chapter 4, sec. 21. Whatever we may say about it, it is clearly more rational than the kolkhoz.

10. So much for those aspects of the kolkhoz that could possibly be subsumed under a generalization, or at least illustrate some principle. But it is of the essence of comparative economics that not very much is comparable. We are forced, then, for a true understanding of the kolkhoz, to add a great deal of strictly unique material.

First, the astonishing separate ownership and management of movable machinery, especially *tractors*, owes nothing to the 'specialization out of agriculture' referred to in chapter 5, sec. 2. For except in this one respect the Soviet-type farm performs innumerable services for itself. The smaller farms of capitalism require, for instance, that combines be owned by service enterprises; but the biggest have their own, and all have their own tractors, the sizes of which are tailored to the size of the farm. But in USSR sovkhozy have always had their own tractors, while the rather larger kolkhozy did not. The separation owes nothing, again, to the Yugoslav/Polish idea that co-operatively held tractors will persuade the peasants to join co-operatives: the Soviet peasants had already joined them, and that was just the trouble.

The tractor was to be the great persuader, showing the peasant the advantages of collectivism. So obviously it must be too big for use on small farms, or it would show him the wrong thing. Even Yugoslavia was very late in producing small tractors. Characteristically until 1970 the Yugoslav peasant's son earned enough money in West Germany to remit a small tractor. In Poland both production and import were prohibited until the fall of Gomułka (1970); but a mechanically minded peasant could legally put one together out of spare parts, for his own use.

But wherever there is forced collectivization the peasant will treat the tractor as a symbol of the kolkhoz; he will wreck it out of ignorance like all peasants everywhere, but he will also wreck it out of malice. So in the early 'thirties Stalin formed state-owned and managed 'machine-tractor stations' (MTS) and thus nationalized the tractors he had just so proudly supplied to his new kolkhozy.[22]

The administrative complexity of a farming system in which very large farms do not own their tractors is now happily a historical subject, marked 'Ph.D.s only'. The inefficiency may be imagined. But it did at least prevent sabotage, and it did give the government a powerful lever: all misdemeanours could be met with a refusal to plough or harvest. Moreover the Party, at that time extremely thin in the countryside, was centred on the state employees, often of urban origin, in the MTS.

Kolkhoz amalgamation (1950), the firm rooting of the Party in the kolkhoz, the growth of milking and other non-movable machines that *must* be kolkhoz property, and the mere passage of time made the MTS unnecessary. In 1958 Khrushchev liquidated the MTS, selling the tractors to the kolkhozy. The satellites have nearly all followed him.[23]

As in most co-operatives (but very few communes), the Kolkhoz permits *outside income*. In this case it is a very big factor. The STE has arranged this matter in a way highly counter-productive to its own aims. Not only does the low procurement price depress the value of the trudoden'. Food produced on the private plot is the kolkhoznik's absolute property, and he can sell it on the free market without any turnover tax.[24] For the turnover tax is 'ideologically loaded': it is the profit margin of the socialist state, whereby it exploits non-socialized elements that buy from it, and so must only be charged when a socialized product is sold to a consumer – or a kolkhoz! Therefore there is no indirect tax on private sales. Therefore the kolkhoznik sells in competition with heavily taxed 'socialized' food, and pockets the difference. Add that excess demand is normal and state prices are inflexible; so he normally gets more, and occasionally very much more, than the state price.[25] *A fortiori* if he eats what he grows he pays no tax. About one half, then, of the kolkhoznik's real income from agriculture used to come out of the miserable one acre that surrounds his house. Here he worked late and early. To this he carried out his night soil – and the crop stood visibly taller than in the neighbouring collective fields. An astounding one third of all Soviet agricultural production was private.[26]

The private plot is essentially a sop to the peasant Cerberus. It was legalized not at the moment of collectivization but after the famine, to assure him he would not starve again. It is in direct psychological continuity with the old private farm. An equally ineradicable part of the past is the winter migration to work in industry, which also contributes substantially to the family's total income. Indeed to be a member of a suburban kolkhoz, i.e. to sell early geraniums off the private plot in the central free market of a great city after a short 'bus ride,[27] and to commute to a good factory job in the winter from one's own rent-free house, was the *summum bonum*. Only top industrial managers were so fortunate. But under Khrushchev procurement prices rose steeply, so that collective work became more profitable, and sundry administrative chicaneries were introduced against the private plot. Its importance has somewhat diminished.

The *kolkhoz sector was more like a foreign country*, or rather a colony, than a part of the socialist state. There are many different reasons for this:

(i) The NEP tradition of so regarding private agriculture (chapter 5, sec. 1) was not dead.

(ii) Since the country had a dual economy (chapter 10, sec. 18), even normal Western development theory expects that co-operative agriculture be treated as an internal colony.

(iii) The kolkhoz paid turnover tax on its inputs and interest on its long- as well as its short-term capital (above). This was precisely and explicitly because it was not part of the socialist sector. We can therefore regard the turnover tax as an export tax, and compare the interest with that charged on foreign aid (there used to be no long-term interest within the socialist sector).

(iv) The kolkhoz received no agricultural subsidies, in stark contrast to the sovkhoz, which from the moment of its foundation tended to make large losses and so bore witness against the falsehood that 'Communist agriculture is not subsidized'. Alone of Soviet citizens, the kolkhoznik had not a guaranteed income.

(v) It received indeed tax advantages, but only vis-à-vis the private peasant, who was a citizen of the same 'colony'.

(vi) Only its compulsory deliveries were included in the annual output plan of the state (but the whole sowing plan also figured – chapter 11, sec. 20).

(vii) Its members could not travel on ordinary passports, but were treated, when 'abroad', as tourists with only the right of transit (chapter 8, sec. 10).

(viii) Its members had no right to the social services of the state, except education and medicine.

Point (viii) needs elaboration. First it is of the essence of a community that it provides its own social services: the idea is reasonable. Secondly, it is very common all over the world to begin social insurance only in towns. Thirdly, ideological blinkers were clamped on as usual. Soviet social insurance went with trade union membership, because the trade unions were originally supposed to run the whole socialist economy in every respect. But kolkhozniks have no trade union! Later even Khrushchev, so pro-peasant but so erratic, tried to make collective farms erect (residential) school buildings at their own expense.

But Khrushchev also gradually opened up the social services to them, and in this the satellites, inheritors of a more civilized tradition, had long preceded him. He also abolished the turnover tax on state inputs into co-operative agriculture; introduced a virtual wage in place of the trudoden', with virtual Gosbank guarantee as in the socialist sector; abolished the MTS, and sold the tractors to the kolkhozy; greatly raised compulsory delivery prices; sold a vast supply of new fertilizer; and generally elevated the kolkhozy to a par with sovkhozy. All this was an enormous and wholly admirable social reform. The kolkhozy no longer suffer much injustice, but they remain very inefficient.

11. The collective ejido is extremely similar, indeed in part a copy.[28] Fundamentally, however, like the individual ejido, it is in law a credit society. In the latter case this is not surprising; for would not indeed a revitalized loose traditional community take on this function above all others? Marketing, supply, technical advice and enforcement of the land regulations are all less important to a small peasant.

So the collective ejido undertakes to give credit only for collective operations, and to refuse it for individual operations; and on this proviso all rests. It is a legal gimmick, arising from the circumstances of 1936. Its consequences for internal structure are, however, smaller than for external structure. For since all ejidos are credit societies all are controlled by a specialized bank (the Banco Ejidal). So oddly enough it is in turn the bank that provides technical advice, and enforces the regulations, including those for collective operation. Indeed the bank deals with each individual member (ejidatario) directly. Not even the French banking system (chapter 12) has so much detailed power through 'qualitative controls'.

How does the collective ejido differ from or resemble the kolkhoz?

(i) It is voluntary, or at least a governmental response to popular pressure for something radical. But enthusiasm is by no means great enough to save labour discipline (xii).

(ii) It rests on the acquisition of others' land. Thus its historical origin is in class-war against large land-owners, who were not however killed but retain portions of their land right in the neighbourhood, as they were entitled to do under the law. Indeed they chose to retain the best bits, and that is one of the problems, at least in the Laguna region. The kolkhoz on the other hand incorporates only a minority (c. 20 per cent) of confiscated land, but this was taken without compensation from rich peasants in an act of factitious class-war (sec. 17). 'Dekulakization' weighs heavily on its moral origins.

(iii) Members usually belong to an existing ordinary ejido nearby, and need not bring in their own land but continue to work it separately. They also work on the remaining capitalist farms, and in factories in the slack reason. This is as big a distraction as the kolkhoznik's private plot and winter factory job.

(iv) The collective ejido has never been in any way unpopular. Members are, for instance, proud to introduce tractors, which needless to say belong to the ejido and not some state body. The contrast is striking between the early tractor sabotage on the kolkhoz and the joyous introduction of a garlanded machine to the ejido.

(v) In both systems there is a general assembly and elected officers. In STEs of course the Party decides every detail of these elections. But in Mexico the Party is tolerant and the ejido very small; so democracy is not merely formal. Indeed the ejido is the stamping ground of the tolerated minor left-wing parties. Of course corruption and petty oppression are rife, perhaps all the more so. But amalgamation or nationalization, for instance, could not possibly be imposed from above, as they are in STEs.

(vi) But there is a very powerful specialized state organ to deal with the ejido: the bank. In an STE there is always a separate agricultural bank or a specialized part of the Gosbank, but this is, by the nature of the system, not the main thing. We have not space to pursue the dull, shifting and complicated subject of the agricultural planning hierarchy in an STE. Sometimes it is the ministry of agriculture through its local branches, sometimes the ordinary organs of local government, sometimes even the MTS. But in each case the whole system always works badly, so the authorities are for ever reorganizing it.

(vii) Politics plays an enormous part in the internal functioning of both systems. In Mexico a left-wing president founded the collective ejido, and forced the officials of the Banco Ejidal to find the money and take on these new functions. In the following three moderate-to-right-wing presidencies the bank was instructed to lend more economically and permit subdivision into individual plots. At the same time a Communist-influenced league grew up which promoted subdivision into smaller collective ejidos (formally called sectors); a process much aided by family quarrels and the like. Collectivism, rightly or wrongly, lost much ground. Under López Mateos (1958–64) the bank spigot was turned on again, and new collectives were founded, though nothing was done to reverse the individualization that had occurred on existing ones.[29] By 1964, for instance, there were 264 collective ejidos recognized by the Banco Ejidal in the Laguna region, plus 1,216 'sectors', making 1,462 'operating units' with 25,340 members; plus a few ejidos otherwise financed. As to the kolkhoz, it is of course pure politics from top to bottom. Its operation is so unsatisfactory, and its violent origins so blatant, that the Party is for ever meddling. It is generally characteristic of single parties that they replace the state machine wherever there is a crisis, and Soviet-type agriculture is a perpetual crisis. However Communism permits, at least in this field, a certain pluralism: periods and styles can be detected within each country, and of course countries differ.

(viii) Indebtedness is endemic in both systems, and leads to centralization in state hands. Notably the ejidos could not pay for their tractors, however popular they were. Many were originally held by voluntary super-co-ops consisting of many ejidos. But when Cárdenas ceased to be president and the Banco Ejidal was forced to collect some debt it repossessed these, and something suspiciously like the Soviet MTS came into being. Kolkhozy could not afford to buy tractors in the very early days, and again got into severe financial difficulties in 1958 when they were forced to. When Brezhnev acceded to power he forgave much kolkhoz debt – a gesture reminiscent of any new-crowned king.

(ix) In what is fundamentally a populist régime the collective ejido is ideologically the highest form of property. In an STE the kolkhoz is more like the ordinary ejido: a 'native reserve' in which to keep unproductive and uneducated people until something better can be done with them.

(x) Both systems show a natural tendency to individualistic erosion. We postpone this important matter to sec. 15, where it is treated more in general.

(xi) The ejido is much smaller than the kolkhoz: about 120 adult members (before the division into *sectores* mentioned above) to 500 (in the amalgamated kolkhozy that characterize USSR and Bulgaria).

(xii) Labour discipline is very bad and incentives ineffective, in both systems: in the one because it is unpopular and founded on violence, in the other because it is genuinely democratic. In both the personality of the brigadier or labour overseer is of first importance. Indeed, in the matter of getting a labour gang together in the morning the kolkhoz *is* democratic: owing to the formalities of the statute, the traditions of the village, the lay-out of the housing and the personal relations of those involved the members are not bound to go to work on a given day, and the brigadier must make do or use 'persuasion'. No capitalist factory could survive on such a system: it is practically an idiorrhythmy (chapter 4, sec. 23).

(xiii) Ejido labour is paid by the piece where possible, as on the kolkhoz. In the former there were experiments with time payments, but the temptation to idle was too great. In both the principal beneficiaries from timework are the administrators. In the kolkhoz payments were for long made in kind (chapter 21, sec. 15), never in the ejido.

(xiv) In a fundamentally democratic system it was necessary from the start to make a monthly advance of pay (*anticipo*), and settle the member's full claim at the end of the year. This was a great gain, *ceteris paribus*, over the individual peasant's uncontrolled withdrawals from his business; for the individual is much more likely to mortgage the future than the ejido treasurer. Several systems have been in force: *anticipos* according to work and bonus either equal or in proportion to *anticipos*, or according to days of work done; *anticipos* equal and bonus on a Soviet-type trudoden' system. Many more systems could be thought of. By contrast, under Communism it has been possible to keep a poor man waiting for his income twelve months. This is one of the greatest and least appreciated scandals of the STE. Its rationale is quite simple: the kolkhoznik is a co-operatized peasant, and peasants always cast their accounts once a year. This is, however, not right, since individual peasants can also help themselves currently from the business, i.e. make private *anticipos.* In this respect then the Soviet peasant loses, and the Mexican peasant gains, from collectivization. Under Khrushchev however this fault, like so many others, was rectified. Nearly all kolkhozy went over to making monthly advances with a settlement at the end of the year (both on the trudoden' system).[30] But the advances must bear some relation to sovkhoz wages, so if the kolkhoz cannot pay the bank must lend. Shades of the Banco Ejidal!

(xv) The kolkhoznik is – or was – *adscriptus glebae*, but in the quasi-democratic society of Mexico this is unthinkable: there are no internal passports at all, let alone ones that discriminate between classes.

(xvi) The Soviet townsman and state farmer despise the kolkhoz. The kolkhoznik has the lowest prestige. The Mexican despises peasants but is simply ignorant of the ejido. It has not captured his imagination; it is studied by Israelis and Yankees, but not by him. The information clerk in a certain Mexican embassy asked me if the word meant some kind of cigarette.

(xvii) Despite the Marxist government Soviet collectivization had no technological excuse. There were no economies of scale to be reaped, and precious few new machines were supplied to justify the action *ex post facto* – and most of them were out of order. But Mexican collectivization had above all a technological excuse, as we have seen: the fact of irrigation by river and ditch. This at that time made individual ejidos impossible. But much of the disaster the movement has subsequently undergone is due to the cheap well and pump. Whole areas have reverted to individual farming just because of this – with the Banco Ejidal putting up the money. There are few more brilliant confirmations of basic Marxism – except that technical progress has *de*concentrated capital! The Soviet government would of course have refused to supply drills and pumps, as it has refused to supply small tractors.

(xviii) Theory is almost useless for both bodies. But the theoretical maximand of the collective ejido would have to be Illyrian, with or without 'demographically determined labour-supply' (chapter 4, sec. 9). And the kolkhoz is best dealt with as a queer kind of sovkhoz, maximizing plan fulfilment.

12. As to the commune, we shall confine ourselves, for serious factual

detail, to its best known form, the Israeli kibbutz. This is not a very common form in the real world, nor even statistically important inside so small a country as Israel. Members and their families number about 80,000 – about as many as the members of collective ejidos. There are about 300 members per kibbutz. But the thing is a perfect paradigm, and has been well described.[31] There have been many other communes, notably the various experimental ones, founded by Owenites, Transcendentalists and sexual pioneers, in USA;[32] their successors the hippie communes of the 1970s (chapter 21); the experimental Soviet communes that Stalin liquidated when he collectivized agriculture (Wesson, op. cit.); the various monasteries and nunneries of Christendom; and the two principal Protestant orders of commune, both of which grew in USA and one of which remains, the Shakers (Noyes, op. cit.) and Hutterites.[33] These we shall mention only in passing.

The commune socializes consumption too. There is only one dining hall and one crèche, though exceptions are made and rules vary. So the housewife is simply another member of the work force, who happens on the days when she does housework not to be directly engaged on saleable production – but for that matter the tractor repairman is never so engaged. She is moved from task to task – baby care, hoeing, administration – just like anyone else. There are, then, no housewives, only housework, and these activities should rather be treated like the auto-consumption of the peasant farm.

This makes auto-consumption an important concept in the study of the commune. Then too there are its sheer size and its autarkic policy. It does a great deal for itself, on principle, even though it might save labour to buy and sell more in the market. So the metaphor of international trade is very useful. Over-consumption shows up in the employment of too much 'non-export' or 'non-import-saving' labour; the commune must watch, indeed need only watch, its 'balance of payments'; it is highly protectionist, so subject to some uniform 'tariff' it should, or possibly should not, allocate resources internally according to the law of comparative costs. It also suffers emigration, especially a brain drain.

The theoretical maximand of the commune is the same as that of the co-operative: average income per head, but with special stress now on auto-consumption. The further we get from capitalism the further we get from all maximization – nor were we ever very near it. Yet the 'Illyrian' analysis does explain much about the commune. It sheds light, for instance, on its restrictive membership policy. But the main factor here is that the commune needs social homogeneity, as we have seen.

Like other Illyrian enterprises the commune is tempted to hire for wages at more or less than the internal rate of income (chapter 4). Like them it finds this incompatible with its ideology. But the kibbutz, unlike the Yugoslav factory, is not protected by law, so instead of the old capitalist Adam seeking to cheat the Illyrian government from below we find violation imposed on an idealistic minority by a government only partly sympathetic. This government has to find work for poor immigrants, and imposes this duty on kibbutzim as on all other enterprises. Hence the rash of light industrial plants, with hired labour as well as members.

For the rise and fall of the kibbutz, and its banking system, cf. sec. 15.

13. The shift from 'housework' to 'auto-consumption' has social effects. The change in women's economic status has obvious connexions with Women's Lib., and the irreligious commune, like the kibbutz, was indeed a forerunner of that movement. So even were the fundamentalist Protestant Shakers, who were founded by a woman whose unsatisfactory husband drove her to religious innovation. Not only did Mother Ann Lee completely prohibit sex – a rather Victorian approach to Women's Lib., but still an approach – she also made women hierarchically and administratively equal. Other communes, however, have retained male superiority, mainly by inertia.

The commune raises, but does not always solve, the question, should women's work be sexually distinct but equally honoured, or should the distinction be abolished? The zealots of Women's Lib. demand the latter verbally, but their practice very much confuses the two ideas. They demand that men should do housework and that women should perform bourgeois labour, but they press very little for a redistribution of paid manual labour. This is not merely because such zealots are all bourgeois themselves: it has a sound physiological basis. Besides, the whole movement is based upon the claim to parity of esteem, and if the husband's work is repetitive and manual there is that already. Even so the husband, as the 'exporter', is more honoured than the 'importer', even if she does also produce import substitutes. On the kibbutz the honour of producing saleable goods is on the whole reserved to men. But Mother Ann provided equally honoured work for both sexes while retaining a rigid sexual distinction; she saw to it that women, through their specialization in textiles and pharmaceuticals, should produce saleable products in great quantity.

So the commune is a household. But most other households are nuclear families. Exceptions are monasteries, officers' messes on active duty, old people's homes, residential schools, and the extended family when and where it lives together (e.g. chapter 21, sec. 16). What do we notice about most of these exceptions? – there is either no sex on the premises or highly structured sex. People living together are going to have to take a strong stand on sex, and the commune is no exception. The bold experiment of the Shakers came to its predictable end, when the supply of adoptable children dried up. Oneida struggled forwards on free love, which is *par excellence* a strong stand on sex, and on that rock it eventually foundered. After a few initial experiments with free love the kibbutzim have settled on fairly normal monogamy, but this has its price. Nubile bachelors and spinsters are frowned upon. They may well not be admitted as members, and if, being adult children of members, they cannot be kept out they are under severe pressure to marry.[34] Note the curious disconnexion of this whole question from Women's Lib., i.e. women's work.

For despite its surpassing interest the sexual life of the commune is almost without influence on its economic behaviour, so we must regretfully pass it by. But we must spare a paragraph for the corollary: the almost totalitarian social pressure on the individual, especially – and obviously – for the purpose of extracting work. In this respect the nuclear family is perhaps better; for while the commune gives the child more parents to play off against each other it is much bigger and more autarkic, so it gives the adolescent less chance to get out. For the deviant adult of course the commune has no room at all – and divorce from *this* family entails loss of job and residence. Hence a certain hostility to higher education. For this loses the commune its best young people. While this may not surprise us in Hutterites or Shakers, it may be objected that kibbutzim must be different, owing to the Jewish obsession with higher education. But we must remember that Israelis of the second generation are not 'Jews'.

The habit of conformism leads to splits. Serious communes must have ideologies to keep them going, so they naturally quarrel. The Hutterites quarrel about dress, and have three sub-orders. The kibbutzim quarrel about politics, and belong to three federations attached to three centre and left parties. They also have a young reform movement (below). Monks, for that matter, divide into orders: contemplative, teaching, missionary, etc. But in each case the groupings take more or less strict attitudes to equality and collectivity of consumption, which is at once the glory and the stumbling-block of the whole concept. Even the ejido colectivo indulges in political splits; indeed it is quite peculiarly subject to them.

The commune is not just an enterprise, and like other communities it must provide for the young, the old and the sick. To be unemployed within a commune is hardly possible, since it is a small command economy: one does what one is told, however democratically, to do. There is seldom a shortage of effective demand since there is no internal money and outside sales are a small part of all effort (including housework). Only technology or leisure preference could create even the simulacrum of unemployment: a commune is a smaller and more perfect STE. The state of Israel does not provide social services within the kibbutz (but it does within the moshav). Even the police rarely intervene; partly because there is so little crime, partly because the police are always chary of family quarrels.

For consumption decisions, cf. chapter 21.

14. Genuine co-operation is impossible in a command economy. Their shared hostility to capitalism, their common historical origin, do nothing to mitigate this contradiction. For both the co-operator – whether labour

or capital or land be his e.b.f. – and the capitalist must run their enterprise; but in a command economy the state does that. It makes no difference if there is a 'funny' maximand, or no maximand; the point is, who decides? This is, moreover, a tautology: precisely and ineluctably to the extent that the centre commands, there is neither capitalism nor co-operation.

The history of command economies is littered with attempts to square this circle. The retail co-ops have compulsory membership and obey a state plan no less detailed or obligatory than that for state shops. Communes were tolerated for a while and then liquidated. Above all the kolkhoz – compulsory to its members but formally democratic, its vestiges of workers' control a standing reproach to the socialist sector, subject to the annual command plan but only in respect of sowing and the state procurement, providing its own social services, a colonial reserve officially condemned to liquidation – is a veritable hippogriff among economic forms, but no myth. In industry even the mild 'workers' audit' of 1917 (so much less strong than workers' control – chapter 7) could not survive against the command economy. For that system is like a pine-tree: however tall and handsome, it permits no undergrowth, not even trade unions.

There is no better example of this contradiction than the history of Poland in 1956–8. Gomułka returned to power on a wave of popular, anti-Soviet but not anti-Communist, enthusiasm. An example of a nationalist and more liberal Communist state was ready to hand in Yugoslavia. Workers' councils sprang up, not merely because of this example, but as expressions of political discontent: the factories of Warsaw were organized by dissident Party members in Gomułka's favour. Thus workers' councils were a grass-roots movement, in stark contrast to Yugoslavia, where they had been imposed from above.

Politics has no room for gratitude. Gomułka kicked away the ladder up which he had been forced to climb. There had been too much spontaneity about October 1956, and the workers' councils were a political threat. Besides Gomułka was, if labels are permitted, a Bukharinite and not a Titoist: he wanted to reconcile the peasants, to compromise with the intellectuals and the Church – and *not* to abandon the aim of central command planning.[35] Having already achieved 'socialism' in industry, Poland was not to go a-whoring after strange gods. Nothing was done to moderate the claims of the Planning Commission and the ministries to make detailed decisions. The newly articulate and highly competent economics profession was brushed aside. The old state bureaucracy took every trick.

The workers' councils were therefore left functionless. A number of weird and wonderful compromises were worked out whereby they shared certain minor powers with the local trade union and the local Party. These finaglings are now of historical interest only, if that. The powers concerned were on the whole normal ones for the local branches of Soviet-type unions (chapter 7), and the workers' councils gradually faded from existence. They could only have continued to live in a market.

So the more powerful the workers' council the more total the freedom of the market and the weaker the planner. Capitalism itself, even petty capitalism, is easier to control from the centre than workers' councils. It follows that a government of the moderate left, concerned for both grass-roots democracy and 'planning', will rationally choose co-determination (Mitbestimmung, chapter 7) and French planning. For now the director, who is *rather* free of the planner, can sit down with the workers, who have *quite a lot of* power, and they will not be *completely* wasting their time.

15. But given a market within which to live, these forms have a strong tendency to capitalist erosion. For them, convergence means capitalism not socialism. Let us examine the technical reasons for this.

First is the brain (or at any rate competence) drain. It is nearly certain that somewhere on the market our best members can earn more money. The absolute egalitarianism of the commune and even the more modest egalitarianism of the co-op make it very improbable that we could match the highest outside salaries. A commune, for instance, could only do so by simultaneously paying unskilled labour, say, five times its outside rate; but it is probably less, not more, efficient than other enterprises, and could not possibly afford it.

We see this force at work even on the kolkhoz. Whatever the internal passport system decrees, young members can and do move out. So to keep them back we reintroduce the ideologically suspect 'link' (sec. 9). Now to entrust several fields to strong young technicians, and to separate their account from the rest of the farm, is to exclude grandmothers and other hangers-on. For on the ordinary kolkhoz one of the most inefficient and socially just features is the way in which *babushka* can stand around with a fork, watch the combine go by, and collect half a trudoden'. The young thrusters in the mechanized link are not going to stand for this: *their* work decides the value of the trudoden' and they don't want the capital watered. Thus the ancient and beneficial Communist principle, that socialism means paying incompetent people to stand around, is violated – and fantastic increases in productivity result. And even though the outside economy is socialist it is towards capitalism that the forces of the labour market, no doubt temporarily, push the kolkhoz.

The same tendency towards inequality, in order to keep the skilled happy, is evident in Yugoslavia. The originally Soviet-type society was, *pace* Djilas,[36] quite egalitarian except for a few top Communists. The mere decentralization of 1950–2 permitted more open competition for skilled managers and workers *between* co-ops. A market automatically differentiates incomes from work, whoever is competing. But on top of that the more liberal economy and society caused emigration to be allowed. A skilled man must be paid enough to keep him in, or get him back from West Germany – minus whatever margin patriotism contributes. Residual egalitarianism causes some to protest, but it is much eroded. Beside Djilas's New Class of top Communists has grown a New New Class of managers, professionals and entertainers.

The kibbutz suffers similarly, even though it is based on more genuine idealism. For this was no imposition from above. It originated with Russian Jews, of whom it would be difficult to say whether they were Socialist Revolutionaries or Marxists. Their Gentile equivalents stayed on and founded the ill-fated Soviet communes (sec. 9). But they, being Jews, had to emigrate. Unusually intense external challenges have kept the movement going until now: the pioneers' lack of skill and Arab hostility produced siege conditions, then followed distinguished military service for the new state. The present relaxation and success are a serious threat because they are no challenge. The very fact of prosperity, even egalitarian prosperity, weakens ideals that were partly a rationalization of its absence. A reform movement has arisen to embrace pioneering and Our Lady of Poverty all over again, just like a monastic reform: the Organization of the Spoilt Children.[37]

But most spoilt children present other problems. The kibbutz is mainly agricultural and Israel is industrializing. So there is a natural drift from the land. But each kibbutz is a national monument and must be preserved. So incomes must be raised to keep the young from leaving. Now no kibbutz has seriously sacrificed distribution according to need, i.e. near equality; so everyone's income has to rise; so labour is diverted to housework and auto-consumption; so the 'balance of payments' is permanently adverse. And this brings us to that seemingly inevitable *Doppelgänger* of a producers' co-op: a bank prepared for losses. In the case of kibbutzim it is the federations that act as investment bankers. They get money from Jews overseas, and from such members as are profitable. Originally founders and starters, they have become preservers and subsidizers.

So the kibbutzim have basically retained their equality in face of the brain drain, but at the price of their independence. To be precise they have paid in managerialization, in the growth of expert visiting administrators, good accountancy and rational allocation. For the federations must economize, and 'the world has grown grey at their breath'. Ordinarily we only speak of technocratic convergence between capitalism and socialism (chapter 20), but it does not spare the co-op or the commune. Ejidos too suffer from just such pressures (the Banco Ejidal).

Another source of inequality is the sheer individualism of the members who do not intend to move. This has hardly affected kibbutzim, but in ejidos members simply will not work enough without individual reward, and it is this that has worn down over the years the collectivism of their more conscientious colleagues, in the absence of government pressure to the contrary. Some slip back into private individual operation (*ejidatarios libres*) and some into 'semi-collectives', in which certain cultivating operations only remain collectivized, and members receive credit for the harvest from 'their' land in severalty. These 'semi-collectives' are too varied and fluid to deal with here. As this is written the *ejido colectivo* is in a severe decline through idleness, corruption, divisive politics and governmental bungling (Reyes Osorio *et al.*, loc. cit.). It is a wonder that in face of this tragic story other Latin American governments are repeating the experiment.

Stalin, paradoxically, realized all this very well, and in collectivizing he tried only to bring people under control while precisely not extinguishing what he called their 'material interestedness in production'. Indeed he only finally settled the internal structure of the kolkhoz after his great denunciation of 'petty bourgeois levelling' in industry in 1931. Inequality is great among those who stay in the kolkhoz, perhaps quite as great as among individual peasants. He achieved this end by central regulation of the number of trudodni to be allocated to each job. But against pressure to raise the size of private plots he was adamant. There was such pressure, and indeed it succeeded (during 1941–5, when the government's back was turned).[38] After the war these encroachments were reversed.

16. As always, we must also be cynical: the co-op is an evasive device in many societies.

In Britain the retail co-operative's dividend on purchase is not subject to corporation tax or income tax. Yet the purchaser has lent to the shop, and a bank or private person lending at short term would expect to pay company tax or income tax on the interest. The dividend is assimilated for tax purposes to a trade discount, so it is not income. This is not so much wrong as arbitrary; for the retained profit is subject to tax.

In Britain again building labourers form co-operative itinerant gangs in order to qualify, as 'self-employed', for the lower unemployment insurance and the freedom from the trade unions' restrictive practices.

In USA the farmers' co-ops distribute most of their profits in dividend; indeed they are legally compelled to distribute 20 per cent. But distributions over 20 per cent are made in scrip, which is virtually irredeemable. They retain the cash counterpart of the scrip and plough it back into the business, along with their formal ploughback. Meanwhile as co-ops they are exempt from all corporation tax (but the members pay income tax on the scrip). So the co-op exploits its members, i.e. its managers use the ploughback to forward their own private purposes. It gets the members by monopolizing what they want.[39]

In Poland kolkhozy are formed by peasants out of their bad land: the principal crop is tax relief. But the peasants retain, at least in the family, their better land for serious cultivation. The collective ejido is similarly used, by members of normal ejidos nearby.

In USSR in the NEP the least collective form of kolkhoz, the TOZ, was regularly preferred. It brought in the tax relief and the preferential commodity allocations, but demanded little. At all times under Communism peasants have chosen the least collective form permitted – and then violated it.

In STEs urban building is often done by co-ops consisting of the prospective owners. They provide much of the unskilled labour themselves, while they may hire the skills they lack. The scheme enables the state, which makes big advances to the co-ops, to charge interest on its capital,[40] and rents, or their equivalents, to be raised without scandal. This too, then, is an evasion, but an extremely sensible one, by the state. These same building co-ops permit a good deal of finagling by the more enterprising members: the law is twisted so that flats are rented or sold at an enormous profit, and the original member makes a capital gain.

17. Let us sum up on the political economy of these forms. They are meant to be joined voluntarily, already under capitalism, which provides the free market in which alone they can live (a fact they are most reluctant to admit). They offer beyond any question less alienation, and a smaller (but not normally a zero) yield on capital. But they are so inefficient that the promise of higher wages and lower prices, skill and quality being equal, is never kept. They make a major point of avoiding violent revolution. When it comes – as it does in certain theorists – to taking over capital instead of building up one's own, the plan is always to compensate, though seldom beyond one life-time.

In 1918 USSR made membership of consumers' co-operatives (*sel'pos*, sec. 3), which had survived the revolution, compulsory. A thrill of disapproval passed through the international co-operative movement. Compulsion was abolished in 1921 but reimposed in 1935. The kolkhoz, again, is unique in being a co-operative based on class-war – to a genuine co-operator a contradiction in terms. The collective ejido and the Yugoslav factory are similarly based, but after all capitalists form a very small class, and comparatively liberal régimes have let scar-tissue form. But in the Soviet countryside in 1929 there were a million or so rich peasant households, who were not perceived by the other peasants as being a different class, let alone a hostile one. But Stalin so defined them – and about a million other households refusing to go along, making about 10 per cent.[41] They were deported and their agricultural property was confiscated and given to the new kolkhozy as a bribe. Compulsion and confiscation are *principles* of Communism. Spontaneity and free will are bad; they may even avert a revolution.[42]

But the massive expropriation of not very rich people is fearfully counterproductive. Socialists ordinarily expropriate very few people, since they wait until the concentration of capital has done its work. For in matters of expropriation mere shareholders don't count; they are passively fobbed off with half the value in bonds (which inflation then depreciates). It is the owner-manager who reaches for his gun, for he will lose much more than capital: his salary, his power, his way of life. Moreover the state will lose his (very efficient) labour. So by a paradox socialist expropriation is painless, it is co-operative expropriation that hurts. Therefore co-operative expropriation is only practised by socialists, who do not understand co-operation!

On the other side a genuinely co-operative system is genuinely unstable. It veers back to capitalism, through the free market, the survival of small-group interests and the generally tolerant atmosphere. It shows no tendency to develop into socialism, as many thinkers from Marx to Hayek have supposed; for men are bad and socialism is unnatural. It has difficulty even in maintaining equality, which is part of its official goals; for men are bad and equality is unnatural. There is therefore something to be said for the violence and compulsion of the only successful socialism we know.

Notes

1. In particular Marx and Engels denied it the accolade of socialism, but Engels did say – quite falsely – that it was the dictatorship of the proletariat. There was, of course, no proper Parisian proletariat at that time.

2. It lingered in Scotland, and some of the English retail societies continued the bonus awhile for their own shop assistants. But since most of these employees had votes only if they were shareholders it is better to describe labour as residual-bearing than as equity-bearing.

3. Excluding alcoholic drink, cars, motor accessories and newspapers.

4. All over the world husbands allow this bonus to their wives in respect of trading stamps. Thus the family acts irrationally in preferring shops that give stamps but the wife who receives a fixed housekeeping allowance does not.

5. Cf. my contribution to ed. G. Ionescu, *Populism*, Oxford 1969.

6. Small tractor imports, strip consolidation with state help, sale of public land, and the end of the compulsory deliveries, the profits of which used to go straight into these co-ops.

7. *Encyclopedia of the Social Sciences*, 1935, 'Co-operative Production'; Benjamin Jones, *Co-operative Production*, Oxford 1894; Beatrice Webb, *My Apprenticeship*, London 1948 (esp. the appendix); George D. H. Cole, *A Century of Co-operation*, Manchester 1944. There is even a fair amount of voluntary collective farming in France and Spain: OECD, *Group Farming*, Paris 1972. These small groups are highly reminiscent of the Celtic run-rig (chapter 5, sec. 5).

8. Cf. Charles Gide, *Consumers' Co-operative Societies*, Manchester 1921, ch. 15; G. D. H. Cole, op. cit.; A. M. Carr-Saunders *et al.*, *Consumers' Co-operation in Great Britain*, London 1942, pp. 43–5, 328–56.

9. An astounding amount of non-farm petty capitalism is, however, permitted, principally in transport, building, tourism and crafts (not shops). These employ 8 per cent of the non-farm labour force. On the practical as opposed to the Illyrian side of Yugoslavia cf. Jiri T. Kolaja, *Workers' Councils, the Yugoslav Experience*, London 1965; Adolf Sturmthal, *Workers' Councils*, Harvard 1964; Jan Vanek, *The Economics of Workers' Management*, London 1972.

10. Not obviously bad, but thought to be so by Soviet observers – as if they themselves did not have different retail prices in each republic, and totally irrational discriminations in farm prices.

11. But not amalgamated or unitary monopolies, since the system is hostile to these (see v). However in a small country with balance-of-payments difficulties there are always *de facto* many unitary monopolies, since imports are always restricted.

12. Cf. Meir Enzer, *The Moshav*, Israel Digest, revised edn., Jerusalem 1973.

13. Salomon Eckstein, *Los Ejidos Colectivos en México*, México D.F., 1966; Nathan Whetten, *Rural Mexico*, Chicago 1948; Clarence Senior, *Democracy Comes to a Cotton Kingdom*, México D.F., 1940; idem., *Land Reform and Democracy*, Gainesville 1958; Henry A. Landsberger and Sandra Hofferth-Emmi, *Political, Social and Economic Determinants of the Success of Mexican Ejidos*, London University (Centre of International and Area Studies) 1972; Sergio Reyes Osorio *et al.*, *Estructura Agraria y Desarrello Agrícola en México*, México D.F. 1974, chapter 6.

14. Joaquín Costa, *El Colectivismo Agrario en España*, Madrid 1915.

15. In the 1920s Mexican populism took on a racial tinge. Populism, as we know, seeks the source of virtue in some defined popular mass. In this period all good things were Indian, especially the ejido and the great mural-painters. All bad things were Spanish or Yankee, especially capitalism and Catholicism. Such racial theories are endemic in populism.

16. Already the law of January 1915 required that land returned to ejidos be cultivated collectively until it was legally split up. Circular 51 of the National Agrarian Commission, in October 1922, recommended collective ejidos outright, but had no practical consequences.

17. Cf. Robert Wesson, *Soviet Communes*, New Brunswick 1963.

18. Cf. Yu. Mironenko in *Munich Bulletin*, November 1964.

19. Cf. Audrey Donnithorne, *China's Economic System*, N.Y. 1967, chapters 2, 3.

20. There have been two historical waves of links. Up to 1949 unmechanized ones, such as the piggery example, were common. The link was then officially banished as being too right-wing. It revived in the 1960s in mechanized form in the virgin lands, even on sovkhozy. Its object is to keep young and vigorous people on the farm by assuring them a good income. Mechanized links even take over whole grain fields for a number of years, on contract. Cf. Dimitry Pospielovsky in *Soviet Studies*, April 1970.

21. Everett Jacobs in *Ost-Europa*, 10/1969. Nádudvar being the name of a particular farm, other Hungarian farms do not use this name!

22. Cf. Naum Jasny, *The Socialized Agriculture of the USSR*, Stanford 1949, chapter 12. It follows that horses and oxen, nature's small tractors, are 'right-wing live-stock', in the sense of chapter 5, sec. 3. Good left-wing livestock yield products other than power – and even then they may be too individualistic.

23. Cf. Everett Jacobs in ed. P. J. D. Wiles, *The Prediction of Communist Economic Performance*, Cambridge 1971. For the ideological difficulties of selling tractors to kolkhozy cf. chapter 3, sec. 7 here.

24. There is however a rather severe income tax on private agricultural income, in so far as it is ever reported.

25. Price controls in the free market are never imposed in principle, and seldom in practice.

26. Private working. This includes the produce of workers', especially sovkhoz-

niks', plots. On the far greater labour input and the relative efficiency of the private sector cf. chapter 15, sec. 21.

27. If distances are long to market the private plot loses its value, and this is another instance of the failure to charge land rent in an STE. The ride should be a two-way shopping trip, or it is very wasteful of time. One may do errands for one's neighbours, both buying and selling, but it is illegal to take a commission. For that is no longer 'individual labour' but 'speculation'. Similarly one may not pay non-family-members to work on one's plot, for that is 'private labour' and so 'exploitation'.

28. We are entitled to make this controversial statement because the first collective ejidos were founded in 1936, by a President who was fairly sympathetic to USSR and won the Stalin prize; and because the local Communists had requested it. But there had been also non-Communist demands for such a thing since 1921.

29. The best book (Eckstein, op. cit.) was written by an Israeli during this period, under the auspices of the Banco Ejidal. It has a mild but persistent bias in favour of collectivism: so to speak Cardenista not Communista. I have not found a Communist or right-wing source.

30. Recently the trudoden' was abolished in USSR. For the new 'bonus-cum-piece-work' (*akordno-premialni*) system cf. Karl-Eugen Wädekin, *Die Bezahlung der Arbeit in der Sowjetischen Landwirtschaft*, Berlin 1972, chapter 4.

31. Eliahu Kanovsky, *The Economy of the Israeli Kibbutz*, Cambridge, Mass., 1968; Leonard J. Fein, *Politics in Israel*, N.Y. 1967; Haim Darin-Drabkin, *The Other Society*, Tel Aviv 1961.

32. New Harmony, Brook Farm, Oneida, etc. Cf. John H. Noyes, *History of American Socialisms*, N.Y. 1966; Arthur E. Bestor, *Backwoods Utopias*, Philadelphia 1950.

33. Paul K. Conkin, *Two Paths to Utopia*, Nebraska 1964; Victor Peters, *All Things Common*, Minneapolis 1965; D. Barkin and J. Bennett in *Comparative Studies in History and Society*, September 1972; Henrik F. Infield, *Co-operative Communities at Work*, London 1947.

34. The same even applies to the moshav ovdim – surely unnecessarily, for there are no such pressures in the kolkhoz.

35. Bukharin, the prophet of the NEP, remained entirely orthodox in his vision of socialism. It had no room for a market. He would have condemned Tito as a revisionist.

36. Milovan Djilas is the great renegade Titoist who has condemned the society he helped to found in his *The New Class* (London 1957).

37. GILAT. See Geoffrey Moorhouse in *The Guardian*, 20 January 1968.

38. Also in occupied territory the Germans kept loose kolkhozy going, since they too needed the 'grain pump'. Cf. Otto Schiller in *Land Economics*, 1951 (twice). But they permitted a great deal of individualism, and on reoccupying the farms Stalin had to 'restore order'.

39. William M. Blair in *New York Times*, 27 September 1967.

40. Socialized housing, like all other socialized investment, is financed interest free. There is also a formal housing subsidy. Rents are also a small part of income simply because people live in one-room flats.

41. These numbers are my personal estimates.

42. So Marx was virtually guilty of these sins in his letter to Zasulich in 1876, as again was Engels in *Neue Zeit* in 1894 (chapter 5, sec. 7).

7
Trade Unions and Hired Labour

7

1. This is one of the very few areas in which comparative economics never ceased to be respectable. There is thus good work to build on,[1] and we may proceed more rapidly – and dogmatically – with many but not all types of union.

A trade union is not an enterprise but an agency (chapter 4, sec. 1). That is, it is so permanently conscious, even in the short run, of its members' interests that *it* cannot be said to be maximizing anything: *they* are maximizing – if indeed, our usual qualification, anyone is. Other similar bodies are a cartel, which is a trade union of enterprises selling something in common, and an employers' association, which is a trade union of enterprises buying labour.

All useful definitions are, of course, blurred. It belongs to the pathology of trade unions that they often behave like enterprises, acting in their own, not their members', interests. This is above all the case with the business unionism of North and South America. Leaders are very often simply corrupt: they invest in the equities of small firms and then sign 'sweetheart' contracts with them, they grant themselves mortgages out of the pensions fund, they recruit members by force simply to get the dues, etc. These then are in part the private business enterprises of the leaders. Then again the ideological unions of Western Europe sacrifice their members' direct economic interests under capitalism for political goals that, no doubt more strongly and consciously held by the leaders, must yet be presumed to appeal to most members.

In this case the agency function is not denied: it is merely politicized. Nor is this phenomenon corrupt unless the members truly have other political goals, but are unable to govern their own union. But that is not uncommon: it is as easy to set up a breakaway union as a new daily newspaper, so one belongs to the 'best union we've got'.

We also use the words 'trade union' of bodies that, while preserving this name and origin, are in fact agencies of management: company unions – or of the government: in STEs and, with more qualifications, in UDCs. Our excuse is that these positions are fundamentally unstable, and that unions always tend to revert to their eponymous role of workers' defence when the lid is taken off.

The basic role, then, is the historic role. The proletarian is alienated and, on his own, powerless. Yet work remains vastly important to him, as a matter of self-expression as well as income. So he forms unions to regulate and stabilize, by collective bargaining and strikes, his conditions of employment. This is the virtuous *Idealtypus* of the union under primitive capitalism. Generations of labour historians, economists and socialist politicians have conspired to present this as the current picture; if some of the facts have altered, at least the moral balance is the same. But even in its time this virtuous union was in many respects a mere *pis aller* for the yet-to-be-founded welfare state: labour monopoly, fortuitously successful in this or that sector of the market, always was a most inefficient and unjust substitute for regular nation-wide social services. It is even more than doubtful whether it ever for long raised its members' real wages, then or now.[2] If its wages-and-hours claims had been met immediately in full the economy would indeed have collapsed, just as contemporary employers claimed. It was the merely partial meeting of these claims made in market places that kept the economy going. The growth of restrictive practices has of course retarded economic growth, whereas most capitalist monopolies have not. The new era of cost inflation is exclusively caused by unions (chapter 14). On the other hand if early unions were violent – and they were very violent, and oppressed non-union workmates shamefully – capitalist opposition to them was still more violent, and must take most of the blame. But picketing, sitting-in, and sending to Coventry and declaring black are inherently on the border-line of violence.[3] The closed shop, the preferred weapon of the professional unions, is a gross violation of civil liberty. We cannot imagine such things away without imagining trade unions away. There are no trade unions in Utopia, however it is constituted in other respects. Their self-righteousness and solidarity rest on no solid ethical base.

2. Later, as the law turns from an enemy into a friend and the worker becomes rich enough to form strike funds and pay for competent representatives, union types diverge. In North, and occasionally in South, America socialism and class solidarity take no root, and so we find the *business* union. From 1850 until about 1890, when socialism came along, the British unions were also of this type. The union turns into an aggressive and restrictive cartel. It often opposes technical progress or throws non-members out of work by insisting on high minimum wages. It has even been known to use its political influence against social services, for that is state competition against one of its own functions (UK, 1910). It has also been known to engage in racial discrimination, and to prevent remedial labour in prisons, lest the product compete.

The business union tries to avoid politics, but so powerful and numerous a body is willy-nilly political. All it achieves – and not always that – is to avoid permanent identification with a single party.

3. Where Communism is weak and social democracy strong (North West Europe, Australasia), there is only one real union movement, professing social-democratic values with varying sincerity and nuance, and infiltrated here and there by nuisance Communists too weak to found an independent movement. Such a group, having no great revolutionary goal

immediately before it, but strongly tinged with idealism, shades off in practice into business unionism. The public stance on peripheral issues like racial discrimination and prison labour is unselfish, and even on the central market issues of collective bargaining it is at least less unfeeling about other workers. We cannot, for instance, imagine many miners' unions consciously and openly causing unemployment among unorganized miners as did the American UMW.[5] What social-democratic unions at least have is class solidarity.

Thus the pure business union is a most unlovely instance of 'group Benthamism' (chapter 2), fortified by traditional self-righteousness – but outside the Americas this self-righteousness has some continuing basis in fact. Nevertheless idealism can degenerate, leaving only self-righteousness behind. The first and worst case of this is the new British *left-wing business union.* Growing out of the old political traditions, but animated by much more radical aspirations, such a union is *militant, but for money not ideals.* It becomes a powerful engine of cost inflation. It can also be manipulated by Communists for almost any purpose: they have but to make more extravagant wage-claims and work harder, and the leadership is theirs.

In Latin Europe, on the other hand, Catholicism and Communism dispute the field with, indeed predominate over, social-democracy. The union movement is split into two or three politico-religious segments, and the unions are competitive, poor and ineffective, enrolling small proportions of the labour force even when added together. A seemingly separate point is that the predominant tradition is revolutionary syndicalism: mistrust of state, bureaucracy and parties, including left-wing parties, unwillingness to set up a bureaucracy of one's own, accumulate funds and bargain collectively, obsession with 'revolution at the point of production'. None of the three political parties has overcome these habits, incompatible as they are with all three ideologies and also with effective support for the workers' day-by-day demands. Strikes are short and sharp, and tend to be rather general; whereas business unions tend, far more rationally, to strike particular firms for very long periods of time. The Latin strike is a gesture; unbacked by strike funds, it is too often a futile gesture. Latterly the workers have turned to the French state to fix wages by law – a clear admission of the ineffectiveness of their unions. Such unions are not unknown elsewhere: the International Workers of the World in USA repeated the whole syndrome.

In no country hitherto mentioned is there any distinction between public and private enterprise: collective bargaining and strikes are normal in nationalized and municipalized industry. But there are a few hold-outs in public service employment: even such non-essential occupations as teachers, railwaymen and civil service clerks are occasionally denied the right to strike. The consequences for labour morale are disastrous. Such workers normally suffer most from wage-freezes and deflationary fiscal policy. They eventually erupt into unofficial strikes of great bitterness, in which the law, being unenforceable, is brought into contempt. With policemen and firemen anti-strike laws are far more common and far more rational. Such cases must await the discussion of the company union, below.

4. So far we have mentioned unions, and social systems, that accept the *fundamental disharmony of interests* between employer and employed. The fact of basic disharmony, in any field, is a bitter pill to swallow. Medieval society would have none of it: we were all children of God and society was an organism. The Enlightenment would have none of it: we were all equal social atoms governed by reason and therefore better understanding would make us agree. The early capitalist would have none of it: posturing as a medieval master craftsman, he was a just and generous patriarch over the segment of the proletariat in his care (much like a modern Japanese corporation). The Communists will have none of it: they are children of the Enlightenment and also the Vanguard of the Proletariat themselves, so how can the workers' interests differ from theirs? To use the Marxist jargon, contradictions within socialism must be non-antagonistic.

It is cynical to accept a fundamental social disharmony as ineradicable. It means you think human beings cannot be perfected. The employer-employee conflict is the greatest and most permanent of all social disharmonies, and its open but peaceful expression is the litmus test of democracy. Capitalism has been dragged, kicking and screaming, into an acceptance of all this. Even its co-operatives and its trade unions,[6] in their capacity as employers, have followed suit – also kicking and screaming. Other social systems, however, continue to 'say it ain't so'.

Beyond the question of harmony stands that of political power. A trade union is a large body of well-organized people, with strong common feelings and a sizeable budget. It would be preternatural if it did not exploit this strength to influence the use of state power, even in spheres unconnected with its members' economic interests. It would be even more preternatural if it were not exploited by other political forces. The politically neutral union is a rarity, even in parliamentary democracies.[7] In other polities the union is *invariably* under the control of the state, or at least of its single party. This control is instituted to preserve the in-group's monopoly of state power, but slops over into an attempt to influence the unions' economic behaviour. But whether any state can really achieve this is another matter. It is one thing to get party members into top union posts, and to be cheered at speech-making time; it is another to enforce an incomes policy.

5. To turn to the other extreme, there is the company union. Statistically so insignificant as to rate no mention in textbooks, the company union

has after all existed and it does throw a flood of light on the whole subject. The key motive in setting up such a union is to forestall, to tame the inevitable: since there must be a union let it be under our control. The company union, therefore, like the Soviet-type union, is a sop to Cerberus.

Mostly company unions have just withered away under the hostile competition of genuine unions, but some have undergone a more interesting evolution. For there is, as we keep asserting, an inexorability about unionism that no one can wish away. Start employees meeting to discuss conditions of work, and they will make demands; and eventually they will back demands by a strike. Moreover a company union is in a strong position, since it can always say *Après Moi Le Déluge*. The existence of genuine unions strengthens its hand so much that it becomes a genuine union. This is particularly common among the 'professional associations' of senior employees, policemen and firemen. Renouncing the right to strike, they renounce virtually nothing. For a strike would be uniquely awful for their employers, so it is enough for the union to threaten that it will collapse while its members strike.

The classic case of the company union that becomes a Frankenstein's monster is that of the unions founded by S. V. Zubatov, a senior Tsarist police official, in 1901. The Ministry of Interior was at that time Slavophil (i.e. both reactionary and Populist). Sentiment among these powerful officials ran against capitalists as mercenary, probably foreign or Jewish, and the carriers of various alien trends such as logic, law, civil rights and democracy. So knowing unions to be inevitable, and feeling a genuine sympathy with the Russian proletariat, and willing to interfere with the 'bad' urban social structure as he would never have been in the countryside, Zubatov founded his unions. They belonged, of course, not to the companies but to the Tsar: much as under left-wing Fascism (sec. 7), employers and managers were excluded. Meetings began with prayer. Official strikes were not unknown. The thing got quickly out of hand and the revolution of 1905 was the result.[8]

Then again in a business civilization, where everything has its price and even a union is a sort of private enterprise, the basically genuine union can constitute itself, at least in a few branches, a company union. For one of the possible equity shareholders in a business, which we did not enumerate in chapter 4, is the, or a, trade union or senior official thereof. So the powerful business union, which could easily crush so small an enterprise, signs instead a 'sweetheart' contract, because it is more interested in the dividend than in the wage: a conflict of interest indeed! We think here of the US Teamsters and Mining Workers in recent years.

6. Above the company union in this case there stands the *union company*. Now we saw in chapter 6 reason to think that participation in management is the solution to the problems of alienation. So we cannot object to union companies in principle. Take, then, a more honest case:

the so-called Jewish needle trade unions of USA – founded by socialist Jews, and poles apart from business unionism – used to operate (*c.* 1900) in an industry of very small firms, the masters of which were also immigrant Jews. Any man might become a master, and vice versa, much as in the British building trade. Class solidarity was great, but so was national solidarity. Everyone wanted better conditions, but no one wanted another Lithuanian Jew to go bankrupt.

The result was persistent attempts to take over managerial prerogative, notably by controlling the big putters-out who distributed contract work to the small masters. There was also one of the very first formal grievance procedures, and an attempt at arbitration. At least one ex-union leader became an acceptable arbitrator. One cannot however actually point to a union-owned employer, though there were a great many co-operative ventures outside garment-making, such as a bank, summer rest-homes and the like. In three words the Jewish needle unions were constructive, not restrictive. Their members were after all transplanted Bundists;[9] however socialistic they were a national movement.

In Palestine the same Bundist culture, again in the situation of an impoverished and threatened immigration, reacted to the absence of a Jewish state machine and a shortage of capitalists by founding a great many union companies. This was via the Histadrut, which is fundamentally a labour union but has become also a conglomeration of enterprises, some co-operatively managed, some managed by appointed experts. In other words the Histadrut has achieved what the British co-operative movement set out to do after Rochdale (chapter 6), but failed in. Since the kibbutzim too were nominally under its umbrella the Histadrut was a real museum of non-capitalist forms. General membership, whatever that may mean, covers 65 per cent of Israel's population. The Histadrut is of course succumbing to its contradictions and size. It is somewhat of a *lusus naturae* and we do not pursue it systematically.[10]

Finally affluence produces union *pension funds*, and not only among business unions. Strike funds must of course be kept liquid, but pension money is invested at long term, and therefore according to someone's judgement. Now judgement may be conveniently deflected and yet remain defensible before an auditor. Perhaps a mortgage on the general secretary's son's house really is a very good investment. Mortgages can also be taken out on union hospitals and union apartment blocks: by ordinary judgement these may not be good mortgages but the very purpose of the pension fund is to help those who benefit from these facilities. Again the idealistic unions of Europe have long resisted buying equities, as it compromises them with the system. But their power to do good to their members varies with the yield on their funds. In particular an employer often offers his own equity to the pension fund on advantageous terms. Without such terms it could be an unwise investment, just as in the case of co-ownership: for the worker's savings depend now on the same enterprise as his earnings. But in this way too the 'union company' becomes a possibility.

There is, then, no one reason for union companies.

7. There is little about *Fascism* in this book because it produces little new in the way of economic institutions. Like parliamentary democracy it appears to be compatible with all of them, except possibly the STE. The failure of Fascism to produce an STE may be historical chance, but it may also be due to Fascist empiricism in economic matters. For Fascists may be very left-wing by ordinary standards, nationalizing and equalizing as no Social-Democrat would dare: e.g. Perón or the later Mussolini. But they are fundamentally interested in other topics, such as race or militarism or war; and this economic empiricism induces a certain moderation.

Left-wing Fascism deserves, however, a cursory description. After the Nazis sprang him from captivity, Mussolini refounded Fascism in German-occupied Northern Italy (the Republic of Saló, 1943–5). He turned decisively leftwards. The Republic was 'founded on labour'. Capitalist ownership continued, but some important things were nationalized. Everything, however, was 'socialized'; the workers, meaning all employees, had power within and shared the profits of all enterprises, however owned. Food procurement at low prices was administered by 'the workers', and in this connexion very many food retailers and even wholesalers were subjected to compulsory co-operatization. The system was non-Communist, since both capital and labour collaborated with the state, and were not commanded by it. It was non-capitalist, in that there were no 'plutocrats'. I.e. it was in opposition to the 'Judaeo-Bolshevik' enemy. Naturally, in the disturbed condition of the times and in view of Mussolini's certain defeat, these principles were very imperfectly implemented. But they are a reasonably consistent set, and the paradigm for left-wing Fascism everywhere.[11] The very radical provisions for workers' control bear a most embarrassing resemblance to the initial arrangements in Tito's Yugoslavia – four years later, in a country with strong Italian connexions, and in similar circumstances of a strong government casting about for new internal allies during a sudden crisis.

In one respect, then, Fascism has shown originality: the corporatist union. Like any other undemocratic system it can tolerate neither antagonistic contradictions nor independent power centres (sec. 4); so it can and often does leave capitalism alone, since capitalists, whatever Marxists say, never form a threatening power bloc. Any dictator, already possessing the state machine, can buy them off or arrest them one by one. But all dictators, even very left-wing ones, must liquidate independent trade unions. It is perhaps this circumstance that causes Marxists to misinterpret Fascism as basically capitalistic. But in the hands of Perón (before 1955) these state-run unions almost ruined Argentine capitalism – quite deliberately. This is because he was a left-wing Fascist, unlike, say, the early

Mussolini, who did indeed use state power to help private capitalism.

The orthodox corporatist union includes all ranks, even the managing director; and hopes in so doing to abolish class war. Collective bargaining is legally controlled. But in the most left-wing versions (Perón) it organizes only the 'workers', defining that ambiguous term much as do other unions. Perón had a deliberately inflationary incomes policy – which worked! Others (Franco, Hitler, the early and the late Mussolini, Salazar) have tried with varying success to enforce restraint. Their record is at least far better than that of capitalist ACEs.

8. So far the union as spontaneous grassroots defence mechanism (the basic concept), and the union as lightning rod. Finally the other *de haut en bas* form, the mobilizing union. People do not like to be mobilized and have their productivity increased for them. They do not willingly listen to lectures on what they really want, or vote *en masse* for wage-scales they have not discussed, which will probably depress their earnings. The mobilizing union, then, is also an outgrowth of the historic union, and would never have come into being without it. In the Soviet-type case this should not surprise us. On the one hand the words 'trade union' are good: the well-dressed polity should have some. Furthermore Communism is a labour movement. On the other hand an economy which reduces enterprises to branch establishments *must* reduce unions to productivity councils: economic systems have not much logic but they do have some. The Soviet-type union, then, is the company union of the single great state enterprise, and Zubatov never died. Stalin loaded the unions with the functions of the Ministry of Labour (safety, technical education on the job, etc.) and the administration of social services. Only one element of a capitalist trade union did he retain: grievance procedures and appeals against dismissal remained a serious function right through the worst period. He abolished central collective bargaining (see below). but retained and enhanced Lenin's idea of the union as a 'trasmission belt', operating between government and labour; i.e. as a political mobilizer, wage-freezer and productivity raiser. Just as in the corporatist case, the highest managers belong to the union; for after all it is an industrial union, and they are employees, indeed 'working class'.[12]

A less well known case is the union in the UDC, which bears a striking resemblance to a Soviet-type union. Only it engages in political, rather than economic, mobilization. Indeed sometimes accident gives it historical precedence over the national liberation party, which then originates as the creature of the union, much as did the British Labour Party. So long as foreign capital and a foreign government are dominant employers, such unions combine easily the economic and the political roles required of colonial liberation. But when that is achieved government and unions are much more difficult to hold together. The Jewish Bund and its descendants (sec. 6 above) were perhaps the first such case.

Since UDCs are less totalitarian than STEs their unions conform far more closely to the classical pattern. They seldom include managers, and they are much harder to buy off. Cost inflation is often even worse than in ACEs.

9. For the name and the origin have an inexorable weight, and everyone knows that unions 'ought' to defend the worker at the point of production, against whoever is in charge. As workers become more prosperous and educated, as colonial liberation recedes in time, as Communism becomes less paranoiac, this ancient verity inevitably raises its head. No economic system has yet been invented that does not require the worker to be defended in this way, and this is one of the most certain points of convergence (chapter 20).

We may even offer a generalization on this convergence. The mobilizing state, whether Communist or 'single-party underdeveloped', and the capitalist state interested in current management, are more likely to control the central organs of the trade union. The workers will probably capture or retain the local organs, and the union will be split. The members then more or less identify the central organs with the employer or the state, and take the same kind of evasive action. Thus, and most notably, the British government may impose an incomes policy, and even get the unions to agree with it. 'Restraint' is exhibited for a time, during which nationwide collective bargains are struck not disgracefully far above the maximum the government says it will tolerate. But of course if 'restraint' is not purely otiose it means that fiscal and monetary policy were lax, and higher wage-rates might have been achieved. This is obvious to members, to their shop-stewards *and to their employers*. Of these latter, those who could have paid a higher wage are the ones who want to expand, so all three parties conspire at the periphery to 'interpret' and evade the terms of the central bargain, for all the world as if it were a state price control. The statistician is naïf indeed who judges the success of a period of British 'restraint' by the growth of centrally determined wage-rates.

Similarly in USSR it has been easy to continue the Stalinist prohibition on centralized collective bargaining, and the main union bureaucracy still willingly performs the welfare and propaganda functions Stalin gave it. Indeed the top leaders of this bureaucracy have for many years been imposed from without. Their previous career has been in the Party apparat and not the unions at all. But the all-important enterprise-level branches press harder for whatever advantages their members can legally get. Here the trade-union picture has been transformed, and the worker has recently acquired considerable respect for his local branch. It cannot bargain over wages any more than can its head office – nor can the enterprise director. The so-called collective bargain between the union and the directors is a mere propaganda exercise in *kontraktatsia* (chapter 9, sec. 12). Both sides are compelled to make the contract, and its purpose is, as in all other such cases, only to put flesh on the bare bones of the enterprise plan – which must not be violated and already contains the wage-bill. But the union can insist on favourable interpretations of the labour-plan directives, and it has even more leeway in safety regulation, the allocation of holiday times, etc. It has a virtual veto over dismissals. These powers, being quite over and above the administration of welfare funds, are very respectable. It is beyond doubt that the Soviet rulers wish them to be exercised, but that does not make the concession any less inevitable.

The concession is a return to Lenin. For in addition to his transmission-belt metaphor he bequeathed the notion of 'bureaucratic deformations' in the socialist state. The unions were to fight these, and it was Lenin's recognition of this that separated him from Trotsky, the out-and-out militarizer of labour. It is of course no paradox that Stalin in this, as in so much else, was Trotsky's heir.

The attitude to *strikes* is of course the key. Strikes are not often expressly legal in Communist countries: Hungarians may strike if the director breaks the labour law; Chinese may strike on non-economic issues, i.e. if Mao Tse-tung wants to have another Cultural Revolution. But strikes are never expressly illegal. However Communist law has many loopholes, and the very rare occurrences are always investigated by the police, and one way or another the ring-leaders are arrested. Characteristically, therefore, labour resists management and the state through the go-slow.

10. Logically still more resistant forms than the STE are the *co-operative and the commune*. Surely, such enterprises argue, since we are the workers the workers cannot want to be defended against themselves? Where management is but an emanation of their will, why do they require another emanation to oppose it? (Stalin also used this 'ontological argument', but in his case the hypocrisy was too evident to persuade anybody.) Consequently all such enterprises have opposed unions strongly – though with less violence than did primitive capitalism.

But in a generally capitalist market the 'ontological argument' against trade unions may give way to the 'labour market argument' for them. If elsewhere the same grades of labour benefit from belonging to an aggressive monopoly, they will pay their dues, join the monopoly and drift away. So the co-operatives must allow union membership, or at the very least pay union rates. It is simply not enough to tell its members they are their own employers.

To begin with the most absurd cases, in the nineteenth century the British retail co-operatives opposed the unionization of their shop employees. This was entirely unjust, since the management shared only class origin (in the sociological sense) with its employees and the owners were the customers (chapter 6) whose interest was directly antagonistic. But the employees could and did become customers, and buy the single share that gave them an equal voting right. Needless to say it was they who turned up most regularly at meetings.

Again the Histadrut has never permitted unions in its enterprises other than itself. We are your union, it says, for since you work for us you are members of us, therefore we are your best and only representative.

In the collective ejidos of Mexico unions existed before the co-operative form was introduced – in ordinary ejidos and in the surrounding capitalist sector. Abolition would have been politically impossible. Besides, there remains a standard wage of sorts. But these unions are typically peasant, 'claimants' unions' agitating for favours from the state or the Banco Ejidal. They do not play a large part within the ejido. That is to say, there is a case for a labour agency not co-extensive with the enterprise whenever labour flows are reasonably free.

We turn to industrial producers' co-ops under capitalism (see chapter 6). In Britain the early unions, especially the Owenite ones (*c.* 1834), were particularly favourable, since unclear about their own functions. It was not always easy to distinguish them from producers' co-ops. In particular in building, where any worker can become an entrepreneur, the unions used to set up enterprises to employ their members during slumps. This is virtually the same thing as 'emergency self-management' in Algeria, above. It is being repeated today in the 'work-ins' at British enterprises threatened with bankruptcy, but this is a grass-roots, non-union phenomenon. For modern business unions, with their insistence on the rate for the job and their ruthlessness towards weak enterprises, are the worst enemies of the co-operative. Not merely are they hard bargainers, they have ideological objections. For co-op members, not being employees, should not belong to a union at all. If they strike, it is against themselves. But if they accept low pay they threaten the level of wages in the rest of the market. Moreover, a world of producers' co-operatives would have no place for business unions and above all for their leaders, who must therefore add personal job insecurity to ideological antipathy. It is not too much to say of the leader of a business union, as Baldwin did of the press lord, that he has 'power without responsibility, the privilege of the harlot throughout the ages'. Why would a harlot support Women's Lib.? Communist-dominated unions in ACEs have also destroyed producers' co-ops, simply because all successful reform must be stamped on.

11. Turning now to the same question under socialism, in Yugoslavia the unions had been thoroughly Stalinized during the brief Soviet-type period, and they were retained when self-management was introduced. Voices were raised for their abolition: they had been quite useless for one reason, now they were going to be useless for another. But the Politburo thought otherwise: a Leninist transmission belt might be just the thing under this new and dangerous system. Accordingly no superior hierarchy of workers'

councils was formed. They had no federal chamber, no republican association – nothing but the unions, to whose existing Stalinist duties there was simply added that of fostering workers' councils. Later, as the market developed, that of plan fulfilment dropped away, while the welfare duties went on unchanged.

Thus the Yugoslav unions are the most Stalinist body in the country, right down to the present time. They are a mere Ministry of Labour and Welfare at the centre, and mere productivity pushers at the circumference. For fighting local grievances and 'bureaucratic deformations' the worker prefers the organs of self-management, even though management and not labour defence is their primary task. When, as often happens since the liberalization of 1965, there is a strike, it is needless to say unofficial, nay, barely tolerated. Strikes, we saw, are an awkward ontological problem for all Communists, and Yugoslavia remains very much a Communist country. Both unions and workers' councils are acutely embarrassed, but the latter, despite their managerial function, come out with rather more credit.

Recently, however, say since 1968, Yugoslav unions have begun to cut a better figure at the centre: they try to influence the organs of government by political means (and so are most effective where Soviet unions are least, and vice versa). They agitate publicly, for instance, for lower prices and taxes – both things within the prerogative of government, not management. They have thus aspects of a 'claimants' union'.[13] This is a very natural development in a relaxed Communist society. There are greater public pressures of all sorts on the central power, that is indeed the purpose of relaxation; but the principle of no collective bargaining, no adversary procedures between the organs of the victorious working class, must remain.

Such centralized union pressures are now common in Hungary, too. The Price Office feels them and notably they resulted in the 7 per cent rise of unskilled wages in March 1973. They also largely contributed to the Politburo changes of March 1974. But at local level little has changed, as we saw.

We cannot speak of actual hostility between workers' councils and unions. For Yugoslavia is Communist, and this 'contradiction' too must be 'non-antagonistic'. Also the bodies' functions are reasonably distinct, there is no collective bargaining and the director takes the brunt of union pressure, if any. But *à la longue* self-management has put the unions' nose severely out of joint, and less subservient ones would have made a great deal of trouble.

In *Algeria*[14] however the unions fostered and politically supported workers' councils. The case must be historically explained. Faced in 1962 with abandoned French properties and general chaos, the labour force in these enterprises simply took them over and ran them through committees. This introduces us, incidentally, to the very general phenomenon of *emergency self-management*. Later the government blessed this arrangement and took a good deal of detailed advice from Yugoslavia. But illiterate workers' councils make expensive and incompetent boards of management, and hostility and mistrust developed in government circles, especially the planning bureaucracy and the Ministry of Industry.

Now it happened the TUC had all along, like so many union movements in colonies, been a parallel movement of national liberation, and was jealous of the revolutionary army that had taken power. So it supported the workers' councils, which thus acquired by the back door precisely that centralized national representation that Lenin and Tito had denied them. The councils, instead of weakening the unions, became their catspaw in a fight with the government. The latter won, and has gradually brought this institution to an end, substituting what is openly called 'state capitalism'. None of this would have happened in a more developed country, with greater institutional stability and role differentiation.

The more self-sufficient kolkhoz and (particularly) commune, to which admission is mainly gained by birth, also require some labour defence mechanism. This becomes truer the larger they are: everyone is more or less alienated and in need of protection in a large organization. But as the ease of hiring and firing, and the connexion with a labour market, diminish, the defence mechanism should become confined to the specific kolkhoz or commune. I say 'should' because even such isolated labour unions of kolkhoz or commune members are unknown in practice.

The technical considerations of the previous paragraph are not the main point at all, since both types of enterprises use the ontological argument against unions, given above. In a commune, where the relation is not of comrades but of brothers and consumption is also socialized, there are particularly strong pressures against the recognition of such a thing as management. For instance anyone admitted to be a manager has the same income as the other and is rotated out of office whenever practicable. A trade union has as much place here, the commune's Establishment will say, as in a family. No labourer, on the other hand, so urgently requires an autonomous defence organization as the kolkhoznik. And this is exactly why Communist governments forbid it.

Finally, what happens when capitalist governments nationalize? We saw in chapter 3 that a rather technocratic trusteeship is normal, so that the question of workers' councils versus unions should not arise. Thus in Britain nationalization has been built on anti-syndicalist principles at union request.[15] Until recently all unions have been satisfied with influence over management, and rejected the loss of hold over their members and the distortion of their functions that a managerial role would bring. The classic exception was the Union of Post Office Workers, who were syndicalist. For they had always had to do with the state, and at that directly with a government department (chapter 3, sec. 12), so could conceive of no other way out of their frustration.[16]

Other British unions see in syndicalism a left-wing, semi-anarchist threat to their own respectable central power; and its revival in 1969 has done nothing to change their minds. The same attitude was extremely clear in the very different circumstances of Russia, 1917–18. The unions, promised a major role in the new Bolshevik state machine and virtually complete control over the economy, strongly resisted the many anarcho-syndicalist excesses at plant level. In his attempts to restore order, whether it was a quasi-capitalist order as up to summer 1918, or a fully Communist order thereafter, Lenin had no more enthusiastic backers than the unions.

But to revert to capitalism, a successful and functioning syndicalism is as conservative a force as one can well imagine! This is of course perfectly simple: it gives the workers more dignity, more power, more interest in what goes on, more understanding of the hard necessities of management than any other system. It comes closest – though not very close – to abolishing alienation. It diverts energy and thought from revolution to administration, even to self-enrichment. It reduces class solidarity by concentrating attention on local issues, and on market issues, that divide the working class. All this is evident after a revolution in Yugoslavia, and before one in the West German *Mitbestimmungsrecht* (below), in Oxford and Cambridge colleges – everywhere. What one has to fear from it is inefficiency and inflation, not revolution. When capitalists propose it, as they often do, both British unions and the far more left-wing 'Latin' unions oppose it. The former see a threat to their power, the latter to their revolution. Syndicalism is only demanded with stridency, and becomes itself a great radical cause, when it is absolutely denied.

12. An economist is bound to ask whether unions actually *maximize* something or other – and to receive the usual dusty answer. The following maximands have been proposed:

(i) the total incomes of the existing members;
(ii) the wages and fringe benefits of the employed members;
(iii) the employment of the existing members;
(iv) the number of members.

In what follows we mostly intend the business union. Other unions have beyond doubt no maximands at all, but combine various imponderable objectives.

(i) is the obvious maximand of *sodalitas economica* if it were to exist; note the identity with that of the Yugoslav enterprise. (ii) and (iii) are rules of thumb whereby the maximization of (i) may be approximated in certain circumstances. Thus (ii) is most likely when employment is full or the particular trade the union represents is expanding, i.e. when there is little difference between 'employed' and 'existing'. It implies restraint in respect of (iv). (iii) is most likely in depressed conditions where there are no social services to fall back on; it implies sacrifices of (ii). But if there are adequate social services it is logical to maximize (ii) even in depressions, for a union should never be too proud to take into account the non-work incomes of its members. Besides, wage-rates once lowered are subject to a ratchet effect and difficult to raise again; and this is another argument for preferring (ii) over (iii).

But things are not that simple. First, work is an absolute good on a par with income, and probably ranks above social service income (chapter 2). The union should not therefore use (iii) as a mere proxy for (i): it is also a competing goal. The choice that faces the development planner for the nation faces also the union's leadership when it considers its members' interests. Secondly, unions are sometimes too proud to take the social services into account. Indeed they see them as a threat to their power over members.

Thirdly, the leaders have a special view of mere membership numbers (iv). To an existing rank and file member, the ideal total membership is the one that maximizes the union's monopoly power. He does not want to fritter away the funds built up out of his contribution on peripheral, irresponsible or weakly placed new members. But he does want a closed shop where he works, with perhaps sufficient flexibility to get his son admitted a member. This nepotical aspect must never be forgotten: the freedom to practise a closely monopolized kind of labour is *property*. In the union case the sale of it would be considered too disgraceful, so it can only be inherited. But an exorbitant entrance fee does practically constitute the sale of the right to work by a union. Hence the ideal new member is one who pays an exorbitant entrance fee and then drops out. The leader, on the other hand, sees his prestige and salary as directly dependent on numbers, and therefore indirectly on employment. So it is he who is most anxious to wage recruitment drives and jurisdictional disputes.

All these add up to formidable reasons for preferring stability of, or maximum growth of, employment. And yet the greatest of these reasons has not yet been mentioned: technological conservatism, or the individual worker's vested interest not merely in his job but in the way he does it. This subject very properly obsesses British authors, since for British unions technical change is a minimand. Certain Latin American unions and certain US craft unions share this aim, but other countries are mercifully free of it.[17] The very phrase 'restrictive practices' is untranslatable out of English. Now it is not by any means wrong to wish to control the rate of technical change, indeed much of Britain's social stability may well be due to her economic stagnation. For men are passionately interested in the way in which they perform their work; it is a major preoccupation which orthodox economics leaves quite out of account. A very few, professionals and technicians, are discontented with the *low* level of technology, and will even emigrate to better equipped countries. But for most of us runaway technical progress, that renders our skills obsolete while we stand impotently by, is a primary cause of alienation. Nevertheless, one cannot help feeling that there are limits to technical conservatism, which Britain has widely overstepped. There are, after all, other partial cures for alienation.

13. The union, then, is no simple maximizer but very concerned over details, and so potentially very interfering. The more moderate forms of syndicalism mentioned above shade off into what we shall call the '*union-constrained enterprise*'. In chapter 4 we excluded labour from the category of management, defining the latter as those people able to influence enterprise policy through non-market means. Now this may be good enough in a formal discussion of maximands, but real life is more complicated. We speak in chapter 18 of a military-industrial complex, wherein the weapons-purchasing departments can scarcely be distinguished from the enterprises with which they work so closely; such is the influence of a perpetual monopsonist. We speak here of a union-industrial complex, where the union has a similar influence because it is a perpetual monopolist.

The union cannot, of course, have it both ways. The price of more detailed interference is the attainment of one's market maximum. Greater influence has an opportunity cost. Thus, most simply, if you want a firm to stick to its old location you will probably lose a little in average wages (if the old site is less profitable) or in membership (if there is a more plentiful labour supply at the new site).

We can do no more than give examples of 'union-constrained' behaviour. (i) In labour-intensive industries close to the consumer, like public transport, unions like to dissociate prices and wages in the public mind. They therefore seeek to time price rises as far as possible from new wage-contracts; and this brings them rather deeply into pricing problems. (ii) Unions have an extremely obvious interest in location, as we saw above. As mere agencies for their members they are bound to respect vested interests, including prospects of promotion which relocation would upset. Behind the questions of employment and wages, so glibly set down in geometrical diagrams, lurk the questions, who is employed, who gets the wage? (iii) Unions have above all an interest in technology and the enterprise's departmental organization. The restrictive practice has already been discussed. The abolition of a department, even though total employment remains the same, also greatly disturbs vested interests. (iv) Unions like very much to control, not so much the volume, but the selection procedure in hiring and firing. This is extremely natural. Characteristic constraints put on the enterprise are that it must choose union members (closed shop) and that it must follow union-determined seniority rules. (v) Middle management feels more threatened from below than from above, so splits away and unionizes itself.

These examples, however, are related to the long-run pursuit of orthodox maximands like wages and employment. Unions do have other and more idealistic aims. They often intervene against the political use of profits, they might intervene against pollution, or for various other charitable schemes.

14. This kind of behaviour closely and paradoxically resembles that which Lenin desired of the Russian unions in the first post-revolutionary stage. For he planned to keep capitalism and install over it 'workers' audit'.[18] Indeed until June 1918 this was more or less the Bolshevik system in practice, though in the chaos of the times there were many exceptions. Plenty of capitalist managers were driven out, and factory committees out of central control took charge of management. But the unions and the government asserted dominance over the factory committees (sec. 11) precisely in order to protect such managers, and to limit labour to its auditing function. When NEP succeeded 'War' Communism in 1921 workers' audit was revived for private enterprise.

'Workers' audit', again, is what has been installed by a very unLeninist group of forces in West Germany: the occupying powers and the trade unions. On the very doubtful premise that capitalism had led to Nazism (chapter 18), the unions were given 'legal powers of co-determination' (*Mitbestimmungsrecht*) in coal, iron and steel enterprises so as to establish a political audit over their use of funds. From this the right has broadened out into a general labour-constraint over enterprises in all sectors.

This German experiment has been generally pronounced successful in an uninspiring way.[19] It says much for the intractability of institutions in ACEs that it was nowhere imitated until about 1970. But it is common enough now, and we have one pallid excuse for such inertia: only in Germany did firms have appropriate bodies already, to which labour representatives could be elected. Ever since the nineteenth century German company law has provided for a supervisory council (*Aufsichtsrat*)[20] to represent the shareholders against the management (*Vorstand*); thus anticipating one of the main features of the managerial revolution. The *Mitbestimmungsrecht* of labour was thus easily organized, the representatives simply joined the *Aufsichtsrat*, whose formal powers were not changed.

Meanwhile, the unions' natural antagonism (secs. 10–11) was bought off by providing that they should run the elections, and that mainly union members should be elected. Indeed, it is fairly normal for paid union experts, not employed by the enterprise, to be among those chosen; and since they are experts they dominate the workers' side. This crucial fact has simultaneously denatured the experimented and ensured its success (Biedenkopf, pp. 107, 125, 164, 175).

Notes

1. I have found particularly useful: Neil W. Chamberlain, *The Labor Sector*, N.Y. 1965; Allan M. Cartter and F. Ray Marshall, *Labor Economics*, Illinois 1967; Clark Kerr *et al.*, *Industrialism and Industrial Man*, Harvard 1960.

2. On this controversial topic cf. Chamberlain, op. cit., Appendix to chapter 19.

3. This continuing but unprovoked violence arises in part from administrative difficulties: how else could such large numbers of people be brought to conform? Farmers' unions, whose members are theoretically more respectable but geographically more spread out, are even more violent (chapter 5, sec. 3–5).

4. From 1850 until about 1890, when socialism came along, British unions were also business unions.

5. Who under John L. Lewis forced, by boycott, legislation, etc., such a wage upon marginal mines as closed them down. The employees of these mines sided with their employers. (April 1972: I leave this passage untouched after the British miners' strike of February. This was openly admitted to result in the accelerated closure of mines. One new tactic was to let the machinery be ruined by not sending down the usual maintenance men. On the new mood of business behaviour by not strictly business unions cf. chapter 14.)

6. Co-operatives merit separate treatment: see below. The trade union is a notoriously ungenerous and inflexible employer of its own office staff: it appeals all the time to their idealism and will not pay the market rate for high skill.

7. But only in Britain do the unions have the left-wing party actually in their pay and power. This curious inversion arises from the fact that the Labour Party was founded by the unions.

8. Dimitry Pospielowsky, *Russian Police Trade Unionism*, London 1971.

9. The Jewish Bund was the anti-Zionist Jewish labour and nationalistic movement in the Russian Pale. Cf. *Encyclopedia Judaica*, article 'Bund'. On the needle unions cf. Max Danish, *The World of David Dubinsky*, Ohio 1957; J. M. Budish and S. H. Soule, *The New Unionism in the Clothing Industry*, N.Y. 1920, esp. chapter 7; Benjamin Stolzberg, *Tailor's Progress*, N.Y. 1944.

10. Cf. however: Gerhard Muenzner and Ernst Kahn, *Jewish Labour in Palestine*, London 1945; Samuel Karland, *Co-operative Palestine*, N.Y. 1947; Walter Preuss, *The Labour Movement in Israel*, Jerusalem 1965; Ferdinand Zweig in *Jewish Journal of Sociology*, April 1959; G. Friedmann in *Midstream*, April 1967.

11. Giacomo Perticone, *L'Italia Contemporanea*, Mondadori 1962, chapter 23; Benito Mussolini, *Opera Omnia*, vol. 32, Florence 1960, pp. 41–54, 129–33, 152–4. The programme of the Republic of Salò resurrects the economic parts of the initial Fascist programme at the foundation meeting in San Sepolcro, 1919; but it is shorn of the internationalism. Cf. Ruggero Zangrandi, *Il Lungo Viaggio Attraverso il Fascismo*, Milan 1962, pp. 50–3, 456–7.

12. See, for the pre-Stalin system, Isaac Deutscher, *Soviet Trade Unions*, London 1950; Margaret Dewar, *Labour Policy in the USSR, 1917–28*, London 1956; for the rise of Stalin's system, Solomon Schwarz, *Labor in the Soviet Union*, N.Y. 1952; for the modern position Emily Clark Brown, *Soviet Trade Unions and Labor Relations*, Harvard 1966.

13. Zdenko Antic, Radio Free Europe Research Reports of 5 July 1968 and 11 February 1971: *New York Times*, 15 October 1972. A claimants' union is one

whose members cannot (in this case will not) strike. So it proceeds merely by demonstrating and lobbying the government.

14. Cf. Wiles in *The Soviet Impact*, with a foreword by Arnold Toynbee, Royal Institute of International Affairs, London 1967 (while the facts are accurate this source embodies a grossly false general appreciation!); Wiles in *Weltwirtschaftliches Archiv*, 1968; Ian Clegg, *Workers' Self-Management in Algeria*, London 1971.

15. Union officials often join nationalized management boards, but in industries other than their own.

16. Surprisingly, since the Post Office was 'nationalized' in 1969 the UPOW has turned to the right. This is because its great strike was defeated in 1973. The change of ownership had no effect.

17. The French independent craftsman, shopkeeper and peasant exhibit the same traits, but not the French industrial worker.

18. Usually mistranslated 'workers' control'. The Russian 'kontrol' is a much weaker concept.

19. Cf. Herman J. Spiro, *The Politics of German Co-Determination*, Harvard 1958; X. Herlin, *Les Experiences Allemandes de Cogestion*, Paris 1959: Wilfried Skupnik, *Mitbestimmung in der Wirtschaft 1962–9*, Bonn 1969 (Wissenschaftliche Abteilung des Bundestags, Bibliographie no. 21); *Mitbestimmung im Unternehmen* ('Biedenkopf Bericht'), Drucksache des Bundestags VI/334, 4 February 1970.

20. The Anglo-American 'Board' has similar powers, but not a similar origin or tradition. There is no notion that the Board is there to protect anyone.

8

Slavery and Forced Labour

8

1. We have discussed the use of force on enterprises at a dozen points in this book. It is not, particularly if merely negative, an especially significant phenomenon. In consonance with one of our basic messages, forced labour is far more important, since it impinges directly on people, while enterprises are not people. Despite the death of Stalin it is still fairly topical, since it is from time to time proposed in one form or other for UDCs, and it retains great penological and military significance.[1]

There is no direct force in the free wage-bargain: that is the meaning of the word 'bargain'. Force enters here only in so far as it restrains one from *not* making *some* such bargain. For the next most profitable thing is theft, and that attracts forcibly imposed penalties. Thus the state, which may be defined as that organization that has a local quasi-monopoly of force, makes certain alternative ways of living intolerable by force, and so we work. The main difference between capitalism and socialism is that in the former living off unearned income from capital is not a prohibited alternative. This apart, nearly all human beings are 'forced' to labour: their supply curve of effort runs where it does because of their social circumstances. It is true that in the extreme case there may be no alternative except death by starvation to a *particular* wage-bargain; then we have 'objectively' forced labour, i.e. a totally monopsonistic employer. But this is irrelevant: we mean 'subjectively' forced labour, where there is no wage-bargain at all, but there are immediate penalties, such as a beating, for not working.

Thus we exclude many very disagreeable and unjust labour situations from our purview. Notably black labour in South Africa, denied educational opportunity, threatened with deportation if not employed, and discriminated against at every turn, is not 'subjectively forced'. For the Bantu can always choose not to labour at a particular place or time, unless he has signed an indenture; but he does this as a free contracting party. So he appears later as a normal case of labour having temporarily subjected itself to force through indenture, and he appears again as prison labour, but otherwise he does not figure at all. This is emotionally unfortunate. But the way out is to say that discrimination, which is a very ordinary feature of free market situations, can be much worse than force, which is not a free market situation at all. Otherwise the forced labour concept becomes so vague and general as to threaten to include the author of these lines, who after all has also signed a contract, and faces in the University Grants Committee a monopsonistic employer.

If labour is 'subjectively' forced, in some sense, its marginal disutility must exceed the utility of its marginal income. Define further punishment and the remission of captivity as not part of income, and this becomes a tautology. The classic unskilled slave or penal worker is made to work up to his physical limit.[2] The latter is or should be carefully respected, since he must live to work another day. But his psychological preferences are overcome by the threat of the lash; his choice is between work and pain or early death.

This, then, is the secret of the forced labourer's profitability: he works longer hours, and no actual or implied contract limits his obedience. Thus American slaves enjoyed no public holidays, and Stalin's convicts worked a 3000-hour year while 2000 was about the average for free labour. In theory, then we do not pay the slave for his hours or by the hour. He is our property, so his whole time is our property.[3] These extra hours are costless to the employer, except that he must buy the lash and reward the hand that wields it. There are also the costs of preventing escape. These can be very large if circumstances are unfavourable, and many things can be explained by the search for escape-proof situations: a galley-ship, a black skin in the Americas, vast untrodden fields of Siberian snow.

A second element of profitability is that the forced labourer has no family, which greatly reduces his subsistence cost. But this must be most severely qualified. Procurement (kidnapping, capture in war, judicial sentencing, transportation, etc.) is very expensive; and its only alternative is, if not precisely the foundation of a slave family, at least the rearing of slave children. The latter, it seems, has always been still more expensive, so that peace, or the suppression of kidnapping, reduces greatly the profitable uses of slave labour. Meanwhile the penal labourer's family falls upon the state anyway. It is easy and of course legal to keep up the supply, but one should use only unmarried criminals.

To all these rules the skilled forced labourer presents exceptions. Take a Janissary officer or a Soviet aircraft designer. He can sabotage his work in ways barely perceptible to the overseer, and mere unhappiness or boredom genuinely gets in the way of his efficiency. So we must strike a bargain with him: instant gratification in the commissary or through shorter hours, etc.; a guaranteed *peculium* (slave saving) that will be effectually his;[4] permission to found a family (like a slave overseer) or leave to go and see his family (as in many prisons); the hope of manumission or remission of sentence. The first two items are identical to the incentives offered free labour, but forced labour still comes, or should come, cheaper because of the last two. These are substitutes at the margin for material goods, but costless to the employer, except for the means of depriving the slave of his family or freedom. They are a *costless quasi-wage*, and this, then, is the alleged or potential advantage of enslaving skilled men. Further, since the slave substitutes them, to some extent, for material incentives the employer's expenditure on these latter is also diminished. Even the skilled slave works, or is supposed to work, longer hours than a free man, and he too pushes the marginal disutility of labour beyond the utility of marginal (material) income.

The state that imposes forced labour, then, has abolished *workers' sovereignty*. This concept is the mirror image of consumers' sovereignty, and simply means that in a free market each worker can choose his job and within limits – what he does while on his job.[5] As is obvious from this chapter, it is of far greater social and political importance than consumers' sovereignty. Our textbooks neglect it partly through lack of imagination, partly because of that 'enterprise bias' of which we have often complained, which treats labour like any other input. Anyway, having deprived the forced labourer of his sovereignty 'we' may be presumed indifferent to his marginal disutility of labour.

We may even, like a colonial government, have consciously judged it to be irrationally high; we disregard it 'for his own good'. This is an important possibility in development economics, and in anti-poverty campaigns in rich countries. It is an article of (unexpressed) faith among Communists. Now there is no reason to suppose that people's leisure preference is irrational in the short run; it is really in respect of his futurity discount that *homo sapiens* is to be faulted. For he should above all work harder to provide against illness, children, unemployment and retirement, while he is surely sensible enough to know how hard he must work to get tomorrow's groceries. A respectful government, then, anxious to let people be themselves, will *force saving but not labour*. Of course in reducing current take-home pay it will indeed move people out along their labour supply curves, which, as we saw in chapter 2, are negatively sloped. But this is secondary to the greater personal security that is imposed on the worker. Moreover, it does not force anyone to work: in the market conditions changed by the welfare state's fiscal system everyone can still work as long as he likes, and of course at what he likes. This is not forced labour.

Even if we do neglect the forced labourer's leisure preference his marginal productivity remains important to 'us'. It depends on the freedom of the employer to buy, hire or accept on assignment such labour at the going price, forced wage or maintenance cost, plus security expenses; and on the employer's maximand. He is not necessarily forced to employ such people, and he will certainly bear in mind that their hourly productivity is very low, and take into account any enforcement costs. We have nothing very special to say, then, on the rational allocation of forced labour: it is like any other input, including free labour.

The paradox also holds that prison labour need not be forced. If the prisoner is guaranteed his subsistence, and offered an additional wage for performing work that he can refuse without punishment, he strikes a free wage bargain. But in another sense his supply curve of labour has been forcibly altered. So his movement along the curve is not, in the case envisaged, 'penal', but its general position is. Notoriously the unforced prisoner will settle for quite low rates per hour: he has no union, he faces a monopsonist, and he is bored.

2. The principal and clearest case of forced labour is the *slave*. The ideal slave is the property of his master, and that not on the grounds of criminal guilt or indenture, both of which limit the master's right, but by capture or by birth. The state enforces the property right, and some minimal good treatment, mostly reserving to itself the right to put to death. But where food and medicine are at the owner's discretion, and beating is permitted, this reservation counts for almost nothing.

There are at least two main forms of slavery, though the distinction is obscured by gradations. Ancient and Islamic slavery rests on the slave-holder's aversion from all economic activity, not merely unskilled and repetitive work. It is all undignified, all unworthy of the philosopher, statesman or soldier that a gentleman should be. Below the aristocrat are merchants and petty capitalists not at all averse from work or at any rate money; and these make more obvious use of an institution sanctified by the highest in the land. So slavery is *pervasive*: domestics, bureaucrats (for to be a quite senior manager at the behest of an owner is also undignified), artists, craftsmen, accountants, even certain kinds of soldiers are quite likely to be slaves. Repetitive and unpleasant work on a large scale will certainly employ them, and slaves so employed are vilely treated and erupt in revolts. But this is not the cause of the phenomenon, and domestic and urban slavery is considered natural by all parties. A slave is an unfortunate person: such bad luck can happen to anyone. Interbreeding is common and creates free but inferior offspring. There is not a little naïf racism, but nothing that can be called a systematic ideology.

In Brazil, the Caribbean, Cuba and USA, however, slavery was based on repetitive and unpleasant work, i.e. on *plantations* and mines. The slave was not an unfortunate human being but livestock. In these cultures a gentleman might well engage in any skilled occupation, and above all he was allowed to make money. The ideology was not aristocratic but Mercantilist or even tribal: we, a people of all classes, occupy this territory and exploit it with our special livestock. Of course the really systematic treatment of men as livestock is rendered much more comfortable by racism (below). In defence of this ideology slaves were not supposed to develop great skills or to learn to read. They could become domestic servants but not much more. Slave bureaucrats and soldiers were inconceivable, and slaves were much more hostile to their condition.

These distinctions must not be exaggerated. Athenian or Arabic mines were more atrocious than Jamaican canefields. The livestock attitude was known in the ancient world, and manumission did occur in the Americas. Quite particularly, slave offspring are their owner's property, too, so they are deliberately bred or prevented from breeding, in Arab countries, by castration. Curiously, North and South Americans stopped short of this, and the main reason was surely not some Christian hesitancy about castration as such, but rather the relative costs of freshly capturing an adult and of bringing up a child. The Arab slave-owners were always near their sources of supply, and the slave trade was finally stopped at about the same time as slavery. The Christian slave-owners were separated by an ocean, and had for sixty to seventy years no other recourse than breeding. As a result, in USA breeding became a regional speciality (Virginia, the Carolinas).[6] It follows that the slave nuclear family may be dissolved by the sale of any member at any age. It is this that distinguishes the slave from all other forced labourers. For indentures (sec. 7) do not bind the children of the indentured, nor do their families exist at the will of a third party. And prisoners are separated from their families, rightly or wrongly, to deter, reform or punish them. Obviously, their families are not imprisoned.

But to have the slave is not automatically to make him work, as we have seen. One cannot simply order him or expect him to work because of his status. Like any livestock he must be rewarded or punished *within* his condition. The rewards, as we saw in sec. 1, are quite capitalistic, and imply a great deal of slave freedom. This may seem surprising, but slavery is a profit-oriented institution without even sadistic principles. Oppression is not an aim but a tool, and if milder oppression is more profitable so be it. There is no objection to respecting the slave's leisure preference or feeling of dignity, if it pays.

A further incentive is the promise of manumission.[7] A slave will work extremely hard for that, and pay his whole savings too; and even afterwards some sort of client relationship, profitable to both parties, will survive. Manumission obviously affects the skilled and the domestic more than the unskilled; it is more probable where slavery is a 'pervasive', not a 'plantation', affair, and more acceptable to a society where no racial tensions among free men will result. Hence it was quite rare in the Americas, but common in the ancient world and under Islam. Manumitted slaves became generals, bureaucrats and even Sultans. Sometimes even the formally unmanumitted attained high office.

Why have modern slaves tended to be of different race from their owners? Ancient slavery was not racist at all. One was enslaved by being captured in war or kidnapped by pirates. The best thinkers regretted it when, say, a Greek enslaved a Greek, and Roman law forbade the enslavement of Roman citizens within the whole empire. Also the international character of war led mostly to the enslavement of foreigners anyway, but they were not of very different race, and quite commonly married free (or freer) citizens while still slaves. The same applies to the Slavonic and Caucasian, even partly to the negro, slaves of Islam.

The cause of the racist slavery in the Americas was the availability of quite distinct races, and the combination of empty land, unsuitable climate and labour-intensive crops, or what we shall call the Nieboer syndrome.[8]

Extraordinary quantities of unskilled labour were required, and already in the seventeenth century the forcible transfer of serfs was out of the question. In Britain there were no serfs any more; elsewhere, with the partial exception of Russia, they had all acquired rights in the land on which they were. Prison labour was tried but was quite insufficient in quantity (sec. 3). Free white labour, after having cropped tobacco for a long time, began to refuse to work in such heat. It came to be believed on all hands that white men could not perform hard manual labour in the climate. The thing appears to be a myth conveniently covering up the fact that slaves were cheaper. Hence the subjugation of whole acclimatized races: first the unsuitable native who was too easily able to escape, then the workable negro whose skin-colour made recapture easy.[9]

The origin, then, was the purest capitalist profit-maximization and the superstructure of racist ideology was added later, in the best Marxist manner. The syndrome was avoided in the two other areas of empty land, Russia and Australasia, by the late survival of serfdom and the plentiful use of prisoners respectively (see below).

For the reasons why slavery comes to an end, cf. sec. 6 below.

3. *Prison labour* is by origin a penological device. If not simply voluntary on the prisoner's part, we call it penal. If this sentence involves a journey to a distant prison, we call it *transportation*. This must be clearly distinguished from mere deportation and exile, which involve no prison sentence (sec. 9).

Penology and economics strongly overlap here. The theory of prison labour rests on the positive value of work as such. This is not the same as its pleasurability (chapter 2, sec. 6). It is that work forms character, and prepares a prisoner for his release – things that may indeed not be unpleasant. Therefore, it is very persuasively argued, work is the most constructive of all ways of serving a sentence; so much so that even those who do not wish to work may benefit by being forced to do so, particularly if they learn a trade.

Now prison labour is highly unpopular with independent trade unions, which have succeeded everywhere in regulating it very strictly. For instance, trade unionists have always resisted the sale outside prison of products made within, and are most reluctant to recognize prison apprenticeships. Serious prison labour, then, bringing revenue to prison or prisoner, is of minimal extent in ACEs. Only training and domestic chores remain. In UDCs the administrative resources are lacking to run serious prison enterprises; and in both there are not so many prisoners.

It is to Stalinist USSR and to imperialist Britain that we must look for really serious penal labour enterprises. Note that we do not say 'Communism' or 'Capitalism'. Hungary under Rakosi was one of the worst tyrannies ever, but it had few penal labourers. France in 1820 had only penal colonies like Devil's Island. The numbers were in each case small, because there was no empty land to occupy with labour-intensive enterprise: the Nieboer syndrome again. It seems to be this temptation that accounts for modern slavery and modern prison labour alike; this circumstance and not economic institutions is fundamental. A basically callous and undemocratic government is, however, a further prerequisite: none of this ever happened in Canada, or in self-governing Australia.

The penal labourer differs in many ways from the plantation-type slave. He is a duly sentenced and punished citizen, not a head of livestock. His family is free, and so is he on expiration of sentence. He is forbidden to breed. He is no one's property. But he may not notice the differences at the time. The same incentives – the lash, extra food, money wages – exist for him. There is even the equivalent of manumission: remission of sentence for good work or behaviour.

4. The British venture of transportation to Australia[10] is the one great success story in this field. This may surprise the reader, whose judgement will have been based on vague reports of actual horrors. These reports are true, but success is relative: what horrors would have replaced them, in the Britain of that time? The moment we reckon the social opportunity cost of Botany Bay, we can only be thankful for it. Economically, the region was aptly chosen: it took off into self-sustaining growth. The climate, too, was bearable: it was not a death-trap like Devil's Island or Northern Siberia. This point is vital. Death is a form of labour turnover, and highly uneconomical: if a man is to be killed it is much cheaper not to transport him and feed him for a year. Then again the labour was very inefficient, but things done were extremely useful – farming, road making, public building – and no other labour was available.

On the strictly penological side, the first pre-condition is always said to have been a savage penal code, but with only 2000 a year being transported this cannot be true. Nothing like every eligible criminal was transported.[11] Every sort of atrocity was, again, committed against those who were; especially in the penal settlements run for infractions of convict discipline. At all times in judging penal systems it is vital to distinguish these special horrors from those facing the ordinary prisoner. The actual reformation of character achieved by the sentence itself was minimal. But then it always is in all prisons, and the question is, what were British prisons achieving at that date? The fact is that most prisoners survived to go on 'ticket of leave' (early probationary release) or release at end of sentence, and that 'straight' opportunities were so great that rather few lived thereafter by crime. Female convicts in particular married, or cohabited, well above their station in life. Nor did their children grow up into crime: Australia in 1860 was not a specially criminous place, even though about one quarter of the population were ticket-of-leave men or their children.[12] So this too may be accounted for advantage, that children who would have been born anyway were born into a less criminous environment, in this new and spacious world of opportunity and social (but not economic) equality.

This venture was quite small by Stalin's standards; only 160,000 were transported from 1788 to 1868, or about one eighth of all immigrants to Australia. At first (1788) there was no economic motive. Botany Bay was simply a penal settlement, discouraged from trading. But in 1793 land grants began to be made to officers and administrators, and convicts were assigned to them. A few years later such convicts had to be maintained by their employers.

In detailed economic organization, too, there were few parallels with Stalin. The public works were performed by gangs, to be sure, but there was little piece-work and no detailed accountancy of individual performance. The only incentives to better work were the lash and remission of sentence; both were more concerned with discipline than production. Moreover, guarding was lax and life rather free. Many convicts doing public work had to find their own lodgings and earn the rent by private work after hours.

Again, the great majority of prisoners were not in gangs, especially from 1815 to 1842, but were 'assigned' on arrival to individual free settlers who gave them subsistence and work. Their fate was various and capricious, from worse than in a government gang to far better. Except for £10 p.a. 'overtime', wages were forbidden, and so were gifts in kind above the basic ration laid down. This was very different from USSR, where employing enterprises offer the same incentives as to free workers, and a *peculium* is consistently encouraged.

But the settlers were economic men, and they needed to get things done. So the rule against wages was broken wholesale, and many convicts in fact accumulated a *peculium*, and settled down on release as minor pillars of society. Many, for that matter, had been used by their masters in trade, or hired out to others. Assignment, then, especially on account of its uncertainty, offends many of the principles of penology and all the principles of Benthamite penology, which is mainly deterrent. But all prisons offend against penology anyway, and assignment should be judged by its results. It left a man free, it did not bore him, it prepared him for life after release. It has, of course, no parallel in USSR, since there are no petty capitalists to whom prisoners may be assigned. The nearest approach is the use, under MVD guard, of prisoners in the enterprises of other ministries (below). Since these are also large socialist enterprises, and the security and incentive systems are identical, there is no real difference from work in an MVD enterprise. Assignment on the other hand carried on the tradition of penal indenture in North America, and was half-way over to freedom.

The costs of actual transportation to Australia were of course never recouped; but to this day Australia gives assisted passage to immigrants and does not recoup. The security costs were not recouped: neither the general guarding and administration nor the costs of the penal settlements within the system. But most of these costs would have had to be incurred in Britain, where it was easier to escape. The public works gangs laboured very much more inefficiently than trained navvies would have done, but there were no trained navvies in Australia, and the doctrine of opportunity cost gives us pause again. On the other hand the settlers who took on assignees must have known what they were doing. So in terms of mere economic profit and loss the system was surely no worse than another method of colonization. It was killed, indeed, by the meanness of the British Treasury: the free colonists had nothing against it until they were asked to pay for it. And behind this meanness lay the persistence of crime *in Britain*. Transportation had evidently failed to deter, in a period when all penology was deterrent. That it did reform was not interesting, since the reformed people were not allowed back to Britain anyway.

But Australians, on the receiving end, were interested in reformation. And here the system succeeded as Stalin's never did. This may surprise us, for transportation has had a bad image in Britain. The public remembers the Tolpuddle martyrs (unjustly though not illegally sentenced, and not ill treated) and a few references in Dickens. Publicists and historians have had axes to grind, like Gibbon Wakefield with his competing scheme of colonization or the Benthamite penologists, obsessed with deterrence. They have written as if the penal settlements were part of the ordinary settlements: as if free labour was available to perform the public works that were, after all, performed; as if entrepreneurs hiring assignees did not maximize their profits;[13] and above all as if the alternative prisons in Britain, which all agreed were much more unpleasant, did in fact reform or deter. Our Australian sources, based on what actually occurred, are much superior. But there too there has to be bias: the descendants of the 'ticket of leave' men are bound to say the system reformed sinners.

5. Turning to Stalin, it cannot be too strongly insisted that most of his performance in this field was an aberration from Communist practice. All Marxists believe in 'corrective' labour, and rightly too. But Stalin's was brutal and inefficient, and located in a murderous climate that wasted lives. He recruited by means of a Draconian criminal code that really was heedlessly allowed to generate millions of prisoners.[14] He further imposed a paranoid political security system, blind to questions of veracity, that generated considerably more millions. And all this to no purpose, since the frozen North was not worth developing anyway.

First the locational aspect. We have hitherto found in the development of empty territory by labour-intensive means the principal *raison d'être* of modern[15] slavery. It is neither here nor there whether the territory *should* be developed: it suffices that there it is, inside our boundaries, marked 'Russia' or 'Brazil' in every schoolboy's map around the world – and empty. A market economy (Canada, Australia) will develop what can pay for itself, and its government will bear bravely whatever pangs of conscience should be the lot of states with white spots on their maps. Not so planners: they know their duty when they see it. Better for planned economies that their deserts and jungles and ice-caps should be seas, for then the 'curse of natural resources' would not operate upon them. It sufficed, then, that the frozen North existed: something had to be done. Moreover Engels had repeatedly stressed socialist man's mastery over nature, and Communist location theory had long since inferred that all territory should be occupied with more or less equal density (Wiles 1962, chapter 8).

That explanations in terms of pure fantasy are not frivolous is shown by recent changes. New investment in the frozen North is capital-intensive. Pretences at self-support in food, etc., have been abandoned. The population is drifting southwards. The Soviet North is coming to resemble the Canadian North: a place for highly paid young men who make their pile in a few seasons and get out. Some enterprises of particular importance such as the Northern Sea Shipping Route[16] have always been on this basis.

Two further fallacies contributed to the freezing horror that Stalin produced: that it is cheaper to use penal labour in any place, and so still cheaper in very unpleasant places, where free labour must be paid an enormous wage. A few approximate accountings of particular camps have come out to us. Even in direct money terms, in the distorted Soviet wholesale prices, there is usually loss after we have deducted security costs, and this despite the vastly increased hours of labour. The decent average capitalist rate of return that expectedly emerges from the surviving accounts of American slave plantations is not seen here at all. And we must remember that these latter include transportation or upbringing costs, and even the maintenance of retired slaves, while Stalin permitted almost no one unable to work to remain long alive, and paid his transportation costs out of the state budget. Beyond that again, the slave system, being capitalist, used each man to its best advantage, i.e. according to his skill. Even British penal transportation preferred productivity to punishment – in its system of assignment. But in USSR pains were taken to punish the skilled with unskilled work, and the privilege of skilled work was reserved for proper criminals; that is, for those 'socially near' to the régime, whose guilt was a 'legacy of capitalism' and not specially dangerous or counter-revolutionary. This waste of skills attained massive proportions during the Great Purge, which was particularly directed against the bureaucracy, artists and technical intelligentsia. The rate of industrial growth in 1939–41 reflects this.

So for all these reasons this particular system of penal labour was quite unprofitable on any reckoning. Such, however, is the enormous variation between enterprises in all systems, mainly owing to the accidents of efficient management and the rents of site, that some of Stalin's camps were nevertheless profitable.

But was there really some affinity between unhealthy climate and forced labour? The answer is that obviously the camps would have been more profitable in warmer zones. The guards would have required no Arctic supplement; transport costs would have fallen drastically; prisoners could have been kept in rags, if that was the policy, but in far cheaper rags; and they would still have lived longer and worked more days. If location is a matter of choice, neither free nor forced labour should be placed in unhealthy climates. This, then, is not the same as the racial adaptation of the slave to the work climate: this rational principle is not touched.[17]

Nevertheless it is plausible to maintain that the occasional excess of free over forced labour costs is greatest in climates equally unpleasant to both. If so, then imagine that there is an urgent national necessity to mine the ice or plough the sand; say a strategic imperative, or an inelastically demanded commodity that cannot be obtained by foreign trade. Now in practice everything can be obtained by foreign trade, and we can always make more of our best exports instead. Only strategic arguments against importation hold water; development policy is neither here nor there.[18] So are there military arguments for the use of forced rather than free labour in very unpleasant climatic conditions? There certainly are some on the firing line: very many men will not fight unless conscripted (why die for pay? – you can't take it with you), and Stalin most efficiently cleared minefields by marching conscripted prisoners though them. But no pre-war strategic considerations demanded the colonization of the Arctic (which many ignorant defenders of Soviet economic rationality seem to confuse with Central Asia or the Pacific Coast). Nor is it obvious what strength a country would gain if it did people its strategic borders with prisoners. So if the possibility of a strategic case must be admitted we still await its instantiation. In any case it would have to be shown why the mere direction of civilian labour (sec. 11) would not suffice.

It is an economic flaw of all these penal labour systems that their origin, motivation and essence is – penal. The British government could possibly have used more prisoners, and certainly more skilled men. The Soviet government was swamped with them, and needed especially fewer skilled ones. The Nieboer doctrine applied only ex post: it told the government where to put the prisoners once it had them. It did not, as in the slave cases, apply ex ante, encouraging the active procurement of such labour. Each government stood more or less passive before the functioning of its police and judiciary. There is only minimal evidence for direct interference in these functions, to get more people sentenced with particular skills: it does seem that aircraft engineers and designers were sought after by the economic organs of the MVD in the second World War, and that the security organs responded.[19] But the camps also set up such organizations, and took on the appropriate plan tasks, because they happened to have such experts. There are also well-attested Soviet 'arrest targets', but these quite clearly served to measure, in a statistically minded society, the efficiency of the security organs in their own terms. New York City policemen suffer from similar directives.

6. Slavery is not merely immoral but even revolting. Yet it is or was carried on for profit by people who did in fact make a living. In USSR, for that matter, forced labour was exacted for the sake of output by central planners who did in fact get output. Could some larger cost-benefit analysis show at least that social profitability was negative? So long as the slave is treated as livestock, whose own real income is nothing but a cost of production, it is difficult to see how. Alfred Conrad, in his great work on the prices of slaves and cotton before and after the Civil War,[20] seems to have disposed of this argument in the US case. Slave productivity had not reached its upper limits, nor was cotton a declining industry, nor was the supply of slaves threatened. The ante-bellum rise in slave prices merely matched the rise in productivity. There were serious externalities in the matter of security, but they were not increasing. Regional growth per white head (and indeed per black head, too, but this is irrelevant) was up to national levels. Similarly Stalin's USSR was a great economic success overall, though on the whole his slaves were less well cared for.

Perhaps modern slavery and mass corrective labour present some sort of technology trap, condemning a slave-holding society to the simplest kinds of production? Certainly slavery often results from needs created by a low-level technology. Slavery in the Americas was, as we saw, the result of certain labour-intensive, mass-production crops, in inappropriate climates.[21] New England industry did not need it. The slave craftsmen of the US South were an epiphenomenon. But the Southern factor-productivity residual before the civil war was as high as that of the country as a whole, and not all specialization is a trap. If demand for the crops had fallen[22] no doubt fewer slaves would have been employed, and so fewer kidnapped or bred. A trap is something you cannot get out of. Nay more, if slaves are livestock the number of human beings used on plantations is remarkably small, and we have no right to speak of a backward technology. Nor again is it obvious that in any dual economy the advanced sector is retarded by the existence of the backward one. Rather the contrary: it would be retarded by an attempt to spread capital more evenly. In the US civil war the South did not lack technical ingenuity in weapon development.

It was morality and war that brought down American slavery. The economic argument is still weaker in the case of 'pervasive' slavery. Athens, Rome and medieval Islam evolved the highest techniques of their day, and in these captured craftsmen figured rather largely. Rome and the Arabs employed even slave managers and bureaucrats. History has even known slave soldiers, reliably defending their chains.[23] After all, it was worse to be captured by the enemy. Moreover Islamic slavery has been ended, in so far as it has, by moral revulsion and external pressure.

It was indeed economics that killed classical slavery. But it was hardly economic progress, only the late imperial labour shortage. There appear to have been no moral causes at all: if Justinian had qualms he stood almost alone, while Popes inherited, bought, sold and bred slaves just like pagan gentlemen. But if Nieboer tells us that to fill new land you need slaves, all Russian history tells us (sec. 10) that to keep a sparse existing population on old land you only need serfs. The classical slave was not racially distinct, and he had principally been supplied in large numbers by the wars of the late republican period. In agriculture he now had to be bred, so he became a hereditary fixture on particular estates. Chain-gang labour was inefficient, since more expensive to supervise than small tenant farming, and not conducive to reproduction. The serf worked harder and with less supervision, first to pay the rent and then to feed himself. So as the free tenant declined into a serf the slave rose to the same position. The landlord had the same problem of keeping labour there in both cases, and solved it in the same way: by legal *adscriptio glebae* (binding to the soil).

This case differs from that of the Americas for several reasons. (i) The crops were not mass-products like cotton and tobacco, and the farming was more mixed. Therefore labour supervision was more difficult. (ii) The technology of management was more backward in those days (literacy, numeracy, accounting). So the diseconomies of scale were higher. (iii) No colour distinction hindered escape, manumission or intermarriage. We may not, then, infer that American slavery would one day have evolved in the same direction.

Stalin's case was different again. Even on a direct and narrow reckoning, we have seen his system to be inefficient. But clearly he was in no sort of technology trap, since although slave-cut timber was at first exported he reduced all exports and cut his dependence on foreign trade to levels unknown in the modern world. And if his slave inventors were very few, he did not stint general expenditures on R and D, using free labour. Nor was he backward in founding new industries! It is, after all, commodities that put us into technology traps, but our modern 'plantation' slavery was essentially a device for filling up empty spaces.[24] Like Islamic slavery, his system has come to an end, in so far as it has, through moral revulsion and external pressure.

Still less can it be suggested that Australia's economy suffered in any way at all from transportation. It was, we saw, metropolitan parsimony and ignorance that brought this excellent system to an end.

So even here we should be careful. If slaves are on the whole technically unprogressive, tactful handling and the prospect of manumission transform them. Moreover, so long as the economy has some jobs suitable for unskilled 'livestock' it has a place for ordinary slaves – and that place can be made smaller as time passes. Slavery is uneconomical – if it really is – because it is a 'culture and government trap'. It has a very bad general effect on the slave-holder, *in the disapproving modern world*. If he owes his income to such violence and rapacity, and must be for ever concealing it or defending it, his other attitudes are likely to be irrational. Guilt will corrupt him. The US South fell behind in public education and public order. Its war leaders were notably boastful, emotional and incompetent at long-run calculation. They were too busy defending the indefensible – their 'peculiar institution'. Stalin had to hide his camps in the frozen north, where they were impossibly expensive. His successors, unable to repudiate him, have not been able to liquidate his cultural and political legacy, even though most of the camps were emptied in 1956.

These extremely indirect arguments are tenuous. Guilt has no ineluctable economic effects. Moreover it cannot be certain that men will always feel guilty. They might revert to the regretful acceptance of ancient Greece and Rome. A revival of slavery is, however, rendered improbable by our increasingly sophisticated technology – slaves are at any rate not well adapted to that; and by the exhaustion of empty land. But a revival of mass corrective or punitive labour is another matter.

7. The *indenture*, whereby a man binds himself to work for so many years, was well known in classical and Biblical times as a form of temporary slavery. It need not be said how easy it was to persuade an illiterate pauper to sign such a document. Indeed American slavery began under the legal form of permanent indenture, and once the slave trade was prohibited British colonies reverted to it, bringing Indian or Chinese labour to work on South African or Fijian or Guianese estates in conditions infinitely better regulated than, but still reminiscent of, slavery and the slave trade. It is these memories, and the hostility of trade unions, that have killed the indenture, except in certain apprenticeships.

The racial aspect is also very reminiscent of slavery, and the Nieboer syndrome too: colonies were populated by indenture, and it is a very convenient way of getting labour to move long distances. Indeed the debt was often contracted *ad hoc*, and consisted of the passage money.

There used also to be a similar system of binding oneself over to one's creditor, to work off an unpaid debt.

The indentured man, then, forces himself to labour, and deprives himself of freedom. In this he constitutes one end of the spectrum of free workers,[25] where the other end is the perfect but not very desirable freedom of the hourly 'pick-up' labourer. For to some extent everyone who performs work bargains away his freedom for a period of time, provided his tasks fall within an explicit or implicit 'zone of compliance' (chapter 2, sec. 4). The very richest people, e.g. film stars, bind themselves for long periods and can be sued. Sometimes they bind themselves with very peculiar conditions: Miss America contracts not to marry for a year.

Now any voluntary long-term contract can, if fairly enforced, turn out to the advantage of either party. There is nothing to stop a worker turning his labour contract to 'exploitative' advantage over his employer, provided he was well advised in the first place and the courts are neutral. There are many labour contracts that can indeed turn to the worker's advantage: they are signed by footballers, film stars, musicians, etc. These do not hesitate to cry 'slave labour' when they find they have lost some market advantage, but we hear less when things turn out the other way, and it is they who are the exploiters. It is this same feeling that the worker must always gain from a long-term contract, never lose, if the circumstances change that makes British unions shy of long-term, enforceable wage agreements.

In most modern capitalist countries certain apprenticeships are the only instance of long-term labour contracts outside the entertainment field. But it is only the poor and unorganized, such as coolies, who are certain to suffer from chicanery and oppression as the result of having signed an indenture or similar document.

8. If forced labour has any economically useful, legally practical and morally defensible form it is the *corvée*. I use this word here more broadly than in any dictionary, to cover all short periods of compulsory work by normally free citizens, for instance:

(i) military conscription;
(ii) designated alternatives to (i), for conscientious objectors;
(iii) the compulsory Soviet-type three-year stint for people graduating from higher education, normally in their new speciality but in an outlying place;
(iv) compulsory public works by agricultural labourers in the off season: e.g. road-building by kolkhozniks outside the kolkhoz;
(v) compulsory public work and work on estates by primitive peoples, as in Portuguese colonies until recently;
(vi) compulsory harvesting by students and soldiers, as in nearly all Communist countries;
(vii) the month's manual labour for bureaucrats, for the good of their souls, as in China, Cuba and Albania;[26] the compulsory harvesting for all citizens in Cuba;
(viii) the 'voluntary' overtime demanded of their citizens by all Communist governments in emergencies;
(ix) simple work imposed on the unemployed as a condition of their dole;
(x) work by serfs on the demesne farm of a feudal lord.

The original meaning of the word corvée embraces only (iv), (v) and (x).

We distinguish all of these from the previous types by their greater humanity in principle (often violated in i, ii and v). For they tend

(a) to affect mainly the young and strong;
(b) to be strictly temporary;
(c) to take place not far from home (except i and ii);
(d) to be confined to normal working hours.

They are of course not penal. They are not used for colonization (except iii). But they do invariably imply work for less than what the free wage would be, and so the marginal disutility of labour still exceeds the wage. This, as we saw in sec. 1, is nearly our definition of forced labour.

Why then is corvée imposed? (i) and (ii) are 'youth service' concepts. We have referred to these elsewhere as tribal customs or *rites de passage.* No doubt also they are society's outlet for the very real biological drives of young males. Indeed there have been other, quite different, economic solutions for the 'young male problem', such as the *Wanderjahre* of the newly fledged journeyman, who had to hike from town to town and practise his craft in a wide variety of places. While thinking young males are not a phenomenon allowed for originally in such systems, it might be possible to accommodate them in varieties of (ii), but in less tight and 'tribal' societies it is also possible to dispense with the whole idea. Possible, but hardly desirable. For 'youth service' is a duty antecedent to the rights of citizenship. It is not plain to the elderly author how these rights can be indefinitely preserved, threatened as they are by ordinary human malice all the time, if they are not felt to be earned. The old hate the young precisely because they have performed, and offer to perform, no duties.

On the other hand (iii) partakes of indenture: although the Soviet freshman signs nothing, he is perfectly aware that he will suffer corvée on graduation. Where Sweden (of all countries!) makes many of its students borrow for their higher education and pay back money, Communist countries send them out into the boondocks, to pay back by being village doctors. We are tempted to say that the Soviet-type system is a socially just, but not micro-rational, solution to the problem of shortages of professionals in rural and backward areas. But the incidence of this particular corvée is very arbitrary and corrupt. No doubt a locational subsidy plus a general loan repayment scheme à la Suédoise would be better. Even so, Communism at least does not ignore the problem.

Items (iv) and (v) exploit the low marginal cost to society of labour, already committed for the year but seasonally available. Now psychologically this is very different from extra hours worked at the end of the day: the seasonally idle do indeed, from boredom and excess energy, offer themselves for less, not more, than their average wage per working day. This is the secret of most peasant crafts in cold climates. But it does not follow at all that such labour should be forced, since its free supply curve is in no way irrational.

The compulsory economic work of students and soldiers (vi) does, however, raise larger issues. Both have aspects of youth service (as in items i and ii). But there is also a fallacy: that students and soldiers have time to spare, rather like peasants in the winter. As this concerns students, it is a severe criticism of those who plan their curricula. It is more probable that the training of soldiers leaves them time, once trained, simply to be 'in a defensive posture'; so available on a short-term basis. If the conscription period exceeds the training period, forced economic labour is indeed rational. But the defence ministry that requests so long a conscription period should be most severely cross-questioned.

Corvée of type (vii) is, so to speak, corrective but not penal. It is clearly inefficient and economically irrational, but that is not the point since its aim is inspirational. We postpone it, and the all-important question of the balance between (v) and (vii) in China and Cuba, until chapter 21, sec. 8. Item (viii) is also inspirational, and best dealt with there. For both (vii) and (viii) are supposed to be voluntary, and some people do indeed volunteer.

Item (ix) is the classical work test of capitalist poor laws. We might wish to define it as 'objectively, not subjectively, forced' (sec. 1), since it leaves a man only the choice of not getting the dole. Such work almost has to be rather unproductive, since otherwise it would have attracted regularly employed people. Since it is always on tap for individuals as they apply it seldom forms part of any serious project. It certainly requires no training. Some infer that such work should not be offered, but there is no logic in that. The work might even be of great value to society (hospital portering, street sweeping), but beyond the employer's capacity to pay owing to a minimum wage law, union restriction or shortage of public funds. It is to be distinguished, in any case, from counter-cyclical public works. These may also well be rather unproductive, but they are at least occupationally variegated, serious projects, and they do hire on the open market.

Item (x) is a straightforward part of feudalism, and requires no further explanation here.

9. Slavery and penal transportation are mixed cases in that both type of labour and place of residence are forced. We now examine *internal exile*, which is forced residence only. We have the following types, which we must distinguish by their Russian names since, as in soil science, Russian is the most technically precise language at this point:

(i) *ssyl'ka*: exile to a specified area inside the country, where one must report to the police periodically but may take any job;

(ii) *vysyl'ka*: exile from a specified part of the country, e.g. major towns, one's home county and all border areas;

(iii) *deportation* outside the country.

All these are individual security measures, but there is also:

(iv) *pereselenie*: the movement of population from one place to another, whether on economic or on security grounds.

Ssyl'ka is often confused with transportation, but the victim is never behind bars except for interrogation before sentence. Many grossly exaggerated estimates of the numbers of Stalin's prisoners arise from this confusion. The victims of ssyl'ka were often very miserable indeed, however, since no one guaranteed their subsistence. Both ssyl'ka and vysyl'ka tend, in all societies that use them, to be 'security', not penal, measures; i.e. one is sentenced on mere suspicion, without legal proof, perhaps by the police not the courts, as a 'dangerous person'. Thus imperialist Britain used ssyl'ka on Indian politicians, and Italy uses it for Mafiosi. Deportation, on the other hand, now that the whole world is behind some frontier, depends on the permission of the receiving state.

There is economic ssyl'ka too: the best known case is the South African practice of 'endorsing out' the black man who has no job in the white township any more. His pass is then cancelled and he must return to his native reserve. But here too security is involved. The black man is not being punished, but he will become a security risk if he lives unemployed in a shanty on the edge of the white town. For in strict economics it is a matter of indifference *where* he is unemployed – unless the dole is locally financed.[27]

Another great case of economic ssyl'ka is the 'sending down' of superfluous Chinese townsmen to the countryside.

Pereselenie on security grounds is merely collective ssyl'ka. It has affected various Caucasian peoples accused of having collaborated with the German invader, and above all the Crimean Tatars, who are still under this sentence. It was used in USA in 1941, as a preventive measure, against citizens of Japanese origin. But it has also been used as a purely economic measure, without any accusation of crime or security risk. Notably, any Russian noble could transfer his serfs from one village to another, and the Soviet government retains such powers. It exercised them to move Caucasian hill farmers into valleys in 1940–1 (i.e. before the war).

Clearly these are all ways of populating empty land, while they also serve efficiently enough their primary security purpose. Indeed one can but wonder that such humane and effective sentences are not more often used than prison, which is harsher and yet, by exposing to bad company, less likely to reform. A strong reason may well be the difficulty of enforcement, where no one carries an identity card. Thus Italy seems to be the only free and democratic country to use ssyl'ka: but she has many islands and few Mafiosi. In larger land masses, as the Tsars found to their cost, exiles will not stay put, even if the whole population carries cards. But certainly these help: every citizen of USSR must have an internal passport, and so must every black man in South Africa.

Perhaps, then, it is the constant identity checks, and the totalitarian background and overtones that virtually confine these practices to wartime, Communism and South Africa. Certainly in and of themselves they are not repulsive.

But exile does sharply reduce the victim's choice of employment, driving him towards less skilled jobs. This is because empty land offers fewer skilled jobs, and people under sentence are unacceptable in positions of responsibility. If colonization were the only aim, as usual a straight subsidy to employment would be more micro-efficient, since it would select only the most suitable people.

10. Extremely similar to exile is *adscriptio glebae*, the non-penal assignment of the agriculturist to his place of birth. This was the principal way in which the feudal lord ensured the fulfilment of labour service on his demesne farm, and it originated in the labour shortage of the late Roman Empire (sec. 6). In other words serfdom is essentially an attempt to keep labour on land it has long occupied. The commutation in fourteenth- and fifteenth-century England of labour-service into money-rents put an end to this restriction. For the labour shortage after the Black Death should have restored serfdom, but it led to a great monetization of the economy (the stock of silver and gold per head rose) and landlords particularly hard hit by the plague did not want *adscriptio glebae* on other people's land. Moreover the English monarchy was not strong enough to enforce such a restoration.

Thus feudalism – unconnected as we saw in chapter 5 with the open-field village – came to an end early and painlessly. But in Russia monetization came very late. The labour shortage was chronic throughout history, and the strong autocrat had a personal interest in serfdom: it helped conscription. So strong was the system that it was even used where other nations have had to resort to slavery: the occupation of empty land. A single nobleman could buy a new village and transfer serfs to it from his other properties, and this happened on a large scale in the southward movement towards Odessa, 1780–1840.[28]

Moreover the village community was almost a creature of the state. Since it was responsible as a unit for taxes and recruits it was also interested in the presence of its able-bodied members. When in 1861 feudalism was abolished in Russia, the lord's quasi-police power was legally transferred to the community. Members could not leave now without the council's permission instead (let alone sell their rights to land). Having been abolished in 1921, adscription crops up again in the kolkhoz and the revival of the internal passport (1932):[29] the kolkhoznik might not leave without permission of the kolkhoz, and in place of the worker's permanent internal passport he received only an *ad hoc* travel document (until 1 January 1975).

When in 1956 perhaps the majority of Stalin's penal labourers were let out by Khrushchev, they received ssyl'ka to their present camps. I.e. the barbed wire and guards were removed, and their families could visit or settle with them, but little else changed. Not otherwise could these enterprises have been manned. This, too, was *adscriptio glebae*. The Australian 'ticket of leave' (above) was extremely similar: its recipient was not allowed to quit the colony. So here too economics and penology were inextricably mixed.

11. The *wartime direction of labour* is, for market economies, like any other element of command introduced *ad hoc*. Instant response is more important than rationality, so we can no more wait for the pull of new wage differentials than for the pull of new price relatives to extract more guns and less butter. It is certainly right that prices and wages should make these moves, and it is one of the grossest and commonest errors that the price mechanism should be suspended in wartime; it should be supplemented. Beside speed there is the need to control cost inflation. All relative price changes, when prices are administered, leave the average higher, since it is inordinately difficult to administer any price downward. Methods of command permit smaller price (or wage) changes.

We have seen that the Soviet-type economy does not normally direct labour either. So the phenomenon of wartime direction is virtually the same. It is, for instance, wholly non-penal and wholly economic. But in neither society are these powers, once on the statute book, much used, and the reason seems to be the same: they are too oppressive, and too contrary to the logic of both systems.

Only in Cuba, China and Albania is direction really common, and not confined to wartime.[30] The reasons are ideological and temperamental, and to be sought in the attempt at *premature Full Communism* (chapter 21, sec. 8). But then in these countries there is much more of other kinds of forced labour, as described above.

The directed person also works for marginal pay slightly below the marginal disutility of his labour; and this is as usual true almost by definition. But he remains a normal citizen of his country: he is free after hours, he votes, he enjoys whatever civil rights there are.

Notes

1. On these general aspects cf. Stanislaw Swianiewicz, *Forced Labour and Economic Development*, Oxford 1965.

2. Therefore his labour supply curve is, by exception, positively sloped! (cf. chapter 2, sec. 12). For extra food raises his limit, and he works up to whatever it is.

3. This is what Marx meant by the expression 'wage-slave'. For the wage, he said, the capitalist buys the whole working day. But in fact the pay system

is often by the hour, and in all cases the number of hours is limited by the wage-bargain. The free wage-earner has not an infinite 'zone of compliance' (chapter 2): only the slave has that, and even he only in theory. The expression 'wage-slave' is therefore self-contradictory.

4. In the Caribbean even completely unskilled cane-cutters, being expected to grow their own food from a private plot, were allowed to trade the surplus on the inter-estate Sunday market.

5. Except, as noted above, when he faces an absolute monopsonist. Cf. chapter 11, sec. 1; Wiles 1962, pp. 97, 137, 154, 230; A. Bergson (Berg) in *Quarterly Journal of Economics*, February 1938.

6. In Greece and Rome slave breeding was not recommended in troubled times, when the supply of prisoners was adequate. But it is thought that peace encouraged breeding. Cuba and Brazil bred few slaves after 1807, and preferred smuggling. The Arabs kidnapped rather than bred.

7. Cf. J. E. Moes in *Journal of Political Economy*, 1960.

8. After H. J. Nieboer, *Slavery*, 2nd ed. The Hague 1910, pp. 383–7, on 'closed and open resources'. Nieboer himself unaccountably fails to deal with white slave-holders and kidnappers. He develops his doctrine to explain primitive slavery. His 'resurrection' seems to be due to Evsey Domar in *Journal of Economic History*, March 1970.

9. North American Indians, in contact with white slave-holders, themselves enslaved a few negroes, no doubt runaways. But for the rest these tribes, being poor and nomadic, did not practise slavery. The rich, settled tribes of the Pacific Northwest, however, did. Quite independently of the white man they developed even slave-raiding and trading. Cf. Nieboer, op. cit., pp. 47–69, 201–226, 407–16.

10. R. M. Crawford, *Australia*, London 1952, chapters 3 and 4; W. D. Forsyth, *Governor Arthur's Convict System*, London 1935; M. Barnard, *MacQuarie's World*, Melbourne 1949; Samuel Marsden, *An Answer to Certain Calumnies*... London 1826; M. C. I. Levy, *Governor George Arthur*, Melbourne 1953; Richard Whately, *Thoughts on Secondary Punishments*, London 1832 (the book includes Gibbon Wakefield's 'Facts Relating to the Punishment of Death' as an appendix); A. G. Shaw, *Convicts in the Colonies*, Melbourne 1886.

11. Thus in 1937, to take at random a year with fair crime statistics, at least 300,000 crimes were known to the police in England, Scotland and Wales which would in 1831 have been transportable. But the population was only three times as large. An adequate police force could have generated 2000 transportees on a far milder code. Incidentally, before the 1820s transportation was commonly a commutation of the numerous death sentences for minor crimes. Thereafter it was the original sentence for such crimes.

12. Cf. Marion Phillips, *A Colonial Autocracy*, London 1909, p. 20; Levy, op. cit., chapter 10; Shaw, op. cit., pp. 228, 244–6.

13. Up to about 1820 assignees were not, for whatever reason, very profitable, and the government had to promise settlers administrative favours in order to make them take up assignees. Thereafter scarcity conditions changed and the receipt of an assignee was considered a favour. But no money passed either way, except corruptly.

14. There were about six million prisoners at work, by my reckoning (unpublished) at the pre-war peak of January 1939. About three quarters would be called by us political. About 90 per cent were men, or 10 per cent of all adult

males. Round about this time mortality was about 10 per cent p.a., or 10 times the free death rate in the same age-groups. These figures exclude mere deportees (sec. 9), and prisoners still under interrogation. Apart from a very few in political isolation camps, all sentenced prisoners had to do corrective labour.

15. And of primitive, or 'anthropological' slavery too. Cf. Nieboer, op. cit., pp. 383–7. But clearly 'pervasive' slavery was different.

16. *Glavsevmorputi*: cf. Terence Armstrong, *The North Sea Route*, Cambridge 1952. It is not implied that *Glavsevmorputi* is itself economically justified. On the new attitude to the frozen North cf. Robert N. North in *Soviet Studies*, October 1972.

17. No attempt was made in USSR to confine the coldest work to prisoners from northerly homes. Extremes of cold were seen as part of the punishment for infractions of camp discipline.

18. This proposition cannot be elaborated here. It is true of all countries, and particularly of STEs. Cf. Wiles 1969, chapter 8. Note that plantation slavery on the contrary is export-oriented.

19. Gregory Klimov, *The Terror Machine*, London 1953, pp. 229–230, 338. For similar activities before the war cf. Vladimir Petrov, *It Happens in Russia*, London 1951, p. 163. The great Tupolev himself designed aircraft in a Moscow 'camp' but history does not relate whether he was arrested with this purpose in mind. (This often quoted story rests on a single sentence by the refugee aerodynamics expert G. A. Tokaev, in his *Stalin Means War*, London 1951, pp. 161–162. It has this much support, that a friend of mine once heard Khrushchev ask Tupolev why he had not joined the Party. He replied, 'I am an old Russian anarchist'.) A. I. Solzhenitsyn relates in his *First Circle* his experiences in a similar 'camp', where he solved mathematical problems relating to electronics. But he was quite definitely not arrested with this in mind (cf. David Burg and George Feifer, *Solzhenitsyn*, London 1972, chapters, 10, 11).

20. Alfred H. Conrad and John R. Meyer, *The Economics of Slavery*, Chicago 1964.

21. New England's industry and agriculture were skill-intensive and small-scale. So the higher supervision costs of slavery were prohibitive, and the climate provided no argument. Upstate New York, however, did reach a 14 per cent slave population by 1800. We certainly cannot speak of moral differences, where Northern capital financed the slave trade, and the same religious sects, centrally co-ordinated, covered the whole country.

22. It never has, whether for tobacco, cotton or sugar – but let that pass.

23. Janissaries, and, it appears, certain Roman conscripts, even up to the rank of naval captain. Mamelukes, however, were invariably manumitted after their military training (below).

24. It would perhaps be right to speak of a location trap. A climatically unsuitable or very distant region possesses raw materials or some other specious reason to be developed. We sink capital and 'transport' labour. But the region never becomes self-supporting and it is a political impossibility to cut our losses. USSR and (post-slavery) Brazil have both fallen into this trap.

25. And not only of free workers. The Mameluke soldiers of medieval Egypt and Syria, commonly described as that contradiction in terms, a slave élite, were hardly more than indentured youths. They were sold into slavery quite voluntarily by their Christian Circassian parents, who knew they had a chance of a great career (and on occasion even came to live with them if they made good). Their slavery covered approximately seven years' training in mounted warfare,

from which they emerged, apparently without exception, as Moslems, freedmen and members of the *corps d'élite*. Their brushes with the law while in slavery were not regulated by ordinary Islamic slave law but by a special code. They could later rise to general in the ordinary, Sultan in the extraordinary but not unusual, course of events. Of this 'slavery', then, it is best said that the Sultan and the Emirs needed indentured, foreign, military apprentices to guarantee their power.

26. This is to be strictly distinguished from the permanent 'sending down' to the countryside of Chinese judged to be superfluous in towns (sec. 9).

27. In all Anglo-Saxon countries the poor law used to be locally financed, and this has led as recently as 1970 in USA to the ssyl'ka of recently arrived poor back to their state of origin. This practice survived in Britain until the 1890s: the unemployed were still occasionally shipped back to their parish of origin.

28. Siberia was mainly colonized after 1861, by free labour. Penal labour was numerically insignificant.

29. It is one of Communism's great ironies that Lenin protested against the Tsar's internal passport system, which kept him in Siberian ssyl'ka.

30. Stalin kept his wartime powers on the statute book, but scarcely used them.

9
The Implementation of Detailed Plans

1. Definitions
2. Epiphenomenal and persuasive planning
3. Regulative plans
4. France until Monnet
5. Monnet
6. France after Monnet: the fiscal agreement
7. Taxes, subsidies, qualitative bank controls
8. Licensing
9. Command
10. Coherence and rationality under command planning up to 1921
11. The command hierarchy
12. The formal disaggregation of command plans
13. The 'open-market operation'
14. 'Procurement' and price control
15. Small countries, government departments
16. Implementation systems and the level of development

9

1. This chapter is not about policy, i.e. the contents of plans, except in so far as these react upon implementation. Therefore it is not about development economics, except in so far as degrees of development react upon implementation. It is not about econometric models, input-output, linear programming or any other technique used inside planning offices, except in so far as these techniques react upon implementation. This chapter is about implementation. Even so it is desperately brief.

Plan implementation is an economic institution, and therefore barely part of economics as usually conceived. It is about what the government must do to have its way. If there are no implementation difficulties there is either a one-in-a-billion coincidence or no real planning, and planners are able-bodied pensioners. This chapter then, is unashamedly about government, corruption, police work and administrative law.

But first some definitions. Merely atmospheric or very general government interventions in the market – the rate of interest, the rate of exchange, the budget deficit – are called by us *Keynesian*. Good or bad, sufficient or insufficient to attain their objectives, they are not part of detailed planning, or relevant to this chapter. We are concerned here with rather detailed and with very detailed planning, and we take as examples France and the USSR.

The rather detailed plan should, and the very detailed plan must, be *coherent*. I.e. the planned supplies of each commodity must be adequate for the planned uses of that commodity, which are entailed of course by the supplies of all the other commodities and itself. At its crudest, coherence can be striven for by balancing each row in an input-output matrix separately (*method of balances*, chapter 11, sec. 8), and manipulating all the rows towards an overall mutual balance by chance and rule of thumb. Better, but still only on the drawing-board (despite optimistic reports to the contrary), is *input-output* itself (chapter 11).

No attempt at coherence, no very detailed plan. It follows that Soviet economic historians rightly deny the name planning to the conduct of the Soviet economy in 1918–21 ('War' Communism), when there was not even any attempt to use the method of balances. This was a period we call *planless command*. It is a corollary that a plan must be serious for some time ahead. If it is intended to be altered at once, on receipt of the first small unexpected news, there is no attempt to master the future. Good or bad, that is not planning. It is therefore advisable, but not part of the definition, that the plan provide for alternative actions in case certain events, especially exogenous events, turn out this way or that. An absolutely rigid and univocal plan, like the classical Soviet plan, is certain to be violated since not all events can be foreseen. But this also is not necessarily bad, as we shall see.

Then again the verb to plan – and so by implication the noun, and all their compounds – can be intransitive. The intransitive is the basic sense: we look ahead and work out in advance what we shall do if . . . This is the planning of the general, the master criminal, or the entrepreneur in a market. This procedure too can be rigid and univocal, and lead to great absurdities. Mr. Mark Spade[1] has described it once for all:

> '(1) In an unplanned business things just happen, i.e. they crop up, life is full of unforeseen happenings and circumstances over which you have no control. On the other hand (2) in a *planned* business things still happen and crop up and so on, *but you know exactly what would have been the state of affairs if they had not.*'

Now the general and the master criminal both remind us that there is something transitive about the most intransitive planning. *All enterprises are small command economies:* the manager's intransitive plan is his subordinate's operation order[2] (section 12) or possibly direct order.

Nevertheless for the manager himself the distinction is vital: is he receiving a document, called 'plan', written by someone else and binding on him, or is he thinking it up himself? If the latter we are in China, and there is no detailed planning (chapter 10). But in the former case we have national detailed planning. In theory national plans need fewer alternative provisions for contingencies, since fewer uncertainties are exogenous: only foreign trade, the harvest and technical progress. But in fact it is not administratively possible for the planner to predict or control the billions (to him) of endogenous variables, and the plan he hands down to, or agrees with, the enterprise is no more likely to be viable over a year than the plan the enterprise on the market makes up for itself.

A plan need not be optimal in the short-run, micro-economic sense. The ontological reason here is quite simple: planning isn't necessarily good. It can be as bad and as stupid as human beings or governments can be. *Laissez-faire* can be better, and plan violation the highest patriotism. The practical reason is that such detailed optimality is not[3] administratively possible. The nearest approach hitherto is the mathematical technique rather misleadingly called *linear programming*, which relaxes the assumption of fixed co-efficients made by input-output. In this we can assure an optimal use of inputs, and therefore an optimal set of input prices, for each chosen set of final outputs. But even so there is still an infinite number of coherent solutions, only one of which is optimal: the one in which the prices used to value the final output vector (and the outputs therein) are also thrown into the pot, and brought into harmony with the prices in the dual. No incoherent solution could be optimal, since incoherence is wasteful. But incoherence does generate planner's tension (chapter 11, sec. 14), and this may be dynamically optimal.

Again a plan need not be wise or 'developmental' in its broad outlines: say in major sectoral choices, or in its regional emphasis, or in its policy on foreign trade or inflation, or in its decision on how much to save. The ontological reason for this is the same as before. The practical reason is that macro-quantities cannot be rational unless the micro-quantities that compose them are (chapter 11, sec. 4). This is a necessary but not a sufficient reason for macro-rationality, and detailed national planning cannot, as we just saw, provide it.

Finally plans can be obligatory, persuasive and 'other'. Command and persuasion we have already met, especially in chapter 2. 'Other' consists mainly of negative or inhibitory items: taxes, subsidies, qualitative bank controls, licensing. But these are also 'open-market operations' (secs. 7, 8, 13).

2. In addition to being not worth implementing, and indeed worth not implementing, a plan may not even be seriously intended for implementation: there is not only planless command but also commandless plan. The word 'planning' obsesses people: the well-dressed modern country must not be without its figleaf. Such is human folly that plans really are drawn up without mechanisms for implementing them. The classic case is British:[4]

> To the development under Stalin that under Attlee presents a sharp contrast. The 'Economic Survey for 1947', published in February 1947, had many of the stigmata of a real plan (including of course its arrival after the period to be planned had already begun!). Yet the whole document rested on a basic confusion, as the following passage shows:
>
> > The Government has no direct control over the way in which man-power moves; it can seek to influence the movement in a number of ways, but the ideal distribution of man-power would involve changes of such magnitude that it would be impossible to bring them about by any means short of complete wartime direction. Even if direction were used, the transfer of labour would be limited by lack of accommodation. The following table sets out a distribution of man-power at end-1947. This is neither an ideal distribution nor a forecast of what will happen; it represents the approximate distribution which is needed to carry out the objectives in paragraph 118 and which the Government considers can be achieved if the nation as a whole sets itself to achieve them.
>
> Needless to reproduce here the table of man-power targets. Enough that at the end of 1947 right-wing economists were making fun of the

extreme under- and over-fulfilment of the various targets; a thing far from unnatural since no enforcement mechanisms had been provided. Yet the 'Economic Survey for 1948' continued in the same almost self-contradictory strain:

> Labour is not at present, and is unlikely to be in 1948, the limiting factor in economic activity as a whole. Any projected distribution such as is given in Table XXI is therefore largely a forecast of the results of other factors, and if some figures turn out differently it is not necessarily in every case a matter of regret. But the labour forces proposed for coal, agriculture and textiles are *targets in the full sense*. They are numbers believed to be required to reach specific objectives in the set of output and export targets decided in 1948. The attainment of these man-power targets is agmong the first *necessities* in 1948.

Note the apologetic tone, induced by the failures of the previous year. Note also the ludicrously undefined phrases in italics. In subsequent years the 'Economic Survey for 194(x)' has said more and more about 194(x–1) and less and less about 194(x) itself, until in March 1954 the word 'for' was dropped from the title, so that now in effect 'Economic Survey 1960' merely meant the economic survey *of* 1959, published *in* 1960. Finally after 1960 the whole series was abandoned. This, then, is the history of the Soviet 'control figures' in reverse. Both started as '*epiphenomenal* planning'; the one developed into the operative planning of a command economy, the other withered away into mere undisguised prediction and then ceased to be even that.[5]

Innumerable other plans really deserve the label 'epiphenomenal', since the government that draws them up is not strong enough to use its implementing powers; or is so unstable that it will fall before the time arrives for implementation, to be succeeded by governments with other policies, which draw up other plans, and which in turn fall. UDCs waste much energy on importing experts to make such plans; and since the imported experts have to talk to the native experts, who are very scarce, there is an even more important wastage of the latters' time and effort. After all the foreigners are probably paid by foreign funds, and their time is their own. But the native expert is a very precious resource, so this kind of planning is worse than useless, since it interferes with more basic tasks of government like tax-collecting or public enterprise.

So there must not merely be stable government before we plan; we must also be assured that the plan is better than *laissez-faire* by a margin big enough to justify the diversion of scarce administrative energy. However, a seemingly epiphenomenal plan may not be without some actual effect, intended or not.

(i) First comes the 'Monnet' case. The plan is a well-thought-out prediction (unlike the British ones quoted), based on information and expertise unavailable to the private sector, or to independent nationalized enterprises. Additionally it is widely known that it was evolved by very thorough consultation with independent enterprises, and that the courses proposed for such bodies are profitable. Then these enterprises follow those courses, and prediction has become persuasion. As we shall see, not much is left of the Monnet case in French planning, and the system contained other important elements from the first; but this is the core of that case. During the Czechoslovak Spring (1967–August 1968) the notion of planning as an essentially informational activity underwent rebirth: Monnet's 'road map of the future' was to be computerized. However we may say with great confidence that even without the Soviet invasion little would have come of this notion. Information can easily be abused, markets are not as perfect and people are not as moral as revisionist Communists suppose. Moreover computers and their supporting input systems are by no means so well developed as was supposed.

(ii) Secondly, what appears to be an epiphenomenal plan conceals elements of command. Thus a 'Monnet-type' plan contains a 'prognostication' of government investment and current expenditure and these elements involve its good faith. Moreover the government is less tightly bound to the state of the market, and so can fulfil its part of the plan anyway. The notorious British national plan of 1965, which was discreetly buried after a balance of payments crisis in 1968, was nevertheless borne out in its 'forecasts' of government expenditure.

(iii) What if the plan is a badly thought-out, or at least for some reason a wrong, prediction? Then there will still be people to believe it. If previous plans have been good perhaps nearly everyone will. They will begin on the courses suggested by the plan and find them impossible after a time to pursue. I.e. the plan will still have affected their actions, but not, ultimately, in the way intended. This is 'technically impossible Monnet'. It cannot be too strongly emphasized that this is not necessarily a disaster. It might be an improvement on *laissez-faire*, typically by increasing investment. But the micro-allocation might also be superior, if for instance the badly thought-out plan had been directed against monopoly. And the whole outcome might also be an improvement on case (i), since the ultimate resource allocation embodied in the last year of that plan might be merely coherent, and owe its success to that, while being in every other respect inferior to the allocation actually achieved in case (iii).

(iv) We may go even further. The epiphenomenal plan may be counterproductive. It may cause an explosion of public anger by predicting, say, greater imports or off-farm migration or something else that citizens do not like but ought to have. This in turn will cause *laissez-faire* in the guise of planning to be given up in favour of a restrictive policy. If the government had kept quiet by not pretending to intervene, it would not have had to intervene in reality. But planning forces the government to lay nearly all its cards on the table; in democracies at any rate the whole plan must be published and may be criticized. Consequently everyone thinks harder and sees further. A counter-productive plan too is in no necessary way a catastrophe. How great has been the improvement in urban affairs since it became customary to publish construction plans! The improvement has of course been their abandonment in the face of public anger.

(v) Very different, but at least equally valuable, is the plan drawn up for foreign investors and aid-givers. These people, especially if employed by the governments of Western democracies, like to be reassured that their particular gift or loan truly fits into an overall development pattern. They are apt not to give money for a port unless they are shown a piece of paper saying that there will be a steel mill and a road in the hinterland. Such paper is easy to produce, and is called a national plan. Once the money for the port is committed, the paper can be torn up. And this too is not necessarily a catastrophe, since something other than steel will doubtless be produced instead, to take advantage of the port; and steel was probably a bad idea anyway; and the main thing was to get the money. This, then, is the 'stock exchange prospectus' type of plan.

3. Beyond the epiphenomenally persuasive plan is the plan enforced by regulation but not command; e.g. by qualitative bank controls, by quotas and licensing, by 'open-market operations',[6] or by direct taxes and subsidies. Pure persuasion is very unusual. Regulation nearly always accompanies it. In French planning there is less and less 'Monnet-type' persuasion and more and more sheer detailed regulation (sec. 6). The novel and the intellectually exciting get the publicity, but the work is done by the square and the dull.

Regulation shares with persuasion the extremely important characteristic that the *micro-initiative is left to the enterprise*. It is not told what to do, it is told what not to do (in the first two cases); or exposed to changes in market parameters which leave them after all merely market parameters (in the latter two cases). The plan is what we have called 'rather detailed'. In view of the extreme complexity of any economy (say 15 million goods and services, many strongly interrelated: chapter 11, secs. 9, 10), is it still so lacking in detail that it can hardly be violated, nor can it be seriously incoherent. In terms of the quantity of police work or the powers of the state the difference between this and 'very detailed' is very great indeed. It is the difference between trying to control 100 items and 15 million.

If under *laissez-faire* 'everything is permitted', under rather detailed planning 'everything is permitted that is not forbidden', and under command planning 'everything is compulsory that is not forbidden'. Under Full Communism highly detailed persuasion, of the same degree of disaggregation, is supposed to replace command (chapter 21).

4. The classic case of persuasion, epiphenomenalism and regulation is post-war France. First the background, which is more surprising and worse known than it should be.

France was always very different from other capitalist countries, so different indeed that it should perhaps never have been included in any list of them. France took Mercantilism seriously, under the règlements of Louis XIV and Jean-Baptiste Colbert,[7] and never really forgot it. Free trade was Anglophile; Louis XVI and his minister Vergennes made themselves very unpopular indeed by this policy, which substantially helped to bring on the Revolution.[8] It was the Sun King's minister whom, effectively, the revolutionaries remembered. Robespierre protected French industry against British imports, regulated prices and even forcibly procured agricultural deliveries with the absolutism of a Colbert and the fury of a Communist – which he certainly was not. He also invented universal military conscription. Beneath him, however, there festered the first true Communists, who possibly invented the command economy, and certainly were the first to work it out in detail: Gracchus Babeuf and his 'Conspiracy of the Equals'.[9]

There followed Napoleon, whose attitude to the economy was that of a military quartermaster. This showed itself first and foremost in an exaggerated and uncritical Mercantilism. But in one respect Napoleon does enter the history of planning: he founded the *Grandes Ecoles*, nurseries outside the university system of a *corps* of engineers, a *corps* of inspectors of finance, etc., etc. The idea here was by no means individual advancement or self-perfection, but bodies of trained people at the disposal of the state. They are notorious to this day for their *esprit de corps*, their readiness to help each other, their switches from public to private employment and back,[10] their capacity to put the *corps* above the employer of the moment, whoever he may be. Outside the military sector, they have no parallel in other countries. Characteristically they have always been the nursery of the social élite: in state capitalism such institutions are provided out of the public purse, while under pure capitalism they are independent trusts.

Yet more important than all of these to our understanding of French planning is St. Simon.[11] Principally active under the restored monarchy, St. Simon seemed unable to distinguish between managers and workers. To him they were all *les industriels*, who should govern the economy, while the state was a feudal and military incubus that should wither away. The King should put himself at the head of the economy as *Le Premier Industriel.* The restored Bourbons were on another wavelength, but this is what Louis Philippe actually did: he was himself a true St. Simonian.

Under the Premier Industriel the task of management belonged to the *bankers*.[12] St. Simon does not explain exactly how they are to do it, but it is clear that money and the market are to remain, along with small private property. He is cagey about private property. He was probably opposed to it, like his pupil Enfantin, but feared to say so aloud, and condemned only inheritance. He favoured, however, differentiated wages. His bankers were to live like gentlemen. Had he known about the detailed planning problem, which he did not, St. Simon would certainly have opted for 'rather detailed'. In any case his bankers were to be an openly recognized élite of 'generalists' (*hommes généraux*), and no doubt he had the Napoleonic *Grandes Ecoles* in mind. He is thus the father of qualitative bank controls (chapter 12, sec. 14) and so of French planning. Moreover beneath the bankers come another *corps d'élite*, the engineers. These are to provide what the French today call in franglais an infrastructure, forgetting their own well-rooted terminology of *outillage national* or *équipement public*. From them derive de Lesseps and all the magnificent and less magnificent French canal builders of the nineteenth century: they were overtly St. Simonian. *Equipement public* has never ceased to be an independent element in French planning ideology.

All this amounts to *state capitalism*. From the fall of Louis Philippe until the end of the Third Republic it is possible to consider France an ordinary capitalist country.[13] But the eye of hindsight detects St. Simonism and Mercantilism still alive beneath the surface. The latter survived in protectionism and an imperial preference system much earlier and more thorough than in Britain. The former is more subtly represented in early, almost non-ideological, nationalization; in the companies of mixed private and public ownership; in the strength of the Banque de France and the state extra-budgetary funds, over against the weakness of the commercial banks and the stock exchange (chapter 12); in the government's persistent pre-occupation with, and active financial support of, *outillage national*; in the National Economic Council, founded 1924.[14] The France that emerged from defeat in 1945, then, had the appropriate economic traditions and institutional structure to listen to Jean Monnet. Indeed these almost unrecognized prerequisities made 'French planning' possible and have survived it. Monnet was but an interlude in a long St. Simonian story.

5. For St. Simonism and Mercantilism have no direct intellectual link with Monnet-type planning. In so far as not original, Monnet's ideas may be sought in Roosevelt's USA. Specifically, an agricultural economist administering the new price supports under the Agricultural Adjustment Act, Mordecai Ezekiel,[15] imagined their extension to all products. If each producer knew he had a minimum price guarantee he would produce a lot, and so set up a good demand for current and capital inputs, and so justify the optimistic expectations of all the other producers. So if the government made convincing enough noises about its price supports, and if they were sufficiently general, they need never be involved. Note in particular that this is a way of stabilizing investment too – without any Keynesian weapons. So here is the germ of Monnet's notion that there

can be a non-market conspiracy of entrepreneurs to have full employment. There are no price supports in his version; the government consults everyone openly, and the contours of a feasible and profitable full employment emerge. Once believed in, the prophecy validates itself.

This version is even more non-Keynesian than Ezekiel's. Like the latter, it rests on no kind of monetary theory, but it is also innocent of price theory. Indeed it has precious little economics at all – Monnet was an engineer by training. The essential vision is of a very aggregated input-output table democratically arrived at. Each industrial sub-commission puts up qualitative targets which the planning officials marry off, input against output, complementary against complementary and competitive against competitive, all across the economy. In the pre-computer days of the first two four-year plans the officials worked by rule of thumb, and their 'iterations' were more like horse-trading or diplomacy; compare the Soviet method of balances in chapter 11, sec. 8. Like Monnet himself, they had the most various backgrounds, which did not include orthodox economics. Prices did not figure largely in their minds, and they fully accepted the possibilities of monopoly inherent in the industrial sub-commissions.

Moreover the planners tried to steer clear of all macro-monetary problems such as the wage-price spiral and the rate of exchange. These were shrugged off as 'political' and 'ephemeral': the planners were engaged in the 'real' business of the country, which was 'reconstruction and development', objectives quite above mere party politics, and subject to technological laws. Such notions appealed strongly to a defeated country, suffering grave war damage. Many choices were obvious: the railway bridges had to be restored. Moreover by long tradition the civil service kept the country going, while parliamentary instability showed itself in mere macro-monetary affairs.

Our quotations in sec. 2 show a contemporary British flirtation with physical planning. In the land of Keynes it never got very far, but in France it carried all before it. What does *macro-physical planning* look like to the enterprise? First, it believes more or less in the plan's nation-wide targets, and applies them to its own conduct by means of some estimated share of the market. Secondly, it is in no way penalized for even deliberate non-fulfilment: the actual market still governs what actually it does, and the object of the plan is to influence the market, not regulate the firm. Besides, thirdly, the plan is grossly aggregated, to such an extent that it could not conceivably be called a production instruction, even if it were broken down enterprise by enterprise. Consequently capitalism, which is justified only by decentralized initiative and risk-bearing, feels it can very well survive.

6. Nevertheless the system has broken down. Monnet-type planning is nearly dead. The reasons are many:

(i) When the novelty wore off and the obvious post-war reconstruction was done the institution lost prestige. The degree of aggregation made the whole exercise seem epiphenomenal rather than persuasive. Yet the actual choices implied in the large aggregates were still quite arbitrary.

(ii) The economy was growing fast, but so were others. No one could show that planning had helped – or hindered.

(iii) 'Merely' macro-monetary problems became more and more insistent. In 1958 de Gaulle returned to power and obstinately stabilized the franc. So he had to deflate instead of devaluing, as weaker governments had done. So investment fell, and the Third Plan was destroyed at macro-level. The planners' pretended independence of politics and money was shown up as a chance circumstance, unlikely to recur.

(iv) More 'Westernized', econometrically trained, planners (Massé) took over from the undogmatic pioneers. Both Keynesian doctrine and orthodox micro-economics began to be known inside the planning office. I am very far from alleging that this was beneficial, but it was an important change.

(v) The Common Market took hold, and the planners' grip on foreign trade weakened. Ironically another invention of Jean Monnet, the Common Market is of course utterly incompatible with his type of planning, unless it is practised supranationally in Brussels. There was such talk, but it came to nothing since the other nations would have none of it, whether at home or in Brussels.

(vi) The Common Market is prejudiced against monopoly, and above all against that non-amalgamated, confederal or conspiratorial kind of monopoly that the sub-commissions encourage – nay, that they constitute.

Was the breakdown inevitable? The logic of our six points seems indefeasible, so we are bound, with hindsight, to say yes. Ordinary common sense is against macro-physical planning, however attractive, nay positively virtuous, it seems.

But the Planning Commission is not dead, it has merely restored St. Simon to his rightful place. At the top it has saved its prestige by concentrating on social planning, regional balance, questions of the far future and the like. At a lower level than in the industrial sub-commissions control is as firm as ever. French planning has preserved, even strengthened, itself, by retreating into those financial and banking controls that the Common Market cannot yet touch. Each enterprise is separately subject to a *capital-allocating bureaucracy*. No new issue, no substantial bank loan, can be made without the permission and collaboration of these comparatively junior officials. These men check each investment project for rough accordance with the 'macro-physical plan', and arrange for the appropriate financing by the banks or the stock exchange. The banks are legally bound to do the government's bidding by a detailed system of qualitative controls. Access to the stock exchange is legally free – but it would be foolish to act without the approval of the enormous extra-budgetary funds that dominate it, and whose approval is equivalent to a good underwriting. Their approval depends of course on the opinion of the planning commission (chapter 12).

Nor is that all. Direct and even indirect taxes on enterprises are subject to innumerable remissions, which an enterprise can earn by locating a branch in Brittany, freezing its prices, producing an exportable article, conducting a research project, etc., etc. It can even be persuaded to amalgamate with another enterprise, i.e. sacrifice its very existence. So many and so complicated are these remissions that enterprise *taxation is negotiable*, or to put it in French-planese the enterprise enters into an '*agrément fiscal*' with the state. It negotiates the broad lines of its production, location and employment with that same rather junior official in the planning commission (or, now, Ministry of Finance) against a lower tax bill. The very concept, be it noted, of a fiscal agreement is almost self-contradictory and highly original in a modern state. It opens the widest possible field to corruption and to arbitrary state power. It is spreading to other ACEs, particularly in matters of industrial location and where the entry of foreign companies is concerned. Although it has existed in France since 1945 its 'take-off into sustained growth' coincides with the return of de Gaulle to power.[16]

7. The second way to implement a plan then, is not by persuasion but by monetary reward or penalty. We postpone to sec. 9 the plan-fulfilment bonus from the wage-fund to the Soviet-type manager. We also exclude the border-line case of the bonus which modernized STEs permit to be deducted from profit by enterprises with somewhat more autonomy. Our present subject is the more parametrical interventions of the state on a fully functioning market.

For our purposes there are three types of monetary reward. First comes the 'fiscal agreement' of the previous section. This is a detailed and direct stimulus to do a particular thing. It is indeed a marginal case like the Soviet-type bonus from profit: the reward approximates to a direct command, leaving its recipient few alternatives. If it is negotiated between the (capitalist) enterprise and the fisc, after all most of the orders in a Soviet-type plan are negotiated, and many are precisely couched in the form of a contract.

The next kind of monetary reward is fixed taxes and subsidies. These are entirely commonplace, so however important we pass them over very rapidly. One point of political economy must, however, detain us. *Fixed taxes and subsidies are the only instruments of planning compatible with parliamentary sovereignty*. That is, they are the only instruments that can be imposed at long and regular intervals of time, and discussed publicly by large bodies of men. This does not of course exclude the imposition of such levies by autocracies. Every single other instrument, from persuasion to command, including the fiscal contract and the qualitative bank control, is necessarily 'administrative'. What does this word mean? It connotes bureaucrat's or planner's *discretion*. Those who persuade or command us do so with detailed aims in mind that differ, literally from day to day. Their broad aims may be constant (and also may not be), may even be laid down by public parliamentary discussion. They may even be held to account for their detailed actions, whether by audit at regular intervals or by tribunal in case of scandal. But from day to day they are free, and they can nearly always present parliament with a *fait accompli*.

Fixed taxes and subsidies on the contrary have a quite different original *raison d'être*: the provision of a determinate quantity of money to a rather weak government not interested in planning. So they are not meant to be 'administrative', and often in fact are not. Corruption and excessive complication may make them so, but in this case discretion is not vested in a senior bureaucrat following some public plan, but in a bureaucrat of any level lining his own pocket. This raises two large questions at once: how great, then, can be the role of such instruments in any planning worth the name, and can such planning be compatible with parliamentary democracy? Postponing the second question to chapter 17, we can answer the first briefly in the negative. As we saw in section 1, the detailed planner cannot even predict or control the variables that are nominally endogenous to his plan, for they are simply too numerous. So he spends most of his time simply reacting to the unexpected, even if *per impossibile* he has correctly predicted the exogenous variables. In this situation fixed rates of tax and subsidy, indeed fixed anything at all, are quite useless. They only help the pursuit of permanent and broadly defined objectives which indeed also form a part of the detailed plan. They are irrelevant by their very nature to day-to-day decisions. *Detailed planning is administrative.*

This is even true of the Soviet turnover tax (chapter 11). Its rates are fixed at rare intervals, and it is not the mechanism of short-run adaptation to demand. Indeed how could it be otherwise? In no economy are prices varied from day to day, except on highly specialized perfect markets, where the operators are professional speculators with the requisite time, energy and nerve (chapter 10). The ordinary mechanism of adjustment is and should be quantitative. We 'run out of' things and 'order more of' them: we do not put up the price to see what happens. Day-to-day flexible taxes, therefore, can be imagined, but are not humanly possible. They form no part, for instance, of the French fiscal agreement.

Our third and last type of monetary reward or penalty is the qualitative[17] banking control. Credit is made easy for exports, import substitutes, projects for investment in heavy industry, projects situated in backward regions, etc. This subject is developed at length in chapter 12; our object here is mainly to range it in its appropriate place among implementation mechanisms. Constitutionally the bank, even a nationalized central bank, has much more independence of parliament than the treasury, and so acts administratively. We could imagine a different situation, in which bank controls had legal formality and permanence and were somehow publicly accountable; but this has not developed in practice.

8. Our next mechanism is all forms of *licensing*: quotas or prohibitions, not based on taxes or other monetary disincentives (though possibly enforced by fines in the courts), with exceptions granted to some. In economics licensing and taxation are rather similar, while positive commands, and to some extent fiscal agreements, stand out as something separate. For licensing acts much as a prohibitively high tax. It leaves the person or firm free to do everything that is not expressly forbidden: most initiative remains decentralized, the profit motive is not touched, the market is regulated but not suppressed. No firm is ordered to apply for a licence. What all these instruments share is not their negativity – subsidies are not negative – but their generality. None of them is *ad hominem*. Even a subsidy is quite unlike a positive command since it leaves refusal open. These instruments apply to all and sundry, not to a particular person or enterprise. But a command cannot, by definition, be addressed to anyonc willing to come forward and obey. And if the government approaches a particular unit with an *ad hominem* subsidy offer we are very close to the command economy; the fiscal agreement is such a subsidy.

In law however the usual distinction obtains: licensing is administrative, and not open to much parliamentary scrutiny. It *is* thus a suitable day-to-day instrument for dealing with the minor crises of detailed planning.

Moreover there is one substantial economic difference too: the man who receives the licence makes a monetary gain, possibly a very big one, without having incurred more than a small administrative cost. Broadcasting licences, import quotas, building permits, taxi-operating licences: wherever we turn in a market economy we meet these same windfalls. The possibilities of corruption are evident and enormous, and it is hard to understand why public authorities do not more often turn an honest penny by auctioning off the permissions that they give. Let us briefly speculate on this failure; the matter is of great importance, since it underlies also the command economy.

First, most people are *afraid of the price mechanism*. We have just seen how inconceivable would be, in any society, daily fluctuations in tax rates. We know that neither the Polish nor the Soviet government dares raise the retail price of meat so as to clear the market (chapter 14). A whole system of pricing is described in chapter 10, embracing most of the goods and services in the world, which verbally restricts the role of prices to covering costs – and we have seen reason to believe that these mere words to some extent affect practice. The use of prices as an allocating mechanism is widely held, by the man in the street and by the official, by the socialist and the conservative, to be immoral. Moreover it reduces the official's power, so that, unconsciously aware of this, he redoubles his cry of immorality. Thus the grant of social services in money and not in kind, detailed article by detailed article, is resisted passionately by welfare workers. But these people are astounded when they hear that this attitude is tyrannical, contemptuous of the poor, and self-serving (since it creates more jobs). In the same way the Western broadcasting authority resents the auctioning off of a wavelength as impersonal, as taking away some of its power to decide personally; and Soviet officials who decide between investment projects resent the rate of interest on the same grounds.

But there are also objective reasons for preferring administrative means. There is a real fear that the man who pays the maximum price at an auction for some permission or other will subsequently lower quality, raise prices and generally cut corners in order to recoup himself. If the bidder had been less financially pushed he would have neglected these ways of increasing his profit, still open to him. This is of course an implicit denial of short-run profit maximization – and none the worse for that (cf. chapter 10). Then too auctions keep out poor applicants. This hardly matters where the licence is applied for by enterprises, but it is a genuine objection to the sale of, say, taxi-drivers' shields. In both cases, however, one may reply that the high price of the licence argues absurd over-restriction of the number of entrants, and over-payment of the fortunate insiders.

In a word, administrative allocation is seen as morally superior, windfalls or no windfalls. The basic propositions of economics are simply not believed. And these attitudes affect *a fortiori* the subsequent resale of the licence. For it certainly follows from our argument that the inevitable black market in the product should be mitigated by an official market in the licence itself. Thus if, as in UK, the production of hops is subject to quota the authorities are perfectly indifferent as to who grows them. But resources are better allocated at all times if (as is the case) any farmer can sell the part of the quota that he possesses: this ensures that hops are always grown on the best land.

Note that the thing licensed may be money itself: foreign exchange control, certain qualitative bank controls. There is nothing paradoxical here, since the essence of licensing is the numerical restriction of whatever is being sold or produced, while the essence of taxation is the change in its market parameter. Money to be spent on imports or investments can also of course be taxed or subsidized.

9. Our fourth way to implement a plan is to command people to fulfil it, and to punish or reward them accordingly by law and bonus. This introduces us to legal punishment, which is a simple enough concept. The orders themselves are not, of course, directly governed by parliament. For Communism permits no serious parliament, and, as we have seen, so great a volume of day-to-day legislation could not be controlled by one if it

existed.[18] The command economy is 'administration' *par excellence*. But that does not at all mean that the penalties for plan violation should be administrative, not legal. Legal punishment is indeed very rare, because the mere threat suffices.[19] There is a wide-ranging law of sabotage quite unlike similar capitalist laws. It covers malicious plan violation, but malice is not something the authorities normally wish to prove. From day to day they use the plan fulfilment bonus and even in grave cases they content themselves with penalties like demotion and transfer, exactly as in a large capitalist corporation. We note again the parallel between the capitalist enterprise and the Soviet-type state: both are command economies, so both use the same devices to enforce the commands.

This is a totally different system of plan implementation, with the widest political and social consequences. Only the system of economic motivation itself is of greater importance.[20] For command abolishes decentralized initiative: everything that is not compulsory is now forbidden. There is therefore no market, no competition and no monopoly. There is even no absolute need for money any more (chapter 21): certainly money plays only a passive, accounting role. It follows that prices cease to matter very much. We defer the technical role of prices in a command economy to chapter 11. But we should here enumerate the less technical reasons why command planners do not even use rational shadow prices let alone rational actual prices. Two of them we know already from sec. 8: the planners only want prices to cover costs, and neglect their allocative role; and the politicians who stand above the planners resent 'merely technical' restraints on their freedom of personal choice. But above and beyond this is the coincidence (if that is what it is) that command economies have always hitherto been set up and managed by dogmatic Marxists, that is, by believers in the labour theory of value. This theory is completely incompatible with rational resource allocation, or with the use of prices to that end.[21]

Nevertheless in a purely practical way Soviet planners do use prices to reinforce their commands. In retail trade, where money is active, this is obvious, and the celebrated low meat prices are merely an exception. But also in inter-enterprise transactions goods and services that the planners wish to push are subsidized, even though a simple command to buy them would be enough: machinery in general, canal freights. There have, too, been 'agricultural subsidies' long before the recent 'food subsidies' on meat; i.e. state farms have long been subsidized (chapter 6). This illustrates the first rule of plan implementation: use all the weapons you have, you'll probably fail anyway. These plans, however, the implementation of which is helped by pricing, are not rational.

10. In the command system *it is not very important that the plan be optimal, but it must be very detailed and coherent*, and so here alone coherence becomes an ex ante problem; whereas in the most regulated of

markets there are no precise output targets and it is always possible for decentralized agents to adjust outputs and output prices to changed inputs ex post.

We now trace the painful discovery of all this back to its sources as we did for French planning in sec. 4. We saw there that the first people to elaborate a moneyless, egalitarian, command economy were the Babouvistes.[22] They had much of interest to say about the exchange of detailed goods, regional equality, distribution according to need, reform of criminals by forced labour, etc. In all this the list of anticipations of Marx is astonishingly long and detailed. They also took the essential step of transferring to the economic sphere Rousseau's General Will. We discuss this more generally in chapter 17, sec. 5, and need here only point out what a help this self-contradictory concept is to the detailed planner. For his plan is bound to be very incoherent and arbitrary, and so it requires metaphysical prestige to get people to obey it. Rousseau's rhetoric is ideally suited to this end: the planner interprets what the people 'really' want. It is not too much to say that without this self-protective rhetoric there could be no Soviet-type plan.

After their suppression the ideas of the Babouvistes seem to have gone underground until the young Marx. He added much to Babouvism, in particular historical inevitability, class-war and a suitably confusing Hegelian definition of human freedom. But he in no way elaborated on the idea of the moneyless command economy, not even after, as an older man, he had become acquainted with industry and formulated the labour theory of value and the law of concentration of capital; this latter should of course have helped him to a notion of detailed central direction. His many references to the ultimate form of socialism show no advance whatever in understanding of the functions of the market, or of the stupendous task facing the detailed planner, over Babeuf. And this despite evidence of a good deal of practical thinking on other aspects of socialism.[23] Marx used the word 'plan' very rarely indeed.[24]

Probably Engels was the first person to face the problem, at least obliquely (in 1878). For his genius was not merely inferior to, but also more modern and technical than, that of Marx. Here are his words:[25]

> It will still be necessary for society to know how much labour each article of *consumption* requires for its production. It will have to arrange its plan of production in accordance with its means of production, which include, in particular, its labour forces. The *useful* effects of the various articles of consumption, *compared with each other* and with the quantity of labour required for their production, will in the last analysis determine the plan. People will be able to manage everything very simply, without the intervention of the famous 'value'.

1878 is after the Marginalist Revolution, with which he became familiar though probably only later.[26] Though he verbally condemned it root and branch, we can detect in the above passage echoes of both marginal utility and opportunity cost. There is even the root of the idea of planners' shadow prices. But the complexity of detailed planning is still directly denied, and the word 'consumption' implies that there are no investment goods or semi-fabricates. Coherence, in other words, is still not recognized as a separate problem from optimality.

Engels deserves full credit, but his passage is desperately brief and quite wrong. Also it had no effect on subsequent Marxist thinking. Non-Marxists seem to have contributed nothing either, until the great debate of the early 1900s. In reply to N. G. Pierson's[27] challenge, Karl Kautsky[28] gives four pages to the problem. He concedes the Walrasian notions of general equilibrium and opportunity cost, and that the market solves these problems. He even says there must be a national plan to allow for opportunity cost under socialism. Pierson had nothing on planning, so perhaps Kautsky's reference is the first serious one. Barone (in Hayek, op. cit.) elaborated the idea, and said the complexities were insoluble.

But still the idea did not catch on. It is astounding what a number of responsible sources make no reference to a detailed national plan until very recent date.[29] It is certain that no Russian Communist took power with the least knowledge of this problem, and that 'War' Communism (1918–21) was a period of planless command, as described in sec. 1. Towards the end, however, the coherence problem was rather fully understood by the then chief planner, L. Kritsman.[30] His little work is about the necessity of consolidating and co-ordinating the plans of separate departments. Problems which we would range under optimality have second place in his mind, and it is from this moment that the far more tractable problem of coherence dominates the practical planner's concern. After all Marxism is compatible with coherence (which is only common sense) but not with optimality (which is economics).

The N.E.P. intervened, and the rest of the story is 'post-historical'. It is implicit in our more technical chapter 11, esp. sec. 8; and in our passages on passive money and *khozraschet* (chapter 12, sec. 15).

11. As to the modern *hierarchy of command*, the centre of authority is the Council of Ministers, behind which stands the Politburo. The Gosplan, whose chairman has the rank of a senior minister, is in origin an inter-ministerial committee, but in fact a specialized super-ministry whose co-ordinating function makes it the master, on a technical level, of all the producing ministries.

Beneath the Gosplan the intermediate authorities run as follows:

ministries: these are located in the capital city but quite distinct from the central planning office. An increase in their powers vis-à-vis that office is, therefore, decentralization. Decentralization does not, in this book, have any geographical meaning. The ministry nearly always deals with a product category, like ferrous metallurgy. There might be about 25 such ministries, including agriculture, transport, trade and construction.

bureaux of ministries: are still located in the ministry building, but in large organizations the internal communication problem is very serious, and the bureaux are very difficult to co-ordinate. A bureau in the ministry of ferrous metallurgy might deal with steel pipes.

local political authorities: towns and villages administer in the normal way housing, drainage, local transport, etc. They also administer very 'light' industry using local raw materials (e.g. clothes-pegs). These authorities have no central ministry. But from time to time they have also been used by the Ministry of Agriculture as its link with the kolkhozy.[31]

territorial substitute ministries: these are Khrushchev's celebrated Sovnarkhozy (1957–64), a 'hare-brained scheme' whereby he replaced the 21 ministries in charge of industry and construction by 100 territorial authorities, corresponding to the province boundaries. Each Sovnarkhoz administered whatever industrial or construction enterprises were on its territory, and enjoyed the full powers of a ministry, reporting to Gosplan.[32]

specialist state committees: these give advice on such issues as technology or wages. Nominally they are like 'staff' in a vast 'line and staff' organization of which ministries or Sovnarkhozy are 'line'. Precisely such issues are similarly treated by 'staff' bodies, that can only advise, in capitalist corporations (cf. chapter 11, sec. 9).

provincial and republican political authorities: these cannot be denied, considering the party backing that they have, and the existence of national minorities, considerable power to interfere, especially in matters of location. In a sense therefore, these bodies too are 'staff'. But in locally managed industry (above) they also perform 'line functions'.

Below all these bodies come the trust or association of enterprises, and the enterprise itself. Since it is all part of one vast state machine, and not ideologically different from a ministry (chapter 3), it is not nominally the object, but merely the most junior subject, of planning. When in default of other authorities it plans its own production or distributes[33] its own product it does so in the name of the socialist state, and so in theory not for the manager's benefit.

But in fact such confidence should not be, and seldom is, placed in the enterprise. The organ immediately above it has great powers, such as those of arbitrary and unquestionable profit 'taxation', i.e. of cross-subsidizing from the stronger to the weaker units beneath it – all quite apart from formal taxation by the Ministry of Finance. Whether called trust or association this organ is located outside the capital city, but the trust is a lower level of government while the association is nominally a voluntary union of enterprises. In periods of liberalism and apparent decentralization, when the 'enterprise' is taken seriously, associations are often formed, and informally statified, in order to brake the change. The most astonishing case is the Bulgarian reform since 1965, in which very free sounding arrangements for both finance and output are cancelled by the formation of vast 'complexes', less than 20 of which divide the whole small economy, including collective agriculture, between them. These massive units, based on both vertical and horizontal integration, have such power over enterprises as virtually to be enterprises (cf. chapter 10, sec. 6, chapter 11, sec. 18).

Thus probably the main reason why enterprise size is so flexible and on the whole so big is that size and number must be administratively convenient. We are a world away from stock exchange take-over bids, complaints about conglomerates, etc. Under capitalism the size of the enterprise is judged by the conflicting criteria of monopoly power and economies of scale. But since average cost curves are L-shaped (chapter 1, sec. 5), we should be *indifferent* to enterprise sizes above the minimum. The factor of plannability is probably decisive: certainly so in the collectivization of agriculture, which under the technical and psychological conditions of its introduction leads to severe diseconomies. In this case plannability means ease of procurement, and is all in all.[34] In industry plannability means the ease with which price controls (Hungary) and output targets (STEs) can be enforced. Both cases indicate very large enterprises. Costs are irrelevant.

12. Officially the command plan begins with output suggestions at enterprise level. These flow upwards, being aggregated all the way, until they reach the Gosplan, where the input-output interconnexions are preliminarily solved at a very aggregated level indeed, and counter-suggestions as to outputs are sent down. When these finally reach the enterprise, suitably disaggregated, it sends back up a detailed estimate of the inputs it will require. On these estimates the Gosplan bases its final plan, which redescends in the form of detailed orders that are supposed to be coherent. Optimality is under these conditions a separate goal, not on the whole attempted (cf. chapter 11).

But coherence itself is very difficult, and the habitual failure to reach it, coupled with the optimism and ambition natural to Communists, leads to *planner's tension*, the setting of output minima too high for the planned input maxima. We deal with this at length in chapter 11, sec. 14, except for one aspect, which falls to be discussed here: is tension a way to get results, or a hindrance? Tension is often openly attacked by reformers, who point to the incompetence that gave rise to it, and the absurdity of expecting people to make bricks without straw. It cannot be so frankly defended by the insiders who are responsible for it, since it appears to be an imperfection, and there are no imperfections, no shades of grey, in the Workers' Paradise. But the virtues of tension might well outweigh its faults.

Consider a simple parallel. When the writer was an officer cadet he had a disagreeable sergeant, no less on the make in his sphere of life than the writer in his. The platoon was slow in turning out of its barracks one morning. Our sergeant sent us back in, and said, 'Now when I say fall in again I want to see yer fly through them winders and doors.' We did not fly, for that was technically impossible, and we did not use the windows, for that would in fact have delayed us, but we came out through the doors more quickly. That is planner's tension: demand the impossible, and people give you the maximum. The very slightest acquaintance with Soviet economic literature, particularly at the grass-roots level of the local press, shows the Politburo to be my disagreeable sergeant writ large. The reason why Communist revisionists dislike tension is that they are rational men, who would belong to the Western left-liberal Establishment if they could. So they assume other people are rational, and propose rational plans and rational stimuli for them.

Of course they are not completely wrong. Had the sergeant used that phrase again, or had he actually insisted on our using the windows, he would have lost authority. The advantage of tension is psychological, and profoundly unBenthamite, in the sense of chapter 2. It has nevertheless an optimal level that many, perhaps most, STEs usually surpass. In so doing they encourage directors to hoard raw materials and skilled labour, to under-report capacity, to over-report[35] output, to lower quality and to resist all technical innovation as introducing too many uncertainties (chapter 15). In Soviet-type terms, to demand an output of 101 when only 100 is possible is to get 100; but if you screw the target up to 105 you get only 99 and a lot of lies. But a target of 100, or total decentralized reliance on profit, would both have elicited 99 without the lies. For of course there is nothing like planner's tension in a market. Not even the imbalances recommended for UDCs by Hirschman (chapter 15, sec. 15) constitute tension: they are simply bottlenecks offering a large profit to those who open them.

Occasionally tension is increased from below. This is when an STE goes through a 'Great Leap Forward' (chapter 10, sec. 11). The middle-rank Party and other cadres, caught up in the national hysteria, outbid the demands made on their enterprises from above, and produce 'counter-plans' (*vstrechniye plany*) that exceed the Gosplan's final proposals. But the Great Leap Forward syndrome is for obvious reasons barely compatible with the centralized and hierarchical STE, and more suited to Chinese conditions. The enterprises's ordinary reaction to tension is to cheat and lie in a downward direction, as we saw.

In practice, even in periods of the severest centralization, the enterprise retains a good deal of freedom. Basically, when the planner's appetite for detail fails, the enterprise is *forced to make a contract* (kontraktatsia) with a named supplier or customer,[36] covering much of the remaining detail.

Once signed, the contract has as much force of law as the plan, so that command in some sense has reached down to the least nail.

But just as two STEs engage in an essentially market process (bilateral monopoly) when they work out their foreign trade protocol, so are their individual enterprises bilateral monopolists, albeit within the constraints of their respective enterprise plans, when they work out their micro-contract. The amount of constrained bilateral monopoly is very great indeed. In some cases, too, discretion is very wide, for instance when local light industry, under the command of a local Soviet, contracts to supply clothes-pegs to a shop. For the shop manager wishes to maximize sales in order to get his bonus, which means satisfying consumer demand itself. We are very close here to a free market (Wiles 1962, pp. 171–5).

13. So much for the command economy. Next, all governments buy things for their own use. To produce, as we have seen, is more complicated than to buy, and comes under the general heading of socialism. Most government sales, therefore, have been dealt with by implication under other headings. But the mere resale of what is bought, without further processing, falls to be discussed here along with purchase for own use. Our name for all these activities will be, by extension from the financial special case, the *open-market operation.* We include beside bills and bonds: civil servants' labour, military labour, crops, armaments, new and old buildings, etc., etc. A government that spends only a small part of the national expenditure can make no use of this fact for planning purposes. A thoughtless or disorganized government may be spending a large part, and having large effects unconsciously. The power to create employment generally through the multiplier we neglect as irrelevant to detailed planning: our interest is in the developmental, protectionist and reallocative effects of government spending.

Yet important as the matter is, it is obvious that we can pass it over with a few descriptive instances. The government can locate its military bases (buy land, buildings and civilian auxiliary labour) in backward areas. It can prefer people from those areas for jobs in the civil service or forces. It can establish new industries by refusing to buy its supplies from abroad. It can establish new technology by the local procurement of advanced goods. It can hold back wages (a little!) by refusing wage-claims and defeating strikes in the public sector. It can subsidize agriculture by constituting itself the legal monopsonist of this or that crop, and reselling at a loss. And, of course, it can throw its weight about in the bond and bill markets, where as the major participant it has in any case price leadership. This circumstance is one of the pillars of Keynesian economics.

14. Our first eight means of detailed plan implementation have been fairly simple to distinguish. Our last is very blurred: *price control*, agricultural and weapons *procurement*, etc. Licensing, taxes, subsidies, qualitative

bank controls and fiscal contracts leave the profit motive intact. An open market operation is a straightforward free transaction. The Monnet-type 'confidence trick' is also clear, in that it is intellectual, not moral, persuasion: it informs us where our profits lie. On the other hand commands go with plan-fulfilment bonuses and legal penalties, which are very 'Benthamite'. But what are we to make of governments that keep the prices of some things only below equilibrium and yet expect independent enterprises to supply as much of them as ever, while other things' prices continue to mount? And what are we to make of enterprises that respond accordingly? To what precise incentives do kolkhozy respond, once they have settled their compulsory deliveries?

If they did not respond, the long history of this activity would be much shorter: even governments are not mad enough to engage constantly in an act demonstrably fruitless in the short run. This section, then, concerns the mixture of threats, rewards and moral, rather than intellectual, persuasion. We take procurement (*zagotovka*, *Beschaffung*) first, as being concerned with quantities more than prices, so in line with the rest of this chapter. We define it as purchase by the government at a price below equilibrium of a quantity greater than what it is most profitable in the short run to supply at that price. It is a weasel word, skulking on the boundary between 'purchase' and 'confiscation'.

By this definition most things in a reformed STE are procured. What has happened is that legal threats and output-plan-fulfilment bonuses have been supplemented by a price, i.e. by a profit, incentive. Even the most passive inter-enterprise prices were often used by the classical STE to back up its output orders. For no price was ever totally passive: a higher price meant, even under Stalin, more profit and so a larger enterprise welfare fund, less trouble with the bank, etc. But in the reformed STE, and at all times when a Communist government is dealing with collective farms or peasants, price incentive and output command have about equal weight. The reason for this is also quite simple. In the new slightly decentralized system for socialist enterprises the number of output and (above all) input commands has been reduced and managerial incentive has been shifted from plan-fulfilment bonus out of wage-fund to bonus from profit. In the kolkhoz case all income, including the chairman's, depends, via the labour-day, on value added, while only basic quantities of basic outputs are commanded, and even among them substitution is possible. Even Stalin felt bound to raise the procurement price of cotton in the early 'thirties, since there was no sale for it in the kolkhoz market, so that the Central Asian farms producing it had no way of profiting from inflation and no such price incentive for marginal production as there was for grain growers. Indeed with a fixed procurement price, as for grain, they would probably have died.

Slightly more surprising is non-Communist procurement. This is an obscure mixture of threats and cajolery which mostly succeeds in time of war. But we see in chapter 10 the margin of tolerance or uncertainty as to costs and revenues in markets, which leaves the fixing of a price as something subject to error and calculations of probability. Non-Communist procurement, then, also stresses the *possibility* that prices at the lower end of the margin will do. By cajolery, then, the government appeals to patriotism, and makes out the loss of profit to be smaller than it is. Its threats, on the other hand, are to exploit its monopsony power, and to resort to Soviet-type measures of confiscation and command, and above all to re-examine the firm's tax returns, licences and general 'legal health', if persuasion will not suffice. This is what differentiates 'procurement' from 'French planning' and 'open-market operations'. Nearly all wartime procurement of armaments has these attributes, and so did Finland's post-war procurement of reparations.[37] Most agricultural purchasing corporations operate quite freely on the market, but Robespierre was certainly guilty of 'procurement' vis-à-vis his peasantry.[38] Although he was no socialist he is much admired by modern Communists!

Now procurement aims either to implement some physical plan, and so is adjunct to a command economy, or to stabilize prices. In peacetime the government of a market economy is only interested in price stabilization. Moreover we are not interested here in a pure demand inflation, since its cure is to be sought in monetary and fiscal policy, and price controls simply create black markets. In a cost inflation, however, the government often freezes prices, or rather all wages, prices and dividends together. The hope is not to interfere with relative outputs or employments at all, but to break the vicious spiral. It seems, to the disgraceful surprise of many economists, that this procedure can be successful for a time in its pure form (chapter 14, sec. 4). This then is at first blush something we hardly wish to define as detailed planning but only as price control. However, invariably only some prices and wages are fixed – e.g. agricultural prices but no others are subsidized in a slump, or industrial prices but no others, or public sector wages but no others, are frozen in a boom. So the government must eventually counter the undesirable effects on resource allocation and relative incomes by procedures akin to procurement, or even licensing and outright command. It may succeed even in this, because cost inflation is so very unpleasant for all concerned: the people await a lead.

France also uses fiscal agreements to enforce price controls.

15. Our whole previous discussion has made planning seem in one way too difficult and in another too easy.

On the one hand *small countries* have 'French planning' anyway. It is said that when Mr. Raoul Wallenberg consults the Swedish cabinet, one half of the economy is represented round the table. Any decision they take can be interpreted as a 'democratic input–output table' or the 'concertation of expectations'. Hence, *ceteris paribus*, the stronger smell of corruption in small countries, where everyone knows everyone else. The leader of the opposition is the Prime Minister's nephew because there is no one else to lead the opposition; so naturally the principal private banker is married to the former wife of the chief of the planning commission, because there is no one else to marry. Large enterprises own large segments of the country, because otherwise they would not be large enterprises. Each cocktail party is a conspiracy. Most of this can and should be translated into Communist terms: cf. our reference to Bulgaria in sec. 11. But the smallness of the country hardly helps us to move from 'rather detailed' to 'very detailed', since the number of things produced, and the number of their interconnections, remain astronomical. Thus there are 2 million prices in Hungary, in much the same sense that there are 15 million in USSR. This is still far too many for a rational command economy, as Hungarians know. It is 'French planning' that is assisted by small size.

And yet the assistance is not all that great, because foreign trade both is a larger proportion of the national income of small countries[39] and accounts for a greater number of particular things. Reasons of space have compelled us to avoid foreign trade in this book. But we must pause here to distinguish its role in market from command economies. The market economy is open to every wind that blows. It matters little what Mr. Wallenberg and the Swedish cabinet decided: Sweden trades a third of her national income abroad, and the forces that settle world prices and outputs were not present at the meeting, though they penetrate deeply inside the economy. Only behind substantial protective barriers have such planning decisions much meaning. The STE on the other hand, however small, is protected against this: movements in world markets can only affect its terms of trade, not its domestic prices or outputs, let alone its domestic financial conditions. If it kept its barriers against foreign influences but decentralized internally it would be in a stronger position to practise 'French planning' than France. It will be remembered that the Common Market has almost destroyed France's own ability to do so.

Yet in another way we have made too light of the difficulties of coordinating the few. How does the planner *co-ordinate the separate departments of his own government*? The government even of a small country is large. Its departments are run by jealous senior bureaucrats who feel very competitive towards each other, and by forceful politicians, each out to make his mark in a brief period. Each time we say 'the government' the practical planner winces. For Monnet this was vital: departments were like industrial associations, they were independent powers, to be coordinated with each other and the private sector in the Planning Commission, which was to stand above or at least beside the government. And this applied whether the departments were producing or merely purchasing, taxing and supervising.

Certain it is that a government of adequately co-ordinated departments has immense power over a market economy, and that such co-ordination is a life-time's respectable work for any man. The Mexicans since Cárdenas (1934–40), always modest and realistic, have attached their planning office to the office of the President, and ask of it no more than that that it should do just this.[40] The first Six-Year Plan (1934) was no more than a collection of public sector targets and projects. In a Pickwickian sense, this is also all that the Gosplan does: it too has far looser relations with the private and co-operative sectors; in its origins at least it was an inter-departmental co-ordinator of Mexican type. Its purview was narrower and its status lower than Monnet's Commission.

16. Has the choice of implementation mechanism any stable relation to the level of development? We also assume that institutions, and especially planning institutions, have some simple causal effect on the rate of growth, and to some extent they do (chapter 16). But what of the older, more Marxist, attempt to trace from the level of development as a cause effects on other social arrangements, including the planning system as superstructure? This, it seems, must fail altogether. Planning systems spread by cultural imitation (Latin America) and military conquest (Eastern Europe), almost wholly irrespective of levels of development.

The historical roots of Latin American planning go back to Cárdenas in Mexico (sec. 15 here), but the French example of including private industry was only imitated in the 1960s. We have not space here to trace this story. Enough that this loose type of plan implementation is (1) compatible with parliamentary democracy and of course dictatorship. It is also (2) indifferent between capitalism and non-Communist forms of socialism. It is installed in every single Latin American country, of (3) whatever level of development, from the richest to the poorest. In all three polarities the continent shows the greatest variety. We need only mention the virtually unbroken dictatorship of Argentina (GNP per head $839 in 1965), the clean democratic record of Costa Rica ($415), the Marxist but not Communist socialism of Chile and the aggressive state capitalism of Brazil. There seems to be no systematic relation between any of these polarities,[41] and they all use the same planning system: with the very partial exception of Mexico, mentioned above.

This system is corrupt – more corrupt than the particular form of *laissez-faire* capitalism it has replaced. Though it is more strongly interested in development, its follies have been so great as in certain cases (Argentina, Uruguay) to have actually retarded it; but in general its effect has been positive, even perhaps on equality. However, its success has not been obvious enough to impose it as the only rational form of organization, a novelty with irresistible utilitarian appeal like, say, central banking. No Latin American country has a Messianic urge to export its social system (except Cuba, which is Communist and so irrelevant). Though each subsidizes sympathetic plotters in its neighbours, none is in military occupation of another. So the system has spread without the force of arms or of successful example. It is a case of cultural diffusion among a culturally united but otherwise divided people. The degree of development, and for that matter the strength[42] of the government, tell us how efficiently the planning mechanism works; but that is all.

As to Soviet-type plan implementation, it has spread almost exclusively by force of arms. In fact Cuba is the only country where a non-Communist government (that of Castro during 1959) adopted this system voluntarily, though with many exceptions. In Yugoslavia, China and North Vietnam Communist Parties of strictly Soviet type originally seized power, but without much Soviet help. They have all eventually ceased to be STEs.[43] It is thus obvious that the level of development has little to do with being an STE. Albania, after all, had an average income of *c.* \$300 in 1965, the DDR of *c.* \$1600.

One generalization only we shall permit ourselves: Soviet-type planning is very sophisticated and expensive to administer, so that a country can be too poor for it, and also too big. The great example is China, which on one third of Albania's productivity and 350 times her population felt compelled to abandon the Soviet model after one five-year period, 1953–7. Even during that period the model was a mere preference, with such unSoviet phenomena as a free market in machine-tools, including some of those produced by the socialist sector.[44] We have lamentably little notion of the relative administrative costs of an STE and a market, but:

(i) Communists like to conceal their administrative costs in their statistics, except when they criticize bureaucratic excesses for internal purposes. This they do in a purely literary way, though the self-critical stories they tell are quite scarifying,[45] albeit purely literary, or based on incomparable statistics;

(ii) censuses of occupations are in no country designed so as to reveal the number of people working in marketing or in planning;

(iii) quite particularly, an enterprise must have bureaucrats and clerks whose function (or part of it) is to watch the market or to answer letters from planners. We cannot estimate their respective numbers;

(iv) perfect competition has high administrative costs: brokers, a downtown site for the building, telecommunications, arbitrators, etc. Imperfect competition generates advertising[46] and salesmen.

From this emerges the mere opinion that the STE is indeed more expensive than a market, and that the Chinese were right to abandon it as a luxury in favour of their quasi-market (chapter 10). Scarce Chinese brainpower can be far better used, e.g. in direct management. In particular detailed central planners must be experts in the particular technology they plan, and must keep, if they are to live up to their name, people at enterprises fully employed answering letters and telephone calls. Now these people must also be experts in that technology; so who is left to direct the operations on the shop floor? The notion that the system makes possible a concentration and economy of experts is the opposite of the truth. Of course to the non-Communist the STE has a further disadvantage, that the particular results it delivers are not those he seeks. For he puts a heavy – surely an altogether too heavy – weight on optimality, consumers' sovereignty, wide choice, a smooth flow of supplies: all things an STE is very bad at. We have to give these objectives the low weight a Communist would give them in order to admit an STE at any level of development.

At the other extreme from China is the Czechoslovak opinion that the cost of an STE increases, or the possibility of its efficient operation decreases, with high levels of development, until it again becomes undesirable. This is because product differentiation and sub-contracting grow more rapidly than administrative capacity. The doctrine stumbles on the success of the DDR – and indeed of Czechoslovakia since 1968.

Notes

1. In his *Business for Pleasure*, London 1950, chapter 3.

2. This military phrase is an important concept in the field of planning. A direct order might be 'left turn' or 'fire'. An operation order might be 'Capture Hill 60, unless casualties seem to you likely to exceed 20 per cent; you have 403 medium artillery battery under command.' A pre-1965 Soviet *tekhpromfinplan* is a direct order; a modern one is an operation order.

3. Or, surely, only not yet. Cf. chapter 11, sec. 6.

4. I quote from Wiles 1962, p. 74; as revised for the Italian and Japanese translations.

5. HMSO Cmd. 7046 & 7344 are quoted; my italics.

6. In the broader sense of sec. 13: all government purchases and sales, including those of labour and materials, are meant. For the status of *price control*, which lies between regulation and command, also see sec. 8.

7. 1619–83. Cf. Charles W. Cole, *Colbert*, N.Y. 1939.

8. Cf. J. Holland Rose in ed. Frederick A. Kirkpatrick, *Lectures on the History of the Nineteenth Century*, Cambridge 1902.

9. The conspiracy was scotched by the Directoire in 1794. Cf. sec. 10.

10. This is the *pantouflage* of chapter 18.

11. Claude Henri de Rouvroy, Comte de St. Simon, 1760–1825. Cf. Georges Weill, *St. Simon et son Oeuvre*, Paris 1894; Henri Louvancour, *De St. Simon à Fourier*, Chartres 1913; ed. C. Bouglé and Elie Halévy, *La Doctrine St. Simonienne*, Paris 1924; Alvin W. Gouldner in (ed.) Robert K. Merton *et al.*, *Sociology Today*, N.Y. 1959.

12. In an earlier version to the engineers: cf. *l'Organisateur*, 1819. The bankers, not mentioned in this text, have taken over by 1821, in *Le Système Industriel.* This change is in retrospect absolutely crucial for the future development of France. Cf. Bouglé and Halévy, op. cit., footnote 154; chapter 12 here, sec. 5.

13. Napoleon III made many St. Simonian noises. He supported state banking, but was a free trader. St. Simon would not have approved hostility to trade unions. Had these been a serious problem in his time he would undoubtedly have sympathetically opposed their actual development, and supported all-class corporatist unions on the Soviet or Fascist model.

14. Such consultation, or loose planning, had the support of both the trade unions and the Fascists. Cf. Shepard B. Clough, *France*, N.Y. 1964, chapter 9.

15. In his *$2500 A Year; from Scarcity to Abundance*, N.Y. 1936.

16. The fiscal agreement is most culpably neglected in the literature. We owe our knowledge of it to suspicious French lawyers like Gerard Tournier, *Les Agréments Fiscaux*, Publications de l'Institut d'Etudes Politiques de Toulouse, Paris (Pedone) 1970; Jacques Graindorge and Jean Lanchon in *Analyse et Prévision* 5/1968. The most astonishing case known to me is that of the butchers who co-operated with the meat-price control in 1963: they, but not other butchers, were allowed to advertise on TV. The atmosphere is graphically described by Andrew Schonfield in his *Modern Capitalism*, London 1965.

17. Quantitative controls are Keynesian, and so irrelevant.

18. The citizen of course cannot sue the planner for action *ultra vires*.

19. The Central Committee of the Communist Party, with 100–300 members, could conceivably be a serious parliament. But it sits far too rarely to play that role: say twelve days a year. It discusses the Five- but hardly the One-Year Plan.

20. Cf. chapter 2. It will be recalled that the command economy can operate on the ordinary motivation of direct material individual advantage, through the plan-fulfilment bonus – except in Albania, China and Cuba this is what it does.

21. Cf. Wiles 1962, chapter 3.

22. Georges Thibout, *La Doctrine Babouviste*, Paris 1903, chapter 4; Philippe Buonarroti, *Conspiration pour l'Egalité dite de Babeuf*, Brussels 1828. Buonarroti was himself a Babouviste and his book is our principal source. Note its title, which shows what was really on the conspirators' minds.

23. Notably in his *Critique of the Gotha Programme*, 1875. For the many other references to socialism, and the falsity of the claim that Marx left no socialist blueprint, cf. Wiles 1962, chapter 17.

24. Perhaps only in *Capital*, vol. 1, chapter 1, sec. 4.

25. In *Anti-Dühring*, III/4. My italics. His claim that he had said it all before is a great exaggeration. This work is in *Deutsch-Französische Jahrbücher*, 1844 in the Marx-Engels *Gesamtausgabe*, 1930. Abteilung I, Band 2. Cf. pp. 387, 395.

26. Compare his letters to Danielson, 5 January and 15 October 1888; Sorge, 8 February 1890; Conrad Schmidt, 12 September 1892; Kautsky, 29 September 1892.

27. In ed. F. A. Hayek, *Collectivist Economic Planning*, London 1935. This collection gives the capitalist side of the debate.

28. *The Social Revolution*, 1902, Part II. I have used pp. 130–3 of the Chicago edition, 1903.

29. Here is a catholic but haphazard list of those who have omitted both the word and the concept: Palgrave's *Dictionary of Political Economy*, 1913 and 1926 edns; Otto Neurath in his pathbreaking article on the imminent abolition of money by state capitalism, 'Kriegswirtschaft und Naturalwirtschaft', in *Weltwirtschaftliches Archiv*, 1916; Lenin, *State and Revolution*, 1917; Sidney and Beatrice Webb, *Constitution for a Co-operative Commonwealth*, London 1920 (this was one of the founding documents of the Labour Party; it has long

passages on government control, nationalization and pricing); Angelo S. Rappoport, *Dictionary of Socialism*, London 1924; G. B. Shaw, *Intelligent Woman's Guide to Socialism and Capitalism*, London 1928; *Encyclopedia of the Social Sciences*, vol. PAR–PUN, 1934 edn.

30. In his *Ob Yedinom Khozyaistvennom Plane* (on a single economic plan), Moscow 1920. But he was anticipated in 1919 by the Otto Neurath of the previous footnote, who in March became President of the Central Planning Office of the brief Bavarian Soviet, and took exactly Kritsman's line, using of course the word 'plan'. Cf. O. Neurath, *Empiricism and Sociology*, Dordrecht-Boston 1973, pp. 145–8, 264.

31. Not the sovkhozy. As full members of the socialist sector these have ordinarily come under a Ministry of Sovkhozy.

32. Details in Wiles 1962, chapter 8.

33. This is particularly common; cf. Wiles 1962, pp. 172–6.

34. Though neither are as good as capitalist farms, large kolkhozy are more efficient than small ones: chapter 5.

35. With certain qualifications: cf. chapter 11, sec. 14. On tension in general cf. Holland Hunter in *Economic Development and Cultural Change*, July 1961. On the lack of tension in Romania cf. David Granick in *Soviet Studies*, April 1974.

36. And with the trade union local. This binds the union to help fulfil the plan, and the manager to take such and such welfare measures. The forced contract is a curiosum among Western lawyers, accustomed to liberty of contract between sovereign parties. Cf. Dietrich Loeber, *Der Hoheitlich Gestaltete Vertrag*, Tubingen 1969.

37. Cf. Wiles 1969, pp. 541–2.

38. In conjunction with demand inflation and a price and wage freeze. Cf. Henri Sée, *Histoire Economique de la France*, Paris 1951, vol. II, chapters 1–3.

39. Cf. Wiles 1969, pp. 437–53. This law holds with rich and poor countries alike: one simply defines size as population.

40. Robert J. Shafer, *Mexico: Mutual Adjustment Planning*, Syracuse 1966, pp. 45, 51–60, 66, 78, 121. There has also been co-ordination of public investment by the central bank and/or the state investment bank. On the other hand Venezuela, perhaps the next most successful Latin American planner, moved quite rapidly from co-ordinating government departments (1959) on to a 'French' dialogue with private business (*c.* 1964). In both countries the French example is of course well known.

41. A correlation is presented in chapter 17, sec. 20.

42. Some democracies are strong; some dictatorships are weak.

43. Albania, which remains essentially an STE, went Communist under Yugoslav military occupation during Yugoslavia's brief Soviet-type period. Revolting against Yugoslavia during the Tito-Stalin split, Albania chose Stalin and so naturally remained an STE. She has even continued essentially an STE while being China's ally.

44. Wiles 1962, pp. 173–5, 182–3, 186–8; Audrey Donnithorne, *China's Economic System*, London 1967, *passim*, esp. chapter 17.

45. E.g. for Soviet sovkhozy Lazar Volin, *A Century of Russian Agriculture*, Harvard 1970, pp. 533–4; for industry Leon Smolinski and Peter Wiles in *Problems of Communism*, November–December 1963.

46. About 2·5 per cent of the national income in ACEs is spent on advertising and about half of this is on small ads, playbills and other purely informative

announcements. In USSR the corresponding figure is 0·01 per cent, excluding political propaganda. (Marshall Goldman in *Survey*, July 1965, p. 148). In Hungary expenditure is well over 1000 mn. forints (*The Times*, 8 May 1973), or about 0·5 per cent.

10

Short-Run Optimality in Various Market Systems

1. Some corollaries to orthodoxy; the unimportance of the subject
2. Market forms classified by the nature of the product
3. Measuring sub-optimality
4. Statistical concentration is not monopoly; and administered prices are a third thing
5. Which pricing procedure is most optimal?
6. Capitalist monopoly controls
7. General price controls
8. Public enterprises in ACEs: 'many maximands'
9. Public enterprises in other systems
10. Pannonia, Hungary, NEP
11. China, Great Leaps Forward
12. Illyria
13. The elasticity of co-operative supply
14. Yugoslavia
15. The opportunity cost of an e.b.f.
16. Feudalism
17. The traditional village community
18. The dual economy

10

1. We adopted in chapter 1 a very dogmatic and extremist position on optimal resource allocation: the principles of Western welfare economics are quite universal, and entirely system-free; marginal cost has to equal equilibrium price, whether on a market or in a computer, and there's an end to it. We also warned against the typical Western fetishization of optimality. We devote to it merely two out of twenty-one chapters. Since, moreover, this subject is so extremely well known among economists, we shall abstain from any opening exposition, but note a few disjointed corollaries to the orthodox doctrine which are not so well known.

We discuss in chapter 8, sec 1, the importance of workers', as well as consumers', sovereignty. Allocation is not optimal unless workers have the jobs they most desire, or at any rate least dislike, within the given context of techniques, consumer demand and their own skills. In nearly all institutions discussed here this is at least as easily possible as it is for consumers to exercise their sovereignty. We draw attention to the exceptions.

Optimality is defined, as usual, as without relation to the distribution of income. Strictly this is impossible, since all changes in the relative prices of final outputs change the relative real purchasing power of people's incomes, and all changes in relative factor incomes change people's incomes. This is especially important under capitalism and in Yugoslavia, where changes in output prices are so directly reflected in factor income. For self-managers take most of the quasi-rents generated by the market (chapter 16, sec. 22), and rather more interest or virtual interest than is generated by an STE, since ploughback plays a larger part, and budgetary grants and bank loans a smaller part. Hence there is more virtual interest on ploughback, and most of this accrues to individuals. But even in an STE production changes generate changes in wages and in quasi-rents. And these latter leak out through bonuses and social funds into factor-payments – not to mention the same leakage of actual rents in kolkhozy.

Our excuses for neglecting all this are these. (i) In all these societies changes in prices are but loosely connected with changes in relative wages, and these in turn only loosely (considering the social services) with changes in *relative family incomes.* Of course particular changes are by no means random. If they are serious they cannot be neglected, and optimality must indeed take second place. (ii) The social services exist to establish distributive justice. The market *cannot* do it. A perfect market is no better at all in this respect than an imperfect one (chapter 16, sec. 3). (iii) Men (and therefore their incomes) are mortal, but imperfections of competition are not: the income change should not be pursued beyond the time when inheritance takes place, but the wrong production will last, by definition, until it stops. This last argument carries with it a most severe qualification: since most imperfections are quickly brought to an end by technical progress (i.e. by new ones!) there may be little case for expending governmental energy upon them.

Optimality requires uniform, non-discriminatory treatment of all inputs and outputs, buyers and sellers. The wider, then, the area over which it stretches the better. But this does not mean that prices should be uniform. On the contrary, not to discriminate against great distance or poor quality or inconvenient timing is to discriminate. Basing points, for instance, and uniform resale price maintenance, which make the price everywhere the same, are highly monopolistic. The same applies to off-farm prices and to all 'swings and roundabouts' pricing.

Consumers' sovereignty is a larger concept than consumers' choice. The consumer can freely choose when he is free to spend his money – nothing more is required. He can walk down Gorki Street and push out his expenditures on whatever is available, at whatever foolish prices, until the marginal kopek brings in the same marginal utility all round. Indeed he very probably does. He is sovereign only when the producer reacts by changing the quantities produced. The STE seldom does that, but then sometimes capitalist monopolies do not do it either. The consumer is perfectly sovereign when the producer equates marginal cost with price (mc=p). This, of course, never happens on a universal scale, but again the STE is further away from it.

Externalities are very important, and should be allowed for in each separate decision. But they in no way affect the general principles of allocation. They cannot even affect our judgement between various market and planning systems as means of implementing those principles, unless we know empirically which system masters them better.

2. In another work[1] the writer divided market forms more by the nature of the product than by the degree of monopoly, assigning to the latter a very subordinate role. The idea did not catch on,[2] but nothing since 1961 has occurred, whether in capitalist or in socialist fact or in the further outpourings of theory, to alter his opinion. No one contemplating Soviet-type price reforms, or Hungary's difficulties with the prices of vegetables and houses, or President Nixon's or Mr. Heath's difficulties with the prices of vegetables and houses, or the new wave of cost inflation across the capitalist world, can fail to be struck by the persistence of differences in price behaviour according to the nature of the product. Degree of monopoly and differences in maximand rank junior to them. Even the abolition of the market does not, as we see in the next chapter, obliterate them. Market forms are not bloodless legal abstractions but *separate institutions*, and the comparison of institutions is the object of this book.

Here, then, is a corrected version of my 1961 schema.

(i) *Higgles* are the primordial bilaterally-monopolistic deals out of which other markets have, historically, sprung. They survive in their *primitive* form among peasants in respect of unique articles (e.g. a horse), and in oriental bazaars. In their *advanced* form, with teams of sophisticated negotiators representing the many interests of both parties, they are still very numerous. A collective bargain is a higgle, and so is the negotiation of the annual trade protocol between two STEs; the sale by one enterprise to another, in advance, of a substantial part of its annual output; or the sale of a small business on retirement.

(ii) *Perfect competition*. Nature of product: homogeneous by nature, not art; preferably also output uncontrollable in the short run, i.e. agricultural.[3] There are enterprises, most of which must be small in relation to total output (ease of entry makes no difference in the short run, and very little in the long). Then the market congregates in one specialized place, and assigns price fixing to the higgling of specialized brokers. The procedures through which these brokers go in each transaction are a stylized version of the primitive higgle. The market is an extremely centralistic institution (chapter 11, sec. 1). Producers and users are *price-takers*. The concept of producer includes as always the seller of second-hand goods; where the good is durable these are many, and perfect competition becomes compatible with very few original producers (non-ferrous and precious metals, government securities). The market itself works out quality discounts. The producer is a *quantity-maker*: he impersonally manipulates sales in accordance with a price out of his control. In such impersonal circumstances, notably with a total absence of goodwill, he normally maximizes his short-run profits. Moreover the elasticity of demand, being infinite, is precisely known! So this is the economist's sector *par excellence*.

(iii) *Other price-takers* are all who accept the services of brokers and auctioneers, or set themselves up in that capacity for some nonce-transaction: civil engineers competing by tender, consumers disposing of houses, fur coats, antiques or whatnot, and perfect oligopolists if any. Except for the latter class, which seems to be a null class,[4] all these have a single unique product to sell: singularity is a kind of homogeneity. These people also normally maximize their short-run profits.

(iv) *Full cost*. Nature of product: heterogeneous between enterprises by reason of lengthy human processing,[5] but each batch of goods is homogeneous. Production must be in batches or longer runs, and the goods must be storable. Moreover, being manufactured (by definition), they do not flow towards a central market-*place*, but spread out geographically. Therefore there are no brokers. So heterogeneity of location and quality conspire to make each producer or retailer, in however small degree, a monopolist, who *can* maintain in the short run his price for a single article against the variations of competitors' prices. Now neither he nor his buyers like very flexible prices, for they introduce short-run uncertainty. Indeed he notes that they drive custom elsewhere, and he finds them even administratively impossible if, as is usual, his firm produces many products and uses rather subordinate people as salesmen, who are not trusted to vary prices. So the full cost producer or retailer takes advantage of his possibilities and sets prices firmly for a period. I.e. he is a *price-maker*, and his price is sticky. He may or may not price with regard only to long-run profit maximization, but he certainly does not do so with regard to the short run, since in the short run he does not price at all, but sells on demand – the good, it will be remembered, is storable.

(v) *Marginal cost.* Nature of product: heterogeneous and homogeneous as in (iv), but not storable; so must be actually produced, not merely sold, on demand. The sector therefore includes all services (except some labour, below), and transport and electricity.[6] The producer is therefore very often over- or under-loaded, with changes in marginal cost too great for him to neglect. Marginal cost is as often above as below average cost, so as long as he always charges it he will still break even.[7] Charging average cost or above in rough periods loses money and misallocates resources. So there are several prices, depending on the current level of marginal cost. Each of these prices is stabilized so far as possible, as in (iv). Very often, misguidedly, enterprises or planners settle a single price, exactly as in (iv), on the 'swings and roundabouts' principle.

(vi) *Cost-plus.* Nature of product: unique, goods or services. Instead of competing by tender the producer accepts the offer of a predefined profit plus whatever it turns out to cost him. Examples: buildings, repair jobs, research jobs. This is the only category in which the price is not decided at the moment of contract. Note too that where there is competition the procedure of (iii) is preferred.

(vii) *Wages* are almost always an administered price, but one administered by the buyer. Where there is collective bargaining the long-run terms are settled by an advanced higgle, but in the short run it is still the buyer who administers the contract. On the whole the money costs and benefits of the work are clearer to the buyer than its psychic costs to the seller, and this gives him that short-run initiative in naming a price that normally inheres in the seller (e.g. iv). But while a sort of 'full-cost buyer' is normal, the disutility of labour varies according to the length of the day and the conditions of the job, and in the long run labour supply curves, however subjective, must be respected. So where there is overtime, 'dirty money', etc., we have a sort of 'marginal cost' seller (cf. v). Some labour, however, is still perfectly competitive: this refers to the 'shape-ups' of unskilled labour, where a flat hourly rate is bargained for, and no goodwill or permanent connexion is envisaged on either side. But since labour is (like electricity!) a service that cannot be stored, no futures trading or other sophistication is possible. The managerial labour market is a sort of long-term, very differentiated 'shape-up'; so comes, of course, in the sector of 'other price-takers' (type iii). Managerial hiring partakes, appropriately, of the nature of an auction.

(viii) In a few non-wage cases the buyer similarly dominates: the Dutch auction, the take-over bid on the stock exchange.

These categories exhaust all important economic activity. The orthodox variations of imperfect competition fit in as follows: (iii) is all imperfectly competitive price-takers, except that when the producers of unique goods become monopolists they shift to (vi). (iv) and (v) describe the producers of repeatable goods in all kinds of imperfect competition, including monopoly. Any category accommodates any maximand, just as does any category of competition, but short-run maximands go with (i–iii).

Cost inflation is only possible where prices are 'made': (iv), (v) and especially (vi). This is because where short-run profits are not maximized it is always fairly tolerable to raise prices when costs squeeze profits: the initial price is quite likely no longer the most profitable anyway (if it ever was), so why not try another not-most-profitable price instead? All we are doing is review our price earlier than we had intended. But if our price is wholly flexible and set by brokers, and we tell them our labour costs have risen, they will tell us 'where to put' this information. All we can do is contract output and let supply shortage raise the price, until it is again equal to marginal cost. A price-maker on the contrary would simply set a new price, and let output, given that the price is reasonable, take care of itself. It does not suffer much, since cost inflation tends to be universal, at least in one industry.

3. We can now turn to the main task of this chapter: the comparison of degrees of sub-optimality. Strictly, this entails quantification. Ordinal ranking, genuinely not resting on any numbers, is only possible for the feelings that go on within one person's head: 'diminishing' marginal utility; this noise is 'louder'. The writer's feeling that STEs are the most sub-optimal is not 'introspectively ordinal', and therefore methodologically valid, but 'literarily ordinal', and so the poorest possible substitute for an actual number. The Soviet and, say, British economies do not go on inside the writer's head.

The number we should ideally have is the percentage of national income lost by sub-optimality: i.e. the difference between its present level and that which could be obtained, within a 'short' period and without 'much' investment (both quantified), by optimal reallocation. This percentage should be broken down among its causes: irregular taxation, subsidy, monopoly, 'swings and roundabouts' pricing by large enterprises, cross-subsidization within Soviet-type ministries, tariffs, quotas, trade union restrictions, bad accounting practices, neglected externalities, etc. It must not be the sum of partial gains from individual corrections, but the macro-sum of all the gains to be expected from simultaneously making all the corrections. This is likely to be rather smaller. Thus if all British coal mines cross-subsidized by the National Coal Board from its best pits were closed, the cost of coal would fall sharply. But then either there would be unemployment or this labour would be put to unsuitable work at high cost. And the terms of trade would turn against Britain as she sought other, *ex hypothesi* marginal, fuels.

We are a very long way indeed from such knowledge: anything that at present passes for a number is hopelessly aggregative and speculative.[8] It is not uninstructive, however, to offer some 'literarily ordinal' judgements in places where they can rest at least on more than hunch.

4. First, pure capitalism is covered in all the textbooks. We need only add two things to what was said in the previous section. The first is the role of the large managerial corporation. The view seems almost unquestioned that monopoly and administered prices and large corporations all go together. Historically there is no truth in this: monopolies go all the way back to Adam Smith's forestallers and regraters, and indeed much further. Moreover, bad transport made it quite easy for a firm very small even by contemporary standards to be a monopoly.

Statistics of the concentration of production among few enterprises show a wavering upward trend in USA and UK, but they are of very doubtful relevance if by 'monopoly' we mean the marginalist 'degree of monopoly'.[9] If the product category studied is a broad one, perhaps the number of qualities within it has decreased? Are imports greater? Has the mere threat of new entry risen? Have local transport conditions improved? What is the actual policy of the larger modern firm – is it maximizing market share not profits? Positive answers would indicate that monopoly had gone one way and concentration the other. Naturally if there is a price tribunal or public ownership the degree of concentration becomes quite irrelevant. In particular it is an error to tie too closely the administered price of the price-maker to any definite degree of monopoly. The reasons for administered prices were given in sec. 2 (iv). They are numerous, persuasive, and almost entirely unrelated to monopoly.[10] A minimum of market power suffices. A great deal more market power simply makes possible longer periods between prices changes, less concern for competitors and more concern for our own costs.

This is not at all to say that large modern corporations are not a serious development. Socially and politically they could almost be said to herald a new order of things. War and peace, national sovereignty, the transition to socialism, the status of shareholders, union leaders, white-collar workers and top managers, the use of the computer, investment policy – clearly it is not absurd to be obsessed with the growth of corporations. It is also not utterly absurd to be obsessed with short-term resource allocation. What is absurd is to think that any two obsessions have a necessary connexion.

Yet there is a probable, small connexion. The large corporation produces many products, and uses sophisticated managerial techniques. Therefore it allocates resources well between these products, and it is not believable that many enterprises in the average imperfect market perform these tasks better. The increase of scale, therefore, so long as it rationally exploits the actual usable advances of managerial techniques and does not rush ahead into the premature foundation of STEs, makes little islands of comparatively optimal allocation. Between these islands there are of course greater market imperfections – but so there were between grocers in neighbouring villages.

It is a question of the degree of development. When enterprise is scarce, communications and transport bad, and commercial[11] and elementary education poor, allocation will be very sub-optimal. There is little perfect competition, but a great deal of sector (iii), our 'other price-takers'. Owing to poor communications, too many people are bilateral monopolists and waste time and energy haggling. Against this the ACE has to struggle with a vast diversification of goods and with the steep growth of advertising designed to mislead. But in inter-enterprise markets buyers are expert: so diversification is seldom irrational and advertising mainly informative. It is also generally held, as an educated guess, that development slightly increases commercial and administrative honesty. Putting all this together we obtain a probable rise in optimality as capitalism proceeds, on inter-enterprise or government-enterprise markets. It is not that there is more monopoly – perhaps there is less. But the quality of monopoly improves. Much, too, that used to be bilateral monopoly moves over into full-cost charging (sector iv).

The uneducated and primitive consumer will of course act stupidly, indeed with appalling extravagance and snobbery, in traditional ways. But equally when people are rich they are inattentive, vulgar and frivolous. Furthermore under capitalism their better education would appear to be more than offset by misleading advertisements. We shall therefore take the usual coward's way out and refuse to judge any consumer; except to suppose that the socialist consumer, less bemused by advertising, is more rational.

5. Another question poses itself within capitalism: which of the sectors enumerated in sec. 2 is most optimal? It is curiously difficult to be sure in practice. Probably the perfectly competitive sector comes first, as it obviously should. But we have to consider (a) its unique tendency to generate cumulative speculation over time, and (b) the way it provokes government intervention.

Speculation between places is precisely what the centralized market exists to abolish, and does abolish: it is not part of the pathology of this sector. Nor is such speculation the result of panic. But in order to abolish it the market lays itself open also to inter-temporal speculation, and simply makes it easy for prices to be changed from moment to moment. It must also be geographically centralized at a single place. Now all capital cities and places where large numbers of like-minded people meet are febrile and prone to rumour. The competitive inter-personal relation turns us to gossip, fashion, being 'in', going one better. Individual judgement yields to crowd psychology in a way it never does if the crowd is disparate or the individuals dispersed. So occasionally these same experts, whom we pay to exercise their best judgement on their chosen speciality, all go charging off in the same direction. Moreover the structure of their market, where not goods but documents are bought, so that documents can change hands very many times without a bale shifting in a warehouse, invites the outside gambler. He is of course a destabilizing figure. We must, then, on occasions reject the classic claim that today's perfectly competitive price incorporates the best human wisdom on tomorrow's. As a rule, though, it is not so completely the product of wishful thinking and political pressure as the planner's price, with which it is so often in this context compared.

Price is in any case most unlikely to be equal to marginal cost, since it varies daily, but output decisions are not affected. For agricultural cropping plans or new issues on the stock exchange are decided upon about once a year, on the basis of *expected* average prices. Subsequent fluctuations elicit sales out of stock only. Again when we look at what protection, quotas, marketing boards and subsidies have done to agricultural prices we realize that perfect competition tends to be distorted by controls that make it very much more sub-optimal than almost any imperfectly competitive market. True, these controls are interestingly different from the price and output controls over price-makers: they preserve the ambiance of perfect competition quite unmistakably. But this is an academic point compared with the effect on resource allocation (cf. chapter 5, secs. 12–14). Financial markets, the other large group that is perfectly competitive, are equally subject to government intervention by the same techniques. No one would wish to call the structure of interest rates anywhere in the world rational or optimal.

The full-cost sector (iv) presents us with pricing procedures very inimical to marginalist language, and so at least probably to marginalist behaviour, which is what concerns us. Profits are in many respects not maximized. Fluctuations in demand are met out of stock at the fixed price; while output is somewhat speculatively determined with an eye on the next period's price, on future short-term fluctuations in demand, on the level of stocks, and perhaps on marginal cost.[12] The present price was so fixed as to equate marginal cost and revenue (in some sense, so far as they are understood), *if* the enterprise is a long-run profit maximizer. Indeed this is a tautology. But the premise is not necessarily true, and a positive feature of all administered prices is the human tendency to take, in ignorance of marginalism, 'too' small an average profit per article. So 'too' much is produced, simply in order to satisfy demand. There is something embarrassing about a high price, which inhibits some businessmen; and queues are quite unpopular.

The sector of varying marginal cost (v) struggles manfully with its difficulties: how do we know what the marginal cost of shipping freight to Edinburgh will be tomorrow, since we don't know yet whether there will be any wagons returning empty? It is, naturally, here that marginalist theory has had most impact. But public opinion is very hostile to price discrimination, and the public price tribunals that abound in this sector have been rather against it.

Cost-plus (sector vi) has gained importance with the growth of research and prototypes. Cost-plus is certainly a most sub-optimal pricing procedure, yet it must not be called irrational, for that implies that something better could take its place. In ordinary transactions this is not true, since inexpert buyers, giving the product 1 per cent of their total attention, could not possibly spare the time that a better procedure would require. But where the government is the buyer we do now see a possible improvement: the 'technological complicity' of chapter 18, sec. 6. In this the producer opens his books to the buyer, and this perhaps leads to altogether new relations between enterprise and government (or indeed any other buyer).

6. Capitalist countries control, or try to control, monopolies. Here again, as with banking and trade unions, we find a patch well cultivated by economists who are, but have not dared to call themselves, institutional. We need not even summarize, but shall draw attention only to those features that help us to make the comparison with socialist market economies. We distinguish six traditions of capitalist monopoly control:

(i) break it up and make it compete;
(ii) forbid certain restrictive or unfair practices;
(iii) set up a quasi-legal tribunal to regulate prices, outputs and/or profits;[13]
(iv) beat it with imports;
(v) nationalize it as an independent trust;
(vi) incorporate it, private capital and all, into the state-capitalist machine.

Beginning in the early nineteenth century, the British way was to have pure *laissez-faire* as regards monopolies, except only railways (iii). Free trade, for instance, was not seen as directed against specific monopolistic firms *ad hoc*, but as a broad, historical, once-for-all anti-monopoly move, in the sense that the protection tariffs afford even to a whole industry of small firms can be called monopolistic. In the late 1940s there was nationalization (v). Wisely, this was seen not to cancel the requirement of an independent price control. The Railway Rates Tribunal went right on, the others were added in respect of other nationalized activities. By a singular reversal of philosophy, this was closely followed by the Monopolies and Restrictive Practices Act, and subsequent legislation of the same sort (ii). Thus the native socialist tradition ran in tandem with an American importation – it was a time when the well-dressed ACE simply had to have a monopoly control of type (ii), much as later it simply had to have French planning.

The USA, which originated type (ii), began in 1890 with something different: trust busting (i). There was a real enough problem with over-large predatory firms, but the ideology behind the Sherman Act was populist and therefore unsophisticated and incomplete: the courts, not the state, were to intervene and simply destroy these *unnecessary* monsters. But were they unnecessary? It was rapidly discovered that 'Bigness is no crime', and within twenty-five years the structure was greatly improved by adding federal regulatory agencies (ii and iii). Unfortunately US society is too corrupt for these to have functioned very well; an almost French complicity grows up between the state regulatory organ and the regulated industry. For the supervisory, as opposed to the judicial, relation is an ongoing one, instinct with argument, concession, interpretation and executive action. Beside actual corruption there is the irrepressible practice of *pantouflage* (chapter 18, sec. 4). The same prevalent corruption rules out nationalization, which was in any case ideologically unacceptable. Free imports would have worked, of course, against monopoly in import substitutes – and were duly prevented; but USA is a large, autarkic country where most monopolies are unaffected by foreign trade.

Trust-busting has not caught on in foreign countries, though it is for instance possible under the new British laws. But trust-preventing, by the scrutiny of take-over bids on the stock exchange, is fairly common.

France has scarcely anything that can be called a formal monopoly control – which should not surprise even a careless student of its economic history or its planning. Of course every possible instrument of pressure on a monopolist lies to hand, and many are used, but very seldom in the name of monopoly control. The planner's instinct is to adopt and adapt monopoly, not prevent it. After all his own industrial commissions, where entrepreneurs and trade associations meet to discuss the plan with him, are monopolistic. And all his detailed investment controls serve to prevent 'overlapping' or 'chaotic marketing'. His well-known preference for amalgamations does not promote competition. Besides, many monopolists are state or semi-state bodies. So the small monopolistic practice is 'incorporated' (vi) into the single great monopolistic practice known as planning. Only the High Authority of the Common Market intervenes in France in the classical way: against monopolies that reach across national borders.

Capitalist monopoly controls are notoriously ineffective, despite occasional striking successes against important companies. While corruption and public inertia play their part, the main reason is surely that there is just too much monopoly: too many firms, markets, product-types and monopolistic practices. A state with the detailed knowledge and the administrative resources necessary to control all monopoly would be halfway to a capability for perfect computation (chapter 11): i.e. to nationalize all monopolies and everything else too, and simulate perfect competition. But it can hardly be doubted that, however distant the date, humanity will become administratively capable of serious monopoly control before it becomes capable of perfect computation. For many markets are reasonably competitive in the first place, and may be neglected; while the number of acts of intervention required to prohibit something (enforce a law on the manager) is much smaller than the number required to manage someone (put the planner in his place).

It is a paradox that amalgamation is required for monopoly control. Nothing points up more clearly the comparative irrelevance of trust-busting, which should apply only to a tiny minority of the very largest. The ordinary enterprise, engaged in some restrictive practice, is too small and numerous to control. To double its size would hardly make it more monopolistic, but to halve its numbers would make it more controllable. This is precisely the policy of French planners towards their enterprises, though of course they do not fear monopoly and have quite other reasons (cf. chapter 9, sec. 11).

7. In the past ACEs have only attempted *general price controls*, as opposed to anti-monopoly price controls, in wartime. The latter, as a normal peacetime practice, have been quasi-judicial: therefore slow, careful and public. Wartime controls have been executive and used emergency procedures. They have got, and deserved, a bad name for two reasons. First, in a demand inflation the producer has every incentive to get round the control and make the profit of which it deprives him. He will not even sell less at the black-market price since there is excess demand. Secondly, since everyone's immediate interest is to evade, the number of bureaucrats and policemen required is very large. Clearly in a demand inflation the right way to stop rising prices is to reduce demand.

But now that all market economies, including socialist ones, are the almost permanent victims of cost inflation (chapter 14) there is a new case for price control. The seller does not greatly wish to raise his price, he had almost rather resist the wage-claim. There is competition at the going price; the consumer is not queueing at his door with money to burn; there is the threat of lower sales, since quite simply the seller will be moving from one place to another on his demand curve. So, working in part with the grain, the state needs a smaller enforcement mechanism. In particular it can use, as did the US government in 1971–2, large companies as bellwethers. If a few hundreds only of these are controlled they create competition at the going price right through the economy. So again there is great advantage to the state in enterprise amalgamation.

Price controls, then, are quite likely to work *per se*. Their real *raison d'être* is that they help to curb wage-claims. They render Keynesian policies tolerable again; for with frozen prices excess demand exerts its upward pressure on output, just as Keynes claimed in the days before cost inflation. They are, almost incidentally, an excellent new weapon against monopolists, who can simply be treated more harshly than competitors. And they by no means require the fantastic administrative capacity that we need for perfect computation. So the capitalist world is going to use price control much more in future. The Communist market economies have done this instinctively from their foundation, i.e. this is part of the Soviet-type legacy they have maintained (sec. 10).

But at its very best price control will remain discriminatory, arbitrary and bureaucratic. For to control a price is in practice to freeze it at a date, and thereafter to permit it to rise nearly always when costs rise, but only at long intervals in response to demand. For the most part price-controllers operate on the cost-plus principle of sec. 2 (vi) – for of course any worthwhile schema of pricing policies must include them too. Also they reject shortages as a reason for raising a price, since so long as price covers cost no one will complain very loudly, but their object is not to be optimal but to keep prices down. They only accept the play of demand, then, when it creates a surplus and lowers a price.

Queues are preferred to price rises that clear the market, and this is a consumer preference almost like any other. His preference costs him something, and he should know what it is, in terms of time spent waiting, diminished sovereignty and higher taxes (to pay for the administration). But he should surely be allowed to choose between complete sovereignty with rapidly rising prices, and diminished sovereignty with slowly rising prices. Thus in every way price control reduces the optimality of the system. But it still leaves output free to respond when prices fall, and when on a constant price demand curves fall or rise. This is quite a lot of flexibility, and undoubtedly much more than in an STE.

8. On the borders of capitalism stands the public corporation or other public body: nationalized industries, *compagnies mixtes*, schools, hospitals. We divide them into two types: the essentially market enterprise which is still expected to cover its costs but is somehow queer or 'strategic' (e.g. electricity), and the essentially non-market enterprise, which could only be asked to cover its costs after a veritable Chicago revolution (e.g. hospitals). Both act on the market for inputs, and are subject to no rigid plan, but to detailed yet imprecise operation orders. Very broadly we can say that in the former cost-benefit takes the place of profit: the difference is not very great, and since the product has a market there is an adequate basis for the benefit calculations. But the latter can only be cost-effective, unless very sophisticated calculations are made of the shadow value of output. Too often some intermediate output or 'throughput' (patients *treated*, students *in class*) is substituted for the real output (life preserved, something learned). Both types are under 'disinterested management' in

the sense of chapter 4, sec. 5. Their behaviour cannot be described or judged within the confines of one section of one chapter. It is certainly indeterminate according to the ideas of economists, since, to repeat, 'many maximands are no maximand'. But it does raise one vital issue: should there be a maximand at all? does not the mere existence of such a thing lead to anti-social activity?

The governments of capitalist economies introduce public enterprise for just this reason: they mistrust the profit maximand in the context. It will lead to unemployment (marginal coal-mines), to monopolistic exploitation (suburban commuter fares, main line freight rates), to élitist discrimination (schools), to the neglect of the poor (medicine), to ecological externalities, to price rises during cost inflation. These arguments may be wrong or right – a large and variegated question we cannot here discuss – and we omit a multitude of less rational considerations. But mistrust of the profit maximand is always there.

This multitude continually increases. As regards 'market public enterprises' a fairly good rule used to be: let enterprises have a simple maximand (any maximand, it hardly matters for the argument), and let the government enforce regulations to meet externalities, etc. But we are now beginning to find that this rule is, by a paradox, not too *laissez-faire* but too centralistic. There are simply too many such problems for government to take care of; the enterprise must be directly responsible.

A point will come when public enterprises, without single maximands, will be better. It is in advanced economies that moral incentives (sec. 11) are most desirable, particularly since the urgency of extra output or lower costs or higher wages has much diminished. *Externalities arise because enterprises have maximands.* Profit is one of the best of these, since it internalizes at least some costs, while the Soviet-type emphasis on output externalizes them all – Soviet pollution is as bad as any but Soviet waste of raw materials is worse (chapter 15, sec. 10). It is good to take account of profit but bad to maximize anything, even profit.

9. Just this kind of confusion about maximands used to reign in the British retail co-operative movement (chapter 6). These shops have become maximizers, because of the pressure of short-term competition from capitalism. But they started out as 'voluntary public enterprises'. Perhaps the change in attitudes to economic effort and success in ACEs, discussed above, will have come in time to save something of the Rochdale tradition. This might be thought foolish in view of the lengthy and depressing co-operative experience of what happens to the socially conscious, but this is not really so. For it was by the perpetual pressure of short-run competition from real maximizers that working-class culture and ideals were eroded. 'Social consciousness' rested upon monopoly, i.e. upon the loyalty of the working-class customer to *his* (or rather *her*) co-op. But if now capitalism goes over to a more relaxed style, the co-op spirit can survive.

The early British co-operators saw this clearly enough when they hoisted the slogan 'co-operation not competition'. In other words they rejected the very notion of a maximand, and saw themselves as 'market public enterprises'. In pure theory, it will be recalled, they should have been minimizing net retail price,[14] but any single overriding goal, even sheer output, has the same effect. A maximand is not only an easily administered base for an incentive but also a blinker.

Under socialism all enterprises are public. The lampshade manufacturer is assimilated to the mine-owner, and both alike are 'market public enterprises'. Interest now centres on the 'non-market public enterprise', which embraces about the same sector as under capitalism. Thus Yugoslavia faces the problem and solves it in a similar way. Banks, schools and hospitals are not under ordinary self-management but a mixed system admitting outsiders to the workers' councils, renamed social councils. The argument is that banks (chapter 12) have far too much power, unrelated to the workers' effort or skill; and that schools and hospitals earn no revenue, so that pure self-management would result in unlimited demands for public funds. The British Boards of Governors and Boards of Trustees in schools and hospitals are similar, except that they have foolishly eliminated the employee element altogether.

The STE of course has its own preferred maximand for 'market public enterprises': output. It is very seldom relaxed. 'Non-market public enterprise' is not very distinct in this system. All costs tend to be external in both cases, in the sense that no one's income depends on minimizing them. Targets are in both cases mostly a bundle of outputs or 'throughputs', though a few output-input ratios play a part (kilowatts per ton of fuel, patient turnover per bed). Again, if schools and hospitals must react passively to the supply of children and patients, so must shops to the supply of customers. Crude output targets, such as would never be set in other 'public' sectors, crop up in the most unlikely places: the Union of Writers, the Academy of Sciences. The absurd micro-results of the output maximand, even in its ordinary sphere, are discussed at many places in this book.

10. The easiest system to understand after pure capitalism is that of 'Pannonia': Socialist managers maximizing the total profits of public enterprises on a market. Thus the Pannonian maximand is entirely compatible with optimality – nay more so than under capitalism, since there is no equity-bearing factor to confuse the manager with its vested interests and its lack of a proper price or supply curve (in capitalism equity capital plays a small disturbing part as described in chapter 4, sec. 10). The managers are motivated, of course, by a bonus, which is drawn from the profit, not the wage-fund, just as in the reformed STE. There is no workers' council.

Hungary has gone much the furthest of any country towards this system.

The actual Hungary, however, is not yet a Pannonia in a historical vacuum but an ex-STE with a considerable carry-over. The annual command plan, the rationing of material supplies (chapter 11, sec. 17) and the forint audit of current accounts by the banks (chapter 12, sec. 15) have all gone, but the legal power remains to call them back. The habit of obedience to authority is very strong, and managerial promotion hangs upon the Minister's pleasure. So in matters of investment, for instance, a whisper suffices. Most investment is under central command anyway. In Spring 1974 there was an unexplained political reaction against the founders of the NEM, who were removed from their posts. But the NEM itself unexpectedly stumbles onward, with only a little recentralization.

Above all Hungary fears cost inflation. Her wage-controls date from 1957, not 1969 like the rest of the reform. They are very tough, and little discussed by her propagandists. At present (since 1 January 1971) they rest on an extremely progressive tax that rapidly eats away the enterprise's bonus fund if it breaks the wage guidelines. Since the bonus is about one month's pay on average this is a fairly effective deterrent. The trade unions remain, much as in Yugoslavia, of the inactive Soviet type.[15] There is no formal collective bargaining, and agricultural and private incomes have proved more difficult to control. On top of this come price controls, of which the outside world hears a great deal more. These too are effective,[16] except, as usual, in construction and agriculture. The idea is to abolish these controls and allow perfectly free wholesale and retail price formation. But with both cost inflation and monopoly to worry about, this will not, or should not, happen soon.

Thus the fledgling Hungarian market economy is perhaps the most successful of all market economies in controlling cost inflation. It is done by extensive controls on a basis of total socialist ownership – which leaves us with gloomy thoughts for the future of pure capitalism. But of course price and wage freezes ensure sub-optimality – and this is a trade-off to which also the capitalist world must also accustom itself. As to the degree of optimality obtained by the enterprises on the market, I feel uncertain beyond platitudes. The old irregular Soviet-type turnover tax has not been abolished. A small country with large enterprises has many monopolies, and the idea is to keep them in order by free importation, even from ACEs. But of course the balance of payments never permits this. Monopoly is also countered by the detailed price control described above, and by the 'persuasion' of the Communist Party.

However the opinion of shoppers, managers and economists is unanimous: optimality by every sign has risen dramatically since the new system came in. How sad that such happy events cannot be quantified, and added to the respectable and miraculously uninterrupted rate of growth that the economy has shown in the 'sixties and 'seventies.

Hungary actively wants optimality. Few Hungarians are good Marxists, and this goal is one they consciously stress, though, fearful of invasion, in guarded language. They do not talk so much, like Chinese or even Yugoslavs, about the release of productive forces. They do not, like Chinese, want equality. They do not, like Yugoslavs, think that industry is simple enough to be administered democratically. Seeing themselves as an advanced country with an unlucky economic history, they are preoccupied with criteria, with overloaded administrative capacity, with the quality, diversity and modernity of goods. To some small extent a nation is likely to get what it wants.

The Soviet NEP presents a close parallel to Hungary: socialized enterprises on a market, no effective workers' councils, profits more or less maximized but without ideological recognition, price control, investment planning, a single powerful bank, emasculated trade unions. In the NEP 20 per cent of the industrial labour force was employed by actual capitalist enterprises, mainly making consumer goods. Even that has its Hungarian parallel, in the auxiliary industrial enterprises of the collective farms. These are a disorderly group of intruders, noted above all for violating the wage-norms – upwards, of course. As to monopoly control, both imports and the mediation of the Party were used. The serious divergences are in trade (most of Soviet retail trade was in private hands, virtually none is in Hungary), agriculture (Hungary is collectivized) and political (the Hungarian Party is nearly unanimous behind the reform). These matters are peripheral to our concerns, so we shall attempt no separate analysis, but refer the reader to the literature.[17]

11. One of the most curious questions in all economics is, what is the current allocation policy of the Chinese enterprise?[18] A few large enterprises, especially in military production, the bank, the railways, the airlines, form an archipelago of Soviet-type planning. For the rest Chinese planning moves from the bottom up. Factories announce their plans to counties or provinces, and agricultural producers' co-operatives to People's Communes, which confirm them without trying to dovetail them. They certainly may change these plans, and higher authorities may certainly override them in turn, just as in an STE. But this happens only rarely, and still more rarely on the ground that some commodity balance is out of kilter. Nor is this surprising, since the enterprise's plan targets used to be ranges, and have only recently become single numbers. It is obvious that any enterprise in any market economy could go through this formality without pain, succcessfully fulfilling an approximate plan proposed by itself. But then China *is* a market economy, though she uses the rhetoric of planning.

Clearly this system originates in Mao's passionate revulsion from Soviet-type bureaucracy (the attempt to become an STE was abandoned in 1958 during the Great Leap Forward). But is there anything solid behind the non-market rhetoric? What if any maximand has the enterprise? Is China another Hungary?

The answer is that China is extremely remote from Hungary, and from having abandoned certain basic features of the STE which we have not yet discussed: the campaign, the military metaphor, the enthusiastic and ignorant subordinate Party cadre, the setting of new goals and emphases by leaders in the main newspapers rather than by administrative channels, etc. China did not invent all this. The first such period was the first Soviet Five-Year Plan, and Khrushchev's great territorial experiment (chapter 9, sec. 11) bore some resemblance to it. Bulgaria, North Korea and Albania have also gone through this experience. It is known, however, in honour of Mao and of the compactness of the Chinese language, as the *Great Leap Forward syndrome*. What Mao has now tried to do is to routinize this syndrome.

In a Great Leap Forward a surge of millennial fervour grips the Communist Party. Lower cadres are encouraged to seize command of enterprises and raise production by unprecedented percentages. Produce what, and at what cost? Such questions become counter-revolutionary. Optimality was never a problem, but now neither is the method of balances. The state bureaucracy is by-passed and downgraded. Hours of work lengthen. X-efficiency seems to rise because of a staggering rate of innovation; but actually it falls because the innovations are unsuitable or even bogus. Planner's tension rises, for though state planners cease to matter local Party bosses are making impossible plans from below.[19] Moral incentives replace material ones (chapter 2).

Great Leaps Forward are therefore decentralized. But since each unit exchanges products for money, there is a market. All micro-decisions are made by managers or middle-rank Party cadres, but how? The answer cannot be 'the plan', since they drew that up themselves. It cannot be that they read the little Red Book or the leader in today's Jen Min Jih Pao, for these do not tell us when to substitute aluminium for copper. The answer seems to be that: (i) codes of practice are circulated, recommending input-output ratios to enterprises, (ii) there is no Gossnab, (iii) prices are freely but stickily formed at wholesale as well as at retail, (iv) losses are avoided, under supervision of the all-important bank (chapter 12, sec. 18), (v) subject to these restraints, overall output is maximized, rather than profit, (vi) cross-subsidization, however, is extremely common, and in particular one enterprise may be forced by a local authority to price monopolistically in order to generate funds for another, and (vii) all else is indeed indeterminate. The role of the decentralized annual plans is thus hortatory, indeed self-hortatory.

This is not an unreasonable system. As in foreign, military and development policy, beneath the paranoiac surface of China there is a substratum of hard sense. A proper STE is a very expensive toy for a very poor country (chapter 9, sec. 16); it also spells material imbalances, bureaucratization and inequality. A proper market, as in Hungary or Yugoslavia, is cheaper but spells bureaucratization, inequality and bourgeoisification.

A Chinese Marxist is after all a Marxist: sub-optimality leaves him cold. And he is above all a mobilizer of his people. So the compromise of the 'routinized Great Leap Forward' is very logical.

Can it be properly used? If not pursued to the point of lunacy, surely yes. The universal ridicule of China's economic system confuses its essence with the various faulty development policies that Mao has applied simultaneously. It is not the system as described that caused peasant labour to be diverted from the harvest to the production of unusable steel in backyard blast furnaces; or the mixing, on higher orders, of good rice seed with bad (1958–9); or, later, to the invasion of factories by young thugs in a state of exaltation, or the loss of millions of man-days in meetings and parades. These were all logically separable decisions by the central government; pathological phenomena which could be only the birth pangs of a stable system, the outcomes of psychological drives without which the system would not have come into existence but which it must in turn tame. In the same way we do not judge the modern STE by the chaos, waste and starvation of the first Soviet Five Year Plan.

A larger question is whether China can generate the appropriate social type, 'both Red and Expert', to run her system. This is more doubtful than the technical economics of it (chapter 21, sec. 8). Note also that the Chinese enterprise is a maximizer, to wit of output – only output partially defined by itself.

Variety and informality should inhibit generalization. Most recently (1975) Soviet-type procedures seem to be returning: plan targets in points not ranges, handed down by *provincial* authorities. But Pekin has no direct control over these: hence the stress on planning inter-provincial exchanges (as opposed to provincial outputs). China is now quite like an STE, and will probably become more so.

In these allocational matters Cuba (chapter 2) is like, indeed is, an STE. She uses moral incentives *de haut en bas*, as devices to implement a detailed central plan. They are not there to liberate either manager or worker, but to get him to do what is wanted more cheaply, and for ideological reasons. Their most important application is to labour services, since managerial decisions on product supply are a matter of obedience anyway in an STE. It seems unclear whether moral incentives work better as allocators between jobs or between leisure and work on a job. Bernardo[20] implies the former, but there is no solid evidence. For the most part the literature confuses this important distinction.

Thus Cuba does not have Great Leaps Forward: she is too centralized. Nor do her moral incentives much affect allocational efficiency, since they are mainly a plan-fulfilment device. In so far as they do, they clearly work for inefficiency, since they conceal the opportunity cost of labour from the planner. The disutility cost they of course reduce, since that is the definition of a moral incentive. But being themselves costless they can be attached arbitrarily to any labour, so they enable planners to reallocate from high- to low-productivity jobs at a constant wage. Their relation to optimal allocation (in the strict inter-occupational sense) is probably random, so they introduce yet another element of imperfection into the system, over and above inappropriate prices, etc. (cf. chapter 2, sec. 7).

But it is not impossible that their use in China improves resource allocation, since it enables China to dispense with detailed central planning! That is to say, Chinese moral incentives do not back a central plan, they simply increase the supply and mobility of labour. But material incentives would be a yet further improvement in this respect, since they would attach more correct productivity tags (opportunity costs) to labour.

In China the consumer has, then, a modicum of sovereignty. But the worker has not. The policy of keeping incomes nearly equal precludes sufficient differentials to persuade people, above all, to relocate themselves as desired. Labour direction, especially between places, is very common indeed. Another result of egalitarianism is that most enterprises do not pay managerial bonus on any ground, though workers' bonuses are creeping back.

12. In Illyria there is a single maximand: average income per head. So our knowledge of this Cloudcuckooland is sophisticated and extensive. We have already seen (chapter 4) the sub-optimality that arises even in perfect competition, owing to the enterprise's 'irrational' attitude to labour. Inelastic demand for the product simply cumulates the restrictions. Thus we posit: where Q is quantity produced, P is its price, L is quantity of labour:

(1) . . . . $\frac{d(PQ)}{dQ} < P$ (inelastic demand),

and equilibrium is as usual

$\frac{d(PQ)}{dL} = \frac{PQ}{L}$ (assuming for simplicity no bought-in inputs).

We turn to consider productivity. Suppose there are diminishing returns:

$$\frac{dQ}{dL} < \frac{Q}{L}.$$

Then: (2) . . . . $\frac{d(PQ)}{dQ} \cdot \frac{dQ}{dL} < \frac{PQ}{L}$. There can be no equilibrium, for if assumption (1) is maintained,

$$\text{LHS (2)} = \text{RHS (2) only if } \frac{dQ}{dL} > \frac{Q}{L},$$

or *there are increasing returns to the factor labour in an Illyrian enterprise in equilibrium in imperfect competition*. This is of course not so in a capitalist enterprise, for there marginal cost (*mc*) can be rising, indeed it can be above average cost, when it is equal to marginal revenue (*mr*). And if labour supply is perfectly elastic this means diminishing physical returns to it.

As usual Illyria finds its equilibrium at a smaller output than Helvetia or (probably) Atlantis. For if

$$\frac{d(PQ)}{dQ} \cdot \frac{dQ}{dL} = \frac{PQ}{L},$$

then (3) . . . . $\frac{L}{Q} \cdot \frac{dQ}{dL} = \frac{P}{mr}$

or the elasticity of production with respect to labour $= \frac{\epsilon}{\epsilon - 1}$ where ϵ is the elasticity of demand. Now imagine an absolute profit maximizer facing the same ϵ, and paying a wage W for labour in perfectly elastic supply. How would his *mc* be related to his *mr* at such a level of Q and L? It follows from (3) that

$$\frac{dQ}{WdL} = \frac{PQ}{WL} \cdot \frac{1}{mr}, \text{ or mc} > \frac{1}{mr}. \text{ Therefore mc} < \text{mr.}$$

So *the capitalist firm would still wish to expand at the Illyrian point of equilibrium if both faced the same inelastic demand.*

We have already dealt with the Illyrian preference for capital over labour as an input, and with the consequent misallocations (chapter 4, sec. 18). We have also examined and more or less dismissed the mirror-image of these problems posed for Atlantis by equity-bearing capital (chapter 4, sec. 2). It is tempting to conclude that Illyria is in real trouble with her 'funny' maximand, that restricts output and demands too high capital/labour ratios. But macro- is not micro-, and the situation is not as serious as it looks. Part of the definition of Illyria is that every enterprise has the same maximand; i.e. that the huge private sector of the actual Yugoslavia has been socialized. Then the theorem is relevant that the same degree of monopoly everywhere produces no misallocation. What causes relative unemployment and relative restriction when practised by a few does not do so if equally[21] practised by all. Grant, as we must grant in socialist Illyria, some kind of full-employment policy; then if each enterprise restricts employment there are simply more enterprises than there should be. The energetic foundation of new enterprises is an integral part, indeed a main pillar, of Illyria's full-employment policy, and the 'funny' maximand results mainly in whatever costs this policy may impose (chapter 13, sec. 16).

Similarly each enterprise will undoubtedly seek 'too much' capital. But where, if all seek it, will all find it? Obviously the price of capital rises until all capital and labour available are used. Illyria only uses more capital than Atlantis if the wage–interest ratio is the same. But since Illyrian capital is on a free market the ratio corrects itself.

Thus Illyria and Atlantis both run the risks of misallocation due to market imperfection (and taxation), but only if different rates rule in different sectors. Illyria runs a further risk through her 'funny' maximand, whether or not its observance is complete (because the incidence of sub-optimality differs in any case from enterprise to enterprise).

Clearly, in particular, if there were no legal or administrative restrictions on private enterprise the Helvetian sector of Yugoslavia would use too much labour while the Illyrians would hog the capital. And yet here again the market would supply a corrective: the two sectors would come to resemble two nations, specializing in labour- and capital-intensive goods respectively.[22] Indeed this is what happened, though probably administrative restrictions on private borrowing have been the main cause. We develop this international analogy in sec. 18.

13. The argument that a producers' co-operative has a negatively sloped supply curve is complex, academic and very much exaggerated. It runs as follows. We maximize income per head in the manner of chapter 4, so:

$$\frac{\partial(Xx)}{\partial L} = \frac{Xx}{L} \text{ and } \frac{\partial^2(Xx)}{\partial^2 L} < 0,$$

where X is output, x its price and L the number of workers. This is on the proviso that all other costs are a constant fraction of L. But now let there be (and this at least is realistic) some one fixed external cost. This might for instance be borrowed capital B, at a constant price i. Then we are in equilibrium when

$$\frac{\partial(Xx)}{\partial L} = \frac{Xx - Bi}{L} \quad \ldots\ldots\ldots\ldots\ldots (1).$$

Now let the price rise to $x' > x$. Then if L remains the same,

$$\frac{\partial(Xx')}{\partial L} < \frac{Xx' - Bi}{L},$$

so that in order to re-establish equality and so maximize the right-hand side we must lower L and therefore X.

However, first, it is quite unclear how variable costs (V) behave as L increases, nor have we any practical reason to call them a constant fraction of L, as above. There is a fair chance that their usage per hour of labour rises:

$$\frac{\partial(V/L)}{\partial L} > 0.$$

There is also a fair chance that their price (v) rises as more of them is demanded, so that we can with some probability write

$$\frac{\partial(Vv/L)}{\partial L} > 0.$$

If we enter $-Vv$ into equation 1, short-run equilibrium when x has risen to x′ is where

$$\frac{\partial(Xx')}{\partial L} = \frac{X'x' - Bi - V'v'}{L} \quad \ldots\ldots\ldots\ldots\ldots (2)$$

Now is L still $>$L′? If we adjust by laying off L we reduce both V and v, thus raising the RHS by an unknown amount. We can no longer be sure that the RHS does not rise as a whole. Supply may be positively sloped, even in the one-product case. It is certainly less negatively sloped.

Secondly we have tacitly assumed a single-product enterprise, a thing virtually unknown in the real world. Clearly if X is just one product out of many we will make more of it, and the analysis only begins to be true if the prices of all our products rise, and at that relatively to those of the rest of the economy. But if all our *x*s rise it is likely that there is general inflation, and there is an independent as well as an induced rise in our *v*s, so our first objection applies more strongly than before.

Thirdly if the supply curve of labour is inelastic, and passes through the curve of average value added before the latter's peak, a rise in price *increases* equilibrium employment (cf. Fig. 4/1), since it increases AVA, and the demand curve for labour is identical with the AVA curve up to its maximum. Fourthly, after all the income-per-head maximand is itself a very bold assumption.

Certainly a negative supply curve would be a very serious fault. It is perhaps not enough understood how great a virtue is elastic supply in any system (chapter 11, sec. 3). The enterprise's supply curve is not sacred or untouchable but a direct function of the institutional system. The more elastic it is the more responsive the system is (whether to price inducements or to commands), and responsiveness is a good thing. Generally negative supply curves would render any system flatly inoperative.

Whole theories of Illyrian inflation have been built upon the generally negative supply curve. It is unfortunate, then, that all this cloud-capped mountain of theory rests on so many unwarranted premises, and is empirically contradicted by the everyday experience of the Yugoslav economy. We can however tentatively conclude that supply is inelastic compared with other systems – though still certainly positive;[23] and that this has the twin faults of reducing responsiveness to micro-changes in demand and causing inflation.

14. But all this has helped us only suggestively with the actual Yugoslavia. Many other considerations press upon the Yugoslav director, who

is perhaps even more unpredictable than a capitalist. The result is a cross between a capitalist public enterprise (sec. 8) and Illyria (sec. 12).

The main idea in Yugoslavia is that the workers' councils shall release productive forces from the dead and alienating hand of Stalinist bureaucracy (chapter 3, sec. 6). The command planning structure was abolished and the market introduced almost as a mere consequence: indeed until 1950 there was an attempt to keep command planning. Moral incentives, however, only played a role *before* the reforms. In no country calling itself Communist is the appeal to material self-interest more direct.

But the memory of those who lived through 1948–50 is clear: optimality, though hardly at the centre of the reforms, did sharply increase. Nor can we neglect the unanimous opinion of tourists arriving from Bulgaria (a richer country) today. To repeat, every enterprise produces many products, and its labour force can turn its hands to many things, and Illyrian restrictiveness applies only to the total number of employees. The market, then, proves its dominance over the restrictive maximand, and extracts the required positive and negative supply reactions at the level of disaggregation that matters.

Restrictiveness keeps down the size of the enterprise but hardly stops these somewhat larger numbers from forming monopolies. The system has been long enough in operation to develop formal monopoly controls. These used to be the province of the Party, which exercised 'persuasive' powers rather as it does today in Hungary, and by Soviet-type price controls. Today (after the 'second reform' of 1965) the Party has retreated from the economy. But price control, however contrary to the spirit of things, continues. The weak weapon remains of discussion between the Chamber of Commerce (a sort of glorified trade association) of the monopolistic industry and its aggrieved clients. The main stress is now on free importation, the usual recourse of optimistic small countries. But in practice, and again as usual, the balance of payments forbids this and will continue to do so. Probably the mere fact of calling oneself socialist is as important as anything else. Monopoly sets off an in-group, though admittedly not now a capitalist one, against everyone else. This is the reverse of socialism, and ideology still has weight.

So much for producers' co-operatives. As to the farmers' co-operative it has whatever supply curve its members vote that it should have. They supply the produce at the co-op's buying-in price, which is its selling price minus processing and storage costs. If there were no co-op they would bear all these costs, plus those of the diseconomies of small scale, themselves. The co-op is on a perfect or state-monopsony-dominated market, and therefore faces perfectly elastic demand. The farmers force it to buy whatever they produce, and this much, speculation apart, it must sell. Therefore such a co-op hardly alters the supply curve of the product to the market. The difference from the Yugoslav factory is that its value added is small and the employees who add this value are not members and have no vote.[24] The co-op is an agency, not an enterprise: its maximand is the farmers' profit.

15. A major problem for planners is, what is the opportunity cost of an e.b.f.? Under capitalism hired and equity capital are such close substitutes that welfare economists scarcely ever ask this question. Yet when power is involved and a take-over threatens, the difference in price becomes enormous. Even so, however, the nation as a whole may view the matter with indifference, and continue to value equity capital at the rate[25] for loan capital plus a bonus for bearing more risk. Thus local power struggles, not involving foreigners, only alter the opportunity cost of equity capital for those involved in them. The planner of resource allocation should take no notice of this. Moreover he should never maximize average yield on anything, but always aim at the greatest surplus in absolute terms. Therefore he must treat equity capital simply as another factor, with the market price of loan capital.

When labour is the e.b.f., and freely moves in and out of the hired sector, the same applies. Thus under capitalism the small shopkeeper and farmer should be valued at what wages they can earn. But what of the kolkhoznik – an equity-bearing labourer without a shadow of managerial power – who is hindered from joining a sovkhoz or a factory, and kept on a farm where his income is a mere dividend? What of the Yugoslav worker who cannot earn wages anywhere?

Let us first give a Stalinist answer. When we are planning consumption levels we know that the opportunity cost *to the state* of moving workers is their future income minus their present income; and it is this difference also that motivates the individual to move, legally or no. Thus the Soviet planner, considering whether to specialize a particular kolkhoz in a particular crop, wants to know whether this is cheaper to the state than asking a sovkhoz to produce it. He should reckon both kinds of labour at their current income, and decide on the difference between that and productivity.

But today he is no Stalinist: consumption is no longer a cost to the state but a qualified maximand. So he hesitates to value kolkhoz labour at productivity minus dividend, and in practice gives it the shadow-price of the appropriate grade of sovkhoz labour. Now this goes too far the other way. This shadow-price is in no sense an opportunity cost, indeed its use seems partly to rest on the false labour theory of value. As on other peasant farms, marginal kolkhoz labour has low productivity, so there is an argument for giving kolkhoz labour a shadow-price below what it consumes, but none for one above it. Indeed such a practice takes jobs away from kolkhozniki, precisely as uniform wage-rates prevent industrial capital from moving south in Italy or USA. When however the Soviet planner turns from considerations of cost to the state of such non-operational questions as comparing enterprise efficiency in abstract terms, he should indeed use the corresponding sovkhoz wage-rates, skill for skill.

Now while in Yugoslavia there is indeed no market-determined, publishable wage, there is a supply curve of labour (the AC curve in figure 4/1), in that each outside worker is getting an income from some enterprise, which largely determines his supply price. What is again missing is any mechanism to approximate this to his marginal product, either in his new or in his old use. The supply curve, then, exists and slopes upwards: you have to promise more 'income' to get more workers into your enterprise, and the level of income you offer is widely known and attracts applicants. But there is only a general tendency for such labour transfers to make the economy more productive, since incomes do not correspond to marginal productivity, before or after transfer.

So the Yugoslav planner is in the same position as his Soviet colleague: he needs uniform wage-rates to judge the efficiency of enterprises in abstract terms, and for other non-operational purposes. But when it comes to resource allocation it is in the community's interest that between competing enterprises or individuals of equal competence in the proposed job the planner should favour those whose marginal productivity is lowest in their present job, not those who are poorest. In neither case should a uniform wage be used as an allocative device until the institutions have been altered. But in neither case do the current institutions shed any light on marginal productivity, so it must simply be found out by enquiry.

But the two institutions have opposite effects. For in the kolkhoz marginal productivity is usually lower than income except at the harvest peak, since it is a community with a demographically determined labour supply (chapter 4, sec. 9). But in Illyria certainly, and in Yugoslavia probably, present marginal productivity is understated by present income: see figure 4/1. The kibbutz faces the same problem, with marginal productivity being far above and far below income in particular cases. But since the planning unit is much smaller the appropriate enquiries are much easier.

16. More primitive economic systems also raise fine problems of welfare theory. The time is long past when anyone considered an illiterate and ill-informed peasant necessarily irrational or even sub-optimal, provided he can operate freely. He does his best with the time, information, skill and leisure preference that he has. It is often an excellent best, putting more sophisticated operators to shame, as Schultz says.[26] It is not even clear that X-efficiency is low. For changes of technique are risky investments which people at subsistence level can hardly afford;[27] nor can they afford the appropriate technical education. But Schultz's celebrated defence of the 'poor but efficient' hypothesis rests on extremely few empirical examples chosen in a very biassed manner, and omits numerous counter-examples also related in the anthropological literature. It still seems to

me probable on balance that optimality increases with economic development. However the more interesting cases are where the operation of the primitive market is restricted systematically, even legally. We can only deal with the two main ones.

First, feudalism as it operated virtually anywhere, but preferably in Russia just before the emancipation of the serfs (1861). Russia was already an industrializing country, and she has left us full records. Where the land was good and the peasantry not too thick on the ground the landlord stood by his ancient rights: he exacted compulsory labour service (*barshchina*) on the demesne farm, and refused people permits to leave the village. This farm, to be sure, he did not run very efficiently, and that was indeed a psychological consequence of being feudal, and Russian. But in keeping up his rights he was extremely rational. Where the land was poor and the peasants many he commuted the *barshchina* into a money payment (*obrok*), and was free with permission to leave. For the peasant could go into a shop or a factory and pay a very substantial, individually negotiated, *obrok*. He could also buy himself out for a capital sum. There were serf millionaires paying *obrok*. It is probable that in time *obrok* and its capitalization would have eroded feudalism without the Tsar's decree, as happened much earlier in England (chapter 8, sec. 10).

Nor was the *barshchina* inflexible. It could be rendered in produce instead of labour, and in various sorts of produce of labour. The peasant could order his son, or pay another villager, to perform or deliver in his place. Then too the landlord might own a rural, feudal factory and demand that the labour-debt be paid there. Russian feudalism was in no way formally incompatible with industrialization. It even made possible a certain mobility of labour, through the *obrok* and the landlord's legal right to transfer whole villages of serfs from one place to another. Since estates, with their serfs, were bought and sold a landlord could and did own widely separated lands, and move his serfs accordingly (chapter 8, secs. 9, 10).

Of course the worker was not sovereign in this system, only the consumer. The serfs themselves, spending as they wished, exercised their due meed of consumers' sovereignty. Indeed in a market system it is much easier to deprive a consumer of his income – and serfdom did this – than of his sovereignty. 'Consumer serfdom' – adscription to the shops of the master – presupposes industrialized serf-owners and is difficult to administer. But to deprive the worker of his sovereignty (freedom to move and bargain) is a clear interest of any employer. However it is less clear that the serf-owner allocated labour differently from the way in which it would have allocated itself: the main exception being the retention of labour to perform *barshchina* on infertile land. 1861 was indeed a psychological prerequisite for faster modernization, since it shook up people's ideas, and no doubt this promoted X-efficiency (chapter 15). But in terms of allocative efficiency and cold textbook economics the matter is unclear. The *amount* of allocative efficiency lost by feudalism does not appear great, though as usual we have no quantitative estimates. Note the survival of many of these traits in the kolkhoz.

17. Secondly many gross imperfections of the market are produced by the *traditional village community*. These concern, as under feudalism, the factor markets: the consumer remains sovereign and product markets are reasonably perfect. Russia again provides a recent and well-documented example. The legislation of 1861 strengthened the community, transferring to it the landlord's control over movement and confirming its powers over the way the peasant cultivated his own land (chapter 6). Of course the community, being owed neither *barshchina* nor *obrok*, was more generous about emigration. Indeed its demographic interests were quite opposed to the landlord's. It wanted a monopoly of the jobs on his demesne (which the decree had not touched), and the fewer the people the higher the wages. And of course it wanted fewer people per acre on its own ('allotment') land. The main 'irrationality' of the post-1861 system was that no one might sell allotment land. To protect the peasantry against their own improvidence, this land was inalienable to the community as a whole, and allotted by it to each family. Many villages even periodically realloted it, on the basis of need.[28] So again there was administrative misallocation: partly of labour, mainly of land, while the mix of final products was not specially irrational.

For yet again there were innumerable mitigating factors. A household was not compelled to cultivate its allotment but could hire it out. Another, land-hungry, could also rent or even buy from the ex-feudal lord, the church, the state or any other landowner: for these, not being members of the community, could sell. The peasants bought or rented the majority of this land.

The situation of private and ejido farming in Mexico is similar (Weckstein, op. cit.), for the ejido, it will be remembered (chapter 6), was also founded for the protection of primitive peasants, and its land is inalienable. Mexico differs from Russia in that the large private farms are the expanding sector, and it is the ejidos that need protection. So their members do not go out and buy or rent other land to cultivate in addition: they go out as labourers. But this still serves to even out the labour–land ratio if we count hours of work, not people – as we always should.

18. Much more generally, economic systems co-existing within one country are the main cause of *dual economies*, and these should be subjected to the analytical tools of international economics. We normally think of a dual economy as the co-existence of 'Helvetian' and 'Atlantic' elements: of underdeveloped and developed capitalists, separated by a gross imperfection in the labour market. The barriers of labour movement are geography (very poor people cannot afford even short journeys,

especially if they face a fair chance of unemployment), education (urban schools turn out quite enough labour, even for unskilled jobs, so why employ a peasant with even fewer appropriate skills?) and culture (the less hardy souls are too frightened and bewildered to migrate). But above all, the marginal worker in the Helvetian sector receives as income the average, not the marginal, product of labour. So it simply does not pay him to migrate, unless the 'Atlantic' sector is so much more productive that his marginal productivity there exceeds the average productivity at home.

In fact capitalism plays no necessary part in this analysis. Both parts of the duality might be co-operative. In USSR one part is co-operative, the other an STE. Anyhow, where there is an income difference but little or no migration there are by definition two nations, even if both are capitalist. The additional definition of a national boundary, that there *must* also be a barrier to capital flows, is laughably unrealistic, quite unnecessary and indeed self-contradictory.[29] But there *can* be such barriers, especially where land is inalienable. It is at this point that differences of economic system are added to, or even replace, differences of culture and wealth. If the countryside is full of ejidos and the like capital clearly cannot flow in, for where land is inalienable only crops and livestock can be mortgaged. Neither can an emigrant peasant take his capital out, for he normally gets nothing for abandoning his aliquot claim to the community's land. And this is an important limitation on his mobility, which probably outweighs the protection afforded against his own improvidence.

A different barrier to factor movement is presented, as we saw in sec. 12, by the self-managed enterprise. The quasi-Illyrian enterprises of Yugoslavia tend to absorb capital and repel labour. This creates for the 'Helvetian' sector – a considerable one in practice – an unusual interest–wage ratio, so that it employs less capital and more labour than the nationwide scarcities of each would indicate.

But the product markets, just as in the case of international trade, are much more perfect than the labour market. Crops and crafts are exchanged freely for urban goods and services, and compete freely with the produce of state farms or private latifundia, and of factories producing consumer goods. When in international trade we speak of consumers' sovereignty we mean the world consumer; so here we mean the national consumer, never mind to what sector he belongs. Poor consumers are, we have seen, as sovereign as rich ones.

Pursuing the international analogy, we see that the two sectors should specialize, each in the techniques and products requiring the appropriate factor-intensity. This is a distinct improvement on random specialization, though the country would do still better if its labour and capital flowed freely. For the Heckscher-Ohlin theorem only establishes equal relative factor prices, and at that only if technology fulfils very special conditions: it does not establish equal real productivities in the two 'nations', as would free factor-flow (Wiles 1969, pp. 335–8).

The importance of workers' sovereignty, insisted on in sec. 1, becomes ever clearer. Dual economies, national boundaries and the co-existence of ownership systems all violate it. Nay, this violation is an important part of the definition of a nation or ownership system. But it is not, in the latter case, a necessary part. For only those systems are meant that do not pay labour its marginal product in the outside world. These are co-operatives, communes and peasant families. It is, be it noted, far from uncomfortable to be paid *more* than one's marginal product, which is what these latter systems usually do. But it is sub-optimal. Optimality is a stern goddess, and those who worship her need strong stomachs.

Notes

1. Wiles 1961, *passim.* This section and sec. 5 are heavily dependent on that work.

2. But, as I pointed out in the preface, no reviewer had come to grips with it in the first edition. Clearly, then, it has no *obvious* fallacy.

3. Minerals and forestry, therefore, are less perfect examples.

4. The few big non-ferrous metal producers sell on a market, the London Metal Exchange, rendered perfect by the very many sellers of scrap.

5. Homogeneity of manufactures is highly artificial, and means spending a great deal extra to imitate the rival's product. It is unfair competition or 'passing off'.

6. Looked at carefully, these too are immaterial. Transporters sell no material object, but relocation. Electricity is not matter but a type of behaviour in matter. Gas and water are storable and belong in (iv). So public utilities are not a valid class by this schema.

7. Declining *long-run* marginal cost, over an average of peak and trough, as capacity expands, is no more common here than in sector (iv). It poses a problem for investment policy, not for current pricing policy. It is simply untrue that short-run marginal cost is usually below average cost in a public utility.

8. Arnold C. Harberger estimated, to his own surprise, 0·1 per cent of the US national income lost through product monopolies in 1925 (*AER*, May 1954). David Schwartzman, no enemy of orthodoxy, confirms this order of magnitude for 1954 (*JPE*, December 1960). These estimates have not been refuted, but cf. George J. Stigler, in *JPE*, February 1956. Harry Johnson, in *Econometrica*, July 1966 arrives more speculatively at the same order of magnitude for monopoly in the supply of labour or capital to one industry out of two. Cf. the collection of such estimates by Harvey Leibenstein in *AER*, 1966. For misallocation due to trade unions cf. A. Rees in *Journal of Law and Economics*, October 1963; P. Scherer, *Market Structure and Economic Performance*, 1971.

9. This is (p−m.c.)/p, or simply the reciprocal of the elasticity of demand, provided that m.r.=m.c.

10. They are at least as old as the seventeenth-century Quaker shopkeepers, who astonished the world by refusing to higgle. Cf. Arthur Raistrick, *Quakers in Science and Industry*, N.Y. 1968, p. 42.

11. Note, not 'technical'. For that would be a question of X-efficiency (chapter 15), not allocative efficiency, as here. The distinction is of course question-begging, since transport and communications themselves depend on technology. But we argue there that it is valid in the short run.

12. In so far as it is known: a thing too easily assumed. We have no space here for the complicated and uncertain relation between the economist's marginal cost and the average cost of the businessman and administrator.

13. For general price control by the executive arm cf. sec. 7.

14. Cf. chapter 4, sec. 11; chapter 6, sec. 3.

15. But this is changing. Cf. chapter 7, sec. 11.

16. Cf. Richard Portes in *Soviet Studies*, April 1972; Peter Wiles in *Economie Appliquée*, 1/1974.

17. E. H. Carr, *Socialism in One Country*, N.Y. 1958, vol. I, Part 2; V. N. Bandera in *J.P.E.*, June 1963; Raymond Hutchings in *Soviet Studies*, July 1961.

18. Audrey Donnithorne, *China's Economic System*, N.Y. 1967; Barry M. Richman, *Industrial Society in Communist China*, N.Y. 1969.

19. 'Tension from below' characterized the first Soviet Five-Year Plan. During the Cultural Revolution Mao almost abolished the Party in its turn, for being nearly as bureaucratic and inert as the state machine. With such a great administrative load put upon it, this would not be surprising. The role assigned above to middle-rank Party cadres was in fact played by Red Guards, while *military* men restrained their worst excesses. This naturally reduced production. Now the Party is back, but it has not recovered its élan.

20. Roberto Bernardo, *The Theory of Moral Incentives in Cuba*, Alabama 1971.

21. This little word contains some big assumptions, not all of which, perhaps, have been clearly seen by the writer. It means at least this, that every enterprise must seek without compromise to maximize only one thing: value added per head.

22. Cf. Richard S. Weckstein, 'Evaluating Mexican Land Reform' in *Economic Development and Cultural Change*, April 1970, pp. 395–8.

23. The supply of labour by nearly all individuals is negatively related to wage increases. But this, as we showed in chapter 2, sec. 17, is irrelevant to enterprises and industries.

24. Cf. chapter 4, secs. 10, 11; chapter 6, secs. 4, 5.

25. Net, in both cases, of the expected rise in the general price level. The principle has finally been grasped in practice that fixed interest must be settled in this manner.

26. Cf. Theodore W. Schultz, *Transforming Traditional Agriculture*, New Haven, 1964.

27. Cf. Sipra Dasgupta, 'Producers' Rationality and Technical Change in Agriculture. . .', London Ph.D. thesis 1964. This is fundamentally an elementary proposition in portfolio management: the poor cannot afford risky 'holdings'.

28. The three-open-field system with strips was usual. Cf. chapter 5, sec. 4.

29. See Wiles 1969, p. 39. The higher rate of interest in the poorer sector is ordinarily due to the lower creditworthiness of the borrowers. Many analysts refuse to say this because the truth, that the rich are less improvident and possibly more honest than the poor, is a 'right-wing fact'.

11

Short-Run Optimality and Economic Administration in the STE

1. Perfect competition is very centralized, and not a myth
2. Planless perfect computation
3. The priority of output orders over price orders
4. The fallacies of aggregation –
5. the market avoids them, and –
6. so would perfect computation, were it technically possible
7. Input-output incoherence is not a separate allocation problem –
8. except under the rigid planning
9. Administrative capacity and ex ante hierarchical disaggregation
10. The 'partitioning' of the STE
11. Some general theories of bureaucracy
12. Functionalism in the STE
13. The Soviet-type price mechanism
14. Tension in Soviet-type plans
15. Criteria in the classical STE
16. Decentralized exceptions within the classical STE
17. The Gossnab
18. Semi-decentralization on principle
19. Price Reform
20. Co-operative agriculture
21. The costs of command planning

11

1. Perfect competition sheds a flood of light on the STE. The perfectly competitive market (chapter 10, sec. 2) is a highly organized, expensive and artificial institution, somewhat comparable to a planning office. In origin merely the coming together on a vacant plot of primitive higglers, who want to reduce the risk inherent in decentralized pricing, it has come to own an expensive downtown building with paid officials, professional brokers who have bought themselves a seat and subjected themselves to the rules, and modern communications terminals (all paid for by a levy on the product). From here it fulfils a most important social function: it centralizes information, digests it, and issues a 'planning criterion' to anyone who can afford the *Financial Times* or a teleprinter. This is the single price. This price has been worked on, if in a strange fashion, by many acute, well-informed and utterly sceptical minds. It takes the future as fully into account as any planner's decision. It is of course subject in practice to mood and speculation, but these things also affect planners, in smaller degree but more secretively. Although referring to a particular grade of the product delivered to a particular place, the price is used by buyers and sellers all over the world, let alone the country. They agree (by imperfectly competitive methods!) on discount factors for quality and distance from the 'middle price of the day'. Only a tiny percentage of national, or world, turnover actually passes through the central perfect market.

Thus perfect competition is highly centralized, but only as to the upward flow of information and the setting of the price. Moreover it still pays brokers and their principals to monopolize upward information before the price is set: the centralized information is not rationally used at all. But we shall see almost equal reason to doubt whether any feasible central planning office could consolidate the information better. The only downward flow of information is the price itself, though more than that can be bought from brokers. Reaction to the price is left to the producers and users. This all-important element is still wholly decentralized. What flows downward is information, not orders – an elementary distinction blurred by too much of communication theory. Still it is undeniable that perfect competition is the most centralized allocation system in the world, except for the crucial production decision.

Moreover perfect markets in several industries are very satisfactorily interconnected. Even though there is a special building with special experts for each basic price, nothing at all stops producers or users from knowing other prices and so from substituting other materials. A system of many perfect markets sets up no 'partitions' in the sense of sec. 10

below. All we need to do is buy the *Financial Times*. The knowledge these markets provide is very incomplete, but supremely accessible.

2. Centralization, then, is part of perfection. This is a vital point to have established before moving over to non-market systems of allocation. These are so peculiar to the Western student that they deserve a chapter to themselves. To begin with, perfect computation is a much less realistic category. There can be and is perfect competition for individual commodities, and the absurd notion that this category is a myth rests only on the absurd demand that all markets be perfectly competitive. But there is not – yet – perfect computation for anything so broad as a single commodity. For all the talk and the promises, all that can actually be dealt with by linear programming, when we allow for the difficulties of getting good data, is a single enterprise with, say, 40 inputs and outputs. The co-existence of many such 'computed' enterprises is of course competition, not computation, since only a market can link them effectively (sec. 4). However the possibility of perfectly computing, from a single centre, every detail of an economy remains in my opinion real, and worth discussing as a reality. Moreover, while it is still only a potentiality it is already an intellectually necessary myth.

The big difference between computation and competition is that the former simultaneously centralizes prices and the optimum production from each enterprise. It may or may not be necessary (sec. 3) for it to send out these production orders, but they need no more be exactly right than the perfectly competitive price need be exactly right; both systems can proceed *à tâtons*. We believe the opposite because we further assume a rigid plan. But *perfect computation need not be planned at all.* It can be simply reacting all the time to changes in supply, demand and technology at the periphery of the sphere, big or small, that it controls. The 'computed' enterprise of today remains firmly embedded in a market. The perfectly computed economy that most of us imagine is equally firmly planted between a labour market, possibly a capital market, markets for consumer goods and arms, and a foreign market. This economy is simply a large enterprise. Then if it planned it would do so 'intransitively' (chapter 9, sec. 2); trying to foresee, making provisions against events, etc. Planless perfect computation, then, has logical priority.

Planless perfect computation (whether by prices or by outputs and prices) has certain virtually definitional advantages over a market. It eliminates the cobweb. For it proceeds more directly, and less *à tâtons*, from one supply and demand equilibrium to the next. It could only hit an intermediate disequilibrium, whether threatening explosion or convergence, by mistake. Even if it did, it would not explode or even converge, but continue by the shortest path towards equilibrium. Perverse elasticities, which are nevertheless of sufficient normality to produce a stable equilibrium, have now no effect on the approach to equilibrium.

Speculation is also eliminated. Speculation is a bet on what other people will do; it may even involve anticipatory action by the bettor that makes them do it. This, the worst form of speculation, is self-validating. But there are no other people inside a computer: it knows what it is going to do.

For these two reasons planless perfect computation could not generate Keynesian unemployment, or a trade cycle: unless the computer was instructed to ignore total employment.

The computer, again, internalizes all the 'externalities' of which it is appraised, provided it is instructed to do so. We use inverted commas because there are by definition no externalities in an economy run from a single centre.

There would be no need to enforce anti-monopoly rules with a powerful police or judicial apparatus, for there would be essentially only one entrepreneur, the central computer.

3. Perfect computation (planned or planless) might set prices or outputs or both. And here there is a fallacy to dispose of: that somehow centralized[1] price setting is less sub-optimal and disaggregated, or in some unspecified way better, than centralized output setting. If you solve the primal you solve the dual: there are as many prices as outputs. It is possible, of course, to set only one price in each sector, and hope that the others round about will fall into line. But equally we might set only one output in each sector – and the hope would be as vain. As far as optimality goes there is no advantage at all in setting prices rather than outputs. Indeed all systems are subject to cost inflation, and the suppression of this is likely to bring quite extraneous considerations into the setting of prices, while leaving outputs rational.

So if one has the information to do one accurately one can do the other, and should settle for outputs. Output, after all, is what economics, and quite especially the optimality problem, is about. We do not eat the price of bread or roll the price of steel. Every enterprise, we saw in chapter 4, sec. 1, is a command economy – that is the definition of an enterprise. It does not influence its employees by telling them the prices of products, so why should the planner necessarily try to influence subordinate establishments by such means? We are more likely to get the output we want with an output order, because orders increase the 'elasticity of supply' of such establishments.

There is this difference between labour supply or consumer demand and enterprise supply or demand. We respect the former as part of consumers' or workers' sovereignty: they are as elastic as they are and we are not playing God with that (hence we should condemn most advertising under capitalism). But a capitalist enterprise and still more so a socialist establishment is only a social convenience, and we should be able to dictate not only its maximand but also its elasticities.[2] It is a seldom asserted but very obvious fact about the price mechanism that it is most effective where elasticities are highest. The corollary is that enterprises in all economies *should* have as elastic a supply curve as possible, and that institutional systems should be judged on this basis. Now in a command economy we cannot, of course, by definition, speak of elasticities since price is not the causative variable. That is now the command itself, and we must go behind the elasticity concept to what in any case is there: reaction time plus percentage fulfilment of order. It scarcely needs proof (and it has not been proved!), but it seems obvious that 'equivalent' output orders elicit more 'elastic' response than 'equivalent' price changes, provided that some cost-covering mechanism or other is guaranteed. Why otherwise do enterprises exist? Why do belligerent ACEs switch to a command economy?

Note that both kinds of planning have the advantages of sec. 2. Both kinds eliminate the cobweb and the planners go directly, and not *à tâtons*, for whatever price they choose. Perverse elasticities cannot produce a cobweb, since there are no intermediate stages. In the same way both kinds eliminate speculation; and both kinds internalize all the externalities of which the planners are apprised.

4. Suppose the price-planners just set a price for grain as a whole? Would not this be very flexible, while remaining effective? No, *for there is no such thing as 'grain' or 'steel'*, and so no such thing as the price of grain or steel. Furthermore, of course, if these metaphysical abstractions did exist, it would be as easy to order quantities of output in respect of them.

We come herewith to the '*curse of aggregation*'.[3] In a market economy 'grain' and 'steel' are the concepts of statisticians, journalists and economists. We know how many tons were produced, and the average price per ton, ex post. Serious people are not interested in this, but operate with far more disaggregated concepts: Canadian durum c.i.f. Liverpool in November, steel bicycle spokes 30cm. long from the factory in Novosibirsk (and not from the one in Vinnitsa, which is inferior). And not only are these the things producers produce and talk about and earn their living from, these are the things consumers substitute for each other. These are the 'scarce resources', and these substitutions constitute the allocation problem that is allegedly the prime concern of economics.

We do not substitute grain for steel or guns for butter, since there are no such objects. We do substitute one kind of wheat for another, and for specified grades of rye, and soya-beans and potatoes. We even substitute it in the longer run for specified grades of steel (fewer bicycles and more bread), while perhaps making opposite substitutions in allied fields (less oats for horses, more of another grade of steel for tractors). And quite far-fetched substitutions are also brought about by switches in technology or supply: plastic plumbing for copper plumbing. These especially have made difficulties for the STE.

It follows that a central computer talking to other computers, each representing an enterprise, is not perfect computation. For the central one either can or cannot disaggregate as far as 1cm. copper pipes or Canadian durum. If it cannot, there is no computer that can substitute plastic pipes or Aroostook potatoes, and resources are not rationally allocated. If it can, there is no need for other computers or for enterprises.

Why do economists and top administrators not talk in these detailed terms? Alas, it is all too plain: disaggregation is boring. You have to know about some actual industrial process, to get, if not your hands, then at least your mind, dirty. We are no longer in a one-product, two-factor, economy. We can no longer talk big. We are not intellectuals any more, the Freudian Omnipotence of Thought is lost. So we avoid the question of disaggregation, and imply possibilities of rational planning or of relevant econometrics which simply do not exist.

When they are without power or influence, intellectuals do not matter. In market economies resource allocation merrily pursues its sub-optimal way, beginning and ending with the tiniest details. *The macro-categories are the ex post results of all these prior micro-decisions.* This is a very powerful proposition, a veritable joker in the pack of economic ideas. Not only does it destroy a great deal of planning theory but – incidentally for our purposes here – it threatens the Keynesian macro-economics. For it follows that this too must rest upon some micro-foundation or other. In its original formulation this was perfectly competitive, and therefore the macro-theory could not explain cost inflation (chapter 14).

It may be objected that laws and taxes do use foolish words like 'grain' and 'steel' – but they must be painstakingly defined by delegated legislation, or case law, or a fat appendix to the act.

5. Soviet economists estimate that there are about 20 million commodity-types, final and intermediate, in USSR.[4] The equivalent Hungarian figure is 2 million.[5] These staggering figures exclude grades of labour, agricultural land, forest, water and mineral seam; also services both final and intermediate, especially repair services and R and D projects. They do not allow for the diversity of buildings – nearly each building is a grade to itself, and there are more than 20 million in USSR. Even within the categories of industrial and agricultural commodity referred to, it is impossible to lay down what is not a different commodity from another. Perhaps the best criterion is that the elasticity of substitution is infinite. Let us assume that this is what figures rest on. As to the excluded categories of economic object, listed above, there can surely not be less than twice as many of all these. But linear programming can only cope with about 1200 rows and columns![6]

The market solves this problem by having something like one 'entrepreneur' to 40 types of economic object, where 'entrepreneur' means a person entitled to decide on price, technique, input, purchase and sale.[7]

Indeed clearly the number of types is limited by the number of 'entrepreneurs'. Unmanageable diversity does not pay. A fairly intelligent person, spending much but not all of his working day on these questions, can manage 40 goods and services (inputs as well as outputs, and the techniques that connect them) tolerably well. After all he does not make many decisions a day, he has employees to advise him and trade literature to reduce search costs. He can also use linear programming, since his problem is well within its capacity.

Each of these 'entrepreneurs' has access to virtually the whole market. He may well not have freedom to produce very different things, the 'free entry' of the Western textbook. But that, on an inter-system comparison, is a trivial drawback: he has freedom to know what there is and what it costs, and freedom to buy it. His money is active, it motivates suppliers. Moreover if he is already a producer he can sell virtually anywhere. Therefore all substitutions are possible, all scarce resources really are comparable with all others (e.g. plastic plumbing with copper plumbing, electricity with oil). No one is limited, as in the STE, to a single macro-category of products. If the market solution is highly imperfect and slow-moving, it at least exists.

6. Now under perfect computation all of this information would be equally available. There is now only one entrepreneur: the computer. All these substitutions are proposed to him alone (the actual initiatives must mainly still come from people), and he decides between them on a simulated perfect market. Could it happen, such a thing would be a great improvement on the many imperfect markets, and capitalism would surely die (chapter 20). However there are many technical reasons why this will not happen soon, though I personally feel it is only a matter of time:

(i) market research has quite insufficient information about the demand curves of consumers and producers;

(ii) supply curves and capacities are even less well known;

(iii) suppose that the national output plan were recalculated fortnightly – a length of interval that would necessitate vast stocks to tide us over *ad interim* – there are no communications channels that could convey all the data in (i) and (ii) to a single place, or convey the orders away again;

(iv) there is no archive or electronic memory that could store so many data and retrieve them in time;

(v) computers are not big enough to perform the required operations in time;

(vi) any trivial error like a misplaced decimal or a single piece of wrong information is dragged through the computer again and again; the resulting error may be explosive (while in a market the particular entrepreneur suffers alone);[8]

(vii) it is possible that the growth of the volume of production and the diversity of products may outstrip market research, communications and/or computer capacity (not likely in the writer's opinion, but recorded as a widespread opinion).

Let us repeat that optimal allocation by computer does not require a rigid plan. The computer could proceed more or less *à tâtons*, and roll with its own mistakes. It would still be able to deal better with cobwebs and speculation, and internalize more externalities, than a market.

7. We discussed above the problem of competitive products, needing to be substituted for each other. What of complementary ones? The great case of complementarity is an input and an output.[9] Now since intermediate goods can be inputs and outputs of each other some of these millions of types of economic object are circularly interdependent: if we want more steel we must have more coke, but coke ovens use steel, so we must have 'more more' steel, and so 'more more' coke . . . This threatens us with disproportions between intermediate goods, of a kind seemingly different from sub-optimality vis-à-vis final demand. But, first, an infinite regress is not a disaster if, as in this case, the series is heavily damped. Then again disaggregation is less of a problem, since fine detail in output is largely independent of fine detail in input. Thus all the millions of grades of steel (and iron) require coke, of a few substitutable grades; and all grades of coke require a fairly uniform oven made of one or two grades of steel only. However our habits of aggregation do shield us from some of the most complicated cases. Within the columns and rows we so gaily baptize 'agriculture', 'engineering', 'education' and 'chemicals' there lurk really serious circularities: fodder-livestock-manure-fodder, bearing-lathe-bearing, teacher-pupil-teacher. These represent large input-output ratios, so the circularities are not well damped. Moreover no serious planner would operate with so gross a category as 'agriculture' or 'engineering' – to use our pet phrase, there are no such activities. Forced to disaggregate, he would meet the circularities head-on. There are also certain very widely used inputs which cannot be triangulated away even by aggregation: fuel, power, transport, lubricants, unskilled labour.

The market glides easily down these infinite regresses, obtaining 'more more' steel only when the original 'more steel' has revealed the necessity of more coke ovens. It reacts by raising prices, by importing and running down stocks. It does not matter if there is an error in the first place, for since the reaction to demand or technology change comes *à tâtons* anyway, the whole economy is functioning *à tâtons*. These interdependencies are simply swallowed up in the general maze of unpredicted interactions. So is the much simpler kind of disproportion resulting from a wrong estimate of an input-output ratio, say due to misinformation or to ongoing technical progress.

Planless perfect computation would solve these problems in the same way as the market. For the computer would proceed similarly *à tâtons* against what would now be internal inconsistencies produced by such circularities and errors. If its orders to the branch establishments were self-contradictory, i.e. involved input-output incoherence, it would correct these too as it went along, simultaneously with its reactions to changes in demand. But it could probably make one or two iterations in the first place, and hit a truer initial balance than the market. This recalls to us its superiority in dealing with the cobweb, which is also a matter of a few iterations.

Indeed input-output incoherence is only a kind of sub-optimality. It results only in excessive or insufficient demand for particular intermediate goods, which are cured by price changes in the usual way. We do not need this concept until we come to the rigid plan.

8. To the Soviet-type mind, tâtonnement is anathema. The central authority should always get everything right and never have to adjust for any reason, be it faulty market research (sub-optimality) or faulty estimates of required inputs (input-output incoherence), or mere subsequent historical accident, such as a bad harvest, a new foreign tariff or an outbreak of war. Therefore we must solve these problems ex ante, with fair exactitude, by a *rigid detailed plan*, alterable only by central authority and then only in emergency. Note the crucial distinction between centralization and (rigid) planning: we can have even planless centralization (above) and decentralized planning (below).

But first, why have a rigid plan? Let us begin on a high ideological and psychological plane, and descend gradually. (i) The proletariat's victorious government can predict history – its victory shows as much; so how can it not predict trivial and philistine things too? The Party is always right: it makes no mistakes in any matter. The plan is its prediction, so it is correct. And in a deterministic system all rational predictions are orders anyway. For reason rules everything, only it is dialectical Reason, of which the Party has a monopoly. But the plan is itself a piece of Reason. (ii) The system is totalitarian. Orders may be indeed arrived at after consultation, and they often are. But once they are given they must be followed. They are proven to be scientific by receiving Party blessing. There is no latitude in execution, that is not what 'democratic centralism' means. (iii) There is nothing about optimality or consumers' sovereignty or scarcity in Marx. Even demand and supply, which he correctly described for capitalism, refer only to capitalism. (iv) Moreover there is no tension in tâtonnement: it requires no effort of subordinate units. There may be orders, but they are tentative, liable to revision; they stretch no one. But a rigid plan can be screwed up, and tension brings about growth. So the plan substitutes tension for tâtonnement and introduces us to a whole new world.

But above all, in the world as it is, the market cannot be abolished in any other way. The whole weight of orthodox Marxist tradition is against the market as a form of capitalist anarchy, and against an even partial return to it as a political and social threat to the system's foundations. So here we stand, in 1928 or 1973 as the case may be: what can we put in place of the market? Yugoslavia, China and Hungary have not replaced it. Perfect computation is technically impossible, and in any case centralized tâtonnement is hardly good Marxism, hardly the abolition of the market. A large number of small authorities, each as big as computers permit, each beginning from the bottom with the operational fine detail, and co-ordinating themselves laterally, would simply be a number of socialist enterprises in a market. If there were a hierarchy of authorities, the upper ones could only register and accept the macro-results of micro-decisions already taken. Clearly, then, all alternatives are excluded. The centre must have the initiative, and it is only capable of a few decisions. These must be aggregative. The micro-decisions must *follow from* these, whether or not the result is rational, and must *consist in* disaggregating them. Therefore these decisions constitute a rigid *a priori* plan. Such planning is the technically necessary result of trying to abolish the market before central computation is technically possible.

If the disaggregated instructions seem sub-optimal, those who receive them cannot alter them at will, because that lets the market back in. They must go back up through channels, and there is no reason why they should get satisfaction. How do they know, down there in their little enterprises, what is optimal? Besides, optimality is, or was, ideologically suspect, even an unknown concept (iii above). But if the instructions are materially impossible, something must be done higher up. Here is something an enterprise incontestably knows about. Hence input-output incoherence is taken far more seriously. Long before there was input-output there was the *method of balances*.[10] This consisted and consists in adding up each row (the columns do not matter) of an input-output table in physical units (which need not be the same throughout the table), and making sure that the 'budget balances'. This is when global output (planned output+imports+net movement in stocks) equals the planned uses. In the absence of matrix algebra, the rows are adjusted against each other by rule of thumb, with very few and very crude iterations.

The pursuit of mere coherence, then, is very sub-optimal. But it has been mitigated even within the classical STE. Attention is drawn particularly to the possibilities of *re*-trading and *re*-exporting described in sec. 16 (viii and ix). Coherence is an absolute value only in the first quadrant of an input-output matrix. Once goods leave the quadrant it does not matter much where they end up; the output plan is fulfilled. So if the consumer forces a revision of the trading plan this is painless. There can even be unplanned international trade between two sub-optimal first quadrants.

9. There are, of course, millions of coherent plans, especially if un-

employment is permitted, but only one is optimal. Every sergeant knows not to issue grossly self-contradictory orders: a little planner's tension is good, but a lot ruins discipline (chapter 9, sec. 12). But not every sergeant knows which set of orders is best. It is also computationally easier to use input-output; modern techniques can invert a matrix 4000 square, which is far more than the 1200 square matrix amenable to linear programming. But 4000 is also a far cry from 20 million!

Nevertheless it is the 20 million that must actually be produced, and eventually plans with that number of products must be handed out somehow. The solution is, of course, to plan what we have condemned as metaphysical abstractions ('grain', 'steel') at the centre, and to pass these targets down for *a priori hierarchical disaggregation* to intermediate authorities. First, through how many separate stages should the disaggregative process go? Now 4000×4000 is 16 million, so it might seem to be barely possible to have the Gosplan matrix in the middle and 4000 large trusts, each with a good computer, giving the orders directly to workmen. But more stages are needed for several reasons:

(i) subordinate matrices are uninteresting and hardly exist. Subordinate authorities give output *orders* and make input *requests*. Their intermediate outputs are seldom their own inputs. Such circularities do not affect them much,[11] but each must spend much energy in persuading others to deliver inputs. Only the single general authority is sovereign over nearly all its inputs as well as its outputs, and faces squarely the circularity problem.

(ii) the plan-disaggregating authority should also be the line[12] authority. Technological change, personnel promotion, labour relations, investment expenditure, legal representation, prices: management has many, many other interests than mere output decisions and input acquisition. The 'span of control' is not so large in these other matters. But the Gosplan, as we saw, is mainly an input- and output-decider. Having little to do with these other matters it can deal with more commodities. Indeed it began as an inter-ministerial committee, without any line responsibilities at all.

(iii) each planning level should have reserve planning capacity, and some capacity[13] at least to interfere with the major sub-allocations going on at the level below.

(iv) each level should also have some capacity to adjust its plan to those of other authorities, not in its line of command, at all levels. This point is dangerous, however, since it threatens the authority of the line superior (sec. 1).

(v) many enterprises must produce the same commodity-type, if only because of transport problems. The whole aspect of location multiplies the problem of choice. There are many more than 20 million products in appropriate places, since there are thousands of places.

So in practice the Gosplan at the top level uses the best computer and orders as many commodities (or metaphysical abstractions) as it realistically can: say 1000 absolutely, with fairly active interference into 10,000 more. The other levels – Ministry, bureau of Ministry, trust, enterprise – complete the task of disaggregation with worse or no computers but little strain. For if each disaggregated only 30 times, i.e. could develop 30 orders out of one, there might be 121·5 million commodities at the bottom.

We substantiate this claim with the very *a priori* and schematic example of Table 11/I. Only the top row and column 2 pretend to rest on known fact (there really are about 30 ministries and 49,900 industrial enterprises, with about 400 production workers each). Column 3 makes the important allowance for the fact that more than one authority produces each commodity. Clearly we are 'home and dry' with only three intermediate levels: there lurks some exaggeration in our guesswork.

Note that the enterprise itself 'plans' the last stage of disaggregation. In an STE, its decisions are also planning (chapter 9, sec. 11).

TABLE 11/I

A Schematic View of the Industrial Planning Hierarchy

Orders flow		1[e]	2	3	4[c]	5[d]
From	To	Commodities	Subordinate authorities per authority	Authority/commodity ratio	Total orders	Orders per subordinate authority
Gosplan	Ministries	1000	30	1·2	1200	40
Ministries	Glavki[a]	18,000	11	2·0	36,000	109
Glavki	Trusts[b]	360,000	11	3·0	1·08 mn	298
Trusts	Enterprises	8·1 mn	11	4·0	32·4 mn	649
Enterprises	Workers	121·5 mn	400	8·0	972·0 mn	49

a These are the specialized commodity bureaux within ministries
b Or associations or combines: these authorities are physically located in the provinces
c = (1) × (3)
d = (4) ÷ the cumulative total in (2)
e E.g. 18,000 = 1200 × 30 (the assumed order-disaggregation factor) ÷ 2.0

A priori hierarchical disaggregation is a vital concept for understanding the STE. It applies, too, as already hinted, to location. For a perfect computer would also locate every activity optimally, and in so doing produce a perfect transport plan. But in practice the centre can only locate activities within large areas, and subordinate authorities must take the final decisions (we postpone to the next section the question whether these decisions should be taken by territorial or production-branch authorities).

The same problem arises within the kibbutz, and especially a literature on the 'consumption tree' is developing. The consumption committee decides on a 'healthy' or 'rational' consumption pattern in aggregated terms, and then allows free individual substitution within these *a priori* categories, but not across them.[14] This procedure is sub-optimal to a Stalinist degree.

The opposite of '*a priori* hierarchical disaggregation' has already been described in sec. 4: in a market there is 'ex post aggregation from below'.

10. So this process hopelessly divides the economy into information- and decision-tight partitions. It produces decentralized command planning, or one of the many sorts – in practice the most important sort – of imperfect computation. Is this phrase more than a pun on 'imperfect competition'? Are there genuine resemblances? One resemblance is that certain goods and services, falling naturally under capitalism into this or that type of market classification, present similar problems to other systems, and specifically to the STE (chapter 10, sec. 2). Another is that at any rate some of the false allocation criteria used are the same.[15] But what concerns us here is another resemblance: imperfect competition also decentralizes and partitions information. It leaves indeed a theoretical power in the entrepreneur to decide to do almost anything, but it puts him into blinkers. This aspect is not enough stressed. It is not so much the occasional legal barrier to entry, or the (now mostly illegal) private barriers; it is not so much consumer fidelity and inelastic demand (what is 'imperfect' about them anyway?); it is sheer ignorance of what is happening that justifies the pejorative adjective. Opportunities to save resources or to use them better are continually passed up because they are not known. The beauty of perfect competition lies here.

How, then, reverting to the similar problem in the STE, do we coordinate the, say, three enterprises in the Ministry of Non-Ferrous Metallurgy that produce copper pipes of 1cm. diameter for plumbing with: (i) each other – they may be under different trusts and in different regions; (ii) the ten copper ingot producers under a different bureau of that ministry; (iii) their electricity suppliers in the Ministry of Electricity Production; (iv) the thousand construction enterprises needing the pipe; and above all (v) the single experimental producer of plastic pipe in the Ministry of Chemical Industry?

Only the Gosplan can cross all the partitions – its choice of 1000 key commodities does do this. But it is entirely incapable of the degree of disaggregation required by real economic life. Of the commodities we have discussed, its 1000 include electricity and copper ingots – certainly not copper pipe, let alone 1cm. copper pipe. It has power to reach that far down, but not capacity. Below the Gosplan there may, with luck, be a single bureau in the Ministry that is cognizant of all the 1cm. copper pipe. It will be able to reach down, perhaps informally, to allocate zones of delivery, say, or guarantee long runs. But this is fairly trivial, and the very fact that it is close enough for that puts it a long way from electricity and chemicals.

The partitions, however, are indispensable to achieve any disaggregation at all; though each principle of partitioning (production-branch, territorial, other) imparts different biasses to the decisions of the subordinate line authorities.[16] On the whole very disaggregated but cross-partitional initiatives are either never taken at all or eventually forced, by public-spirited citizens or the Party, right up back through 'channels' to the Gosplan and then down again. Few have the time and energy. The official bodies may have some administrative capacity to do this (sec. 9, iv) but are afraid to use it, owing to the system's strongly hierarchical nature.

What is missing, of course, is the free lateral links between bodies on the same level that exist in any reasonably relaxed bureaucracy. Many things should be decided by meetings of subordinates *from different departments* without consulting much their different hierarchical superiors. And here a glance at administrative theory is indispensable. As a first approximation we can call the bureaucracy of an STE 'Weberian': information flows upwards and instructions downwards. Everything works in practice according to the theoretical organization chart, everyone is blinkered and obedient. No account is taken of the informal network that grows up in all social groups, still less is it given any formal recognition. Max Weber's idea of how bureaucracies work would seem to us totally unrealistic today, a mere *Idealtypus* in his phrase, had we not USSR to look at.

In the language of administration theory, Henri Fayol's lateral 'gangplanks' are forbidden by the jealous superior.[17] And no wonder, for independent lateral links, forged without a superior's permission, will not merely erode his hierarchical power. Meeting without power over each other, these independent subordinates must *bargain*. Their lateral contacts will probably degenerate, in the context of economic life, into a free market. But the whole object of the Revolution was to suppress the market, therefore Communist bureaucrats must behave in a Weberian manner. Not only orders but even information is partitioned. For while orders tend only to flow where there is information, the reverse is not true, and purely informational gangplanks could easily be set up. This is never done, however;[18] for undoubtedly the monopoly of information bolsters the authority of the upper hierarchy.

11. Behind Fayol's gangplanks, which he did not himself over-emphasize, lurks a wholly different theory of bureaucracy, which we may justly call St. Simonian. It is perhaps above all here that the differences between French and Soviet planning become clear. The former merely brings to life St. Simon's administrative theory.[19] The latter accepts surprisingly much of it as an ultimate aim under Full Communism, but is in practice Weberian. Hence their extremely different attitudes to the market, and to democracy. Let us try to set this out in scandalously schematic form (each row starts with St. Simon, and shows how other systems vary from his):

'St. Simon'	'Weber'	the STE	Perfect competition
the hommes généraux[20] rely on knowledge, not power at all	power is more important and is unitary	(St. Simon ideally, Weber in practice)	the power of each owner is supreme in his sphere
economic life should be the administration of things, not the government of persons[21]	no such distinction	(St. Simon ideally, Weber in practice)	no such distinction
would undoubtedly have encouraged Fayol's 'gangplanks', had he heard of them; even had they led to a market	would certainly have rejected them, had he been planning an economic administration	'gangplanks' are confined to supervised *kontraktatsia* (see sec. 16)	only gangplanks, no administrative superiors
information ascends, mainly information but also orders descend	information ascends, orders descend	(Weber)	information between enterprises, orders within
informal	legal	informal, but authoritarian in a legal manner	legal
voluntary	compulsory	(St. Simon ideally, Weber in practice)	voluntary outside the enterprise, compulsory within

Tabulation, however, is too crude to answer the question, how is this superior hierarchy organized – line, line and staff, or even pure staff? The question concerns optimality very closely, since resources are allocated, i.e. sovereignty is exercised, under pure 'line' by the line hierarchy, and it will, as we have seen, be biassed according to the principle on which it has itself been organized. But if the functional authorities called staff have more influence, the allocation differs again. Thus a capitalist firm influenced by its sales staff will probably oppose technical change and charge low prices, and vice versa if influenced by its research laboratory. So long as losses are not threatened, the 'style' of the enterprise will be very different, and fairly substantial differences in allocation, including that of investment funds, will emerge. These differences are much larger in an STE, where losses do not matter very much and there are very important line or staff offices at the highest national level.

A line authority exercises the principal prerogatives of economic power: outputs, inputs, production schedules, managerial selection and promotion. Other functions – for of course these basic matters are also functions – are technology, sales (including short-run pricing), personnel (including short-run hiring), accounting and law.[22] Line authority passes down from level to level without let or hindrance, staff authority passes from specialized office at one level to another, but staff at either level cannot command line below unless backed by line above. In an emergency there is clearly no distinction: any function can become basic, but if that function has previously been 'staff' there will be trouble converting it *ad hoc* to 'line'. Such an emergency might be a strike, or the introduction of new technology.

St. Simon, had he known of all this, would have backed 'line and staff'. Nay he might have experimented with pure staff. And certainly there is no shortage of influential functional bodies (especially locational) in French planning. A firm in a market may organize itself internally how it wishes; externally it faces no authority at all. Weber of course was a pure 'line' man.

12. But paradoxically the Soviet tradition gives enormous power of interference to 'staff' bodies, and so is not strictly Weberian. The first reason is the out-and-out functionalism of the administrative theorist Lenin most admired, F. W. Taylor.[23] Taylor was the great prophet of 'scientific' labour, i.e. of the stop-watch, piece-work and the view of the worker as a machine, and it is this aspect of him that Lenin, most curiously for a Marxist, embraced. In fact Taylor's views on the stop-watch and piece-work have been utterly rejected by capitalism and – much more reluctantly, in view of Lenin's canonical status – by Communism. But Taylor also interpreted 'scientific' to mean 'functional'. His stop-watch holders were functional, after all, so why, he asked, should not also the planning department in a capitalist enterprise have total power within its sphere? He ended up with no 'line' management at all,[24] an entirely mad solution.

The other source of this extreme Soviet functionalism is, surprisingly, totalitarianism itself. 'Line', and preoccupation with hierarchy, suits a society in which state and other power has limits and must therefore be reinforced. Pure functionalism is a total disregard of the realities of power. This might result from mere stupidity, as with Taylor, or from a mushy assumption that we all love each other and are reasonable and won't rock the boat, as with some 'systems theorists'. But it might also result from the assumption that the main political authority is so strong, and incorporates Rousseau's General Will so clearly, that it can have its way through any channels. No wonder, then, that the Communists have ended up accepting that many enterprises shall be under 'dual subordination':

one man with two masters (three including the Party), the very thing that every administration theorist, except Taylor, condemns.

One reason for dual subordination within the state machine is to pay lip-service to local nationalism:[25] the enterprise is placed in a production-branch and a territorial hierarchy. But another reason is to make sure that various allocation criteria really do get a look-in. For beyond formal subordination are all the means of pressure usable by 'staff' bodies at higher level. To give but the simplest examples, an STE whose intermediate units are territorially defined will locate things less rationally, on the principle of one of everything for each territory. It will also build smaller factories, which is very inefficient. But it might well be able to tackle our copper-versus-plastic-pipe problem. The State Committee for Technology, and its lower organs, will be almost alone in pressing for the adoption of new techniques (chapter 15). The Ministry of Finance wants reduced costs while the line Ministry is interested in output, etc.

13. We can now, after all this preparatory matter, describe the allocation mechanism in the practice of the classical STEs outside co-operative agriculture. It has often been done before, it has become a part of 'what every schoolboy knows', so we may be brief.

Between enterprises, then, or in the first input-output quadrant, there is passive money and detailed command planning. Enterprises are told exactly what goods and services, including capital ones, to pass to each other, and are given land and money capital as free gifts. But workers are not so commanded, and must be attracted hither and thither on a free labour market. Nor are consumers, who must be induced to buy this or that by prices. So the great state monolith is an ordinary monopsonist of labour and an ordinary monopolist of consumer goods, and money remains active in these markets.

But why passive money elsewhere? Let us state it historically. When in 1928–9 Stalin reintroduced the command economy the Trotskyites, who hankered after 'War' Communism, demanded the abolition of money again. This was quite unacceptable: there had still to be retail prices and wages. It would have been possible simply to give enterprises directly from state funds enough money to pay workers with, and simply to confiscate their revenues from retail sales, while going moneyless everywhere else. But this would have led to too much financial centralization. All money transactions would have gone through the budget, causing immense administrative strain.[26] So Stalin simply froze inter-enterprise prices and continued to insist on full normal accountancy. Enterprises selling (by command) to other enterprises had a cost built up in the normal manner (except that there was no interest or rent), and were supposed to cover it out of the prices they charged. And these prices could not be other than passive, since they corresponded to commodity transactions that had been commanded. But ultimately these passive prices built up to the active prices charged in sales to the population, which is how the wages were spent.

Stalin's motives, and the preparatory discussion if any, have not been fully researched. But I am convinced that administrative feasibility was uppermost: as many things as possible should be on *khozraschet*, so as to minimize money flows. The bank should audit (chapter 12, sec. 15) but not actually administer as much as possible. The frozen passive prices very rapidly lost contact with the changing active prices,[27] and the Commissariat of Finance found itself paying large subsidies to some enterprises while it collected fantastic taxes from others. These great discrepancies of fortune in the inter-enterprise sector continue to this day.

There was no sense that passive prices should allocate things, i.e. influence actual outputs or output plans. Passive prices were there to cover costs and to make possible 'ruble audit'.

Now if wages are to attract labour they must be at least as high as market-clearing wages, and if prices are to attract consumers they must be at least as low. To pay more or charge less would be wasteful, and the Ministry of Finance has the most ordinary reasons for opposing such waste. Therefore these wages and retail prices are or should be exactly at market-clearing level, for the quantities that happen to have been hired or produced. But the planning system described above is gloriously and shamelessly sub-optimal from the broadcast categories down to the tiniest detail. No output is necessarily such as would, say, equate average cost with the market-clearing price, or marginal cost with marginal revenue, let alone marginal cost with price. There is therefore need of a *variable indirect tax*, which shall take the passive price c.i.f. last factory[28] and, subject to the retail margin, raise this price to market-clearing level for the given output. In rare cases, for 'raise' we must read 'lower': the tax becomes a subsidy.

This is the celebrated Soviet turnover tax on manufactured goods leaving the socialist sector. The method of calculating it, described above, is officially called the 'method of differences', and it applies to the majority of turnover-tax rates. So it is not an *a priori* tax of so much per cent on such and such a large category. It is a set of highly individualized rates for narrow categories, that go limping after changes in the retail market. Since costs, market demand and planned output targets all change, and the rates are set once a year at budget time, they usually fail to build a market-clearing retail price, and queues and surpluses are common. But this is equally the fault of the price setters: for they could make adjustments more readily than the Ministry of Finance, but they do not.

Signals that this or that is being under- or over-produced are passed up the planning hierarchy, along with many other signals. But they are swamped in volume and urgency by the signals that inputs are in short supply, so the output plan cannot be fulfilled; i.e. tension and input-output incoherence overwhelm sub-optimality as an immediate concern.

Moreover if there is under-production a queue can be tolerated – it only wastes the planners' wives' time, and that is no one's prime responsibility, nor indeed a waste recognized by Marxism as on a par with the destruction of a material object. Also in the longer run we can ask the Ministry of Finance to raise the tax-rate and the price. It will hardly object to greater revenue, but the general fear of rises in the cost of living restrains us here (chapter 14, sec. 7). Over-production, however, leads to surplus stocks. This is a much more obvious waste, and it affects the plan-fulfilment and bonuses of shops. It is more probable, then, that the planners will react quickly with a new output order.

Clearly in an STE indirect taxes are after all part of the state's profit under another name; they are only levied with a different periodicity, and by different administrative means. Therefore in keeping these rates unequal the state may be said to impose different degrees of monopoly, and so in a very striking and simple way to fail to optimize allocation. The rates are not on the whole differentiated in favour of the poor, except for black bread, children's clothes and children's shoes. This is because the proletarian state must have got the gross distribution of income right in the first place (chapter 16, sec. 16). Apart from these few categories, and an obvious and necessary discrimination against the national hard liquor, the rates are random with respect to social purpose. They are there, as the phrase 'method of differences' implies, to balance supply and demand. They should be equalized by output changes, like the monopoly profits they are. But there is amazingly little evidence that this is being done.

The rates are all a state secret. A shop assistant posting them on the price tags would be fired, possibly arrested. This is only in small part due to their manifest sub-optimality; for as we have seen Communists do not feel very strongly about this. The main reason for secrecy is that most of the rates are very high – which is not surprising or disgraceful since the income tax is very low and the state is very expensive. But the Party likes to give the citizen the impression he is little taxed, that the income tax is the only 'tax on the population', while all else is surplus value, generated by material production, that would have gone to capitalists had it not been for the revolution. On the whole this operation has been successful: Soviet citizens are amazingly ignorant of the turnover tax, and of the very substantial profits that constitute a tax almost as heavy.

14. Input-output incoherence, then, is far and away the main concern at all levels. Below, it affects plan-fulfilment bonuses. Above, it is an open reproach to competence. Of course if it produces a material surplus at any point the lucky receiver will hold on and conceal it. In the prevailing input-starvation he will not complain: such things always come in handy, if only for secret deals along some illicit 'gangplank'. There are two sorts of deficit: those produced by the general ambitiousness of the Politburo and top officials, who always try to extract more output than the system

can easily produce, and the random material deficits produced by sheer incoherence. These shortages are the curse of the system, and unlike 'monopolistic' prices have no parallel in market economies. Together they constitute *planner's tension.*

The random material deficits have a theoretical cure: a good input-output table on which one could pursue everything down to, say, the third iteration, and substantial stocks to take care of everything else. These stocks would include gold or foreign exchange, convertible into all needed items. In their absence, the planners use merely the 'method of balances': they consider only the rows in an input-output table, in physical units, and juggle them by rule of thumb so that not only each sums to zero but also the major column-wise discrepancies are removed. It is mathematically possible to invert a matrix in which each row is in a separate physical unit, since the column sums are not required. It is not, then, the fact of physical measurement that inhibits the use of input-output,[29] but – of course! – the fact of its extreme aggregation. The rule-of-thumb juggling is more or less equivalent to the first iteration: it leaves substantial discrepancies which are the tension-through-incoherence to which we have referred.

Some authorities[30] seem to be so attracted by this intellectual problem as to forget that even if the planners could perform three iterations managers would still not be allowed to carry large stocks. The ambition of the Politburo would still cause a *generalized* tension; everyone would have a slightly greater output plan than his input plan made possible, so that in the absence of more irrational forms of incoherence there would still be tension, though more evenly spread. Whatever subordinate administrators and mathematical economists think, top people view tension as an incentive to greater output. They have not been proved wrong.

Tension leads to various sorts of re-insurance:

(i) Intermediate officials add tension of their own as they disaggregate. For they too are responsible for the taut plans they have received, and stand to lose promotion or even bonus. So they give their subordinates still more unreasonable disaggregated plans in order to assure at least the fulfilment of their own aggregated ones.

(ii) Everything that can be hoarded is hoarded (above). The Politburo and topmost planners are of course extremely hostile to this, since it weakens discipline, assists evasion and makes informal lateral deals possible.[31]

(iii) Lower levels lie to higher levels, understating their output capacity, so as to receive plans they can fulfil.

(iv) They also lie about their output achievements, but this is more complicated. The big bonus comes with bare plan fulfilment: call this output X. Then at an actual output of 0·99X it pays to lie 'upwards'. But at 0·97X it is not so clear. The auditors might detect a 3 per cent lie, or someone might squeal. Besides, next year's target is normally screwed up by 5 per cent on what is reported. If we report fulfilment now it will be 1·05X, so it will be necessary to lie by 3 or more per cent again. So there is much to be said for reporting the truth, taking no bonus, receiving exceptional help in labour, materials and machines, and standing a chance of fulfilling next year's 1·02X. Now suppose we made 1·02X this year? Then perhaps report 1·01X: you get the bonus and a little more beside, and next year you only have to report 1·06X. Whatever you produce, that should not be impossible. In this extremely simplified account, we leave out several possibilities. A director retiring, or being promoted or transferred, may well report 1.00X on a reality of 0.97X; his successor can worry. A director who sees a present prospect of the Order of the Red Banner, or a place in the Supreme Soviet, may report 1.03X on a reality of 1·02X. Much again depends on his personal relations with the chief engineer and the accountant.

(v) Output and productive activity settle into a wasteful rhythm of peak effort before the target deadline (*shturmovshchina*), and exhausted inertia after it. There is nothing like this in a market economy. But schoolchildren and students live in a command economy, and they reproduce the rhythm of *shturmovshchina*. The thing is virtually inevitable, and once started can hardly be broken. Besides shorter periods, some claim to detect such a rhythm even with respect to five-year plans.

(vi) Every enterprise and higher authority tries to make itself independent of outside suppliers, especially of suppliers with other customers likely to enjoy some informal or formal priority. This had particularly serious effects when the 'line' authorities were territorial: each territory became a small autarkic nation. Organization by production branches confines this sort of 'subordinate autarky' (Wiles 1962, chapter 8) to ancillary enterprises: repair, transport, small building. But kolkhozy have such low priority that they branch out very widely, into building materials and electricity, for instance. And this means the spread of co-operative property into industry, which is a hot ideological issue.

All these factors affect not merely what is reported, and so statistical measurement, but also what is done. They are 'allocation criteria' (below). They also lead to the vast parallel bureaucracy of material distribution, known in USSR as Gossnab (sec. 17). Again, they showed their power when they brought to nought one of the earlier Soviet attempts at reform. For a few years after 1959 output was dethroned, and cost minimization became the principal, bonus-carrying, goal. But it did not work: managers became too choosy over inputs, and were less punctilious over delivering outputs that might raise costs, so that they delayed supplies to the next enterprise more often even than usual. In a few years output was back on its throne. Even after the 1965 reforms it is still there, since the fulfilment of a taut plan remains the pre-condition of all bonuses, out of whichever fund and for whichever indicator they are paid.

There is no more serious case of planner's tension than the system of compulsory deliveries from collective farms. Every feature is present though magnified: the Politburo's greed for output that is the *fons et origo mali*, the planners' consequent annual panic, the producers' concealment of both output and capacity, the mendacious statistical reports of both parties.

15. What then actually are the short-run allocation criteria of the STE? They are many, curious and conflicting, and their bald enumeration comes as a shock to the tidy mind. I try to list them in order of importance.

A. *Criteria of the Politburo.* The Politburo deals only with investment, so strictly speaking it has no short-run criteria. But some of the things it is known to want influence the planners, e.g.:

(i) more exports and fewer imports;

(ii) more heavy industry;

(iii) probably some current pet idea: Kaganovich disliked diesel locomotives, Khrushchev wanted maize and later mineral fertilizers, Gomułka liked very cheap housing.

B. *Criteria of Planners.*

(i) repeat last year's mix, with a few per cent more;

(ii) widen bottlenecks (and don't question the output targets that gave rise to them). This is as much as to say, arbitrarily fill the gaps indicated by the method of balances, without disturbing the main items already determined;

(iii) give current effect to long-term Politburo directives and whims;

(iv) follow local market research;

(v) as regards new goods, imitate consumption structure of ACEs (this is quite openly confessed).

C. *Indicators for Enterprise Directors.* An 'indicator' (*pokazatel'*) is a criterion dictated by the planners.

(i) surpass each detail of the output plan;

(ii) fall short of each detail of the input plan;[32]

(iii) bring in the newest technology as quickly as possible (mainly a long-run indicator);

(iv) profit, albeit in passive money and at fixed prices.

D. *Criteria of Enterprise Directors* (i.e. their private maximands). The Soviet-type enterprise director has one maximand: his bonus. Owing to the way the planners set up the conditions for reward, this meant in the classical STE output, and to this he sacrificed all his other indicators. The planners were perfectly well aware of this – many of them had been directors – but they never seriously tried to 'promote' the other indicators. Even so these did act as constraints, so the director habitually cheated. He cheats, however, in ways too numerous to describe: by padding output figures, by acquiring inputs on the side, by concealing stocks and capacity, etc. Some of these were mentioned above, but for the whole list we must refer to the specialized literature.[33] Plan evasion, like tax evasion, is not a subject for generalization. We can only insist here on how common it is. There is cheating in all enterprises under all systems where there is subordination, and men are not principals on their own behalf. But planner's tension greatly increases it.

Simplifying, the answer to the question, how are scarce resources allocated from day to day in an STE, is: according to criteria B(i) and B(ii). It is the planners who make most of the decisions, and this is how they make them.

16. Decentralization was always present, it has merely grown. Let us list first the old elements, present in the classical STE. We define 'classical' as meaning up to the end of 1962, excepting the brief interlude of workers' audit in Poland, 1956–7.

(i) In innumerable minor matters the director wrote his own plan. After all he was a state official in the same administrative hierarchy as the other planners, so why not? Furthermore in a planned economy everything is planned![34] – for it is very bad Party manners to draw attention to the distinction between transitive and intransitive verbs. The usual case was *kontraktatsia* (chapter 9, sec. 12). The director tried to arrange the terms so as to maximize his bonus, i.e. so as to maximize his overall output. But since he had no exterior plan to back him he was up against the equivalent freedom of his client, who could not be compelled to accept articles not yet laid down in any state plan. Most usually the plan, at this level of detail, specified only the client. So a constrained bilateral monopoly was very common, with both parties looking over their shoulders not at the profit from this transaction but at their overall outputs.

(ii) The nearer the commodity got to the retailer, however, the more we see real consumers' sovereignty (at the fixed price) acting upon the producer. In so-called local industry the market was never far away, since effective planning was in the hands of trade organizations (Wiles 1962, pp. 171–2). Traders never had the least bonus-incentive to go against consumers; their output plan was a sales plan.

(iii) Sometimes consumers', or at any rate retailers', sovereignty was formalized for important and centralized articles such as cloth. Within a broad category the producer received no output sub-targets at all, but had to fulfil the 'orders' of the retailer (*sistema zakazov*). But the plan-fulfilment bonus depended on the output of the whole category alone, and profit was a very weak incentive. So the system offered the producer nothing extra for doing as he was bidden.

(iv) But in Hungary after 1956 consumer goods industry was instructed outright to maximize its profits within output targets for broad categories, and bonus was made dependent in part on profit. This seems to have worked.

(v) Buildings, being unique products, were mainly planned in money terms. Although detailed physical specifications also existed, variances were easily come by. Within the overall money output target, builders substituted material inputs according to their relative prices. This meant, of course, a special flexibility on the part of producers of building materials, or withdrawals from stock.

(vi) Czechoslovakia made a more foolish experiment in 1958, decentralizing investment decisions, especially in the social and local government sphere. Everything else remaining centralized, this naturally did not work. Building materials continued to be planned in the old way, so these unco-ordinated expenditures led to more starts and fewer completions (chapter 14, sec. 5).

(vii) Co-operative agriculture is of course irrelevant, but state farms were allowed many substitutions, this time on the output side. One crop could replace another in satisfaction of delivery targets, at physical 'barter' rates centrally laid down.

(viii) Trade organizations could get together at 'trade fairs' and sell very large quantities of goods that were hanging fire in one corner of the country to other shops willing to buy for another area. This was felt to be only geographical redistribution of goods already nearly in the hands of consumers, and so nearly in the sphere of active money (Wiles 1962, pp. 179–80).

(ix) Trade organizations were even permitted international leeway. For, to repeat, once the goods have left factory and farm they are virtually out of the first input-output quadrant: it does not matter very much what happens to them, since we do not pretend to control consumers so rigidly. Why then should not the unplanned consumer be a foreigner, against an equivalent import of consumer goods?[35] Why not even let the tourists of one STE purchase freely up to a certain limit in another?[36]

(x) As premia to encourage exports, enterprises were allowed to retain and freely spend a small percentage of their hard currency earnings on foreign machinery. I.e. this money went into an earmarked fund, like so many other such funds drawn from profit. But the difference is that the domestic funds could not be used, even for their earmarked purposes, without a planner's order that the goods in question be produced – a problem that still afflicts the much larger post-1965 funds (chapter 13, sec. 7).

(xi) Shipping and actual foreign traders had of course great latitude.

(xii) Lastly there was the occasional romantic exception, the foreign body within the system. Stalin ran a private Klondike-type gold rush in Siberia in the mid-'thirties. When the prospecting had been done the discoveries were nationalized.[37] He also encouraged his Polish fellow-travelling Catholic organization, the PAX, to set up many businesses within the Polish STE (chapter 3, sec. 13). The object seems to have been to finance pro-Communist activity within the Church, but the PAX also supported its Soviet masters against Gomułka.

Dull stuff, the writer is fully conscious of it; above all very disaggregated! But if we cannot play the standard variations we do not really know the tune. Moreover there is method in all this madness: none of these exceptions touches heavy industry or armaments. These are ideologically and politically the ark of the covenant. They are also mostly easier to administer. Numerous enterprises, uncertain costs, the weather, the consumer, the foreigner: these were the factors making for exceptions. However difficulty of administration must have ranked below ideology, for the activities we have listed are not more diversified, nor do they produce more prototypes, nor are they freer of input-output circularity, than chemicals or engineering.

17. In place of a free wholesale market the STE must allocate administratively semi-fabricates between producers and users. This is done by the 'organs of material supply', which constitute the Soviet-type wholesale sector. Although there are many such organs run by Ministries, etc., we refer to them here generically by the name of the biggest one, that of the central Soviet government, *Gossnab*. The subject used to be disgracefully neglected by Sovietologists, and continues to be so by writers in STEs.[38]

It is sometimes suggested that this administrative allocation is solely the product of taut plans: it is a rationing device in a condition of excess demand through tension, just as ordinary rationing is necessary when there is excess monetary demand. This is only slightly misleading: there would invariably be excess demand for the best qualities of everything, were the plans never so relaxed. Thus the Gossnab is an administrator of heterogeneity, where the plan assumes homogeneity, in addition to administering sheer absolute scarcity. But it is also an ideological necessity, for otherwise there would be a market.

The textbook categories of competition apply loosely to the activities of the Gossnab. Where a market has bilateral monopoly the STE has two enterprises with plans that dovetail directly. Thus the Gossnab does not intervene at all when a large turbine is made *ad hoc* for a dam, or in any case involving *kontraktatsia*. Where the product would have been perfectly competitive in a market the Gossnab collects it from producers according to their plans, stores it and hands it out to users with valid claim forms (*zayavki*) according to their plans. These storage costs are borne by the Gossnab itself: it intervenes as a principal.[39] In intermediate cases it may be principal or agent. If a principal, it again collects from various producers, stores and must now somehow allocate. So, to repeat, it has the task of administering unplanned heterogeneity.

In this latter capacity the Gossnab is an extra planner, attending to the fine detail not covered by actual plans or by *kontraktatsia.* It has no instructions as to how to proceed, and is thought to do so by accepting bribes or by favouring with the best qualities the users with the most (Wiles 1962, pp. 169–70) political pull.

These functions can be classified another way. The most important commodities, like all kinds of wheat and steel ingot, are 'funded': directly administered, in accordance with a conscious Gosplan scheme, by the central Gossnab, which is a State Committee attached to the Council of Ministers. Less important ones are administered by regional Gossnabs or even by ministerial ones. It should not now surprise us that the producing ministry is entrusted with the allocation of its own product. It may indeed favour its own consumption of this product, if any, but it is a planning as well as a producing body. All economic organs are planners, and so are supposed to take national interests into account.

There are two litmus tests of serious decentralization: has a country abolished the one-year plan and the Gossnab? Only China, Hungary[40] and Yugoslavia pass these tests. But experiments with partial abolition continue in STEs, sometimes in favour of a market, sometimes of *kontraktatsia.*

18. Since the early 'sixties there has been serious reform in principle, as opposed to hugger-mugger exception-making. Each STE has gone rather its own way, but the 'starter's pistol' was E. Liberman's article in *Pravda*, 9 September 1962. With this article, in its principal paper, the USSR gave the Comecon countries[41] licence not merely to act but also to think. It would appear from the Hungarian case that USSR sets no limits, except public ownership and the acknowledgement of Marx; Czechoslovakia went no further, so her main offences must have been political. Nevertheless there is a very great weight of conservative opinion in each country's Party, except Hungary's.

Now in fact Liberman, a professor of business economics in the very provincial city of Kharkov, belongs to the practical and unsystematic wing of the reform movement. He was put up to it, and protected, and found space for in *Pravda*, by the mathematical economists. These are the intellectual, mainly non-Party élite of the two capitals, Novosibirsk and the Academy generally.[42] These people have played a far more creditable role than in the West. After a few brief years of unrealism in the late 'sixties they have not on the whole been super-centralizers, nor grossly overrated the computer, not forgotten the facts of aggregation; but have rather cast a scientific and mathematical glow over very ordinary economic concepts, thus winning the adherence of science-struck Party bosses to all kinds of reform. Effectually they have demanded the same things as the practical people. As in other countries, linear programming has helped the planners with manageable allocation problems such as: how shall a railway serving several cement works and building sites map out its pick-ups and deliveries? It has also been used for long-term planning, and the five-year plans have been partly based on much more disaggregated input-output tables. But the crucial one-year operational plan is still based on the method of balances and rule of thumb.

The reform of STEs has inspired a vast literature, more theoretical than practical. Here we shall confine ourselves to what administrators do, not what professors write. Outside Hungary they do not do very much, so we may be brief. The *Leitmotiv* everywhere else has been (i) to decentralize outputs only a little, since this is the ark of the covenant. But the bonus system must be changed so as to direct managers to more rational ends, including (ii) honest dealing with the planners, (iii) cost cutting and (iv) a warmer welcome for new techniques. It is also possible (v) to decentralize the financial system a good deal, since the output plan and the Gossnab are almost intact (chapter 13, sec. 7); in putting more weight on ploughback the authorities give another incentive to cost cutting. Thus (as always) *X-efficiency* (chapter 15) *is the reformers' main aim: allocative efficiency is a side-show.*

But how can we cut costs if we cannot freely choose our inputs? And how can we be allowed to do that if these inputs are some other enterprise's outputs, and so still laid down by a central plan? Again, the new financial system allows the enterprise to retain a great deal of its profits in earmarked funds. One of these is the development fund, for ploughback. But how can we spend it on, say, bricks, unless we get our prospective supplier's plan changed, or at least receive a *zayavka* from the Gossnab (it may be in stock)? Everything we want to buy with such a fund – it is not a retail fund – is still planned. Where there is vertical disintegration, A's inputs are B's outputs. The new freedom of the director is only meaningful in so far as the lessened details in his suppliers' output plans gives him a little user's sovereignty.

Then again we cannot deal honestly when we propose plans to the planners while tension remains. But at least the proportions of the dishonest proposals are improved by the price reforms, discussed below. These further make directors behave more rationally to the extent that they have decentralized powers and are now more interested in profit. But are they? In USSR at least the principle continues that bonus is not payable until the output plan has been fulfilled: even though it is now paid out of profit not the wage-fund, and is a function of the amount of profit. All this raises the status of profit, but the output constraint is crippling so long as tension remains – and it does. It means that most enterprises maximize output as before. (On the obstacles to the application of new techniques cf. chapter 15, sec. 17.)

One input there is that really can be decentrally economized in an STE, without upsetting the whole fabric: labour. Labour is the only input bought on the market, the only one that is not some other enterprise's output. But here we come up against the government's full employment policy. This is to compel directors to employ unskilled people they do not want, and in most STEs there are plenty of these. Plenty of candidates, then, for the sack. So Party and trade union deny the director the power the new model formally gives him. This leads to an interesting social cleft (chapter 14, sec. 10, chapter 16, sec. 20).

From about 1970 there has been retreat from reform nearly everywhere. The most face-saving way back to centralization is via the administrative amalgamation of enterprises, notably in USSR in 1973. On the mainly administrative reasons for setting the size of the enterprise cf. chapter 9, sec. 11.

19. We have seen that the computer has not yet bitten really deeply. The practical optimization of plans is a matter of price reform. Is this a refutation of what we have said earlier (sec. 3) about the priority of outputs over prices? No, for that was about a completely centralized system, in which they were genuine alternatives. But where the very drawing up of the plan is largely decentralized, as it has always been in STEs, prices matter a great deal: for the enterprise, in so far as it has freedom and profit is important, and for all the various planners in any case. The planners cannot help looking at these prices; the managers even look across lateral 'gangplanks' at the prices of substitutes – this much they can do without illicit contacts and actual bargaining. A rational price is a beacon, spreading its light in all directions. If the planners are asked to rationalize their prices and to pay attention to them, they will plan far better allocations.

First, financial capital and land have eventually received prices. As we see in chapter 13, sec. 15, Marx forbade a rate of interest, so the authorities have had to call it a tax. This is not unimportant, since it does not function exactly like a rate of interest. As to land, it is added to capital at a valuation, and the same capital tax is levied also on it. But this does not apply to kolkhoz land.

Western welfare economics and marginalism have not been accepted by practical price setters, even though they were pushed hard by the Polish economic community in the late 'fifties,[43] and are weakly implicit in linear programming.[44] But prices are rearranged so as to diminish subsidies to cover the average cost of the nearly marginal firm, and to correspond to relative world prices where exports and import subsidies are concerned. These are all good principles, and output plans are at last being changed as a result of these prices. This is of course what prices are for.

Marginal cost within the enterprise, however, is never calculated. Disgraceful as this seems, we may fairly ask how often a capitalist, let alone a Yugoslav, enterprise makes any serious estimate. It is at this point above all that orthodox micro-theory has something to contribute to practical affairs, under all systems.

It is not in the sphere of manufactured objects with stable average costs that marginalism makes its heaviest demands on the Marxist conscience.

The sensitive sectors are, as elsewhere, agriculture (next section), and the sector of variable marginal cost. The laws of production being the same everywhere, the Soviet-type railway system must also cope with returned empties, seasonal peaks, odd lots, etc. It does so with even less flexibility than capitalist railways since it is not merely constrained, like them, by public policy but also deprived of any motive (such as profit) or theory (such as marginalism) to do otherwise. Nevertheless in recent years enormous progress has been made here. The 'Railwayman's Economic Handbook'[45] makes blatant use of the marginal concept (p. 643), albeit in algebra (△) not Russian (predel'ni)! It lists a number of presently valid discounts for the use of wagons returning empty, for customers who allow the railway to ship their freight part way by canal at its own discretion, and for tourist and educational groups (pp. 603, 616, 625–6). It also lists, of course, discounts on the grounds of public policy, having nothing to do with cost or demand: coal and iron ore freights actually rise, instead of tapering, after 2500km. (this is to counter the planners' bad habits of locating steel plants in the wrong places!), invalids go cheap on social grounds, mineral fertilizers go cheap to make farmers use them, etc., etc. (pp. 605, 616, 626). Such things are also common in ACEs.

Then, again, since the laws of production do not vary, the cost-plus problem does not vary. When we build a building or repair a car, eventual total cost really is uncertain. In this case, however, there seems to be only one answer to the problem. The pricing procedure remains cost-plus, regardless of systems. The only difference from the market economy is that there is now no competitive tender at all.[46] All 'contracts' are administratively allocated by the planners.

Next, the STE has great difficulty with the pricing of new goods, particularly in the full-cost sector. These will under *laissez-faire* begin with a high monopolistic price, though quite possibly not with a high monopolistic profit, since the bugs still have to be taken out of the production process. Later mass production and new entry will lower the price to competitive levels. The STE must reproduce this sequence artificially, and is now taking trouble to do so (chapter 15, sec. 19).

Finally seasonal prices and sale prices. In many full-cost products (skis, summer clothing) that are both seasonal and durable production is lowered in the off season, and the peak season is the period for which the price is frozen, i.e. 'administered'. There is then a clearance sale, where full-cost discipline breaks down, shops charge very different prices, higgling is tolerated. I.e. there is a perceptible approach to perfect competition.[47] Of course goods that are seasonal but also in any case perfectly competitive (fruit, vegetables) also show marked seasonal swings in price. All this too the STE must deliberately reproduce. It is now gradually doing so, after the long inconveniences and wastes of year-long price rigidity.

20. Soviet-type agriculture preserves most of the traits that make it

perfectly competitive in market economies: many enterprises, easy entry (each crop is an industry, and one can easily substitute crops), homogeneous product. The marketing system is very unlike that for non-agriculture, just as it is under capitalism: a procurement agency, which goes out and collects things, is a far cry from the Gossnab, to which they must be delivered according to plan. Indeed the procurement agency resembles most suspiciously its Western counterparts, the marketing boards.[48]

The old Stalinist system laid down three prices for kolkhozy: one for compulsory deliveries (*zagotovka*), very low, 'in the nature of a tax'; one for nominally voluntary deliveries to the state, a simulacrum of a state market price (*zakupka*); one on the kolkhoz market, where the free remainder of the collective produce was sold, along with members' private produce, directly to consumers. This latter price was entirely free (though there have been local price stops), and attracted no turnover tax. In inflations it was very high indeed, bearing the brunt of all the active monetary overhang in the entire economy (chapter 14, sec. 6).[49] For state farms there were two prices: one, between the *zagotovka* and *zakupka* prices, for the nationalized output, and the kolkhoz market price for the private output of state farm employees. Naturally there was no *zakupka* for state farms, any more than for state factories, for they do not perform 'voluntarily'.

After Stalin died – and now we speak of USSR alone – much effort was spent in raising the *zagotovka* price. It was one of the very few passive prices that directly affected income distribution, and its freezing during a period of gross inflation caused terrible poverty among grain-growing farms with no access to a kolkhoz market (chapter 16, sec. 17). Eventually the *zagotovka* was assimilated to the *zakupka*, and the sovkhoz delivery price slowly approached this level too.[50] It seemed that the obvious goal of a single state off-farm price was near. But prices were also differentiated according to regions, and that not always wisely: the regions were too big and the gradations too few to skim off rent (or to allow for transport cost) at all fairly. They also encouraged production in the wrong places. Moreover the erstwhile 'voluntary' *zakupka* became in effect compulsory: i.e. the Communists predictably found themselves unable to give up methods of command in matters of procurement.

However, there was to be no single price. The state cannot afford – or rather, since it refuses to collect agricultural rents as such, it thinks it cannot afford – a price covering the average cost of the marginal farm, especially as, with increasing acreage, marginal cost rises. Moreover, it needs an incentive price for extra output, much like an overtime payment for extra work. This too is more a subjective than an objective need, if the experience of the rest of the world's agriculture is relevant. But it is certainly traditional in STEs. So a higher state price for above-plan output is now customary again; the basic price applies to effectually compulsory deliveries; and the kolkhoz market continues. So there are three prices again for the kolkhoz, with the very important distinction that the compulsory delivery price is now quite profitable. Sovkhozy that operate on the system of the 1965 industrial reforms do now at last enjoy the same prices as kolkhozy. But the more backward ones, that require more intimate state financial intervention, still get lower prices!

There is precious little optimality in all this. Occasionally such issues are raised: for instance when one crop is substituted for another to fulfil a delivery quota (sec. 16); and no doubt in the minds of planners. But optimality, we have to repeat even at the risk of wearisome iteration, is a matter of output rather than price. How, then, are outputs decided? The basic sowing plan of both sovkhoz and kolkhoz used to be set directly by higher authority, but this is clearly contrary to the basic fiction that the kolkhozy is a voluntary co-op. So in 1955 the kolkhozy were allowed to settle their sowing plans according to their procurement plans. This, had the authorities adhered to it, would have allowed great internal autonomy. The sovkhoz is of course under direct command like a factory, and simply hands over whatever it produces. It presents no 'procurement' problem since that confusing word implies a change of ownership. So one way and another prices only influence farm production decisions in respect of unimportant crops, or marginal quantities of important ones; and the issue that they really decide is income distribution and incentives.

As to the contents of plans, the operative one-year plan very sensibly includes only the sovkhoz sowing plan and the *zagotovka* or *zakupka*. The gross harvest from the collective fields, and the output of the private sector, figure only in five-year plans, i.e. as predictions – and these days only as five-year averages.

21. We have already asked in chapter 9, sec. 16, how expensive the Soviet-type system is in direct administrative terms. Since detailed plans have to be drawn up and implemented, it is probably much more expensive than a market, even allowing for non-informative advertising. But, we saw, there are no good figures and all this remains mere opinion. Another 'literary' opinion, for which there is better evidence, is that the detailed and the broad allocations are much more sub-optimal than in a market. This follows immediately from the preceding sections. It can also be observed at once by any tourist – who should of course make comparisons with a capitalist country no richer than the STE he is visiting. It can also be confirmed as to the broader allocations by perusing even superficially the technical press, which is always full of Communist self-criticism as to choice of location, choice of technology, etc. Precisely where capitalism is wasteful – subsidized farms, cross-subsidized mines, failure to import, unprofitable location – the STE is also wasteful, and more so. But it also pullulates with other wastes the market has never dreamed of. The impression that the system is very sub-optimal rests upon a mountain of evi-

dence; it is more reliable than the impression it is more directly expensive to operate.

So the STE is using up more administrative resources than capitalism in order worse to misallocate factors, goods and services. Therefore it is a very bad system which should be abolished? If the reader is not a trained economist he will not even contemplate drawing such a conclusion. If he is, he probably needs to be reminded to consider also X-efficiency, income distribution, inflation, unemployment and the various other economic topics raised in the rest of this book. We do not ourselves offer any conclusion on grounds of economics, believing that not enough is known.

Notes

1. I emphasize this word. In a market, or in decentralized planning (sec. 19), prices have priority.

2. The system most threatened by this proposition is not capitalism but co-operation (chapter 10, sec. 14).

3. In much of what follows I was anticipated by Aleksy Wakar and Janusz Zieliński, *Zarys Teorii Gospodarki Socjalistycznej*, Warsaw 1965, p. 91.

4. V. F. Pugachev in ed. J. Los and M. W. Los, *Mathematical Models in Economics*, Amsterdam 1974, p. 477.

5. This is the number of prices for which the price office says it is responsible. Information from the director, Dr. Bela Csikos-Nagy.

6. Information from my colleague Dr. Stanislaw Gomulka, November 1971. Input-output (capacity 4000) is of course irrelevant, since it does not pretend to achieve optimality.

7. This is almost but not quite wholly a guess. Unfortunately we have no capitalist figures, but at least Hungary is a recent recruit to the ranks of market economies. Put the total number of types of economic object in Hungary at 6 million (three times the number of industrial and agricultural objects, above). State industrial enterprises are very large, and under capitalism probably each establishment would have been independent: 5600. There are 800 industrial co-operatives, 1000 building enterprises and 25,000 retail outlets (a better figure again than that for retail enterprises). There is one post office, with total control over all its outlets. There are 1600 state and collective farms: put 16,000 for a capitalist Hungary. Guess 5000 foreign traders and wholesalers and 1000 small transport organizations. There are 1000 hospitals and 20,000 schools. There are 50,000 independent or collectivized professionals, or 25,000 allowing for the partnerships they would form in a capitalist Hungary. Now let every enterprise thus defined have on average two people entitled to take 'entrepreneurial' decisions, except for professionals (1), farmers ($1\frac{1}{4}$), retail shops ($1\frac{1}{4}$). Total 144,000 'entrepreneurs'.

8. But there are a few errors that can be made by a whole market-place of experts. These are mainly those associated with speculation and the cobweb (sec. 3).

9. Indeed all complementarity is of this kind. Bread and butter are complementary because they are inputs into the output bread-and-butter. Basic

complementarity does not, however, exclude competitiveness over a range. Bread can be buttered thick or thin, and price relatives affect this. But it is the existence of the defined output that makes the inputs complementary.

10. It was first seriously used in the second FYP (1932–6), while Leontiev first published proper input-output in 1937. Cf. Wiles 1962, Chapter 10; Nicholas Spulber, *Soviet Strategy for Economic Growth*, Indiana 1964; ed. Nicholas Spulber, *Foundations of Soviet Strategy for Economic Growth*, Indiana 1964.

11. Except, as we saw in sec. 7, agriculture, engineering, education and chemicals.

12. The 'line' is the main direct operational authority, as from division (general) to brigade (brigadier) to battalion (colonel), etc. 'Functional' and 'staff' are often interchangeable words for specialist officers attached to each HQ, junior in rank to the commander, and advising him. The 'line and staff' principle gives staff at one level direct authority over staff at the level below, without going through line. 'Staff' in the sense of very junior personal assistants is not meant. Cf. any textbook of administration, for instance ed. E. F. L. Brech, *The Principles and Practice of Management*, London 1953, pp. 29–31.

13. This being Communism, the *right* to interfere in this way is undisputed. Indeed in Hungary and China it is fully preserved, and this is one of the main things distinguishing them from Yugoslavia (chapter 3, sec. 1).

14. On utility trees cf. L. R. Klein and H. Rubin in *Review of Economic Studies*, 1947–8; P. A. Samuelson, ibid.; R. H. Strotz in *Econometrica* 2/1957; W. M. Gorman in *Econometrica* 3/1959.

15. Notably Soviet-type planners (and even, at first, French planners) often have engineering backgrounds and so use engineers' criteria (chapter 4, sec. 12), which neglect total cost. There is also a common reluctance to vary prices with seasonal or hourly peak and trough.

16. Cf. sec. 12; R. W. Campbell in ed. Henry Rosovsky, *Industrialization in Two Systems*, N.Y. 1966; Wiles 1962, chapter 8. Occasionally capitalist corporations also have a territorial 'line'. In China territorial, or 'horizontal', is almost synonymous with decentralization.

17. Cf. Bertram Gross, *The Managing of Organizations*, N.Y. 1964, pp. 133–134. On Weber cf. ibid., pp. 139–43.

18. It was one of the key economic ideas of the 'Czechoslovak Spring' (1967–8).

19. On this cf. Alvin W. Gouldner in (ed.) Robert K. Merton, *Sociology To-day*, N.Y. 1959.

20. These are St. Simon's wise men, principally bankers, who co-ordinate everything.

21. His phrase, not Marx's, by the way!

22. These things are not widely different in an STE. Personnel, however, is a Party prerogative, and we must add plan formulation to 'line'.

23. Cf. Gross, op. cit., pp. 121–8; V. I. Lenin, *State and Revolution*, 1917.

24. Cf. his *Principles of Scientific Management*, Harper and Row edn. 1967, pp. 118–30.

25. The most perfect case is Slovakia. Cf. Wiles 1969, p. 302.

26. To accept this strain is Guevarism. For Guevara's hostility to *khozraschet* cf. chapter 2.

27. In 1928–41 these rose rapidly under inflationary pressure. In more settled periods retail prices have risen very slowly, and wages more rapidly, while technical progress and the economies of scale reduce inter-enterprise prices.

28. I use this word advisedly, since all food so taxed goes through a stage of manufacture: baking, slaughtering, etc. Fresh fruit and vegetables pay no turnover tax, for whatever reason, nor do retail transport services. There is, however, an entertainment tax, but since this is a tax on services it bears a different name from the ideologically loaded tax on (goods) turnover. The latter tax is the sacred accumulation margin of the socialist state, or non-exploitative surplus value. Its formal incidence is on the factory, not the shop, since Marx held that surplus value is generated only by material production!

29. It is widely used in STEs for long-term planning and academic work.

30. Notably Herbert Levine in his classic 'The Centralized Planning of Supply in Soviet Industry' in Joint Economic Committee of Congress, *Comparisons of the US and Soviet Economies*, USGPO 1959. But Communist planimetricians are equally at fault: they seem to think the authorities *want* to abolish tension.

31. Among the things that can be hoarded is money: chapter 12, sec. 15.

32. Since not every input is specified, this amounts to minimizing only a few input-output ratios: the engineer's criterion denounced in chapter 4, sec. 12.

33. Joseph Berliner, *Factory and Manager in the USSR*, Harvard 1957; Janos Kornai, *Overcentralization in Hungarian Light Industry*, Oxford 1959; Barry M. Richman, *Soviet Management*, N.J. 1965; David Granick, *Management of the Industrial Firm in the USSR*, N.Y. 1954.

34. The Chinese make full use of this equivocation: chapter 10. So do the Yugoslavs.

35. A Sino-Soviet example in Wiles 1969, p. 330: the retail co-operatives of both countries met to do a barter deal in 1959. Again, I know a Bulgarian official who deals with such barter: she works for the Ministry of *Internal* Trade.

36. The greatest case was Poland and the DDR in 1972: tourists could change as much money as they pleased at the non-commercial rate, and shop freely. Needless to say the Poles spent overwhelmingly more than the Germans, and the scheme had to be abandoned on balance of payments grounds.

37. John D. Littlepage, *In Search of Soviet Gold*, N.Y. 1938.

38. Thus Mikail Z. Bor's popular official textbook, translated as *The Aims and Methods of Soviet Planning*, N.Y. 1967, has only one effective (and very brief) reference to the Gossnab (pp. 199–200). Hungarian writers however are very conscious of it, and emphasize that their reforms have abolished the organ. On the Western side cf. Levine, op. cit.; Wiles 1962, chapter 9.

39. The main case of this is agricultural procurement. These important organs go under separate names, but fulfil functions like the Gossnab's (sec. 20).

40. The Hungarians keep a formal and very aggregated one-year plan, and allocate a few commodities administratively in order to ensure export commitments to Comecon countries.

41. Albania, Cuba, North Korea, North Vietnam and China were already wholly independent. Of these China has most ostentatiously gone its own way since 1958. But the first three have been influenced by the reforms – which is not surprising, since they remain STEs. The details of the reforms are summarized on a comparable basis in ed. Wiles, *The Prediction of Communist Economic Performance*, Cambridge 1971; ed. Hans-Hermann Höhmann *et al.*, *The New Economic Systems of Eastern Europe*, London 1975.

42. Cf. Richard Judy in ed. H. Gordon Skilling and Franklyn Griffiths, *Interest Groups in Soviet Politics*, N.J. 1971. The story that Liberman was more directly the mathematicians' stalking horse is of unofficial origin.

43. Compare the Theses of the Rada Ekonomiczna (Council of Economic

Advisers) in *Dyskusja o Polskim Modelu Gospodarczym*, Warsaw 1957, pp. 261–78. The Council was subsequently suppressed, not least for its marginalism. Marx and Engels dealt in averages, and Engels flatly condemned the differential calculus. Cf. Wiles 1962, pp. 50–3, 63.

44. Each straight-line facet of the production possibility curve represents the average cost of one enterprise or process. Thus linear programming deals precisely with the average cost of the marginal firm, somewhat as in the text here. Since it does not actually use the margin it is more acceptable to the orthodox: cf. Oskar Lange, *Political Economy*, vol. I, N.Y. 1963, pp. 197–225.

45. Ed. B. I. Shafirkin, *Ekonomicheski Spravochnik Zheleznodorozhnika*, Moscow 1971. Note that this work is a practical guide for operating officials, not a theoretician's pipe-dream. It sets out currently valid standards for actual management. For the problems that railway pricing used to set the good Marxist cf. Wiles in *Oxford Economic Papers*, October 1953; Wiles 1962, pp. 123–6.

46. In chapter 10, sec. 2 we showed that quasi-perfectly-competitive procedures take over if more than one producer is available.

47. It is not paradoxical that prices become more various. For the goods remain heterogeneous by nature and location, and their previous uniformity of price was artificial, not perfectly competitive.

48. Minerals were never an open-and-shut case for perfect competition. In STEs they are assimilated to manufactured goods, with special provision for rent. This is normally taken out by a special tax, forming an exceptional part of the turnover tax.

49. Therefore technical crops, the free remainder of which had no outlet on the kolkhoz market, had much more profitable *zagotovka* prices. Otherwise it would have been impossible to persuade kolkhozy to produce them.

50. A handy source for these details as to the later period is Everett M. Jacobs in *Jahrbuch der Wirtschaft Osteuropas*, vol. 111, Munich/Vienna 1972 (in English).

12

Banking and Monetary Systems

12

1. Here too, as in the case of trade unions, we stumble on an area in which rigorous institutional economics never ceased. For this reason we can move much faster, assuming far more institutional knowledge in the reader. Even so, much that we say will seem very elementary indeed. But the ordinary textbooks omit not merely French planning and Communist banking but also the basic principles that these reveal to underlie all banking. This chapter, then, has nothing very remarkable to say: it only shows where and how everything fits together.

First we list and define our institutions. There are many forms of bank, and of institutions that can substitute for banks.

2. The basic form, of which we all instinctively think first, is the *deposit bank*. The depositor takes the initiative, wishing to store his cash. So the bank *stands permanently ready to borrow*; and lends only afterwards. But equally important, and for our purposes equally part of the definition of a bank, is that *its debts are negotiable and accepted as money* (except by other banks).

Now since cheques drawn on or notes issued by a deposit bank are money the bank can 'multiply', i.e. create much more 'money' than the 'cash' their depositors have left with them, according to some informal or legal liquidity ratio. Note the plural: one deposit bank alone cannot do this, since its cheques or notes, being presented to be cashed at other banks, are not accepted as money by them, but will drain away its cash to other banks. But all the banks can achieve this together, if they move in monopolistic concert, or in a uniform speculative mood, or under the encouragement of a powerful central authority that undertakes to bail each of them out if it suffers a drain. For in these cases the net balances presented to be cashed will be very small.

3. If there are many deposit banks they will need a clearing house for the majority of the cheques drawn on each other, and a *money market* to finance the net balances. The clearing house is on the whole merely technical, and we pass it by. But the money market is very important indeed. It arose historically before there were ever banks, out of the domestic trade bills generated by inter-enterprise credit (sec. 8). Then the new commercial banks became major operators on it as described. But its main modern importance is that it has made possible the market-type intervention of the treasury and/or central bank, which would otherwise be confined to administrative means, as in Yugoslavia. This, then, is the primordial 'open-market operation'.[1] By deliberately buying and selling

money the 'authorities' (see sec. 6), who are far the biggest operators in the market, make cash scarce or plentiful for the deposit banks. These accordingly find it difficult or easy to finance their net clearing balances, and must in future be more or less careful about permitting overdrafts or issuing notes.

If money markets arise from deposit banks' needs to borrow or lend at short term, and are themselves peculiarly suited to interventions by the central authorities, they have many other uses. One can hardly create such a market without other lenders and borrowers intervening: the Treasury again (on its own behalf this time, in the hope of lower borrowing rates than on the long market), the local gold mines, the merchant banks, bill-brokers, stock-brokers, various foreigners, etc., etc.[2] On the whole we must pass this by as a mere detail, but note particularly that 'various foreigners' includes the whole effect of the balance of payments, and 'the Treasury' that of the budget deficit. I.e. there are other macro-influences in the money market than the exogenous or at any rate policy-determined influence of true open-market operations.

4. A *unitary central bank* has been added in most cases in the course of history. Its definition is that its debts are accepted as money by other banks. So, being single, it fears no presentation of its debts to be cashed, since there is no one *inside the country* to whom they are not cash *per se*. However vis-à-vis the rest of the world it is in no such position, and must maintain some sort of liquidity ratio, however informal. But a central bank is no necessary part of the arrangements described in sec. 3, since the money market will work perfectly well *qua* market without conscious human direction; indeed it has done so, especially in the very early nineteenth century. If, furthermore, central banks have at least always acted to stave off the bankruptcy of deposit banks, they have not by any means always been wise or succeeded in damping cycles.

Such banks are not structurally very different from deposit banks. They dispose of more money market assets (but are not otherwise bigger); they are more under government control; they definitely do not maximize profit while deposit banks may; they often but not always monopolize the note issue; they are often but not always sole deposit and investment bankers to the government; they eschew private depositors with few exceptions; they hold a great deal of foreign exchange but are far from monopolizing it. In a word the central bank carries very strong traces of its origin as a privileged deposit bank. There is more than ample discussion elsewhere of the behaviour of capitalist central banks, and we shall not pursue this matter here at all.

5. But we must note the *branch central banks* of the 1820s to 1840s. In USA, France and Britain the central banks had branches all over the country which practised private banking as well as note issue and the

control of the (still localized) money markets. Different as these central banks were from the Soviet-type monobank in function, their structural similarity reminds us that the admirable Soviet-type banking system is compatible with free markets and capitalism. The paraphernalia of money markets, separate deposit banks, liquidity ratios and open-market operations is not necesssary. Branch central banking declined in USA and UK in the 1840s, owing to local business ambition (the country bank lobby) and abstract devotion to *laissez-faire*. President Andrew Jackson actually destroyed his central bank along with its branches. Such a total monopoly was never anything like complete in any country, and it must be said that capitalism never gave it a fair trial. There had certainly not been greater mismanagement than by country banks, quite the contrary. In a period of endemic corruption, when all business was heavily politicized, branch central banking certainly concentrated overwhelming power in very dubious hands. Today, however, and with the Soviet example before us, it may be time to resuscitate this notion.

The ACE where it would be easiest to install a monobank is of course France.[3] The Banque de France is a monobank manqué, and the idea of a monobank is the logical conclusion of St. Simonism.[4] While England was contracting its operations into one building, and the Second Bank of the United States was being liquidated, the Banque de France stretched out across the land. It founded 15 branches in 1836–46, and in the crisis of 1848 absorbed all the nine independent state banks of issue in the provinces, and monopolized the note issue. Under this pine-tree among central banks scarcely any other banks grew until the 1850s. It played its part in bringing down its first serious competitor in fields other than those of merchant banking, the Crédit Mobilier (1871). It continued to expand the number of its branches, and has now 247 of them.[5] But it was unable to resist the growth of private deposit banks (three of the five big ones were nationalized in 1946!), and it has almost abandoned the private deposit business. Nevertheless it remains enormously large in comparison with other banks – and of course enormously influential.

The main functions of the branches are to inform headquarters and to influence the local lending policies of other banks. The director of a *succursale* is a very important local personality. He 'watches in a general way' (mission de surveillance générale) over other local banks, especially the weak ones. He makes liberal use of the threat that his bank will not rediscount paper. He 'enjoys incontestable moral authority', he 'knows the people as well as the documents'. The literature of the Banque de France does not, however, mention planning or the Commission du Plan, and presents this, like other aspects of its activity, as a purely bank matter. My inclination is to say that this is departmental jealousy, not fact. Certainly qualitative bank controls are essential to French planning, and branch central banking is essential to them.

The quasi-monobank is not unknown in developing, 'middle-class' capitalist countries, let alone in underdeveloped ones. Thus the Banco de España,[6] facing the same problems as earlier the Banque de France, supplied Valencia and Alicante with local banks of issue in 1858 because private enterprise had not done so. The year 1874 was Spain's 1848: the Banco de España received a note issue monopoly, and many of the private banks affected availed themselves of the favourable merger terms. These *sucursales* developed in number and function after the modern French model. There were 69 in 1962.

But the most striking case is Tsarist Russia.[7] Not only was banking at all times virtually a state function, but when eventually experiments ceased and the Imperial Bank was founded (1861) it quite outdid the Banque de France. It was little more than a department of the Treasury, it had many very active branches which in Russia's 'banking deserts' were local monopolists, its investment and foreign exchange policies were wholly those of the government, etc. The Imperial Bank is yet another of the many ways in which Communism was anticipated by those *animae naturaliter Marxianae*, the officials of the Tsar.

In STEs the deposit and central banks are invariably merged into a monobank, for many obvious reasons. The first is that a money market would be worse than markets for semi-fabricates: it is in Marxist terms unthinkable, since high finance is not exploitation but super-exploitation. The second is the Marxist belief in the economies of scale. Third comes the love of centralization and the total acceptance of monopoly so long as it is public. Finally a technical point: where most money is passive there would be great difficulty in having a money market (sec. 15 below). The Soviet-type monobank, however, differs in many ways from all capitalist banks. Notably, it does not stand permanently ready to borrow. For it does not handle the active money deposits of the population (see below under savings banks), and there are no random and unpredictable depositors of passive money.

Thus the monobank is ideologically essential to genuine Marxism,[8] and practically almost essential to passive money. But when, as in China, Hungary, and the Yugoslavia of the 'fifties, an STE goes over to the market there is no particular reason to destroy the existing monobank. Indeed in the USSR of the NEP period this was precisely when it was built up.[9] The ideological reasons in its favour remain, and if the market is to be tightly controlled it has also substantial practical conveniences.

Whenever in a market system the central bank, or 'the authorities' generally, use non-market means to influence deposit banks, and in particular force them to impose qualitative controls on their customers (below), we approach a monobank situation. It is no accident that France, which went further than other capitalist countries towards a monobank in the 1830s, and retreated the shortest distance thereafter, has now the kind of planning that it has.

6. The *State Treasury* is not a bank. No one deposits with it, so it operates no liquidity ratio and cannot directly create money in this way. But it resembles a bank in that its credit is so good that its debts are money anyway (e.g. British Treasury Bills, which are so fully monetized that deposit banks treat them as the basis of a secondary, non-cash, liquidity ratio). A Treasury, with the force of the state behind it, can even issue non-interest bearing debt (Treasury notes)[10] and cause them to circulate as legal tender. This is the paradigm of so-called 'fiat' money.

The Treasury can also operate, just as easily as the central bank, on the open money market. At certain times of year it has a great deal of cash, and a budget surplus may even give it this advantage throughout the year; so it often has the choice of whether or not to redeem the national debt, and that is the quintessential open-market operation. But at all times, whatever its cash position, the Treasury can sell one kind of debt and buy another, thus altering the structure of yields. This is less a manipulation of the quantity of money than mere 'debt management'. But if, as in the UK, deposit banks treat the shorter forms of government debt as a secondary liquidity reserve, 'debt management' can have strong quantitative effects by changing the proportion of short debt to a constant total.

In the case of a budget deficit the Treasury has no choice: it must borrow. If it does so exclusively from the deposit banks and the public the macro-effects of the deficit are sharply reduced, unless they in turn borrow from the central bank. If it wants the deficit to work in a Keynesian manner the Treasury may have to borrow from the central bank, i.e. increase the quantity of money itself. This of course is not an open-market operation but a closed transaction shrouded in questions of influence and legal power.

These personal and legal considerations ensure that the Treasury and the central bank are seldom at odds. The days of the independent watchdog central bank are practically over, and the rise in the price level all over the capitalist world bears witness to this simple fact. The bank has everywhere lost its 'trustee' status, and if it retains power as part of the state machine it is only because its top people happen to be more intelligent or personally influential than those in the Treasury. We speak of both bodies together as 'the authorities'.

In primitive conditions the Treasury and especially its local subtreasuries have been known to function like a central branch bank, accepting deposits, discounting bills, etc. This is particularly true if tax revenues have seasonal peaks and the money is not immediately required at the capital city. This happened, notably, when the Second US National Bank was destroyed.[11]

7. Investment banks, merchant banks, discount houses, finance houses and the like are *funds not banks*:[12] they do not normally create money. Their essential tasks are to manage the investment affairs of their clients,

advising them on financial and other matters, and issuing and underwriting their borrowings on the stock exchange; or to discount bills of exchange, hire-purchase paper, etc. For these operations, as for a business in material production, they require a cash float, which will bear some ratio or other to their liabilities. But this is not technically speaking a liquidity ratio, since the fund is not, so long as it sticks to its true nature, accepting deposits or making advances (which is virtually creating deposits). It borrows only in order to lend; it does not borrow (accept deposits) simply to do customers a favour. It only lends what it has borrowed; it does not lend customers its own IOUs, to use as money, against their own illiquid collateral.

All this is most clear and definite in STEs, which normally have an investment bank, a foreign trade bank and an agricultural or co-operative bank (for the kolkhozy, not the sovkhozy). Such 'banks' are mere administrators of money granted to them in the budget. They are not allowed to run overdrafts at the monobank, from which they are administratively separate.[13]

8. *Ad hoc banking.* Our brief dogmatic distinction between a fund and a bank could be faulted a million times over in practice. But it is not meant to describe totally the actual institutions that call themselves investment banks, etc.: it is meant to separate out the *function* of such institutions. Thus in capitalist practice deposit banks advise on new issues and German deposit banks also underwrite them; or again investment banks grant all normal deposit banking facilities to their own employees. It is in particular open to almost any financial intermediary, not merely investment banks, to create new money by turning its customer's bad credit into its own good credit, without any increase in the volume of real assets. I.e. the customer exchanges some acceptable though not readily negotiable collateral for the intermediary's IOU – and the latter is money for most purposes and may circulate a great deal, and facilitate many speculative or productive transactions, before being finally presented to the intermediary to be cashed. A good modern example is hire-purchase finance: the customer's original debt is amalgamated with others into a negotiable short-term security by a financial intermediary specializing in this branch of business. In order to do so the intermediary indeed only lends what he has borrowed, but he has borrowed, at long term, inactive liquid funds the customers could not have mobilized. So the growth of intermediaries raises the ratio of near-money to both real assets and money; and thus the liquidity of the economy as a whole.[14]

Nay more, one does not have to be a specialized financial intermediary at all to monetize others' debt. Thus a spinner with good credit can let a weaver with bad credit have his yarn on exceptionally long terms. Then the weaver can satisfy other more urgent claimants such as his employees, while the spinner runs up an overdraft with his bank. The spinner is then a financial intermediary, monetizing the weaver's debt. This kind of thing is enormously common, and led the Radcliffe Committee[15] to believe that no quantitative credit squeeze would ever work; people will go for '*ad hoc* banking' so long as they have confident expectations, whatever the authorities do to the quantity of money. The monetary system is like a soggy balloon: squeeze it here, it will bulge somewhere else.

Certainly this is true of bank strikes under capitalism, but perhaps that is a too exceptional case. It is also, more convincingly, true of Poland, though possibly not of other STEs. For one of the monobank's main aims is to keep productive enterprises on a short leash where short credit is concerned. 'Ruble audit' (sec. 15) is made very difficult by the presence of spare funds in the system. Indeed this is an obsessive preoccupation, and inter-enterprise credit is forbidden. Yet in fact it flourishes in Poland, particularly during financial squeezes![16] Judged by its price index, Poland is easily the least successful in matters monetary of the orthodox STEs: this is an undisciplined people, hating the whole system as Russian, and claiming its historic *liberum veto* where it can. Its attachment to inter-enterprise credit should not surprise us. After all, such credit is older than banking itself, and gave rise to a reasonably satisfactory system, the internal bill of exchange, which is not yet dead under capitalism. Such bills exceeded in volume total bank deposits in most countries until late in the nineteenth century.

9. The next important institution is the *extra-budgetary fund*. This is only a special case of our general concept of a fund. It is fed by fees or taxes not included in the general budget, and used for defined purposes under the control of the government. Like all funds, it must balance; it is not normally permitted either to run a deficit or to create money by acting like a bank. Indeed the power to run a large arbitrary deficit (i.e. to issue money uncontrolled – the difference is slight) is by definition vested in the sovereign government of any country, and not in any branch thereof. The issue of money is the power to bid away indefinitely many real resources from all other uses. A government must monopolize this much as it monopolizes armed force: indeed the latter depends on the former. So it is the 'consolidated fund', or budget, that normally runs the deficit. But if the funds are very numerous and scattered, like enterprises in an STE (below), or if overt central budget deficits lead to electoral or legal problems, the deficit is 'decentralized'.

The classic country of the extra-budgetary fund is France. No description of the French financial system is complete without this element. The funds are larger than the commercial or investment banks, and though they do not dispose of anything like the same net inflow as private savings they are an overwhelmingly dominant *masse de manoeuvre* upon the stock exchange. They have always been responsible for debt management, as indeed they are in Britain, but they are also permitted to buy new private issues. It follows that their refusal to buy is tantamount to a veto. Therefore the government, i.e. the Commission du Plan, has a veto on new issues of the most informal sort, immune from inspection or appeal.

The Soviet-type enterprise may be regarded as an extra-budgetary fund. This is certainly the implication of Communist works on finance, which set 'the population' against the monobank, the Treasury and the enterprises, and present these three as a planned monolith working together in the sector of passive money. Again the relation of enterprise to Treasury, with its automatic clawback of profit residuals and its interest-free capital grants, is very much that of a capitalist extra-budgetary fund to its Treasury. Above all this parallel throws light on Soviet-type inflation: the budget is always balanced, so how does the new money get in, and how can the state possibly not be responsible? Guilt lies with the deficits of extra-budgetary funds, of course: only in STEs these are the enterprises themselves, which state policy virtually forces into deficit. The virginity of the Minister of Finance is preserved simply by debauching other state bodies.

10. Our last financial institution is the *savings bank*. This body is virtually identical in all economies. It stands open to borrow like a deposit bank, receiving whatever the population may bring in the way of small savings. But it pays interest on all deposits, and in revenge will not return them on demand; whereas the deposit bank, rendering far more services to customers, and obliged to hold cash sterile at the central bank, cannot meet its costs without an actual charge to customers. There is an upper limit on savings bank deposits under capitalism, simply because other means of saving exist and the savings bank enjoys tax privileges. In STEs there is no such limit, and here again we run up against the logical but inaccurate assumption that all incomes legally earned in a Communist state are just, so that no further privileges should be accorded to the poor. The debts of the savings bank, however, are not negotiable (sec. 19): consequently it can no more create money than any other person or organization – but we have seen that this is not to say too much. For instance a cheque on a savings bank, though administratively more troublesome to draw, and liable to an interest penalty, can scarcely be prevented from circulating under capitalism, though in an STE each cheque not for cash transfers cash only from one named depositor to another. Again the savings bank chooses not to allow overdrafts or make advances, or is forbidden to do so: otherwise it easily might. On the other hand its liquidity ratio is quite low, since it lends the cash deposited with it only to certain safe borrowers, mainly the government, and need neither keep any cash at the central bank, nor – since its cheques are costly – much in its tills.

Thus the savings bank trembles on the brink of being a deposit bank, and is only prevented by regulation. Otherwise it would have to participate in the money market, and obey the rules of the game for money-creators. Even as it is, it offers 'unfair competition' to deposit banks. But here at least the STE is different, since the savings bank has a monopoly of dealings with the public, and the monobank deals with enterprises and institutions only.

11. The types of money correspond to the types of bank, and both together form a monetary system. The system in turn corresponds to a certain typical relation between the state and the non-financial enterprise, or degree of central planning. But these correspondences are neither historically nor logically precise or inevitable. In any examination of them, history is inextricable from logic. In what follows, then, we show the important combinations only; we do not pursue every by-way.

Let us look aside from primitive money and begin with the system of *gold and silver coins only*. The 'only' implies no banks, and the main influences on the quantity of money are domestic mining, the balance of payments, and currency debasement. The first is obvious. As to the second, the whole of Mercantilism was based on the recognition that in the absence of its own mines a country could only acquire specie by an export surplus, though it might retain it by an export prohibition – of specie itself. Neither concept presents any trouble to a modern economist. He is only reminded that exchange control is very old.

Debasement is more complicated, but also quite relevant to the modern world. Often it means that the government actually forges money and lies to the people. A smaller weight of gold is said to be a larger weight, and is passed off at the value thereof. Then when the deception is discovered the two kinds of coin invariably diverge in purchasing power. Either the prices of goods and services in full gold coins do not change, the debased coins circulate at a discount and the government has made a once for all profit at the expense of those holding them; or the latter are made legal tender at par for certain taxes, so that general prices come to be constant in debased coin, and full gold circulates at a premium; i.e. the numéraire follows one or other coin, but the premium is the same as the discount. Modern governments are, surprisingly, more honest. They announce the debasement, and, since coins are now so trivial a part of cash, easily ensure by fiat that the debased coin shall have the same relation in purchasing power to, say, the bank-note as did the full-bodied coin. The latter is hoarded or withdrawn.

The issue of money at high purchasing power but low minting or printing cost leads to the state profit called *seigniorage*. Thus the minting of precise weights of the metal, with a confidence-worthy stamp on them, raises the value of metal; and the issue of notes that really are redeemable at par, but are not redeemed in fact, is obviously very profitable. A fiat currency like a Treasury note is a pure case. The note issue of all central banks is in fact of this sort, since one way and another the notes never will be redeemed. So the profit of the issue department of the bank is seigniorage, and the Treasury always takes it. Debasement only increases dishonestly the amount of seigniorage.

As in all other monetary systems, the public in the pure metallic system create near-money for themselves when, as is normal, transactions outrun cash. The commonest near-money is inter-enterprise credit (sec. 8), and specifically that negotiable type of it, the trade bill. Money markets began with trade bills, before there were banks, as we have seen. Granted downward flexibility of prices, and sufficiently extensible inter-enterprise credit, the pure metallic system would still be practicable today.

Moreover, Mercantilism reminds us that the system is entirely compatible with central planning, nay positively generates its own variety thereof. For it virtually restricts the government's intervention to the foreign exchanges, and this has led in the past to a quite remarkable amount of such intervention. The notion that pure metallic systems encourage *laissez-faire* is laughable: the nineteenth century is an exception after all the 'metallic' centuries. It was indeed a rather complicated exception: *laissez-faire* produced first the competing country banks and the uncontrolled issue of paper; this was succeeded by the great acts of intervention which stabilized and centralized paper. But monetary *laissez-faire* persisted now in another form: the gold standard and the refusal to intervene on the foreign exchanges. These were in their way a prime weapon against the over-issue of paper.

It is quite important for Marxism that Marx best understood, and mostly assumed, this combination of a nearly pure metallic system with *laissez-faire*. Marxists' understanding of capitalism, and especially of Keynesian economics, is severely limited by this fact. They even carry over their nineteenth-century addiction to the crude quantity theory of money into their analysis of Communist monetary systems.

12. Now superimpose a number of independent deposit banks. There is no central bank, but as explained above the private banks become major operators on the pre-existing money market. Bank-notes compete with metallic coin as a new form of cash, and bank deposits become a more efficient kind of near-money than trade bills, but are not called, or treated as, cash. The very phrase 'currency and credit' recalls this phase. Inter-enterprise and state-enterprise transactions are now, physically, marks in ledgers while transactions involving individuals are still in notes and coin. This physical distinction is preserved for us by the Soviet-type monetary system (sec. 15 below): not merely, then, for convenience of administration but also because of the phase in capitalist development that, historically speaking, Russia had reached in 1917.

The domestic trade bill is an amateur kind of near-money. Its issuer is a manufacturer or tradesman and he backs it with expectations of resale of the goods whose purchase the bill financed, rather than with a liquidity ratio. He does not think financially – a fact that often causes bankruptcy. The independent deposit banks begin with equal crudity, relying on 'trade conditions' or 'the needs of trade' rather than hard and fast liquidity ratios. This generates waves of speculation followed by bank bankruptcy. Since a defaulting bank deprives people not of long-term assets but of money and near-money, our second monetary system turns out to be highly unstable and inefficient, and it is in this atmosphere, we have seen, that the first notions of a monobank were born.

But it was not to be so, and instead such concepts as the liquidity ratio took root. We shall pass over the multiplicative character of these ratios as too well known. But note how little a matter of chance it may be that precisely this monetary system is associated with *laissez-faire*. Independent deposit banks represent *local* interests, as recent Yugoslav history rather comically reminds us (sec. 20). The long failure of USA to evolve out of this system leads to the same conclusion. The system creates separate power centres, which are very likely not to agree about the government's balance of payments policy, which, it will be remembered, was the main instrument of monetary control under a pure metallic currency. There is always some region that feels itself aggrieved by any particular foreign economic policy: e.g. the Southern states before the US Civil War. And the easiest way to settle such grievances is to opt for no central policy at all, i.e. *laissez-faire*. Precisely this claim was repeated by the Croatian dissidents in 1971–2.

There is, therefore, an affinity (we cannot put it more strongly) between *laissez-faire* and the system of gold coin with independent deposit banks. This system has also much affinity with populism: for neither its currency nor its credit is much amenable to central manipulation. I.e. the system is elastic and capable of inflation (which populists, as small businessmen and peasants, approve), but cannot be controlled by city slickers or the nascent financial establishment.[17]

13. Add a central bank, and we have two-tier banking. The deposit banks continue to treat their money-market assets – principally bills of exchange and Treasury bills if any – as a secondary reserve, which may or may not be formalized in a secondary liquidity ratio. But their primary or cash reserve is now not only coin in their tills but also the new 'super-cash': the short debts of the central bank. These are its notes in their tills, and their own deposits in its ledgers. These pieces of paper and marks in ledgers drive out the inconvenient gold, which however must be retained by the central bank. For gold remains the only international 'super-cash', and central bank notes must be tied to it by a liquidity ratio, for the sake of foreigners. This ratio is likely to be informal, but the primary liquidity ratio of the deposit banks becomes highly formal if not legal, and forms the fulcrum upon which open-market operations act as a lever,

This is the monetary system of our textbooks, and it will receive here no further discussion, except to emphasize one 'non-classical' possibility that brings us some way towards the fourth system (below). Instead of selling bonds on the market the central bank can freeze the other banks' deposits with it; even require, perhaps by legal as opposed to market force, such deposits to be raised and then frozen. In highly imperfect money markets, and above all in Yugoslavia (sec. 20), this is the preferred way.

Historically, though not logically, local banks begin at the same time to exploit the economies of scale by amalgamation: sleek City bureaucrats replace the thrustful amateurs, and the formidable local families supported by the local magnates. In any case, combined, the Treasury and the central bank form 'the authorities'; a truly overwhelming *masse de manoeuvre* that dominates the money market. Thus this third monetary system is very centralistic. 'Keynesian' policies become so easy to pursue that their pursuit is inevitable. If ever a man with his ideas was engendered by a situation, it was Keynes. More detailed 'banker's planning' (chapter 9) also becomes a possibility, desirable or not.

But before it becomes an actuality we must (a) cut the link with the balance of payments and (b) establish qualitative controls. For although highly centralistic in some aspects, yet in its relation to the state and to non-financial enterprise the third system is entirely compatible with *laissez-faire*. Even Keynes must be classified as a *laissez-faire* man, at least at the micro-level; for he assumed perfect competition, and limited himself to such general controls as the rate of exchange, the short rate of interest or the budget deficit (as a whole, and without regard to specific taxes or outlays).

The worm in the apple of the third system was the balance of payments. It is the curse of all these first three systems that the quantity of money is so vitally dependent on foreign deficits or surpluses. The addition of one and then two tiers of banks only aggravated this dependence, by bringing in the multiplicative effect of one and then two liquidity ratios. The earlier reaction of these fluctuations was one of 'macro-*laissez-faire*': preserve the rate of exchange and let prices, income and employment rise or fall. The rise automatically corrects the inflow, and the fall the outflow. This policy was so successful that individual countries seldom had balance of payments crises, but rather the whole world was subjected to a simultaneous cycle, starting in one place and transmitting itself rapidly via the free trade in money. The vehicle of transmission was as often speculation and hot money flows as changes in trade balances.

Domestic full employment was thus systematically excluded, as a matter of principle. When finally it became a goal of central bankers it was at first thought sufficient to 'sterilize' international money flows by open-market operations. But this is contrary to the logic of free trade in money: if when gold flows out you substitute domestic 'super-cash' at the base of the pyramid you threaten its convertibility and create speculation. Also by maintaining full employment in a world slump you add a trade deficit to whatever kind of deficit began the trouble.

So capitalist central bankers stumbled into another within-system change: devaluation and floating rates,[18] to back up the sterilization of money flows. The trouble here is that, men being what they are, when the last anti-inflationary fetish is removed rates float mostly downward. And this very downward movement adds to cost inflation, via import prices, and to demand inflation, via the (probable) increase in export volume. Nothing in the vast well-meaning international superstructure of IMF and Special Drawing Rights fundamentally alters this simple fact. Indeed SDRs, as the first man-made international super-cash, can only aggravate it: *homo sapiens* is by nature inflationary, and cannot be trusted with a cheque-book. Keynes, by promising full employment within the system, put upon it a burden it could not carry, and destroyed it.

Our third system, then, operates mainly by quantitative bank controls. These are any means whereby a central bank changes only the quantity of money. The most important case is an open-market operation, but the administrative freezing of the reserves of deposit banks is another, and a change in the budget surplus is yet another. All these are blunderbuss affairs; for instance when we inflate we give people money without telling them what to do with it. Of course things are not quite so simple really, and all such quantitative moves have a qualitative or discriminatory side. The open-market operation lowers the short rate of interest more than the long, and so helps industries, such as trade, that borrow more at short term; the freezing of reserves hits some banks, with more free reserves, harder than others, and this may discriminate between regions or even between industries; above all, the general budget surplus cannot be changed without changing particular taxes and outlays, etc.

14. It is no accident that at just this moment of history cost inflation, generated by trade unions, should have become an endemic international phenomenon (chapter 14). So the capitalist world is, as this is written, in a painful and confused oscillation between this degenerate form of the third system and the fourth, that of *qualitative bank controls.* This is a mild form of banker's planning, especially by way of exchange control. For to isolate a country from international disturbances one needs a new monetary system, one not based on free trade in money. The writer can make no prediction. He would like the transition to be made, but there is life in the old system yet, particularly in its new international superstructure.

In our fourth monetary system people are told what they may do with their money. Deposit banks may only make advances or sell foreign exchange to clients for purposes specified by the central bank, Treasury, Ministry of Trade or planning office. In the mildest form these controls are enforced upon the deposit banks and other financial intermediaries by the 'devil they know', the central bank. Thus the US Federal Reserve announces that it will no longer discount paper based on mortgages of less than such and such a length (Regulation W). This lowers the finance available for housing, and house prices respond quite smartly. But the same effect can be produced more directly by government regulation: the British Department of Trade and Industry simply orders that hire-purchase contracts shall include such and such a minimum down payment – and consumer durable sales respond quite smartly.

Notably, such restrictions affect advances to importers, exporters and the producers of import-substitutes, and the sale of foreign exchange for all purposes: visible imports, invisible imports and capital exports. We can almost say that balance-of-payments policy is the heart and the origin of qualitative banking control, though it is used much more widely than that in France and in any capitalist war economy. For instance such controls are used to favour backward regions or the production of armaments, and to enforce price restraint.

The system does not require a monobank, or new forms of money, or any other organizational change. Yet it is still an enormous institutional change, since it profoundly restricts the market and introduces detailed planning. The intervening money market hardly blunts the controls, since the central bank can threaten to discriminate against the disobedient precisely on the money market, as the instance of Regulation W makes clear. The market can in any case be avoided by direct executive decree under enabling legislation. But the system does establish a general atmosphere hostile to two-tier banking: if the deposit bank is the agent of the authorities in such detailed affairs why leave it a merely nominal independence? Indeed why subject it to the temptations that such independence on a market offers, in the form of the profit from breaking regulations?

We have already considered the working of this system in France (chapter 9, secs. 7 and 8). We remark here again the flexibility, speed and secrecy of such arrangements, compared with the constitutional obstacles to continual changes in taxes by the government, let alone a command economy.

15. Now let this sequence be interrupted (there is no historically appropriate point) by a Communist revolution. Then we must introduce command planning and passive money. In an STE, as we have seen, these are confined to inter-enterprise and state-enterprise transactions. There is even a physical distinction. Passive money is bank money, cheques and marks in ledgers. Active money, in which virtually every labour income is paid, is notes and coin (sec. 12). The basic system, including the market-clearing turnover tax, has already been described in chapter 11, sec. 13. What is its effect on banking?

First it is desirable that there be a monobank, for many reasons already given. The bank reflects and audits but does not initiate. Its function is to clear those cheques only that correspond to physical transactions laid down in the plan, or to tax payments and subsidies sanctioned by the Treasury. This is of course the very essence of passive money. It is called *ruble audit*.[19] The bank itself is on *khozraschet*, so it must charge interest to cover its expense, though naturally not at anything that could be called a market rate.

For although these rates of interest on short-term advances are also meant to deter borrowers this is after all a command economy, and if to fulfil his physical output plan a borrower must have money he will have it.[20] So another principal concern of the bank is simply to refuse short credit, or to claw it back if it appears not to be necessary for plan fulfilment. It is through short credit, as we see in chapter 14, that inflation arises. In their pursuit of excessive short credit, furthermore, the authorities give the monobank a monopoly of it, and forbid inter-enterprise credit. But in this, we saw, they are not particularly successful (sec. 8): the Soviet-type monetary system appears also, at least in Poland, to be a Radcliffian 'soggy balloon'.

There is of course an overall financial plan, determining the quantities of both 'currency' and 'credit' and the velocity of circulation. Now these overall quantities are built up enterprise by enterprise, on the basis of the production plan and the pre-set prices; and the velocity of circulation of 'credit' is therefore also simply the result of the plan. Quite unlike the physical macro-quantities, which are settled ex ante and help to determine the physical micro-quantities (chapter 9), the macro-financial plan is the ex post sum of all the micro-financial plans – which in turn are translations into money of the micro-physical plans – plus some such balancing item as extra direct and indirect taxes on the consumer/wage-earner. So there is no call for quantitative controls. Indeed since there is no money market, and each enterprise is in its own monetary slot, so to speak, a quantitative control over credit cannot even be imagined. Credit inflation occurs, of course, but only as a result of specific plan violations (chapter 14).

But a quantitative control over currency, i.e. active money, would be highly desirable. For the outflow of this, in payment for socialized labour and co-operative agricultural deliveries, can only be planned in part; since the harvest cannot be predicted and the supply of labour is under almost no control. And its inflow cannot be planned at all, since it is open to individuals to spend in state shops and to deposit in the savings bank (thus returning the cash), but equally to hoard and to buy from each other on the black and kolkhoz markets. Hoarded money, and even officially saved money, can suddenly come alive to lengthen queues in the state shops, divert resources to the black market and raise the legitimate cost of living in the kolkhoz market.

The STE has developed an immensely laborious system of monitoring the flow of cash: the 'Balance of Money Incomes and Expenditures of the

Population', which is broken down even by counties (*rayons*). But all this detailed knowledge gives rise to very few effective actions. These are in the nature of 'open-market operations'. The most obvious case is the rapid transfer of goods between shops, to the regions of greatest monetary overhang. Next comes the quasi-compulsory, Party-supported sale of bonds: very unpopular and now suppressed. Another is the special ('commercial') state shops that sometimes crop up, selling at inflated kolkhoz-market prices. Similar to this is the 'Volkswagen tactic':[21] get people to save by selling durables to them only after they have bought specific state bonds to the value of the durable. The switch from state housing (subsidized rents) to co-operative housing (full rents including an interest component) is really the 'Volkswagen tactic'. And finally, but less successfully, one can raise the rate of interest at the savings bank – which reminds us that a savings bank conducts a kind of open-market operation also in an ACE.

Reverting from currency to the 'credit' side, how closely does ruble audit resemble, say, French qualitative controls? Historically there seems to be no connexion at all. Moreover the French controls are the planners' only means of implementation, while the Soviet-type audit is precisely an audit: a making sure that other means of implementation (planners' commands via production ministries) have worked properly. This is, reflection should make clear, precisely the difference beetween active and passive money. Then again, ruble audit is far and away more detailed: yet when an STE is decentralized (sec. 18) ruble audit quickly and easily becomes qualitative control, for the banks are accustomed to this sort of thing.

16. Passive money has many parallels in market economies, particularly in their public sectors. In the British Army there are *imprest accounts*: money given to subordinate units that may only be used for defined purposes, such as the sergeants' mess. Indeed virtually every military account is imprest in fact if not in name. British universities are similarly plagued with *earmarked grants*, whereby the authorities seek to promote this or that highly specified activity. In all walks of life there are *trust funds*, which are confined to certain types of expenditure laid down in the trust deed. In each case the money is confined within this narrow range of uses by law.

One cannot transfer money from one of these accounts to another, or to the *general or free account*. Sums underspent in a particular line may be left there perhaps for one more year, but are then *clawed back*. The art of evasion consists principally in moving objects of general expenditure into earmarked accounts, so as to unburden the general account of everything possible. In this way we do not underspend the earmarked accounts, which is always a danger. On general account there is of course always something we want to buy, so there is less danger of underspending and consequent clawback.

The general account is 'all-purpose money' and the earmarked accounts are precisely parallel to the 'special moneys' that anthropologists observe. But they are not quite the same as passive money. For their aim is to define a range of purchases within which the spender is still free and the money still active, while the aim of passive money is to reflect in accountancy a transaction already precisely decided in physical terms by higher authority. In other words capitalist earmarking is qualitative control by the Treasury. It is exactly the same sort of thing as French qualitative banking controls, and we have already seen how different these are from passive money.

But if an STE decentralizes a little (not a great deal, as in Hungary), its passive money becomes active within limits, like an earmarked account. The great case was always the construction industry, even during the classical period. Each building is a prototype;[22] no one knows what it will cost, or what quantities of specific inputs it will require. So the construction enterprise is given a rough physical description of the building and a global maximum cost in money terms; and is permitted to choose and substitute its inputs within these limits. The wholesale prices of building materials and the wages of building labour have always had allocative significance.

In a still looser way, the very existence of the extra-budgetary fund imposes earmarking on the Treasury itself. It cannot spend exactly as it pleases, by passing revenues into the *consolidated fund*, which is British Treasury language for the general or free account (above), since some of its revenues are permanently earmarked for extra-budgetary funds, to cover specified expenditures. Sometimes this is an absurd electoral gimmick, as when the unpopular British whisky tax was earmarked for the popular item of technical education (1890), or the petrol tax to road-building (1909; in the first case the tax, in the second the outgoes, were far too small). Sometimes it is a very necessary administrative convenience, like the great French financial funds. Sometimes it is the businesslike decentralization of a productive public enterprise, like all Tsarist and Bolshevik uses of *khozraschet*.[23]

Large capitalist enterprises also earmark, some with great precision. A particularly common form of loose earmarking is to distinguish capital and current expenditures, allowing the branch manager to decide only the latter. Though administratively convenient this is by no means economically logical; it prevents good substitutions unless carefully watched.[24] The retained profits of the Soviet-type enterprise are also always most strictly earmarked by the superior authorities, both before and after the 1965 reforms. There are and were three funds: for incentives (bonuses), for fringe benefits and for investment. The reforms made them larger, but changed little else.

17. The balance of payments must continue to obsess us. The monobank

has a total monopoly of foreign currency. In commodity trade, and in invisibles connected with it such as freights, the domestic currency is passive as usual. The producer for export delivers to the Ministry of Foreign Trade according to detailed physical plan as to any other customer, and receives passive domestic money. The Ministry keeps a separate account in this money, which it feeds by sales of imports – the import-user is ordered to accept the goods and pays for them in passive money. The export-producer and the import-user never handle foreign currency. The ways in which the Ministry balances this account with Treasury subsidies, and the criteria of what to import and export, do not concern us, since there is unfortunately no room for foreign trade as such in this book: we confine ourselves to its financial effects. Note how little these procedures resemble exchange control, i.e. the rationing of active money in the foreign trade of market economies.

But in foreign retail trade (tourism, emigrants' remittances, etc.) money is as usual active. One really does slap down a ruble note on a bank counter and receive 90 cents for it. So naturally one is subject to exchange control! The privilege of tourism is severely limited. As to financial flows, there are no negotiable securities, so no spontaneous or speculative flows are possible, so long as tourists are rationed and the officials of the Ministry of Foreign Trade obey the law.[25]

All financial transactions – export credits, foreign aid and the settlement of short balances between central banks – are highly official.

Thus the currency has *administrative convertibility* in retail trade. Between monobanks there is also now *transferability*, which is virtually the same thing: any number of such banks can cancel their mutual debts multilaterally, but only by arrangement with each other or with IBEC, the Comecon bank. No technicality prevents the participation here of other central banks. But there is not what the experts now call *commodity convertibility*. No foreign wholesale trader, given a ruble, can spend it as he pleases on Soviet semi-fabricates or finished goods – except when he does his personal shopping. He must go through the planners and get a physical claim (*zayavka*). It is clear that commodity inconvertibility is nothing but the passivity of money. Short of abolishing money altogether, it is the most effective 'sealant' against international disturbance.

How much does all this add to exchange control? We can see that it is all necessary in order to keep money passive, but is it necessary simply to prevent hot-money flows or the importation of inflation? Our answer must be yes and no. Behind exchange control, as even Soviet tourists remind us, there is active money, plunging about, outside all central control. Such money may permanently, and must from time to time, build up pressure behind the barrier. This pressure may be purely financial (we see a good speculation in a foreign country) or even political (we want to emigrate). It may have nothing to do with inflation at home, but so long as there is pressure active money is very troublesome. Excessive passive money simply lies about – it is passive! It follows that exchange control is much more likely to be violated in a market economy, though it certainly suffices as a 'sealant' in theory.

18. Decentralization is all the vogue in certain STEs, notably China and Hungary, which nevertheless retain a monobank.[26] In Hungary since January 1968 the enterprise maximand is profit, output and quality decisions are largely free, price decisions partly so. The Gossnab (chapter 11) and the one-year plan have been virtually abolished. So the monobank has given up 'forint audit' since there is nothing to audit. All of this applies to China since 1958 (chapter 10) with two very crucial differences: there has been no ideological adjustment or serious attempt to define what has happened, and the enterprise maximand is, if it can be identified at all, the local Party cadre's idea of how the general line in Pekin should be applied in particular. Hungary's is a revisionist, China's an extreme leftist, decentralization, but both promote the monobank to new power. In China it was even protected, as ordinary enterprises were not, against the worst excesses of the Cultural Revolution – and so recognized as a commanding height like the army.

For take away the command hierarchy, as these countries have done, and what lever is left in the hands of a government that is after all a Communist government, believing in strong central power, national unity, independence from foreigners, etc.? By mere elimination the monobank stands out. Moreover the removal of the one-year plan and the Gossnab activates all the passive money in the inter-enterprise sector – but the monobank has always administered this money. It continues to restrict or grant short-term credit, but now according to looser criteria handed down from above or worked out by itself. It continues to worry – neither more nor less effectively than before – about cash in the hands of the population, and to monopolize foreign currency.

In a similar case before all this was properly understood, the Soviet NEP, the monobank's credit restriction brought about a recession (1923, end of Scissors Crisis). That is to say, not merely the micro- but most of the macro-laws of the market hold good, whoever owns the enterprises that operate upon it. If, as in the NEP, the monopoly of foreign currency is abandoned, the monobank must even keep to an international liquidity ratio, just like any central bank that enforces no exchange control.[27] Actually the Gosbank had an internal propaganda reason for doing so which had little to do with the balance of payments: it had to restore faith in its notes, after the astronomical inflation and the grain requisitioning, among the peasantry.

19. *Debt under socialism.* It is impossible to stop socialist enterprises, especially collective farms, and individual citizens from getting into debt. The government also borrows, notably through the savings bank, from

the population. Foreign aid gives rise to long-term international debt, and foreign trade, principally through the under- and over-fulfilment of plans, to short-term international debt. This short debt, just like the short debt of all enterprises, can easily cumulate if the lender is indulgent.

All this debt is non-negotiable, though some of the short international debt is now administratively transferable, in the name of multilateralism. Therefore capital gains are impossible. The lender may easily make a capital loss through default, but never through a movement on the market, since there is no market. Therefore the yield to redemption is always the nominal yield. This may surprise the sophisticated, but it will be a relief to beginning students in economics who, familiar in their tender years only with savings banks, are mostly unable to grasp 'the' relation between interest rates and bond prices. The simple reason is that textbooks do not distinguish savings from bonds negotiable at variable prices. The textbook relation does not apply to non-negotiable debt, which is the only kind most people know about. Now socialism holds capital gains to be the abomination of desolation, while it cannot do away with debt as such. So non-negotiability is an excellent ideological compromise.

For capitalism differs greatly. Nearly all the debt is negotiable, and there is much more of it, mostly held by individuals or organizations who are entirely free to dispose of it tomorrow.[28] There is therefore a vast debt market, which is also perfectly competitive. It could not be otherwise, given the innumerable homogeneous pieces of paper, and the innumerable people and institutions buying and selling them. 'Free entry' is of course ensured merely by having a stock of a particular security: it is not necessary to make a new issue, and the volume of new issues is a tiny fraction of the turnover. But what is perfectly competitive is speculative.

Moreover the accidents of budgetary history leave the government as far and away the main debtor. So it is almost duty bound, for budgetary reasons, to manipulate security prices in its own favour, by open-market operations. It tries by these to induce speculation in the appropriate direction, but in so doing it must inflate. So debt management normally runs counter to monetary management.

It is hard not to condemn the very existence of the typical capitalist debt market, as both unstable all the time and inflationary much of the time. Moreover the possibility of capital gain causes many intellectual and physical resources to be wasted in the market, instead of being invested in factor activity. When Yugoslavia teeters on the brink of bond and equity markets we must share the Maoists' concern that she is going capitalist.

20. Certainly her market banking system[29] reproduces innumerable features of, say, the US system. But on closer examination this turns out to be, not capitalism, but federalism. For Yugoslavia is the only Communist country to be federal and mean it, and although her workers'

councils arose from other preoccupations her federalism rapidly exploited the idea, and blew it up into the 'self-managed society'. The banking system is an expression of the localism, rather than of the workers' councils, inherent in the idea of self-management. Indeed the banks are not self-managed but 'socially managed' (chapter 10, sec. 9). Formally they are managed by the enterprises that 'founded' them (i.e. deposited with them), and under the guidance of the political authorities at various levels. The bank workers have only one seat on the board of management. The founding enterprises dispose of the profits. But this also means that 'merely financial' windfalls do accrue eventually to individuals – those now working in the founding enterprises.

Up to 1954, then, there was a normal monobank, investment bank and savings bank. But further changes were occurring in Yugoslav society and ideology, less well publicized than the original ones but of equal importance. For if workers' councils in enterprises began in 1948 and were the offspring of Tito's misunderstanding of Marxism,[30] the idea of a whole *self-managed society* began with the new constitutional law of 1953. Already this law gave the lowest unit of local government, the *Komuna*, financial and regulative powers over the enterprises on its territory.

For what is a self-managed society but a *locally* managed society? And what country in the world is more a prey to localism than Yugoslavia? – with her eight republics or autonomous regions, her five or six languages, her eight or so nationalities,[31] and the traditional fourfold spread of regional incomes. The very word for self-management (*samouprava*) is of pre-war, non-Marxist, origin – there used to be a Croatian populist journal of that title.

Banking change, then, followed constitutional change, and has continued to do so up to and including the final decentralization of the state in 1971, when a collective State Presidency was set up, exclusively on localist lines, to take over when Marshal Tito eventually dies. Useless to go through the intervening steps – the instability of institutions characterizes Yugoslavia even more than Khrushchev's USSR. There can be very few native banking officials who could recite so complicated a history, yet the drift is clear. We end, as this is written, with a *unitary central bank*, the National Bank of Yugoslavia in Belgrade; this is the bank of issue and foreign exchange control, and it holds the compulsory deposits of the other banks and acts as lender of last resort. The Yugoslav Investment Bank continues to administer the old federal investment fund, which was much the largest of the extra-budgetary funds that grew up after 1954. Then come the *republican national banks*, one for each republic and autonomous region. These are mainly agents of the central bank, since they are but its republican branches renamed. But they have some independent powers within their territories; notably they administer the erstwhile investment funds of the republics. Below these are the Communal banks, which conduct both a deposit and an investment business.[32] They may (since 1965) operate anywhere in the national territory, with any customer they please, no matter where they were founded. Thus there is a three-tier banking system! But the middle tier is purely a concession to national sentiment.

Note that we cannot in this case distinguish banking from investment finance, since Yugoslav banks, like West German ones, deal with both investment and deposits. There are indeed three specialist investment banks: 'Agriculture', 'Foreign Trade' (i.e. the promotion of exports and import substitutes) and 'Investment'. Nor are the independent extra-budgetary funds quite dead.

This extreme formal decentralization took place in response to the Croatian near-secession of 1970–1. Banking was at the epicentre of that storm, and Zagreb University must have harboured the first student revolution ever to be ostensibly about (and of course to misunderstand)[33] exchange controls. But Yugoslav Communism continues to show a very firm grasp of essentials beneath its Protean surface. The Croatian secessionists have been suppressed, and we may be sure the banking system still does not defy Belgrade on what is essential. This last episode goes but to confirm our rule (sec. 18) that banking is the most commanding height in a decentralized STE, by whatever precise means that height is occupied.

There is still no money market, and so no open market for the national bank to operate on. Undoubtedly this is because it would not appear 'socialist', even though capital gains are very small on money markets, and are only made by banks, never by individuals.[34] The present control system, as we saw, is that the central bank freezes the deposits of the other banks. It is not clear to the writer, as it is to the OECD (op. cit.), why this is so greatly inferior. Surely so long as the markets for goods are so very imperfect, regional incomes so very unequal and the balance of payments so uncertain, a discriminating central bank control is, in theory, even better than a more purely quantitative one. In any case investment projects are still subject to qualitative control by banks at all levels.

Notes

1. We speak of quite different ones in quite different markets in chapter 9, sec. 13.

2. If, as in USA, there are still unit commercial banks in a large country, they will have to use corresponding banks in metropolitan areas where there are money markets. This makes little difference in principle.

3. Cf. Rondo Cameron in ed. Rondo Cameron, *Banking in the Early Stages of Industrialization*, London 1967; George Garvy in *The History of Political Economy*, Spring 1972; *La Doctrine St. Simonienne*, ed. C. Bouglé et Elie Halévy, Paris 1924, pp. 267–73, esp. footnote 154; Alex Gerschenkron, *Economic*

Backwardness in Historical Perspective, Harvard 1962, pp. 22–5. Gerschenkron however most curiously fails to notice that the Banque de France was a St. Simonian quasi-monobank, and Cameron asserts quite falsely that the French rate of growth was lower than the British in the nineteenth century. Taken *per capita*, his own figures show the opposite. It is clear that much work remains to be done on the relation between French growth and French banking. I do not deny certain restrictive features of the latter, and propound, in the absence of study, no view at all except scepticism. On the Bank's branches, I have been privileged to see various non-confidential documents of the bank itself.

4. The idea of having branches was not new, or due to St. Simon. It is contained in the Bank's charter of 1808, and was at that time practised in England. St. Simon was not yet interested in banks at that date. But when the branches were founded (1836) we may fairly allege his influence. The original technical need was to implant the paper currency habit in the provinces, and to unify the issue of this paper.

5. On 1 January 1973: 173 *succursales*; 74 mere *bureaux*, including 3 in Paris. The peak was reached in 1928, with 260.

6. Ed. Felipe Ruiz Martín *et al.*, *El Banco de España*, Madrid 1970.

7. George Garvy in *Journal of Economic History*, December 1972.

8. It is indeed rendered so by figuring on the last page of Lenin's *Imperialism*. This passage contains a well-deserved compliment to St. Simon, and foreshadows the banking system of the NEP. St. Simon was already popular among Tsarist bankers.

9. In the previous period, of 'War' Communism, there had been in principle no money, so no need for a bank. The old Tsarist bank of issue was, however, used to print notes and bring about an astronomical inflation, quite deliberately. Later, in January 1920, the People's Commissariat of Finance took over this function, and the ruble note became a 'Treasury note'; cf. sec. 6 below.

10. We have seen that the inflated ruble notes of the later months of 'War' Communism were formally Treasury notes (sec. 5 above). The one ruble note remains so to this day. The higher denominations are bank notes. The UK had Treasury notes, worth 10 shillings, in the first World War and for a few years thereafter.

11. Cf. Esther R. Taus, *The Central Banking Functions of the U.S. Treasury*, N.Y. 1943.

12. In saying this I slightly distort normal capitalist and Communist terminology. The IMF is a 'fund' because it can only lend what it borrows, *at short term*. The equivalent long-term institution, the IBRD, operates of course under the same restraint, but is called an 'investment bank'. This phrase always implies the quality of a fund in my sense. The IMF is further restricted by not being allowed to borrow over certain limits. But it also operates as a bank, under another hat, when it administers the new Special Drawing Rights. These are not governed by the IMF's original charter at all, and the accountancy is quite separate.

13. But this is a *purely* administrative question. Sometimes these funds are merged into the monobank, becoming functional departments of it. Even so they are limited to their budgetary allocations.

14. Richard S. Sayers, *Modern Banking*, 6th edn., Oxford 1964, pp. 218–27.

15. Committee on the Working of the Monetary System, London 1960, Cmd. 827.

16. T. M. Podolski, *Socialist Banking and Monetary Control*, Cambridge

1973, pp. 137–51; Andrzej Brzeski in ed. Gregory Grossman, *Money and Plan*, Berkeley 1968.

17. Cf. Wiles in ed. Ghita Ionescu, *Populism*, London 1969.

18. The rapidity of the exposé blurs much important detail. The devaluations and floats of the 'thirties were succeeded in ACEs by a partial return to a virtual gold standard, but it was in the 'thirties that the Nazis experimented, quite successfully, with the fourth monetary system, of qualitative banking. Britain imitated the Nazis, again quite successfully, from 1940 to about 1952; and then turned her back on this achievement.

19. The Russian word *kontrol'* is correctly translated by a weaker word than the English 'control' (cf. 'workers' audit' vs. 'workers' self-management', chapter 7).

20. For a general view of the rates of interest in an STE cf. chapter 13, sec. 15.

21. The reference is to Hitler's pre-war bond sales for Volkswagens on this pattern. The outstanding bonds caused the company and the West German government a lot of trouble after the war.

22. Chapter 10, sec. 2; chapter 15, sec. 6; chapter 18, sec. 6.

23. Cf. chapter 3, secs. 4, 12. The success of *khozraschet* warns us not to condemn earmarked funds too soon. The fiasco of the British 'Road Fund' deflected attention from the genuinely constructive notion that there should be a road-building corporation, drawing its revenue from vehicle and fuel *levies* set by itself, and quite separate from vehicle and fuel *taxes*.

24. Thus my own institution, the London School of Economics, is compelled to spend millions on a new library building in a prime down-town site, when the interest on half the sum would improve services beyond recognition, including a twice-daily van to the out-of-town repository for rarely used books. Different higher authorities are responsible or the School's capital and current expenditures.

25. If they did not, they could engineer, not indeed a flow of funds but a speculative balance in foreign currency, built up out of a doubtless temporary export surplus.

26. Which Yugoslavia has not done: cf. sec. 20.

27. The ruble was convertible in 1926, and the Gosbank supported the rate in Berlin. Cf. Wiles 1969, pp. 123–9.

28. This extremely simple but important contrast was drawn to my attention by my student Mrs. Carol Nussey.

29. George Macesich, *Yugoslavia*, Charlottesville 1964; Peter Dobias, *Das Jugoslawische Wirtschaftssystem*, Kiel 1969; OECD reports, Yugoslavia, November 1970, March 1972; Egon Neuberger in *QJE*, February 1959; John C. Waller, M.Sc. essay for Bradford University, 1973.

30. Especially of the purely tactical concessions made to syndicalism by Marx in respect of the Paris Commune and by Lenin in 1917–18: cf. Wiles 1962, chapter 18.

31. By my controversial count. I put Serbo-Croat as 1½ languages in order to give as little offence as possible. I count the Bosnian Moslems and the Hungarians of Vojvodina as separate nationalities.

32. To lend long one must borrow not too short: these banks have few 'funds' to administer, but they do have long-term deposits, and the permanent capital subscribed by the enterprises and local authorities that founded them.

33. The Croatian complaint is that the exchange control regulations pool

most of the foreign currency earned by Yugoslav exporters under the control of Belgrade banks. Possessing most of the coastline and beauty-spots, Croatia does export more than her share. But if she had to pay foreign currency for the import component of the goods delivered to her by the sister republics her balance might be negative.

34. Except very indirectly, by members of the founding enterprises, as described above.

13
Investment Finance, Thrift and Risk

13

1. As we move from short debt to long, the question of investment criteria arises. But this book is not about development policy, so we confine ourselves to a few scattered remarks where the criteria or the policy are very intimately connected with some institution. But more inevitably the balance now shifts slightly away from technical management questions towards large issues of ownership and the sources of thrift. Nevertheless many of the last chapter's *dramatis personae* reappear: long debt becomes near-money as it approaches maturity, default on short debt turns creditors into owners, etc. All dividing lines between this and chapter 12 are arbitrary. But this is surely the more important subject of the two. For the slow pressure of new savings alters the social structure of ownership under capitalism, and even in Yugoslavia. Nay, the same can result merely from the growth of a new intermediary, selling bonds to new savers and using the proceeds to acquire equity. Moreover at this point the differences between market socialism and capitalism become very great, and lose altogether the aspect of a mere formality.

2. Alex Gerschenkron[1] lays down the following connexion between investment finance and the sources of thrift. In the beginning was the United Kingdom, with an extremely rich land-owning nobility and a large number of Caribbean slave-owners and plunderers of India. These people were far from snobbish as to where they put their money, just as they had always been willing to marry into the bourgeoisie. One landed estate was *de rigueur*, but for the rest one ventured one's savings much as one ventured one's younger sons. So the needs, first of Mercantilist foreign enterprise, then of government, and finally of the industrial revolution, were met spontaneously, the first two by a *stock exchange*. For the extreme inequality of wealth provided large packets of risk-bearing thrift, that needed no mobilization or special treatment. Reliance on the stock exchange was so complete that the investment, or merchant, banks did not actually invest: they only underwrote new issues. It was not necessary to *mobilize small savings*, though this did come about through the independent action of the working class in savings banks, co-operative societies and building societies. The *government provided no savings at all*, not even for railways. The *deposit banks* were able to keep clear of investment finance, confining their assets to personal advances, bills of exchange and government securities. The Netherlands had anticipated UK in most of this, and remains to this day similarly dominated by its stock exchange.

Gerschenkron proceeds to ring the changes on the four sources of thrift italicized, in respect of other European countries with different degrees of development and income structure. But first let us note how right he is not to over-emphasize the London Stock Exchange. The industrial revolution, as opposed to the state and the great trading companies, was not financed through the stock exchange, but by an astonishing variety of makeshifts. The new industrialists borrowed privately from their families; they took inter-enterprise credit; they wrote 'finance' bills, i.e. bills of exchange appearing to be in respect of raw materials but actually designed only to be renewed indefinitely, so as to obtain long-term finance; they paid labour and local tradesmen in their own private scrip, i.e. effectually they borrowed cash from them; and they ploughed back profits. These makeshifts recur in virtually every country's economic history. They make us wonder whether Britain would have rejected the Crédit Mobilier or the Tsarist budgetary advance if they had been available.

Meanwhile until after the first World War, the London Stock Exchange looked not northwards but overseas; London is a Mercantilist city. And this leads us to a further point Gerschenkron under-emphasizes: individual thrift has tastes. People, and even London merchant banks, are very sensitive about handing over their savings, and do so only where traditional trust or special knowledge gives them confidence. The same point is evident in British working-class thrift, with its tropism to mortgages and co-operative trade; and in the Frenchman's preference for foreign bonds (below). Only a rather dense network of financial intermediaries produces a reasonable perfection in the capital market. In an STE all thrift is at the disposal of the Politburo, which is again a collection of a few individuals. The perfect capital market disappears, and the new 'savers'' tastes are referred to as an investment policy.

3. We may now pursue the Gerschenkron thesis more rapidly. France, it runs, had a more equal distribution of income, or at least the very rich were less adventurous and preferred the socially correct investments of rural and urban land. So the savings of poorer people had to be mobilized for general purposes, and the Crédit Mobilier, the first deposit-cum-investment bank, was born. And the government took a great deal more part, especially in financing the transport infrastructure (chapter 9). In a St. Simonian country the weakness of the stock exchange was the strength of the authorities. Indeed it so remains; taxes are used to feed certain extra-budgetary funds (notably the Fonds de Développement Economique et Social) whose purpose is direct investment. This is quite over and above the portfolio investments, nay the scarcely more than underwriting role, of other, non-tax-fed, extra-budgetary funds (notably the Caisse des Dépots et Consignations); which can nevertheless make or break any given new issue because of their immense size and switching activity. France not only was, but is, a different country. Thus Table 13/II shows an immense 'budgetary' contribution to private investment. And although the stock exchange did comparatively well with 10 per cent, this is because

1964 was an off year for London. Even in this bad year London's stock exchange *turnover* was 71 per cent, Paris's 9 per cent, of the national income.

The USA faced originally the same problem of a weak stock exchange and few really rich men, but had no St. Simonian tradition. One may imagine what Andrew Jackson or his Populist successors would have said of such a thing! But it had a Mercantilist tradition (Alexander Hamilton), in the name of which a state-supported infrastructure spread across the country. Government units of every size from federal to municipal provided finance and, more importantly, free land most of which the contractor could afterwards sell. Nothing in any part of the American tradition opposed such participation by non-federal government. But much of the states' debt that was counterpart to these loans was very unwise, and had later to be repudiated. The states borrowed largely abroad, and so after them did the early industrialists. With increasing development (and probably increasing inequality of income) the stock exchange took over its British role – or rather the domestic role so commonly attributed to the London Stock Exchange, which, however, it did not play until about the same late date. Hampered by populist legislation, the US banks played no great part in investment finance. Thus the populists 'objectively' preferred the stock exchange.

4. In Germany however the same gap in capital sources and institutions was met by the deposit banks. This caused considerable tut-tutting in the nineteenth century: was this not the sin of borrowing short to lend long? Was it not worse even than banks' buying equities? But the big amalgamated deposit banks went right ahead, making scarcely-negotiable advances of permanent capital to industry as orthodox banks did to individuals, and appointing directors when their loans were endangered.[2] No bank bankruptcies resulted; the rules of the game had simply been wrong. Observing this tendency, German Marxists after Marx's death founded a whole doctrine of *Finanzkapital*, whereby these deposit-cum-investment banks would be the instrument of the final concentration of capital that would herald the revolution. Echoing Thorstein Veblen,[3] they distinguished between the producing and the banking capitalist, to the latter's disadvantage. And in this at least the writer is disposed to follow them, but not in their prophecy, which never came true. For all they were really observing was one of the many ways in which other ACEs fall short of being perfectly British. With further development (West) Germany too has come to rely more upon its stock exchange for new capital; the banker's hold has been relaxed, and the large producing capitalist is beholden to no one, except possibly the state.

In all these cases the pressure of borrowing on lending led to new financial institutions, but also, and much more simply, to foreign loans. These must be described as part of the system, as an 'institution'. Even Britain borrowed heavily from the pre-industrial Netherlands. Early colonial incomes too were, though strictly personal to individual exploiters, a kind of foreign borrowing, or at least theft. In contrast to later imperialism (chapter 19) capital tended to flow inwards.

5. What, now, of the altogether more backward capitalist country, for which no mere bridging institution suffices? which will not develop German banks, or US local government, or French small savings, in a century, let alone an adequate stock exchange? There are not enough banks – though 'underdeveloped' banks are characteristically adventurous and unorthodox; local government has not tax revenues enough to secure a loan with; and small savings means notes and coin under the mattress. We must add the extraordinary general corruption of society, which militates perhaps most against a stock exchange. A stock exchange depends on inside information, which it is scandalously easy to obtain for money. The London Stock Exchange, the great cynosure of them all, was not free from gross corruption until the 1920s, if it has ever been. We cannot then be surprised that the public is unwilling to buy stocks and shares.

Gerschenkron takes as an example his native Tsarist Russia. But if we add public foreign aid any of today's capitalist or state-capitalist UDCs fits his pattern. Which makeshifts do such countries prefer? First, of course, foreign capital. This may bulk as large as one half of all disposable savings. Secondly, the budget. Theoretically this is admirable; for each marginal ruble or rupee of tax replaces say one quarter as much voluntary saving, and three quarters as much consumption. In practice however the budget cannot be balanced, and inflation takes the place of taxes. For the rest, there are no new devices: we have already exhausted the list.

It follows that a sufficiently poor country, developing sufficiently fast, cannot develop much native capitalism. Foreign capitalists, foreign states and its own state are the most serious contenders for ownership. Native capitalism will be more or less confined to its existing volume, and probably to backward sectors. It is simply a matter of where the thrift comes from.

Later, when native thrift has sufficiently developed, the government and the foreigners can sell their property to native capitalists. Thus the British sold their rubber estates to Malayans in the 1950s, and the Japanese government used to sell its state-financed factories to the public. And here we note, for the first but not the last time, the extraordinary role of the equity share. It is not after all necessary to wait for very much development. Minute quantities of equity can be created, and huge enterprises, still owing fixed debt to the state, moved into the private sector. For this and other curiosities, see sec. 13.

6. The STE, however, escapes from Gerschenkron's net. In its classical

model it mainly accumulates through a balanced budget. Being a strong government it is well enough able to tax, and so covers not only recurrent but also developmental expenditures. There is, thus, no 'line' as in the British budget, outgoes below which are covered by borrowing. Note the deep difference, which can only be called ideological, between the STE and a system which implies that developmental expenditures are not recurrent, and that borrowing is *a priori* the appropriate way to finance both public and private accumulation.

Investment finance is a free gift of the Treasury. It passes out through 'funds' known as investment banks, which are merely administrative entities. These were described briefly in chapter 12, sec. 7, and we need say nothing more. But the provisions for debt amortization do require notice. The Soviet-type financial system is even more heroic than we have implied. Amortization provisions, or roughly corresponding depreciation rates on fixed assets, are built into all prices, and these sums are properly set aside by the accountants of enterprises. But they do not go back to the Treasury! – not even in the new decentralized system when Treasury grants attract a capital charge, for that charge corresponds to interest alone. If the grants were amortized they would not be free gifts, so the quotas pile up in special accounts all the way up the planning hierarchy from enterprise to ministry (but not above that). They must only be spent on capital repairs or new investment, and of course the central planners have total ultimate control over this, since they allocate the relevant physical goods.

Only when investment finance flows outside the socialist sector is it really a loan. Only then is actual interest, under that name, charged and amortization paid back into the Treasury (sec. 15).

Again the Treasury only pays interest on money borrowed from abroad or from the small savings of the population. For the population too is strictly outside the socialist sector; or at least the attraction of their thrift is a market operation. So all deposits in the savings bank (chapter 12) are a budgetary revenue, and all withdrawals and interest a budgetary expenditure. Moreover the net disbursal by the monobank of notes and coins into the hands of the population is effectively a (negative) revenue of the authorities. The sum of these two items is the population's 'net acquisition of financial assets', most of the rest of personal saving being the construction and improvement of dwellings. Personal saving in STEs is important and interesting, and deserves an excursus. In UK personal savings are divided about 50–50 between 'finance' and 'dwellings', whereas in Hungary before and after the reforms much the major part went into private buildings.

Nevertheless we know that the growth of the liquid assets of the population (the figure 3098 in Table 13/I) runs at 3 or 4 per cent p.a. of disposable personal income in all STEs and Hungary, and a question that worries all monobanks is whether this perpetual pile-up of liquid assets is not inflationary. It is very hard to tell. Since private supplementary pension schemes are virtually unavailable and equity shares completely so there is little to keep the money invested. In UK on the other hand the net increase in private pension funds is counted as personal thrift. It exceeds the net personal acquisition of financial assets, i.e. we borrow from other sectors to buy private pension claims, and our net acquisition of other financial assets is negative. Thus no disorderly monetary overhang arises out of personal saving in UK.[4]

TABLE 13/I
Personal Saving, Hungary and UK
(mn. ft., mn. £)

	Hungary	UK
Money expenditure of population	148,486	40,045
Increase of cash in hand and savings deposits	(3098)	—
Net borrowing from state (negative means more indebtedness)	(−1497)	—
Net acquisition of financial assets (of which net increase in private life assurance funds)	1601 (0)	1238 (1755)
New private dwellings excluding land	? 6155	666
Purchases and sales of existing land and buildings	?	−239
Other personal business investment	?	662
Increase in value of stocks and work in progress	?	205
Total of above personal savings	(7756)	2532

Sources: *Statistical Yearbook 1968*, pp. 155, 158, 354, 325; *National Income Bluebook 1971*, pp. 27–8. Workings available on request. Other countries, East and West, seem to have less good statistics.

But *per contra* Communist populations are always *in the process of* building private houses, and many run little 'grey' businesses; even perfectly legal private enterprise may not use the monobank but must use cash or the savings bank; and all this activity needs a fairly stable cash float. So we need not share the extreme sensitivity of monobanks, but we must certainly admit that private thrift flourishes greatly in STEs, that its cumulative sum is very great, and that it may at any moment come 'unstuck'.

The role of small savings probably varies, but in general the STE's peculiar institutions do not express any particular stage of development. Rich or poor, all STEs act in the same way: this is simply the way that suits them. When they decentralize, they naturally de-emphasize the budget in favour of ploughback and the bank. And this has indeed been part of the universal 'post-Liberman' wave of decentralization since 1962 (chapter 11). But the movement has no connexion with stages of development. Reliance upon the budget signifies underdevelopment only under capitalism. The country to decentralize most, and to put most emphasis on banks, local authorities and ploughback, is China! The next in line is Hungary. In other countries the new financial arrangements differ greatly, although the degrees of relaxation of command planning is about the same (Table 13/II). I have added UK and France, but their statistical comparability with each other or with the other countries can by no means be guaranteed. In these two cases, and no doubt in all the others, definitions differ markedly. The years chosen may well be exceptional and comparison is in its infancy.

7. Yugoslavia has also its Gerschenkron problem – no country more so. She feeds extra-budgetary funds from taxation, especially but not only for large federal and military projects, and for projects in the under-developed South; where ploughback and bank advances will not meet the case. In accordance with their decentralized ideology, the authorities are for ever expressing the pious hope that eventually these latter sources will suffice.

We come in sec. 10 to the special Yugoslav problem of thrift, i.e. of the motive to plough back. We note here that in matters of sheer financial flow Yugoslavia is merely the first of the STEs to decentralize. They all go the same way, whether or not there are workers' councils, and whether or not there is a free market in intermediate goods. But the Yugoslav budget, since the 1965 reforms, confines itself to urgent and unprofitable projects of national importance. It leaves the rest to ploughback, and to the bank or banks. These receive permission to lend at long term, at interest and repayably, money not received free from the budget (notably amortization quotas). They thus become deposit-and-investment banks, of the old German type.

In Yugoslavia and Hungary there is no parallel system of physical controls over capital goods, so financial decentralization means what it says: no longer the planners or the government but the banks decide investment. Hence arise complaints against what we may call 'socialist *Finanzkapital*', with impassioned denunciations of a remote financial establishment. During the Croatian near-secession of 1971–2 things were said about Belgrade banks that remind one very much of William Jennings Bryan denouncing Wall Street.

But where an STE does not re-establish a free market this decentralization of financial flows is rather pointless. If machinery and bricks and labour can only be got with planners' permission, what does it matter that we can sometimes get the money without Treasury permission? – especially if our prices are controlled and our profits heavily taxed. Certainly it is enormously frustrating to scrape together the funds and then find that they cannot be spent, and many complain of this. But at least one bureaucratic hurdle has disappeared, and the enterprise director has more influence over the planner if he comes waving a cheque-book. Moreover

TABLE 13/II
Sources of Finance for Gross Fixed Investment
(In Communist countries, state sector only, per cent)

	Budget[b]		(Ploughback including depreciation)		Banks		Other	
	1965	1969	1965	1969	1965	1969	1965	1969
Bulgaria	63	32	30	38	7	30	0	0
Czechoslovakia	69	35	23	42	8	21	0	0
DDR	40	27	35	50	25	23	0	0
Poland	46	28	45	36	9	36	0	0
Rumania	61	44	37	41	2	15	0	0
USSR	61	50	39	49·5	0	0·5	0	0
Hungary	86	51	13	37	1	12	0	0
Mongolia	87	—	13	—	0	—	0	—
China[a]	?98	—	?2	—	?0	—	?0	—
France[d]	18·8	—	49·5	—	4·4	—	27·3	—
UK Public[e]	90·5	—	52·6	—	1·8	—	−45·0	—
UK Private[f]	0·5	—	79·7	—	5·9	—	13·9	—
Yugoslavia[c]	57	16	28	29	9	49	6	6

Source: First eight rows: H. F. Buck in ed. Yves Laulan, *Banking, Money and Credit in Eastern Europe*, NATO, Brussels, 1973, p. 136. Presumably excludes co-operative farms.

a. My approximation for 1957, from varied sources. Note that in this very centralized early arrangement depreciation funds went to the Treasury.

b. Including net current subsidies.

c. John C. Waller, *The Yugoslav Banking System*, University of Bradford M.Sc. thesis, 1974, p. 158. 'Budget' is split thus between federation, republics and communes: 1963: 27/10/20, 1969: 9/3/4. 'Other' includes bonds sold to the population, and various foreign borrowings. Note it is 1963, not 1965.

d. My working, from the end paper in Jean Marchal, *Monnaie et Credit*, Paris, 1967, for public and private non-financial enterprises, 1964. 'Other' includes 4 per cent from abroad, 4 per cent from bond issues, 6 per cent from the issue of ordinary shares. The main extra-budgetary funds are in 'budget', the minor ones in 'other'. The concept (=100) is long-term borrowing of all kinds (including net acquisition of financial assets, movements in stocks, foreign transactions). Of this gross fixed capital formation was 101 per cent.

e. Fuel and power, iron and steel, transport and communications; average of 1963–5. Most borrowing from the Treasury corresponds to the big redemptions on the Stock Exchange (−45·0) which accompany actual acts of nationalisation. So a more normal period would be about: 45·5, 52·6, 1·8, 0. But it must not be forgotten that the Treasury itself borrows on the Stock Exchange. Subsidies, discreetly called 'capital transfers' and included in 'budget', were 9·9 per cent. Source: *National Income Blue Book 1969*, p. 43. Concept as for France; gross fixed investment was 90 per cent of the total.

f. Kindly culled from various sources for me by Prof. A. D. Bain. Concept as for France; gross fixed investment was 59 per cent of the total. The year (1964) does not seem to be exceptional.

heavy ploughback means large profits which mean low costs: the new system is an incentive to economy.

Ploughback by enterprises, then – the point is sufficiently obvious – decentralizes a planning system. And this is much more true where there is no physical allocation. Conversely, if for any reason there is very little ploughback the centre has more influence. This simple rule applies also to state capitalism: precisely the growth of ploughback (and of Eurobonds) has weakened the French plan.

Moreover current and long-term finance can be quite separately decentralized. Technically the one affects the other only in so far as it is difficult to prevent slop-over: the 'finance bill' masquerading as a trade bill but always renewed, the bank advance that is never repaid, the long bond approaching maturity, the stock exchange issue or budgetary grant applied to the financing of stocks, etc. Just as of old the discount houses tried to detect and prevent finance bills so does the monobank limit the periods on its advances. In France and in Hungary the banks or the monobank are free to determine short loans, and little plan control applies, precisely on condition they are not disguised long loans. Long loans are far more carefully controlled at the centre. This is then normal in all systems, but the reasons are twofold. In pure market systems the banks watch merely liquidity not current production, but a new issue means a detailed prospectus. In systems planned even a little like the French investment is simply considered more important than current production. The classical STE is an exception; it retains detailed physical controls over all goods, so must control long- and short-term finance with equal strictness.

8. Ploughback is also quite a feature of primitive capitalism. Since competition is (or is thought to be) nearly perfect, and profits are normally maximized, there is not much choice about prices, and the entrepreneur either happens to or happens not to be able to plough back. If the latter he is simply forced to borrow, and the thrift of others is available to him on the stock exchange, or whatever alternative to that the country offers. The difference between the ploughback and the borrowing of small firms is interesting but is not thought to be crucial. It does not, for instance, affect resource allocation.

But it is part of the ideology of this system to mistrust both monopoly and hired managers. So as enterprises expand the opinion grows, as part of the obsolescent ideology, that they should not plough back. They should return their profits to the shareholders and re-borrow them through the stock exchange; this will both ensure that resources go to the most profitable uses, instead of the pet schemes of the management clique, and stave off the managerial revolution. When companies with limited liability first ploughed back they were even legally challenged by minority shareholders.[5]

This view is still common. It neglects the administrative costs of paying out dividends and of re-borrowing. It neglects the costs of borrower's and lender's risk. It either is indifferent to a fall in investment volume, or assumes that 100 per cent of marginal dividends is saved. It assumes that projects financed by new issues really are superior to those entertained by existing, and profitable, firms. Since it is clear that all these points are doubtful or false it might seem that there was nothing to be said against ploughback in advanced capitalism.

But not quite so, for primitive capitalist ideology also holds that even large monopolists charge only one determinate price. Maximizing short-run profits by means of flexible prices, even monopolists have little choice. They set the price they must, and so *find themselves* able or unable to plough back. This doctrine I flatly reject on factual grounds.[6] In fact monopolists neither desire to maximize short-run profits, nor know exactly where marginal cost equals marginal revenue. Therefore they must choose within a wide band of possible prices; indeed all imperfect competitors have this choice in limited degree. Nothing more natural, then, than to follow a qualified cost-plus policy at all times, and in particular to pitch the price high if ploughback is the preferred method of finance. For clearly otherwise we must simply wait too long or borrow. For a single great act of expansion the likely rise in price is uncomfortably great: say 20 per cent over four years. Demand is seldom inelastic enough to tolerate that, and on grounds of public policy it is most undesirable in an age of cost inflation. On the other hand a long-term policy of ploughback and moderate regular growth would necessitate at most a 10 per cent rise in prices in a normal case. Moreover in all cases when growth ceases the ploughback margin is deducted from the price, which sinks to about what it would otherwise have been, since the saving on interest must in the long run be balanced by a higher dividend, to keep shareholders happy and takers-over away.[7]

It is obvious that the choice between ploughback and borrowing has minimal direct effects on the volume of current output. It affects investment, however, by saving certain administrative costs, reducing the risk premium, and ensuring part of the supply of thrift. It affects, as we saw, resource allocation to whatever extent the expansion of firms really does go in different directions from the foundation of firms. It raises the size and reduces the number of firms. It raises real incomes only indirectly, in so far as it raises investment volume. It redistributes income from potential new bond- and share-holders, bankers and underwriters to old shareholders – not a very exciting social event; and away from the consumer of the product during the period of ploughback.

The policy of ploughback under advanced capitalism, then, has one main motive: to preserve the power of the in-group. It has a number of minor economic and social advantages and one substantial drawback: it raises prices. There is also a substantial point of justice. The saver for the future project is the present consumer, who is not consulted and has, if his elasticity of demand is low, no veto. The actual consumer of the project's output does not pay so much.

9. We saw earlier that in an STE reliance on ploughback decentralizes, if only a little. But if we look at the matter from the point of view of the price system and the ultimate sources of saving, we find that budgetary finance itself is ploughback. An STE can only choose between kinds of ploughback. The voluntary savings of the citizens do indeed flow directly through the savings bank into the budget, but are far too small to cover national investment (section 6). Income tax is negligible too. But indirect taxation is hardly distinguishable from profit. A tax is a margin imposed by the enterprise (which is after all itself an extra-budgetary fund – chapter 12) in accordance with a financial plan agreed between the central planners and the Treasury. And in any case most of it goes to the Treasury in 'deductions'.[8] This is, moreover, entirely official doctrine, and not mere snide Sovietological comment.

So in no case can the saver avoid ploughback. Apart from the distinction between its centralized and its decentralized administration (sec. 7), this raises again the question of price policy. So large a monopoly can choose which prices to make 'profitable', whether by indirect taxation or by planned enterprise profit margins does not matter. In this as in so much else it resembles the large capitalist corporation: it is not maximizing its short-run profits. Nay it is not even following, item by item, the principle of cost-plus.

We have seen how in practice the STE, and especially USSR, allocates the burden of financing new investment: on consumer goods, in a highly irregular way (chapter 11), so as to balance the irrational *a priori* supplies with consumer demand. However irregular, the turnover tax is also substantially positive or average. Planned profit rates (it is the planned, not the actual, rates that enter into price formation) are much less irregular, but hit semi-fabricates and capital goods more lightly. They now yield no less overall (in 'deductions') than the turnover tax. Hence in comparison with capitalism the Communist[9] price level is high for consumer and low for producer goods.[10]

By the pure theory of economic models all this is quite unnecessary. In a command economy any price level will do in the inter-enterprise sector, since money is passive there. Nothing prevents us from raising more taxes on such transactions and fewer on final sales to the population, since such a shifting of taxes back down the vertical chain of production will not alter the general level of retail prices, which are the only active ones; nor will it lower investment, since everyone still does what he is told, and everyone still has enough money to buy capital goods with, as profitability in the strict sense need nowhere have been changed. But the practice of two differing price levels in USSR has behind it both history and ideology.

Historically, money was not really passive nor the plan all-embracing and enforceable in 1928–32. If investment was to be encouraged investment goods had to be subsidized and consumption goods taxed. And this was the psychologically formative period. Ideologically indirect taxes are a very sensitive affair. They are the means whereby the workers' state realizes the surplus value generated by its productive labour. Under capitalism the surplus is realized each time the commodity changes ownership, so it is appropriate to apply this rule under socialism: ownership changes only when semi-fabricates and tools are sold to co-operative farms, and when consumer goods are sold to the population.

In other STEs all this has long seemed too theological, and turnover tax has always been more evenly distributed between goods sold to collective farms and the consumer and other goods. The theology has now been eroded also in USSR, especially in favour of collective farms, which are treated more and more like state farms (chapter 3). But the irregularity of the turnover tax remains in all cases; it still serves to balance irrational supply against demand.

10. Turning now to Yugoslavia, we can no longer speak of an identity between federal indirect taxes (especially the substantial remains of the old Soviet-type turnover tax) and high enterprise profit margins. For the latter are not determined by the state at all, but by independent enterprises, which set (subject to maxima in the worst periods of inflation) their own prices.

We are thus back in a familiar world, where the whole normal analysis applies; only the means of obtaining outside capital are very slender, and ploughback is peculiarly important. What we have to study instead, is first the will to plough back of a labour-managed enterprise. This we have already done in chapter 4, sec. 18: workers' interests are not consilient with those of the enterprise, since the latter is enriched but the former cannot 'take it with them', e.g. by selling their aliquot portion of the ploughback. This leads us to the second question: the appropriate socialist forms which would make this possible.

The obvious procedure is to issue every worker annually with a bond to the value of kP_i/N_i, where i is the year in question, P the ploughback, N the number of workers and 1-k (where $0<k<1$) is the agreed general fraction that shall belong to the enterprise. On retirement, or in other defined cases of great need, the enterprise must redeem these bonds, which should be insured by a special federal office. This insurance policy, and the paper work, would not be light expenses for the enterprise. Nor is it clear that the workers' increased will to plough back would offset their actual withdrawals on retirement. Indeed one can bet that the insurance scheme would simply become another of Yugoslavia's deficitary extra-budgetary funds.

Like all other bonds in this inflationary economy, both interest and principal would have to be indexated. But the scheme would preserve the basic principles: no capital gain since the bonds are always redeemable at par, and no dilution of self-management by outside interests, since these ex-workers have only bonds not equities.

11. This however is not all. Equity shares, i.e. claims on profit however defined, that convey a modicum of control over the business, have also been proposed for Yugoslavia, in at least three different cases.

(i) Individual rich people – engineers, pop singers, American Slovenes retiring in the old country – might wish to lend their private accumulations to a particular enterprise rather than to the state. It might for instance be a local enterprise, or the one in which they were working. The tastes of savers (sec. 2) must always be taken into account, lest society lose the savings altogether, and this applies especially to a country with open borders and a tradition of emigrants' remittances. For instance a resident can ask his émigré relative to accumulate the usual remittance abroad, since on its conversion into dinars he cannot place it as he would like. But with all deference to the strength of the argument and the flexibility of mind shown by its proponents, this is simply capitalism. Even if the share is not transferable it is still capitalism. But if it gives its possessor no control it becomes an inferior version of an indexated bond. Few things are indexated in Yugoslavia, and one wonders whether the lack of such an obvious precaution in so inflationary an economy is not the 'onlie begetter' of this curious proposal.

(ii) In order to save a weak enterprise from bankruptcy,[11] a strong enterprise is often persuaded to merge with it. The means of social persuasion must be strong indeed to cause a group of working men to dilute in this way their claim to the value added of a profitable concern. Nor are they likely to meet gratitude. The case was reported to me of a weak enterprise, taken over in this way, whose workers rioted against the workers in the enterprise that took over, and threw stones at them as exploiters. But short of complete merger is the (non-transferable) inter-enterprise equity investment. The profitable enterprise buys a certain amount of control in return for a limited injection of capital. Now every socialist system has to have a bankruptcy procedure, and this is bound to, nay is meant to, prove unpleasant to the enterprise proceeded against. In an STE there will be a change of management and cuts in bonus: why not in Yugoslavia a suspension of self-management? Our doubts only concern the body that suspends: if it is itself a labour-managed enterprise then a small group of individuals is making losses and hoping to make profits where it has not worked – and that again is capitalism. This is supposedly illegal, though it does in fact happen: the laws seem to conflict.[12] It is surely more socialistic to install a bank or government department as liquidator – but then that way it is far less likely that the ailing enterprise will be set on its feet again, and it is a greater violation of the principle of self-management.

(iii) Finally a foreign capitalist,[13] possessing some advanced technology that we must urgently acquire, may insist on an equity share in the technique-importing enterprise. Yugoslavia is not merely socialist but positively Leninist in permitting this; for she is not going so far in temporarily recognizing necessity as did Lenin, who gave long-term concessions to full-blooded capitalism on Soviet soil during the NEP. It is obvious that the Yugoslav enterprise or state will eventually buy out the capitalist: this is a *smaller* deviation from ideology than (i) or (ii). Such a kind of enterprise is now permitted under Yugoslav law, and some are working. In each case the foreign and the domestic enterprise sign a contract, giving the foreigner a non-transferable equity share and limiting the rights of the workers' council.

12. The STE cannot offer a foreigner a meaningful equity share. For every enterprise on its territory is subject to detailed price and output, and therefore profit, control. No effort, merit or good fortune of the foreigner can prevail over the planners' decisions, and to them the temptation to reduce the foreigner's profit will be irresistible. They have but to raise a single railway freight rate, and save their balance of payments the whole dividend transfer.

The apparent exceptions are not exceptions. Lenin gave concessions involving equity, indeed direct investment, during the NEP – when USSR was not an STE. Stalin's satellites 'borrowed' from USSR after the war in what appeared to be equity form: the mixed Soviet-satellite companies. But it was not so: their planning offices were under Stalin's command, so that it was he who arranged the freight rates and everything else, to ensure a profit on his mixed companies. The recent Fiat deals with Poland and USSR are sometimes presented as direct foreign investment, just as is the joint Polish-Hungarian enterprise Haldex. But closer examination reveals them to be without exception trade treaties: the STE on whose territory the enterprise sits undertakes fixed obligations, usually to deliver so many units of the product of the enterprise, in return for the technology and perhaps some capital.[14]

Unless complete *laissez-faire* is accepted, it is always better to borrow abroad without relinquishing control, whatever the domestic system of institutions – saving only the planned sacrifice of sovereignty to some supranational body. All market economies, and not merely Yugoslavia, *can* borrow abroad by means of bonds, or by the Soviet-type promise to deliver a named quantity of a product. A mere quantitative shortage of home thrift can always be overcome in this way. It is the attraction of foreign enterprise and technology, i.e. the importation of uncertainty-bearing factors, that makes foreign equity acceptable. In theory it is only an added attraction in a market economy that it can offer a meaningful equity to a lender of ordinary capital in a particularly risky situation, or to a lender who insists, in order to preserve a technological lead, on retaining control.

In practice however many ACEs and very many UDCs have been negligent, and sold away control over their economies to foreign capitalists by permitting foreign equity where it was not really necessary. The most notable case of this is portfolio as opposed to direct equity investment. All this preceded the formation of STEs, and what we now see as an optional advantage was taken to be almost a necessity. It was not suspected that a foreign capitalist would come in for less than total control. A Soviet-type incapacity to borrow in certain ways would have saved the world much pain.[15]

13. The transferable equity share is in fact a powerful, Protean and probably undesirable institution. Consider what one can do with it:

(i) a syndicate can buy control of an enterprise without the knowledge of its existing management: perhaps by treaty with a large shareholder, perhaps gradually and in small lots, through men of straw, on the stock exchange.

(ii) the management can create new blocks of shares and give them away for considerations other than monetary:[16] say in a take-over bid, in exchange for the shares of the object of take-over; or to a creditor, to induce him not to press his debt; or to an unpopular manager, in exchange for the cancellation of his contract of employment; or as a bribe.

(iii) a capitalistically minded UDC – Japan once, now Pakistan comes to mind – can create new enterprises out of budgetary funds or foreign aid, and then sell their control, in the form of minute quantities of equity, to a favoured few. Admittedly such enterprises will be highly 'geared', and the shares risky, owing to the huge fixed debt outstanding to the state; but the capitalist is risking very little in toto, and he may easily win a great deal.

(iv) the independent auditor's clerk knows the dividend in advance. He can tell his wife's aunt to buy or sell.

(v) the knowledge that all these things are so keeps off ordinary investors.

(vi) fantastic capital gains can be made, especially by insiders and in high-geared stock. Nearly all the really great capitalist fortunes are made in equities, or in the outright ownership of land and buildings, which is similar.

(vii) in an age of inflation, when however bonds are not indexated outside Latin America, very ordinary people and organizations are virtually forced to buy little else.[17]

An important feature of capitalism is the take-over bid. It is often argued that this is a rational institution that should be encouraged: there being a very imperfect market in managers, and managers being extremely important, it is good to have a market in the results of management, i.e. equity shares, as well. Also assets at present being wasted by inexpert managers can be 'stripped' more easily by buying control – they will not sell off these assets separately. Asset stripping is good: all actions undertaken by rational and intelligent men are likely to lead towards optimality.

But all this is to overlook the corruption and dependence on corruptly gained information that is the essence of the take-over bid. It is not at all efficient to enable insiders, just because they are insiders and not because they are good managers, to oust the present management and install their own protégés for reasons that may well have nothing to do with optimal resource allocation, indeed may only concern some tax fiddle; and at that in circumstances of maximum public excitement, verging on economic war. The take-over bid is far too chancy in matters of optimality, and in all circumstances flouts distributive justice. Administrative solutions to the problem of inefficient management seem preferable; i.e. let the state or some para-statal efficiency auditor pronounce on the tenure of managers.

One qualification must however be made. The take-over and the exchange of shares are very flexible instruments that make possible all sorts of experimental amalgamations and hivings-off, of which a more bureaucratic system would be incapable. The 'conglomerate', which simply relies on good management in bringing together units not otherwise related, is not known in STEs. The STE is a great amalgamator, but only along the lines it finds orthodox: geographical propinquity, horizontal similarity, close vertical relations, or simply the planner's convenience. Also the fanatical belief in the economies of scale causes altogether too many and too big amalgamations.

It is difficult to generalize or develop a theory. But we can see that the equity share contributes mightily to corruption, speculation and inequality. Yet the residual capital and income of private enterprises will necessarily belong to someone, and title must be somehow transferable. It is not at all easy to think of an alternative to the equity share short of nationalization by a *central* authority. For to leave the equity in the hands of local authorities or groups of workers is hardly to make a great change: the Illyrian solution perpetuates inequality and monopoly on a smaller but significant scale, while generating problems of its own. But central ownership of equity need not disturb the market: the 'Pannonian' solution appears to be the best.

14. Now how is the role of interest changed by these various systems? Let us remember the essentially modest role that it does play under capitalism, compared with that claimed for it. Take a long-term rise in the real rate, unaccompanied by speculation. It does not increase thrift, it reallocates it between savings media. Indeed it would quite likely expose a backward sloping supply curve of thrift, just as the general rise in real wages has undoubtedly diminished the supply of labour. It does not much diminish investment, since it is so small a portion of the cost of most products, and it is the profitability of the ultimate product that makes us invest. But it

is about one half of the rent of a house, so it does choke off private house-building.[18] It does not substitute labour for capital, since their elasticity of substitution[19] is quite low: the best technology is, in most lines of business, sufficiently outstanding to remain best despite a change in the wage/interest ratio.

In a word, the long rate of interest in a real capitalist market is the classic victim of inelastic supply and demand curves. It is important for speculation and wealth distribution, but not for resource allocation. If it has always fascinated intellectuals, that does not enhance its practical role. Prices matter when elasticities are high.

In an inspired moment Keynes is said to have dismissed the rate as an ancient monument. In so doing he must have meant, as a resource allocator. For the *General Theory* makes all too much of it as a governor of liquidity preference, and indeed of the overall volume of investment; though it leaves vague whether this is through feelings about liquidity or as a direct cost of carrying on business. We are not required here to say what does determine the overall volume in a market economy. We must note however that our obsession with the multiplier effects of changes in this volume blinds us to the importance of changes in the composition of the volume. Specifically, it is not only in UDCs but also in ACEs that new techniques put labour out of work. Capital-intensive trends in the composition of investment have rendered whole classes of people unemployable except in conditions of demand inflation.[20] Most likely direct controls, not interest changes, would be required to thwart a trend in capital-intensity. But at least classical interest theory found this sort of problem congenial; whereas if we stick to macro-effects it is possible for us to delude ourselves that technological unemployment is impossible, and that more investment, of any sort, will restore jobs for all.[21]

Thus it is not true that Keynes re-established a close link between macro- and micro-economics. He talked a lot about it, but failed completely.[22] But in STEs there is no macro-economics (chapter 14), and in a reformed STE the government might *make* the rate of interest very important indeed. The overall volume of investment, the choice between projects and the degree of capital intensity might all be profoundly affected by raising the rate of interest to a level, doubtless, picked out of the air, or a computer. This would be so because the revisionist Communists who are *ex hypothesi* in charge decide that this is the scientific way to do things: they order the economy to be interest-elastic. This is the essence of the Warsaw-Cambridge[23] vision.

In the real life of STEs, including Poland, investment is decided by ideology (heavy industry should grow faster), by the political pull of *local* Party bosses (each seeking to industrialize his own bailiwick), by military needs, and by a dozen more directly economic considerations. Many of these are very arbitrary: the Politburo wants to be autarkic in a particular line, or the planners are using the method of balances. But one is precisely the interest-type calculation. So rather as under capitalism, the rate of interest or its equivalent plays a minor role among many factors. It does *not* decide, or even help to decide, overall investment volume. But it is naturally open to a theorist to infer ex post a change in the Politburo's rate of futurity discount! Reasons of space preclude us, as always in this book, from any deep consideration of policy matters.

15. Marx was led by Nassau Senior's abstinence theory to associate even a thorough understanding of interest with the defence of capitalism. He therefore, in a rare burst of flat statement about socialism, said there would be no interest under it (*Kapital*, I/22/iii). It follows that in the classical STE there was no long-term rate payable in active money by an enterprise in the socialist sector. Such an active, normal rate, coupled with normal amortization, is payable as follows:

(i) by private and co-operative borrowers, to the socialist sector (investment by kolkhozy and housing co-ops, hire purchase);
(ii) to private savers, by the Treasury (the savings banks);
(iii) to or by ACEs, in foreign capital transactions.

In transactions with UDCs and STEs a below-market rate is charged, in further deference to Marx. Indeed if we emphasize 'within the socialist sector' the only ideological violation is the fact that in short transactions with the monobank there reigns a complicated variety of penal and non-penal rates (chapter 12, sec. 15).

But the original prohibition on interest and amortization between Treasury and enterprises could not outlast 'War' Communism. Amortization, as we have seen (sec. 6), came first. It has entered into price formation from the beginning of the NEP, though the funds are not paid back into the Treasury itself. Then came a shadow rate of interest, the 'co-efficient of relative effectiveness'. This was confined to technological choice, i.e. between more and less capital-intensive ways of performing a task already decided on: in other words a rate used only for micro-purposes, within the planning office or (above all) the local project-making office. Since like all shadow prices it attracted no payments, little attention was paid to it by planners or enterprise managers. It was usually overridden by other criteria, and it was even permitted to differ between ministries; in other words the notion that what was being allocated was abstinence, and that this, being mediated by the Treasury, should have only one price throughout the economy (subject to risk), was rejected. The formula had also technical defects: it did not allow for the reduction of the interest bill by the amortization of the principal, and it could not cope with fixed assets of differing durability.[24]

In the mid-'sixties this co-efficient was replaced by a *tax on capital*. Now this really is close to a violation of Marxism, and has given rise, no doubt because of the ideological strain, to much unclear thinking. The very name 'tax' is simply whitewash for a fairly straight interest charge. In Hungary the tax is a cost, and planned profit is set without reference to it, so the tax influences prices. In other words prices embody not merely labour values but also interest charges.[25] This can be defended ideologically by reference to Marx's posthumous (and dreadfully confused) *Kapital* vol. III. It contradicts vol. I, which is more canonical and the sole source of orthodoxy in Moscow.[26]

Moscow has its toe in the hot bath: a capital tax yielding substantial sums. But it is deducted from unchanged, or theoretically unchanged, planned profits, precisely so that it shall not influence price formation. Soviet economists have insisted passionately on this to the author; they had no reply to the query whether the new incentive role of profits would not gradually establish planned profit rates that were in fact reckoned net of the capital tax, so that it would come to influence prices after all. Even as things are, however, the Soviet capital tax does discourage waste of capital, since it cuts directly into retainable bonuses. But it only influences the manager, not the consumer of his product.

Meanwhile the fact that the thing is a tax and not interest has irrational consequences. It is levied only on completed assets in working order, not on borrowed money, so it does nothing to relieve that curse of all STEs, excessive gestation periods (chapter 14, sec. 5). In Hungary if the completed asset was financed by a bank loan the tax is payable on top of the bank interest! On the growing role of interest in Soviet-type house-rent, cf. chapter 20, sec. 10.

The final erosion of Marx's prohibition is the straight and unblushing provision of long-term capital, within the socialist sector, at interest. Here, as we saw, Yugoslavia led the way. Lest anyone think it comes easy to a Marxist, here is how it happened:

The Yugoslav trade union leader Vukmanović-Tempo relates in an autobiographical article in NIN, 3 May 1964: 'I remember a conversation at the home of Kardelj about the economic system then in force, which was based on the principle of the financing of economic enterprises on the basis of their budgets. I spoke of the difficulties in building key projects and expressed doubt whether we would succeed in completing them quickly since up to this point a tendency had been observed to extend the deadlines for delivery to the users and to make the construction as dear as possible so as to be able to build under the same title a series of objects which appeared from the point of view of local interests to be more useful. That evening I openly affirmed that we must work out another system: in exchange for the existing budgetary one we must finance the enterprise in such a way that having received credits it would return them within a period of time along with a payment of interest – then they themselves would control the way in which this capital was invested. I remember that the late Boris Kidrič said, "But that is capitalism. Credits, amortization, interest: all that is the most perfect capitalism." And gradually a very serious discussion flared up on the theme, was that capitalism or not? That evening I felt myself pretty much isolated. I thought about these questions all night, not sleeping a wink, and tormenting myself with doubts whether I was right or not. In the morning I decided I was wrong. The moment I got to the office I called Comrade Kidrič on the telephone and declared to him, "Boris, I worried myself sick all night, and now I have to say to you that you are right, all that is capitalism." To which he immediately replied, "I also worried myself sick all night about it, and you know to what conclusion I came? That is not capitalism at all. All that has got to be really put into practice, that idea was extremely interesting. By God, you were right yesterday evening!" '

16. While high theory discourses endlessly on the factor enterprise, more earth-bound students of socialism avoid it.[27] Let us enter this subject via the mechanics of founding new firms.

Where enterprises are small (primitive capitalism, Yugoslavia, Kibbutzim) it is extremely urgent to have a vigorous mechanism for founding new ones. Indeed co-operatives and communes actually refuse to grow, for reasons given in chapter 4, even to the most profitable size for a monopoly. In their case reasonable market performance is almost wholly dependent on new entry. The textbook assumption that 'firms enter the profitable industry, provided that there are no artificial barriers' can hardly be true here – if it is anywhere. But where, as in advanced capitalism or in Hungary, enterprises are large[28] and accustomed to branching out, the matter is slightly less important; for of course a new branch is much less risky than a new enterprise. In a classical STE the founding of a new branch already is difficult, and a whole new enterprise requires intensive lobbying on all levels. The inhospitable climate for initiative is one of the main drawbacks of the STE.

It is impossible to found a new enterprise out of ploughback. This is of course a tautology, but like so many an extremely informative one. For the tautology is a crushing argument in favour of some central arrangement, be it a Gosplan, the Crédit National[29] or the Stock Exchange, that shall decide about the sizes and numbers of enterprises, and finance or otherwise facilitate new ones. It is not enough that enterprises should be guided by profit: there must be a mechanism whereby enterprise founders can be too.

The foundation of a new firm is a matter of initiative, and initiative can have a fixed 'wage'. Examples of this are the officials of Yugoslav banks and capitalist merchant banks, officials of existing productive enterprises, especially in Yugoslavia, and the 'civil service entrepreneurs' of capitalist countries, who sit on the committees and do the leg-work. The actual makers of new proposals are often also salaried people. Under capitalism they could, and sometimes do, receive a residual income for their services, e.g. stock in the enterprise they found. But it is not necessary, and mostly they do not get it. This is because under no system do initiators *have* to bear risk – that is a separate function: maybe of the state, as in Hungary and the STE, or of some factor of production (elsewhere).

The Illyrian (and the Yugoslav) worker-partner has no share in the original initiative that founds the firm. Neither has the small capitalist investor who buys an ordinary share; for even when it is newly issued all the crucial decisions and most of the crucial expenditures have already been made. But the law is such that subsequent decisions, even ones involving very large initiatives for expansion or liquidation, are made by these seemingly inappropriate e.b.f.s. More exactly, they must now be consulted by the true initiators.

Under capitalism this distinction between founders and subsequent partners is not a great matter, but with workers' self-management it has the following curious effects. The founder is often the state, and its wish is on the whole to create employment; so it often chooses a capital-extensive technique. But the new partners proceed first to underman the enterprise handed over to them and then to capitalize the technology. For the state thinks of society, the partners only of themselves. On the other hand if the founder is another enterprise innumerable motives operate: to secure cheap components from an 'independent' enterprise that pays lower incomes; to get ambitious senior employees an outlet for promotion; to place liquid funds, etc., etc. The new partners find themselves bound by marketing arrangements, royalty payments, etc., in lieu of the straight founder's equity holding that would be normal under capitalism. This is of course ideologically unacceptable, and probably illegal (Sacks, op. cit.).

In all systems the founder or initiator of a new enterprise must push his proposals through a planning or financial bureaucracy, or both. If the bureaucrats agree to support him, he or they must now get money: in the STE from the budget, in market socialism from the banks at long term. Under capitalism one normally borrows from the banks at short term before a tidying-up operation on the stock exchange, i.e. a new issue designed to pay back whatever, ex post, turns out to have been borrowed at short term.

In all types of market economy syndicates and consortia are common as founders. The risk has in any case to be spread, but it is not enough that small savers pool their capital in the hands of an enterprising individual. Large organizations must also contribute their specialized connexions, manpower and knowledge. One or more of these organizations is normally a bank. In addition to connexions, etc., it provides, not long-term capital (except in West Germany), but bridging loans, as just described.

This even applies in a classical STE, *mutatis mutandis*: the investment bank manages the budgetary grant, and gives payments on account or even short loans in anticipation to the construction enterprise. But there are no syndicates or consortia, since there is no sharing of capital risk: the STE is, after all, one enterprise, and capital risk is wholly consolidated. But collective farms do form syndicates to set up industrial, service and insurance enterprises. After all, they are not strictly part of the STE.

17. Turning now from initiative to risk, we note two kinds of 'residual risk':

(i) that the enterprise will make a loss through general bad luck and miscalculation. This is nowhere insurable, partly because the future is unlike the past and it cannot be calculated, partly because 'general bad luck' tends to be, in market systems, very widespread indeed when it occurs. No insurance funds are ever big enough to cope with it. Risk (i) is also called uncertainty. In its nature economic activity is subject to *some* uncertainty. It therefore generates a residual income. Some person or organization must receive that income, and so bear the uncertainty. Under primitive capitalism and state socialism the bearer is also the owner. In Yugoslavia and under state capitalism the matter is less clear.

(ii) that there will be a loss through some defined and calculable cause like fire. This is insurable in advanced countries. Even cessation of profits due to fire is mostly insurable. These 'residual risks' hit either the state or the capital employed, but may be borne by labour if it is paid by bonuses or on the Yugoslav system.

There are also three kinds of 'personal risk', which primarily hit labour, but also hit capital if they have not been insured against. Note that bad luck under case (v) virtually entails bad luck under case (i).

(iii) Labour takes physical risks with its health. This problem is the same in all systems. It is dealt with by legal actions for compensation or (better) direct insurance. In the former case, the employer in turn can insure against losing the case; but a large employer sufficiently consolidates his risk by being large. So the risk is in any case insurable. But the basic reaction in all systems is to reduce the risk, not insure against it. Hence the vast network of administrative rules for industrial health and safety.

(iv) Labour risks dismissal or low income through its personal circumstances. This may be because of (iii), or because of disease and misfortune unconnected with the job. In both these cases the risk is again insurable, and policies of this kind are indeed written – but not very often. There is, for instance, insurance against loss of earnings through sickness in ACEs. On the whole the state again provides non-insurance remedies, which differ according to system. Thus restrictions on dismissal are easiest under capitalism, but become ever stricter.

(v) Labour risks dismissal or low income through the circumstances of its employer. We discuss this at length in dealing with unemployment (chapter 14). It partakes much more of uncertainty than of calculable, and so insurable, risk. So the capitalist welfare state meets it with a system of hand-outs that is still indeed called insurance for historical reasons but is based on other principles. It also tries to abolish the causes of the uncertainty themselves. Socialism, even market socialism, greatly reduces this uncertainty. The STE, with excessive confidence, has even abolished the dole. But it creates at the same time a similar uncertainty: by overdoing piece-work and output-plan-fulfilment bonus, as under Stalin. The risk, not of dismissal but of low income, is very great under such systems of payment, and it must be classified here since it is mainly caused not by personal ill-health but by the breakdown of machinery and the non-arrival of supplies. The worker most at risk in the STE is of course the director. It is important for comprehension to see that he is just a particular kind of worker on a particular kind of piece-work. Capitalism, which is subject to great macro-fluctuations, often threatens a worker with dismissal, and so performs less well than the STE, which however constantly threatens him with loss of bonus through its various micro-inefficiencies. But in addition to piece-work and dismissal there is the profit-related bonus, whether in the Soviet or any other system. Now no one who has read this far will automatically impute profit or residual income to capital. If, therefore, the bonus to any worker, including the director, comes from the residual income of the enterprise, and is unrelated to any saving or ploughback by that worker, it is a residual paid for his 'investment' of labour only.

Who takes risks under socialism? In classical Marxism there is no risk, but Marxism is false. The short practical answer as to risk (i) is, ultimately always the state (and the same under state capitalism). Never mind law and ideology in, say, Yugoslavia or Hungary or France: this is how it is. Only under primitive capitalism is the capitalist seriously and alone at risk. For after all, if in any system an individual seriously risks his own capital, rather than the state's, we are inclined to call it capitalist. This, then, is another of those highly revealing tautologies. In the three countries named, the state always comes to the rescue in the end. Therefore it retains much of the power *de facto*, whatever the ideology says. I.e. there is in practice no distinction of equity from residual. To be responsible for the residual but to have no power is merely a logical possibility: the body so exposed would be subjected to indefinite drains of money.

As to insurance (risks (ii) to (iv)), under no system are its possibilities exploited to the limit. In particular, Marxists suppose that insurance will disappear under Full Communism and that risk is essentially capitalist. So their use of insurance is sluggish and unimaginative, being confined to injury, fire, theft and natural disaster. There is calculated insurance in these fields even for state property, and a wider range of coverage for collective and private property: the state is very rightly held to be big enough to insure some things without formality. Social insurance, however, against illness, old age, industrial accidents, etc., is as in most capitalist countries merely a name for a particular budgetary fund. Even the formality of individual contributions is dispensed with. Scarcely any supplementary life assurance or pension schemes, financed by voluntary extra payment, are available. Yugoslavia is intermediate between this and capitalism, with competing socialist insurance companies.

At the other extreme from the muddled actuality of capitalism stands the Chicago School, which would have us insure (privately of course) against virtually everything, and substitute this for social services. They would also, through futures markets, make it possible to insure capital against price fluctuations. We cannot pass judgement here, but we note that the strength of the Chicago case is much underestimated by those who neglect the potential of private insurance. In particular, while the very young cannot insure themselves against poverty or the need to be educated, any person already at work could be expected, if not over-taxed or the victim of some great misfortune, to insure himself against all the remaining risks of life.

Socialism, then, has little effect on 'personal' risk. As to 'residual' risk, it is not abolished but consolidated, while some of its causes are strengthened, some weakened. In market socialism there need be no less risk at all than under capitalism: that depends on the imperfection[30] of the market, the stability of prices, the success of counter-cyclical policy, etc. The greater likelihood of state intervention will create some new micro-risks, but it does abolish the great macro-risks. Thus Hungarian builders have to predict the many new government measures that are always being taken.

When we said above that the socialist enterprise is not really risking its capital we only meant that it is risking the state's capital instead. There is divorce of initiative from risk. No one *feels* the risk any more. It is 'borne' by impersonal organizations. But it is nonetheless objectively there, and very great. And all this applies *a fortiori* to the STE, whose various self-contradictory authorities put its own capital to severe 'planning risk', but which *eo ipso* abolishes market risk. It is hard to tell whether a given project is more or less likely on balance to fail. Certainly the STE wastes much more capital (investing about 50 per cent more for the same rate of growth), but other reasons contribute to this.

What socialism does reduce is capital-risk-*bearing*. This very genuine subjective burden on economic agents can be depersonalized, and a disincentive to invest removed. Certainly no one fears bankruptcy, since whatever the law says (above, and chapter 14, sec. 5) there is never any bankruptcy. Indeed even state capitalism is opposed to this. So all capital losses are paid by the banks or the budget, not individuals. But socialism cannot do without personal responsibility, so *the 'personal' risk of the director is substituted for the 'residual' risk of the shareholder.* A very considerable subjective burden in the form of risk (v) continues to attend investment, and in particular people are unwilling to innovate, because they cannot be sure of their bonuses when new techniques are introduced (chapter 15, sec. 17).

Innovation is a cause of risks (i) and (v). The actual innovator can be salaried, like the supplier of any other service. He need not bear the risks he causes. He need not, of course, be the director of the enterprise. He may well be a distant bureaucrat, or a pushy scientist.

Contrariwise if we put the director on bonus he shares the risk of an innovation with the state or shareholders, whether he or someone else thought it up. If in the STE there were less emphasis on bonuses people would *bear* less risk, and they would be more willing to *put* the state's capital *to* risk. So the state insists on individual responsibility in order to diminish its own risk. But by sharing the risk with actual individuals it revives the subjective disincentive to take risk that characterizes capitalism. This hits innovation particularly hard, since it is a risk produced not by organizations but by the nature of things.

It may appear paradoxical that the STE generates considerable capital risk. Let us recapitulate on this:

(i) there is less risk subjectively borne by individuals. But it is still very much there;
(ii) price fluctuations almost disappear;
(iii) macro-fluctuations in output and employment almost disappear;
(iv) micro-risks, due to non-arrival of supplies, greatly increase;
(v) there is far more risk from the government, which as always often changes its mind but has now much more say;
(vi) the fact that the risks are all consolidated means that they are in a sense 'insured' by the budget; but insurance does not lessen the probability of accidents occurring. On the contrary it makes people more careless. There is a socially optimal level of insurance, which in respect of capital risk may well have been exceeded in STEs and in all public sectors everywhere.

Except for (iv) these points apply in lesser degree to market socialism and state capitalism. But Yugoslavia is as usual rather special! For in all systems *capital must be there first*: the labour can only be hired when the money and indeed the plant is there. Since this is perfectly clear in Marx it presents no ideological difficulty to an STE, but it does complicate the status of the Yugoslav self-managing workers' collective: however ideologically prior they are, they cannot be chronologically prior. The self-managers can only bear the risk after they have been constituted. Since it exists before they do it must be borne first by others. These are the founding sydicate described above.

The Yugoslav self-manager is in a very complicated position. He is subject to all the ordinary labour risks but additionally the whole capital (not only the ploughback) of his enterprise belongs in some sense to him. Certainly his income is in part an income from this capital. Except for the ploughback, he has not abstained from consumption in order to accumulate it; it is a gift. But since he draws the only residual income from it he is subject to its risks. This does not prevent his labour income from also containing a residual element. His is a 'mixed income' just like a peasant's or a professional man's. Therefore its residual part can easily be mixed too.

Notes

1. *Economic Backwardness in Historical Perspective*, Harvard 1962, the title essay. I have silently supplemented his account here and there with further facts tending to support it.

2. This is one of the reasons for the superimposition of the *Aufsichtsrat* (chapter 7, sec. 14); and of the growth of cartels – the banks did not want their protégés to ruin each other.

3. Cf. his *Theory of Business Enterprise*, N.Y. 1904. The best German Marxist author is Rudolf Hilferding, *Finanzkapital*, Vienna 1910. Nearly all his examples are German, and he admits things are different in Britain (p. 283), without understanding how damaging this is to his thesis. Veblen, the founder of Technocracy and not a real Marxist, imparted a strong moral tone to the distinction between producers and financiers.

4. I.e. the velocity of circulation is not continually falling, as it is in STEs.

5. Adolf Berle and Gardner Means, *The Modern Corporation and Private Property*, revised edn., N.Y. 1968.

6. Cf. Wiles 1961, chapters 5, 11. The point is also important in connexion with cost inflation (chapter 14).

7. These approximate figures rest on private workings, available on request.

8. It will be remembered that 'deduction' is more ideologically correct than 'tax', when we speak of profits. Cf. chapter 3, sec. 14.

9. I use this word in order to include China, Hungary and Yugoslavia, which have not abandoned the heavy and irregular turnover tax on consumer goods.

10. An effect exaggerated in the Soviet, but not in other, cases by the decades of priority in investment and R and D which certain producer goods have enjoyed. Cf. Wiles in ed. Wiles, *The Prediction of Communist Economic Performance*, Cambridge 1971, pp. 386–8.

11. Bankruptcy is abhorred as capitalistic waste, much as in STEs. Most of the rare bankruptcies affect the small private enterprises. Cf. chapter 14, sec. 11.

12. Stephen R. Sacks, *Entry of New Competitors in Yugoslav Market Socialism*, Berkeley, Calif. 1973.

13. In principle it might also be an STE, which can behave like a capitalist abroad. Cf. sec. 12.

14. Note that in the Haldex case the foreign lender is Hungary, at that time an STE. This makes no difference. Cf. my op. cit. 1969, p. 321.

15. The political economy of this subject is called Imperialism (chapter 19).

16. It is amusing that just this attribute used to lead to corruption in the allocation of labour-days on kolkhozy (the labour-day was a sort of annually varied equity share in the income of the kolkhoz; cf. chapter 6). Suppose the

chairman's nephew has a camera, and photographs the annual harvest dinner: why should he not get ten labour-days, since this unusual service has no centrally regulated rate?

17. The compounded yield of non-indexated bonds usually rather exceeds the rate of rise of the cost of living, so that we may speak of a very low positive real yield of bonds. Equity prices are driven up so high that good ones have about the same very low yield; but in terms of present, not future, dividends. A dividend freeze – not an uncommon event – makes them far less attractive than bonds at a low enough price, but the dividend will rise again while the interest cannot.

18. And one or two other curious industries, notably water-works, which are also nearly all capital and no labour.

19. I refer to real ex ante elasticities of substitution by actual entrepreneurial decisions on the ground. The macro-elasticity in two-factor, one-product growth models concerns ex post substitution, due to investment and population growth. It is of as little real interest as any other aspect of such highly aggregated models.

20. Sometimes the trend is simultaneously skill-intensive, and it is the unskilled who suffer; sometimes it is skill-extensive, and it is middle management and craftsmen who suffer.

21. The intertemporal effects of investment, in increasing the stock of capital, and so changing the size of full-employment income, were also neglected in early Keynesian writing. But this defect was easily corrected within the system, and macro-theories of growth were born.

22. Not only in connexion with technological unemployment but also in the case of cost inflation: cf. Wiles in *E.J.*, June 1973.

23. The role of Warsaw, in particular of Michael Kalecki, may easily be understood. Like most Polish economists he was never a Marxist, but wished to rationalize, not to abandon, Soviet centralism. But it is paradoxical that the Cambridge of Keynes and liquidity preference should contemplate growth models so heavily dependent on the allocative role of interest.

24. Cf. Wiles 1962, pp. 126–7 and the references there given; Abram Bergson, *The Economics of Soviet Planning*, New Haven 1964, chapter 11.

25. Amortization is payment for dead labour, part of the c in Marx' c+v+m. Marx himself gave it an influence on price.

26. So the Hungarians, combining vols. I and III, defend a 'two-channel' system of pricing, in which both labour and capital yield a 'surplus', represented by a social-security-type tax on labour and the aforementioned capital tax. Cf. Vaclav Holesovsky in *Jahrbuch der Wirtschaft Ost-Europas*, Munich, no. II, 1971; Bela Csikos-Nagy in *Acta Oeconomica*, Budapest, vol. I/3–4.

27. Except my colleague Stefan Markowski (see chapter 4, footnote 7a). The factual background is excellently set out by Jozef Wilcynski, *Profit, Risk and Incentives under Socialist Economic Planning*, London 1973, chapter 3; and Sacks, op. cit.

28. The Yugoslav enterprise is indeed quite small: in 1966 socialist industry and mining had 2281, averaging *c.* 550 workers each, and of these 101 had fewer than 30, so that everybody was on the council (*Statisticki Bilten* no. 452, February 1967, pp. 10–11; as the enterprises employing under 10 people are omitted, I have made an arbitrary small deduction also from the labour force). In Hungary in 1968 there were 811 industrial enterprises averaging 1873 workers (Statistical Yearbook). But each enterprise averaged seven establishments, and these formed no technical unity. In UK in 1963 in manufacturing there were

7540 enterprises and 24,347 establishments, with 884 employees per enterprise and 273 per establishment (Census of Production 1963, p. 132–8).

29. This is the French government-banking-planning committee that deals with bank advances and new issues.

30. Note 'imperfection'. Perfect markets destabilize prices. Imperfections are introduced by human beings precisely in order to reduce risk.

14

Inflation and Unemployment

1. Introduction
2. Demand inflation and the capitalist trade cycle
3. The non-Keynesian character of the STE
4. Cost inflation in capitalist countries
5. STEs: inflation through tolerated cost overrun
6. STEs: demand inflation in retail markets
7. The lessons of (6) for capitalism and market socialism
8. Unemployment in market economies: the importance of money
9. Unemployment in the classical STE: the irrelevance of money
10. Unemployment in the reformed STE
11. Yugoslavia: inflation
12. Yugoslavia: unemployment

14

1. This chapter deals with two related topics: rising prices and surplus capacity in men and machines, their causes and cures under various systems. We concentrate on the STE because it is so much less familiar, particularly in these aspects. Demand inflation means excess demand at current prices, and is normally, but not quite inevitably, associated with rising prices, of both inputs and outputs in no particular sequence. Cost inflation means that output prices rise because and after input prices (costs) have exogenously risen, say import prices after a devaluation or wage-rates through trade-union pressure. Unemployment is slightly increased, in a market economy, by cost inflation and much diminished by demand inflation; in an STE it is unaffected by either, since employment is always what the planners order it to be – or more. But STEs certainly generate price rises and excess demand independent of output movements: demand inflation in respect of active money and a special sort of cost inflation, the 'tolerated cost overrun inflation' (TCOI) in respect of passive money. By unemployment we mean equally that of men and of machines, though neither is clearly measurable. Early retirement, malingering, housework, official courses of study and long unpaid holidays are all apt to show up as unemployment, and indeed they may be in small part a reaction to a slack labour market. A necessary reserve of machinery is virtually impossible to distinguish at the margin from unwanted machinery.[1]

2. Of demand inflation in market economies we need here say very little. It arises from investment booms and budget deficits. It could also arise, in days of affluence and consumer durables, from a consumption boom; and in earlier days it did arise from a simultaneous speculative expansion by uncontrolled country banks. This too was not necessarily connected with fixed investment, but rather with speculation in commodities. The banks were overdiscounting trade bills in pursuance of the doctrine of 'real bills'. This says that no amount of genuine trade bills can be inflationary, since they represent actual production *ex hypothesi*, and will liquidate themselves when the product is sold. So the doctrine implicitly encourages a speculative price spiral.

But demand inflation is never really serious without a big budget deficit due to a near-collapse of state power. In such cases, with the government too weak to tax but still strong enough to print bank-notes, we arrive at the celebrated galloping inflations.

Demand deflation in a market economy is nearly but not quite the mirror-image of this. An investment slump, a budget surplus, a consumer durables slump, a simultaneous loss of confidence and contraction among country banks: in these cases we simply reverse the sign. But a galloping deflation cannot be produced by human contrivance; and while a stock exchange collapse can cause a slump a stock exchange boom has little effect. Indeed in 1928–9 Americans were not absurdly complaining that the stock exchange boom was drawing bank loans away from the rest of the economy and deflating it.[2]

Implicit in these paragraphs is the view that unitary endogenous explanations of the erstwhile capitalist trade cycle, depending on consumption, investment and the budget, are worthless. In part this is because, as the monetarists so justly complain, these explanations leave out capital values and monetary institutions, and their probably destabilizing role: let us add, the *changing* monetary institutions, and the *new* ways in which they produce instability, even when centralized. In part it is because, owing to Keynesian remedies, however unskilfully applied (and so not to the accuracy of Keynesian econometrics!), there is no endogenous trade *cycle* left to explain. My own view, however, while being scarcely at all Keynesian, is profoundly anti-monetarist: the quantity of money, or changes in it, or changes in the changes in it, is not a powerful explainer either. It fails in UK because the econometric techniques used to support the notion that prices follow money actually indicate more strongly that money follows prices – if only the possibility is honestly posed. This is for 1952–72.[3] It fails for North America in 1928–32.[4] The theory fails nearly everywhere through the necessity to vary the lags and parameters *ad hoc*: i.e. it is not a proper theory.[5] Indeed it fails even where it succeeds by its inability to go behind econometrics to causal explanation. Notably it cannot break up the national income into a price part and an output part.[6]

It is no part at all of my intention to substitute institutional for Keynesian or monetarist explanation. Monetary ups and downs are not only due to the endogenous interplay of real magnitudes, e.g. to the multiplier and the accelerator. They are not only due to varying forms of monetary mismanagement. They are still more certainly not only due to institutions, except perhaps to the existence of a market as such. There is room for all three lines of thought and for much else besides. My proposition is much simpler: demand inflation and deflation in market economies is a complex and highly irregular historical phenomenon. Anyone proposing a unitary explanation should have his head examined. Each moment of inflation and deflation is unique. There is no substitute for economic history.

We need spend little time here on so well-worn a topic as cures for demand inflation in market economies. Let us only observe that normal fiscal and monetary policy do not exhaust the list. There is also the regulation of amortization rates (chapter 12, sec. 14). Either the government or the central bank can one way or another determine the percentage down payment in a hire-purchase or mortgage contract. Powers also exist, though they are never thoroughly used, to regulate the length of local government bonds, and the same could in theory be done to the bonds of private corporations. Considering how effectively these measures increase the saving of would-be borrowers, it is a surprise that they are less used than the older, weaker and more difficult weapons. The cause is undoubtedly the horror of discrimination brought about by market theory: amortization control would not hit all enterprises and industries equally.

3. The STE has nothing remotely resembling a trade cycle, or any other endogenous mechanism that accelerates or moderates demand. The time series of macro-aggregates are all remarkably smooth by capitalist standards,[7] with the single natural exception of agriculture and agriculture-related industry. Dreadful kinks do happen on rare occasions, but they are without exception of political origin. Those who claim to the contrary have utterly failed to prove their case on the simplest level, that of inspecting time series. Their motivation is plain: they are Western econometricians trying to expand their intellectual empire, or Communist revisionists over-anxious to 'apply the conquests of the most advanced economic science' to their special case. And the reason for their failure is plain: most money is passive, excess demand in such money cannot raise output. It is true that a shortage of passive money would eventually halt the movement of goods between one enterprise and another; and since they would all continue to produce according to plan as long as they could it would lead to intolerable stockpiling. But the case is entirely theoretical: the monobank never permits it to happen, since it is forced to prefer TCOI.

In real terms the multiplier is always equal to one in an STE. An order goes out, say, to erect a new factory or pay higher wages on the strength of a budgetary or extra-budgetary deficit. The financial part of the plan accompanies the order, and the extra money is made available. It goes round and round in the usual way. So long as it is in the passive circuit the 'leak' through which it seeps away is the Treasury's deductions from profit, or in the reformed STE also the permitted savings of enterprises. But eventually all production generates wages and the money enters also the active circuit. The worker in an STE has a low marginal propensity to pay direct tax (chapter 16) and to save (chapter 13, sec. 6), but a very high one to pay indirect tax; and so the flow continues to leak away in the normal manner, generating a monetary multiplier of an ordinary kind. But since all output is commanded no real change occurs, except in the black and free markets (sec. 6). And this would remain true if there was unemployment.

The accelerator on the other hand retains whatever (low) degree of validity it has in a market economy, since it is an input-output, or engineering, relation. But it has no macro-economic significance, since if the planners order more of output A, and therefore much more of machine B, they must order less of something else. Macro-accelerator-effects will not cause the planners to command more employment, since if there is any under-used labour they will in any case command it to be employed, so far as they can afford to educate it or construct capacity for it. To repeat, if all output and all employment is by command, full employment in the Keynesian sense must be expected all the time. It *could* be otherwise, but a planner who planned it would be dismissed.

Perhaps, then, there is a psychological or political cycle with real or monetary effects? There are, certainly, lurches to left and to right. In those to the left (Soviet first Five Year Plan, Chinese Great Leap Forward, Rakosi's reign in Hungary, Bulgaria 1959, Albania most years since 1965) investment and hours worked rise, incomes, though carefully controlled, outstrip consumer goods and there is a black market. In the lurches to the right (Malenkov, Nagy's first premiership, Gierek) investment lags or is financed by foreign loans, hours of work fall – and incomes, being carelessly controlled, outstrip consumer goods and there is a black market! (or consumer goods are imported and state reserves of gold and commodities are run down). So much one cannot deny, but these lurches are not of a regular pattern and certainly not to be explained by any endogenous model, even a political one. We discuss below the inflationary mechanism only, without relation to 'lurches'.

Diseases that it does not have, the STE need not cure. But TCOI does leak out into demand inflation at the level of retail trade, and we return to this topic at that point.

4. It is still possible for monetarists, nay even for the less dogmatic Keynesians, to assert that cost inflation is not possible. In this book I have taken throughout a high-handed line with such ostriches, flatly asserting that outside perfect and quasi-perfect competition prices are *normally* determined by costs, at least within a zone of tolerance (chapters 10, sec. 2; 13, sec. 8). Now in the context of this chapter such a zone of tolerance, say 5–10 per cent of the present price, makes it possible to raise prices enough to cover rises in costs, without any reference to short-term profit maximization; and this in turn allows cost rises to precede and (more or less) determine price rises. All competitors (who are ex hypothesi imperfect competitors) face similar cost rises, i.e. in materials and labour. So they are likely to raise their prices by about the same amount at about the same time, and this gives us further confidence to raise our own prices first. So enterprises become mere administrators or registrars of cost rises forced upon them by, notably, trade unions.

Enterprises use their own powers to re-establish (i.e. defensively – and often they do not quite re-establish) their profits in real terms. Public bodies are of course particularly weak, since they cannot go bankrupt. Meanwhile the unions pass from beating the cost of living to beating each other, i.e. they set up a wage-wage spiral, to which there is no conceivable end. Only two forces can stop this cumulative merry-go-round: a shortage of demand, reducing output and employment, or direct controls over incomes and prices.

The governments of capitalist countries hesitate to create unemployment, for obvious political and moral reasons. There is also the point that if trade unions do not mind unemployment it will take too long a time. But for what it is worth demand can shrink in two ways. First the natural forces of the market can reduce real demand, since the money income of the perfectly competitive sector, of bondholders and pensioners, and perhaps of public employees may be fixed in money terms. But today, with cost inflation endemic in the capitalist world, only bondholders are unlikely to be baled out by the governments. So the only remaining procedure is for the government to create yet more unemployment, by freezing the quantity of money.

Slowly, then, and with extreme reluctance, capitalist countries are moving towards direct controls of incomes and prices. Unable to emasculate their trade unions – even in Hungary and Yugoslavia these are showing increased vitality – and so strike at the root of the problem, they are abandoning the market instead. Nor is this illogical: no one ever argued that a market was desirable if it contained a powerful and unscrupulous monopoly, facing no countervailing power. If cost inflation cannot be contained, the weapons we must use against it will destroy the market system. But to help our understanding we must first compare Soviet-type inflation.

Since the Soviet-type rate of exchange plays no part in pricing imports (chapter 12, sec. 17), neither rises in foreign prices nor devaluation can start off a cost inflation. Since there is no collective bargaining (chapter 7), neither can trade unions. But the theorists of cost inflation tend to forget that in primitive countries which depend greatly on the domestic harvest, and are unable to import much, a harvest failure produces cost inflation in the non-farm sector. For the price of food rises and so, since food dominates the consumer's budget, wages must rise, even without union pressure, lest people die. This presses up non-farm prices in turn, and, since there is no more demand in the whole economy, this causes unemployment. Such a syndrome was noticeable in eighteenth-century France and in Russia until 1929. So long as people have to buy food on the kolkhoz market, and food bulks large in their budgets, 'harvest failure cost inflation' is not excluded even from an STE. But its period is now past.

5. On the other hand we have seen that Soviet-type inflation is not of the orthodox demand variety either.[8] Its fundamental cause is something almost without parallel in market economies: the tolerated cost overrun, or the reluctance to bankrupt state enterprises.

Now in market economies there are of course tolerated cost overruns in the public sector, that lead to budget deficits. Concorde, or almost any building project, springs to mind. But the thing is simply not of major importance. It becomes that, and a whole separate source of inflation, when:

(i) there is no private sector, intolerant of cost overruns and insisting on bankruptcy instead;

(ii) there is very ambitious physical command planning, setting improbable cost targets in all fields and successfully insisting that violators be financed when they overshoot;

(iii) the opinion reigns that passive money is 'only credit', and so doesn't really count, since inflation is a 'currency' matter.

All these conditions apply in an STE. Thus the bank and the Treasury have less political pull than the planners and factory directors. For it is upon output that bonuses, and even Party secretaries' promotions, depend; and behind that again lies the pro-output, anti-money, Marxist ideology. Under Full Communism money will wither away, and whatever can be produced must be financed. The bank fights back and quotes strictly formulated regulations, but is eventually overruled.

The most frequent types of cost overrun are:

(a) there is a shortage of skilled labour, so the *wage maxima are violated* in order to get the required people on what is after all an ordinary competitive labour market. Mostly this is done by the bogus upgrading of skills and the manipulation of fringe benefits, rather than by direct and open overpayment. This process is well known in the public sectors of capitalist countries;

(b) goods, whether final or intermediate, are produced at too low quality owing to the tension in the plan. The customer (resisting much political pressure) exercises his right to reject them, and *stocks pile up unplanned*. Deprived of price flexibility, even for final goods, the producer cannot dispose of them;[9]

(c) *Investment overstrain:* projects are easier to start than to finish, let alone to finish on time and within the estimates. But until they go into production they yield no revenue, so their unplanned costs to date must be met from unplanned finance. This is a surprisingly important special feature of the STE. As in all systems, once a project is started it is morally very difficult not to finish it, so the ambitious people most personally involved cause a start to be made. This was nearly always the case with cathedrals in the Middle Ages. Since all projects are unique no one knows what they will cost or how long they will take anyway, so it is easy to make specious promises, which get written into building plans and financial plans. In this way the authorities are induced to commit finance without actually paying it out now, and the capacity of the building industry is overloaded, as workers scurry between uncompleted sites. The thing is common enough, as anyone will know who has had the plumber in. But the ambition of Communist planners and the tension of Communist plans make it very much worse. Very approximately, instead of projects taking twice as long and costing one and a half times as much as planned, as under capitalism, factors of about three and two should be applied, but to longer planning periods.[10]

In each of the above cases the producing or building enterprise initially asks the monobank for an unplanned short-term loan. The bank protests, and is overruled as shown above. For a time everyone pretends that the short loan will be paid, but often it never is. It is then transferred to the category of the enterprise's 'permanent circulating capital'. Now normally this is a sub-category of the permanent capital that is – in the classical STE – a gift from the budget. So if the Treasury repays the bank out of a budget surplus money is withdrawn elsewhere from the economy, by an act of nearly Keynesian fiscal policy. But normally it does not do so (sec. 6), since the Treasury recognizes no Keynesian duty to keep the economy on an even keel. So the authorities, in making the transfer, simply write off the loan.

6. Thus the quantity of money is increased, and it does not remain passive for long. For in every case there is a wage bill to be paid. In (a) indeed this is all. In (b) and (c) there is not merely the enterprise's own wage bill, but the wage component of all the materials and machinery it has bought in: for only the unplanned loan makes it possible to pay these bills either.[11] Thus passive money cannot be separated from active. Indeed it creates active money, while the reverse is not true, whatever Communist monetary theorists may say.[12]

Note that wages are guaranteed by the state, and specifically by its bank. This is an important and inflationary feature of the STE's socialist sector. Kolkhoz incomes on the other hand used not to be so guaranteed, and suffered most severely (chapter 6, sec. 10). Now that a minimum is guaranteed, it is again the bank that is responsible. So we have yet another reason for kolkhoz indebtedness, and the habit of write-off persists (chapter 3, sec. 8).

When the money becomes active the main effect is a straightforward demand inflation in retail markets. There is no theoretical obstacle to reducing this by the orthodox Keynesian use of the budget surplus. But Communists are hostile to this. They make only minimal use of budgetary means, such as forcing parents to pay for school books or other peripheral fiddles with the social services. The general attitude is staunchly pre-Keynesian: budgets should be balanced, a surplus is a real magnitude that can really be carried forward for use next year, etc. Hence the undoubted possibility of countering demand inflation by a budget surplus, and so in a less discriminatory and arbitrary way, is simply neglected. But there are also practical reasons. Direct taxes, visible to the payer, are held to be highly disincentive. The highest marginal rate of income tax on socialist income in USSR is now a magnificent 13 per cent; and in Hungary there is no income tax. These situations would rapidly worsen if budgetary policy became a major weapon. For of course indirect taxes are excluded anyway – they raise prices and cause riots. Indeed in market economies also they must be excluded, for to use them is to substitute cost inflation for demand inflation.[13] It follows that a deflationary budget surplus could only be achieved by reducing expenditure. But the Soviet-type budget is like any other in keeping expenditure down all the time anyway: such a reduction would have to mean some new state policy.

So the authorities have renounced control through the budget, and they have no quantitative control over passive money through the bank either. For passive money is very particular, and arises from the plan for each enterprise separately. The bank can be told to be tighter on each separate enterprise and enforce each separate plan, but that is all. Interest is of no effect (chapter 12, sec. 15). But a serious rate, chargeable on finance borrowed rather than on assets brought in to use, and deductible from profits rather than from profits tax, would help a little.[14]

The main weapon in the investment sector, the Communist equivalent of raising the bank rate, is not strictly monetary, and so is rarely mentioned in this context: one simply prohibits new starts for so many months. Such a move is of course quite beyond the political powers of the monobank: only the Politburo itself can chop the pet projects of all the local and central bigwigs.

Now state retail prices are sticky, so in a demand inflation the black and kolkhoz markets boom, and draw a little extra supply from the population, in the form of moonlighting or of goods stolen from the state. This is the sole Keynesian phenomenon in an STE: imports are, as we have seen, quite unaffected except for smuggling (which is very considerable, by tourists). In normal times kolkhoz market prices can fall temporarily below those in the state shops if private supply is great enough, though eventually the switch of buyers from the major to the minor market will bring the latter back into line. But the converse does not hold; inflation can raise kolkhoz market prices above state prices for as long as it lasts.

Meanwhile queues form outside state shops, and the rules of the game indicate a rise in retail prices. But rising prices are more unpopular than queues, and in an STE there is only one body to blame for them: the Politburo itself. The Politburo has, after all, nominally complete control over the single state price. In a market economy at least half the population will – correctly – blame the trade unions, and about a quarter each the capitalists and the government, and this division of opinion makes serious popular reaction very improbable. But in STEs rising retail prices have very often triggered off the perpetual discontent of the population into serious rioting, nay revolution.[15]

As to other weapons, fiscal and monetary policy are out, as we have seen. Moreover the authorities have, as we saw, good long-term reasons not to raise direct taxes, though they usually do cut a few marginal expenditures. So incomes and prices policy are the main thing. On the income side the authorities further dispose of the magnificent weapon of lowering compulsory farm delivery prices, and raising labour norms. It certainly shows the remarkable strength of a Communist government that it should even contemplate such steps, but the risks of rioting are by now too great here too.

Besides, a little excess demand was always openly recognized by Stalin and Mikoyan as a good thing (Wiles 1962, p. 261). For – though this is not how they put it – it persuades the consumer to buy whatever we choose to sell him; it lubricates our creaky planning. Indeed they went further and, from 1947 to 1954, actually lowered state retail prices in discrete annual steps (by about 50 per cent all told). This is the most striking of all proofs of the efficiency of the Soviet-type financial system. The resources for so doing were of course available in the post-war recovery: as consumer good output rose efficiency rose and turnover tax rates could be lowered. But no other government or system was able to put a similar situation to such a use.

Such a lowering of prices is clearly inflationary, since it creates excess demand! It must be added to our other sources of inflation, and is paradoxical only because in a market we cannot conceive that prices might fall except under some deflationary pressure (including competitive pressure, which is deflationary).[16] But a large vertically integrated monopoly, that is not maximizing its profits, might easily lower one or two prices off its own bat, and this gets us very close to the STE. The system was abandoned after 1954 on social grounds, as a too random way of distributing the increase of wealth. Khrushchev preferred to raise low wages, pensions and agricultural delivery prices (chapter 16, sec. 16).

7. More discreetly applied, the remarkable anti-inflationary armoury described above remains very effective. Retail prices rise much more slowly in all STEs, even Poland, than in ACEs. The contrast is becoming yearly more pointed, and driving mere quantitative performance from the centre of the state. These discriminatory micro-measures, used by STEs against demand inflation, would be still more appropriate against the cost inflations that plague advanced capitalism. Thus price control is much more likely to work in a situation of fundamentally inadequate demand, in which enterprises raise prices unwillingly, only after costs have gone up. And to abolish collective bargaining, and to screw output norms upward, would be to strike at the root of the evil.

Capitalism has been caught quite off its guard by cost inflation. The US and British governments have from time to time operated general emergency freezes of everything. They have also used appeals for restraint.

These measures have not proved worthless, but they are too temporary and have far too shallow roots in law, habits and economic institutions (chapter 10, sec. 7).

Only France and the Communist market economies have a solid substructure on which such controls can be permanently based. In China and Hungary this substructure is the Stalinist tradition: the state controls everything in principle but has relaxed its hold as a matter of expediency. It retains full residual powers and keeps their memory green by using them, precisely for wage and price control, now and again. France is not widely different, though she uses the fiscal contract instead of the direct order. Price control is now one of the main objects of the fiscal contract (chapter 9, sec. 6).

Yugoslavia has formally abandoned many of the Stalinist residual powers, and her gross failure on the inflationary front occupies secs. 11 and 12.

Whatever the success or failure of Communist market economies, that of STEs is undeniable. No wonder then that their ministers of finance have been, after the ideological conservatives, perhaps the principal obstacle to decentralization. Nor are they wrong, for it is precisely the central detailed control over prices and wages that causes the success of the system. And they have direct experience of this, for it must not be thought that there are no direct upward pressures on prices as such in a classical STE. Quite the contrary, quality is misrepresented in order to claim higher prices, and bogus innovations are reported in order to claim the cost-plus prices normally accorded to genuine innovations, etc., etc., just as in a market economy. Nor is it at all easy, during the periodical general wholesale price reforms, to get anyone to accept a lower price. Profit was always at least attractive enough for that, and there is a sort of managerial cost inflation at all times. Uninhibited by competition, it requires the constant vigilance of the State Prices Committee.

8. Unemployment in a market economy is or is thought to be connected with wages and prices: perhaps the movement of prices in general (demand deflation), or the movement of wage-rates relatively to other prices (cost inflation), or the wage–interest ratio (Malthusian unemployment). If there is insufficient demand, there is Keynesian unemployment and simultaneously all prices tend to fall; until perhaps they hit rock bottom and there is a positive monetary effect. If wage-rates rise exogenously and other prices can be administered there is cost inflation, which produces classical or union-induced unemployment. And both these phenomena can be abolished by policies that intimately affect prices; for reflation affects prices as a whole, and in the restraint of cost inflation prices are the actual lever of policy. In the Malthusian case, a maladjustment of population to capital, pretentious theories have been developed that suggest cure through a more appropriate wage–interest

ratio, but as we have seen (chapter 13, sec. 14) interest rates do not in practice much affect investment volume or choice of technology; the ratio could only work in this way if it were made to, say by being a shadow price set by a Polish central planner who had been reading Kalecki. But there is in the Malthusian case an important price relationship actually at work. It is the price of machinery, not that of saving, that counts: wages and machinery *are* important costs, and technological choice *does* depend on the machine-price/wage-rate relation. Technologies totally unsuited to Malthusian countries are forced upon them by trade unions, while the poor remain unemployed.

9. Though still controversial, these cases have been often enough discussed. We cannot add to that discussion here. The STE differs in that prices hardly matter: technological choice, the price level, the volume of employment and individual prices are what they are ordered to be. The limitations are technical knowledge, previous accumulation, the number of jobs currently created by investment, and demography. Passive money cannot, above all, alter the volume of employment. Even the fact that all plans are violated, and none more than labour plans, even the numerous black markets, make no fundamental difference.

At only two points is money active in a relevant way, in both cases micro-economically. First, on the supply side, relative wages must be such as to attract the right people to the right jobs. This is not a small matter, and much frictional unemployment could be cured by more flexible and better publicized rates. Stalin's myth that he had abolished unemployment, and the Marxian pretence that under socialism there cannot be a labour market, persist to hamper the development of labour exchanges, regional wage differentials, etc.[17] Moreover all STEs, and not merely China, Cuba and Albania, still use campaigns, appeal to the idealism of youth, etc. in order to fill undesirable posts. It is not obvious, however, why such campaigns, mildly directed at the genuine but temporary idealism and availability of the young, should be a bad thing. No doubt higher wages could substitute for them, but is it desirable? A better case for the more consistent use of differentials is that there is still often forced labour (chapter 8).

Secondly on the side of the demand for labour, a free enterprise might well not employ the people brought to its door by force, campaigns or state promises of high pay. And at this point the STE has a great advantage: the enterprise is under orders, and its wage-fund is guaranteed by the monobank. This, then, is the basic full employment policy: specific jobs are created and paid for. The system is unpopular with managers, who are forced to make work for old women, youths and the unskilled generally. This is bad for the morale of the essential labour force, and for efficiency and financial indicators. But it does assure to each person self-respect and a living, and is thus surely superior to even generous unemployment pay, or to make-work schemes that segregate their beneficiaries under *ad hoc* employers.

10. Decentralization of course affects this adversely. Gaining power, and told to seek efficiency, the manager lays off labour. Indeed, except in Hungary and China, what other power has he gained? The new system of investment finance amounts to very little (chapter 13), all prices and outputs are still centrally decided, and therefore all outputs other than labour have to be too, for one enterprise's input is another's output. So the whole movement towards more managerial rights amounts to freedom in respect of the one input bought on a free market: labour. Naturally the manager wants to fire the unskilled and use the money to bid competitively for the skilled. Inequality and unemployment threaten simultaneously.[18]

The STE has no separate macro-policy for full employment; as so often, its macro is merely the sum of its micros. But it does have the usual macro-problems: what shall be the rate of labour force participation, and how shall we govern the rate of migration off the farms (chapter 8, sec. 11)? Participation is as elsewhere a matter of women's attitudes, the length of schooling, the date of retirement, demographic movements, and the general supply curve of labour in respect of real hourly income. This curve slopes, of course, backwards (chapter 2). The situation differs only in that the government is particularly anxious to maximize participation.

So we meet again serious arguments against the reform of the STE. Its policy for full employment is very successful. 'Unemployment' as defined by the statisticians of ACEs runs perhaps between 1 and 2 per cent, and is mostly frictional.[19]

The idea of tackling even Keynesian unemployment by discriminatory micro-controls has some support in France, where enterprises investing in backward areas are persuaded to include in their fiscal contract an undertaking to use labour-intensive techniques. Indeed French planners have no particular snobbery about capital-intensity,[20] so do not commit the ridiculous error of installing the latest machinery and then surrounding it with unskilled labour.

One such discrimination, however, is rather common in market economies: restraints upon firing. Jobs are protected not merely by collective bargaining but increasingly also, as for a long time in STEs, by law (chapter 7, sec. 9). Probably as yet this has little effect on the volume of employment, since it makes firms more reluctant to hire, and the laws have many loopholes. Indeed by stabilizing the employment of senior workers such laws destabilize that of junior workers. But it is not implausible to look ahead to more complete coverage, coupled with tax relief or subsidy to firms hard hit by the working of the prohibition.

11. Yugoslavia is a most inflationary place: it has easily the worst record in Europe. There are many candidates for an explanation:

(i) the Illyrian inelasticity of supply (not negativity: chapter 6, sec. 8). Increases in demand do not result in great increases of supply even where there is unemployment:

(ii) the Illyrian reluctance to plough back (chapter 13, sec. 10), which throws too great a burden on the budget and the banks. These therefore resort to inflation;

(iii) the cost inflation inherent in workers' councils (see below);

(iv) the inflationary consequences of decentralizing an STE (sec. 7 here). The simple fact that Communists are ambitious and wasteful has not ceased to be true in Yugoslavia. But decentralization has gone much farther than in China and Hungary, which seem to have taken adequate precautions. The Yugoslav state has given up its Stalinist powers legally; it can be sued for *ultra vires* action;[21]

(v) the federalization of the banking system (chapter 12), so that there is no monobank any more.

(vi) the legacy of depressed agricultural prices with which the system began. The necessity to raise these prices a lot, while it was impossible to lower any others, was long urged as an excuse, but over 15 years now agricultural and other prices have marched in step;

(vii) the pressure of backward areas for development funds and the unwillingness of advanced areas to provide them. The regional income spread is fourfold, and some regions are more hostile to each other than foreign countries. But Yugoslavia is after all a state, and must come up with these funds. So again she has resort to inflation. Even once started, the 'political factories' require constant subsidy;

(viii) a more general reluctance to bankrupt loss-makers, inherited from the Soviet-type period;

(ix) sheer incompetence and over-confidence. Certainly the Hungarian authorities make a better impression. The mere instability of the monetary institutions argues incompetence.

Yugoslavia is a market economy. What she has is mainly demand inflation. Her trade unions have preserved Stalinism more perfectly than any other institution, and do not engage in collective bargaining (chapter 7). Wages are not even formally a cost. But in a small country with many monopolies prices are very much administered. Again the foreign trade system is quite different from that of an STE, and import prices are set by importing enterprises on the basis of the foreign price and the rate of exchange. So despite the tight exchange controls, the frequent devaluations of the dinar also lead to cost inflation. Moreover in the workers' council we have a combination of labour emotion and managerial power ideally suited to creating cost inflation. The mechanism is alleged to be that the large profitable enterprises pay more out in recessions, maintaining their previous prices; the small unprofitable ones raise their prices in booms, so as to be able to pay more too, and retain labour.

Such conditions urgently demand an incomes policy. But the whole ideology of self-management rests on the proposition that workers should distribute the value they have themselves generated between ploughback and take-home pay according to their own lights. This is the key article of faith. The authorities, therefore, can only preach restraint.[22] This is particularly serious since they do not use the budget to cut consumption, for Keynesian fiscal policy remains taboo, and the budget is supposed to be balanced, just as in an STE. However we saw in sec. 6 reason to be sceptical about Keynesian remedies for cost inflation. A general price freeze is more promising, and this, with their Soviet background, the authorities do often use.

When we turn to demand inflation, we note again the refusal to use the budget – more culpably, this time. But another habit has also carried over from the STE; that of investment overstrain, greatly aggravated by politically powerful localism. It has, then, become an accepted instrument of policy to postpone all project starts by central fiat. At least, then, investment can be manipulated, even if consumption cannot. For quantitative bank controls see below.

Yugoslavia is a country of heavy unemployment. In 1971 more than 6·7 per cent of the active population was employed temporarily abroad, 39·7 per cent in the self-managed sector, 6·0 per cent in various public institutions and 1·0 per cent in private enterprise; 41·0 per cent was self-employed in agriculture and 3·0 per cent in crafts, transport, trade hotels and building. This leaves 3·3 per cent registered as unemployed, and a −1 per cent discrepancy. It is on the one hand fair to apply the unemployment figure to the whole active population, but on the other hand it is harder to get on to the unemployment register than in an ACE.[23]

This unemployment is mainly Malthusian: a poor country, skimpily endowed by nature and devastated by war, has few places of work to offer a burgeoning population among which peasants crowd off hill farms into towns and Moslems breed with Central Asian rapidity. But it seems to be generally agreed that Illyrian restrictionism plays a part (chapter 4). The foundation of new enterprises is a very poor way of offsetting the unwillingness of existing ones to expand. Moreover the Illyrian enterprise has another defect in this connexion: it prefers capital-intensive techniques (chapter 4, sec. 18). On the other hand in outlying areas restrictionism leads to nepotism, so that instead of too few too many people are employed, and in practice the self-managed sector is a surprisingly small one in Yugoslavia, so its effect cannot be big.

Pressures remain, therefore, to make enterprises take on too much labour, but they are very weak compared with those of an STE. The enterprise has of course great difficulty in getting rid of labour, and is supposed not to do so without taking social consequences into account. Certainly it would receive bank support if it kept labour on. Such devices are of course more appropriate to Malthusian than to Keynesian unemployment.

The great long-term device is temporary *emigration*. This is something that no STE has until recently contemplated, on both security and ideological grounds; but now there is growing temporary and permanent emigration both among STEs and to ACEs. Yugoslavia has specialized in temporary emigration to ACEs for many years, and profited enormously by the emigrants' remittances, while losing substantial skills and expensive training for at least a period. Migration, however, is less an institution than a policy.[24] It is certainly a humane and efficient one, that stands much to the credit of pragmatic rulers who suffer much ignorant abuse for it. We should be more critical of Poland and Bulgaria for not following suit.

But there is also Keynesian unemployment, though the authorities have been extremely unwilling to learn the pathology of that disease. Yugoslavia excellently exemplifies what one would *a priori* suppose: a market economy remains a market economy, never mind who owns the means of production or what professors teach or what politicians were brought up to believe. So perforce a monetary device has had to be developed for the short-term regulation of unemployment. There being no money market and no publicly held national debt this cannot be open-market operations. So it is the other quantitative device: central regulation of bank liquidity ratios by fiat. This is, all visiting Western experts agree, clumsy and arbitrary. With their limited ideological insight and institutional imagination, they hanker after a money market and a negotiable short bill; but one wonders whether simply more finesse could not be shown in handling the ratios. When we add a more flexible fiscal policy, and take account of the admirable control over project starts, do we need a money market? Yugoslavia lacks not the means but the will to stop inflation.

Notes

1. The unemployment of the other factors of production does not count. Land and raw materials, of a sub-marginal sort, are present in great abundance. It is a prime fallacy that they should be employed (see Wiles 1962, chapter 8, sec. 4). Underused thrift is of course the Keynesian phenomenon *par excellence*, and is discussed implicitly in the text. Underused entrepreneurship is perhaps a feature of, say, the STE (chapter 15) but we shall not bother too much with it, since potential entrepreneurs can always do other work. Underused knowledge is also lightly dealt with in chapter 15.

2. Indeed it was in this context that Americans revived the doctrine of 'real bills': finance should be directed towards production, where it would not be inflationary but would expand output. To keep down loans to brokers qualitative controls, even, were proposed. Cf. Milton Friedman and Anna Schwartz, *A*

Monetary History of the United States, Princeton 1963, pp. 254–66. From this controversy in turn arises the not very helpful notion that Soviet-type banking rests on the doctrine of 'real bills'. On the doctrine from start to finish cf. T. M. Podolski, *Socialist Banking and Monetary Controls*, Cambridge 1973, pp. 12–18.

3. Albert G. Hines and Carol Nussey, *The International Monetarist Theory of Inflation*, Birkbeck College, London 1974, p. 42.

4. This is asserted for USA and Canada separately by Nicholas Kaldor in *Lloyds Bank Review*, July 1970. Alan Walters, perhaps Britain's leading monetarist, correctly objects that Canada is too dependent to be treated separately (*The Banker*, October 1970). But he tacitly admits that monetarism fails when Canada and USA are combined.

5. It follows that monetarists cannot both object to 'fine tuning' and claim they have a reliable theory, or even one that was specified in any way. If they had, there could be fine tuning.

6. Harry Johnson in *AER*, May 1971, p. 10.

7. On the comparative instability of smaller aggregates, cf. George Staller in *AER*, June 1964; Colin Lawson in *Soviet Studies*, April 1974. On Soviet-type fluctuations in general cf. Bohdan Mieczkowski in *East Europe*, 11/1967; Josef Goldman in *Economics of Planning*, Oslo 1964 and 1965.

8. Except that Lenin's and Rakosi's 'gallopers' were quite orthodox: the central bank simply printed notes to fill the gap in the budget deficit.

9. Attempts have long been made to *re*distribute unsaleable consumer goods between regions, at the old fixed prices, at annual 'fairs'. These are not unsuccessful: cf. Wiles, op. cit., 1962, pp. 179–80. Doubtless the Gossnab and its sister organs do the same more informally for intermediate goods.

10. On investment overstrain under Communism cf. UN Economic Commission for Europe, *Europe in 1962*, pp. 16–23; Oldrich Kyn and Jiri Slama in the *Forschungsbericht* of the Ost-Europa Institut, Munich, 1973. The ratios in the text are my guesses, except that 'Time taken to construct objects of comparable complexity is 3–5 times longer than in USA or England' – P. Kuznetsov in *Problemy Funktsionirovaniya Ekonomicheskikh Sistem*, Moscow 1967, p. 264.

11. Cf. Bronislaw Oryzanowski in *Mysl Gospodareza*, Cracow 1957.

12. Their views are summarized by George Garvy in ed. Alec Nove and Jane Degras, *Soviet Planning*, Oxford 1964, p. 62.

13. This was hardly true in Keynes' day, since the budget took a far smaller part of the national income, and trade unions were not strong enough to raise wages unduly when indirect taxes rose.

14. To raise such a rate increases project completions and reduces project starts. This gives the paradoxical appearance, even under capitalism, of increasing investment – if investment statistics are wrongly collected.

15. The whole DDR in 1953; Novocherkassk 1962; the Polish Baltic ports 1970. These issues were to the fore, but not actually dominant, also in Kronstadt 1921, Poznań 1956, and in the Hungarian Revolution of that year. Pilsen 1952 was mainly about monetary reform, another draconian deflationary measure.

16. We may however compare the 'positive monetary effect': this too describes the inflationary effect of lower prices.

17. For unemployment in the first Soviet FYP cf. Raymond Hutchings in *Soviet Studies*, July 1967. Since Khrushchev abolished the Siberian differentials there has been net migration of labour out of Siberia, clean contrary to government policy. Labour exchanges, abolished in 1933, began to be restored on an experimental local basis in 1966.

18. Hence in USSR the freedom to hire, fire and reallocate the wage-fund, duly legislated for all managers in 1965, has been exercised very rarely and only under the strictest Party control, notably in the fully employed region of Shchëkino (Jeanne Delamotte, *Shchëkino*, Paris 1973). In Czechoslovakia Novotny tried to use these aspects of the reform, of which he disapproved in toto, to rouse the proletariat against Dubcek.

19. Cf. Wiles in *Soviet Studies*, April 1972.

20. On the role of this snobbery among STEs cf. Wiles 1962, chapter 16; Wiles 1969, chapter 8.

21. Actually only republican governments have been sued – but successfully.

22. Cf. OECD, *Report on Yugoslavia*, March 1972, p. 9. But the OECD confess they have no hard evidence for cost inflation.

23. Workings available on request.

24. Cf. my op. cit. 1969, chapter 13; Ivo Baučić, *The Effects of Emigration from Yugoslavia* . . . The Hague 1972; Robert P. Gallagher in *ACES Bulletin*, Winter 1974. Poland and Bulgaria have every demographic reason to imitate Yugoslavia. Mongolia used to import Chinese labour, and was thus a strong exception to the rule that STEs dislike immigration. Cuba has liberally allowed its pre-revolutionary bourgeoisie to leave.

15
Technical Progress and Productive Efficiency

15

1. This chapter discusses what Harvey Leibenstein (*AER*, June 1966) calls X-efficiency (the use of the most input-saving technique 'available'), not allocative efficiency (optimal use of resources at given techniques, to satisfy competing ends). The former, he says, causes incomparably greater losses, even between enterprises within one country. Now is such a thing logically possible? Abram Bergson,[1] for whom all economics is welfare economics, goes so far as to deny the existence of technological gaps, and asserts that virtually all technical knowledge is available simultaneously to all humanity. It follows that for him international productivity differences are virtually the same as differences in allocative efficiency – so that India and China have to rank below USSR, one might comment! We must concede him this much, that dynamically, the two concepts merge. Every improvement in short-run static allocation *constitutes* a growth of output from the same inputs. And more importantly, one of the competing ends that concern allocative efficiency has always been admitted to be net investment – is not saving a resource? But net investment could well be into technical education and R and D: very small sums can buy revolutionary quantities of foreign R and D. Therefore the present level of technique depends, *inter alia*, on past allocations of savings, and X-efficiency is *inter alia* a result of past allocative efficiency, and the past will to save, indeed of past leisure preference too. Since the Fall men could have worked harder, saved more, used their time more wisely, been more inquisitive, etc. All this accounts for their present endowment with technical knowledge and capital too; indeed it also explains international differences in this endowment.

Bygones are bygones. What the present generation possesses as a result of its forbears' allocative efficiency is X-efficiency. Moreover all this is not in any case the whole truth: workers must also *wish* to work well and managers must *seek out* better techniques, not merely *be able to use* them. Not differences in skill, education or even leisure preference, but differences in will-power, whether among individual workers or among individual managers, produce the extraordinary differences in cost recorded by Leibenstein, even within one country. But is will-power a valid concept? It is unpopular with psychologists, though not for any obvious reason, since it is clearly a large part of Freud's ego, and a large part of Adler's whole theory. Further, it is a good stick with which to beat Behaviourism. It is unpopular among social scientists, however, for a very obvious reason: it varies, and this makes people unpredictable and unmanipulable. Notably, Leibenstein's variations in X-efficiency leave cost, output and therefore price indeterminate. Economists are exceptionally obsessive about indeterminacy, so no doubt this is why his important article has had so little *retentissement*.[2] Leibenstein, however, refrains from using such an old-fashioned explanation. As a result, indeed, he has no explanation, and merely correctly concludes that from such poor data as we have, X-inefficiency causes much bigger losses than allocative inefficiency. He might have said, indeed, that technical progress is by far our most important source of wealth. It easily outweighs capital accumulation, allocative efficiency, and economic systems.

On a national level, allocative macro-efficiency differs from the sum of all micro-efficiencies by reason of externalities; and on this we have nothing to add to the orthodox position (chapter 11). X-efficiency shows a similar externality: the enterprise should employ the best technique merely for the resources it decides to employ, but the market or the planner must generate employment for all who wish it, and this may affect the choice of techniques (sec. 8).

Now in chapter 11 we agreed to treat allocative efficiency statically and narrowly. The short-run choice of what to do with existing capital, let alone techniques, is a vitally important issue. And if allocative efficiency is so defined, X-efficiency is indeed something distinct. Thus perfect competition ensures the former, but ties up risk-bearing and enterprise in current speculation on flexible prices, and reduces the profits that might be spent on R and D. But imperfect oligopoly, which offends against the Lerner Rules, reduces price speculation and ensures profits. We are therefore entitled to ask as separate questions: who spends most on R and D? who spends most wisely? who makes best use of the results? who permits least unemployment? We are, quite separately, entitled to ask, who *wants* technical progress?

2. X-efficiency is defined by the way in which it is measured. An enterprise or an economic system is more efficient than another one by the proportion that its average total cost is lower for the same quality of output. Its rate of technical progress or regress is the rate of change in cost. The usual qualifications apply:

(i) the measurement of the output must take account of all ecological and other externalities (sec. 11);

(ii) if the input is another enterprise's output, the externalities of producing it should be applied to that other enterprise. But the disutility of labour must be counted in the reckoning of the labour-using enterprise (sec. 8);

(iii) inputs, and especially labour, may not be a minimand at all. In that case technical efficiency is only a maximand in respect of non-labour inputs (sec. 8);

(iv) as aspirations level off, or Full Communism approaches, X-efficiency ceases to be a maximand (sec. 12);

(v) since the costs must be taken at constant input prices there are important problems of substitution and index numbers. These affect output measurement in exactly the same way, and the matter is no less important in considering efficiency (sec. 3);

(vi) unemployment of labour and capital brings about a difference between enterprise and national efficiency (sec. 9);

(vii) superfluous labour must be valued at its marginal productivity, not its price, which is higher. But the computational difficulties are overwhelming (sec. 4).

3. Let us begin with the problem (v).[3] Two enterprises or systems are of equal technical efficiency if given the same inputs they can produce the same outputs. But this does not necessarily mean that the points representing the present input-mix of each must lie on the same iso-product curve, for there is nothing to stop the actual iso-product curves of enterprises or systems from cutting each other. I.e. the efficiency of a particular group of people may depend on their knowledge: they can make better use of some patterns of inputs, and worse use of others, than people differently informed. But our main problem is that these curves are simply not available to us at all. Our statistics give us only points and prices. The temptation is to use index-number techniques on these, and we have to see here how dangerous this is.

First, however, while it is obvious that prices are not the same over time or between countries, and an adjustment must be made, within a single country we usually base inter-enterprise comparisons on simple average total cost at current prices. We have thereby assumed reasonably perfect competition. This is the only way of avoiding the index number problem that is present by definition in all other comparisons. The matter is of practical importance where regional wage-levels differ, and above all in comparing farms, or agricultural ownership systems. For land rents are settled on a very imperfect market, and systematic differences in the rent of land of one quality between, say, an advanced and a primitive agriculture are all too possible. The straight monetary comparison tells us the competitive situation on the market (or in the ideal planner's eye) of two enterprises or systems; it does not necessarily tell us which is more efficient, since the answer to the latter question excludes luck and discrimination.

The index number problem is therefore universal except in perfect competition: our costs must be made 'real' like our output values, which means that we must use fictitious prices! For of course constant prices are always fictitious for one place or time, if not both. Moreover they are fictitious in a very important way: they misrepresent the real possibilities of substitution open to an enterprise. Thus in the following example three enterprises A, B and C are of equal X-efficiency, i.e. they make equally good use of the technical information, all of which is available to all of them; so they all lie on the same iso-product map. They are all represented on the same curve only for convenience. A faces one set of prices (Latin letters), and B and C another (Greek letters). Both sets are 'rational', though they may be only 'shadow', in which case there is detailed planning, and it is in the mind of the planner that the comparison is being made. A and C are of equal, and indeed of maximal, allocative efficiency, since they have both reached optimum input-mixes. But B has made an allocative error, given the prices it faces. D is more X-efficient at least than C since it produces the same amount with fewer inputs, i.e. lies on a separate iso-product map, of which the curve representing output ABC passes through D. But since D is only a point we cannot say whether it has optimized its input-mix. The two inputs are called X and Y, not 'labour' and 'capital', in order to 'dehydrate' them. The shift from one set of prices to the other has nothing to do with economic development, and the supply of each input is independent.

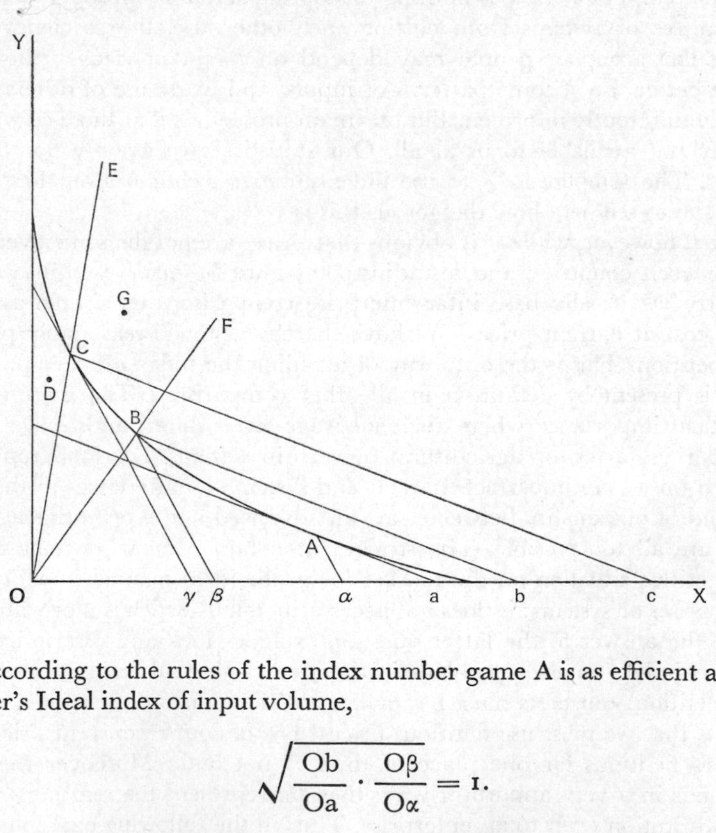

According to the rules of the index number game A is as efficient as B if Fisher's Ideal index of input volume,

$$\sqrt{\frac{Ob}{Oa} \cdot \frac{O\beta}{O\alpha}} = 1.$$

Let this be in fact the case, so that $Ob/Oa = O\alpha/O\beta$. Now it is obvious that B can be drawn, irrespective of its relation to A, more efficient than C. Indeed we have done so, for $Oc/Ob > O\beta/O\gamma$.[4] It is clear that index numbers and constant, i.e. partly fictitious, prices put us into a wholly different world from iso-product curves. For we began with the data that A, B and C were of equal technical efficiency and B of lower allocative efficiency. But the most advanced index number technique tells us that A and B are both more 'efficient' than C, and fails to distinguish technical from allocative efficiency. This is because it proceeds from points, not curves.

Moreover all this applies to outputs too. For it is clear that our iso-product curve might be an indifference curve, and X and Y two consumer goods. It is not at all clear why the whole distinction between points and curves, the acknowledgement that index numbers are insufficient, and the complicated mathematics of substitution elasticity, have been confined to inputs.

However, iso-product curves are, to repeat, flatly unavailable. We must live with the data that we have, and prefer probable statements to none. How likely is it that Fisher's Ideal would make so great an error as that illustrated? Let us itemize:

(i) we are very often in practice in the situation D<C (i.e. D uses fewer inputs for the same output), which is unambiguous by any technique. This is particularly common in short temporal sequences, which are our main concern;

(ii) Fisher's Ideal is always superior to Paasche or Laspeyres alone;

(iii) B's allocative inefficiency would have counted against it if it had settled north-west of C, since $\frac{Ob}{Oc} > 1, \frac{O\beta}{O\gamma} > 1$;

(iv) a narrower price spread or a more angular curve would bring A and C closer in the figure, and so lessen the efficiency gap A–C (which need not >O). As drawn, C's price (tan CyO = 2) is four times A's price (tan AaO = $\frac{1}{2}$), and the arc elasticity of substitution at A is 1·23 ($C_y = 5$, $C_x = 1$, $A_y = 2$, $A_x = 5$). Although σ is thought to be normally close to 1·0, certainly a fourfold change in a relative price would be ordinarily held to render two economies or enterprises incomparable;

(v) If then in ordinary cases Fisher's Ideal really would bring C and A close together, such a point as D, being undeniably more efficient than C, would tend to show the same relationship to A, even if C were unknown;

(vi points (i) and (v) apply *mutatis mutandis* to a point G lying north-east of C.

We shall therefore recommend, with extreme caution, to measure X-efficiency by Fisher's Ideal indices of inputs and outputs. It follows that the change of X-efficiency between places and times is the Cobb-Douglas factor-productivity residual (FPR), defined so as to include returns to scale, but using Fisher's Ideal index for both outputs and inputs. Cobb-Douglas, it will be recalled, sets σ arbitrarily at 1 throughout, and so imposes constant weights, as in single index-number formulae. Fisher's Ideal of course averages two such sets of weights; and this allows to some extent, over short periods, for substitution.

Strictly the FPR should be zero along any isoquant. But not even a CES production function would yield that result, since isoquants are not of constant elasticity. But the whole subject is in such rapid movement and conceptual disarray that we can only present our comparisons of FPRs between systems in the diffidence of an appendix.

4. Those who calculate these functions tend to assume that marginal productivity equals factor price, or perfect competition for inputs. The measurement of output is as usual not discussed in this connexion: though it is at least highly probable that marginal utility equals product price in most markets. Most imperfections of competition are unbiassed in this latter respect, so irrelevant. But the STE provides either no price or too low a price for capital and land, and UDCs and poor STEs pay wages to unskilled labour that exceed its marginal product, since otherwise it will die. This is particularly true in agriculture. For the peasant patriarch supports his superfluous children on his farm though there is little for them to do. Similarly the kolkhoz admits to full membership the children of members, who have the right to perform work and so to receive the unit value of the duly accounted claim on collective income. These are both cases of the demographically determined supply of labour to a commune or a co-operative (chapter 4, sec. 9). They result in payments much above marginal productivity. The same is likely to be true in Yugoslav co-operative enterprises, albeit on a smaller scale since they are (just) able to fire labour, and under no compulsion to hire it. Soviet-type industry, too, being compelled to hire unwanted labour as part of the state's full-employment policy (chapter 14), pays more than marginal productivity. This should lead to surprisingly low weights for certain kinds of labour.

The importance of this is that a perfect market for inputs does the statistician's work for him. He does not need to put output and input series through a computer to establish marginal productivity: he just reads it off from the shares of the factors in the national income. No one who has not tried to establish a production function directly can imagine the gain in certainty and ease from this indirect procedure. The writer for one much distrusts the computational, or direct, method: to the extent that he would always present alternative exponents (weights) for capital and labour in cases where factor-shares are plainly wrong, so that the limits of likely error can be seen and judged by the reader.

5. Auto-consumption characterizes the peasant and above all the commune. Auto-consumption is an infinitely efficient system of retail distribu-

tion on top of a rather costly production process. Neither can exist without the other: it is a particularly strong case of vertical integration. Unless we are for some reason interested in the separate efficiency of the production process, we should value auto-consumption at retail prices. This activity is undergoing a considerable revival in advanced countries: do-it-yourself, home repairs, etc. This is because high wages and high taxes on employment have raised the cost of services, where there has been little technical progress.

But a further, and extremely important, case of auto-consumption is the housewife. In the commune and in most primitive societies there is no conceptual distinction between housework and other work (chapter 6, sec. 13). The farmer's wife, who bottles fruit, dresses meat, harvests carrots in the kitchen garden and collects eggs from under hedges, also fits very ill into a set of definitions devised for industrial and urbanized but pre-affluent capitalist economies. For serious comparisons of output, input and efficiency we must count not merely her bottling but also her cooking and bedmaking. Nor is it clear that she is producing less efficiently than workers in the market sector, or increasing her efficiency less rapidly. In other words we can, in our present ignorance, say nothing about the effect of her inclusion on intertemporal or international comparisons of output or the FPR.

6. A second underrated problem is the increasing part of output that must be reckoned at factor cost. This is not the same as, though it overlaps with, the increasing weight of services. 'Factor cost services' include the expanding fields of public health and public education. But many services have good enough market prices, and the big new phenomenon is the prototype good, which is sold at cost-plus. Now the prototype includes construction jobs of all sorts: a sector neither new nor technically sophisticated nor expanding. Cost-plus is and has always been rampant in the building industry, and this fact has long plagued statisticians measuring its output.[5] But a new and expanding kind of prototype is the sophisticated weapon or aeroplane. These things are, to be sure, subsequently reproduced at a strikingly low marginal cost, but these runs are much shorter than they used to be when technical change was less rapid, and the prototypes themselves are very costly indeed, out of all proportion to the costs usual two decades ago. Indeed it is within living memory that the most sophisticated weapons were cannons, and had a world market price, so that advanced military technology was not in the factor-cost sector.[6] Then too R and D themselves require prototype machines and materials (sec. 17).

The expansion of the factor-cost sector is important generally, but also for the comparison of STEs and ACEs. It unfairly downgrades the latter, for their productive advantage is exceptionally great in this sector, so far as is known. Obviously productivity, although unquantified, is 'there'.

For if it were not there would be no product, and so no point in spending anything. So if a sum spent on, say, R and D or space travel is converted into rubles or dollars by an input deflator instead of an output deflator – i.e. by a purchasing power parity over scientific workers and laboratory instruments – we use about \$2·5=R1·0, owing to the lower wage level and the quite exceptional productivity of USSR in machine-making. But those same dollars converted by a parity that reflected the utility and speed of research output might be worth \$0·9 or even \$0·5=R1·0. The same may well be true of medicine, where the exorbitant monopolistic salaries of US doctors similarly devalue the dollar, and make an input deflator quite unsuitable.

In intertemporal comparisons a large factor-cost sector is equally distorting, since changes in productivity are implicitly set at zero again.

7. We pass to some difficulties posed to statistical measurement by the consumer market. An example of *minor quality discount* is the strengthening of orangeade concentrate in a bottle of unchanged dimensions: it should not be, indeed often it is not, beyond the wit of a statistician to vary the cost-of-living index accordingly. In theory these changes are duly made in all countries, since they present no conceptual difficulty. But having myself calculated purchasing power parities[7] I am more than sceptical. Quite apart from the magnitude of the task, governments cannot be trusted with cost-of-living indices. At least the British government has deliberately and notoriously manipulated the index (during the second World War).

Passing from intertemporal to international comparisons, most Western economists or other travellers, trying to reckon purchasing power parities for the currencies of STEs or UDCs with their own, simply dare not make the appropriate minor quality discounts. How often and how fast does this 'bus run? Electricity is cheap, but how often are there power cuts? How old are these eggs? How truthful is this newspaper? Does the rent include lift maintenance, and how often is the lift out of order?'[8] All these questions must be truthfully answered before we arrive at a purchasing power par (or a cost-of-living index). I am certain that everyone leans over backwards to exaggerate the purchasing power of the ruble and the rupee. I further suspect that at the other end the dollar would suffer from such 'full disclosure'. For one of the greatest drawbacks of so-called affluence is the decline in service standards: doctors' and plumbers' house-calls, crime prevention.[9]

So much for the extraordinary, and always neglected, difficulties of minor quality change. Now going to the other extreme we meet the 'hedonic' issue. The advent of television presents us with such vast problems of philosophy and data-gathering as: do we count the man who used to spend £2 to go to the races by train, but now sees them better, without catching cold, for 0·3p? *The TV set is a means of consumption not an object of consumption*, not a product innovation but a process innovation. The products it purveys are the same, indeed distressingly the same, as those previously purveyed by cinemas and race-courses. It is clear that mere changes in the price or quality of TV sets, once they have become articles of mass purchase (not consumption!), are a trivial issue besides the change-over from no TV to TV. It is also clear that, controversial as they would turn out to be, large 'hedonic' allowances should indeed be made, shifting the indices from the means to the objects of consumption. All consumer durables would disappear from the cost-of-living basket, to be replaced by a costing of the services they provide. After all, this is already done for houses and, in some countries, for motor-cars.

I have nothing else to add to my previous remarks on this,[10] so shall merely repeat that such a necessary step would depress prices and raise outputs by uncomfortable amounts, especially in connexion with wage claims. Also, hedonically STEs and UDCs are farther behind ACEs than an orthodox comparison of income levels would imply. But the rate of change is quite another matter. We cannot quantify it for any country, and have no reason to believe that it is, in particular, slower in STEs. Perhaps it is slowest where consumer durables have either not yet begun to sell or already satiated the market. If so, hedonic considerations would raise growth in most STEs, since they are countries of middling wealth.

How, next, do we allow for the different degrees of diversity within a product category? Clearly STEs and UDCs are much inferior in this too, but again the rate of growth is another matter. Furthermore it is easy to overdo diversity, since it leads to endless search procedure (so both time and therefore loss and neurosis) for the buyer, and deprives him of the economies of scale. He might well prefer the package deal, of less diversity and lower prices, which planning can offer him. Indeed the imperfect competition of many enterprises virtually guarantees too much diversity. A monopoly too, not maximizing its profits and subject to public pressure, may well prefer an unprofitable diversity of products that keeps its customers quiet.[11]

A further factor promoting unnecessary diversity is fashion. Fashion is the preference for novelty, even cyclical novelty, for its own sake. It is not obviously irrational, since we cannot simply condemn a preference for novelty, in comparison, say, to a preference for alcohol. Nor does it appear that the very fluctuating course of fashionable prices invalidates index numbers. Indeed on consideration, to condemn fashion is precisely that kind of Puritan moralization that economists are supposed to eschew. Communist (except Yugoslav) morality is hostile to fashion and diversity. In a literary way we can be sure that STEs have too little of both, whether or not market economies of all sorts have too much. For such is the constant and very loud complaint of everyone who lives in an STE.

The next of these 'consumer' items is the genuinely new product (object of consumption), previously unavailable even in substitute form. Since new means of consumption like TV sets are excluded (above), it is curiously difficult to think of really new products. But contraceptives seem to be a genuine instance. I can propose no procedure for valuing the gain in welfare during their introduction. But, as with TV sets, once they are fully established we can treat their mere rate of increase as indicating the increase in our welfare.

Lastly, the sheer unavailability of many products counts against the STE and the UDC in a comparison of absolute levels, and orthodox measurement errs greatly in making no allowance here. The price of an unavailable product is infinity, so we must clearly use instead the price of the closest substitute, multiplied by a quality discount. Moderate unavailability, i.e. queues, is also a great feature of the STE (not the UDC). The appropriate discount here is the most probable queuing time multiplied by the hourly wage. Intertemporally, it is anyone's guess in which kind of economy the rate of introduction of new products is greater, i.e. how growth comparisons are affected.

8. But even if we could make all these corrections we should still face the question, do we really want to maximize X-efficiency as defined? First come several arguments connected with the special status of the input labour.

Labour is human. Raw materials, semi-fabricates, capital, land are all inanimate: to endow them with feeling or value *per se* is anthropomorphism or fetishism.[12] They should be coldly 'economized' in the short and the long run. They have the value human beings set on them, and that is that. 'Benthamism' (chapter 2) reduces labour to virtually the same level. It has disutility at the margin, and so should be 'economized'. It is scarce just as other inputs are scarce, so it is another commodity on another market.

But the moment we admit that intra-marginal labour may have positive utility we are in difficulty. *Some* work is better than *more* income because it is part of a man's self-respect, and a guarantee against boredom. Leisure, including higher education, sickness and retirement, cannot always be distinguished from unemployment: we would often accept less 'leisure' at the current wage or even a slightly lower one. Work with an obsolete technology is often a joy: not only an uneconomic amount but also an uneconomic kind of work may be demanded. For all these reasons X-efficiency, which means economy of work, is actually undesirable. The 'right to work', however vague and impracticable that notion, outweighs efficiency, provided the work is human.

Here the market economy does not come out well. Theoretically perfect competition in the labour market could depress wages enough to find every unemployed man, however unsuitable, a job, and every technically obsolete worker a niche suiting his skill. Indeed, labour-saving techniques would be automatically disadvantaged by the price mechanism. Given flexible wages and a suitable monetary policy,[13] it might seem that there was no problem. But so long as social services come in lieu of, not in addition to, wages, and people are supposed to live *either* off wages *or* off the dole, there is not perfect competition. There is on the contrary a highly effective minimum wage, preventing the unsuitable and the obsolete from lowering their price. Trade unions of course make this much worse, so the marginal worker is in fact laid off and efficiency grows by means of unemployment. It is for this reason that we speak of the extraordinary technical progress (high FPR) in US agriculture: we only mean that marginal farmers are being ground out of business, indeed that marginal black tenant farmers in the South multiply their incomes by going North to enjoy the much higher social services. Take this element away, and the FPR of intra-marginal agriculture is not outstanding. Again British nationalized industry has recently astonished the world by its high FPR; but this is mainly because it did not for decades dare to lay off redundant labour, and eventually plucked up courage to do so in the late 'sixties.[14] But the labour was for a long time not re-employed.

The ideal STE can of course do whatever perfect competition can do. The actual STE, however, is a technological Potemkin village, created by a government that wants to cut a good figure in the world. So it heaps up capital irrationally in particular places, so as to displace labour and look modern. Elsewhere, however, people who would in an ACE be unemployable are forced upon reluctant managers (chapter 14). So actual unemployment is not permitted. There is even an unrealistically high minimum wage, but it is financed by subsidies if necessary. Only man's occasional preference for obsolete techniques is not tolerated. The craftsman must yield to the machine, he has no rights in the matter. If today he can at least carry on until there is enough capital to finance the change, Stalin actually persecuted him, and seemed to prefer to have him standing, rootless and redundant, at the periphery of some inefficient new factory.

We see again that allocative and technical efficiency are closely and paradoxically related. Perfect competition in the labour market would raise the former and lower the latter. And it is the single-minded pursuit of efficient allocation that would in this instance do less damage. For the pursuit of a higher FPR is here perversely related to growth. What heightens it is not the increasing returns to scale, beloved by those who try to analyse the residual into its components, but diminishing returns to labour and land: the smaller the input the higher the FPR. But again, once the decision (if that is the right word) is taken to raise minimum wages and create unemployment it is still important to optimize the use of the factors remaining at work.

9. There is a similar point about the unemployment of capital. We can always raise X-efficiency by writing off obsolete assets and installing new.

But the written-off assets are still 'there' and usable; they are unemployed capital. And this holds whether our decision was micro-rational (ATC with new plant<AVC with old plant)[15] or not (e.g. ATC with old plant>ATC with new plant>AVC with old plant). For we shall nevertheless show a higher FPR, since the old plant no longer figures in the capital stock, owing to the accounting conventions for calculating the FPR, which are to accept actual decisions about obsolescence. For the FPR merely conveys information about current techniques. It does not ask whether these techniques were rationally adopted, so it is right to neglect, at enterprise level, the unemployment of both labour and capital.

As we saw, the FPR of an enterprise is the movement of its ATC between two periods. The enterprise is supposed to 'fire' capital as easily as labour: i.e. sell it or write it off. In neither case should unused capital count towards its costs any more than unused labour. And capitalism, with the accounting procedures that it encourages for capital, and its refusal to accept ownership of or responsibility for labour, approximately achieves this result. But more left-wing systems put obstacles in the way of both redundancy and write-off. Neither the Soviet-type nor the Yugoslav enterprise can easily fire labour, and the former is even compelled to hire it. In both systems write-off is discouraged. Indeed in USSR until 1955 obsolescence was denounced as a bourgeois mystification.[16] It cannot have been very important in an era of extensive investment, but this obscurantism reduced technical efficiency.

This is of course because the Soviet-type or Yugoslav enterprise is 'affected with a public interest'. It is part of a single national system responsible for full employment. It is expected, to this end, to sacrifice enterprise to national efficiency. If it lays off obsolescent capital or elderly labour, they will not be re-employed elsewhere and the national product will shrink. The enterprise FPR rises, but what of the national FPR? For the national capital is at any moment a historically determined fact, and the labour force given by demography, sociology and the structure of the social services. The nation cannot give these factors the sack, so enterprise efficiency is sacrificed instead.

Estimates of the FPRs of market economies seem to fall between two stools. They show the capital-output ratio increasing during slumps which implies delay in the write-off procedure, but the labour-output ratio falling (i.e. increasing productivity); which means that the unemployed are not counted, and are the less efficient workers. This discrepancy is of ideological origin: the capitalist owns the capital, and so feels more responsible for it than the labour.[17] Until better figures arrive, the FPRs of market economies should be measured between years of full employment only.

10. We now consider whether nature, as well as labour, should not be a value in itself, and exercise some constraint upon 'progress'. At this point

X- and allocative efficiency merge. When pollution, etc., were small we dealt with them as errors in static short-run allocation. Now that they are big we call them deductions from, nay reasons against, economic growth. But they were at all times both.[18]

It is certain that the ecologists have unearthed stupendous externalities. Although these are not different in kind from the factory smoke and farm drainage known already to Pigou[19] they are very different in degree, and present an overwhelming argument for more detailed controls. It is clear, too, that output is overstated unless money estimates of ecological damage are deducted from it – this is again an old and perfectly familiar principle, but it is much bigger than until recently suspected. As yet, unfortunately, we have no serious quantitative estimate for this. Experts talk in terms of deducting 1 per cent per annum from US growth rates.[20] There would be more in Japan, less in UDCs. Wealth, population density and anti-pollution laws are the main factors influencing this quantity. We cannot say, amid the welter of controversy, whether this percentage is now rising or falling. The temptation is to say that it has at any rate risen uninterruptedly until the ecology scare, but the great periods of soil erosion[21] and of big game extermination were clearly peaks of ecological disaster, after which things got better for a while.

The STE should cut a good figure here, since it can in theory internalize all the externalities. But unfortunately in practice even the classical STE had always to decentralize enough to nullify this theory.[22] Moreover, the output plan fulfilment bonus is every whit as anti-ecological as the profit motive; both ensure neglect of whatever is external to the enterprise. Indeed *in the STE all costs are external*, since neither cost reduction nor profit is seriously rewarded. We have then an economy of output maximizers, each decentralized in this almost alone, that he will take every opportunity to produce more by any means and at any cost that his constraints allow. So long as there are maximizers of any sort there will be pollution.

The STE *seems*, then, to pollute as badly as any other type of economy, subject to the handicaps of low wealth and sparse population that happen to characterize it. Its anti-pollution laws seem to be about as ineffective. But in the absence of good quantification this judgement is arbitrary.

11. In addition the STE happens to have an unfortunate anti-nature ideology. It happens – and it need not have happened – that Marx saw human history as man's struggle with nature by means of labour. Labour distinguishes man from animals, labour wrings things from nature, dead labour accumulates as capital, accumulation is technical progress (!), man perfects himself through technology and controls nature; thus history is matter in dialectical motion, and nature is transcended by an emanation of itself. This is a truly great intellectual construct, and much of it is enormously plausible to the writer. But it 'comes on' anti-nature and pro-

man. For instance it embodies such basic corollaries as that there should be no rent to warn us of the scarcity of land and minerals, that the earth should be evenly populated, each area equally industrialized, climate overcome and the difference between town and country abolished.

Another ideology has also inadvertently trapped us in the same way: 'So God created man in His own image, in the image of God created He him; male and female created He them. And God blessed them, and God said unto them, "Be fruitful, and multiply, and replenish the earth, and subdue it: and have dominion over the fish of the sea, and over the fowl of the air, and over every living thing that moveth upon the earth." '[23] It is not thus that Buddhists talk, and we are a long way from the Stoic's 'live in accordance with nature'. The Judaeo-Christian tradition (of which Marxism is but a heresy) should have deified nature more and man less. It is easy to see how Communist and capitalist governments have failed to protect Lakes Baikal and Erie.

But if the psychological advantages of humility before nature are clear, can any logical reason be given for it? *Every single ecological argument appeals to man's future or present convenience.* Even the balance of nature, or the preservation of a large pool of genetic variability, are not ends in themselves. Despite many rhetorical excesses, I can detect in the solid parts of ecology only a very proper anthropocentrism.[24]

In this connexion we must not forget the very common, and equally fallacious, 'inverted ecology'; the doctrine that man must sacrifice himself to nature, not by refraining from exploitation but by an unprofitable insistence upon it. Notably empty land within a nation's boundaries, no matter how barren, and undug mineral seams, no matter how tenuous, are a disgrace to that nation. Knut Wicksell had the last word on this in the 1890s. It was proposed that the Swedish government should prevent emigration to USA, because it was denuding the farms of farmers. 'After all,' he said, 'it is a question of the welfare of people, not acres.'

But 'inverted ecology' is still with us. USSR still exploits her frozen north, though at least with more capital and less labour (chapter 8, sec. 5); Brazil still builds her capital in the jungle. The unknown wit who first spoke of the 'curse of natural resources' can still point to many absurdities. For of course our 'proper anthropocentrism' tells us to exploit only those resources that yield a profit, however defined. They have, by merely existing, no claim on us at all. If Marxism (above) encourages this waste, so do pure nationalism and technological display (sec. 16). Note that this all concerns the STE and the public sector. The market casts a cold eye upon all this, and it is a major advantage of market economies that they leave many natural resources unexploited. Thus the new capital-intensive Soviet effort in the Arctic is a great compliment to the Canadian example.

All in all, it would seem that the relation of economics to ecology was adequately defined by Pigou and Wicksell a very long time ago.

12. This is not so harsh a judgement on ecology as may appear. For if anthropocentrism is proper, it is certainly not proper that men should remain as they are. They should 'consume nature' in a very different way, enjoying its amenities more and its material yield less. It is rather the volume of goods, not services, consumed that ecologists, and others, rightly query. We discuss this in chapter 21, and need only point out here that if consumption levels should not increase indefinitely, either efficiency must eventually be frozen or there must be an indefinite increase in 'leisure'. Clearly, since work has positive utility, the former is preferable. There is here a curious paradox about the STE, since Marxism worships both technology and work, yet despises consumption.

After all, to make anything into a maximand is to fetishize it. It is not 'properly anthropocentric' to maximize the FPR, but a sacrifice of human beings, this way or that, on the altar of technology, much as some ecologists would sacrifice them on the altar of nature.

13. Nevertheless for a very long time to come most men will not be rich enough, and it remains a perfectly valid question which system generates the highest FPR. So let us retain our definition of X-efficiency, but admit that it should not always be a maximand. This seems clearer than trying to revise and complicate it so as to be universally valid. What, then, is the statistical record? Let us begin at the national level. It is a commonplace that growth is most rapid where technical progress is most rapid: in countries which

(i) are rich enough to import technology;
(ii) have enough educated people to apply it once imported;
(iii) possess un- or under-employed people and natural resources;
(iv) are not so rich as to have already imported all the foreign technology they need.

This is simple and standard,[25] except that in view of sec. 9 the third condition must be treated carefully. It implies that extensive investment will do: i.e. no change in the average FPR of the best enterprises. If the wasted resources are quite unemployed there is little change in any enterprise's FPR as new enterprises are set up, but only on the national level. If however, we read 'under' employed we obtain instead a very sharp increase in enterprise FPRs, but a smaller increase in total output!

In any case nations of middling wealth, as today's world goes, have the highest FPRs and growth rates. Now broadly the STE is of middling wealth, and does grow rapidly; up to 1931 and since about 1946 it has imported technology (except the DDR and Czechoslovakia, which were the exporters after 1946, and did not begin to import themselves until the 1960s). It also fulfils, except for the DDR and Hungary, condition (iii). So a bird's eye view might just slot the STEs into the world picture and forget them.

But this is far too crude. For we have omitted the crucial items of defence expenditure and foreign aid, and we have not treated the FPR but only output.[26] *Every one of these countries for which data are available has a low FPR, balanced by a high saving ratio*: though the FPRs are indeed greatest for those of middling wealth. We 'conclude' in this section that this is the primary trade-off of Communist revolutions: will and effort for efficiency, or resource mobilization for resource utilization. We examine the reasons for it in the next section. But although the conclusion rests on far too few, and too bad, data, we must at least pretend to examine the main disturbing factors in each case. In what follows W stands for defence expenditures.

USSR. Very high W/Y, necessitated by imperialist position even though much of this is R and D. Spin-off is held to be trivial. Foreign aid

TABLE 15/I

	GNP per head, annual per capita rate of growth			Productivity growth differs by (per cent p.a.)[f]	
	1880–1913[a]	1950–2 to 1960–2[b, d]	1960–2 to 1970–2[d]	1951–61	1961–71
Australia		1·6	3·2		−0·3
Belgium	1·9	2·5	4·7	0	0
Canada	2·1	1·0	3·6	+0·1	−0·4
Denmark	2·5	3·1	4·1	+0·1	−0·2
Eire			3·6		+0·1
France	2·2	3·6	4·7		0
Germany/FRG	1·8	6·1	3·8		+0·1
Italy	0·9	5·5	4·2	0	+0·5
Japan	2·2	8·0	9·2	−0·4	−0·1
Netherlands	0·7	3·5	4·2	+0·1	0
Norway	1·5	3·0	4·1	+0·1	0
New Zealand		1·6	2·2		
Portugal			6·5	+0·2	0
Spain			5·6	0	+0·1
Sweden	2·7	3·0	3·3		+0·2
Switzerland	1·2	2·8		−0·4	
UK	1·7	2·2	2·2		+0·2
USA	1·9	1·2	2·8		−0·1
Russia/USSR	2·8[g]	5·5[c]	4·2[j]	−0·1[j]	−0·7[j]
Bulgaria		5·5[e]	5·9[i]	+0·6[k]	−0·2[i]
Czechoslovakia	n.a.	4·3[e]	3·5[i]	+0·3[k]	−1·1[i]
Germany/DDR	1·8	5·9[e]	3·6[i]	−0·9[k]	−0·3[i]
Hungary	2·2[l]	4·7[e]	4·0[i]	−0·4[k]	−0·5[i]
Poland	n.a.	3·8[e]	3·8[i]	+0·7[k]	−1·2[i]
Rumania	n.a.	5·4[e]	5·5[i]	+0·1[k]	−0·7[i]
Yugoslavia	n.a.	6·0[m]	6·0[m]		

expenditure trivial: annual net deliveries about 0.2 per cent of national income. Farm labour surplus no longer considerable. FPR mediocre, but her (I+W)/Y is a remarkable effort of non-consumption. Her growth rate only equals that of middling rich capitalist countries (i.e. the poorest ACEs). We may doubt however whether any ACE could do as well, given such a defence burden.

DDR. Clearly a very great success; gives the lie to the notion that STEs cannot be advanced. Only the FPR is mediocre, and balanced by a large S/Y. West Germany does as well, at less cost. However the Soviet prejudice against capitalist technology has only recently been relaxed, and the DDR may well do still better.

Czechoslovakia, the next wealthiest, is far more successful than is ordinarily believed, especially by Czechs and Slovaks.[27] She must surely benefit, like the DDR, from the new Soviet line on importing capitalist technology, and will doubtless no longer be forced to generate her own in every sector.

Poland too is reasonably, especially since Gierek took over in 1970, successful – and Poles do not believe it. Note that this country has not a Soviet-type agriculture.

Rumania is slightly poorer than Japan, but has an almost equal record. Both profit from a very low W/Y. Bulgaria is similar and nearly as successful, but is thought to receive more foreign aid.

Albania and North Korea are the most successful countries on their level of income in the world, particularly in view of their high W/Y. But the Albanian record is marred by stupendous capital imports.

---

a. Simon Kuznets, *Post-war Economic Growth*, Mass. 1964, pp. 139–40.
b. Ibid., pp. 129–31.
c. Stanley Cohn in *Dimensions of Soviet Economic Power*, Joint Economic Committee of Congress, Washington 1962, p. 75; and source (e), p. 104.
d. Modern official sources, unless otherwise stated.
e. Morris Ernst in *New Directions in the Soviet Economy*, Joint Economic Committee of Congress, Washington 1966.
f. Thus if the percentage, labour force ÷ population, fell by 1 per cent in the decade, productivity growth differs from per capita growth by +0·1 per cent p.a. Sources as for GNP.
g. 1897 – 1913: Raymond Goldsmith in *Economic Development and Cultural Change*, April 1961.
i. Thad P. Alton in *Reorientation and Commercial Relations of the Economies of Eastern Europe*, Joint Economic Committee of Congress, Washington 1974, pp. 270, 255, 278.
j. Soviet Economic Prospects for the Seventies, Joint Economic Committee of Congress, Washington 1973, pp. 151, 431, 520–1.
k. Andrew Elias in Economic Developments in Countries of Eastern Europe, Joint Economic Committee of Congress, Washington 1970, pp. 153, 157.
l. Net material product, old kingdom boundaries: I. T. Berend and G. Ranki, *Hungary*, N.Y. 1974, pp. 25, 74.
m. 1950–9 and 1959–72; workings available on request.

Cuba's record is bad, owing at first to the US embargo and the defence burden; but increasingly to her own mismanagement. She is also highly dependent on the Soviet (previously US) sugar subsidy.

Of Mongolia too little is known. Yugoslavia, China and Hungary are not STEs. North Vietnam has been at war.

14. The STE, then, is a better mobilizer than user. The input volume index grows more rapidly than elsewhere; but the FPR is not remarkable. While labour is available and capital can be extensively invested, output grows more rapidly than in other systems. This is, as implied in sec. 1, a matter of will-power translated into politics. On the side of capital, the STE's capacity to tax, as befits a totalitarian state, is legendary. On the side of labour, we have seen (chapter 7) that it uses all means short of compulsion to bring housewives out of homes and peasants out of farms; but that it also does not shrink from compulsion. Again if there is empty land it can be rapidly brought under the plough,[28] and prospecting for minerals is thorough and quick. For to mobilize land is only to mobilize labour and capital. In matters of land use, however, allocative efficiency is of extreme importance, and we have seen in chapter 11 how peculiarly wasteful the STE is at this point.

The STE is, being a good taxer, also a good educator, and education is certainly a kind of mobilization. Education is more specialized, and more specialized in technology; crash courses and evening courses are easily available; the authorities do not quail before that essential preliminary to development, the lowering of educational standards. Those leaving higher and middle education are ordinarily directed to their first jobs (chapter 8). But the allocational efficiency of this forced draught seems to be very low. We have as usual no serious way of judging this. But stories proliferate of more or less correct planning frustrated by individuals (agronomists who prefer urban jobs even far from their speciality, because they cannot bear to live on the farm); and of thoroughly incorrect planning (notably the surplus of engineers, and their use in commercial posts).

But eventually a nation's reserves have all been mobilized. It may struggle for a time to substitute sheer investment for technical progress, but there are clearly limits, indeed limits due quite simply to diminishing returns. Eventually he grows quickest whose FPR is biggest. This is now the greatest obsession of Communist governments. Their R and D is not better, but worse, than capitalist R and D. There is no such thing as a 'socialist technology'. Crises and unemployment – the 'demobilization' of the basic resources of ACEs – have not come in the expected severity. The STEs are not catching up any more. What are they to do?

15. To most Western economists and to many Communist revisionists,[29] the answer is simple: decentralize and revivify the price mechanism (it is particularly important to note that the two things are quite distinct). But

there is such a thing as the dogmatism of good men, and one does not have to be an orthodox[30] Marxist or a Stalinist or just temperamentally conservative to see that the revisionist arguments are very shaky. The system into which Stalin blundered was brilliantly successful. It offered a very different package of faults and virtues from the market economy, a package surely (if we look away from political consequences) more suitable when the chief task is mobilization, and surprisingly able, with few modifications, to support further progress in the DDR today. As we have seen in other chapters, inflation, balance of payments crises and inequality are probably inherent in the market economy, and these are big vices.

In what directly concerns growth, would more allocative efficiency help or hinder?[31] In a general way the questions are distinct, and nothing should be assumed. First, if a sub-optimally allocated economy doubles all its outputs, while an optimal one multiplies them by 1·9, then the former has grown 10 per cent faster. The fact that it remains sub-optimal is quite irrelevant. But a move towards optimality is growth, albeit of a once-for-all kind. Unlike a change in policy or institutions, it does nothing for growth potential. We mean, then, degrees of optimality that change, or do not change, independently of a change in the system. Thus in Fig. 15/1, a move from B to C (more optimality) constitutes growth in proportion to the saving of inputs $O\beta/O\gamma$. But if E and F lie along the rays OC and OB respectively, and OE/OC=OF/OB, nothing hinders that F should be on a higher isoquant than E, or sub-optimal growth greater than optimal, for the same input of resources. For the economy that chose the ray OBF might have greater X-efficiency; indeed the two things might go together.

But this merely establishes the formal possibility. The causal links cannot be shown on any diagram. For the STE at any rate, they are that while factor mobilization is overwhelmingly important, sub-optimality can easily be an inevitable consequence of growth. For mobilization procedures are arbitrary, and haste, or at any rate some haste, makes speed. Nay more, the government ought to be full of 'will-power' and therefore cannot be expected to interest itself in fine tuning as well. For that would be a misallocation of its limited energies! It is not that we could not have pursued an optimal growth path by chance, it is that we are much less likely to. Certainly an actual dedication to a false theory of value, guaranteeing a departure from optimality on principle, adds nothing. On the contrary, decisions should be as optimal as time and resources allow. Prices should be as rational as possible whether or not decisions are decentralized.

Now all this argument is institutionally based: it concerns STEs and the public sectors of governments in market economies. As far as private capitalism goes – and the same surely applies to Yugoslavia – there are other arguments for sub-optimality during the period of factor mobilization.[32] The problem here is a shortage of enterprise, and the solution is so gross an imbalance as to produce bottlenecks one after the other. The bottlenecks are so obvious that they attract the attention even of the 'underdeveloped' entrepreneurs. This time misallocations are not merely an inevitable result we must live with, but an indispensable precondition.

Development à la Hirschman, then, follows from an increase in the number and quality of entrepreneurs. The more there are the more we can enjoy optimality. But in an STE the factor enterprise has a very curious status. The volume of investment is independent of managers, even of ministers. This decision, devolved to many thousands of people in market economies, now rests with the Politburo. There is, then, no problem of insufficient volume, quite the contrary. Where enterprise is needed is in making particular proposals and pushing them through the bureaucracy. It is particularly needed for new kinds of proposal, including technically new schemes. So the STE has less need of the factor enterprise while mobilization is the order of the day.

16. But when technical progress becomes the main source of growth the argument for decentralizing the STE becomes stronger, at least in the modern period. And here we must interrupt the argument simply in order to describe. For the ways in which R and D have been conducted in the West, let alone USSR, are not part of the common stock of knowledge, as they should be.

All pure and applied physical knowledge is internationally valid since physical nature recognizes no human frontiers. Human nature, however, does, and the social sciences are excluded from this analysis. But discovery and testing are expensive, and must be financed by firms or states. Under capitalism large enterprises finance their own R and D: these are oligopolists and monopolists. But small enterprises cannot afford it, so must federate to raise a levy on themselves, or be taxed by the government to support a quasi-public institute. There are also specialized R and D firms which contract to perform projects, or sell their independent discoveries.

Where it is unprofitable (pure knowledge) or impossible (applied agricultural knowledge[33]) to keep results secret they are divulged quickly. This is because of the internationalist ideology of scientists, especially pure scientists, who consider themselves to be citizens of the single world republic of science – a republic, however, in which each speciality is a hostile tribe. They have also a career-motivation to reveal their discoveries, and again they are quite simply proud of their achievements. Even collective pride and curiosity are basic motivations in R and D, and frequently outweigh profit. Obvious cases of this are the state financing of basic research, and the curious behaviour of capitalist oligopolies, which train more apprentices than they can use, and even competitively display their technical achievements.

Curiosity mainly motivates pure research. But pride often motivates applied research, and development (which is by definition never pure). Pride distorts choices, and leads above all to technological chauvinism (applied scientists are less internationally minded). Each nation and each ownership system[34] wishes to show how clever it is. It is difficult to know whether system-chauvinism or national chauvinism leads to greater waste and absurdity, since the nation-state is in all cases the unit of measurement. Enterprises on the other hand are more subject to the pressure of the market than nations or individuals, but how could this not be true also of them, so long as it does not involve them in actual financial loss?

Technological display, *pace* Veblen, is a very inferior criterion for economic activity. It usually means we must *minimize some one input–output ratio* at the expense of all the others. A simple example is pounds of coal per kilowatt hour – as if the more refractory furnace lining and the more efficient stokers required did not cost more. Why not minimize stoker-hours per kilowatt-hour? The answer is, of course, that we should minimize cost, a concept that allows for all these things. These other, fallacious, ratios are known as engineers' criteria. They have small connection with X- or allocative efficiency.

Sometimes technological display requires not that we minimize any particular ratio but that we *adopt the newest technique* – again regardless of cost, or indeed of any particular engineer's criterion. At national level this is evident in every kind of folly, at enterprise level perhaps most clearly today in premature computerization, or – in the Soviet case – a preference for computers that don't work over fork lift trucks and other elementary aids to intra-enterprise transport. Good examples of technological display at national level are Britain's premature specialization in atomic energy, and the Concorde aircraft. Note that both are non-market, public decisions, like the Soviet ones. Competition on a rather perfect market is perhaps the only way to dampen technological display.

But display and chauvinism leave room for secrecy as to how the thing actually works. This secrecy characterizes primitive capitalism, in which *knowledge is property*, and is guarded by the law of patents, copyright and licensing. Now this law is inordinately difficult to enforce: what is to copy, what is originality? how much may my employee take away in his head, in his briefcase? which of these two scientists had most of this idea first? So theft is enormously common. Therefore the patent system was never a very good idea; indeed it used to be highly controversial. The Netherlands rubbed along without patents from 1869 until 1912, though perhaps their industrial backwardness weakens this argument.[35] Switzerland never had a patent law until 1888 (very partial) and 1907 (complete). Here neither industrial growth nor inventiveness suffered in any way and both countries gave in only to international pressure. But Switzerland was undeniably parasitic upon foreign inventions made under functioning patent laws, notably by German chemists.

For to patent is half to publish: it not only alerts the enemy, it gives him a rough idea. So the Swiss watch manufacturers were rendered more secretive: what they could not patent and license, they tried to conceal (Schiff, p. 91), we know not with what success. So too in the military field the world over there were never patents, but military invention has never lagged. In the first and second world wars the patent-free sector expanded enormously, and with it the public award to the inventor. These awards were evidently incentive enough, and, issued after quasi-judicial proceedings, were far more likely to go to the right person. State capitalism is not incompatible but uncomfortable with patents anywhere.

In the last thirty-five years R and D expenditures have increased astronomically: notably in USA from about 0·4 per cent to 3·5 per cent of national product, 1940–75 – a more than 40-fold increase in volume. As a result, even the FPR has risen a little! It is difficult to establish a serious connexion between R and D and the FPR, and it would divert us from the purpose of this book. We need only list such complications as:

(i) improvements or (in STEs particularly) deteriorations in management, which also figure in the FPR;

(ii) depletion, which raises the need for R and D but depresses growth;

(iii) the distribution between 'catch-up' R and D which is mainly imported and almost bound to pay off, and 'frontier' R and D, about which little can be said.

We do note, however, that most of the finance is now from public sources and is spent on public-sector goals, overwhelmingly defence. In this perpetual avalanche of subsidized novelty, how useful is the patent?

The sceptic must admit that each novelty is at least good enough to render something obsolete. There may not be much social profit in it at all, but there is enough private profit to render it compulsory for enterprises to ride the avalanche. Therefore all patented things become quickly obsolete, and it is more important to be in the technological swim than to monopolize any currently workable object.

Our image of technical progress as a series of discrete inventions, launched into a surprised market place, holds only for the elementary stages. As the flow of discovery quickens and thickens discreteness is lost, and we choose arbitrary cut-off points to take out saleable objects. 'If it works it's obsolete.' Half the point in doing the research for article A was to prepare a knowledge base for the next thing but one (C). By the time A is in mass production B is in prototype, so nearly obsolete, and our minds are all on C. Who cares, then, what our competitors know about A? Yet only A actually works, so only it can be patented.

So legal costs combine with human pride to downgrade the patent. The very numbers taken out are declining. Secrecy there still is, but it concerns laboratory projects. Knowledge is still property, but the fashion is to sell it, not monopolize it. In the above example, it would be excellent now to *license* the production of B, especially to foreign firms. Licensing makes of the contracting parties a virtual consortium, since for instance they must exchange technical information about the product.[36] From the consortium it is an easy step to an equity holding. Hence the importance of the equity share in technological transfer (chapter 13).

17. How then must we organize an economy that has nearly caught up, can no longer import the discrete inventions of intermediate technology but must be part of the flow? First, technology is now so diverse, so complicated and so swiftly changing, that it is an expensive research project merely to understand it and choose between competing variants. The importer's role is active, he must himself belong to the 'world republic' or 'global village'. Flexible institutions are essential. On the research side (whether pure or applied) there must be many free individuals and organizations, able to travel and communicate. On the development side producers must welcome technical progress, nay demand it and pay for it. And both parties must be able freely to order, and the economy quickly to deliver, prototypes and mock-ups.

Such a free-swinging group of researchers is of course anathema to any Communist security police. For research is not nationally bounded, and these people need foreign contacts even more than domestic ones. Technology is developed by a vast international network, which though nationally financed instantly puts new knowledge to use on a world scale.[37] It is useless to wait for the journals: they take too long to print. It is worse than useless if your government centralizes the acquisition of journals. You must establish personal links at an international conference, and thereafter use the international telephone. Basic discoveries are freely communicated, and exclusive behaviour results in exclusion. So the researcher is a security problem. Then too he spends a lot of money, and must be audited. Here he does not differ from researchers in other systems, but the auditor does! He is a Communist auditor, therefore suspicious, niggardly, recalcitrant and slow.

The development problem is worse. The Soviet-type enterprise fears the radical changes in its plan that new products and methods will bring. All projects take longer and cost more than we think; but if we cannot dispose of our own profits and must still justify all this extra expenditure to the authorities can it be worth the spiritual wear and tear? – note that the question of will-power becomes again important. Then when we are ready for output the principle of planner's tension comes into play. We have no experience, we have not taken the bugs out yet, but we shall get the usual taut plan. Therefore our bonus is unusually uncertain. So we have no incentive to develop the researcher's proposal.

Beyond development lies *diffusion*: once inside the country and working at one enterprise, how will the new technique spread? Competition spreads it quickly enough: the rest of us adapt ourselves or go out of business or are bought up and adapted against our wills. But in the STE each separate enterprise can and does resist diffusion just as the original development is resisted. The contrast with capitalism is extreme and devastating. All market forms give an enterprise ample incentive to adopt new techniques. Even the monopolist benefits greatly: he profits by lower costs, and he cannot otherwise preserve his monopoly.

Moreover, prototypes and mock-ups suffer greatly in the STE, which is geared to the serial production of already developed goods. For at this very early stage not only is there no production experience at all on which to hang a bonus, but the researcher or developer can only order what he wants through the central planner. If the request is an odd one, e.g. involving non-ferrous parts for a machine ordinarily made of steel, a whole new ministry is involved.

All these problems clearly call for a market, i.e. for decentralization, not merely rational prices. R and D is the most vital of the sectors that would flourish better in a market (the others, less exciting, have been dealt with in chapter 11). But in order to describe the actual decentralization of Soviet-type R and D we must take the historical approach.

18. In simpler days, Peter the Great started systematically importing science and technology, and Catherine I set up a state monopoly for the scientific side: The Academy of Sciences (1725). It bought journals and sent students abroad, surveyed the vast country, and became the largest and most successful of the many contemporary institutions of this kind. Resisting the individualism of scientists, it survived almost alone of them in its pristine state down to the Revolution. When journals were few, and communications slow and Russia very backward, such an institution was not so much a bottleneck as a pump. But in the modern world, and with innumerable Soviet universities and branches of the Academy itself specializing in this or that, it is an obstacle as notorious as it is obvious.[38] Besides, until recently the connexion between new basic knowledge and new technology was less direct, and the monopoly at the former level did not after all affect the decentralized capitalist importation of technology up to the revolution. Much of this even came in on the back of foreign equity capital as described in chapter 13, secs. 11–12.

After the revolution, however, the Petrine monopoly, instead of contracting, expanded from R to D. The Ministry of Foreign Trade monopolizes the patents and licences as all other imports.[39] Moreover D was almost wholly removed from enterprises to separate institutions attached to the production ministry concerned. This reduced its efficiency very greatly, setting up geographical and psychological barriers to communication. Thus there was a whole Stalinist R and D set-up, closely parallel to the Stalinist production set-up. The Academy was the Gosplan of research, and did literally draw up five-year plans. There was an 'R and D strategy' just as there was a 'development policy'. And one clear message of this book is that where planners substitute themselves for the market things are as likely to go worse as better.

The whole notion of having a general research policy at all sprang from Engels' fascination with the philosophy of science. The more rational Western interest in science policy originated precisely in Bukharin's visit to London in 1931.[40] In Stalin's hands, the policy itself became chauvinistically pro-Russian, extolling Russian achievements and citing Russian sources as much as possible. But it was 'Marxist' in the Engelsian sense Marx never accepted, allowing Party doctrine to influence the direction of research and the acceptance of factual findings. It held that 'socialism' was bound to develop better science than capitalism .Within these bounds, as befitted an heir to Engels's sciolism, Stalin respected and financed much basic research.

On the development side he had to be practical. The Marxian science-philosophers did prevent the application in practice of basic knowledge they had 'proved' to be untrue (plant genetics). But an exception was made for modern physics and the atom bomb, and almost all other branches of natural science turned out by good fortune to be philosophically neutral. Here there was a massive importation by purchase and theft.[41] It was limited by the resources available, but the pro-Russian chauvinism did also lead to much unnecessary duplication of foreign results, and delay in applying them.

The system had also virtues. The only patents were those bought from foreigners. Domestic inventors were rewarded out of fairly substantial central funds, administered much like the similar British wartime awards to inventors. Thus the decline of the patent under capitalism was anticipated and made final. Knowledge was nationalized and freely distributed to those who needed it. A backward country, in a world of still-not-breakneck technical change, could have had a much worse system, and we must distinguish this from the nationalist and Marxist absurdities that marred its use.

19. Reforms in this field have, as we saw, in sec. 16, left the researcher much hampered by various aspects of Soviet[42] *society*, and the developer still in the toils of the command *economy*. Nevertheless much has been done: (i) obsolescence, long rejected as an immaterial cost ('moral depreciation' in the prejudicial Russian phrase) was recognized as genuine already in 1955 (sec. 9); (ii) the Marxist principle that knowledge comes free of charge, being immaterial, has been abandoned. After all 'what Marx really meant' was that knowledge should not be private property, not that it costs nothing; (iii) so international payment, always made to or exacted from capitalist countries, is now also made between Communist countries (the specialized patent trading body Litsensintorg was founded in 1962); (iv) enterprises still receive old domestic knowledge gratis; (v) but

they are encouraged to order new research on their own behalf, and their relation to the research institute is one of *Kontraktatsia* (chapter 9, sec. 12); (vi) large enterprises are being encouraged to develop their own institutes, and the control of Academy and Ministries has weakened; (vii) USSR has signed the international covenants on patents and copyright (1973);[43] (viii) the principle has been introduced that the factory price shall be high for new goods, and be systematically reduced as they get older. This would be a most effective simulation of the free market were physical command planning really dead. But it is not: profits only become important after the basic physical plan has been fulfilled, and that plan is still taut; (ix) even the ideology has been changed: sheer physical accumulation is no longer the same thing as technical progress, indeed the latter must be separately counted as one of the basic 'forces of production'.

Military R and D has always been a world on its own. It attracts huge sums and the best people and supplies. Many also think, but with little evidence, that its institutional set-up is different. At least the central planner probably intervenes less between producer, customer and researcher.

20. Technological transfer by acceptance of foreign equity is continually being discussed, but as we saw in chapter 13 the difficulties are virtually insuperable so long as there is no market. Of course during the NEP, and today in Yugoslavia, decentralization has gone much further. In the latter case R and D was not in the minds of the reformers, and it moved mainly in reflection of the general trend towards a market. But the founders of the NEP certainly had the importation of technology in mind: it was their main concern after the peasant problem. They proceeded at once to admit foreign equity capital,[44] which later had to be expelled when the country returned to a command economy. Latterly Yugoslavia has begun, many years after her reform, to grapple with the same issues. But self-management offers more obstacles to foreign equity than the NEP.

As to the mechanics of knowledge protection and the incentives to discover and apply, little need be said about either case, since the set-up under market socialism differs little from that under capitalism. Thus the Yugoslav patent law of 31 October 1960[45] abandons the ordinary Soviet distinction between 'inventors' certificates' (*avtorskie svidetel'stva*) and patents. Both are possible under Soviet law, but, in the tactful phrases of A. K. Yurchenko:[46] 'Since the patent gives a monopoly right to use the invention, the law forbids the issue of patents for such vitally important objects as medical procedures (*sposoby*), medical, edible and nutritional substances, new breeds of livestock, types of plant and of silkworms for mulberries and oaks. In addition the law does not allow the issue of a patent for an invention made in connexion with the work of an inventor in a socialist organization or at its request, or if the inventor received money or other material help from the organization in working up the invention (section 49 of the Statute).

'A patent is issued for life. The inventor's certificate is valid during the life of the inventor.'

Thus in an STE there are effectively only foreign patents. But in Yugoslavia:

> 'The main feature of the new Law on Patents and Technical Improvements is its rejection of dual protection of inventions (patents-technical certificates) and adoption of the principle of exclusive patent protection of inventions. The Law regulates the question of patents in the classical manner, as a monopoly, an exclusive right of making use of the patented invention. The right of making use includes production and sale of products and any other use of the invention for economic purposes.'

In both systems the patent law also regulates rewards to innovators, i.e. to people who suggest procedural improvements in the enterprises that employ them, without claim to world priority.[47] Just as a large capitalist enterprise regulates such matters, so does the STE, being one enterprise. The fact that the Yugoslav state also regulates it shows again that there are genuine differences between market socialism and capitalism.

21. This chapter has so far avoided agriculture. Here the law of diminishing returns has very special effects. If a particular country engages in foreign trade and begins to import food or fibre, it will abandon its marginal land and gain a higher FPR; i.e. greater allocative efficiency is the main reason for greater X-efficiency. The same applies to a mere opening up of trade within a large country.

The FPR has been negative over time in Soviet agriculture, even in periods when land area has not expanded, so that diminishing returns present no excuse (chapter 5, sec. 9). I.e. there was 'organizational regress'. Such an event is conceivable in industry too, but the 'basic' rate of technical progress is so much higher that it is quite unlikely.

It is also possible to work out an inter-sectoral FPR for both USSR and Poland, comparing efficiency at a moment of time. The descending order of efficiency seems to be: state farms, private plots of all sorts, collective farms.[48]

Notes

1. In his *Planning and Productivity under Socialism*, N.Y. 1968, and more explicitly in *Soviet Studies*, October 1971.

2. Normally, however, we can reconcile an economist to a new idea if we show it to follow from an old one. It can genuinely be argued that when Herbert

Simon substituted 'satisficing' for profit maximization he drew attention to variations in will-power. It is not only time and skill that search procedures use up, but that special psychic energy required of us when we argue or enquire, instead of merely doing routine things. Again a 'shortage of enterprise in UDCs' is a common and acceptable concept; but enterprise is largely will-power.

3. This section assumes a fair grasp of the technicalities. On Laspeyres, Paasche and Fisher's Ideal cf. Wiles 1962, chapter 12; Robin Marris, *Economic Arithmetic*, London 1958. On Cobb-Douglas and CES production functions cf. David F. Heathfield, *Production Functions*, London 1971; Murray Weitzman in *AER*, 1973. On the index number problem in international, as opposed to intertemporal, comparisons, cf. Wiles in ed. Alec Nove and Jane Degras, *Essays in Honour of Naum Jasny*, Oxford 1964; Wiles in ed. Wiles, *The Prediction of Communist Economic Performance*, Cambridge 1970. On weights according to marginal productivity not income cf. Wiles, op. cit., 1970.

4. For the more nearly parallel CB is to the price line Cγ, the smaller is $\gamma\beta$ and the larger bc.

5. It also makes construction an epicentre of cost inflation (chapter 14, sec. 5).

6. On military prototypes cf. chapter 18, sec. 6. On cannons cf. chapter 18, sec. 17.

7. Wiles 1964, op. cit.

8. In the grandiose new high-rise buildings of Moscow University on the Sparrow Hills, lift service to student rooms ceases at 10.00 pm. There are fifteen storeys.

9. During my last stay in New York City (1968) our black hotel maid revealed that she and her husband, also a hotel servant, were sending their elder son to school in a white military academy out of town, to keep him 'off the needle'. Thus inefficient crime prevention cost them $2000 p.a. It is entirely fair to reckon this towards the purchasing power par of the dollar.

10. Cf. Wiles 1962, pp. 242–9. We have not space here to discuss 'important but not radical' quality change, such as nylon for silk.

11. For example the BBC – a case in which this tendency is virtuous. Cf. Wiles in *E.J.*, June 1963. It is there indicated, though probably not demonstrated, that oligopoly tends by comparison to excessive uniformity of product.

12. Livestock forms the intermediate category of animate but not human. It presents great moral perplexities for which we have here no space. The feelings of livestock are in a qualified way an end in themselves, as regulations about cruelty and vivisection confirm. The battery hen and the calf that never sees daylight do raise questions about the size of the FPR in agriculture.

13. We must include monetary policy because perfectly flexible wages would not abolish Keynesian unemployment, they would merely spread it around more evenly.

14. Cf. Richard Pryke, *Public Enterprise in Practice*, London 1971.

15. ATC=average total cost; AVC=average variable cost.

16. Cf. Robert W. Campbell, *Accounting in Soviet Planning and Management*, Harvard 1963.

17. Some Marxists justly but confusingly include the unemployed among the capitalist labour force, and thus reduce, not raise, real wages per hour during slumps. Cf. Jürgen Kuczynski, *A Short History of Labour Conditions under Industrial Capitalism*, London 1942, vol. I, p. 86.

18. On the pricing of land and the 'curse of natural resources' cf. sec. 11.

19. A. C. Pigou, *The Economics of Welfare*, first edn., London 1920, II/vi/8.

However this celebrated passage surely much underemphasizes the problem, even for that date.

20. W. Nordhaus and J. Tobin, 'Is Growth Obsolete?' in *Economic Growth*, NBER, N.Y. 1972. Only deductions from the final product count, and then only those that have not already shown up in prices and quantities. Examples are the pollution of breathed air, and of water bathed in or drunk, landscape disfigurement, traffic slow-ups for private passenger vehicles. These examples are formulated so carefully because, for instance, Arctic air is not an amenity, an enterprise suffering from polluted water reports lower profits, and the slow-up of public vehicles *should* figure in the cost of living index. In addition natural resources are part of a nation's capital, and movements in that capital should figure in the national income. They should be defined as newly proved reserves minus depletion, a sum that is ordinarily positive (improvements to land and water figure in ordinary investment).

21. The primitive slash-and-burn agriculture, the Dark Ages deforestation of the Mediterranean litoral by goats, the Oklahoma dust-bowl of the 'thirties.

22. Cf. Marshall Goldman, *The Spoils of Progress: Environmental Pollution in the Soviet Union*, Harvard 1972.

23. *Genesis* 1/27–8. But atheistical ecologists should also bear in mind God's vision of His ultimately restored peaceable kingdom (*Isaiah* 11), and His assertion of His own transcendence over man vis-à-vis nature (*Job* 38–41.)

24. Exception must be made, as before, for the feelings of livestock.

25. For an excellent recent exposition cf. Stanislaw Gomulka, *Inventive Ability, Diffusion and the Stages of Economic Growth*, Aarhus 1971.

26. Indeed the high growth of STEs was discovered before the importance of the FPR was recognized: notably by myself, in a passage then famous but not now worth re-reading: *Foreign Affairs*, July 1953. My op. cit. 1962, chapter 13, is hardly an improvement.

27. For the two bad years 1962–3, which colour everyone's thinking, cf. Wiles 1969, pp. 112–22.

28. The Soviet virgin lands are an exception to this. They were admittedly ploughed up under conditions of grossly excessive cost and haste, but 25 years after USSR became an STE.

29. Especially in Czechoslovakia, as was made manifest in early 1968. Hungarian revisionists are more sober. The Chinese have not dared to revise doctrine, only behaviour.

30. There is no doubt at all that Marx took a Stalinist attitude to the market under socialism and, especially, full Communism. Cf. Wiles 1962, chapters 3, 17, 18.

31. Cf. Wiles 1962, chapter 11, which I here summarize and improve.

32. Cf. Benjamin Hirschman, *The Strategy of Economic Development*, New Haven 1958. Neither Hirschman nor I was aware of the other's work when we wrote these two arguments! It is perhaps better so, since they are completely distinct.

33. Agriculture is land-intensive, and takes place outside buildings; it tends also to be perfectly competitive. So the costs of concealment are not worth incurring (all this is separate from the point that small firms cannot afford R and D in the first place).

34. Wiles 1969, chapter 8. Cf. Thorstein Veblen, *The Instinct of Workmanship*, N.Y. 1914. It is ironical that, writing at this early date, Veblen held this instinct to be almost wholly good.

35. Cf. Eric Schiff, *Industrialization without National Patents*, N.J. 1971. Dutch industrial growth, however, was not less rapid than in other rich countries either during or after the patentless period. Dutchmen concentrated on trade, finance, land reclamation and imperialism, and took out few patents even abroad (pp. 36–8). The 1912 law certainly stimulated Dutchmen to take out foreign patents (p. 47), but this may well be only because the marginal cost of so doing is small to the holder of a home patent; the law cannot be shown to have stimulated inventiveness. On the contrary perhaps the lack of inventiveness made possible the patentless period.

36. But some licences are of a simpler and older sort, like Coca-Cola. This substance is kept a genuine secret from the licensee, and is delivered to him from a single central source. The reason is that it happens to be 'unimprovable'. On the slow decline of the patent under capitalism cf. Jacob Schmookler, *Invention and Economic Growth*, Harvard 1966.

37. General literature on the STE and technical progress: Jiri Slama and Heinrich Vogel in ed. Zbigniew Fallenbuchl, *Economic Efficiency versus Other Objectives* ..., 1976 (includes bibliography); ed. Stanley Wasowski, *East-West Trade and the Technology Gap*, N.Y. 1970.

38. The other large-scale importer of basic knowledge was Japan. She operated through Tokyo University, but merely by concentrating here a very substantial proportion of the total university grant. Thus competing acquisition was perfectly possible. But all Communist countries have been persuaded to imitate the Soviet Academy. It seems to have no parallel elsewhere any more.

39. Except for the foreign concessions during the NEP. See sec. 20.

40. Cf. Loren Graham in *Russian Review*, 2/1964.

41. We have no reason to think that Japanese or even US companies are less thievish than the Russians. Our obsession with Soviet theft has military origins. Also we dislike the role played by the KGB· why can't they use the decent business thieves, to whom we are accustomed? But of course the STE is both a state and a corporation: we must expect it to use its best specialists.

42. And much less of East European society. These social disadvantages are partly of pre-revolutionary Russian origin.

43. All the other STEs had signed before they went Communist, except China. Kuomintang China has also not signed. Thus the matter is largely historical, but the legacy of history showed a close ideological fit.

44. On the concessions and their systematic connexion with technology transfer, cf. the great but very prejudiced work of A. C. Sutton, *Western Technology and Soviet Economic Development, 1917–30*, Hoover Institution 1968.

45. See the journal *New Yugoslav Law*, Belgrade, January–September 1961, pp. 170–1; also ibid., January–September 1964, p. 86 (on the new patent offices); ibid., December 1963, p. 34 (bibliography); Stojan Pretnar in *Jugoslovenska Revija za Medjunarodno Pravo*, 2/1960 (in French).

46. In his *Patentovedenie*, Leningrad University 1972, p. 9.

47. These, then, are distinct from such 'procedures' (in Russian *sposoby*, above) as are considered to have world priority and be patentable.

48. Private workings of my own. The component data seem reasonably reliable and are almost all official. It is necessary only to guess land quality and the amount of fodder stolen from state and collective farms to feed private livestock.

16

The Distribution of Wealth

16

'If the laws do not oppose [equality], if they do not maintain monopolies, if they do not restrain trade and its exchanges, if they do not permit entails, large properties will be seen without effort, without revolutions, without shock, to subdivide themselves by little and little.'

Jeremy Bentham, *Principles of the Civil Code*
vol. i, chapter xii

1. The message of this chapter is that Bentham, whatever his influence in Chicago today, was quite wrong. One is reminded of Francis Place, who believed that the repeal of the Six Acts, which prohibited trade unions, would kill trade unions. The world is not so simple.

In this book 'wealth' means 'income and capital'. It is seldom necessary to reduce them to a common denominator (sec. 8). Resources are said to be *allocated* between categories of productive use while wealth is *distributed* between individuals or families. Capital is a stock of physical resources, plus documentary or monetary claims upon them. Barring foreign claims, all others cancel out inside a nation. In communes and in Full Communism there is no money, so there are only physical resources. Further, the distribution process is the last stage of the allocation process, and the distinction falls away.

Distribution was to an astonishing extent neglected by modern Western economics until very recently. Indeed its classical, Ricardian predecessor and its Marxist rival (so far as they can be distinguished) are almost equally sinners. For while both of these latter are fundamentally based on a distribution theory, both are merely about factor shares: a question so abstract and general that even a correct answer tells us virtually nothing about any particular person's income. Also, these two answers are wrong!

Modern Western theory also concentrates on the 'Ricardian' question of factor shares, and also utterly fails to explain the wealth of particular people. On the share of each individual factor-unit it is at least right, since each unit of labour, land and capital does indeed receive its marginal product.[1] But peasants own land, film-stars labour: what we want to know is who owns how many of each of these units, and why? The theory does not even pretend to explain why one individual is in a position to supply many units of skill and capital, another hardly any. And what about non-productive incomes like social services, capital gains and lottery winnings? The theory of marginal productivity at least avoids the fallacies of Ricardo and Marx, but it shares with them an obsession with the 'division of the product of industry' among its inputs, which is only a very small part of a total account of income distribution. Above all it does not tell us why a *family* is rich or poor; i.e. it does not cope with the laws and customs of inheritance, or with such demographic factors as who marries whom, and how many children they have, or with the biology of the inheritance of IQ.

2. The economist's fault has been to assume that there *is* a theory of income distribution. But there is not: there is only a theory of the valuation of productive services on a market. There is not, and there ought not to be, a theory of the distribution of the ownership of those services, or of transfer incomes. All that is a matter of economic and political history – three long words for which the single shorter one, 'chance', might be substituted without great loss.

For never was truer (or more often misquoted) word spoken than by Irving Fisher:[2] the distribution of wealth is due to the 'unequal forces of thrift, ability, industry, luck and fraud.' Also we inherit, not merely the tangible means of production – that applies only to capitalism – but consumer durables too. We also inherit Fisher's 'thrift and ability', health, education and the appropriate manners and turns of speech that make us acceptable or unacceptable for promotion. And of these ability and health are partly inherited through the genes.

So long as salaries are differentiated, and the institutions of the family and selective education continue, this remains true under socialism; for educated parents, as is notorious, do more to make their children intelligent and industrious than any school, public or private. Nay more, however seemingly egalitarian the school system, the loving and influential parent will get administrative exceptions made for his child irrespective of intelligence, as Soviet experience shows.

And beyond education stands the tremendous fact of nationality and location. This baby will be poor because it is Indian; that one will be rich because it is Canadian. Even within one country regional origins make vital differences: the baby born in Armagh may expect half as much income as the baby born in London. All this too, of course, is inheritance; but the word is no magic talisman and above all no theory. Coldly considered, 'inheritance' is yet another long word for 'chance'.

In line with this radical agnosticism, I propose no general theory of how wealth is distributed. I can only discuss theories of how it should be distributed, and specific empirical cases, *illustrating some* of the effects that *have accompanied* the economic systems of chief interest to us.

3. As to the normative theories, the medieval theologians made the basic distinction here: normative theories must aim at either *catallactic* or *distributive justice*. Catallactic refers to exchange: it implies that a *just*

price has been given and received in a particular transaction, by a product or a factor-unit. The theologians stumbled badly, however, in defining the just price: it must not include usury, it must be customary, it must not reflect temporary glut or scarcity, etc. These concepts jostled awkwardly with the nascent concept of opportunity cost (*lucrum cessans, damnum emergens*), and fatally obstructed the rational allocation of resources (the theory of which was unknown at that time). Indeed the notion of distributive justice was never really eradicated from the notion of the just price, so that the latter never really stood on its own feet.

Distributive justice meant of course that wealth was 'properly' distributed between people. 'Properly' entails under any economic system a value judgement. To the medieval mind it meant unequally, according to inherited status. Displeasing as that may be to the modern mind, we cannot claim that equality would be any better at all at reconciling catallactic with distributive justice. For *whatever* distribution is 'proper', there is no guarantee at all that just prices will perpetuate it, or unjust ones disturb it. For the just price is received by the unit factor of production, and there is as we have seen no distributive justice at all governing the number of units at the disposition of each person or family. In other words there is not merely a distinction, but an actual contradiction, between catallactic and distributive justice.

Perfect competition is hardly more egalitarian than any other market form. On the contrary we may well have to subsidize or protect an industry in order to maintain or attain a given distribution. In the relation of distributive inequality to degrees of competition three cases stand out. First as supply, demand and technology change labour must resort to all kinds of restrictive practices – which are catallactic injustice, since the employer no longer gets a fair day's work for a fair day's pay – in order to maintain its wages. Secondly monopoly, whether it is practised by inefficient village grocers or by vast corporations, has no predictable effect on distributive justice. It enriches a random group of capitalists, and since employees these days are normally unionized they quickly take their cut. It may enhance equality if these people were poorer than the averages of their classes. It may preserve some traditional income structure against the inroads of competition. And it may do the opposite of either or both these things. Thirdly however, the mere concentration of capital, without increase of monopoly, does increase inequality. For although capital is concentrated without decreasing the number of shareholders, mergers seldom occur without stock-watering and capital gains for those in the know – and that means people already rich. They also create a higher salary pyramid.

Looked at with a cold eye, justice in exchange is a very simple concept. Don't cheat and don't exploit monopoly power: that about sums it up. So the just price is little more than an honest and competitive price, if its sole content is justice in exchange. It will certainly tend also towards optimal resource allocation, provided that we distinguish marginal from average cost, but we need not pursue that here.

4. One way of linking the two kinds of justice was that of J. B. Clark:[3] to define distributive justice as the distribution of wealth resulting from competition in a perfect market. Marginal productivity, he said, represents a man's contribution to society; so is it not justice when he receives that much? 'Functional' productivity – that of a unit of a factor of production – is all, 'personal' productivity is neither here nor there. Socialism is theft from those whose personal productivity happens to be high, theft because it violates the natural law of paying for functions what they are worth.

We have already shown (sec. 1) that this is a disgraceful equivocation, since it begs the question why people are able to provide this or that factor-service. In other words distributive justice is defined as catallactic justice, and that is the end of the matter. We discuss below the various subterfuges whereby the belief is maintained that eventually *laissez-faire* will produce personal equality (sec. 9).

5. The extreme opposite solution is to demand complete equality, or at least only such inequality as arises out of differences in 'need', narrowly and physically defined. Much the easiest way to achieve this is to abolish the labour market and all private ownership and hand out a token income, or even a basket of goods in kind, to each citizen. This income is to be regarded as a social dividend, not a wage. Such is indeed the policy in all communes and from time to time in Communist countries (chapter 2, sec. 11, chapter 6, sec. 12, chapter 10, sec. 11).

In this system catallactic justice in its turn disappears: for exchange does not meaningfully take place within a commune. In particular the man who makes the most valuable inputs is underpaid. As to optimal resource allocation, which is so closely connected with catallactic justice, it is not a question to which the managers of communes are psychologically attuned. But there is no reason why labour, which in a commune is under such strict social control, should not receive a shadow scarcity price and be allocated accordingly, like capital. The equality of the social *dividend*, which is the essence of the commune, implies not so much an equal wage as a zero wage – just like the zero interest one assumes anyway.

But it is usually held (note the cautious phrasing) that perfect equality is bad for effort (sec. 20). Wage inequalities designed to elicit effort from a man already in a job are not the same as inequalities designed to move him into the job (chapter 10, sec. 11). The former alone might suffice, and even be regarded as compatible with a commune. It is the latter that presuppose a market, and really raise the allocation question. But the distinction is often blurred, as for instance when a man is asked to accept promotion within an enterprise.

Nor has the revisionist bloc abandoned its ultimate dedication to Full Communism. Rather does it defend its present policy, however long-lasting, as a transitional stage, and quote Marx's Critique of the Gotha Programme:[4]

> Despite this progress [sc. after the revolution] this 'equal right' is still subject to a bourgeois limitation. The right of the producers is *proportional* to their labour contributions: the equality consists in their being measured by an *equal measuring rod*. But one man is physically or mentally superior to another, so he supplies more labour in the same time, or can work for a longer time; and labour, to be a measuring rod, must be defined by its extent or intensity, or it will cease to measure. This equal right is an unequal right for unequal work. It recognizes no class differences, because everyone is only a worker like everyone else; but it tacitly recognizes the workers' unequal individual talent and so capacity to work as natural privileges... but the unequal individuals (and they would not be different individuals if they were not unequal) can only be measured on one scale in so far as... one looks at them *only as workers* and sees nothing more in them, abstracting from all else. Further: one worker is married, another not; one has more children than the other.... In order to avoid these defects the right must be not equal but unequal.
>
> But these defects are inevitable in the first phase of the communist society.... The right [law] can never be higher than the economic formation and the cultural development of society determined by it.
>
> In a higher phase of the communist society, after the enslaving subordination of the individual to the division of labour has disappeared, and with it the contrast of physical to mental labour; after work has become not only the means of living but the first need of the living person; after the all-round development of individuals has been accompanied by a growth of their productivity, and all sources of social wealth flow more copiously – only then can the narrow horizon of bourgeois right [law] be surpassed and society write on its banners: from each according to his capacity, to each according to his needs!

6. There is another, very different moderate policy: *populist egalitarianism.* In underdeveloped, mainly agricultural countries, where urban enterprises are also very small and the proletariat is insignificant, policies hostile to inheritance and private property have little chance, and government policy is directed towards equalizing private property. We examined the populist syndrome in general in chapter 5, sec. 16. But populism is essentially a policy or group of policies for distribution: to what measures does it lead?

The first and foremost is land reform. What the populist always and absolutely insists upon is the possession of a family farm. Note 'possession' not 'ownership': left-wing populists accept, even demand, 'public ownership' of land, whatever that means.[5] They are not theoreticians, and 'possession is nine points of the law' (cf. chapter 3, sec. 1). The object of their land reforms, then, is to establish family farms, in secure possession with a low mortgage and land tax. And this remains true even of left-wing populists who believe in some form of compulsory co-operation. For the family farm is not incompatible with, but actually in circumstances of land shortage demands, the co-operative principle of an upper limit to property. The Russian village community even periodically redistributed land among families, according to the changing number of 'mouths' in each. The co-operative is seen as a protective matrix for the family farm.[6] The high point of populist class-war, then, is the confiscation, no doubt with very low compensation, of large private land-holdings. But there is also much hostility to state land reserves and state farms.

The principle of an upper limit can be, and sometimes is, transferred to non-agriculture by populist governments. A notable case is the present Indian government's upper limit on urban property holdings. The Congress Party is more populist than 'socialistic', and uses the latter curious word because the former does not occur in the body of political theory the British left behind.[7] And when the British Labour Party legislates for leasehold enfranchisement, and allows owner-occupiers' mortgage interest to be deductible for income-tax purposes, we are bound to point out that protected private house-ownership is urban populism, and quite unsocialistic.[8]

In comparison with all other distribution policies the populist is healthy, practical and undoctrinaire. In particular it legislates directly for the nuclear family, which is in all social systems the relevant unit. Naturally it is easier to do so when the nuclear family is usually an independent enterprise. Secondly it aims at equality of capital not income, i.e. of opportunity not result. It does not protect the absolutely thriftless from current misfortune: it merely protects their children by rendering the property inalienable. Then again populism assumes incomes are mixed; and it is not squeamish about small amounts of unearned income or even sheer luck.

Roman Catholic social doctrine is very populist in the above sense, and both doctrines have relevance, if not to industrial, then to post-industrial societies. For where labour is mobile and independent and rich enough to save large sums there is no proletariat any more; and where substantial social services must be added the income of the nuclear family must be described as a mixed one. So the simple ideas of limiting inherited property and equalizing initial capital but not the resulting income regain interest, and validity.

7. Capital is not only physical objects, or pieces of paper certifying that

we own them or parts of them. Nor do we exhaust the concept by adding to it cash and the ownership of sheer debt. Capital can also be intangible. The first form of this is 'goodwill', the nexus of contact and acquaintance that a business builds up, and can sell apart from its physical assets. A doctor's practice, even a barrow-boy's pitch, is equally goodwill.

Then too there is the fact of being allowed to do something. Thus on the individual level a New York taxi-driver's 'shield', which certifies that he has the board's permission to ply that lucrative and restricted trade, is worth about $20,000. To be sure, he must also pass a test, but basically he buys permission from an outgoing taxi-driver, so permission is capital. On the corporate level 'permission capital' can be worth many millions; planning permission to build in London, licence to broadcast (with advertisements) on a given frequency. And beyond permission the mere fact of being organized already is capital. It is cheaper to buy the name of an existing company than to go through the legal process of founding a new one; so that many British property companies bear the names of Malayan rubber estates.

And all this is a mere *hors d'oeuvre* to the main course of intangible capital: *education*. We need not have any special view of education's contribution to national economic growth in order to admit its central importance in determining individual earned incomes.[9] It is clear that employers value a degree or diploma, and pay accordingly; whether because they are uneconomic snobs, or because higher education genuinely enhances productivity, or because a degree at least certifies its holder to be of originally superior natural intelligence, probably undiminished by schooling. Thus education is, amongst other things, capital yielding an income. The distribution of education is a part of the distribution of wealth. In the absence of public provision education is inherited, depending on one's parents' wealth and attitudes, and the genetical constitution they pass on.

The distribution of education is not so unequal as that of ordinary capital, since one must bring in hard work and talent of one's own, and these are not so unequally distributed as stocks and shares. Again it is physically impossible for any one person to accumulate, say, ten degrees; or to be both a Sumo wrestler and a ballet dancer. Indeed there are sharply diminishing returns to personal capital. Even a Ph.D., let alone two, made no man a millionaire. Or again more professional skills than, say three, can indeed be learned by a few, but 'practice makes perfect', and they cannot be fully exploited. Moreover the time taken to acquire the second skill reduces the time available for exploiting the first. But educational capital is still to a high degree 'inherited', in the loose sense that the children of skilled and educated parents are themselves skilled and educated out of all proportion. One's degree or school-leaving certificate does determine one's initial wage or salary, indeed on any ordinary definition it determines one's social class.

For the extent to which the public supply of education has mitigated inheritance, see sec. 13.

Education gives us knowledge that someone else already knew and was in the public domain. By *research and development* we acquire new knowledge, and in many social systems we are also entitled to keep it out of the public domain. On the extent and legitimacy of such practices compare chapter 15. We have only to note here the effect on the distribution of wealth. The new Soviet charges for R and D are mere resource allocators, ensuring that the right objects are researched and the costs thereof borne by the potential (public) beneficiary. Personal incomes vary only in so far as inventors get bonuses; and as enterprise profits vary and are in fact distributed.

How different are capitalist countries, where a thing can be privately patented and yield staggering sums. In the bad old days, when most inventors were individuals, the system of inheritable private patents was one of the greatest sources of inequality. But now the pace of new invention has drastically shortened each patent's life, and most belong to corporations or governments. The profitability of corporations has rather little effect on distribution between individuals (sec. 3); but this does not prevent licences and patents from fetching astronomical prices, and being the objects of espionage and theft. As to capitalist public sectors, they use more or less the Soviet system of awards to inventors.

Another important distinction for our purposes is between *personal and impersonal* capital. The former we define as embodied in a person: the natural bust measurement of the actress, the acrobat's trained ability on the trapeze, the graduate's degree. All tangible capital, on the other hand, is impersonal, and so are the intangibles of a freely transferable kind listed above.

Personal capital continues to flourish and to be unequally distributed under most forms of socialism. After all, it *cannot* be socialized, though particular systems might ensure that it yielded no income to its owner. Personal capital must of course be individual not corporate, except under slavery.

8. *Wealth* is the combination of income and capital, and the true subject-matter of this chapter. Strictly one could add income to capital according to mathematical formulae, converting the expected future stream of income and capital gain into present value by a rate of futurity and risk discount, and so arrive at an unambiguous notion of wealth. But the purposes of comparative economics would be ill served thereby, for from this view point many kinds of income and capital are quite essentially different from each other.

Capitalism provides many sophisticated institutions for converting some incomes into capital and vice versa. A lump sum paid to an insurance company buys an annuity – and bedevils the tax-collector. The stock exchange capitalizes future income-streams from property. But while identical formulae could capitalize future income-streams from labour, including labour mixed with personal capital, in the market the practice is frowned on. Primitive capitalism did indeed provide the requisite institution: the *indenture*. But slavery grew out of indentures and gave them a bad name (chapter 8). So legal insecurity prevents the capitalization of labour income, and it remains merely a statistical device, notably among education economists.

It is therefore certainly open to a private person to count his own wealth by means of these devices. But even so they are very misleading. For the discounting process must take account of the fact that capital, including personal capital, however risky its own prospects, enables one to take higher risks, both with one's capital and with one's labour. It also confers, especially if it is equity capital in sufficient quantity, legal power; – and illegal power, for a capitalist can corrupt the government with a bribe of a different order of magnitude from the peanuts he could spare out of even a large income. Inheritance again is easy with impersonal capital, while it is an uncertain and difficult process to pass on a job. One can, it is true, build up personal capital in one's heir; indeed this is very common and explains much of higher education. But this capital is useless if he is ill or idle, and in any case quite illiquid, since the heir cannot be sold.

Under Communism wealth is much more nearly equal to income alone: but consumer durables and education persist, as we shall see. The only institution that converts income into capital or vice versa is the state insurance company. Sophistication in this area is frowned upon.

We shall therefore continue to be naïf, and speak separately of the distribution of income, personal and impersonal capital, and capital gains.

9. We may now proceed to actual cases. First, in an ACE the prime distributor of capital is inheritance. Yet this must not be exaggerated. Probably only 46 per cent of the existing stock of private tangible capital is due to inheritance and 13 per cent to savings out of current unearned income.[10] The rest has been saved out of earned income by people still alive. It is, then, a fact with substantial political consequences that 41 per cent of all private capital should have been saved out of earnings, and be still in the hands of the original savers (20 per cent more if we count widows, as we surely should). No doubt, too, we must add to 'justified private capital' the savings that people make out of the unearned income their inheritance yields. To the ordinary person, what he inherits is merely what he inherits, and the savings he makes out of the income it yields are to be counted to him for virtue. If we include such savings, the proportion of 'justified' private property rises, as we have seen, to about 74 per cent (100−46+20). 'Justification' here is to be understood in a

Lockean sense, as property being the product of one's own labour or savings.

But the great fallacy in this reasoning is to assume that earned income itself is independent of inheritance. For personal capital is, as we have seen, the gift of parents who can bestow it. Therefore, though more equally distributed, it is still inherited and still a source of inequality. Statistical evidence for this fact will be found in every sociological textbook, and need not here be repeated. The reasons for it are many and varied, and we shall confine ourselves to listing them uncritically:

(i) parents with much personal capital earn a lot, so can afford the fees and – above all – maintenance for their children while they are accumulating theirs;

(ii) intelligence is in part genetically inherited (sec. 10 here). Intelligence is a sine qua non for the accumulation of personal capital. Therefore those who have such capital tend to have children who can get it;

(iii) parents with personal capital can almost always accumulate or marry impersonal capital. This helps their children's finances;

(iv) parental example and pressure, and a quiet study room at home, are indispensable to forming in the child the all-important *will* to be educated;

(v) parents with good jobs can obtain through influence the superior schooling that it is very often impossible to buy;

(vi) such parents also get their children slightly better jobs than their talents and education warrant.

Were inheritance the only major determinant,[11] and in particular were there no redistributive taxes, wealth under capitalism would become ever more unequally distributed, without assignable end. The conditions required for this are that the rich should (a) have no more children than the poor, (b) save a higher proportion of their income, (c) get higher returns on their capital, (d) be not less competent, (e) have easier access, through education, nepotism or whatever, to high earnings, and (f) like to leave wealth to their children, not holding the only goal of saving to be personal consumption. It is further necessary that (g) the yield on capital not secularly fall.

It is not obvious that all these conditions hold, but they do in fact. If they do, we need no model to demonstrate our gloomy conclusions.[12] Condition (a) is notoriously true; (c) is demonstrated by Meade,[13] (e) is, as we have just seen, as staple proposition in sociology. It is a particularly scandalous defect of most economic models to neglect this point.

The other points merit our attention now. As to (d) the case of incompetence is that a particular rich man has a son with lower earnings than himself. But that son would have capital enough to ensure for his son a fair chance of acquiring again his grandfather's earnings. Indeed even in the interregnum of the incompetent heir the family's capital would probably increase; though at a lower rate than for many poor families – for the thrifty and competent poor, with fortunes much smaller than their annual incomes, are able to increase the former very rapidly indeed. But the incompetent are not black sheep: they still earn a fair amount and are in a far better position to save than the average poor. Again it has been argued that spendthrifts (as opposed to incompetents) occur after three generations or so in all very rich families. The damage they can do is indeed such as no one generation of thrift can restore, so they reduce the inequality of wealth. But do they, indeed do incompetents, occur less often near the bottom? How many proletarian spendthrifts end up on skid row, thereby increasing inequality again? How much *does* a rich spendthrift succeed in getting rid of, what with trusts and entails? Is not the effect of mere incompetence on a small fortune quite disastrous? The incidence of these accidents has to be shown to be biassed against the rich, rather than, as one might suppose, against the poor. No such demonstration has ever been offered. 'Clogs to clogs, three generations' is mere wishful thinking. It helps us, rich and poor alike, to believe we live in a mobile society.

Then as to condition (b) Meade insists (op. cit., p. 43) that capital has a big negative influence on saving, so that the accumulation of capital has an internal braking mechanism. But even if true this is quite irrelevant to inter-class comparisons. For in fact the rich always have more capital *and* more income than the poor, and always save more out of their incomes. No doubt the rich who have high salaries and low capital save more than other kinds of rich. No doubt high saving or capital gains in one year lower saving out of the same income in the next year, among both individuals and nations.[14] But none of this touches the simple fact that most rich people save more out of income than the poor.[15] They also increase their capital more rapidly over a life-time.[16]

Condition (f) is very simply established – by reading a newspaper. Yet the very fact of bequest has been assumed away by distinguished economists.[17]

To discuss condition (g) with the thoroughness it deserves would take us too far afield. We need only repeat our assertion in sec. 1 that the rate of profit did not fall until recently for fully a century, perhaps two centuries. It is however just possible that the recent world-wide cost inflation has permanently diminished it, at least in Britain (sec. 12 below).

To him that hath, then, shall be given, and these results are far gloomier, not only than those of authors with an obvious *laissez-faire* bias, but also than Meade's. The main reason seems to be that my actual data take explicit account of retirement, while his theoretical data do not.[18]

10. If furthermore we recognize – as we surely should[19] – the role of

genetical inheritance nothing is altered. For genetically inherited talent under capitalism (and socialism) brings wealth and social promotion, in just the same way as education and a good home. Moreover mating is assortative. So the old rich, who being descended from nouveaux riches can hardly have been born stupid, marry either each other or the nouveaux riches, who cannot possibly be stupid; and a gene pool of the best talent accumulates at the top. Even if society is very democratic, and mating is not assortative by wealth, still only the talented catch the rich. For people compete for them: adventurers, young employees who marry the boss's daughter, adventuresses are all intelligent. Marriages of two graduate students are on the increase; they produce, statistics show, many children of genius level. But their parents will soon be rich – if they are not so already. The intelligent marry, or have children by, the intelligent, if not the rich – or both.

The size of the family, and the decline of primogeniture, make little difference. In most advanced countries contraception has worked its way through to the bottom, and family size is no longer widely different from top to bottom. Primogeniture was never all that widespread, and the habit of equal division among children, or among male children, does virtually nothing to move property across the boundaries of social classes or even statistically defined percentiles of the population,[20] for it is cancelled out by assortative mating.

11. This gloomy picture of perpetual and automatic polarization has been falsified under advanced capitalism by three things: autonomous, market-induced shifts in the 'Ricardian' distribution, public education and progressive taxation. The first of the Ricardian influences is the increased demand for skill. The supply of skill is determined by genes and education: the one a fixed natural resource and the other costly. So as advancing productive techniques and more sophisticated consumer tastes have demanded more skilled workers they have very simply commanded higher wages. The supply of and demand for labour have filled the middle ground that the inheritance of capital has tended to empty.

There was nothing inevitable about this. Changing taste and advancing technology might have increased the demand for morons, indeed in some areas they have. Thus the comptometer operator is less skilled than the accounts clerk she replaces, the chauffeur is less skilled than the coachman. I only assert that elementary education has so much expanded as to lower the literacy premium that, say, the printer could once command, even though more highly skilled labour has in fact been the general result of economic development, and that simultaneously the yield on a capital-year has fallen relatively to the yield on a labour-year.

The market, that is, decrees wages that correspond to the scarcities of the various types of labour. It would be a fantastic chance indeed that made all these wages equal: there *must* be inequality in a market. But there is no law that says inequality will either rise or fall as a result of the historical operation of supply and demand, as techniques advance.

12. But other long-term 'Ricardian' shifts occur, and are rather mysterious. Thus in Britain there have been very large movements indeed.[21]

The share of corporate profits in corporate value added fell precipitately during the first World War, from 23·5 per cent to 17·1 per cent. It remained at about this level until after the great slump, when it rose to 19·2 per cent in 1935–8. It remained at this level until 1969, when the great cost inflation further depressed it by about 5 per cent of the national income before tax. Although reduced corporate taxes and increased corporate subsidies approximately restored this 5 per cent after tax, the yield on capital as opposed to its share in value added has fallen from a steady 13–15 per cent in 1956–65 to under 10 per cent in 1970–2. And this cannot be explained by any movement in capital-intensity, nor, surely, by those curious macro-economic, ex post, two-sector elasticities of substitution that high growth theory has made fashionable.[22]

This fall in the yield of capital employed is very striking. It is not all. It was preceded by a remarkable event in the replacement-accountancy-yield of bonds. We are allegedly accustomed to interest varying between 3 and 6 per cent. It has taken twenty years for the concept of the real rate of interest to sink in: for twenty years it has been about zero, and it is now (1974) negative! Yet all this time elements of private monopoly, legal restriction (such as the rules for trustee securities) and sheer idiotic habit (banks, insurance companies) have provided a market for bonds. As to dividends, there used before the second World War to be a *customary* rate of corporate profit retention. The war altered this by legally freezing dividends: what force operated to restore the old position when the law was repealed? The answer is that for many years there was no force: the law had established a new custom. A genuine market force has eventually emerged in the takeover bid, but it is not a strong one. The corporate payout ratio has indeed responded to it, but not much, and does not look as if it will ever rise to pre-war levels.[23]

It may be asked how, without a revolution, such large changes in factor-shares could come about. The first answer is that fighting a major war, even when it is won and the country is not invaded, is a virtual revolution. Changes otherwise impossible become easy, are indeed made unconsciously. The freezing of dividends and farm and house rents during the second World War was very redistributive, the high guaranteed farm prices originated in the submarine threat, and salaries would not have lagged so far behind wages in peacetime without violence. It is particularly notable that corporate profit ratios fell strikingly in the first World War in UK, USA and Germany, but not in neutral Sweden.[24]

But why did not the market re-establish the ancient state of affairs? First, after the second war, a few controls remained, notably on rents, and were not ineffective. But the broad answer is that both the old and the new states were the product of chance, not economics. Earned and unearned income belong to 'non-competing groups'.[25] High salaries, low salaries, wages and farmers' earnings each belong to non-competing groups. Depress the macro-share of one such group, and the individuals composing it, being as a whole in inelastic supply, will simply accept relatively lower real awards. The marginal members who switch are very few, even when young. Their individual relative rewards are still determined by marginal productivity: their group as a whole, however, has lost a monopoly, received a negative windfall or whatever.

Britain is now undergoing a remarkable redistribution within the factor labour, with wages gaining on high salaries very rapidly. This is very obviously due to the new monopolistic militance of trade unions, and the connivance of an unusually left-wing government. Neglecting equal pay for women – another non-market phenomenon – the inequality of one union with another has not greatly fallen. It is the high salary that has lost, relatively and absolutely, before and after tax. Higher civil servants and doctors have better resisted this trend, being better unionized. But one does not see much tendency of the market to 'correct' these changes by individual seepage. Rather to the contrary, the large groups concerned go up and down and retain their individual members.

Again, almost no change, and certainly no likely or actual change, in the interest-wage ratio, beloved of simplistic growth-and-distribution modellists, will render the economy actually more or less capital-intensive, for in normal technological calculations interest is too trivial a cost. It is ineffective as a substituter between macro-categories. It is the relation between wages and machinery or building prices, not interest, that mostly determines capital-intensity (and this of course varies mainly with productivity in those particular industries). But changes in this particular relation are not obviously or strongly related to the Ricardian distribution. Capital competes with capital and labour – within certain categories – with labour. Economics tells us the detailed conditions of supply only. The supply price of the macro-categories, and therefore the Ricardian distribution, is a matter of economic history. And that, as we have seen, is an impressive phrase meaning chance. The continued output of two-factor models is a tragic waste of brainpower.

I am therefore far from denying the importance for individual distribution of large Ricardian shifts, or of the market at a more detailed level. I simply maintain that abstract theory cannot explain these shifts, and that in any case other forces – most of them quite foreign to traditional economics – are considerably more important. It follows that each ACE must be studied on its own. We have only space for Britain here.

13. This leaves the role of the capitalist government. Take first public education. Free primary and secondary education *redistribute produc-*

tivity; but not necessarily income, since in general the parents of the promoted child do not gain, and the child's gain is offset by the loss of the child he displaces. Thus if, in the extreme case, the skill structure of jobs on offer remains constant in face of larger and more egalitarian supply, the promoted children become rich and other children, cheated of their expectations, become poor. Since the displaced children will probably inherit impersonal capital, this still equalizes incomes in a small way. Public education continually breaks the link between impersonal (largely inherited) capital and personal capital by subsidizing the build-up of the latter out of public funds. But this is what we call equality of opportunity, and not equality of result. Socially it is of the greatest importance; it may even outrank egalitarianism. It is also something that all but the poorest countries have long had in large measure.

So a mere increase in the equality of opportunity, *ceteris paribus*, is not a very strong equalizer in strict statistical terms. Moreover, we have not yet considered the effect on parents. 'Free' compulsory education still imposes great costs on a poor family, in child maintenance, earnings forgone, and perhaps school equipment. Free but voluntary access to universities is thus not so very egalitarian in any sense, since poor families do balk at the continued maintenance of their children. This problem reproduces itself precisely under Communism. It would seem to follow that as a degree becomes more and more necessary, at least in employers' eyes, public 'free' higher education will cease to equalize incomes or even opportunities, unless there are also maintenance grants for the last two years of secondary education. For the poor, even in rich countries, will hold themselves unable to afford it.

Now suppose that, as is much more normal, the skill and pay structure offered by employers adjusts itself to new patterns of supply. While there remains a pool of uncultivated talent generous public education increases competition at the top and brings down the highest salaries. So it acts to equalize until the pool runs dry, whosever children were in it. At that point the skill pattern of the labour supply becomes stable and equalization stops unless other reasons now induce employers to offer a still more equal skill and pay structure of jobs. We saw above that technology is unpredictable in this respect: it may for all we know be fighting for inequality.[26]

Thus public education is a very uncertain equalizer. There can be no doubt that taxes, subsidies and confiscation are a great deal more effective.

14. Now turning to the other social services, when the capitalist state began to help the poor it tried on the whole to strengthen their position as factor-suppliers on the market: legalizing trade unions, setting minimum wages. Since, to repeat, family incomes are not the same as individuals' wages this 'Ricardian' method was extremely inefficient at

relieving poverty. Indeed it tended to create an under-class of unemployables, who could otherwise have got some work but were not worth employing at the official minimum, and could not afford trade-union dues. 'The minimum wage', as they say in USA, 'is objectively an anti-Negro device.'

So various kinds of social income were added: housing subsidies and insurance schemes against unemployment, sickness, old age, death, maternity and children. In form most of these schemes are compulsory 'horizontal' redistribution: people within a given life-time status are forced to subsidize their ilk who undergo a specified misfortune. The strictly 'vertical' elements are the high minimum benefits, disproportionate to the lowest life-time incomes, and the state subsidy to make the accounts balance. Quite often this element was 100 per cent, i.e. there were no insurance contributions at all. Since all tax systems are progressive, at least at the very top and the very bottom, the presence of a state subsidy makes the schemes progressive, i.e. redistributes 'vertically' between types of life-cycle. Very often, too, a charge would be levied on the employer; but since he treated this as an indirect tax, to be added to prices, it is not obvious that this was a further element of progression.

Pure 'national assistance' or 'relief' – discretionary payments to very poor people as such, and not as an insured right – is much older than capitalism. It is, of course, more fiscally progressive than most of the newer schemes. Other old public expenditures are distributively neutral, like weapons and army pay, or even regressive like the service of the national debt.

Many have been far too impressed by the fact that four favourite modern expenditures are neutral or regressive. These are, first, on higher education – for which mainly middle-class children qualify, whatever the intentions of the state; and secondly on research and development – which raise the salaries of the intelligentsia, but scatter their other benefits at random. Even our road expenditures today are regressive. For the urban throughway goes characteristically through slum areas, so that the rich landlords receive the compensation while the poor tenants have to move; and the motor-cars thus favoured carry the rich. This was hardly true of nineteenth-century traffic improvements.

Agricultural subsidies, again, in so far as they really benefit farmers not shoppers, are normally thought to be regressive, because such large sums go to the richest farmers. But this is not true in proportional terms at all, since the subsidy is often the sole income of the poorest farmer. We are revolted by the incidence of these subsidies because if each farm is a family farm unequal parts of the subsidy will accrue to each family, which is broadly untrue of limited companies. But if for any reason we subsidize production, not poverty, we must take the distributive consequences. Indeed universities, roads and farms have other functions than the provision of social justice, and these remarks are factual, not critical. On balance public expenditures remain highly progressive. Moreover, and above all, taxation has become much more progressive, all loopholes notwithstanding. The undeniable fact that the net effect of a capitalist government's taxing and spending is progressive has been so often questioned in this cynical age that a whole school of quasi-scientific disbelief has grown up. This school's writings do not survive examination, since they rely heavily on the following fallacies:

(i) particular taxes and expenditure are examined alone, instead of all together;

(ii) it is even hinted that no single item should be regressive or neutral – as if the sole obligation of government were to redistribute wealth, and it had not also to provide certain services, moreover to provide them efficiently;

(iii) the effects on the extremely rich and poor are hidden by using too large income brackets. But it is in fact with the top 5 per cent and the bottom 10 per cent that the progression is so noticeable. The intervening 85 per cent are indeed not much equalized by government – nor is it clear why they should be;

(iv) loopholes and anomalies are pointed to but not quantified.

15. Note that the capitalist government operates mainly on the distribution of net income. Minimum wages, etc., are far the smaller part of its total armoury, and the less efficient too: being apt to backfire unpleasantly by enlarging the class of unemployables. Quite often, at the other end of the scale, public servants' salaries are held down as an anti-inflationary device, or even – in the case of the boards of British nationalized industries – on socialist principles. This also backfires, in that good people are lost to the private sector, efficiency falls, there are bitter strikes, etc.[27] Progressive taxes and expenditures are by far the most effective redistributive methods of a capitalist government.

What has been the net result in advanced capitalist countries of these (on the whole progressive) government measures and the other (mostly regressive) forces at work? First take the rich end of the scale. The fantastic multi-millionaires of 1870–1914 have certainly disappeared – from view; but have they disappeared from the earth? Our statistics are so bad in all countries, so shot through with private evasion and official tolerance, that we have no sure way of knowing. The large landed estates, the private, personal business empires, and Veblen's conspicuously consuming leisure class, are gone. But land is too easy to tax, a fainéant shareholder can be as rich as the founding tycoon, and truly massive consumption is easily possible away from envious eyes. Moreover there has been mass migration to small islands that make tax evasion their principal export.

It has *probably* become more difficult to get very rich, or even merely to stay very rich. It has certainly become impossible to do so honestly.

The poor on the other hand have very obviously been helped. The various social services do in fact protect them against the designated disasters, and the long-run tendency is to administer these services more generously. The upshot would appear to have been a certain closure at both ends, but not much net change in the middle. 'Middle' is here understood to include at least 85 per cent of the people.

16. The *Soviet-type economy* is different in every respect. First comes the undeniable fact of revolution, which is an enormous equalizing movement in the Ricardian distribution. To repeat, I am by no means hostile to Ricardian explanations – where they really explain. For Communist revolution sharply reduces or abolishes the following:

(i) dividends – abolished;

(ii) interest from productive enterprises – now paid only to Gosbank (on short loans, ever since NEP began) and to the Ministry of Finance (on long loans, since 1965: but called a capital tax);

(iii) interest on national debt – reduced to interest on personal savings accounts. These savings are automatically lent to the government, and along with withdrawals figure, gross, on both sides of the budget;

(iv) rent of land – abolished. The result is that what would be agricultural rents accrue to collective farms and are paid out, *inter alios*, to collective farmers. The compulsory deliveries of crops to the state, even when they were at very low prices, are never arranged so as to substitute for rents;

(v) rent of house room. Since two thirds or more of town housing, and most state farm housing, belongs to enterprises or municipalities most rent is paid to the state. It is so notoriously low largely not because of a subsidy but because there is no interest (see (ii) above). Interest accounts for about one half of a capitalist house rent. But private housing (nearly all collective farm housing is private, and much other housing besides) can be let, and state housing can be sublet – for what the market will bear. Much new housing nowadays (and also in the late 'thirties) is co-operative. This pays a full interest charge, and in addition fails to qualify for whatever subsidy there is;

(vi) wages, salaries, fees and commissions from private employers – abolished except in the service sector (for according to Marx exploitation is confined to material production). This leaves rather substantial opportunities for side-earnings, especially in medicine, education, repairs and domestic service, and even enables a few to live without 'proper' jobs. Prices are settled by the market. Such incomes, however, attract a very heavy rate of income tax (if they are ever declared);

(vii) income from individual material production – discriminated against. The income tax is very high, and raw materials so difficult to buy that theft is extremely common. However about one third of global agricultural output is on this system, from the large private plots of collective farmers and the smaller ones of state farmers and townsmen. Prices are settled by the market. One may only employ one's own nuclear family on the job, lest there be Marxian exploitation.

But inheritance is, most surprisingly, free and untaxed. The idea seems to be that once all capitalist property has been confiscated only such property remains as is not the fruit of exploitation: consumer goods, savings accounts and the tools of individual labour. And whatever is saved is saved after tax, out of incomes permitted by the socialist state. So it happens that art collections, private houses, savings accounts, jewellery, libraries, durables, cash, even claims on the royalties of best-sellers pass freely down. Certainly this is most illogical, and dangerous to equality in principle. But in practice without items (i) to (iv) the danger is small. No doubt the inheritance of education, a thing inevitable while the nuclear family is allowed, has far greater consequences.

I reckon, very tentatively, the income confiscated under (i) to (v) above to have been 20 per cent of the Soviet national income. Most of it went to the profits of state enterprises, i.e. effectually into budgetary revenue; but some of the rent accrued to the peasants.[28]

As to earnings in the socialist sector, the STE has every power to control gross earnings, so sees no need for redistributive taxation. Now strictly this is a non-sequitur. For labour is seldom directed and so must get a scarcity wage for every kind of skill, with full allowance for unpleasant locations and working conditions. But the centre's monopsonistic powers cannot, in the nature of things, be fully exercised. There has to be some decentralization, so an enterprise might be willing to pay, in competition with others, a greater scarcity premium than the minimum necessary to a true monopsonist. Thus unintended inequality, and doubtless sometimes equality, are generated. At the other end of the scale the scarcity wage of an unskilled man may be below subsistence. But here at least a simple solution has been found: enterprises are compelled by the plan to employ unnecessary numbers of unskilled and juveniles at a minimum wage. This is the Soviet-type full employment policy discussed in chapter 14.

So what with one thing and another, there is in fact no redistributive taxation. The highest marginal rate of income tax on earnings in the socialized sector is 13 per cent in USSR, and zero in Hungary. The turnover tax is, as we have seen, a way of establishing ex post a market equilibrium for whatever the planners happen to have ordered to be produced. It is scarcely used at all for redistributive purposes, even though it would be so easy to manipulate in this way. True, black bread and children's shoes and clothing are cheap, but the other objects favoured with low tax rates are 'cultural', not 'poor men's', goods.

Wages are of course the easiest part of family income to operate upon, and there have been conscious drives to widen or narrow the spread of wages. The succession of such periods in USSR corresponds to great ideological reversals at the highest level.

Thus under 'War' Communism there was virtually complete equality; the whole country was supposed to be a single commune. But the NEP re-established scarcity wages, with the result that by 1928, after seven years of virtual *laissez-faire*, industrial wages were about as well spread out as in USA that year. Then in the first FYP Stalin imposed further inequality, appealing to the necessity of incentives for development and to Marx's distinction between the first and second post-revolutionary stages, reproduced above. Too many economic historians have unthinkingly accepted his judgement in this as in other matters: was the fool who collectivized agriculture bound to be right about incentives? Was further inequality, greater than that known in the West, an obvious necessity? And why was the increase of inequality during the first FYP not enough? Why did the trend accelerate during the second FYP? Above all, how has Eastern Europe managed to develop as quickly, but with much more equality throughout?

From 1947 to 1954 retail prices were reduced (chapter 14, sec. 6); i.e. the growth in real resources was not used to redistribute incomes. But from 1955 Khrushchev did so use it, raising minimum wages very substantially, and even cutting some top salaries.[29] Economic performance has not evidently suffered from this, and I am tempted to assert that Stalin went far beyond the optimal degree of inequality, wasting resources and creating injustice in this as in so much else. Less controversial is the demonstration of Soviet power: the state *does* control the distribution of gross income, in a way no democratic government can.

The social services are also subtly different in a STE. First they bulk larger: perhaps 30 per cent of an urban income as opposed to 15 per cent in a capitalist welfare state (chapter 21, sec. 13). But secondly they are not particularly redistributive, for the same reason as taxation: gross incomes are held to be just in the first place. So many items like paid holidays and pensions are formally linked to wages, and others like medical care have a strong informal link. We may put the same point in a different way: these are not social services open to all citizens, since (especially in USSR, less so in other STEs) peasants and even non-trade-union-members are discriminated against, but fringe benefits for the employees of the single socialist enterprise. Indeed how could they be otherwise, if trade unions administer them?

Perhaps the writer's surprise at this inegalitarianism – which must not in any case be exaggerated – is specifically British. In many capitalist countries the social services redistribute 'horizontally' not 'vertically' (cf. sec. 14). It is perhaps only British to insist that social services be rigidly egalitarian (i.e. vertical): a harbinger of the total socialism to come that remains very much a part of the Labour Movement's hazy vision.

17. Inequality of wealth in Soviet-type agriculture has had ups and downs hidden from the statistician and inexplicable by the economist. The land reform of 1917, virtually the Bolsheviks' first act, permitted an anarchic seizure of state, church and noble lands by 'the tillers of the soil'. In the prevailing chaos populist conceptions dominated, so the kulaks also benefited in full measure. Thus the reform was not re-distributive among peasants – as have been all subsequent land reforms in Communist countries, owing to the firmer hand of the government. In the Soviet case there was not even an upper limit to peasant holdings.[30] Thus in the NEP agriculture was nearly all private peasants, obeying the ordinary 'laws' of capitalist distribution with one exception: they paid no rent to the landlords, the corporations or the state, and very little to each other (for even inter-peasant renting was discouraged).

It is difficult to say how this affected distribution: possibly it benefited the rich, since they no longer paid rent outside the village, but not the poor, since if land could not be rented to them by the rich they had to hire out their labour instead.

Thus the effect of the Soviet revolution up to 1928, quite unlike that of other Communist revolutions, was highly capricious. About collectivizations we may be more dogmatically general. The kulaks are driven out and utterly impoverished, and a new agricultural bureaucracy and technocracy occupies the positions on the income scale they vacate. The middle and poor peasants are collectivized, so their land, livestock and tool holdings are equalized.[31] Moreover they gain from the fact that the kulaks' land, livestock and tools are confiscated by the farm. But each of them is still paid personally for the work he puts in, by the hour and according to skill (chapter 6). So the individual inequalities of labour remuneration in these classes largely persist.

While the net result of all this is probably more equality on the farm it is not certain. Also new differentiation occurs when, as efficiency dictates, small permanent sub-units (links, chapter 6) are formed with special working privileges. Meanwhile just off the farm there grow up yet other privileged groups: specialists, machine repairers – under Stalin even machine operators were not farm members. These are all paid higher, 'socialist' incomes. And finally collectivization lowers the position of the farm in the national scale, because productivity falls and compulsory delivery prices lag behind other prices.

This lag requires explanation. A primary reason for collectivization, as we saw in chapter 5, sec. 13, is to ensure food deliveries in 'reasonable' quantities and at 'reasonable' prices for the towns and for export. These prices are normally fixed, like the rents of controlled houses under capitalism, at the market value at the moment of change. But like other important publicly fixed prices they cannot easily be altered, and meanwhile even in an STE inflation pursues its gay way (chapter 14). Now the private and the collectivized peasant alike live off the net revenue of their enterprise. So the compulsory delivery price, which seems to the Soviet-type government merely one rigid wholesale price among others, has in fact the distinction of distributing income; its rigidity in the face of inflation impoverishes the peasant.

Khrushchev understood this well, raising the compulsory delivery prices to very favourable levels in the late 'fifties.[32] This was a very great event, a veritable Soviet War On Poverty. The East European STEs have all been far more generous to the peasant from the start, and have imitated the Khrushchevian reforms as well. But within-class inequalities seem to be quite big.

However a more radical change is the recent drive, or series of drives, to nationalize, or 'sovkhozize', the collective farm. For in a state farm, as in any other Soviet-type state enterprise, the worker (no longer a peasant) gets a state-guaranteed wage, to which the wholesale price of his product is no more relevant than that of steel to a steel-worker. If necessary the state farm is subsidized. Indeed it normally is (chapter 5, sec. 14).

18. The state-farmer's wage, then, is very much more *stable* than the collective farmer's 'dividend'. It is also very much more *equal*, in that the similar relative income structures on good and bad farms are brought to the same absolute average. That is, the bad farm is subsidized and the good one must either plough back profit or pay it away in tax.[33]

We have here a large general proposition about equality that has no special connexion with agriculture or socialism: *the wage system is a great equalizer* compared with the family business and the co-op. Moreover this applies under capitalism, for there too there are centralizing forces enough: minimum wage laws and trade unions.

We may *illustrate* this proposition with two cases out of very many:

I→II: private peasants are converted into state farmers for ideological reasons, no profit being generated by technical progress or the economies of scale;
I→III: private peasants are converted into landless proletarians by the capitalist system, there being technical progress, economies of scale and new profit.
Small letters indicate individual peasants. They are arranged in alphabetical order of both efficiency and wealth, which are assumed to go together (p. 441).

In both cases the peasants go over to wages more or less suited to their skill. Now it is an important general property of wages that they reward time spent, or at least have a strong tendency to do so. So they cannot reflect every nuance of skill, effort and luck in the way peasant incomes do, and the proportion a/j is automatically diminished. Earned incomes, then, are 'equalized', in one important sense of that peculiar word,[34] in both cases.

I	II		III	
private peasants, mixed incomes	peasants become state farmers		peasants become landless proletarians	
	wage	profit	wage	profit
(a) (b)	skilled	profits lost	skilled	become credit
(c) (d)	semi-skilled	nil	semi-skilled	nil
(e) (f)				
(g) (h) (i) (j)	unskilled	losses written off	unskilled	become debt
	all existing profit or loss goes to the state, so the debts of the poor and the credits of the rich are cancelled. There is no change in the total.		all existing profit or loss is converted into fixed debt or credit borne by the individual. The new capitalist firm takes the extra profit due to technical progress or economies of scale.	

In case I→II a socialist state confiscates private property and its contribution to income. Since probably the skilled have most property and the unskilled are actually in debt, this is strongly equalizing. In case I→III credits and debts are preserved, since the entry into the capitalist farm is a voluntary market process, and the peasant sells his capital. But ordinarily the peasants' private property will have depreciated first, by the competition of the more efficient farm. So they enter their new status trailing a property inequality, and mostly in debt. Moreover the profit from the technical progress goes to the new corporation's owner or owners – who are almost certain to have been richer than any peasant in the first place.

This whole analysis also applies to small shopkeepers and craftsmen. It remains valid if a, b, c . . . are whole collective farms. This is an important case for the classical STE, since collectivization imposes no direct and expensive responsibility on the state for agricultural incomes like 'sovkhozization'. Poor kolkhozy get into debt like poor peasants – and sometimes enjoy similar debt forgiveness when the new king ascends the throne.

Again there have been very embarrassing results in the event that there were, in case I→III, economies of scale but unskilled-labour-intensive technical progress. Mostly, when faced with this embarrassing combination (tobacco, cotton, sugar) capitalism has reacted by imposing slavery. It is worth repeating that this sort of analysis is by no means exhausted by the two examples we have chosen as *Idealtypen*.

The wage system has also a very great interregional effect. Regional wage differences are psychologically intolerable to workers and trade unions, and it requires a very special government to defend them. Such governments existed in the southern states of USA for a long time, when the central government was still truly federal. They stood out successfully against trade unions, and attracted a lot of industry. They thus contributed a lot to the remarkable equalization of regions that characterizes USA. More centralized ACEs cannot resist trade-union pressures, so their poor regions can no longer be helped by market processes. The STE on the other hand forces enterprises to employ people at the nationally uniform wage rates. There remain substantial interregional inequalities of income per head in STEs, and they are due mainly to the kolkhoz system (i.e. to the non-introduction of wages) and to culturally determined variations in family size.

19. We have now discussed the distribution of all kinds of wealth but one: that awkward but vigorous hybrid the capital gain. This is essentially a difference between purchase price and sale price caused by fluctuations on the market that have no relation to the purchaser's productive activity. Capital gains include:

(i) any such difference between security prices. But in the case of equity shares one must subtract the ploughback net of depreciation made by the company during the period, for the shareholder is entitled to the capital value of 'his' savings which 'he' used in the business;

(ii) any such difference between commodity prices, less storage costs and any value added by further processing;

(iii) works of art, jewellery, stamp collections, etc., may be assimilated to commodities;

(iv) land, houses and consumer durables are like equity shares, with improvements playing the role of ploughback.

The 'normal' earnings of professional jobbers in these markets present peculiar problems which cannot detain us. They differ only in degree from the problems of the 'abnormal' earnings of ordinary retail and wholesale traders. Changes in the purchasing power of money should also be allowed for. Even from this truncated account the definitional difficulties are plain, and there need be no wonder that capitalism, baffled by the administrative difficulties of taxing capital gains, objectively favours them over income though most people regard them as morally and economically inferior. Quite small in volume, they are most unequally distributed, being the privilege of those in the know, indeed very often those corruptly in the know. When we add the fact that by definition they do not reward labour or saving, the case against them is very strong.

The STE is very hostile to capital gains. They are almost impossible to make, except under heading (iii), owing to the institutional set-up, and they are prohibited legally as well. The difficulties of definition are solved by extreme looseness and inclusivity. Capital gains are lumped under the general heading of 'speculation', which includes black marketeering and various other activities.

20. Again and again East Europeans of the sort one meets – i.e. members of the socialist intelligentsia, indistinguishable from their imperialist opposite numbers – will tell you that 'incentives' must be increased.

TABLE 16/I

Per Capita Income from All Sources after Income Taxes[f, a]

	UK 1969	USA 1968	Italy[c] 1969	Canada[d] 1971	Sweden[e] 1971
P95/P5	5·0	12·7	11·2	12·0	5·5
P90/P10	3·4	6·7	5·9	6·0	3·5
P75/P25	1·9	2·6	2·5	2·4	1·9

	Hungary 1967	Czechoslovakia 1965	Bulgaria 1963–5	USSR[b] 1966
P95/P5	4·0	4·3	3·8	5·7
P90/P10	3·0	3·1	2·7	3·5
P75/P25	1·8	1·8	1·7	2·0

a. Omits owner-occupiers' imputed rents.
b. Excluding families headed by kolkhozniki.
c. Also omits auto-consumption, rents and dividends.
d. Privately communicated by Statistics Canada.
e. Swedish Survey on Relative Income Differences 1972, Statistiska Centralbyrån 1974, p. 22, as reworked by me.
f. Source except for d and e: Wiles, op. cit., 1974, p. 48. P5 means the income of the fifth person from the bottom out of a random sample of 100, and so on. Income is the average family income from all factor activity and social services, net of income tax and employees' contributions, per family member.

Pressed, they admit that Stalinism, with its large plan-fulfilment bonuses, was a highly incentive system. It emerges that East European Stalinism, unlike Soviet, was highly egalitarian (Table 16/I), and that they mean that their own salaries, as professional workers, researchers, teachers, etc., are only a very small multiple of the average wage. But why shouldn't they be? Where are supply and demand? Have the attractions of this sort of career *in fact* been so small as to put off one's interlocutor? Is not higher education, on which his government has spent so much, turning out his like in very large numbers? Does he not himself work hard?

This archetypical conversation then moves on to the general will to work in a Communist country. Let us allow that, so far as it can be measured, it has fallen in recent years. Can we possibly explain why, say, a fitter works less hard in 1969 than in 1952 by saying that in *both* years he earned no less than half as much as a professor? Clearly the fitter's own personal opportunities for bonus will affect his work many times as much as his knowledge of a professor's salary; and the professor's opportunities for side-earnings are what concerns *him*. The reason why both of them work less hard is doubtless that they are both richer than they were, and both fear less the sack and the police.

Incentives and inequality have almost no relation. An incentive system of payment faces a particular person in a particular situation within an income-band, and lets him choose between work-and-wealth, idleness-and-poverty. A person in a wholly non-competing group (sec. 12) faces a similar income-band; and the relation between these two bands, which determines most of what we call inequality, may have any value. It may for instance satisfy egalitarians, by approaching unity: the professor and the fitter face the same band. Or it may satisfy traditionalists by leaving the professor's band three times as high. Moreover this applies to capitalism and STEs alike. And in so far as macro-supply and macro-demand play a role, the history of economic development everywhere is that education rightly or wrongly expands, and brings the differential of the educated down.

A much more serious problem is that of a particular sort of competing group: one's own hierarchical superiors. If we were all rational differentials would depend on the attraction of sheer power and prestige, offset by the unpleasantness of taking responsibility. The net effect *might* be so great as actually to lower salaries on promotion. But something else intervenes· subordinates' values are believed to make it necessary to buttress hierarchical with monetary superiority. However great the supply of candidates for power, those who have it must be paid more in order that they may exercise it effectually. *So large administrative units create inequality*.

Or so it is argued. But businessmen take large cuts in incomes to become politicians and civil servants, and enhance their prestige thereby; and barristers do the same to become judges. In universities again hierarchical salary differences do not confer, though they may result from, prestige. They are certainly not what causes one's juniors to obey one. In the artistic and literary world and in the cultural Bohemia there is no need for power, and the status hierarchy is voluntary and fashionable, so people's incomes may have any relation. In USSR up to 1925 Party members exercised power over higher paid bourgeois specialists; the former were proud that it was so and the latter were afraid. In China and Cuba today a somewhat similar situation prevails (chapter 2, sec. 11; chapter 10, sec. 11).

It is more probable that the powerful within any organization occupy a 'quasi-Illyrian' position: they employ everyone else at market-determined wages, with regard to productivity; but they hand themselves out the residue, and so force the same on competing organizations. If the distribution within all competing hierarchies were flattened at the same time, who can doubt that the supply of candidates for promotion, and the authority of those promoted, would stay the same? Note that even those more interested in money than in power (a type we might particularly wish to promote) would also stay where they were, since they would have nowhere else to go.

To repeat: the relations of non-competing groups are very arbitrary. Shifts in supply and demand may alter them; and so may shifts in custom and public opinion, or government intervention. It is only within a competing group that factor rewards are rigorously determined by supply and demand, and hierarchies of power probably present an exception even to that.

Such doctrines are not popular with East European, or even Soviet, intellectuals. There is in the whole recent reform movement an element of 'rebourgeoisification'. Being very often of bourgeois origin[35] and nearly always of bourgeois aspirations, the technocrats, scientists, doctors, teachers, etc., have quite simply wanted to re-establish the income differentials their fathers enjoyed; and they have tried it on in the name of incentives. But this, we have seen, is largely illogical. Nay more, the recent (1965 and after) reforms are objectively anti-proletarian; for however little else is decentralized one function always is – the employment of labour. The manager, possibly in consultation with the (Soviet-type) trade-union leader, is no longer compelled to take on unwanted labour for the sake of full employment (chapter 14); he may hire and fire more freely than of old, and is freer to strike a wage bargain. Labour, after all, was always on a market, unlike intermediate materials or machinery; it was much less of a wrench to decentralize further in this field than to begin decentralizing elsewhere.[36]

So, under Communism as under capitalism, the poor clerk with the good grammar and the collar and tie has superior status to, but about half the income of, the muscular young manual worker who is prepared to rough it, and at higher income levels the cultured professor stands in the same relation to the publisher of pop music. There is nothing wrong with this, morally or economically. Indeed it is surely the mark of a civilized society that money should not buy status, nor status money; and it is certainly good economics that agreeable occupations – which include, of course, status-conferring occupations – should be less well paid. To think otherwise is, quite literally, medieval (see sec. 3).

21. Is inequality necessary for growth? If Stalin's excesses be put aside, we can only generalize as follows:

(i) STEs other than USSR have grown very rapidly while reducing inequality from its pre-revolutionary level. They have nothing in common with USSR and are also more equal than ACEs or capitalist countries in rapid development (iii).

(ii) UDCs have very various degrees of inequality, according to their social systems.

(iii) After entering the capitalist growth path countries do in fact incur great inequality, though probably smaller than what some of them had in the first place. Under *laissez-faire* this is inevitable, but that does not make inequality a necessary condition for growth. A sufficiently egalitarian government can prevent large concentrations of individual capital and substitute its own savings: while we have just seen that extreme differences of pay are simply wasteful. The problems here are those of political power and of the corruptibility and competence of tax collectors.

(iv) In ACEs governments do develop an egalitarian bias, and their fiscal machines are reasonably efficient. So they are as a rule more egalitarian than middle-class capitalist countries. Comparing the more and the less egalitarian at this higher level (Sweden, USA), we see no reason to suppose that growth is affected.

(v) Very large concentrations of individual capital are in no way necessary. Millionaires have no economic function whatsoever, since corporations are better risk-takers and savers.[37]

(vi) But in one way the pursuit of equality must surely retard growth: it diverts administrative and municipal talents from constructive tasks to tax collection and tax evasion respectively. This could not, of course, be quantified, but it is tempting to point at India's stagnation and Pakistan's success in this context.

There is then solid middle ground between those who insist on incentives like Stalin, Dubček and all capitalists, and those who insist on equality, like Lenin, Mao, Novotny and kibbutzniks. An incentive income structure is one that presents each person here and now with the chance of making more money by longer or better work within his present field. Non-competing groups can be kept fairly equal. Power, promotion and status are rewards in themselves; they will still be pursued for little more money, and they are at present so well paid because it is the powerful who set the pay scales.

The question remains how disastrous for the will to work would be complete equality not only between but within each occupation, and the prohibition of production bonus and overtime. The answer seems to be that only careful selection, novitiates and even brain washing can combine hard work with perfect equality (chapter 2, sec. 7; chapter 6, sec. 13).

22. It was no part of Yugoslavia's intention in 1952 to allow the market to generate inequality, and those who think it does not do so have to explain the Yugoslav case away. Broadly, an economic dictatorship can produce the distribution it wants. One can use it for inequality, as did Stalin, or for equality, as did Khrushchev, and all other rulers of STEs. But the socialist market entails a certain inequality, depending on such supply and demand factors as those enumerated in sec. 10 and 11.

We have few figures for personal income distribution. They became so sensitive after 1965 that many ceased to be published. Earlier data show greater inequality of earnings per earner than in the East European STEs. With so great an emphasis on profit sharing, and profits made in a market, our surprise must be that the difference is so small. Inequality appears to have been static over time.

The system has also totally failed to reduce regional inequality. This has always been extremely heavy in Yugoslavia, with Slovenia enjoying four times the per capita income of Kosovo-Metohia.

Market economies are less willing to waste money, and better able to detect its waste. They therefore invest less in poor regions, and rely more on the slow process of emigration. But between what are psychologically separate countries there has been little migration.[38] This is by no means to say that Belgrade has been ungenerous to its poor regions: only that the problem is quite exceptionally acute and that the market precludes many kinds of special assistance.

But the main rule that Yugoslavia demonstrates is of wider application: simply that the market differentiates personal incomes to an unwelcome extent. This is particularly true of professionals and entertainers – both nominally part of the socialist sector. The undoubtedly increasing inequality between workers and management is at least directly due to other causes: to sheer corruption and to the director's capacity to browbeat the workers' council. But the marginal productivity of a good director on a market is very great (under self-management, he promises a great addition to average member's income); and it is not impossible that by turning a blind eye to his peccadilloes the council are recognizing this fact in the only way they can.

Yugoslavia also demonstrates, by default, how equalizing is a nationwide system of wages (cf. sec. 18). The self-managers absorb the enterprise's quasi-rent, and prevent others from joining them. Nevertheless incomes from work per recipient in the socialist sector remain far more equal than peasant and professional incomes. As in USSR, regional inequality per head of consumer is mainly due to variations in agricultural incomes and family size.[39]

23. Since books can only be so long we cannot venture far into true political economy. The influence of wealth on political power would take

us into another book, but there is room for some of the direct influences of political power on wealth.

The essential difference between capitalism and socialism, as we have already seen many times, is precisely the simplest and oldest one: the private or public ownership of the means of production. Wealth under socialism is present income, present bureaucratic status and the future prospect of each; also consumer durables and bank deposits. Wealth under capitalism is all that plus securities, notably their future income prospects. Moreover since marginal productivity is a flow theory, we tend to neglect the stock aspects of capital. Capital is useful to us also as a disposable lump sum. First it can actually be sold, to make a capital gain. Secondly the *potentiality* of selling it gives us security, and enables the rich man to take risks the poor man cannot.

Also, within the capitalist system, some capital means economic power, since equities confer voting strength. And in another way: government, especially local government, can be bought with a sufficient sum; but only under capitalism has any non-governmental agency such sums, or could any corrupt bureaucrat safely accept them. So here again capital means power: again essentially of an economic sort. Such major bribery is possible only under capitalism.

Under all systems one can influence government by blackmail, browbeating, libel, intrigue, etc. This use of power is non-market bribery. We threaten the administrator corruptly with some adverse consequence, and his advantage in obeying us is simply to preserve his position (negative bribery). Or we may be forced to promise him some improvement in his position (positive bribery). Note that market bribery, the ordinary kind that uses money, goods or services, is far more humane. It can only be positive. However the use of such power is not costless to the user. Power is, so to speak, a depletable stock: we can threaten our subordinates so often that it becomes a scandal, they pick up courage and report us to our superiors; or such overuse annoys and infringes upon the 'rights' of other powerful people. But metaphors are treacherous: power is also like a muscle, which must be used a little lest it atrophy. For it is only by convention that others respect, and indeed create, our power. They must be given sufficient opportunity to learn this convention or it will not establish itself.

So if wealth is power under capitalism, in a non-market economy (note the asymmetry) power is wealth. This is simply because administrative allocations are made by the politically powerful. Thus the story has been told me by a Rumanian refugee of a provincial Party boss who had a suit made for himself of good imported English worsted – and forbade any more of that cloth to be sold in his province. The boss did not have all that much money; indeed he may well have felt sincere ideological inhibitions about money. But he did have great power, and he used it to create a scarcity in the commodity he coveted, while buying it himself at (no doubt) the usual price. In this way he exercised a privilege inaccessible to any Rockefeller.

Akin to physical allocation is dual pricing, and here too political influence plays a large part. For it is an administrative decision to have two prices, and someone has to say who comes under which heading. So one can use power to lower the prices one pays, and raise the prices one is paid. Thus a capitalist tradesman can 'get it wholesale', at least in his own trade, for personal consumption. The distinction between wholesalers and retailers, although based upon the realities of supply and demand, is nevertheless administratively determined in the short run; it is therefore a matter of status and seniority whether a particular transaction is *defined* as wholesale or retail. It is not to be doubted that the innumerable double prices, and multiple exchange rates, of Communism provide a similar field for the exercise of political power. The most obvious example is access to the special shops for privileged people (*zakrytie raspredeliteli*).

Similar again is sheer information, a commodity in very short supply everywhere. Information is extremely valuable: it gets you to the head of the queue, it warns you not to buy because a new regulation is about to come out, it tells you today what speculators will think tomorrow, etc., etc. To be sure, wealth can buy it, and this is why the rich do well on the stock exchange; but political power can extract it for nothing, or in exchange for other information. In an STE the most valuable information is about the incredibly inefficient distribution system: when to queue or where to go for it. Note again the comparatively trivial sums at stake in the non-capitalist case.

Again all detailed interpretation of a tax law is administrative, and therefore subject to political power. Whether such and such a revenue is 'income' or 'expenses' or possibly 'capital gain'; whether such and such an expenditure is investment or a current business cost; whether my imported cloth is a raw material (so free of tariff) or a finished product; whether my personal vehicle is a van (so free of purchase tax) or a passenger car – the questions are endless in all countries, and the answers to them depend on the status and powers of those who ask and answer.

We have already seen what striking redistributive effects public expenditure has even when honest; but it is even easier for the powerful to pervert it than to evade taxes. The state can be charged exorbitant prices for one's products (a trick confined to capitalism); roads can be laid to suit a local councillor's private convenience; universities can be made to admit the children of Party members; M.P.s can jump the queue for appendectomies on the National Health – but this list also is endless. The public officials concerned always have more administrative discretion than tax collectors, and so are more open to improper influence.

The market, then, is no respecter of persons. It is democratic and egalitarian: nor is this simply a paradox, but a genuine and important truth which cynics living in market systems must accept and bless their lucky stars for. It is mostly in other systems, or part-systems like the government sector, that power is convertible into wealth, and the more government interference there is in the market the truer this is. When finally we arrive at the STE we find that power is the royal road to wealth, a far broader and smoother one than mere economic competence, though heaven knows top managers are paid a great deal. But in the end the truly fantastic inequalities of power are not fully reflected in inequalities of wealth, for the system is after all 'socialist'.

In all societies top people try to defend their children against whatever equalizing processes there are. Let us sum up the differences and the similarities. In all systems the labour market judges the children of the rich harshly: how do we prevent that? First we can get them a privileged education. We have probably given them good genes in the first place (sec. 10). Then in all systems we can give them a suitable home for learning in; and we can use power to influence the decisions of educational administrators in their favour. If power fails we can also bribe, and such bribes are well within the range a rich Communist parent can afford. Moreover under pure and state capitalism we can simply buy a private education. Nor is this unknown under Communism, where private tuition at free or black market rates is commonplace. The chances of a child getting to a university in Poland and USSR are much more unequal by social group than in UK, though the proportions in higher education are about the same.[40]

Thus favoured, the rich child arrives on the labour market. Commonly no further help is given, and he makes his own not unsatisfactory way. But hiring is also an administrative process, and a matter of judgement. So power can also be used to influence the hirer's judgement, and this can also happen at each stage of promotion; and bribery can take over again where power fails.

But in the end when it comes to nepotism capitalism bears off the palm easily. Many enterprises are family enterprises, so management *must* pass by inheritance. Many publicly quoted companies have overwhelming family traditions and concentrations of shareholdings. Quite anonymous security holdings, conveying no power, still convey wealth by inheritance. All this is abolished under all forms of socialism.

24. It need not, then, surprise us that many people want political power only for the wealth it brings. In the comparatively honest politics of Northwest Europe, Canada and Australasia, where also private business provides a quicker and legally safer road to wealth, this is not so. But where standards of honesty are lower (USA), and especially if in addition private business is the football of government (most UDCs), the man greedy for wealth must seriously consider a political or even a civil service career. In countries where these conditions are extreme – much of

Africa and Latin America – the whole tone of government is set by such people. These are the so-called *kleptocracies*.[41]

We lack altogether a political or economic theory which may describe a state which is really an estate; where the ordinary attributes of sovereignty – courts, police, laws, parliament, diplomacy, armed forces, taxes – are not the parameters of but the variables in the economic model. Somehow crime is not academically respectable. On a low enough level it is fine, and we call its students criminologists. But when it gets too big it blurs the edges of university departments, so it is not studied at all. Nor is this for lack of evidence; for when the particular kleptocrat has made his pile and been thrown out his successor often publishes fairly full documentation of his crimes. For in this way he covers his own.

It can hardly be the task of a general survey to repair this omission. Let us only make four points. First, kleptocracy is not an ideology nor yet a new economic system – it is only a way of using an ideology or a system. Its exponents usually believe, in a moderate but genuine way, in the ideology they manipulate. The robber barons of German feudalism were 'convinced kleptocrats'. The many Caribbean rulers who install in their islands a sort of semi-colonial state-welfare-capitalism, are 'convinced kleptocrats'. So was Field-Marshal Goering, who stood on the capitalist wing of German Nazism. There were 'convinced kleptocratic' elements in Argentine 'Justicialismo', which based itself on trade unions and hostility to foreign capital; and in Ghanaian 'Afro-Marxism' – which for all its pretensions boiled down to a type of British socialism. There are also innumerable straight and unblushing kleptocrats. But at least some of those mentioned have a claim to economic originality. After all, why not? – respectability is not a precondition for importance.

Secondly kleptocracy is very inefficient. Decisions taken for the wrong reason are apt to be wrong. But it is not necessarily hostile to innovation – nearly all innovations yield pickings. Nor, aside from the very top, is it necessarily inegalitarian. Rather the contrary: everyone has to be squared, and discontent is particularly dangerous.

Thirdly, *laissez-faire* is unsuited to kleptocracy. The ruler must in that case help himself directly from public funds, which is dangerous and limited. Paradoxically, the same applies to complete socialism; for then too there are only public funds available. The mixed economy is best, in which the ruler can own private enterprises and help them in this way or that, or can accept bribes from other private entrepreneurs. State capitalism tends strongly to kleptocracy.

Lastly under Communism economic corruption is very widespread in small matters, and the politically powerful are certainly not innocent of it (except in China). But in large matters power is used with striking honesty and dogmatism, partly because large corruption is as we have seen technically impossible. The system retains its ideological drive: it is quite certainly not a kleptocracy, though nearly all its citizens are black-marketeers.[42]

Notes

1. Marginal value product when competition is perfect, marginal revenue product only when it is imperfect. But the distinction is trivial and need not detain us.

2. In his *Elementary Principles of Economics*, N.Y. 1912, p. 482.

3. *The Distribution of Wealth*, N.Y. 1956 (first edn., 1908), *passim*, but especially pp. 5–9.

4. Written as a letter on 5 May 1875. I have occasionally translated 'Recht' by 'right [law]'. The German word means both, and to an English-speaker Marx is almost punning.

5. The classic case is Lenin's land reform immediately on seizing power in 1917. The decree was copied out of a populist newspaper, and designed to catch peasant support. A few days later he took some Socialist-Revolutionaries (populists) into his cabinet, and one of them willingly administered the decree as People's Commissar for Agriculture. It 'abolished private ownership in land for ever', but was extremely vague as to what took its place. Down to this day only state farm and urban land is state property: kolkhoz land is 'public' (*obshchestvenny*) property. Other Communist countries perform similar equivocations.

6. The classic case of this too is Russian. With full populist support Russian law regulated, both before and after the Revolution, the disposition of each peasant family's land-holdings. The head of the family was a trustee, not an owner. Cf. D. J. Male, *Russian Peasant Organisation Before Collectivisation*, Cambridge 1971, pp. 67–71.

7. Cf. Wiles in *Journal of Constitutional and Parliamentary Studies*, New Delhi, April–June 1970.

8. Leasehold enfranchisement is when a house or flat on a long lease may be bought outright, contrary to the private contract and in conformity with subsequent state legislation, from the owner by the tenant at a price favourable to the latter. It is thus the equivalent of an anti-capitalist land reform. Mortgage interest is like hire-purchase interest: a cost of consumption. No consumption costs should be deductible from revenue subject to income tax, and the allowance is very clearly regressive. But the Labour Party also exhibits socialism in refusing to allow the sale of public housing, say to its present tenants.

9. This is as much as to say that I reject the calculations of Christopher Jencks *et al.*, in their *Inequality*, N.Y. 1972, which claim the opposite. They have not troubled to say why they contradict all other workings, and these are preferable because they make due allowance for *sickness and age*, which the authors do not. Cf. Wiles in OECD, *Education, Inequality and Life Chances*, Paris 1975, vol. 2, p. 160; and Henry Levin in *Saturday Review*, Education number, 11 November 1972. Jencks's reply (ibid., 9 December 1972) is extremely obscure on this point. I am far, however, from rejecting the authors' major conclusion, that education is not as good a weapon of redistribution as income-tax and death duties, i.e. that equality of opportunity will not bring equality of result (cf. sec. 13).

10. I derive these approximations from a model for UK with many plausible but unproven parameters; actual data from USA do not badly upset them. Workings available on request.

11. The influence of inheritance on great wealth seems not to have changed in UK between 1924–6 and 1956–7: C. D. Harbury in *E.J.*, December 1962, esp. p. 866.

12. There are many such models, built very airily on false assumptions and bad data: for example J. E. Stiglitz in *Econometrica* 1969 and F. W. Pryor in *AER*, 1973. For whatever reason they tend to gross optimism, assuming that earnings are not positively correlated with capital, and the rich get the same yields as the poor. Pryor at least recognizes what he has done (p. 64) but he commits a new optimistic error on pp. 56–8: assuming that inheritances are all used up, and do not influence their recipients' bequests.

13. Cf. J. E. Meade, *Efficiency, Equality and the Ownership of Property*, Harvard 1965, chapter 5.

14. But there are many exceptions to this rule. In one third of Mr. Watts' social groups thrift is positively correlated with existing capital (Harold W. Watts in Thomas F. Dernburg *et al.*, *Studies in Household Economic Behavior*, New Haven, 1958, p. 133. Mr. Watts used a sample of 7983 spending units from the Michigan Survey Research Center's observations in 1948–51. He divided them into 187 groups, by age, occupation, region, etc.). In any case very rapid increases of capital are compatible with a negative influence of capital on saving, if the parameters and initial magnitudes are right.

15. Watts, op. cit., p. 140, plots the life-time S/Y against the life-time income of 34 social groups to obtain this result. He has thus standardized for both age and social status. The near-constancy of national S/Y in face of rising national income does not of course contradict this.

16. Workings available on request.

17. Notably by Franco Modigliani and Richard Brumberg in ed. Kenneth K. Kurihara, *Post-Keynesian Economics*, New Brunswick 1954, pp. 394–5. By pp. 421–2, 430 they have come to 'proven' conclusions without relaxing this assumption.

18. Cf. J. B. Lansing and J. Sonquist's results for the US white cohort born in 1885–94, in ed. Lee Soltow, *Six Papers on the Size Distribution of Wealth*, N.Y. 1969, pp. 35, 50. Between 1952 and 1961 these people retired, and while the rich increased their capital as usual, the poor dissaved.

19. M. Young and J. Gibson in *British Journal of Statistical Psychology*, XVI, pp. 27–36; A. Jensen in *Harvard Educational Review*, February 1969. Note that no racial distinctions are implied by my argument, nor do I necessarily accept them. We are concerned with hereditary differences within one race alone. If I have to quote authors who think otherwise it is an implicit criticism of the orthodox liberal position, which confuses belief in the genetical inequality of individuals with racism.

20. We neglect the tendency of the infertile to be rich, and so of infertility genes to accumulate at the top (R. A. Fisher, *The Genetical Theory of Natural Selection*, N.Y. 1958, chapter 11). It has evidently had very little effect.

21. I take the figures from my *Distribution of Income East and West*, Amsterdam 1974, Appx. II, and G. J. Burgess and A. J. Webb in *Lloyds Bank Review*, April 1974. The latters' yield figures are based on replacement accountancy (p. 16, col. 4).

22. A true elasticity with explanatory force would be ex ante and micro-, a parameter in the mind of a particular entrepreneur contemplating the prices of many inputs and a highly specific new technology.

23. Emile Primorac, Ph.D. thesis at London University, 1966.

24. E. H. Phelps Brown, *Pay and Profits*, Manchester 1968, pp. 18–19.

25. Cf. my contribution to ed. A. B. Atkinson, *Personal Distribution of Incomes and Property*, London 1976.

26. As is suggested, but certainly not proved, for USA in the last decade by Peter Henle, in *Monthly Labour Review*, December 1972. The wage and salary structure has indeed become more unequal, but he forgets that his figures exclude agriculture ('immigration' of poor negroes), and he does not allow for Puerto Rican immigration.

27. Compare the capitalist failure to control wages in the private sector in order to prevent cost inflation (chapter 14).

28. Workings available on request.

29. Cf. Wiles, op. cit., 1974, Lecture I.

30. Nor is there, except informally, in Poland down to this day. But in the peasant periods of other Communist countries there was an upper limit from the very start.

31. But in the transitional phase in many Communist countries the kolkhoz pays rent on capital.

32. Along with his freezing of retail prices, above. Strictly, he abolished compulsory deliveries (zagotovka) and fell back on the government's second line of defence, its quasi-voluntary procurement (zakupka). Zakupka prices now vary about world prices at the (not unreasonable) official rate of exchange. But the zakupka has become unofficially compulsory.

33. A further important point is that state farmers have smaller private plots, so their access to the kolkhoz market is restricted. This reduces the incomes of suburban farmers.

34. I am implicitly using a definition of 'equalization' and 'more equal than' which stresses the semi-decile ratio and is insensitive to redistribution within the middle 80–90 per cent. For the logic of this cf. Wiles, op. cit., 1974, Lecture I.

35. Except in USSR, where a generation has intervened, it is noticeable how often the children of white-collar pre-revolutionary parents have the best jobs. While it is not surprising that such people should have outdone the children of capitalists, high functionaries and peasants, it is that they have kept ahead of proletarian children. Such are the necessities of having a career open to talent.

36. The former Czechoslovak President Novotny, himself a genuine proletarian, tried not unsuccessfully to arouse the manual workers against the economic reforms of 1967–8 because they threatened full employment and equality, and favoured the 'bourgeoisie'.

37. Cf. chapter 13, sec. 1–4. But they may possibly have a political function, as angels to the press and the opposition (chapter 17, sec. 3).

38. There are, indeed, Kosovar street-sweepers in Ljubljana. But most migrants, especially if qualified, go abroad instead: why should a Croatian fitter earn 50 per cent more in Slovenia when he might treble his earnings in W. Germany? Thus if we lump internal and external migration together it has no great equalizing effect.

39. Cf. Wiles, op. cit., 1974, Lecture III; Wiles in *La Distribuzione del Reddito nella Pianificazione Economica*, ISDEE, Trieste 1976; Iwan Koropeckyj in ed. Zbigniew Fallenbuchl, *Economic Development in the Soviet Union and Eastern Europe*, vol. I, Praeger 1976.

40. Cf. my contribution to OECD, op. cit. 1975.

41. Cf. Stanislaw Andreski, *The African Predicament*, London 1968, chapter 7; Paul Harrison in *New Society*, August 1973.

42. All this is evident from, though not made clear by, Steven J. Staats, 'Corruption in the USSR', in *Problems of Communism*, January–February 1972.

17

Political and Economic Freedom

1. A working definition of political freedom
2. Capitalism accommodates itself to virtually all politics
3. But its ideology, if any, is weakly liberal
4. Serious socialism is technically incompatible with liberty
5. Serious socialists have never liked liberty
6. Social transformation and conflict
7. The road to serfdom?
8. Cases of freedom under socialism
9. Freedom and state capitalism
10. France
11. Detailed planning and the constitution
12. State capitalism and false consciousness
13. Co-operation and freedom: general
14. Yugoslavia: the origins
15. Yugoslavia goes liberal
16. Self-management among intellectuals
17. Forced labour
18. The freedom of slave-holders
19. Economic freedom
20. Freedom and development
21. Conclusions

17

A man is seldom so innocently employed as when he is making money

Samuel Johnson

1. We mean in this chapter the ordinary philistine definition of freedom: doing what you like, and changing your mind about it, without human restraints. Freedom is not taken to mean Hegel's or Marx's 'realization of necessity', for that can also mean doing whatever the KGB tells you (sec. 5). Willing slavery is slavery. Perversely used freedom is freedom. Freedom is not necessarily good; quite the contrary, it can be very bad. There is no reason why everybody should have it, since most people are rather bad. Give it to them without restriction and they will kill each other: so they cannot all have it, since they will restrict each other's. Anarchy and chaos are excess of freedom, and therefore a kind of it. The common distinction between liberty and licence is highly misleading and prejudicial, since it too serves the notion that freedom must be good. Finally, material incapacity to do what one likes, though untrammelled by human restraint, is poverty, not freedom. The terms are quite distinct (sec. 19).

I choose the following empirical criteria for the existence of *political* freedom:

(i) the electorate can change the government at not too long intervals, by peaceful voting;
(ii) therefore, as a corollary, political opposition not engaged in physical violence can operate unhampered;
(iii) nearly all adults have the vote;
(iv) civil rights and freedoms are effectively guaranteed to all;
(v) one can effectively sue the police and the executive (this is the essence of the rule of law).

Parliamentary democracy (i, ii and iii) is identical to *some* of the preconditions of freedom. It is neither a guarantee nor a definition.

A depressing list. France does not really qualify, and the USA barely. Mexico, much praised in this book, does not begin. Trinidad has recently become doubtful. Chile and Uruguay have dropped out. In the whole of Africa only Ghana ever approached 'doubtful'. The Arab and Communist worlds know nothing of it. With what are we left?[1] – Canada, USA, Australasia, N.W. Europe, Austria, Italy, Japan, Costa Rica, Venezuela, Barbados, Jamaica, Bahamas, Iceland, Israel, and perhaps

France, Trinidad, India and Ceylon. And even in these states our conditions are often grossly violated.

2. Now, turning to the relation of economic structure to political freedom, we postpone the major aspect, the government's control over the individual, and take first the effects of enterprise structure and government-enterprise relations.

Political freedom as defined is evidently something to do with private capitalism (the least capitalist states in this list are India, Israel, and Ceylon – the latter perhaps going Communist). Taking a historical view, we get the same impression. Capitalism began, crudely speaking, in medieval Venice, which was and remained a tyrannous oligarchy, invariably contemptuous of civil rights. But it spread across Northern Italy, where at the time of the Renaissance political freedom made its first appearance since ancient Athens (also essentially capitalist, but a slave state). In Florence, fitfully, most of our conditions were fulfilled – and Florence was run by bankers. But the whole set of conditions was first systematically imposed in capitalist Britain, followed by capitalist North America, Scandinavia and the Low Countries (France contributed only the theory, not the practice). The presence of UDCs in our list is exclusively due to British imperialist conditioning. No ex-French, Dutch or Belgian colonies have made it.

Venice reminds us that very narrow oligarchies can rest on capitalism, too. The US South rested on slavery, while trying, like Athens, simultaneously to fulfil all our conditions for free men. Pre-revolutionary Mexico, under Porfirio Díaz, was a dictatorship by a man who favoured capitalism, including foreign capitalists. He had no special ideology, and thus stood in contrast to *Fascism*, the really controversial case. Italian Fascism originated in the defence of capitalism threatened by Communism and anarchy, though it moved very far to the left before it ended.[2] But the German Nazis began and ended in a more populist position. They had few capitalist backers (cf. chapter 19). Even after murdering their own left wing (1934) they kept German capitalism at arm's length. They were no dogmatists – they tolerated whatever they found.[3] Spanish Fascism (the Falange) is distinctly anti-capitalist – it is other pillars of the régime that represent the large corporation, the Common Market, foreign investment, etc. Argentine 'Justicialism' or Perónism is a rather pure 'labour Fascism'; it is very much opposed to large foreign corporations.

Summing up, capitalism has almost no ideology and tolerates virtually all political movements not actively bent on its destruction. Slavery, racism, civil rights, protection, free trade, peace, war, imperialism, isolationism, Fascism, Venetian oligarchy, Swiss rule by referendum – this pliable and amoral system can fit in. It has even adapted itself to trade unions, and made money out of the Soviet NEP.

3. But capitalism does occasionally throw up an ideologist: Smith, Jefferson, Ricardo, the young J. S. Mill, Cobden, Bastiat, Hayek, Robbins, Friedman. Strong advocates of private ownership and free markets, insensitive about equality[4] and full employment,[5] these people have invariably defended political freedom with passion. The captains of industry for whom, objectively, they spoke have been far less scrupulous, but broadly speaking they have mainly leant this way. The German capitalists opposed Hitler, Mr. Oppenheimer opposes *apartheid.* All in a very gentlemanly way, of course, and without personal inconvenience: but this is the preponderance of the record for *private* capitalism.

Why? Basically it is because economic freedom is both a precondition for and a stimulant to political freedom. It is difficult to distinguish these relationships, so let us simply lump them together. People who wish to resist or change their government must dispose of certain goods and services without consulting that government. Freedom to buy and sell includes traffic in information. Freedom to hire and be hired includes freedom to migrate. And all these freedoms imply a weak government, which can be sued. But if it can be sued in this field, why not in others? It is technically possible to draw lines through the law and the market. Steel can be uncontrolled while long-distance 'phone calls are censored. The movement of labour can be free within a country while all migration is forbidden. But the lines are not easy to draw. Private capitalism calls for a free market not only in steel but also in wrapping paper and newsprint for advertising and trade circulars. This makes it less easy to control newsprint for printing news on. It calls for free foreign trade in goods and services – but this means that an unselected group of our citizens shall have physical contact with undesirable foreigners. It calls for free economic migration, and political migration is very easy to disguise. It calls for unlimited private accumulation. But this generates private charitable and economic trusts, whereby the dead hand of the eccentric tycoon prevails over the state's educational or artistic policy. Of course trust law can be changed and trustees pressured, but not without difficulty. Nay more, the mere fact of greater inequality produces a number of people willing to work at political opposition. Without financial angels, opposition crumbles.

One does not envy the security policeman or censor who operates in such an economy. It can be done: the Doges and the Greek colonels have proved it. But freedom has a weak tendency to be indivisible.

However this indivisibility does seem to be only technical; an ideology hostile to freedom certainly can grow in such a soil. The ante-bellum South in the USA developed an intellectual defence in depth for racism and slavery. Weimar Germany sprouted Communists and Nazis. The economic system of private capitalism weakly ensures intellectual and political freedom, and does not mysteriously impose on people, say in the Marxist manner of the base determining the superstructure, any particular way of thinking. On the contrary the freedom is often used to propagate anti-democratic doctrines, and anti-capitalist ones too.

4. Socialism is quite different. I exclude, as usual, West European social democracy from this concept, but I include Arab, African and even Chilean socialism along with Communism. True socialists, then, talk big about freedom while in opposition (who does not?), and even sometimes while in power: but they invariably suppress it. History provides not one contrary example. This is very striking, indeed it is perhaps the principal question in political economy.

Why? First a point of overwhelming simplicity: socialism is collectivist, political freedom is individualist. The latter is all about single persons doing what they like: if they can't, there is no freedom. The former is all about preventing that same thing, either for ever and on principle or in order to restore it later on a higher plane. But policies of retreating in order to advance are rightly very suspect, and it is not only the simple-minded who prefer to advance in order to advance. The mildest forms of socialism threaten the individual through the closed shop; the more rigorous through state control of newsprint. Inequality and unemployment on the other hand, the scourges of the market place, are genuinely smaller threats to political freedom. What they are is unpleasant in their own right, and perhaps it is worth our liberties to be rid of them. 'Freedom under socialism' logically entails a caesura between the political and the economic orders. One need not be Marxist to appreciate the difficulties of this. No wonder either that Marxists invariably weasel out of the dilemma by redefining political freedom.

Coming down to particulars, we must next invert the foregoing technical argument. Clearly a system of central controls over purely economic objects facilitates censorship and the persecution of the opposition. Since by the nature of civil society there is going to be a security police, it is going to use these weapons. Moreover there has also to be an 'economic police', i.e. some branch or branches of government that audit accounts and check material stocks, not merely against tax evasion but to see that the plan is fulfilled. These tasks are extremely detailed and far-reaching. These authorities are quite unable to avoid collecting masses of economic information that is of use to the security police. The STE is automatically, and always has been, a 'data-bank society'. Yet again the absence of great private wealth makes professional opposition a heavy sacrifice. True, all politicians of all parties should be financed out of taxes, but who is to administer such a law? What compromises would politicians be forced to make to come within its definitions? Again public education is not at present used as a vehicle of official propaganda in ACEs – for teachers' unions are both independent and internally divided. But in the long run a competing private sector is a bulwark simultaneously of liberty (this is obvious) and of inequality (because only the rich can afford it, whatever its philosophy; and it must ensure jobs for their children). So freedom as we have defined it is almost inconceivable in an STE, on technical grounds. We shall see below reason to be almost equally gloomy about state capitalism and market socialism, on the same grounds.

5. Technical difficulties in exercising freedom, however, have never existed on a large scale or for a long time without the concomitant – and vastly more important – will to suppress it. No truly socialist government has been without this will, so any empirical evidence as to the effect of such technical economic difficulties on their own must be drawn from non-socialist cases (e.g. the opposed cases of Venice and modern France).

But we can say something on the socialist will to suppress freedom. It is undoubtedly present except in the Fabian tradition.[6] Primarily responsible is the vast and unfortunate historical chance, which disposed that Marx, not in practice an enemy of our kind of freedom, nevertheless accepted and bequeathed to his followers both the Hegelian definition of freedom and the Rousseauian definition of democracy. He thus bequeathed an ideology totally opposed to freedom in our sense, which has had its effect far outside Marxist circles. It has even begun to penetrate that last bastion of pragmatism, the British labour movement.

Rousseau and Hegel are the staple of all political theory textbooks, but their connexion with modern economics is so little studied that I make no apology for going over this well-trodden ground. Rousseau's General Will, then, is the real will, the real interest of the people. In small communities the General Will is probably observable in the actual decisions of democratic bodies if the people are uncorrupted, for they will then be unanimous. As to large communities, they are inherently tyrannous and corrupt. The will of all, the will of the majority, the will of a representative body, are no substitute for the genuine article. But it was not left clear how the General Will could normally be ascertained in a large community – until Robespierre ascertained it in the Jacobin Club and enforced it with the guillotine. We are free of course only when we act in accordance with the General Will. We can therefore, when we err, be forced to be free.

To this Hegel added a suitable new definition of reason. Rousseau had rather weakly substituted sentiment for the unsympathetic individualist reason of the *philosophes*, which kept tripping him up in his self-contradictions. But Hegel's dialectic enabled a properly educated philosopher to contradict himself with impunity under set conditions. For things have essences, and their 'scientific' relations of cause and effect are but the superficial reflection of the mutual entailments of their essences. These entailments are the real basis of historical development, and they are of a logical character. To the motion of phenomena corresponds the self-contradiction of essences, in accordance with the dialectic. Strictly, then, it is only the essences of things that contradict themselves. But the philosophers, not least Hegel himself, less so Marx, more so Marxists, have taken this as licence to practice self-contradiction on their own.

Thus, and most relevantly for our purposes, Hegel called freedom 'realized necessity'. In so doing he followed respectable precedents. The Stoics recommended that we 'live according to nature' in order to be free. The Anglican prayer book informs us that God's 'service is perfect freedom'. This is very disputable. Such actions are not free, but wise or good. And when we replace nature with history, or God with men, as did Hegel, we have called slaves free. Rousseau, even though 'forcing people to be free', would probably not have welcomed this self-contradiction. But the beauty of Hegel's formulation is that since all great social developments are logically entailed they are inevitable. We do not even have to force freedom on people: we simply explain what is going on (dialectically of course), and leave them to 'realize' it. The scale of the organization under which they live no longer matters; large units are no longer inherently corrupt, and their inability to engage our sentiments is irrelevant. For sentiment itself is irrelevant, now that reason has swung into Rousseau's camp.

Freedom, then, has become a logical matter. Under Lenin (who was to Hegel what Robespierre had been to Rousseau) it comes to mean that the prisoner awaiting execution quietly in the Lefortovo prison is free while the guerrilla on the run from the Cheka and the stockbroker complacently taking orders on Wall Street are in chains. Philosophers are apt not to accept the natural consequences of their words in action; indeed Rousseau was a man of many facets, all of which no pupil could actualize in practice. But I do not think Hegel was misinterpreted. His definition of freedom was, quite without irony or perversion, used to justify the invasion of Czechoslovakia.

We saw in chapter 9, sec. 10 the relation of this philosophy to the detailed central plan, and especially to its moral status. This is of course an extension of the doctrine, since neither Hegel nor Rousseau was a socialist. Even if they had been born late enough, it is not clear that they would have been. But their political and moral collectivism is not in doubt, and it drew sustenance from their confusions about freedom. With that kind of contradiction it is possible to make individuals obey the representatives of groups against their will, persuade them that this is what they really want, or what is going to happen anyway, and tell them that they are free. Now a Marxist is a Hegelian socialist. Therefore in non-economic matters, *a fortiori*, all Marxists are opposed to most freedom under socialism; but nearly all socialists in power are Marxists. Perhaps a little academic discussion might be excepted, but the policy of the particular clique in power is the General Will. It is therefore right, logical, in the interests of all, inevitable and irreversible. Anyone who opposes it is insane, corrupt or obsolete.

6. History, then, has not been kind to socialism in this respect. It did not have to be the case that socialism should be introduced by Hegelians – or did it? Could a less determined group have introduced something so uncomfortable? But there is also a more endogenous tension between socialism and freedom: the socialist government, even if not Hegelian, has a practical mission to transform society irreversibly. So it is almost bound to be intolerant if there is serious opposition in principle. But since some of its ideas are always unpopular there is always such opposition. For a capitalist government is just a government. Its mind is not on the transformation of society, though it tolerates spontaneous transformations. Most of the time it just runs the economy as it finds it, accepting the amount of socialism or co-operation or what not that there is, and reacting to the day's happenings. In so doing it may well provoke riots and shed blood. But a serious socialist government, even if not Marxist, is the handmaid of history, which is moving in a known direction. It does not tolerate spontaneous social transformations but imposes its own; while fitting in the day's happenings as best it can. Thereby it adds a whole extra reason for riots and bloodshed, and makes resistance certain instead of probable.

This harsh judgement will certainly be misunderstood. So let me repeat that the question is not what policy or institutions are more efficient or more just: for socialism is certainly more economically just, and surely no more inefficient in the larger sense. The question is which government is heading for more conflict as a result of its economic policies. Because it is on conflict, not injustice or inefficiency, that freedom's fate depends – that is, where the government has any intention of preserving freedom at all. To put it another way, the consent of the governed is somewhat less likely if the government is seriously socialistic, and where this consent is absent freedom is impossible.

7. Friedrich Hayek's *Road to Serfdom*[7] is a different proposition: all attempts at planning and intervention by social democrats lead to initial failure and are variously counterproductive; so the government does more of the same in greater detail, in order to correct its initial errors; further disappointments lead to still more far-reaching and detailed measures, until total socialism and total tyranny are reached. With hindsight it is clear that there is hardly one word of truth in this. Social democrats are not Communists. They react to their first disappointments by retreating, not advancing, *lest they lose elections.* I.e. they accept, if only under protest, the priority of freedom and this ensures the reversibility of their policies. They also consist of more tolerant and compromising (if you will, dishonest and unstable) characters. Moreover, the mild controls they initially impose are not all that unsuccessful, and tend to be accepted by their political opponents. Freedom has not suffered in this way in any ACE at any time. But it has suffered from Communists,

who take over with wholly different intentions from the start, and quickly fulfil them; and from Fascists, who also wish from the start to abolish freedom while leaving a market economy – a goal they also achieve! In truly democratic societies left-wing parties do not stumble into the loss of freedom; they stumble into the loss of socialism.

However in UDCs there is surely some truth in Hayek's doctrine. Governments really cannot be trusted with mild powers to regulate the market: exchange control is used to deny newsprint to the opposition, qualitative bank controls prevent lending to the businesses of opposition leaders, labour legislation is bent to favour the unions that support the government. Strict *laissez-faire* really would protect freedom. Even here, however, there is no gradual cumulation of controls as the first ones fail in their goals. There is no slippage into the command economy. That is still something that governments either do or do not want; no one stumbles into it. Indeed non-Communist UDCs also stabilize the level of government intervention short of this level, quite intentionally They use their powers corruptly, but they do not increase them indefinitely.

The real point is that fundamentally most societies are incapable of political freedom. They are corrupt and violent. Their governments pursue incompatible goals – which are often better ones for their peoples, since the freedom would be misused anyway. They are not on the Road to Serfdom, they never left it.

8. So is political freedom possible under socialism, if both are fairly strictly defined? Hardly. The conclusions of both *a priori* and empirical reasoning are strong and pessimistic. The fact that Hayek *also* agrees with this proposition must not put us off! We pointed out above that there must be a divorce between the collectivist economy and the individualist polity, both being necessary by definition to 'freedom under socialism'; and that the means of communication form a practically awkward no-man's-land. Has this divorce ever happened, and how did the no-man's-land fare?

We may say that it did in Czechoslovakia, from January to August 1968. A people with a deep parliamentary tradition but a numerically strong socialist, nay Marxist, movement, revolted by its recent past, more or less threw off Soviet control. Simultaneously the degree of socialization was higher than anywhere, including USSR. For the free peasant market was smaller, and so were the possibilities for professional men to moonlight. Moreover this was not yet market socialism, and the means of communication continued under a tight government monopoly of their material inputs; but the 'message' as opposed to the 'medium' was very free. So freedom preceded the market. However the authors of the Czechoslovak spring remained, despite their abandonment of Leninism, Marxists. They insisted that changes in the economic base must eventually underpin the new superstructure.

This state of affairs was clearly unstable. But it was not allowed even to demonstrate this instability, owing to the Soviet invasion. My personal opinion is that Czechoslovakia would have gone the way of Yugoslavia (secs. 14, 15). That is not a way that can be simply described, but freedom, the market, inequality and petty capitalism have in fact increased together. Indeed we have already questioned Yugoslavia's claim to be socialist at all. *Socialism*, that is to say, *is hardly possible under freedom.* Hayek was too pessimistic, since he forgot that cause and effect might be inverted.

In Hungary however the market has preceded freedom. Indeed there is none, except that of the director to decide price and output! It is important for the reader to pause and sneer here, for there are many on the Right who really do equate such managerial powers, an almost purely administrative matter, with serious political, social and moral freedom. However the existence of such powers is a stepping stone to other things, and once we have relegated them to this lowly role it is important to examine the stepping stone.

The introduction of a market economy has removed the technical obstacles to political liberty mentioned in sec. 4. Since Hungarians are more fond of freedom than most people they have certainly used their new opportunities. There have been a very few hippies; effective mimesis of sexual intercourse on stage; importations of foreign literature for tourists; free speech in private; much travel to the West; lobbying on behalf of particular interests; printed criticism of the Party line, etc. But note that there is in no case a necessary relation to the free market. It was not some change in employment policy that created hippies, they were not directly born of the reforms; and it was the police that eventually liquidated them. The stage has been 'cleansed' again by a simple act of censorship. Foreign currency shortage persuaded the exchange control authorities, who had at no time been abolished, to curtail tourist allocations.

It is rather that in STEs relaxation of economic controls is often part of a *political* syndrome that includes other controls too. Or as it has been put: 'you cannot have freely formed wholesale prices for six months without getting a grand décolletage at the opera'. Government and people agree on this; the unusual thing about Hungary is that later the government covered up the décolletages but left the wholesale prices free. The syndrome applies also to Yugoslavia (sec. 15) and, in the inverse direction, to France: what the Commission du Plan did to the wholesale prices Mme de Gaulle did to the décolletages. But we must be very careful with it. It is clearly invalid for China. Indeed the Great Leap Forward syndrome (chapter 10, sec. 11) shows exactly the opposite relation: cultural and political freedom are still further decreased by the substitution of independent fanatics for law and bureaucracy. Syndromes are not laws of nature. It must also not be forgotten that Mussolini on first taking power 'tidied up' the cultural scene but introduced free trade.

9. Now private capitalism has developed everywhere, even in UDCs, into monopoly and state capitalism. One can but wonder that this spontaneous change is nearly everywhere considered to have reduced freedom. It certainly should have, since capitalism now switches from neutrality to complicity with the state (chapter 18), threatening some of the material preconditions of freedom: the unquestioned mobility of goods, services, information and people. Private accumulations of capital, even by individuals, become more monstrous than ever: but at no risk to the state since their 'complicity' has increased. Trade unions go the same way, and it becomes genuinely difficult to work without a union or professional ticket. Technical progress, a presupposition for all these changes, also improves information retrieval, and so brings the threat of an involuntary data-bank society scarcely less oppressive than that consciously aimed at by STEs.

Fine arguments, and convincing were it not for the facts. For the growth of state capitalism has been accompanied in all ACEs except France by: gay liberation, women's liberation, tolerated student rebellions, laws against race discrimination, an 'underground' press, above-ground pornography, a counter-culture, the end of capital punishment, Ombudsmen, protection for conscientious objectors, prison reform, voting at age 18 ... It is this period that has seen parliamentary democracy imposed on West Germany, Austria, Italy and Japan by conquest, and apparently taking successful root. It has seen the tradition of one-party dominance broken in Norway and Denmark. It has seen nowhere any unusual persecution or chicanery against legal opposition. These same countries have all grown to accept and tolerate legal Communist and Fascist parties; i.e. the very extremes have been almost tamed. Only in France can we detect a serious backsliding since 1939.

Yet simultaneously the pathology of the capitalist market has waxed almost without check. Monopoly corrupts and penetrates its government controllers in the USA, and elsewhere escapes more or less unpunished. Pollution has increased a hundredfold. Commercial broadcasting debases the minds of the citizenry. Unions cause rampant cost inflation, etc., etc. No one can deny the economic evils of state capitalism. How then has it managed to realize its potential for evil in every direction except one: the suppression of political freedom?

The answer is irritatingly simple. Outside the fields of their direct concern these mammoth organizations want and have very little influence. This even goes for trade unions, which are, of the various monopolies, the greatest threat to the individual. For the union is not a whit less interested than the capitalist firm in who is employed. Each is likely to operate a political blacklist, discriminate racially, discipline unjustly and the like. Yet not much of this occurs, and surely not more than in the past. Even the union sticks more or less to its sphere. It is individuals that demand more non-economic freedoms than they used to, and allow more of them to others; so, in a fairly responsive political system, they get them. They happen to be doing so during a period when economic organization is pulling the other way. So they win. The priority of politics over economics was never more clearly demonstrated.

There is special interest in the cases of pornography and sexual permissiveness. These involve *laissez-faire* in the use of paper and pharmaceuticals, hiring and firing, the renting of premises and much else. They presuppose tax laws that cannot be stretched by authority. Given that all governments are puritanical, they could only have arisen in a free market. A more convincing instance of the essentially market character of state capitalism could scarcely be wished. The corporations that could have stopped the sexual revolution by deprivation of materials had no monetary interest in doing so. The state, however, responded reluctantly to the pressure of the very small interest groups that favoured the revolution.

10. Nay more: France is an exception. The country is prosperous, yet civil rights decline, the police behave worse,[9] pornography is less tolerated, journalists are more often assaulted, the press is more seriously manipulated, etc.

It can surely be no accident that France is the extreme example of state capitalism: not a 'military-industrial complex' but a 'state-industrial complex', leaving out no branch of state or economy (chapter 18). It has the public broadcasting system and the higher educational system most blatantly manipulated by any capitalist state. Nearly all intellectual activity, from the supply of newsprint for *Le Monde* to the teaching of Maoism at Vincennes, is subsidized and regulated by the state. Moreover this complicated and interlocking system is quite efficient: its various branches really can conspire to get the results they want. There is thus at least a *prima facie* case for saying that if state capitalism goes far enough it does diminish political freedom. For, first, the plenitude of weapons is so great and tempting that someone eventually uses them. And secondly the radical opposition to this Argus-eyed monolith becomes more and more paranoid, and so more and more frustrated and provocative, with that resulting escalation of repression that all radicals need. State capitalism is not quite the system Hayek attacked in 1944, but the French case does give him some colour of veracity.

On the extreme left, then (beyond the Communists, of course) this situation is welcome. But to what extent has any other Frenchman intended it? It would appear, not at all. The French love their liberty as much as any people on earth. They simply grudge it to each other, and have an étatist tradition more inimical to freedom than they realize.

11. Economic planning has grave constitutional effects, which make Hayek's theory again very plausible. For the more there is of it the more the executive dominates the legislature. No legislature – not even its

finance committee – can seriously debate the whole of a budget, yet a budget is something every government must have. When we look closely at the detailed process of defining who is liable for a tax or who is entitled to a benefit, it is an executive matter. But in its broad and even its not so broad outlines a budget really is the legislature's achievement. So strong is this tradition that Communist governments always submit budgets to their puppet parliaments, and in this revisionist period the parliamentary finance committee is a body of genuine importance, which even occasionally puts through minor amendments.

But the budget is an extreme case. How much less can the legislature debate a detailed physical plan, or supervise an exchange control system from month to month? Time and skill are lacking. Physical planning, French planning, nationalized industries, exchange control, price and wage control, rationing, operations in the open money market – all these alike are run by bureaucrats on the basis of enabling legislation, or by central bankers who need not even that. They are subject only to occasional check. Thus the Fifth French Plan was submitted to parliament in three versions: high, low and medium growth – but only three! And the general proportions were similar in all three versions except the investment/consumption ratio. This then was but the faintest beginning of legislative control.

Socialism, then, even a hypothetical non-Communist but still highly centralized socialism, means a powerful executive, beyond legislative control; and the same is true of state capitalism. Yet economic theorists still talk as if all economic controls were interchangeable, at least short of Soviet-type planning. Thus in international trade theory there are three alternative weapons: tariffs, devaluation and exchange controls. They have this or that effect on the balance or the terms of trade, and that is that. But in real life the tariff is a nineteenth-century device, passed at rare intervals by the legislature and more suited to development policy than to monetary management. Devaluation is Keynesian: it is a simple overall monetary measure affecting all equally. But it is the executive decision of the central bank, or the cabinet and the central bank. Already popular control is slipping away. And exchange control is Schachtian: administrative, detailed, discriminatory, privy, personal and *ad hoc*. True, it is in the hands of the same central bank, but the details now escape even the cabinet and there is no popular control at all.

Why, then, have our liberties not been threatened? First because all this has been simultaneous with a move to strengthen people's rights against the state: Ombudsmen, *ad hoc* tribunals, etc. The thing has produced, to some extent, its own antidote. Secondly because the executive branch of an ACE's government consists of fairly average citizens in the first place: they find no pleasure in destroying our liberties, which are also theirs. Thirdly because this is all mainly economic. Cultural liberties and control over the police have seemed more important, and have increased (above). Our economic liberties *are* threatened, but there is no reason to take an inverted Marxist view and to expect the political and social 'superstructure' to collapse as well. For Marx was wrong: this is not the superstructure, nor is economics the base. Only control over the means of communication need worry us.

12. Not merely politics but also culture is autonomous. It is a passionately held New Left belief that under state capitalism an undifferentiated state and economic Establishment, controlling education, advertising and communication, washes our brains, *making* us desire the kind of material success it offers, at the expense of justice and enlightenment. The people who do this are only semi-conscious themselves, and act as partial prisoners of their own system, while the rest of us are totally sunk in False Consciousness. That is, we see reality through the categories provided, so we kiss our chains and call them freedom.

Note first that we may be only partially deceived. Political freedom is not all a subjective matter, nor is its existence called in question by the fact that people have moderate delusions about it. On the contrary it rests upon the five entirely objective conditions enumerated in sec. 1. The extent to which economic institutions generate these conditions is our principal subject; the extent to which they generate delusions about them is secondary. Then too the concept is a very dangerous one: I have insight, you have False Consciousness, he is a liar. Anybody can accuse anybody of using the wrong categorial spectacles, but he exposes himself to the question, through what categorial spectacles did you look in order to establish the existence of *any* categorial spectacles? If I said Marx was a prime victim of False Consciousness how would you refute me?

Epistemological argument may be short-circuited on this occasion by putting it thus: a 'good citizen', who does not think deeply, can be so sunk in his/her daily life of breadwinner or housewife as simply not to perceive poverty, inequality, injustice or the true basis of the power under which he lives. Such a person does, as a matter of brute fact, refuse to register inconvenient phenomena, be a non-Party[10] member of the town Soviet or an Elk. He is also provided by his education with a number of pat apotropaic phrases, whereby he interprets away whatever he really cannot avoid noticing: 'it will be all right under Full Communism', 'niggers won't work'. He is even without a vocabulary to describe some of the things which he 'should' not notice. Thus, the exploitation of man by man is capitalism; but we have socialism, so no one is exploited. Or, the free market establishes justice in exchange, and that *is* distributive justice (as in chapter 16); so again no one is exploited.

Such a citizen naturally regards himself, in particular, as free. Under Communism he accepts the Hegelian definition, so he thinks everyone else is free too. Hegel's definition imposes a truly Orwellian reversal of vocabulary and perception, as we saw: it is the perfect example of False

Consciousness. Under capitalism also we have our pat apotropaic phrases about freedom: 'they have the vote, don't they?', 'let him win an election, then', 'so if he likes China let him go there', 'why shouldn't the public get what it wants?' Our problem is, do these latter phrases too merely characterize False Consciouness, or are they true and deep arguments, unanswerable on any level?

My reply is, the latter. We do not refute a position by saying it is a cliché. Our obvious deficiencies and smugness have not in fact clouded our judgement on the essence of the matter. We know what freedom is, and we know where it is and is not to be found. So long as we accept that freedom is neither Hegelian nor necessarily good, this is hard to get round.

Why are so many reluctant to admit that in fact there is freedom only in ACEs and a few British ex-colonies? In part, because they are extremists of right and left who have failed to persuade the majority. If you are an ideologue yourself, and need this light to live by, it is difficult to admit that others are differently constituted. So you posit a conspiracy and present the majority as victims of False Consciousness. All this is especially true of Marxists, for whom opinions and laws are necessarily the superstructure on the economic base: since the base is so clearly recognizable how can there not be the appropriate superstructure?

Let us however see how False Consciousness affects our attitude to other matters. We must expect various forms of it everywhere, since men are stupid and inattentive, and avoid intellectual disturbance. But how much of it is propagated, consciously or otherwise, by the systems under which they live, and especially by the economic systems? Under capitalism, notably, the economy generates, independently of the government, a vulgar and materialistic advertising for goods and services which surely instils, not merely its own overt 'pig' values, but also a capacity for inattention to 'irrelevant' matters. This indeed is False Consciouness as far as it goes: a vast externality of the system, a moral pollution for which no one is directly responsible, since competition forces our hands. But how far does it go? Nearly everyone everywhere is materialistic and unwilling to think, and it is questionable whether advertising has much increased any vices so quintessentially human. Indeed the reaction against advertising has become so great that one must doubt its influence.

What then of the more directly governmental parts of the advanced capitalist system? Here countries must be distinguished. I would deny that in Scandinavia, the Netherlands, or Britain at any time since the war, public broadcasting or education were other than sceptical about the social system, and quite particularly about its rampant materialism. Or consider Japan, Italy or France, with their immense Communist presses and numerous fellow-travelling littérateurs and professors. Where there is cultural opposition on that scale the pro-régime culture can only survive by direct and open dialogue. Of this there is plenty on all levels, and people simply choose the culture that seems to them the lesser evil –

or retreat into scepticism, which is not False Consciousness. Of course in both kinds of country groups may live on incapsulated in some ideology, and shelter themselves from dialogue. The French Communists are the best example. But they are not majority groups, and above all they are not the élite or the floating voters. Their False Consciousness is undoubted, but not decisive and clearly not always of a type helpful to the system.

The obvious positive example is USA, and no one who knew that country between 1776 and the beginning of the civil rights movement will deny it was a classic case of False Consciousness. No official scepticism, and no fundamental opposition, existed on a scale enough to count. Conspicuous consumption, getting ahead, *machismo* – these were both the values the people held and the values the Establishment needed. They were also actively inculcated in schools, comic strips, films, etc. But since about 1965, i.e. since the doctrine of False Consciousness came to be sharply formulated and widely accepted, all that has ceased to hold.[11]

Note above all the diversity of national reaction to what is broadly the same system. For the truth seems to be slightly different. Just as advertisements cannot sell an individual product if it is really unwanted, so propaganda cannot sell a system if it is really unwanted. After all Communism has tried much harder for a sufficient time to instil a different False Consciousness into its subjects, and has failed miserably. Conspicuous consumption, getting ahead, *machismo*: how else would you describe a Pole or a Hungarian? Russians, after a longer period, seem as devious, orthodox and hierarchical as they were in 1913. National characters differ, and largely determine 'Consciousness'. These characters are traditional and intractable, though they do change. They also make us more or less willing to accept this or that economic system, this or that degree of freedom.

That a small élite, within the system of state capitalism plus cultural pluralism plus political freedom, can *deliberately* 'deceive all the people all the time' is obviously false. This is only the vulgar version of the doctrine we are refuting. But it is in any case obvious that, since most ACEs are also democracies, there is rather less such manipulation than elsewhere, since the legal and economic means are to hand to oppose it. Besides, 'False Consciousness from above' is what we nowadays call an official ideology. There must be then an official journal or organization laying it down: but none can be identified in any parliamentary democracy. On the contrary advanced and state capitalism accept human beings the way they are. So far from having an ideology, they have not even any ideals.

13. How do co-operative forms show up? Within the enterprise or community, particularly if it is a small commune, the individual is hardly free. But all these units together are on a market so in theory they can

be very diverse: each of them[12] is free to differ from the others. If then the individual is free to move he can enter the unit of his choice. So he too is fairly free in the longer run, vis-à-vis his immediate surroundings. Then, again in theory, the state's power is reduced by the independence of these units on the market beneath it, much as under private capitalism (above). Indeed nothing prevents the co-existence of capitalist and co-operative forms on the same market under the same state. Further, co-ops and communes resist amalgamation and cling to small scale, which makes difficult a 'state co-operative' system parallel to state capitalism.

There is no tolerant, totally co-operative state. The Israeli state tolerates all forms of enterprise and lays down no rules for their internal structure; so not surprisingly it also permits political freedom (in so far as its belligerence allows). But moshavim and kibbutzim between them account for only 8 per cent of the population: Israel is not, then a co-operative society.[13] Nay more, the state regulates parliamentary elections within kibbutzim. As we saw in chapter 6 sec. 13 each of them is in principle politically unanimous. Political divergence within the kibbutz, with the 'scandal' of multi-party voting, has come to be tolerated because the state insists upon the secret ballot.

We saw reason in chapter 6 virtually to exclude the kolkhoz as un-canonical. That leaves us with Yugoslavia. Here a co-op of a fixed form is indeed compulsory for about 40 per cent of the labour force, and there is a one-party régime: both bad signs. But there is a great deal more freedom in Yugoslavia than there used to be, and this prompts a longish digression.

14. The Tito-Stalin split of 1948 was essentially on the issue of the sovereignty of the new Communist states, but immediately there were libertarian stirrings. For, first, the rhetoric of national liberation is apt to slop over into individual liberation. Secondly Yugoslavia is a gaggle of small nationalities, the largest (the Serbs) being only 40 per cent of the whole, mostly on very bad terms with each other. Indeed the Communist Party was the only truly national party before and during the war. The minor nationalities began stirring too, and breathing life into the formal Communist federalism that Tito had indeed taken over from USSR. There was also genuine moral revulsion, not against the terror (Stalin's supporters were pitilessly terrorized) but against the servility and hypocrisy of Stalinism.

The command economy came under questioning along two lines: decentralization (Kidrič) and workers' participation (Tito). I repeat here a passage from my earlier work.[14]

> 'When Tito split from Stalin in 1948, the Yugoslav Communists faced the question, "What went wrong?" It is as much as to say, Stalin died in Yugoslavia not in 1953 but in 1948.

'The first advocate of economic reforms was Boris Kidrič (1912–53). At the time of the break with Stalin he was president of the Economic Council and of the Federal Planning Commission. As late as April 1948 he had, it would appear, no special quarrel with the system.[15] A year later in his speech to the second plenum of the Central Committee,[16] he was half way over to market socialism. In a long passage he wrestles with what we may call "administration versus law of value", and concludes emphatically that in all small questions of consumer goods supply and demand is better than any kind of central planning. There is not one word or hint about workers' councils. The same omission is still more glaring in Kidrič's much later and more defensive piece on the new economy.[17] Not to mention them at this date was surely to imply disapproval. Indeed in the great discussion on the introduction of the workers' councils in the Skupština (June 1950) Kidrič also spoke, but characteristically avoided the councils themselves, concentrating on the reorganization of the state machine.[18]

'Thus it was indeed practical questions of choice and planning, and not the larger ideological questions, that first roused Yugoslavia from her dogmatic slumbers. With his doctrine of 'socialist commodity production'[19] Kidrič did try to provide an ideological underpinning for his views on a freer market. But that is dry stuff, far less exciting than the ideological innovations served up by Tito himself. These were two in number: the doctrine of the withering away of the state, with its un-Marxist assertion that the planning bureaucracy forms part of the state *proprement dit*,[20] and so may be asked to "wither away"; and the doctrine and practice of workers' councils.

'The workers' council came in quite suddenly, and without the longer gestation period to which the free market itself was subjected. By the end of 1949 the first experimental councils had arisen in the larger factories, with an advisory role alone, and in the latter half of 1950 all enterprises, including state shops and farms, were handed over to councils with much the powers they have today. Also in 1950–52 (mainly August 1951) price and output decisions were devolved to enterprises, in accordance with Kidrič's original preoccupation.

'The intellectual origin of the workers' councils was perhaps with Kardelj. But it was Tito himself who introduced them to the Skupština on 26 June 1950.[21] He could quote no Marxist source for them, except Marx's purely tactical pronouncements on the Paris Commune, which are not about socialism; he derived them directly from the "withering away of the state", which he misunderstood (Wiles 1962, chapter 18). Tito's new doctrine on this latter point was the third great Yugoslav innovation. It is plain that in practice without Kidrič's advocacy of a freer market there could have been no workers' councils, for they would have had nothing to administer – as later transpired in Poland. Without Tito, Kidrič would have seemed ideologically unattractive, without

Kidrič, Tito would have had no substance with which to back his dreams.

'Yet both these innovators had essentially the same thing in mind: neither the withering away of the state (as a Marxist ideologist might presume) nor the rational allocation of resources (the obsession of a Western economist),[22] but *the release of local energies.* Not enough people, they felt, had really been putting their shoulders to the wheel. Not merely initiative but also enthusiasm and sheer hard work at all levels had been damped by the centralized state machine. Whether decentralization emphasized the free market environment in which the enterprise should work (Kidrič) or its democratic internal structure (Tito), its object was to set energy free; indeed in philosophical terms to reduce alienation (chapter 21 here). Thus the Yugoslav economic revolution really concerned the activation of economic effort; the changes in management, etc., followed from this.'

Kidrič, then, was a practical administrator, but Tito was a charismatic Communist leader who had hitherto been on the left of the movement. But he was without deep knowledge of Marxism: there is nothing in Marx, Engels, Lenin or (of course) Stalin that supports workers' control except as a tactical device for taking power. Tito's 'error' was to attribute *spontaneous* socialism to his workers: socialism had been virtually suppressed by the dead hand of Stalinist bureaucracy, and must now be released. This belief in spontaneity reminds us of the Soviet 'Workers' Opposition' under 'War' Communism, and is at the opposite pole to Gomułka's right-wing caution.

15. Spontaneity, however, as we saw in sec. 5, is not freedom to Marxists. The Revolution had rendered people unanimous and uncorrupt, and that was why they were free. Neither workers' councils nor the market led at once to any increase in cultural or political freedom. Nor were they meant to. The Yugoslav Party had been especially left-wing, and did not change all its spots at once. On the contrary 1949–52 was a period of extreme political tension, with a cold war against Stalinists outside the country and repression of those within. Simultaneously collectivization was pursued with violence, in order to prove Yugoslavia's orthodoxy. But from 1953 liberalization sets in.

The remaining history of the enterprise-planner relationship, and of the growth of the market until 1965, is only of technical interest. But the slogan, 'the *factories* to the workers' (far from being Marxist, but at least likely to figure among the pre-occupations of a Marxist) was rounded out in 1953 by the idea of the self-managed *society.* A new constitutional law established the bottom-most local authority (Komuna) as the basic unit of society. It was given strong powers over the enterprise at once, and promised increasing status vis-à-vis the republican and federal organs above it; disappointingly little, but still some, of this status has also accrued.

Although this was a logical extension of the workers' councils, it was distinctly non-Marxist and much more directly Yugoslav. A Croatian populist journal before the war had been called 'self-management';[23] neglecting workers' councils in factories, it had asked for that sort of local autonomy that was now promised. Yugoslav Communism had thrown off the pope in a traumatic schism and, in a brief four years, gone native. Simultaneously, and by no accident at all, collectivization was declared voluntary and nearly all collective farms thereupon disappeared.

Another event from about the same period[24] was the admission of the Western pop culture. Thus the Yugoslav Communists were the first to draw in their horns and refuse to censor the purely aesthetic life of the masses, short of downright pornography and narcotics. Simultaneously the demand for socialist realism in highbrow art was dropped, though political censorship remained very strong. Now these early acts of liberalism cannot possibly have been dictated by the new market system, which was itself not complete until 1952; if a market can be called complete in which foreign currency and some basic materials are rationed, more of the latter are subject to price control, there is a variable turnover tax, and nearly all capital is centrally allocated. This was still a period, too, in which citizens were extremely frightened of the security police, and it was particularly unsafe to discuss workers' councils! In 1955 Djilas was arrested for his excessive liberalism: specifically for attacking the manner of life of the Party élite in the press, but also after he had advocated the withering away of the Party as well as the state.[25]

It is thus evident that one can introduce a market economy without substantially lessening tyranny, *in the short run*. Indeed in Yugoslavia in 1957 there was to my eyes far less freedom than in Poland. Poland had all Yugoslavia's freedoms, in the early years of Gomułka's reign, plus a certain liberty of political and economic discussion. Above all the Party line was not sacrosanct, and people were not afraid. The principal difference was the will of the government, not the structure of the economy. But by 1970, even in 1971 after Gomułka had fallen, the situation was quite different. Gomułka re-established a centralized STE without workers' councils (chapter 6, sec. 14), suppressed the student press, expelled the Jews, offended the Church, pleased the Russians, invaded Czechoslovakia – and only left the peasants uncollectivized. Meanwhile Yugoslavia, in the so-called reforms of 1965, anchored the principle of self-administration everywhere more firmly. These reforms devalued the dinar (again), relaxed various controls including exchange control, turned the management of banks over from politicians to enterprise directors, and reduced officially the role of the Party in the economy. I.e. the country ceased to play at being a market economy and really became one. Concomitantly, the government let Djilas out of prison, permitted him to publish abroad, sold *Le Monde* in street kiosks,[26] sacked her security police chief, permitted a government to lose a vote of confidence and resign,[27] decentralized the Home Guard to republics, gave autonomy to her Albanian minority, sprouted a small hippie movement, a little nudity and quite a lot of student revolt – and nearly tore herself apart in strife between the constituent nationalities. The astonishing re-growth of petty capitalism (chapter 20, sec. 10) somewhat pre-dates 1965.

That disorderly and charmless state of affairs is freedom – one-party freedom of positively Mexican dimensions. Did it happen because of the market, or did the market happen because of it? We can only be sure that the League (Party) wanted a free market – indeed a still freer one than it has, with a wholly convertible dinar; and that it has always trusted the masses more than other Parties. Since the early 'sixties Yugoslav freedom and the Yugoslav market have grown together. Before then the market grew while freedom did not. While one cannot see the detailed connexions, the general outline at least is persuasive: the market was not merely chronologically prior, it encouraged freedom.

16. Yugoslavia is liberal enough to have a small New Left. Partially contained by Party discipline and state censorship, this tendency grew up long after self-management. The New Left is certainly dedicated to self-management in all countries, but only in a disruptive and impractical way. For instance in Yugoslavia it demands small enterprises, direct democracy and the downgrading of the technocratic 'business committees' (chapter 20) and simultaneously less market![28]

Certainly self-management, involving millions of people in the hard practical conduct of day-to-day business, is deeply conservative wherever it really works, even if inefficiently. Hence the lack of interest in Yugoslavia among foreigners demanding workers' control. This conservatism applies even in organizations where the New Left congregate: universities, publishing houses, broadcasting, sometimes museums and newspapers. When the thing is here to stay, more patient and practical people take it over. However self-management in the means of education and communication poses a special problem: freedom of opinion in general.

If in these organizations self-management is replacing an existing capitalist set-up by violence, there is of course an interval when freedom at best changes sides, more likely diminishes for ever. But once it is fully installed what have we gained or lost? Let us set aside the universities as too peculiar and too often discussed elsewhere. Then on a newspaper the proprietor or his appointed director is out, and we must obey the committee of self-management instead. In terms of working conditions this is clear gain, since in these matters this system is more democratic by definition – and therefore, as we have seen, probably more free.

But as to freedom of opinion (including here the artistic policy of the museum), those who aspire to leadership in settled systems of self-management are likely to be socially homogeneous: middle-aged, neither rich nor poor, organization men who have worked their way up – and more than a little opinionated. They are likely to give the views of misfits short shrift, and sharply to lessen that capitalist diversity and spontaneity which have been the life-blood of free opinion. Thus in modern British circumstances each journalist would feel about as free as he does today, if self-management delegated choice of a newspaper's political bias to a committee of journalists, to the exclusion of printers and charwomen. But this would be because he had exercised his new power, so changing the editorials and news selection in favour of what happens to be majority opinion among journalists. So the tabloids would move towards the centre, and leave the Tory working class without their pabulum; for the Tory worker is never a journalist.

There are, that is to say, blocs of opinion that the amoral capitalist system is willing to satisfy, since nearly anyone can persuade a capitalist to sell him what he wants. But in a marginally more moralistic system producers would impose their own values, yet there is no reason at all to prefer these values. Thus the market forces journalists to satisfy the reader's bias, not their own; and this is less disreputable than the other way round. For there is no capitalist *class*, but there is a journalistic *profession*, with a very definite *déformation professionelle*. Thus to take other examples, the official Stalinist newspaper would quickly go Trotskyite, and the various trusts that protect and more or less stabilize the political identity of *Le Monde* and *The Times* would yield to rapid and unpredictable change. A small movement of journalistic self-management would increase diversity, a large one would diminish it.

It is not possible to generalize, in our present dearth of evidence, on the net effect of all this homogeneity on our press and cultural institutions. The pessimist will point not merely to the power of professional homogeneity but also to the baleful influence of printers' unions everywhere. These unions are constantly tempted to censor anti-union material, especially about themselves; and in revolutionary times they censor much more. They could hardly be kept off the boards of political self-management, and their influence would be extremely illiberal. The optimist will recite the invariable and more far-reaching censorship and the positive bias of capitalist proprietors.[29]

There was surely never a sector in which institutional *laissez-faire* was more in order. Every system has its evils. The essence is to preserve diversity, and no one system can do that.

17. More decisive, however, is the relation between political freedom and the status of the individual labourer. We have pointed out before (chapter 4) how wrong is the emphasis of economics in beginning with the enterprise. We find that it leads here to the implicit doctrine that political freedom is something to do with government controls over

enterprises. But ultimately these latter are metaphysical abstractions: only people are free or not free.

What, then, if the main incentive to work is not monetary gain but force, i.e. physical threats?[30] Then, first, if the state not the enterprise applies this force it obviously has an economic stranglehold over the individual, which his political freedom is unlikely to survive. For if the authorities can compel a man to work in a particular place, they can tell him how to vote, and when to keep quiet. And if they can, they sooner or later will. This is the *a priori* argument from the direction of labour in originally free societies. It is purely *a priori*, because there is no historical case of such a sequence. Direction of labour is so unpopular that it is practised only in wartime, even in STEs. Since it is never imposed on a large scale in peacetime, except in Cuba and China, we have no evidence to back our argument, but it appears solid all the same. It is confirmed by the fact that there is even less freedom in Cuba and China than in other Communist countries: a sign, doubtless, of the converse proposition, that only governments radically hostile to individual freedom of any kind will abolish this elementary economic freedom.

However a partial and controlled use of such force is quite compatible with political freedom. Most countries compel children to go to school. Many almost compel, and some quite compel, prisoners to work. In peacetime many, in wartime all, countries compel young men to join the forces (chapter 8, sec. 8). All this has proved its compatibility in the long run with freedom. But note why: prisoners and children are not free anyway, while young men are perpetuating unthinkingly an ancient tribal custom, during which they perform no economic task. The exceptions are, by no accident, Cuba and China, where military service includes labour service: why not, since the whole of life is labour service? – and the military metaphor is commonly applied to it. Even so, conscription is a marginal case; indeed when young men cease to think tribally it becomes a freedom issue. Nevertheless the commonplace example of military conscription shows that we cannot safely infer political consequences even from something so overwhelming and elementary as forced labour. After all, conscripts vote.

18. What, next, if the enterprise has the power to exact forced labour, but is itself on a free market? This is the case of *slavery* under capitalism; the enterprise now owns the labourer, while the state merely protects this form of property by its usual means of coercion. There is no direction of labour, not really even for slaves: there is a new right of property. In this case it is crystal clear that the non-slave population can enjoy political freedom. All that nineteenth-century US rhetoric about a country not surviving 'half-slave, half-free', about no man being free until all are free, was – rhetoric. The birthplace of political freedom, after all, was

also a slave-holding society. There is nothing paradoxical or unstable about a restricted franchise.

Opinions to the contrary rest ultimately on the notion we have rejected: that freedom is necessarily a good thing. Not so: the slave-holders will exercise it to reinforce slavery. Precisely their freedom is what is wrong:[31] some higher tyrant must move in. The most one can say is that in the modern world as a whole external pressures on slave societies are too great. They become paranoid and persecute the slightest deviance on this issue, and so destroy the individual freedom of the slave-holder and his hangers-on. But relax that external pressure, and freedom for slave-holders will return.

Similar kinds of slavery can and have easily existed in STEs. Except for legal and ideological trimmings, there is nothing contradictory between socialism and slavery (chapter 8). But there is between co-operation and slavery, and this stands highly to the credit of the 'third way'.

19. What relevance has *economic freedom* to this subject? We have already said so much implicitly that we may be brief. As a corollary definition, it must be the absence of human restraint over individual economic activity. This is not *laissez-faire* as ordinarily understood, since that is a typical concept of that 'enterprise-based economics' for which we have tried throughout to substitute individual-based economics. Besides, if an enterprise is a metaphysical entity, and cannot have a leisure preference or a futurity discount (chapter 4), how could it enjoy being free?

The most workable definition seems to be that labour and consumers must be free, while the status of the enterprise is a purely instrumental matter. Its freedom may help or hinder, but is in any case only the freedom of its managers to take decisions *in that capacity*. They would have to take similar decisions anyway in a hierarchy, and none of their human rights would be violated by such a subordination. There is no right to take decisions about other people; that is simply something you get paid for. We have, then, to do with a civil right: the individual should freely dispose of his own labour, income and savings. The dividing line between individual and enterprise freedom runs approximately between 'populism' and 'capitalism': the essential freedoms of the many and the peripheral freedoms of the few. But whether good or bad in itself, the economic freedom of the enterprise clearly overlaps with the political freedom of the individual, in that the press, the broadcasters and the political opposition must, as we have seen, freely dispose of goods and services, and form enterprises for that purpose. Political freedom requires the economic freedom of both individuals and some enterprises.

Does co-operation or self-administration increase the economic freedom of the ordinary worker, vis-à-vis his position under capitalism or socialism? Clearly it gives him more control over his own conditions of labour, and indeed over all the other decisions of the enterprise, less directly related to his working conditions. This means a lower degree of alienation, and is *par excellence* an instance of that 'control over what nearly concerns us' demanded by the theorists of participation. If ever the 'absence of human restraint over individual economic activity' had meaning, it is here.

Therefore Yugoslavia is easily the country with the most economic freedom, for it has substituted for the 'peripheral freedoms of a few' corporate executives the far more central freedoms of every working man.[32] The nearest equivalent under capitalism is the 'labour-restrained enterprise' of chapter 7; but union bureaucracy and centralization often alienate the individual member completely. In an STE there is really no equivalent, since the *local* branch of the union cannot influence the central planner; moreover the highly centralized Party interferes very thoroughly with union affairs.

But the Yugoslav citizen still has very little political freedom as defined in sec. 1. So economic freedom as defined is fairly separable. This is an obvious point, since intellectuals, priests, artists and politicians are not interested in the same things as workers. The latter will on the whole tolerate whatever political power permits them to work, earn and spend. The former (an overlapping category, of course) need such economic freedom as allows them to pursue their other aims, but they must have political freedom as well.

Even so, economic freedom virtually entails inequality. There is no force equalizing private fortunes, even under workers' self-management, if accumulation and inheritance are free (chapter 16), and a free labour market fans out our earnings too. So is there perhaps a contradiction in the very concept: can the poor be economically free? Can they, indeed, be politically free? The double answer is yes; for just as freedom does not have to be good so it does not have to include other good things, or to be particularly precious to us or worth preserving. If I am without wealth or skill economic freedom means a choice of doss-houses, a choice of unskilled jobs, etc. It is wholly unparadoxical to wish I was both richer and compelled to work at a particular, interesting and permanent, job. My economic freedom is not worth having, but it is certainly there. 'Anyone may enter the Ritz, and anyone may sleep under a bridge' – the *pons asinorum* of our subject is the perception that this splendid piece of rhetoric entails a straight fallacy. If not anyone is allowed under a bridge, and not anyone may enter the Ritz, there is less freedom. If anyone *may* do either we admit *ipso facto* that there is economic freedom, and not just the uninteresting sort that applies to enterprises, but the important kind that individuals enjoy. If not everyone *can*, there is inequality. Equality is often preferable to, and sometimes incompatible with, freedom. Freedom is often a mockery. The rich are usually hypocritical, and by definition selfish. None of this alters the meanings of words.

20. Finally, what is the relevance of the level and rate of economic development? Since both political freedom and economic development result from the chances of history, we should expect a low level of correlation. It so happens that at the end of the eighteenth century, when economic development for the most part began, parliamentary democracy was *à la mode*. The connexion was not fortuitous; since all governments, with their various economic regulations and ideologies, were at that time 'objectively' opposed to development, only *laissez-faire* could favour it. But as we have seen, *laissez-faire* sits easiest with civil rights, and certainly at that time to reduce the power of the government one had to extend the franchise. So development needed *laissez-faire*, and *laissez-faire* needed political freedom.

Western capitalist economics has never really surmounted this syndrome. But Communist governments are actually favourable to development, while under *laissez-faire* neutrality is, by definition, the best we can expect. So the *rate* of economic growth (a subject we on the whole avoid for reasons of space) tends now to be faster under governments opposed to both *laissez-faire* and political freedom. This is also natural in that only strong governments can extract from poor people high expenditures for investment and R and D, or impose sharp changes in the manner of life.

But the *level* of development is different. If government influences the rate, the level influences government. Those countries[33] that by embracing *laissez-faire* originally attained the highest rate, have now of course the highest level. They tend to be satisfied with political freedom. By colonization or conquest they have imposed their system on others with a different history.[34] Osmosis and chance account for a few more cases.[35] In these two latter categories almost any level of development is possible. Indeed India, worth about 25 ordinary countries by sheer population, is one of the poorest in the world.

It seems that any correlation between political freedom and the level of development, where historical chance had been eliminated, should be very small. The only case where various political systems compete in a fluid situation, while neither history nor culture differ much from country to country, is the countries of Iberian culture, and the relation there is:

$$P = 0{\cdot}1627 + 0{\cdot}003Y + 0{\cdot}0134L$$
$$(R^2 = 0{\cdot}269)$$

where P (for parliamentary democracy) was set at 3 for Uruguay, Costa Rica, Chile and Venezuela, 2 for Mexico and Colombia, 1 for all the other fourteen countries (including Portugal and Spain) in 1969; Y is GNP per head and L literacy over thirty.[36]

These seem to be the best data and the fairest comparison. They show almost zero correlation. But the numbers are so small that the subsequent defections of Uruguay and Chile have radically changed the parameters. I am tempted nonetheless to infer that economic institutions have more influence than real incomes on political freedom.

21. What are the basic lessons of this chapter? First, the subject-matter is infinitely complex, we have scarcely grazed its surface. For it is really a part of political economy, not comparative economics, and therefore beyond anything properly to be called social science. All the connexions we claim to have perceived are exceedingly loose. Secondly politics dominates economics. We get freedom if those who have political power want us to have it, or are adequately controlled. Some economic systems expose us to more, others to less, danger. But the former do not so much stifle freedom of themselves: they are chosen by those who, seeking power, are hostile to freedom anyway. Thirdly the individual has primacy over the enterprise. We do not really care who runs very large corporations, but we do care who tells the individual to work. Indeed this third point can be put in another way: the system of incentives is the most important aspect of the economy. It is perhaps tolerable to order enterprises about, it is not tolerable to order individuals about. The direction of labour is poison, whereas Soviet planning is acceptable outside the communications sector – though of course French planning, with its negative stimuli and essentially market-oriented enterprises, is preferable.

Is it, then, the market or is it capitalism that forms the true economic substratum of political freedom? Evidently, a labour market is enough to avoid the direction of labour – other markets are unnecessary. But in the communications sector we need a great deal more. It is not enough that we can freely dispose of the goods and services currently required, though this is already a great deal. We need an ownership system that can live without subsidies and cope independently with bankruptcy: i.e. a capitalist or a co-operative system, or preferably both.

Again we have seen state capitalism posing a weak threat to French freedom, and on the other hand Yugoslavia and Hungary stumbling away from totalitarianism after the market had been introduced. In Yugoslavia this was a matter of time, and freedom was hardly intended. In Hungary freedom was the sly main aim, and the market little more than a stalking horse. If there have been many capitalist and only one co-operative countries, that is due to historical chance or even to the lower economic efficiency of the co-operative form. The Yugoslav and Hungarian instances confirm what one would suppose *a priori*: the market is crucial, but ownership is, so to speak, *secundus inter pares*. Without ownership changes the market will not function for long, but co-operation is as good as capitalism. Nay, in one way it is better for freedom, since it produces fewer capital transactions, and so less major gross corruption. But the inequality of capitalism is in this context a virtue, since it produces trusts and very rich men, who are necessary for the defeat of a government. Co-operation on the other hand must be expected to reduce intellectual diversity, since it is not cynical and individualistic enough.

Notes

1. As of April 1973! Cf. my 'The Chicken and the Egg' in the *Journal of Constitutional and Parliamentary Studies*, New Delhi, April–June 1970. I have dropped the Philippines, Ghana and Singapore from that list, and added Barbados and Bahamas. The qualifying population is 100,000.

2. I refer to the Republic of Saló, under German occupation in Northern Italy. Mussolini justifiably called this socialism; cf. chapter 7, sec. 7.

3. Including even the kolkhoz! – in the occupied Ukraine (chapter 6, sec. 16).

4. The almost populist Jefferson is an exception here, though visitors to Monticello may question his sincerity.

5. This question reminds us of Keynes. He never presented an ideology.

6. Many will protest that this too is wrongheaded about freedom, being élitist and technocratic. While this is true, we must not be too particular. Few non-socialist traditions come off any better on balance, and it is clear from experience that freedom can live with Fabianism.

7. The book was published in 1944 (Chicago). Cf. Wiles in *History and Theory*, 1/1972.

8. In the form of mildly dissident limited editions, printed at author's expense (James Feron in *New York Times*, 7 December 1972).

9. In other countries the counter-violence of the police is of course greater in quantity since it is more often attacked; but it is much milder in quality than before the war. There can be no question but that police behaviour has improved, even under very severe provocation, along with the growth of all other civil rights.

10. Party members think harder. Many of the most disturbed and sceptical Russians are Party members.

11. I have deliberately passed over other ACEs, feeling uninformed about them.

12. If not, as usual, in debt! Cf. chapter 6, sec. 16.

13. I rule out the Histadrut as essentially a consumers' co-op owning ordinary factories. It is also too governmental and too large.

14. Wiles 1962, pp. 36–8 (amended).

15. Speech on the budget, *Borba*, 24 April 1948. There is a longish passage on the standard of living where the question of 'administration versus law of value' would have fitted in very appropriately, had he wished to raise it.

16. *Komunist*, March 1949.

17. 'Theses on the Economics of the Transition Period in Our Country', *Komunist*, November 1950.

18. *Komunist*, July–September 1950.

19. Cf. Wiles 1962, chapter 3, sec. 2.

20. See Wiles 1962, chapter 17.

21. *Komunist*, July–September 1950. Djilas, in his *The Unperfect Society*, London 1969, pp. 157–9, says the originators were Kidrič, which is certainly

wrong; and Kardelj, which may well be right. On the possibility of Italian Fascist influence cf. chapter 7, sec. 7 here. Djilas's own originality, while he was still a Marxist, lay in his doctrine that the Party must wither away simultaneously with the State. But this came after the economic reforms, and did not affect them.

22. For instance Kidrič had never read Oskar Lange. Cf. I. M. Maksimović in *Essays in Honour of Oskar Lange*, Warsaw 1964, pp. 349–50.

23. *Samo-uprava.* The post-war word is *samo-upravljanje.*

24. This paragraph is from my personal experience in 1957. Cf. my 'Voyage to Laputa' in *Encounter*, London 1957.

25. But his idea lived on after his arrest. The Party was renamed the League of Communists, and after the 1965 reforms it really did retreat from interference in the economy.

26. This is a basic freedom. In Hungary or Poland today one can only buy *Le Monde* in the lobbies of grand tourist hotels. The staff could report and the security police could identify buyers from off the street, but this is thought not to happen. Western non-Communist newspapers are very much more expensive than others. They may also be subscribed to privately and by institutions.

27. To be sure, only in the Slovene republic, and only on the issue of social security finance; but still . . . !

28. For a good example of the Yugoslav New Left cf. Mihajlo Marković, *The Contemporary Marx*, Nottingham 1974.

29. Also they are amenable to advertisers. The influence of advertisers is a logically separable matter. Presumably their influence over the self-managed press would be as great as it is over capitalist ones unless the sources of newspaper finance were changed. But they could be changed anyway.

30. This does not exclude substantial appeals to self-interest once one is confined to one's place of work: cf. chapter 8, sec. 2.

31. One of the principal instruments of tyranny in the US South until about 1965 was trial by jury, the palladium of our common Anglo-Saxon liberties. For no matter how the judge summed up, the white jury convicted the negro.

32. It furthermore ensures more decentralized power to local government, which is much the same thing.

33. Canada, USA, Australasia, UK, Belgium, Netherlands, Scandinavia (incl. Iceland). Finland is not Scandinavian.

34. West Germany, Austria, Italy, Japan, India, Ceylon, Israel, Jamaica, Barbados, Bahamas, Eire.

35. Finland, Costa Rica, Venezuela. Note that France is unclassifiable.

36. Wiles, op. cit., 1970. Cf. Irma Adelman and Cynthia T. Morris, *Society, Politics and Economic Development*, Baltimore 1967.

18

War and Economic Systems[1]

18

1. Do economic institutions cause war? Do they generate, that is, internal pressures for which war is a preferred outlet? Do they tempt us into war for economic gain? – a motive that might, of course, sway us irrespective of our system. Are they themselves the expression of messianic, imperialistic economic cults? Have some systems more of these tendencies than others?

There has been war under every economic system – against entities with the same and entities with different systems. There was nothing so like the domain of one Chinese warlord as the domain of another Chinese warlord, yet they fought – for the greater power of the warlord, but also for personal plunder. This latter was an economic motive indeed, but one quite unconnected to systems. Similarly the Vikings were essentially robber bands, seeking to become kleptocrats (chapter 16, sec. 24): they fought for plunder and dominion, but also because they liked it. The Mahrattas fought for the same purposes. Both, then, accepted the social systems they found: all they demanded of any conquered system was good tax discipline. The role of economics and ideology is even slighter when one tribe of New Guinea cannibals fights another – yet these people live to fight. *Their* chief motive appears to be simply and straightforwardly the proof of the warrior's manhood. Economic gain is neither sought nor made. Very similarly in the nineteenth century, from Napoleon inclusive, European capitalist and semi-feudal powers fought several wars against each other, to expand boundaries or suppress new nationalisms. They were certainly not after economic gain, whether of the rulers or the ruled. The tincture of ideology was also very slight.[2]

The Crusaders on the other hand, and the Moslem conquerors before them, had genuinely ideological motives. They fought to impose a religion. Both plunder and the love of war were important but secondary. The economic *situation*, though probably not the *system*, of Arabia may well have played a role in launching the Moslems. But even this is not true of the Crusaders: their aggressions were surely the most purely idealistic of all history. It is worth remembering that we industrialized Western capitalists are descended from those agrarian, feudal Crusaders. Their monuments embellish our churches, their deeds our history books. We sing hymns in their praise at Matins.

Less strong, but occasionally convincing, instances of ideological warfare are provided by the USSR. The nascent Bolshevik power faced a civil war and a (very half-hearted) capitalist intervention. It has fought and beaten nearly every small nationality and country within its power that has tried to throw off its system. Of these it has annexed, except for

Finland, every single one to which the Romanovs had a claim. It fights – very circumspectly – its Chinese comrades. It is always near the brink of war with the USA – praise or blame are out of place here. It is constantly in a state of economic war with some country or other (Wiles 1969, chapter 17). In all this, ideology is inextricable from Russian imperialism.

2. What is it, then, that history teaches? It teaches that men make war, full stop. Unlike all mammals except, it seems, rats,[3] men have few inhibitions about intra-specific killing. Any motive can overcome these weak inhibitions: fear of aggression and the wish to pre-empt it; sheer plunder (called today, more nicely, reparations); the genuine need to move to better land (or, today, to improve one's terms of trade, to get access to raw materials, markets, warm-water ports); religious mania; irredentism or other territorial injustice (e.g. anxiety about people across the border who speak our language); boredom; the love of fighting *per se*.[4] This chapter puts the question, must we add to this list of motives strong enough to overcome the inhibition, any internal pressures brought about by economic systems as such? Such might be the imminent collapse of profits, the search for full employment, or a messianic opinion about the economic system one's neighbour ought to have. They include also economically induced civil strife, e.g. class-war. But we exclude such economic motives as plunder and getting better 'land', which operate under all systems.

Before we answer our question a more fundamental issue must be faced. The lesson of history, drawn above, is that men are bad. They like to fight, they do not mind killing each other, so long as there is a reasonable excuse. It is not necessary to postulate *any* defect in a social system to explain why its denizens make war: it is enough that these denizens are human. If the system itself does not give them one reason they will find another for themselves.

Indeed throughout this book certain assumptions – I am too certain they are right to call them prejudices – have been latent. They were probably unimportant elsewhere, but must now be made explicit. Selfishness and even aggression are instinctive, like mother-love and the sexual appetite. They are *to some degree* genetically determined. The three qualifying words are added to allow for variant individuals, in whom these instincts are very weak or very strong, like any other inherited characteristics. They also allow for the possibilities of overlaying instincts with training, and of stifling more specific ones by denying them opportunity.[5] But the suggestion that free trade or Communism or what not might abolish war is absurd. Similarly an economic system that makes no use at all of selfishness will fail, as indeed many have (chapter 2).

This is as much as to say, I hold that biology is peripherally a social science; that to deny instincts and assert that man's character is infinitely malleable is as absurd and dogmatic as to deny inherited inequalities of intelligence (chapter 16). But in so doing we must not revert to biological determinism. What biology does is to set limits to the range of human temperament. They may be rather narrow, as in the case of aggression, which is the subject of this chapter; or quite broad, as in the case of economic motivation (chapter 2). In any case the position of these limits has not yet been established scientifically, since there are so many variables in the study of man, and passion and prejudice run so strong. But that biology sets no limits has been virtually disproven, and it is always best to take as provisionally true that which is most probable.[6]

3. To many people, and to many social scientists (though I can proudly report that few of these are economists), such a view is anathema. The social sciences have a very bad record of not recognizing genetics and instinct. So far as a mere amateur like the writer can determine, human evil comes with the genes. Better social science, and better systems, can only mitigate it; *pro tanto*, the salaries and numbers of social scientists might as well be lower. All this is particularly true of war and aggression, where also economists have a bad record. For these are primary social phenomena, that do and should obsess thinking people. Yet since about 1800 economists have left war out (Wiles 1969, chapter 18). If from time to time they have been serious about its conduct, they are still very innocent about its causes. This is because of their residual Benthamism, and their instinctive aversion from the irrational. But at least Bentham, though foolish enough to believe that men were rational, never said that they were good – such super-naïveté is implicit, however, in several of our sister sciences.[7]

But such people are not truly scientists, who 'put their hand into the hand of fact, and let it lead them like a child'. For the attitude here recommended accepts without sophisticated evasion the verdict of history and of each day's headlines. It looks straight and cool at that frightening monster, the baby in his cradle. It avoids, too, intellectual imperialism, the omnipotence of thought and wishful thinking: i.e. it is modest about the possibilities of social science. In particular as to my own speciality, I just do not think economic systems are that important. We have seen that nearly any system can grow quickly; we now see that no system, taken as a social whole, can prevent war. Probably only the fear of national extinction, or the discovery of a reliable psychological substitute for war,[8] can do that.

4. But at least systems can and should be improved: perhaps some of them do generate removable internal pressures leading to war? It seems to me that of all purely economic systems, capitalism is the one that generates most such pressures. We now turn to *specify* these, and a word is in order about that desiccated little verb. Too often – indeed almost invariably – Marxists and left-wing Keynesians have contented them-

selves with bare asseveration; have failed to contrast hard-headedly the behaviour of systems they may be presumed to prefer; have not connected their empirical suspicions with existing theory; and have neglected contary evidence. All honour, then, to pioneers;[9] but in a matter so desperately serious it is important to be serious oneself.

We postpone Mercantilism and modern imperialism until the next chapter. More precisely, we consider here only wars with opponents of equal power, in which there is no hope at all that reparations or a protected market for one's exports or capital will recoup the military outlay. In other words, our concern here is with wars, or preparations for war, for which the economic reward is reaped by a part of the nation at the expense of the rest. This includes civil wars and strife.

What precisely *is* a military-industrial complex? Let us define it as a group of (a) senior general officers, (b) middle-rank supply officers, (c) civilian defence experts, (d) selected politicians, (e) militaristic propagandists lodged in the communications media, (f) international traders in arms, (g) managers and trade-union officials in weapons factories, (h) weapon technologists wherever located, and (i) shareholders, if any, in the firms of (f) and (g). These people know and meet each other. They have a common interest in a large defence establishment, and in minor wars wherein arms and tactics may be tried out, promotions won and expenditures justified to the taxpayer. Major shareholdings may be held by anyone in groups (a) to (h), thus intensifying their interest. Groups (f) and (g) have an additional interest in wars purely between foreigners. None of them, of course, wants to involve his own country in a major war, since that means and has long meant rationing, crippling taxation and sudden, personal, death. Mere profiteering out of war, however often unearthed and condemned, is irrelevant. People profiteer out of everything. The question is, do they influence their government to make war?

A special word about some of these groups, less obvious than the rest. (c), the civilian defence experts, includes the ordinary civil servants in the defence ministries, many diplomats who have despaired – why should they not? – of diplomacy, and the new breed of conflict resolvers and atomic games theorists, sitting for the most part in universities and independent think-tanks. (d) refers to such politicians as have belonged in their time to the other groups listed, or have thrown in their lot with them for the sake of power, or have been bought by capitalists offering them shares, or by soldiers offering them bases and ordnance factories in their constituencies. Members of group (b), if denied promotion in the forces, are extremely valuable to the suppliers as negotiators with government purchasing agencies on retirement. So they switch and become (g), negotiating with their previous colleagues. This is a very old practice, reaching back to before the first World War. It is indeed of such sovereign importance in the study of state capitalism that it requires a name. The French, feeling most the need, have provided us with the single word – *pantouflage*.[10] This practice affects also group (c). Group (e) are a necessary and powerful element in any such complex. Some are strictly incorruptible, romantic volunteers, like those many British authors of novels about German invasion in 1890–1914.[11] Some are journalists who insensibly slip into accepting favours, such as prior information, in return for slanted articles. Some are bought outright, like public relations firms and professional lobbyists.

5. We can now turn to the mechanisms themselves. Capitalism is more prone to this kind of aberration than Communism because:

(i) the multiplier is greater than one (cf. chapter 14, sec. 3). This means that there is often unemployment, and that military expenditures create jobs not only directly – as under Communism – but also indirectly. Hence on a national level it is always difficult to reduce public expenditures – but under capitalism military expenditures are a large part of them. Not only profits are concerned but also wages. So trade unions tend to support the military even on a national level, and apart from the localization of the multiplier, to which we turn.

(ii) The multiplier has a particularly strong local action. The people who benefit directly from a military base in the Charleston, South Carolina, constituency of Mr. Mendel Rivers,[12] chairman of the House Armed Services Committee, are soldiers from all over USA; but the shopkeepers and local tax collectors are his constituents. In nearly all cases, much of the second round of the multiplier series is localized near the original expenditure.[13] When Mr. Rivers collects an ordnance factory, however, he captures both the first and the second rounds for his constituents. The local value of the multiplier is more important than its larger nation-wide value. For since all political systems and trade unions alike have a local hierarchy local influences are always very strong indeed.

It is difficult altogether to imagine away the local action of the multiplier even in an STE; for instance a local military base means promotion and bonuses for retail trade employees. It might seem to follow that certain first secretaries of provincial party units, senior enough to sit in the Central Committee, are the Communist equivalents of Mr. Rivers. But none such has been, to my knowledge, identified. After all, in an STE any new project is as good as a military base: see (vi) below.

(iii) The shareholders (group (i) above) are the only ones with absolutely no counterpart in an STE. Shareholding is *the* great source of conflicts of interest. It ensures that any member of any of the other groups in the complex might have a conflict of interests, for any might own shares.[14] Undoubtedly very many conflicts of interest arise in STEs – nepotism is merely one obvious case – but never on so large a scale. Small corruption is surely more rife in so controlled and contrived a society, but large corruption is just technically impossible. I.e. in a very general way –

(iv) under capitalism bribes can be very much bigger. Far larger personal interests are at stake when a contract is awarded – not salaries alone, but capital gains and take-over bids hang on the issue. Moreover people have the technical means to make such large payments, and to receive and to spend them, and to conceal all these operations. Therefore larger issues are decided in a corrupt manner (chapter 16, sec. 24).

(v) Then, too, capitalism has fewer ideological defences against this sort of thing. It is founded, as we saw in chapter 2, on a principled amorality. Greed is *meant* to motivate it. Naked pursuit of one's own interest, in conflict with social interest, is not supposed to be possible in STEs. Of course it happens all the time, but it is automatically disgraceful, and this makes its practitioner uncomfortable.

(vi) Public expenditures under capitalism are traditionally confined to certain areas, and this is indeed part of the definition of capitalism. Therefore public favours and state manipulation of the economy, whether honest or corrupt, are confined to the same areas. Some of these areas are electorally or politically popular: e.g. roads and health research. So too much gets spent on them. The assertion that the public sector is starved at the expense of the private in an ACE[15] is false over a great part, perhaps the majority, of it. In periods when defence is popular it also is over-financed. But a socialist government, and also the French government (sec. 10), is responsible for everything; so there are at all times more claims, whether honest or corrupt, upon its resources and attention. Defence is never so dominant, or at least not for this reason.

But a number of other propositions on this subject seem to be false: (a) The need for foreign raw materials or other supplies is more pressing because of the capitalist system (Lenin). In logic, of course, mere input-output considerations know no ideological boundaries; any advanced economy might experience such pressure. Soviet behaviour in Eastern Europe amply confirms this logic (chapter 19). (b) Arms have to be exported in order to reap economies of scale. This applies to all systems (sec. 16). (c) Arms are exceptionally profitable to make. This is not false, but doubtful. Capitalist governments are hard and unfair bargainers, who often use their monopsonistic and legal superiority to revise contracts. The arms producer makes less profit on sales than the producer for the civilian market and his is judged an unstable trade by security analysts and the stock market. But – and this is the main thing – owing to the extraordinary amount of government capital advanced to him he turns his smaller profit on sales into a larger profit on his own net worth (*Newsweek*, loc. cit.; Weidenbaum, op. cit.). (d) The international connexions brought about by capitalism are all of a kind to cause war. On the contrary some of them operate powerfully for peace *between equipollent nations*. Foreign holders of land, bonds, insurance policies and equities on the territory of a potential enemy, want their property undisturbed. The banks fear speculative movements of hot money. The arms manufacturers have strong, sometimes treasonable, international connexions.[16] Though feudalism generated similar problems of divided allegiance, socialism, with its completely sovereign state machine, is much more nationalistic. But contrariwise these same mechanisms operate powerfully for domination and colonial wars, *when the nations are of unequal power*, as the next chapter shows.

6. This leads us to the 'technological complicity' of the producer and the consumer. In the modern world, the argument runs, all important weapons, attracting most of the large expenditures, are prototypes.[17] In no field is technical progress so rapid or cost so uncertain, so here buyer and seller enter into an unavoidable technological complicity. The buyer cannot simply pay on 'cost-plus' principles, or he will run through his money very quickly indeed. This remains true if the usual cost-plus fixed fee yields to some form of cost-plus incentive arrangement, like agreed fines for late delivery, etc., etc. If the customer went over to an unchangeable price, fixed in advance by competitive bidding, he would get no bids, so great is the uncertainty. There is no substitute, then, for a close informal relationship based on confidence and open books.[18] It ceases, then, to be clear who owns what, or who is the ultimate 'sovereign'. Indeed while the customer is interfering in every minor detail of enterprise activity[19] the producer is largely designing the product – but if that product is a weapon then he is also determining a weapons system, and so in turn a foreign policy. Thus had Skybolt worked, *or been made to work*, bombers would not have become obsolete so quickly, Britain's 'special relationship' to USA would not have been exposed as one of such utter dependence but something of value, and de Gaulle might have let Britain into the Common Market.[20]

This is a very old situation. Civil engineers and the private corporations or local authorities that buy their dams, viaducts and aerodromes have long since made confidence and open books a standard procedure, available to the client among other contracting procedures.[21] The reader will probably have enjoyed a similar relation with his watch-repairer, his doctor, his lawyer or his architect. These people also dictate to him what he can and cannot buy. Why, then, has Galbraith, rediscovering it in the case of sophisticated weapons (op. cit. 1967), been so impressed as to found on it a new economics and almost a new society?

All prophets are difficult to understand, and the necessary pedant who clears up after them is often unfair. The point may be that if some 5 per cent of the US national product[22] consists of manufactures procured *by the federal government* under these conditions, the world is turning upside down; a new kind of implicit socialism, or rather state capitalism, is emerging. If so, the doctrine is strained and apocalyptic: the first breath of peace will blow it away, and in any case the present situation is quite stable so far as economics goes. Only *larger* military and space expenditures would make such a sector expand.

Or the point just might be – but certainly is not, in Galbraith's own view – that here is extra evidence that capitalism means war. Quite the contrary, of course: we have to do here with a form of state capitalism or socialism. It is just precisely the retreat from ordinary capitalism that presents the danger. What is shown is not that capitalism means war, but that war means socialism – a very valid point, indeed a cliché, but an old one.

Or again, and most plausibly, so let us hope that this time we draw the intended conclusion, we are faced with a *descriptive* statement. This *is* how governments procure sophisticated weapons, and it *does* lead to 'technological complicity'. It is certainly the same in an STE, where government and enterprise are part of one complex anyway. So here we have a true element of convergence, though more with France than with USSR, as we see below.

7. There can be no doubt that in USA today this whole syndrome exists, and that foreign policy is influenced thereby. Indeed the syndrome seems to have been named by that most unmilitary general and unpolitical politician Dwight Eisenhower, in his farewell speech from the presidential office (op. cit.).[23] But is that enough for a large generalization about capitalism? It would seem, as we go through our other examples, not to be so. Capitalist societies are, as societies go, rather peaceful. They contain and repress for the most part the bellicose pressures their strictly economic system generates.

Thus the syndrome is quite new in USA itself. The *federal government* since 1776 has spent mostly very trivial sums on war: it has a deep-seated tradition of civilian control over a small standing army. No Communist government, indeed no government, has such an anti-military tradition. But then no body of men was ever more unAmerican than the Founding Fathers. The US *people* have cleared a continent by genocide, and restocked a quarter of it with kidnapped black slaves. They have settled their internal differences with a bloody civil war. They have waged several wars of aggression against their weak southern neighbours, mostly without federal approval. They buy personal fire-arms as if they were hats; and resist strongly their government's attempt to check this addition. They elect military men of small ability to their chief office again and again. It was geographical isolation and overwhelming relative power in the hemisphere that stunted the growth of a military-industrial complex, and kept intact until 1940 the fragile integument of eighteenth-century illumination and anti-militarism. In 1938 the defence expenditure was

1·5 per cent of national income. As late as 1935 Senator Gerald Nye, with huge popular support, was not only castigating the 'merchants of death' (sec. 16), but also restricting the federal government's power to make war.

But when war technology broke the isolation, and relative power was no longer overwhelming, isolationism disappeared virtually without trace and a military-industrial complex sprouted, seemingly, out of nothing. It appears to be genuinely self-generating, just as its critics claim; manipulating politicians and communications media, influencing foreign policy and all the rest. Yet the New Industrial State is not so very different from the society of the late 'thirties. *The economic institutions have not changed at all.* They 'generated' isolationism and then they 'generated' war; i.e. they generated neither the one nor the other.

What US economic and social institutions *have* done is to put 'industrial', 'business' or more generally 'civilian' on a par with 'military' within the complex. Civilian control over these vast forces has been repeatedly and triumphantly asserted: most notably and publicly with the dismissal of General MacArthur in 1951, the unification of the services, the growth of civilian strategic think-tanks, and the appointment of Mr. McNamara as Secretary of Defense (1961–8). The Cuban missile crisis of 1962 was run by President Kennedy and his cabinet. It is said even that President Johnson chose individual bombing targets in North Vietnam. That a major power should be militaristic in the age of ultimate weapons and messianic ideologies is inevitable. What shocks the outsider, however, is revealed on closer inspection to be *civilian militarism*,[24] the assertion of civilian control, in accordance with their best constitutional traditions, by a fundamentally bellicose people. This has nothing to do with capitalism, or with economic systems. Its closest modern parallel is the control over and involvement in the armed forces of all Communist Parties without exception. Civilian militarism is one of the oldest strands in Communist ideology.

8. Another undoubted case of our syndrome is Germany, 1890–1932. The Germans had perhaps the first capitalist military-industrial complex, and it was naval; for in those days sophisticated modern hardware was mainly a naval requirement. Like other armies, the German army had an established system of state ordnance factories, and drew very little on civilian production. More tradition-bound in every way, it stood at a greater social distance from the new capitalism, and was truly involved only in so far as its mobilization plans necessitated certain railway building, and the direct operation of the railways in wartime. It was the navy, too, that developed special popular associations for mobilizing the civilian population behind its claim for expenditures.[25]

Certainly to read Grand Admiral von Tirpitz[26] is to agree that there is nothing new under the sun:

'. . . It was very often a difficult part of my duties to prevent myself, as Secretary of State, from getting agitated by the impatient throng of inventions which came rushing in from all sides during this epoch; but it was also a very important one, if we were to set up a first-class navy with our limited means in the short time instead of a museum of experiments. We were overwhelmed with unripe inventions which had first to be sifted by instinct, so as not to fritter away and overburden the energies of the authorities. Once I was unable to put on the brake, and the success of the construction of the fleet was endangered by haste, which was our greatest enemy in the whole undertaking.*

'In my work in the torpedo section I first set myself to perfect the technical accuracy which is necessary in everything connected with shipping, and which in all my labours I continuously kept in view. The Whitehead torpedo was all right as far as the idea went; but it still had too much uneven engine work, and consequently lacked the necessary clockwork precision. The same occurred in the case of the submarine, which likewise requires work of the best quality. For the first time in Germany we obtained this workmanship, upon which serviceability in time of war depends, in the torpedo arm, and even the English did not quite reach the high level of our torpedo firing. When I gave a demonstration of the Whitehead torpedoes before the Crown Prince in 1879, in spite of many weeks' preparation, it was still a toss-up whether they would reach the target or ricochet wildly. Fortune smiled upon us, but I afterwards said to Stosch that now we must get to work on our own standard of precision.

'The Admiralty next approached the German factory of Schwartzkopf, which had been advertising so widely the merits of their bronze torpedoes that the Admiralty wanted to give it a monopoly. I opposed this; in the first place because a public company which has a monopoly easily pays too much attention to its annual dividends and not enough to the development of the product; secondly, because I was convinced in this case of the advantages of steel over bronze; again, because in the tendency towards home-production that was growing in the bigger foreign navies, no foreign money would have come to Germany as a

* 'An example of this. When wireless telegraphy came in it promised to fulfil a long-felt need in the navy for the transmission of orders from ship to ship at long distances. Everybody pressed therefore for its introduction on a grand scale – the navy, the firm directly interested in it, and of course the Emperor. And yet it was not ripe for use at sea, nor was the introduction of business competition at all desired. During my absence in America, however, its installation was carried through in spite of the opposition of my deputy. The consequence was that the necessary development came to a standstill for the time being; moreover, we had to spend a great deal of money quite unnecessarily on the installation, and had endless trouble with these technical difficulties. Naturally I got the blame and I was now attacked because of its ineffectiveness.'

compensation for us; and finally, because the most important experimental work on the water could not be done by the firm, but was our own special prerogative. Thus I succeeded in calling into being State torpedo-workshops; the progress of the torpedo arm is indicated by the increase in its range, which only amounted to 400 yards at the time of its general introduction to the navy, but rose to 12,000 yards by the winter of 1915–1916. The nationalization of torpedo-production did not affect the opinion I held that State workshops are only suited for special and limited purposes, and that repairs are generally carried out better, and certainly more cheaply, in State workshops than in private concerns.

'In order to avoid as far as possible the accumulation of expensive war supplies, I followed the principle when I was Secretary of State of keeping private industry, and contractors generally, prepared for the event of war. At that time I gave out our contracts, including those for provisions, clothing, coal, etc., on the condition that the contracting private firm made arrangements to proceed forthwith to an increased output in the event of mobilization. For these preparations for mobilization we had to pay rather higher prices in some cases. I have often been attacked for acting on this principle, but it was only by so doing that we were able to help out the army with 2,000,000 kilos of gunpowder up to the beginning of 1915. The army was supported far more than we were by State workshops, but it was not prepared for the enormous requirements of the world-war – and at that time it had emptied its magazines, and was saved by the navy from the gravest danger.

'In spite of the military advantage of a recognized, uninterrupted mobilization, the navy system of supply had possessed the great economic advantage that we were able to keep the unused stores quite low in times of peace and consequently lay out to productive ends the small amount of money which Germany could spare us; and further, if it came to the worst, we could only rely on carefully considered peace-time arrangements, and were thus relieved of the danger of over-hasty war-contracts.

'I have often been attacked in the Reichstag because of my attitude to private enterprise and contractors generally. Parliament begrudged the private firms the big orders and, with one eye on the State-socialism of the future, inclined more to the principle of State factories. Even in future wars any overstraining of the State-mechanism or any check upon private industry would lead to the most dangerous crises.

'I mention here a small matter which I would not broach if the Revolution did not threaten to change so fundamentally our old conditions.

'Schwartzkopf had explained to me the advantage which would accrue from the purchase of some of his shares which, as was to be expected, had trebled their value in consequence of the naval contracts. Naturally I did not buy any shares, and would have dismissed any official who acted otherwise. Our State always premises in its servants that nobility of feeling by which it had risen to greatness under the Prussian kings. I am reminded of the Finance Minister who arranged the purchase of the Prussian railways, and on resignation left his own office in the most unsatisfactory condition. The salaries in certain high offices were not in just proportion to their importance and the expenses they incurred. When I was Secretary of State I had to draw on my own income at first in order to meet the calls my office made upon me. It goes without saying that our officials worked for the honour of the thing. With a minimum of expenditure we performed a maximum of creative work. Thus the State administration in the old Prussia-Germany was cheaper and cleaner than anywhere else in the world. After the expenditure of State money, and the creation of innumerable sinecures, which are bestowed upon persons more for their politics than for their fitness for the posts, it is to be feared that the new State will not be like the old. The old German State has been weakened and broken by a period of mediocrity at a time of the greatest danger; but the German nation will never be lost so long as it does not lose the clean character of the old administration. The corrupt German is worse than the corrupt Italian or Frenchman, who at least never betrays his Fatherland.

'The German cannot afford to abandon that uprightness which was the palladium of his old civil service, for he lacks the other political qualities which help to render almost all other foreign nations immune from the poison of corruption. Even during the last generation one could notice the harmful influence of the materialism which was penetrating into the upper classes of Germany, in the shape of a weakening of character, a diminution of that positive idealism which the German nation will always have to exert in the interests of its own self-preservation. For it is only by proud, unselfish devotion to the State that it can counterbalance the deficiencies of its geographical position, its bad frontiers, its limited area, its jealous neighbours, its religious differences, and its too young and too uncertain national sentiment.'

Von Tirpitz was of course a great imperialist in the sense of the next chapter, where we return to him. And there can be no doubt at all that he, not his capitalist suppliers, made the running: there was by no means so much 'civilian militarism' here. It is not only British authors who regard the whole venture of the German deep-sea fleet as a purely aggressive initiative, without redeeming features (Ritter, op. cit.). But Hitler's Germany was far more complicated. It seems safe to assert that the old military-industrial complex continued to exist – its most remarkable achievement in the 1920s had been the technical collaboration with the Red Army – but it had little influence on Hitler. The weak position of the armed forces has been amply documented in many places, but simplistic Marxist rumours still circulate about the role of heavy industry. Fritz Thyssen, the steel manufacturer, was almost alone in financing Hitler's rise to power, apparently from 1923. Most of his great industrialist colleagues were like him good Bolshevik-fearing patriots, but up to 1931 they financed the traditional conservative Nationale Volkspartei, and included the Nazi Party in their contributions only one year before its assumption of total power.[27] Even so great a giant as Krupp exercised, and tried to exercise, no special influence at any time. He paid from 1933, and for the rest he merely collaborated, *after* Hitler got in. Hitler, we must remember, differed in social origins, ideology and domestic policy from both generals and capitalists. It should therefore be no surprise that he kept them at arm's length when making war. Notoriously, 1914–18 was the war of the Kaiser's military-industrial complex; but 1939–45 was Hitler's war. When the Prussian military caste threw up, *per impossibile*, members prepared to break their military oath and make a revolution, it was not against the Kaiser.

9. The British people (Clarke, op. cit.; Noel-Baker, op. cit.) had much of the same psychological background as the American, though circumstances have enabled them to grow away from it. They developed a military-industrial complex of the type generated by great-power conflict only once since 1800: in 1900–13, in connexion with the Anglo-German naval rivalry. This reproduced faithfully the syndrome outlined above. Ship-building unions and employers collaborated with naval purchasing officials and admirals to increase by any means the demand for naval hardware. The Navy League beat the patriotic drum, and lied about the Germans. Retired officers joined engineering firms, certain MPs became naval lobbyists, elements of the popular press collaborated, etc. No doubt there was less actual corruption, for the British people, less honest than the Germans, are by fairly long tradition more honest than the Americans or the French.[28]

But then in the 1930s, faced with a far more menacing German government, an equally capitalist Britain failed to reproduce the syndrome. It is not that its elements were absent. The Navy League was still in business, and several new air force counterparts were vicious and vocal. But the daily press was almost conspiratorially silent, while Stanley Baldwin and Neville Chamberlain, each in person the very quintessence of capitalism (Baldwin was a *steel* magnate!), simply failed to react 'properly' by rearming. Even unemployment – never greater in British history – did not move them, though by personality and by family tradition they were extremely sensitive to such issues. This is a tremendous fact which theoreticians of warfare capitalism must somehow incorporate into their systems or perish.[29]

For my part, it is enough to say that Britain and USA are both democracies, in which the – no doubt manipulated and gerrymandered –

electorates are beyond the slightest doubt sovereign. In the 1930s the British people showed in every conceivable way, in and out of Parliament, that they wanted peace at any price – and they got it at the price they deserved. In the 1950s and early 1960s the American people wanted foreign adventure and world supremacy – and that is what they got, too. No one familiar with public opinion could say they got something they did not ask for. Representative democracy worked admirably on both occasions, and the capitalist economic system, responsive as ever to consumer demand, provided the quantities of weapons that both government and people wanted.

The British Left has not used since 1914 the kind of rhetoric now being used by the US Left. Where even they can see no smoke, we may safely assume there is no fire. In other words the most charitable and probable assumption is that the difference in rhetoric corresponds to a difference in fact. Every institutional and technological prerequisite exists in Britain today as in the 'thirties for a self-generating military-industrial complex à l'Américaine. But a perpetual balance of payments crisis and an insatiable demand for social services are just as much a part of the New Industrial State, and in this particular country they have tipped the balance towards peace.

10. The desire not to have or to pay for war has been for an even longer period determining in the French case.[30] As we have seen, a true modern military-industrial complex can scarcely be conceived of before the von Tirpitz era, when weapons became sophisticated and expensive. Since France never sought world naval leadership, she can really only enter our enquiries in the 1920s, with the Maginot Line. This line was never finished in the North, i.e. in the most dangerous place, and there was no public outcry to have it finished, despite its fantastic importance in the contemporary self-image of the patriot. After the Line came the tank and the aeroplane: but the generals refused to believe in them, and therefore did not order them. Industry made little protest. Indeed in 1936–7 much of the aircraft industry was nationalized by the Front Populaire – and that also made no difference. Yet all this took place in the midst of severe unemployment. The fact is that the defensive mentality of the General Staff determined the military budget. Unable to forget Verdun, and too right-wing to wish actually to attack Germany, they dragged their feet over these new, allegedly offensive, weapons. They were helped by the left-wing parties, which resisted all new hardware as necessitating a professional army – whereas traditional Jacobin doctrine substituted equal and universal conscription plus revolutionary élan for mere technology.

This is not to say there was no corruption: indeed the French arms manufacturers' cartel secretly bought outright no less a journal than *Le Temps*.[31] But the General Staff simply was not moved – and it is even doubtful if the arms manufacturers tried very hard to move them. France had a pacific military-industrial complex! Those who believe capitalism means war have much to ponder here too.

Since 1946 French planning has added a new element; and here, as usual, we refer to the fiscal agreement and the negotiability of taxes rather than to the formal process of 'democratically' working out the input-output table. Of course France, being capitalist, produces a far better parallel than USSR to the US phenomenon. But the very important difference remains, that there is nothing special about defence output in France. All of industry is a government-industrial complex, 'complicity' describes the system as a whole. If the local action of the multiplier is important to a politician he does not have to have a military base in his constituency – anything will do. Is corruption rife? – it can batten on any activity, and peace does not harm it. The evil of the US military-industrial complex is very much bound up, as we have seen, with the limited economic role of the federal government.

Furthermore the aircraft industry and now also the Renault works (which produce tanks) are nationalized; and this at least takes the shareholder out of the picture – if that is indeed, in the French or any context, an important question.

More practically, France was engaged until 1961 in two enormously expensive wars of decolonization. There was no money for sophisticated weapons, and anyway then and there numbers and morale of infantry counted most. Even the military doctrines of Vo Nguyen Giap and Belkacem Krim were in part adopted by French military thinkers. This was the period of 'guerre révolutionnaire', 'guerre psychologique' and 'action psychologique (cinquième bureau)'. Always anti-bourgeois and anti-parliamentary, the French officer corps developed a light tincture of upper-class Maoism, in which man and his ideology, land reform, etc., far outranked mere hardware. No doubt, too, the similar Jacobin tradition had prepared their minds. It is not too much to say that nuclear weapons were at an ideological discount. Only one aberrant general, who had never fought in the colonies, and whose arguments in favour of the tank had got him into trouble in the 1930s, was seriously interested in nuclear weapons. He was in a position to put down a military revolt in Algeria, put an end to the war there, bring back the army and give it the consolation prize of anti-Americanism and independent nuclear arms. Great leaders have their own momentum: it is improbable that he consulted any industrialist before or afterwards.

11. Japan, however, is the perfect and uncontroversial example. The object of the Meiji Restoration (1868), it would appear, was solely and precisely to create a military-industrial complex in place of the previous feudal isolation. Success was complete; only among the very many things carried forward from the Tokugawa era was the dominance of govern-

ment. Capitalism simply happened to be the available foreign model, but it was a very submissive capitalism that got transplanted. There were hardly any unions, and the new parliament hardly brought democracy, or powerful members lobbying for their constituencies. So many elements of the orthodox syndrome were absent. In another era Japan would have taken over a socialist model, but that is not the point: she wanted militarism and industrialism, and she got them.

12. Do we find military-industrial complexes in capitalist UDCs? The answer is a clear yes: UDCs tend to be militaristic, indeed unself-critically so, and local procurement is eagerly and corruptly sought by local capitalists who therefore give such militarism support in politics and in the communications media. The multiplier, of course, operates just as under advanced capitalism, and the trade unions are even more selfish, restrictive and corrupt. Who can blame them? – they have more at stake.

But there are also substantial differences. Local procurement is of simple goods. That 'technological complicity' that characterizes an advanced military-industrial complex is absent, and with it disappears a powerful link between the state and the firm. Sophisticated weapons are an import, so the forces become the client of some advanced country – a very interesting and widespread feature of the modern world that is beyond our scope. Secondly the officer corps is always the best organized, often the best educated and not seldom the most radical body of professionals in the country. In Burma in 1962 they reached out via local procurement into the socialization of defence supplies; strengthened by this experience, they made a coup and socialized everything else too. Such an event would be difficult to imagine in, say, Britain.

Burma, then, is now a single, total, socialist military-economic complex. Algeria is not very different, and several other Arab states show traces of such a system. Enough has been said here to open vistas, which however others must explore.

13. But if capitalism has this to be said against it, we must nonetheless admit that the STEs and Yugoslavia have spent slightly higher percentages of national income on defence than most contemporary capitalist countries,[32] while exhibiting a much higher degree of militarism in education and propaganda. Nay more, one whole period of pure capitalism (1815–70) was a uniquely peaceful interlude in world history. Whole areas of it – Scandinavia, Canada, Australasia, even Latin America – remain so to this day. All its great ideologists (chapter 17, sec. 3) were men of peace, while all Communist ideologists except Bukharin and Gramsci have been men of violence.

Indeed both these sets of ideologists attacked the same thing: Mercantilism and state capitalism. The Marxists, thinking in terms of the violence of their own creed and temperament, were unable even to imagine a peaceful world which they did not themselves control. They foresaw imperialist war where there would be only minor incidents, overlooked the peaceful interlude of 1815–70, and misleadingly overlooked the much more bellicose imperialism of the Mercantilist period.

True, the ideologists of capitalism inferred that it was a peaceful system mainly because they falsely identified it with free trade (i.e. overemphasized the 1815–70 interlude), and identified that in turn with peace; again they did not consider unemployment and the Keynesian case for small wars; and were quite blind to 'objective' imperialism (chapter 19, sec. 2). But none of this can outweigh the pacific temper of the vast majority of books advocating capitalism. Even Keynes, upon whose work rests so much of my own argument that capitalism encourages war, was a profoundly peaceful thinker who never understood war. Indeed even capital*ists* tend to be men of peace. 'A man' – how often must we repeat it? – is seldom so innocently employed as when he is making money.' Greed is not lethal, merely disgusting. Greed gives us a positive incentive to avoid war: it is expensive. But pride, loyalty, conviction, idealism – these are lethal. And socialist governments not only prize these emotions, they are also better tax collectors and resource mobilizers.

For if the objective logic of economic institutions impels men to do certain things, whatever they think, it does not compel them. A country is warlike for a hundred reasons of which its economic system is but one, probably a weak one. Communist countries as a whole are much more militaristic than capitalist ones, despite the more peaceful logic of their economic institutions.

The reasons for this bellicosity lie in the chances of diplomatic history,[33] in the violence of the ideology and in the violence of the temperaments attracted to it. We must regretfully turn aside from these large matters to the economy: has the STE a recognizable military-industrial complex?

14. Of the nine social groups listed in sec. 4, only (i) the shareholders are absent from the STE. It would be paranoia indeed to imagine that this single change could abolish the syndrome. It is doubtless much more significant that of the six mechanisms that make capitalism so war-prone, listed in sec. 5, none operates in an STE. But our ignorance is a potent barrier to analysis. The civilian members of the complex, and the factories in which they work, can hardly be named. The question put here seems never to have been put before. Might there not be other economic mechanisms or social groups, as unknown to capitalism as is the shareholder or the multiplier to the STE?

There might, at least in USSR, about which alone I feel competent to make guesses. First, *senior ideological officials* are not to be confused with mere journalists and propagandists. Such people as A. A. Zhdanov and M. Suslov are the cardinals and *periti* of the new theocracy: their attitude for instance, to the 'doctrine of just war' is as practically important as the archbishop's in a Catholic country. We should think back especially to the medieval church. A medieval crusade was the product of a military-theological complex, while 'industry' merely tagged along. Economics[34] was a mere constraint, or as de Gaulle is alleged to have said of the French economy, *l'Intendance suivra.* Or a more strictly relevant theocratic parallel is late-nineteenth-century Russia, from which Communism as we know it derives so unfortunately much. Foreign policy was in the long run very much dependent on pan-Slavism and the support of Orthodox churches abroad. Konstantin Pobedonostsev (the great obscurantist theoretician, chief Procurator of the Holy Synod, 1880–1905) was the Suslov of his times. These crusading models are surely more apposite to USSR, North Vietnam and Cuba than any purely economic model. If the ideology were peaceful everything would be peaceful. Indeed other Communist countries, not actually engaged in wars of re-unification, are quite peaceful.

The directly economic part of the ideology makes at least one contribution to bellicosity: the emphasis on heavy industry. In pure theory a gun or a bomb is an 'object of consumption', while an armoured vehicle is a 'means of production'; so if heavy and light industry are to be defined on strictly Marxian lines weapons of war belong to both departments.[35] But in practice the means of production are confused with 'heavy industry', and this in turn is confused with defence industry, which has thus acquired an ideological sanction that logic and Marx himself would have denied it. Having this ideological weapon to hand, and seeing it attacked, the generals and the arms manufacturers have often leaped to its defence. Thus they have at least to this extent entered the 'ideology business' on their own account.

15. There is further the matter of political promotion within the Party. There are good figures for the Central Committee membership of generals and arms manufacturers. They show a steady rise, as a percentage of the whole, except perhaps for the Khrushchev period.[36] In April 1973 the Minister of Defence even re-entered the Politburo.

But Soviet weapons manufacture has not hesitated, over and above that, to single itself out and defend its own perimeter within the State machine. This brings us to the sole *known* event which indicates the existence of a military-industrial complex in the strict sense. In 1957, as we saw in chapter 9, sec. 11, Khrushchev dissolved the product-based ministries in Moscow that commanded industry and construction and put all enterprises in these sectors under territorially defined local councils (Sovnarkhozy) with similar powers. But the weapons ministries put up resistance; at first exempt from the reform, they followed it very slowly. In the civilian sector the Ministry for Product A was replaced by a State Committee for A, which was genuinely confined to the technical coordination of enterprises now genuinely under command of the 100 local

Sovnarkhozy. But the State Committees for military products retained or regained most of the powers of ministries, and overrode the Sovnarkhozy. Atomic energy, in particular, never bowed its head to them.

Khrushchev put his coping stone on this structure in November 1962: a USSR Sovnarkhoz to 'manage' industry and a parallel body (Gosstroi) for construction. Their functions were current management, while Gosplan continued to plan – whatever that distinction might mean. The chairman of the USSR Sovnarkhoz was V. E. Dymshits, a well-known personal protégé of Khrushchev from out of the Party apparatus, with a background in the control of consumer goods production.

In March 1963 yet another body was created, evidently without Khrushchev's approbation:[37] the supreme Sovnarkhoz under D. F. Ustinov. In the charts this body was set over Gosplan, Gosstroi and the USSR Sovnarkhoz. *It also had the military State Committees under its direct, unmediated control*, while the civilian State Committees were subordinated to its nominal subordinate, the 'Dymshits' Sovnarkhoz. But what it was actually supposed to do was never clarified! Ustinov had an arms-producing background, and had made his career in the state not the Party. The relations of the two central Sovnarkhozy and the Gosplan were never made clear, though surely every Soviet manager and planner must have wanted to know. But the 'Ustinov Sovnarkhoz' slightly outshone the 'Dymshits Sovnarkhoz' in the press. In 1964 Khrushchev was dismissed, and in 1965 all Sovnarkhozy ceased together. The hostility of the armed forces to Khrushchev is a matter of much notoriety, and well documented.[38]

16. One exception, however, we must make in all these cases: the export trade. All great capitalist states mentioned, and every socialist state there has yet been which could make arms, and neutral, peaceful, holier-than-we-all Sweden as well, have engaged in export. The economies of scale are ample explanation, and – as we are not tired of repeating – the laws of production operate under all systems. In 1934–6 the US Senate under Gerald Nye[39] moved against private foreign trade in arms. Restraints on such trade were everywhere a popular left-wing cause, under the slogan 'Merchants of Death'. But since that time state trade, wholly eclipsing private trade in all countries, has taken on monstrous dimensions. In other words neither Communism nor state capitalism has improved things one jot. We are all merchants of death, because in international trade we maximize profits, and death is profitable. However discreditable the government that buys, there is always some government that will find it diplomatically appropriate to issue an export licence.

17. So before there were 'military-industrial complexes' there were 'merchants of death'. I.e. before there was state capitalism there was pure capitalism. Let us end this chapter by examining the arms business

before there was state complicity. Weapons were expensive, but nothing like as much as now, not even as a proportion of national income. The industrial revolution had already happened, and metallurgy was in its prime. Technical progress was very rapid, but nothing like as rapid as now. Above all, large capitalist arms manufacturers were independent of governments. They went their own sweet way in the sacred names of free trade, free enterprise, and business as usual. This was the state of affairs, very approximately, from 1850 to 1940, with the exceptions, principally naval, noted above. For it was in about 1850 that technical progress became so rapid in large and small *guns*.[40] Yet however big, a gun is a compact and easily tradeable object. It is, or was, not a weapons system, and it requires little servicing after purchase. So much was the convenient gun the principal stock-in-trade of the merchant of death that his French name was *marchand de canons*.

The arms manufacturer regarded all governments equally (including potential enemies) as his clients. He readily formed international cartels and combines, even with firms belonging (if such firms really did 'belong') to potential enemies. Hence he stood more at arm's length from his own government. In this context the most fantastic feat was that of Guy de Wendel, the French arms manufacturer whose blast furnaces lay at Briey on the German border in 1914. Retiring a few kilometres in good order to their planned defensive position, French troops left the furnaces untouched. This is by itself highly suspicious, but beyond doubt due to the assumption then prevalent among European armies that the war would be short and sharp, that one needed large stocks and good mobilization plans, but not current industrial production. A spadeful of iron-ore at Briey could not become a gun until victory or defeat, so Briey was unimportant. 'Asked,' relates Mr. Challener,[41] 'by the commission's presiding officer if men of his acquaintance in the iron and steel business had ever discussed or thought about the possibility that the French metallurgical industry would play an important part in a future war, de Wendel responded, "In all sincerity, no." '

This alone suffices to destroy the notion of a French military-industrial complex in 1914. We may contrast the care of von Tirpitz (above) to assure himself long-term supplies. But Tirpitz was a sailor. What is really striking, however, is that once the Germans had occupied Briey, and everyone agreed that the war would be a long one, it was recommissioned and formed an important part of Germany's steel supply. Though at all times within aerial bombing and artillery range it remained untouched throughout the war, despite the protests of many junior French officers (Noel-Baker, op. cit., pp. 42–6). In that cruder age state and capitalists often had starkly opposing interests, so there was less complicity and more bribery. Supply officers and newspapers, especially French newspapers, were simply bought, and the panaceas of the Left were export licensing and nationalization, as related above.

The evolution of Krupp[42] best exemplifies the change from capitalism to state capitalism. In 1865 Bismarck, that moderate man, refused the firm a loan when it was in difficulties.[43] Krupp turned, successfully, to a French bank. He also tried to sell his best and newest gun to Louis Napoléon. But by 1913 we find the Kaiser a principal stockholder and godfather to a child; and a terrific scandal over corruption in Berlin, with Krupp employing ex-officers as salesmen, and bribing civil servants. With all the extreme unpleasantness of these earlier incidents, however, it is evident that pure capitalism, quite unlike state capitalism or socialism, could be a force making for treason, and so for peace.

Notes

1. A preliminary version of this chapter appeared in *Mélanges en l'Honneur de Raymond Aron*, Paris 1971.

2. No one acquainted with Napoleon will pretend to detect serious differences of ideology and motive between him and the other kings and generals. Only the first French revolutionary wars, in 1793–5, were ideological. When Metternich fought Kossuth it was indeed Hapsburg legitimism against Hungarian nationalism; so that perhaps qualifies as an ideological war (especially the Romanov legitimist intervention). But Bismarck and Cavour, again, were not ideologues, nor seriously different from their opponents.

3. Konrad Lorenz, *On Aggression*, N.Y. 1963, chapter 10. The importance of the rat is to show that intra-specific killing *can* be common among mammals. It is sometimes argued (Sally Carrighar, *New York Times Magazine*, 10 September 1967) that aggression in rats is artificial, since they are peaceful until crowded together by experimental biologists. But Lorenz quotes a convincing example of intra-specific aggression in nature, and in captivity with little overcrowding. Anyhow this qualification is quite untrue of human beings, who have always committed war (inter-tribal killing) in all circumstances, and also commit murder (intra-tribal killing) – a thing absolutely unknown among rats. Overcrowding and other rational causes are merely an additional factor in both species.

4. It is of course very common in the animal kingdom to love a fight but to refuse to kill. Many men, too, are like this. But others like to fight *and* to kill.

5. If a linnet is brought up apart from other linnets it must still sing, but the song it chooses is the one it happens first to hear. However, if it then hears the song of the linnet it sings no other. That is, an exceedingly specific potentiality is inherited, but circumstances must trigger it. For the rest a more general potentiality is also inherited, which either needs no triggering or can be triggered by nearly anything.

6. Works on human aggression, comprehensible to non-biologists: Lorenz, op. cit.; Anthony Storr, *Human Aggression*, N.Y. 1968; Lionel Tiger, *Men in Groups*, N.Y. 1969; Geoffrey Gorer, *New York Times Magazine*, 27 November 1966; Carrighar, op. cit. It is customary in such brief bibliographies to quote also Robert Ardrey, *The Territorial Imperative*, N.Y. 1966. I hesitate to recommend this book because of its total failure to recognize that territorial political units

mostly grew out of semi-nomadic tribes, in which kinship was surely a greater bond. It is not obvious how a genetically determined territorial imperative, similar to that observed among birds (which do not recognize kinship) could have operated among nomads. On the late development of a territorial ideology among modern states cf. Henry Maine, *Early History of Institutions*, 4th edn., London 1885, chapter 3.

7. It is of interest that the New Left, which admires violence so much in its heroes and practises it when it is more or less safe to do so, is ambivalent about the origins of violence. For instance Frantz Fanon, *Les Damnés de la Terre*, Paris 1961, takes the violence of colonizers and colonized completely for granted, and regards the latter as a psychological necessity – though he would probably reject a biological origin.

8. As preached by William James, in his *Moral Equivalent of War*, N.Y. 1910.

9. I have found the following particularly useful, whether for good insights or for factual discoveries: Marc Pilisuk and Thomas Hayden in the *Journal of Social Issues*, 3/XXI; John K. Galbraith, *The New Industrial State*, Boston 1967, chapters 27, 29; Fred J. Cook, *The Warfare State*, N.Y. 1962; Walter Adams in *AER*, May 1968; *Newsweek*, 9 June 1969; Dwight D. Eisenhower, speech on relinquishing Presidency, 17 January 1961; Murray L. Weidenbaum in *AER*, May 1969; Daniel Ellsberg, *Papers on the War*, N.Y. 1972. Most of the voluminous new US literature on this subject is beneath contempt. On the right it bypasses all the issues and deals very scientifically with marginalia; on the left it is as described above.

10. Cf. also chapter 10, sec. 6. *Pantouflage* is also common among tax-collectors who retire early, on much increased pay, to become tax-evaders for large corporations.

11. Cf. I. F. Clarke, *Voices Prophesying War*, London 1966, chapters 4.

12. Cf. *Look*, 26 August 1969; *New York Times*, 12 August 1970. Mr. Rivers died in 1970.

13. Strictly the multiplicand is an injection of income, and the multiplier describes round by round the income that accrues to others therefrom. I refer here instead to the money, whether it purchases intermediate goods or ultimate factors of production. The money from off the base flows mainly through local shops. Certainly shopkeepers buy goods not made in Charleston, but their gross turnover is chronologically the first to benefit, with great psychological effect. My 'rounds', then, refer to the crude posssession of the money, and not to the generation of actual income as eventually certified by an accountant. Expositions of the multiplier culpably neglect this distinction. Note too that one of the first-round 'leaks' is into *local* taxes – and therefore from Mr. Rivers's point of view no leak at all.

14. Cf. chapter 13, sec. 13. We extend the concept for this purpose to include stock options, convertible loans, ordinary loans upon which default is expected, mortgages exceeding the value of the property, and all other legal and illegal devices that resemble equity shares.

15. Cf. John K. Galbraith, *The Affluent Society*, London 1958.

16. Cf. Norman Angell, *The Great Illusion*, London 1914 and my comments thereon in Wiles 1969, chapter 18. Cf. also sec. 17 below.

17. For the neglected place of the prototype in Western value theory cf. Wiles 1961, chapter 8; and chapter 15 here.

18. 'You know how we bought the F-86?' a former civilian procurement

officer at the Pentagon asked ... 'Lee Atwood came to see Hoyt Vandenberg [Air Force chief of staff]. Atwood said, "We've got a hell of a good fighter 'plane here, and we need the work." Vandenberg said to him, "Build it." If we hadn't had that 'plane when the Korean War hit we'd have been in a hell of a shape.' How did Vandenberg know the F-86 would work? 'North American always built good fighter 'planes,' the ex-official said. How could Vandenberg order the 'plane (which ultimately cost $299,000 a copy) so simply in the face of 3000 pages of procurement regulations and without competitive bidding? 'Faith,' said the former official. 'Trust. In the end. that's the way it has to be done – with a lot of faith and trust on both sides.' – *Newsweek*, op. cit.

19. Many fantastic examples in Weidenbaum, op. cit.

20. De Gaulle finally decided to exclude Britain after the US decision no longer to proceed with this air-to-ground missile upset all British defence plans (1962).

21. Notably Bovis Holdings Ltd., the British building firm, base their advertising on this fact. The 'Bovis System' of pricing dates from 1927.

22. This is my guess as to those *parts* of weapons and space hardware production that are relevant. It is noticeable that Galbraith offers no estimate of his own. He adds to his list of sectors in technological complicity with the government atomic power; but this is surely untrue – atomic power is a highly competitive business, like coal-mining.

23. But C. Wright Mills, to name only one, got there first, in *The Power Elite*, N.Y. 1956, chapters 8, 9, 12.

24. Cf. James A. Donovan, *Militarism USA*, N.Y. 1970; and chapter 19, sec. 13 here.

25. Albeit the British Navy League was the model and precursor of the Flottenverein. On this period cf. Gerhard Ritter, *Staatskunst und Kriegspolitik*, Bd. II, Munich 1965. Ritter is however very weak on the collaboration of industry, but he refers us to: E. Kehr in *Die Gesellschaft*, Bd. 2, 1928, pp. 221. sqq.; idem, *Schlachtflottenbau und Parteipolitik*, 1930, esp. pp. 93–119; W. Marienfeld, 'Wissenschaft and Schlachtflottenbau in Deutschland, 1897–1906', Beihang 2 to *Marinerundschau*, 1957. I have also found Philip Noel-Baker extremely useful: *The Private Manufacture of Armaments*, Oxford 1937, vol. I.

26. *My Memoirs*, N.Y. 1919, vol. I, pp. 48–53.

27. Alan Bullock, *Hitler*, London 1962, pp. 173, 196; Fritz Thyssen, *I Paid Hitler*, London 1941, pp. 46, 132–5; Hjalmar Schacht, *My First Seventy-Six Years*, London 1955, p. 301. Thyssen quarrelled with Hitler, incidentally, and left the country in 1939.

28. This assertion is based on no statistical finding or proper research; but on hunch and fairly wide reading and experience.

29. Their most profitable line of argument would be that (a) Chamberlain feared above all Communism, (b) he saw it as an internal threat of revolution and correctly estimated at zero the likelihood of the Red Army landing at Hastings, and (c) he hoped to tempt the Nazis to invade the Communists. But his refusal of Soviet help over Czechoslovakia kept USSR *out* of danger for the time being.

30. Ritter, op. cit., chapter 1; Paul Reynaud, *In the Thick of the Fight*, London 1955; Pierre Cot, *Le Procès de la République*, N.Y. 1944; George A. Kelly, *Lost Soldiers*, MIT 1965; Heinz Pol, *Suicide of a Nation*, N.Y. 1940, chapter 5; Richard D. Challener, *The French Theory of the Nation in Arms*, N.Y. 1955.

31. Noel-Baker, op. cit., Part II, chapter 7. They also lobbied successfully against the purchase of foreign aircraft.

32. Frederic Pryor, *Public Expenditures in Communist and Capitalist Nations*, Illinois 1968.

33. Notably the long cherished memory of the feeble Allied intervention in 1917. There was not until the Bay of Pigs (1961) a single other case of aggression in principle by a capitalist state upon a Communist one, just because it was Communist.

34. Except when the already post-feudal Venetians diverted the Fourth Crusade (1204) against Constantinople, their trade rival. This was surely the first act of capitalist imperialism in history.

35. For a general discussion of the heavy industry concept in Marxism and in practice cf. Wiles 1962, chapter 14. The whole concept is Leninist, i.e. Tsarist, and has no justification in Marx himself.

36. Gerry Hough in *Problems of Communism*, March–April 1972, footnote 10. For a recent more general statement of the position of the military within Soviet society cf. Roman Kolkowicz in ed. H. Gordon Skilling and Franklyn Griffiths, *Interest Groups in Soviet Politics*, N.J. 1971; W. E. Odom and E. L. Warner in *Problems of Communism*, September 1973, March 1974.

37. The usual 'speech by Comrade Khrushchev', laying the groundwork for the innovation, was not reported this time after the Central Committee meeting. For the various supreme Sovnarkhozy see E. Zaleski, *Planning Reforms in the Soviet Union*, Chapel Hill 1967, pp. 22–3, 37–41: Wiles in *AER*, September 1968, p. 996.

38. Cf. David Burg and Peter Wiles in ed. Sidney I. Ploss, *The Soviet Political Process*, Waltham, Mass., 1971; Kolkowicz, op. cit.

39. The Special Committee on the Investigation of the Munitions Industry of the US senate. The result was the arms export licensing act of 1935.

40. J. U. Nef, *War and Human Progress*, Harvard 1950, p. 365.

41. Op. cit., pp. 95–100. The commission of enquiry sat in 1920.

42. Noel-Baker, op. cit., here and there.

43. Bismarck is all too often misrepresented as aggressive. On the contrary he was cautious and conservative, not only in foreign policy after establishing the German empire, but most particularly in his relations with the military. Von Tirpitz complains of his small-minded, pre-industrial attitude. Like a good Junker, Bismarck believed in a military-agricultural complex.

19

Economic Imperialism[1]

1. Definition
2. The definition explicated
3. Mercantilism
4. The free trade era, 1815–70
5. State capitalism, 1871–1914
6. All systems are variously guilty
7. State capitalism and the STE compared: raw materials, terms of trade, imperial preference
8. The same: export of goods and capital, tribute, export of labour
9. The same: economic warfare
10. Economic imperialism and the domestic performance of ACEs
11. 1945–date: the liquidation of capitalist empires
12. The Portuguese exception
13. The US exception
14. French 'neo-colonialism'
15. Foreign aid and the system of the giver
16. The liquidation of the Soviet empire?
17. Internal imperialism, Soviet and other

19

1. Generally, in order to keep this book within bounds, international economics has been avoided. But where war and investment finance figure in the titles of chapters economic imperialism imposes itself. It is, however, extremely difficult to define. How, then, do we normally use this phrase? Abstracting from Marxist paranoia and loose emotive talk, we mean roughly this: economic imperialism is the international use by the strong on the weak of:

(A) political and military power for economic ends, as when Britain forbad India to place a tariff on British cloth, or when Germany exacted a tribute from conquered France, giving herself an indefinite line of credit with the Banque de France (1940), or when Commodore Perry forced his way into the Bay of Yedo (1854), so as to open up Japan to trade, or when Stalin established his mixed companies in Eastern Europe. Note that in very many of these examples one dispenses with formal annexation.

(B) economic power for economic ends. And here we must be careful. If we are offered a low price, and refuse to sell, and are strong enough to outsit the buyer, who is so weak that he must eventually settle on our terms, that is not imperialism but mere monopoly. Consequently imperialism B is a matter of judgement. An international cartel, mainly based inside strong powers, restricting output and raising prices to buyers mainly situated inside weak powers, would be economic imperialism.

(C) economic power for political ends: a different case altogether. An excellent case is if we lend excessively to a feckless government and thus lure it into a bankruptcy that we can exploit. This is what happened to the Khedive of Egypt in 1875; the British government settled its part of the debt in Suez Canal shares. A quite different example is when the USSR stopped buying Finnish exports in order to change the Finnish Cabinet (1958), or when Germany financed the Baghdad Railway (from 1889) in order to obtain a Turkish military alliance. Mostly case C corresponds to economic warfare (Wiles 1969, chapters 16, 17).

Economic imperialism aims at power and profit, by no means at impoverishing the exploited. Quite the contrary, it has been considered wise, at least since the stage of mere robbery and tribute exaction was passed (say 1815), to leave a little profit. Therefore there has to be considerably more production than before. Therefore modern empires have always tried to be economically progressive. Of course they have often failed, and it is easy to guess who in that case bears the loss. But the principle is crystal clear: it ought 'to pay to be exploited'. The political force is meant to ensure the smooth running of the enterprise, while the enterprise is meant to enrich one and all. On the whole recent imperialism has achieved this aim. There have, however, been deliberate harkbacks even in very recent times. The Germans in S.W. Africa cleared the Hereros off their land and killed them (1904–8). The South African government is still clearing Bantu townships in this manner, and leaving the inhabitants to starve in the bush. The genocide of aborigines continues slowly in South America. It only stopped eighty years ago in North America. On the other hand in certain ex-colonies the mere achievement of order and a little net investment has proved beyond the capabilities of the successor régime, and things have slipped backwards. Indonesia is the classic case: it has not paid her to cease to be exploited.

We speak of *inverted imperialism* when the metropolis sets out quite deliberately to lose money, in order to retain power (secs. 14, 17). *Internal imperialism* is what is found inside the boundaries of one multi-national state (sec. 17). Empire can also be *formal and informal, subjective and objective* (sec. 2).

2. Let us next consider what this definition does and does not include. Not all acts of economic warfare are imperialism, since an imperialist power must, by definition, have a larger national income than the country it attacks or exploits. Thus the Arab League blacklists British companies that deal with Israel, which comes under (C), but the British national income is about as big as that of the Arab League, and whatever our views on the rights of the issue Britain could protect these companies. This is not the strong bullying the weak; or was not until the oil embargo of October 1973. *Per contra* however, if China were to cut off her vegetable supplies to Hong Kong this would be imperialism, even though average income in Hong Kong is four times, and in Britain twenty times, as big as in China.

Without a state machine, without legal military force, there can be very little imperialism. But this was not always true. In earlier days a mere company, the East India Company, using its own troops and in no way subsidized, conquered a sub-continent. Until at least 1940 the United Fruit Company dominated the governments of several Central American states without much diplomatic help from Washington, and without its own military force, simply by its monopsony. Such activities could indeed be pursued in opposition to government policy, if the metropolitan state were liberal and the laws permitted it. The lesser crime of 'objective imperialism' (below) is quite easy without government help.

When, as is far more usual, the imperialist state must act it need by no means go as far as annexation. *Informal empire* is extremely common: the imperialist state leaves the colony's constitution in being and imposes a treaty with a few vetoes built in.

The mere possession of economic power is not *subjectively imperialistic*, since it results from nothing more than being rich and big, or happening to monopolize a raw material, or sitting across an international canal, or a river approach to a landlocked country. Notably it is possible for US capitalists to buy up Canada piece by piece, on pure profit criteria and without engaging in any monopolistic conspiracy, or even consulting each other, or even knowing what is happening. No political motive and no contempt for Canadians need fire this movement, but the end result is objectively hard to distinguish from imperialism. It acquires that character subjectively only when the Canadian government passes a law about it, which offends US nationalism, which stimulates a countermeasure, which leads to a spiral of escalation. This kind of unconscious or *objective imperialism* is common between neighbouring states and the unequal regions of multi-national states (sec. 17); and for many purposes Canada is three or four such outlying regions of USA. Mostly the US domination of Cuba was also of this 'objective' character, especially after the repeal of the Platt Amendment (1934).[2] The bankruptcy of the Khedive, referred to above, came about through objective imperialism, though Disraeli then exploited it subjectively.

The mere ownership of foreign assets is not imperialism: it must be by the strong in the weak. The vast Cuban holdings of real estate and cash in Miami, of which Castro so greatly disapproved, were not imperialistic. Nor do we speak of Swedish or Swiss imperialism, even when these countries invest in UDCs. Indeed it is difficult for a small ACE to be imperialistic, unless it annexes territory outright: e.g. the Belgian Congo. The notion that its investments are as such imperialistic rests squarely and solely on the Marxian theories of surplus value and non-equivalent exchange, which are false (Wiles 1969, chapter 1).

The mere collection of debt is not imperialism. Most debts are perfectly fair, and their collection is not only good business morality, but simple morality. The world has become so soft-centred and hypocritical as virtually to deny the sanctity of debt; and on the other hand so lazy and cowardly as not to study or lay down guide-lines for scientific repudiation. Yet repudiation is also morality and good policy, under certain conditions. Our question must always be, *how* was the debt incurred? *How* is it being collected?

The manipulation of the terms of trade in favour of imperialists is imperialism. It is true that only large powers are capable of such manipulation. But even before 1945 (sec. 11) the terms of trade were nearly always manipulated, if at all, in favour of the poor. The days of international steel or chemical cartels are long gone. The only remaining cartels are interstate schemes for raw materials, and these have been for the most part exported by poor countries to rich ones.[3] Certainly these cartels were arranged to benefit also the domestic producers in ACEs, and certainly the exporters in UDCs were usually large foreign capitalist firms.

But these firms were taxed, even before the war, by colonial governments for local purposes, and they incurred heavy local expenses, notably flexible wages; so that if we ask what nations benefited it was almost invariably the UDCs.

The colonial status, even, made little essential difference. We can find no evidence that the ACEs *manipulated* the terms of trade in their own favour; nor that they in fact moved in their favour. So we must fall back upon some other doctrine of unfairness.

Rejecting the Marxist theory of international value,[4] which sees an inherent unfairness in free exchange between the poor and the rich, we can still find a common injustice. It is imperialism when the strong manipulate the factor endowment of the weak, and this they have until recently continued to do. We mean here by refusing to invest in the manufacturing industries of UDCs, lest they compete with their own; and confining their foreign ventures to the production of raw materials for their own use. There is no doubt that in the colonial period investment, and so the factor endowment, was consciously manipulated so as to prevent industrialization. We may, then, fairly compare the actual terms of trade with those there would have been, though both terms were fairly settled by open competition. The Bengal cotton industry, which the British refused to protect, is the classic case. Since the end of the empire, however, this argument has become quite unsustainable (sec. 15). Foreign aid has been repeatedly poured away on attempts to change the recipient's factor endowment, by heavy industrial ventures incompatible with his present or likely future situation. Either way, the manipulation of colonial factor endowments can be seen as a form of 'external French planning'.

3. Ancient economic imperialism consisted almost only of type A: political power used for economic ends, to wit the exaction of a tribute. Tribute, the tax paid by one state to another, has, as we shall see (sec. 8), persisted into the modern world. As the basic and simplest form it could hardly have died out.

The next important form is Mercantilism (*c.* 1600–1815). From the point of view of modern economic institutions, and of the at present fashionable Marxism, Mercantilism is of great importance. For it can only be described as pre-industrial state capitalism, and like all state capitalism it was imperialistic. Marx and Marxists fail at every point to distinguish it from feudalism, and implicitly, sometimes even explicitly, date capitalism from the industrial revolution.[5]

Mercantilism produced vast chartered companies to engage in foreign trade; a tight network of state regulations, internal and external; a degree of complicity between the state and the capitalist not since regained even in France; a full employment policy (capture the foreigner's gold and have inflation); a welfare system; and a shameless and utterly exploitative imperialism that included the slave trade. If 'imperialism is the highest stage of capitalism', the latter has been declining ever since 1600. Capitalism entered history as state capitalism and imperialism.

4. In nearly all countries the industrial revolution was itself a state capitalist affair, as we make clear in chapters 12 and 18 for the nineteenth century, and as every newspaper reader knows to hold for the twentieth. What really has to be explained is how there was ever pure capitalism, free trade and anti-imperialism: these are the strange phenomena, and they have no right to dominate our textbooks. The answer is of course that this exceptional period (*c.* 1815–70) was dominated by one industrial country alone, Britain. She at any rate, as the pioneer, had had to weaken the state in order to abolish the old Mercantilist technological restrictions and give capital free play. Thereafter other states might be expected to take a more enlightened view of the new industry, and restrict it in more appropriate ways. This indeed is what happened.

Looking now abroad, for Britain, as the overwhelming front-runner, free trade *was* Mercantilism. She needed, like all Mercantilist powers, to reserve a colonial market as her very own. This market simply happened to be, at that time, the world. But cynicism is never enough. There was also a very genuine ideological movement, engendered no doubt by the objective fact of the American defeat. Its first move was the forcible abolition of the slave trade (1807), but it gathered strength with the defeat of Napoleon, the arch-Mercantilist (1815). Notions of free trade gained more with the enfranchisement of the bourgeoisie (1832), the liberation of all slaves (1834), and the devolution of power to Canada (1840). With this background free trade was inevitable, though the actual abandonment of imperial power over other races in, say, India was not on the cards.

So free trade co-existed with imperialism and then, when other countries had industrialized and begun annexing new empires, faded away again (*c.* 1870). Except for Britain, the whole period of capitalism has been one of state capitalism and imperialism, from 1600 until 1945. And the British exception does not amount to much. After all, within four years of the advent of free trade even in agricultural products (the abolition of Corn Laws, 1846, the great climax of the whole movement), the Royal Navy was sent to Greece to enforce the debt claims of a man who may not have been a British subject (Don Pacifico 1850).

What are we to make of this record? – that imperialism is a necessary emanation of capitalism? Surely not, for there has in all world history been only one brief period of pure capitalism in one country that had the strength to be imperialistic, and that brief period marked a most distinct retreat from empire. Moreover the ideology of pure capitalism is exceedingly peaceful (chapter 18, sec. 13), as indeed befits an ideology of pure economists. There can be no doubt at all that imperialism is what *states* make of capitalism, and that as a system on its own it is internationalist (chapter 18, sec. 17), and positively resistant to such ideas.

5. It is not only the period 1815–70 that provides evidence for these propositions. The years 1871–1914 have been well studied by Eugene Staley (op. cit.), investment by investment and incident by incident. He concludes that the mere migration of private capital never caused inter-power rivalry, since international syndicates of private capitalists were the order of the day and incidents were just what these people did not want. Most imperialist incidents were purely inter-state (e.g. Fashoda 1898). But occasionally the German investor acted hand in glove with his government, and thus lent himself to imperialist designs (the Baghdad Railway);[6] and these occasions created the desired incidents.

Staley's work is far too little appreciated. It destroys, even for that earlier and more plausible period, the Marxist notions that the export of goods and capital, and/or the search for secure raw material supplies, would lead to a great war between capitalist countries. This was the essence of the original Marxist doctrine of imperialism, and it was still being promulgated, in flat defiance of all evidence, by Stalin in 1952.[7] Such wars had often occurred in the first Mercantilist age, but that was long past. The powers long knew roughly who was to have what, in the Caribbean and the Far East. These were never hot spots after 1815. It was the carve-up of Africa that now led to such tensions, notably Fashoda, Algeciras and Agadir. But this is the nearest that Africa came to causing European war. Moreover secure and agreed African frontiers had already taken the heat out of the situation by 1914. War came, in 1914 and in 1939, out of much more old-fashioned imbroglios: unagreed European frontiers, with plenty of nationalist tension but scarcely a touch of economics in them.[8] After all why should anyone get himself killed for a little of someone else's money? The mere private interests of companies were simply too trivial to set conscripts marching. On the contrary foreign investors form international syndicates and settle their differences. Capitalism, to repeat the previous chapter, makes for peace between equipollent parties.

But Staley confirms the Marxist analysis of colonial war. This was not, in the first half of the twentieth century, a prime Marxist preoccupation: the theory dealt with the breakdown of capitalism through internecine war, not its spread through easy victories. Cecil Rhodes, who shared most of the Kaiser's preconceptions but operated out of the way of other powerful states, succeeded in his annexationist policy where the Kaiser failed, and he used every trick the Marxists list (but caused no major war). For capitalism, even without state support, is often 'objectively' imperialist (sec. 2), and so generates the conditions for subjective imperialism; i.e. for the often unwilling intervention of the state. This is what Rhodes so successfully, and consciously for his own part, relied on.

6. The record is confused by the fact that Britain was top nation during her pure capitalist period, and retained an extremely substantial empire of Mercantilist origin. But history seems to confirm these propositions, which knowledge of economic systems makes plausible: capitalism as such is not ideologically or institutionally compatible with subjective imperialism, but it is very liable to generate it objectively, and so lay an unfortunate groundwork; serious, i.e. subjective, imperialism can hardly happen without the initiative of a state machine, so requires state capitalism or socialism; and it is peculiarly likely when strong states are in rivalry – why should a single strong state bother?

Societies based on other economic systems are equally imperialistic, *ceteris paribus*. Feudalism produced the Crusades, Communism the USSR, imperial China its expansive dynasties: can we make of this more than that economic systems are irrelevant? Indeed, why not, since all factors except sheer military strength are more or less irrelevant? For the Marxist analysis of capitalist colonial wars only sets out the many detailed ways in which capitalism objectively and subjectively generates them. But the Communization of Mongolia was equally inevitable, and came about by other means. 'Truth to tell,' as I have put it elsewhere (Wiles 1969, p. 534), 'the history of sovereign groupings of men is largely that they attack their neighbours when opportunity offers, and the attacker's stage of development, rate of growth, or absolute level of productivity would seem to be related to this tendency in no way whatsoever. What does matter is that the neighbour be held to be weaker, and the campaign technically possible. A good ideological pretension helps, of course: Liberate the Holy Places, *Drang nach Osten*, White Man's Burden, Manifest Destiny, Permanent Revolution. But such ideologies have a way of appearing when needed, and disappearing when the policies they indicate become too expensive.'

7. Such total agnosticism is not enough. At least the state capitalist system has a different detailed relation, a different set of causal connexions, to imperialism from the other systems. To begin with, what has it in common? What economic goals is a strong state-capitalist country likely to pursue by imperialist means, thus coming under our rubrics A and B?

First, all systems need foreign raw materials, and if they are important enough, may feel compelled to take ownership of them, or to reduce to satellite status the country possessing them. What USSR did to East German uranium Britain did to Persian oil.[9] In the period of her pure capitalist grandeur, of course, she did not need to. The raw materials came in anyway, the navy ensured the supply, and it did not matter who owned them. Foreign capital was even allowed into British colonies. But then pure capitalism and *laissez-faire* are a historical oddity.

An economy under any system needs better terms of trade. Capitalist imperialist powers used to manipulate these by imperial preference, but since the preference was mutual it cannot have greatly altered the terms of trade to either party's advantage. It seems that the system was exclusive rather than exploitative, except in so far as it fossilized the colony's factor endowment, as described in sec. 2, in a structure favourable to the metropolitan power. USSR on the other hand uses a system of physical trade agreements more consonant with her domestic economy. She seems to use fair, i.e. 'world', prices, or at least equal deviations from that level when buying and selling, but to demand exorbitant quantities of specialized goods which a non-satellite would have refused to deliver, or for which it would have properly demanded a bonus above world price, to cover the high marginal cost and the risk of specialization. There is thus a quantitative, as opposed to a terms of trade, preference (Wiles 1969, pp. 238–44). But we have just seen that ACEs arrive at the same type of preference by other means: so the difference is interesting but not important. Moreover, much like any other imperial power, USSR returns such preferences, providing minerals at 'world' prices which, she claims, cost her far more. These claims and counter-claims are extremely hard to judge, but it is undeniable that by pressure of these agreements, by diplomacy and by the plans drawn up in the Comecon USSR influences her satellites' investment. Therefore she manipulates their factor endowment contrary to their will.

8. In other respects we note more divergence. Any capitalist system requires to export, indeed prefers exports to all but essential imports. This is simply because in each short run exports yield incomes while imports reduce them. Nearly all lobbying of governments in market economies is on this basis; only if a whole region suffers from import restrictions is there an effective counter-lobby. But to the STE exports are first and foremost a drain of resources. They are a necessary evil, of course, since imports, especially developmental imports, must be had. But since profit is not a motive exportation is not a motive. The STE takes an 'input-output' view of foreign trade, the ACE and even the UDC a 'Keynesian' one, except for strategic imports (Wiles 1969, chapter 4). There is therefore no special desire to monopolize export markets in an STE. The Comecon itself is a device for assuring supplies, not outlets.

The same applies to capital. An ACE, functioning in a Keynesian way, is apt to generate investment funds that have no outlet, or only disadvantageous outlets, at home. Saving cannot exceed investment ex post, but it certainly can ex ante, especially within a given territory. Unequal income simultaneously generates saving and diminishes the consumption that could justify investment. $S=I$ ex post is a law that applies only to the world as a whole. In an STE on the other hand $S=I$ ex ante (in the plan), and it would be an absurdity to lay upon people the duty of saving more than the plan required (including any foreign component). It is true that private accumulation in savings accounts cannot be planned, but its unpredicted component is a tiny part of national saving, and can be easily offset. Above all, neither planned nor unplanned saving can flow abroad, because of the state's foreign exchange monopoly. So there is no inherent uncontrollable tendency to buy up foreign assets in an STE. When Stalin wanted to own things abroad he grabbed them.

There is a loose formal identity between a goods-and-services export surplus and a savings export surplus:

$$X - M = S_h - I_h + R$$

where X and M are all visible and invisible exports and imports, R is the net inflow of gold and foreign currency, S_h and I_h are saving and investment within the territory. We call the identity a loose one because of the balancing term R. Contrary to what is often said, there *can* be an independent movement in S_h, which *can* exhaust itself simply by transferring reserves abroad (e.g. after a foreign flotation on the stock exchange), without affecting the export surplus or even requiring such a thing to exist. In the longer run however, as reserves are exhausted they deflate the economy and so bring about a roughly corresponding $X - M$. I insist on this point in order to maintain that there are two causal mechanisms at work in an imperialist ACE: an inherent preference for exports over imports and an inherent tendency to oversave. These things are not identical; but they react closely on each other. Both are absent from the STE.

On the other hand the STE is, as we have seen, better at importing. So it has no 'transfer problem'; it can easily absorb tribute or reparations or whatever they may be called. There is no Keynesian absorption problem, only the technical difficulty that the specific goods chosen for the tribute might be inappropriate. But that is an administrative problem that always affects the import decision in all systems.[10] The unpopularity of tribute absorption in the victorious ACEs contributed greatly to the scaling down of German reparations in the 1920s. Stalin had no such motive to scale down East European reparations in the 1950s. That he did so simply demonstrates a rough political wisdom. So in this particular the STE is more prone to economic imperialism.

Commonly discussions of this kind forget labour. But empire generates very many lucrative posts at all levels, paid for by the colonial inhabitants but occupied by people from the metropolis. Marxists, whose labour theory of value surprisingly attributes everything to capital, have forgotten the imperialist drive generated by a labour surplus in a rich country. It has political consequences when the younger sons of English peers or French postmen cannot find a job commensurate with their social status. We include here not only administration but business and the professions, including very humble business and white-collar occupations. Often even the armed forces, and certainly officers seconded to the native forces, are paid out of colonial taxes. And this too is in part a Keynesian tendency: the inability of the ACE to provide work adds itself to the simple search for better pay. Of all this the STE is very markedly less guilty, provided we do not count internal imperialism (sec. 17). Soviet citizens scarcely ever move outside USSR, mainly owing to security paranoia. Also Soviet-type employment policy is more effective.

9. So far we have referred to economic imperialism on our definitions A and B (sec. 1). Type C, the use of economic power for political ends, or economic warfare, is observed among strong countries. It would take us too far afield to discuss this at length, so let us give a summary dogmatic view:

(i) Communism is much more aggressive as an ideology than anything that can plausibly pass for a capitalist ideology (chapter 18, sec. 13). So economic warfare is a preferred Soviet weapon where USSR is strong. It is usually used against other STEs, since in all religions the heretic is worse than the infidel. Yet since he is after all some kind of socialist it is very bad manners to attack him militarily. Moreover vis-à-vis capitalism as a whole, and specifically NATO, USSR is weak. The boot is on the other foot, and we have the CoCom embargo on strategic goods.[11]

(ii) As the more disciplined and centralized organization, which can ride roughshod over all vested interests, the STE is far superior at the conduct of economic war – or at least it should be. Certainly most ACEs are reluctant to engage their undisciplined troops in these ventures.

(iii) But an ACE is more likely simply to fall into unintended trouble. For its economic power is more likely to generate objective imperialism (sec. 2), the simple infiltration of a UDC by capital and technicians without government connivance, a thing impossible in an STE. Now UDCs, as chronic debtors and debt repudiators, are very often engaged in economic war with some creditor or other. If this normally begins without a political purpose, it always ends up with one, moreover one that was not desired by the 'imperialist' country. And here too Marxist ideology, being opposed to debt collection, is more peaceful. UDCs can more safely repudiate Communist than capitalist debt, or expel Communist than capitalist technicians: Communists never 'send a gunboat', except of course against each other.

We conclude that, as in the case of domestic war preparation, the Marxists are right: the ACE has more internal *economic* forces impelling it to economic imperialism than the STE. The reason is as before the 'Keynesian' nature of the ACE, which adds special motives to those that it shares with all states and systems.

10. But if economic imperialism is inherent in ACEs is it also necessary to them? Could they perform so well without it? Some small ACEs have done precisely this, even in the nineteenth century, and prospered more than the big imperialist ones. Table 15/I musters the available figures. Before 1880 little is reliable, 1914–45 is bedevilled by war and slump, 1945–date covers the end of empire but is of great interest. Let us divide countries in accordance with their status in 1880–1914, the classical period, into fully imperial, half imperial,[12] 'new land' and definitely non-imperial.

If these figures show anything it is that other factors, such as the uncompleted industrialization of Italy, Sweden and Germany, or the still overwhelming weight of an inefficient agriculture in Russia, greatly outweigh imperial status. They certainly make it plausible to believe that the lack of empire did not hurt Scandinavia in any way. But the Marxists, and indeed the erstwhile advocates of imperialism, have a satisfactory rejoinder: the capital of the international bourgeoisie is essentially one mass, certain states secure empires for it to operate in, but this gets the capital of their residents very little special advantage. And this argument held well enough even for the capital or the exports of rather large ACEs in 1815–70, when there was less imperialism than usual. The Royal Navy did indeed protect all capital and all exports, and no doubt British capital, being taxed to pay for it, suffered slightly in comparison.

Nay more, even after 1870 there was a reasonably perfect world capital market, so that if a particular colony was reserved for, say, French capital other projects *in France* were deprived of it, and had to use foreign capital. So in this way the capital of non-imperialist ACEs shared in the benefits of imperialism. But not, it may be replied, the labour. There was no free market for that: a Swede could not make a better living in Saigon or Paris and then retire to Malmö. The whole vast opening up of lucrative posts for labour – including, in the French case, masses of very humble workers – was confined to the labour of the imperial power, even in 1815–1870. But where the Swede could and did go was USA; his emigration did relieve overpopulation and his remittances did directly raise both consumption and saving. This was an effective substitute, though not connected by market flows, for the role of the French empire in the French labour market. Moreover the direct settlement of North America, Australasia, and Siberia was also a form of imperialism, ideally suited to the inherent biases we have found in capitalism.

Therefore the success of small non-imperialist ACEs is no refutation of the view that empire was essential to capitalist growth. But neither have we confirmed that view. For the costs of empire were enormous, and just as unproductive as all the defence costs in the previous chapter. And the initial costs were the heaviest, and were invariably borne on the metropolitan budget, so that if empire be treated as an economic venture it always started with an outlay to amortize. It seems indeed very improbable that after the early phase of sheer private robbery (as by the British in India or the Dutch in Java, up to about 1850) imperialism paid any *state*. It was only thought to pay, especially by ignorant and envious Germans and Italians. For these, however, in the brief period 1885–1914 when they were 'in the market', the costs of 'pacification' and administration much exceeded the 'opportunity yield' in dividend, interest, salary, pension or protected export markets; i.e. the net yield from each activity after deducting its likely yield at home. Subsequently too, Mussolini poured subsidies into North Africa and fought another expensive war in East Africa that again wiped out many times over whatever 'opportunity yield' there may have been in Eritrea since 1914. But in all cases there were great divergences between private and social profit, and imperialism surely paid quite enough influential people to be kept going. State capitalism is peculiarly susceptible to rich sectional lobbies, and among these the defence lobbies of the previous chapter were closely bound up with empire.

11. From 1945 comes the liquidation of empires. The growth of all ACEs is superior to that in 1870–1914, as our table shows; and no special distinction marks those that lost empires. Substantial capital losses were suffered in colonies by Belgium, France and the Netherlands, but as percentages of the national capital they were trivial. Portugal retained her empire until 1974 at the cost of perpetual war, France has retained a strong neo-colonialist position – and this too fails to show up. It seems that other factors have again been overwhelmingly more important. Of these I would single out increased R and D and Keynesian fiscal and monetary policy.

Can we at least say that the liquidation of empire had economic causes – since it seems to have had no such effects? This is not true for the liberation of the actual colonies that there were in 1945. The main new factor was the much greater self-confidence and aggressiveness of the colonized. But on the imperial side the British liberation of India was a moral movement, into which some military but no economic calculation in fact entered. France and the Netherlands were faced, after the Japanese withdrawal, by strong military resistance to reoccupation. Themselves both recently defeated powers, they succumbed to this degree of force. It is unclear that the Dutch had to use more violence than during their original conquest: their heart was not in it. The French, facing a resurgent China across their northern border, did indeed face greater resistance, and did indeed use more force than during the original conquest. But they never dared to send conscripts, and made tactical errors, and so were defeated.

Economics played a very secondary role in Indonesia and Indo-China, and the liberation of Africa simply followed from these Far Eastern events. France, above all, became gradually converted to a moral revulsion from colonial war during the Algerian struggle. This again was not smaller than the original wars of subjugation, but she had more hope of winning it than in Indo-China, and she did generate the required finances, and send conscripts. Here at least there were economic motives aplenty: the recent discovery of Algerian oil, and the jobs of very many Frenchmen. No doubt all this accounts for the tougher fight put up.

Perhaps, then, there has been at least some change in the domestic economic structure of imperial powers, to account for the more or less voluntary end to imperialism? First there is less unemployment, or at least its burden is less keenly felt, because of the rise in family incomes. Secondly there has been a notable reduction in the pressure to export private capital (net of its importation). This is very clearly due to more equal distribution at home, and to clamant demands for still more equality. It is just the sort of structural change an economist or even a Marxist would seek. But the existing stock of private investment is very large, and well worth defending. Indeed this is a much more important matter than the placement of the new flow. Moreover politics plays here at least an equal role. The direction of private investment has also changed – away from the Third World, but that is due to the sharply increased danger of repudiation. Moreover it has been replaced by the astounding habit of public foreign aid at low interest or as a gift. This is quite unprecedented in world history; it would have been rejected out of hand by any pre-war government, capitalist, Fascist or Communist. It is clearly of moral origin and that is why it is so small. Thus the sheer proportion of national income flowing out to the Third World has fallen, while the general savings proportion, supported by a new growth of state saving, has not. Moreover the defence proportion has risen, and so the resources available for crushing colonial revolts have also risen, only they are not so used. And this is not because they were at any material time immobilized by the new Soviet military threat, since NATO opposes that as a whole, while colonial revolts are against individual countries. NATO has consistently turned a blind eye to localized wars of colonial repression by its members. The refusal to use military measures against colonies is thus not attributable to the world military situation, nor yet again to economics. It is of course true today that in many parts of the world Soviet or Chinese power would prevent colonial repression if it were attempted. But this was not actually true at the time of any act of retreat from empire, and if it had been true it would not have been an economic explanation!

Economic causes of the retreat from empire are thus of very uncertain, but probably small, weight.

12. That these retreats were not an economic necessity is also evident from the Portuguese case. Portugal, by far the poorest and smallest imperial power (she crops up sometimes in lists of UDCs) had not just

come out of a military defeat and was isolated from the moral movement in the Western world. But her contribution to NATO is more in geography than in manpower, and she benefits from its 'blind eye' described above. Her military operations in Africa were alleged to cost metropolitan Portugal but 4 per cent of the national income[13] – a trivial price for prestige, military glory and the profit of powerful economic lobbies. Yet these lobbies were surely not more powerful than the Belgian ones that failed to activate the Belgian army in the Congo. The important thing is that they behaved very differently. The Union Minière du Haut Katanga hardly tried to bring in metropolitan troops, but preferred the subtler and less violent – and less successful – course of promoting Katangan secession. But it appears that the Portuguese equivalents always successfully appealed to militarism and glory in defence of their own short-term interests. They succeeded of course because the Portuguese government had different moral standards from the Belgian government.

Latterly however these lobbies at length found an economic motive for disengagement, and carried a part of the army with them. The motive was the fear for Portuguese industry's competitive position when, in 1977, associated status with the EEC comes into force; their wish was to use the money at present spent on killing Africans (to defend Portuguese capital in Africa) on new investment at home (to defend Portuguese capital in Portugal). This is the *Leitmotiv* of General Spinola's book,[14] and this is why he was fired by more traditional forces.

Thus in this backward imperialist country there really were economic forces now bolstering, now threatening imperialism. But this is not exceptional. The exception was the country's isolation from world currents of non-economic opinion. When in 1973–4 the break came, it came through the Church (missionary witnesses to atrocities) and the Army (which despaired of victory). The Portuguese economy itself, be it noted, had grown quite rapidly since the 1950s, a trend quite unconnected with, and prior to, war in Africa. But of course Portugal as a nation was by no stretch of imagination drawing any net yield from her colonies. As this goes to print Spinola's counter-coup against the *communisant* Armed Forces Movement (11 March 1975) has failed, and a quite other epoch has begun. It has sufficed to shift the tenses of certain verbs in the above account.

13. USA resembles Portugal at least in this, that until very recently she was comparatively untouched by the shift in world opinion. There are three sorts of imperialism at work in USA today: the old-fashioned 'subjective' economic variety (types A, B and C in our definition) in the old Caribbean stamping ground, the 'objective' economic variety (types B and C) in many places, mainly in the Americas, and the cold war, which is not properly imperialist at all, as in S.E. Asia. No one privileged, as was this writer, to visit Miami shortly after Castro took over Cuba will

deny the strength of US economic imperialist feeling towards the Caribbean. It is a regional phenomenon – foreign policies traditionally have regional support in USA – Miami having taken over from New Orleans, the nineteenth-century centre of plots against Cuba. These people felt their property threatened. It was an extremely small part of the US national capital, but it was big enough to have political weight.

Simultaneously however there has been a retreat from formal empire in the Philippines and from informal empire in South America. Things have been done in Peru, Bolivia and Chile to the substantial US assets there that would not in the past have been permitted. It is the extreme propinquity and military weakness of the Caribbean countries that has kept a more aggressive stance alive there.

No country can be held responsible for 'objective' imperialism. The 'radiation' of a major culture, technology and capital market is a fact of life. But 'objective' escalates into subjective in at least one case. Many capitalist corporations are interested in securing their mineral supplies, perhaps even exist only to supply minerals. This leads to the buying up of all even potential mineral deposits round the world and the consequent transfer of little enclaves of the investing country's culture and technology. The metropolitan state's interest, however, coincides so absolutely with the corporation's that it is certain to lend it tacit support in the end.

The Vietnamese war was from beginning to end political. There was virtually no private US capital in Vietnam in 1964,[15] and certainly no influential company at work. Towards the end there was only public capital, of the sort one hopes to write off. It was not a sought-after market for US labour; quite the contrary, people had to be ordered to go there. It was a negligible civilian export market. The major US economic interests nearby are in countries still too far away to be threatened by the 'domino effect': Malaya, Indonesia, Japan. The notion that this war was economic imperialism has only to be examined to dissolve into ridicule. But we may be less sure that it was unconnected with domestic pressures to spend on arms (chapter 18). Even here, however, capitalism seems to be innocent, for the only serious accusation is that branches of the armed forces wished to have the war for a testing ground.[16] After all it did not generate expenditure on the large sophisticated technology that mainly concerns the 'military-industrial complex'. The main causes of this war must of course be sought in the obvious places: US Messianism, US phobias about China, the world-wide cold war, and until latterly – the will of the South Vietnamese people to resist their attackers.

14. The phrase neo-colonialism is so Protean as to be almost meaningless. It has also a bad origin: in the paranoid Marxist view that no good can come of capitalism, and the desperate search to prove that something quite contrary to one's predictions was foreseen all the time. For of course the liquidation of the British and Belgian empires at least, and the

US retreat from the Philippines and South America, are clean contrary to all Marxism. So the usual tactic has been pursued by pretending that nothing has really happened: the superstructure has been replastered while the base is unchanged. If, above all, the ownership relations are the same who cares about the government? In non-Marxist language, the formal empire has been shifted to the informal column, and carries on.

This doctrine is in any case refuted by the nationalizations of imperialist property throughout the allegedly now informal empire: the Suez Canal, Libyan oil, Argentine railways, Chilean copper, Algerian oil ... how can there be empire where there are neither troops nor experts nor property? In any case in the course of time Soviet Marxists, at the service of a less isolationist foreign policy which wishes to influence UDCs directly, have abandoned the doctrine of neo-colonialism except in respect of UDCs that are particularly hostile to USSR. Independent Marxists continue to use it more widely, and we need not follow their arguments here. For our duty is to recognize the essential kernel of truth, and to analyse for ourselves the prime case: France.

France spends a far greater percentage of her national income on foreign aid than any other ACE, and it nearly all goes – in tied loans – to her former empire.[17] The governments of these new states are weak, and leave immensely many administrative decisions to Paris. They receive not merely project aid but direct budgetary support. They send students to France and use French news services. They continue even elementary education in French, and use armies of French teachers. France has veto powers within their universities. In a word France is buying what she can no longer command. The fact that she pays so heavily at once disproves the Marxist notion that the continued ownership of capital assets is decisive for government. Neo-colonialism, then, does not mean that nothing has happened. These countries have sold themselves dearly; the new French system is *inverted imperialism*, and redistributes from rich to poor, from metropolis to colony.

What does France gain? First she preserves her cultural position, a matter of fantastic importance to Frenchmen, and genuinely affecting foreign policy and finance. Secondly and surely still more important, she preserves existing private and public capital holdings, and the free transferability of interest and dividends. For the franc CFA is rigidly tied to the metropolitan franc, since the new African banks of note issue are fiercely restricted by treaty and by 50–50 French representation on their boards. There is thus neither exchange control nor devaluation within the franc zone, but completely free trade in capital, including even the export of native capital to France.[18]

What France does not appear to gain is control over foreign policy. She demonstrably does not dispose of the votes of her ex-colonies at the UN (Scherk, Annexe I). Her military presence is also ebbing. It is impossible to agree with Scherk's conclusion (p. 149), a conclusion shared by most simplistic and patriotic French writers, that these states are sovereign. If a foreign power has veto rights in one's university, and above all one's central bank, one is not sovereign. But neo-colonialism is almost confined to the two fields of currency (not finance) and education. And it must be said that each state actively and consciously chose its treaty relationship: Guinea freely chose to reject it, and Mali freely experimented with rejection. Neo-colonialism, then, is not a mystical Marxist concept, describing exploited nations caught in a dialectical trap they did not make. Neo-colonialism is a bargain: pieces of sovereignty are sold, at freely contracted prices, to an inverted imperialist power. Within this latter the taxpayer loses and the teacher, the technician and the exporter of capital gain. It is quite uncertain how the ex-colony or the ex-metropolis fares on balance.

It may be that genuine neo-colonialism is compatible only with a genuinely state capitalist metropolis.

15. From the genuine to the false accusation of neo-colonialism. First it is alleged that ACEs are still simply incapable of fully employing their own capital and labour: that the nineteenth century is still with us. My first comment is that if this were really true, and foreign aid sprang irrepressibly from the cornucopia of capitalist budgets, accompanied by technicians seeking work, the UDCs would be in a very happy position. For having gained political independence they would face the competition of many ACEs and also STEs to help them, in place of the old bilateral relation. But unfortunately it is not true. Incomes are more equal and trade unions more insistent, and this offsets our greater affluence. Britain and USA at least are often in balance of payments difficulties. We think (sec. 11) that the sum of private and public capital exports is not much smaller today; but we know that private capital rightly fears repudiation and that the slightest relaxation of fiscal policy will stop the flow of public capital. No one can dispute that all competing budgetary appropriations in all ACEs could easily be much bigger, and that ministers of finance resist much pressure. Yet it is essential to the doctrine that the defence and foreign aid funds should be overflowing out of a buoyant revenue.

Secondly the new public foreign aid of ACEs and of the International Bank is said to be slanted towards the wrong kind of investment, in order to distort the economies (i.e. the factor endowments) of UDCs, and keep them dependent. Since this is a policy matter, virtually unconnected with institutions, we may be brief and dogmatic. In the bad old days this charge was exactly correct: we have already instanced the strangulation of the Bengal cotton industry. But today this simple charge cannot be sustained. Light industry grows very rapidly indeed in UDCs, and their light industrial exports to ACEs are one of the fastest-growing items in world trade. Much of this is with foreign capitalist participation. Foreign public aid, too, goes largely into industry and its infrastructure.

So economic imperialism now becomes a refusal to invest in the UDCs' heavy industry, or in their machine-building and metallurgy, or in their sophisticated technology. To invest as suggested would of course violate the rules of static comparative costs. And it has never been shown how such an undoubted waste of resources on a static calculation would be other than a waste also on a dynamic one.[19] Many authors write as if it were enough to show that static and dynamic criteria often differ. What has to be shown is that they differ in this case, and in the required direction. How can a country enhance its rate of growth by spending its scarce savings on dear machines it cannot use when cheap machines it can use are available? Or by withdrawing its resources from its traditional exports, which are ex hypothesi its most efficient sector?

Nor is it even clear why it is in the interest of ACEs to prevent such development. For it is in light industry that they suffer serious competition. Clearly all switches out of this sector would take off the heat. It is pitiful to see how such views are accepted unanalysed, when the last imperial power to tamper with factor endowment, the USSR, demonstrably harmed her Czechoslovak colony by causing her to specialize in machinery. The whole crisis of 1962–3 arose from this (Wiles 1969, chapter 5, sec. 13). Perhaps the success of the oil cartel since 1973 will teach us a little realism on commodity structure.

It is certain on the other hand that aid-giving is not free of political motivations and prejudice. No country aids one hostile to it, and if that be defined as neo-colonialism it characterizes all public and private capital transfer without exception. USA will assist in erecting a public infrastructure, but not normally nationalized factories. No Communist country gives any aid to capitalism, though deals of mutual co-operation with multi-national corporations are common and sometimes spill over into UDCs. Both sides officially avow a wish to build up societies in their own image. Other aid givers, mainly the IBRD and other ACEs, are more pragmatic, and largely neglect questions of ownership. Communist aid concentrates on heavy industry, while capitalist aid is dispersed across all sectors. This again reflects domestic policy – but also the very narrow range of Communist technical competence. Finally it seems that Communist aid givers are paradoxically less inclined to question the whole concept of the particular project, and its place in the national plan. They provide the customer with what he wants: normally a 'latchkey factory'. The reason is doubtless that public expenditure abroad is not carefully scrutinized by democratic bodies at home, applying their own notions of effectiveness. More is left to diplomats. The result is to give less offence, to make stable long-term commitments more possible, and to get out again at the end with minimal entanglements.

Quantitatively, it should not surprise us that capitalist aid should be many times as great: the ACEs are much richer; the tradition and the inclination are there; if it is easier than it used to be it is still less easy than in STEs to find domestic uses for capital; the fact that public aid creates export markets for private enterprise creates a powerful lobby. Also there is a fair-sized public opinion in favour of aid. In STEs public opinion has no weight, but is opposed to it.

Finally ideology but not economic institutions make the Communist country a bad debt collector, and dictate a low rate of interest.[20] The latter is probably compensated by high prices or poor quality, but it is sincerely meant. A low rate is an important way of avoiding the curse of over-indebtedness among UDCs. This has now risen to proportions as alarming as in the prototypical case of the Khedive (above). It says much for the change in the world as a whole that no defaulting country is likely to be occupied during this century.

16. In matters of aid to UDCs, then, USSR has a good record of non-imperialism. Her behaviour within her empire is extremely different. **How then, on her own stamping ground,** has USSR reacted to these great movements of opinion and policy? Clearly she thinks them irrelevant to socialism, and so, secure in her innocence, exercises a great deal more power than even France. But of what nature is this power? Our previous analysis showed the STE as such to be far less inclined to economic imperialism than the ACE; the fault lies with the traditions of the Great Russian people, the exigencies of the cold war and the Communist capacity for self-deception.

We may go further. The Communist hostility to exploitation and dedication to universal brotherhood are perfectly genuine. To be sure, it is not everyone's idea of brotherhood:

> Und willst du nicht mein Bruder sein,
> Dann schlag ich dir den Schädel ein.[21]

But after all that is what family life is often like, and oppression is not a negation, but a perversion, of fraternal feeling. Marxian ideology is extremely explicit on international equality, and this is not one of the canons that the faithful have called in question.

The era of bare-faced Stalinist robbery was soon over, but not that of military invasion to enforce ideological and diplomatic conformity. As a milder substitute for such invasions, economic war is very common, nay almost endemic. But its ends are political: this is economic imperialism of our type C, it does not make the USSR richer but more powerful. We find, then, an inordinate amount of complacency and self-deception, leading to 'objective' Great Russian[22] imperialism. Location decisions, investment decisions, quantities traded all somehow fit a large Russian design. But the terms of trade are another matter (sec. 7). Things not in the interest of the satellites are forced on them, but no vulgar economic profit accrues to the USSR. Quite the contrary, this is probably a case of 'inverted imperialism' *à la française*. Poor STEs get a great deal of aid, mostly Soviet.[23] The USSR is a better debt-collector within the bloc, but still not really ruthless. The bloc's defence burden is quite disproportionately borne by USSR. And yet she is not at all the richest STE.

17. Lastly we have to consider internal imperialism: the economic domination of national minorities within state boundaries. The great case is by chance Russian, so Communist. The accidents of geography spread the Russian Empire over land, with unbroken territorial contiguity from Kishinev to Magadan. It is a well-known fact of human psychology that aggression across water is more sinful; so the British had to lose their empire but the Russians could keep theirs. They are allowed (except by China) the same right to Vladivostok as the USA has to Seattle; little criticized for being in Georgia (annexed 1801, reoccupied 1921 after three years' independence); rather severely criticized for being in Latvia (never an independent state until 1918, reoccupied 1940); and universally condemned for being in Czechoslovakia (still a formally independent state, but after all also contiguous).

With this background the Great Russian people would have been complacent and aloof from modern criticism of imperialism, even under another régime. But add the facts that USSR is nominally federal and includes these places on an equal footing, that the 'exploitation of man by man' has been declared abolished, and that Central Asia has most genuinely developed, at Russian expense, to somewhere near the national average[24] – and we can see that it is useless to tell a Russian Communist his is the most imperialistic nation in the world. No movement of opinion is shortly going to federalize USSR seriously like Yugoslavia (i.e. federalize the Communist Party), or set minority languages on a genuine equality in higher education; let alone allow talk of secession.

But what would it mean in economics, to end internal Russian imperialism? As before, imperialism is essentially about power. To end it would be to give the minorities control over their own development, an increase in power for which they would pay very dearly indeed. For it would also mean to withdraw Russian experts and to deprive them of capital and technology at present freely given. Only the Baltic states are definitely richer than RSFSR (they always have been); only this small area is even a candidate for gain through decentralization, i.e. for seceding from a redistributive system of public finance that works against them. Note, then, how exceedingly 'objective' is the economic side of Russian internal imperialism. Whatever we may say of security and linguistic policy, economic policy means well.

This leads us to a generally reliable law of internal imperialism: it redistributes from rich to poor, not sparing the imperial nationality (which may not be the richest). It is not difficult to see why: all states within one boundary are welfare states, all redistribute, with very varying effectiveness, to poor from rich: be the latter Balts, Czechs, English or Catalans. It is almost a matter of accident whether the rich are also the imperial nationality. To include people within one's boundaries is in the modern world to accept their racial and legal equality, and so to acknowledge a minimal economic and educational responsibility for them, just as if they were 'people like us'. From this it follows instantly that the welfare state will grind away automatically at the regional or racial extremes of poverty and illiteracy.

A centralistic or not-very-federal state can only avoid this consequence by systematic *racism*. In South Africa the income gap between white and black has broadened of recent years. Liberal economists, who correctly point out that average income would rise more rapidly if, for instance, there were less job discrimination, miss the point. The imperial nationality wishes to raise its own income, and has no identifiable self-interest in the national average. The yield on capital might indeed rise, but capital is in the hands of only a minority of whites, and the labour interest of the other whites prevails. Racism has to be found to be morally intolerable; it is seldom against the economic interest of the dominant group. A similar situation holds in Rhodesia, Ethiopia and certain South American countries, and it has not been completely liquidated in USA. In each case internal imperialism is the consequence of a previous external imperialism.

So if the imperial nationality is not particularly racist, and the richest group concerned, its internal imperialism works against its economic interest. With this in mind we should not be so surprised to find that French neo-colonialism is also a way of taxing the imperial nationality for the benefit of the rest. The thing is not absurd or paradoxical, merely extreme. Power, whether in nation-state or in empire, is something one may prefer to buy than to seize.

The less centralized the state, of course, the less the likelihood of internal imperialism, inverted or plain. The multi-national federal state is unable, and maybe unwilling, to effect much redistribution. Thus Yugoslavia and Canada have succeeded so little here because they are so very federal. Czechoslovakia and USSR have succeeded better: being STEs they are institutionally incapable of true federalism. It is also surely important that they are willing to waste money, having no sound investment criterion; this makes them capable of pouring money into Slovakia and Central Asia.[25]

Notes

1. The following are recommended: Eli Heckscher, *Mercantilism*, tr. Mendel Shapiro, London 1955; J. A. Hobson, *Imperialism*, London 1902; V. I. Lenin, *Imperialism*, London 1928 (written in 1910); Rosa Luxemburg, *The Accumulation of Capital*, London 1951 (written in 1913); Lionel Robbins, *The Economic Causes of War*, London 1939; Edmund Silberner, *The Problem of War in Nineteenth Century Economic Thought*, Princeton 1946; Eugene Staley, *War and the Private Investor*, N.Y. 1935; Alan S. Milward, *The New Order and the French Economy*, Oxford 1970, chapter 1.

2. This gave USA the treaty right to occupy Cuba when government broke down – in Washington's judgement.

3. The great exception was wheat. But then wheat was both produced and consumed by rich countries.

4. And its 'Prebischian' counterpart in Western economics: cf. Wiles 1969, pp. 182–4.

5. There is practically no mention of Mercantilism in Marx. His 'feudalism' seems to consist of feudal landlords and a free peasantry. His historical stages of foreign trade begin with free trade: cf. Wiles 1969, chapter 1. It may be that Marx supposed a proletariat to be a precondition of capitalism. But this is almost wholly false. Serfdom, which was indeed necessary to feudalism, was not destroyed by the growth of a dispossessed proletariat but of a free artisanate and peasantry. Several centuries of capitalism intervened, in which the capitalist was only a financier, putter-out or a ship-owner; i.e. in which there were rich and poor but only small pockets of proletariat (miners, sailors). Lenin sanctified this fallacy by also failing to refer to Mercantilism in his *Imperialism*. So the omission became canonical, and the independent US radical Scott Nearing even got into trouble for mentioning earlier imperialisms in his *Twilight of Empire*. At the time a member of the CPUSA, he submitted the manuscript to International Publishers, who turned it down on Moscow's orders, saying that Lenin had not begun so early. The book was eventually published by Vanguard Press, N.Y. 1930, and Mr. Nearing resigned from the Party on this issue. Cf. Scott Nearing, *The Making of a Radical*, N.Y. 1972, pp. 149–52.

6. The Mannesmann iron ore concession in Morocco is often instanced, too. But Staley points out that the German government had excellent diplomatic reasons for keeping these aggressive private capitalists quiet; it was reluctantly pushed along by public opinion, which Mannesmann manipulated.

7. In his *Economic Problems of Socialism in USSR*, Moscow 1952.

8. It is true, however, that Hitler personally was a great economic imperialist: he wished to turn Poland and the Ukraine into German colonies. But the animus of the German people as a whole was directed against the frontiers of Poland, resulting from the 'Versailles Diktat'. And even Hitler's motives were mainly racist.

9. Thus Lenin pre-figured his own system more truly than he knew, when he confined the causes of imperialism to a search for assured material supplies (op. cit.). In so doing he precluded 'Keynesian' causes, unlike Rosa Luxemburg; but no doubt quite unconsciously.

10. Cf. Wiles 1969, pp. 482–9.

11. Cf. Wiles 1969, pp. 521–3; Wiles in NATO (Directorate of Information), *Technology in the Soviet Union*, Brussels 1976.

12. Germany: colonies totalling 8·5 million people, mostly very ill subdued,

from 1885–90, on a metropolitan population of 60 million. Italy: Eritrea very ill subdued until after Adowa (1896), and this costly defeat by Ethiopia must be reckoned against any 'yield' from Eritrea; North Africa not subdued until *c.* 1913. Spain: Cuba a colony in 'good' standing until 1898. Belgium: the Congo 'well' exploited but not until 1885. Russia: much 'new land' expansion, and much territory taken before 1870 that can only be described as 'old colonial'; but capitalism itself scarcely rooted.

13. One half of the total defence budget, which was 7·9 per cent of GDP in 1970 (OECD, *Portugal*, Paris 1972, pp. 51, 60 (putting the budget on a national accounts basis).

14. Antonio Spinola, *Portugal e o Futuro*, Lisbon 1974. The general was for a time on the board of a major steel company. Cf. *Sunday Times*, 24 March 1974.

15. About seven parts in 100,000 of all private and public capital held by Americans at home and abroad, according to my estimate, was invested in Vietnam.

16. James A. Donovan, *Militarism, U.S.A.*, N.Y. 1970, pp. 72–4, chapters 5, 8. The author is a retired colonel in the Marines, with some inside knowledge. His book is largely about Vietnam and the military–industrial complex, but makes no suggestion of imperialism in that particular country.

17. For a truly excellent summary see Nikolaus Scherk, *Dekolonisation und Souveränität*, Vienna 1969. The countries that threw off French economic influence are (1972) Algeria, Cambodia, Guinea, Laos, Tunisia, N. Vietnam. Morocco, an ex-protectorate with an unbroken record of statehood, takes an intermediate stance. S. Vietnam has changed masters. The rest accept 'neo-colonialism'. The distinction between the French Community and the others is not important. Some countries outside the formal Community are bound to France by tight bilateral 'neo-colonial' treaty. Congo-Brazzaville is at present Maoist, but still in the Community! Mali has more or less returned to it, after a flirtation with China.

18. But the Côte d'Ivoire prevents by fiscal law the repatriation of foreign profits unless a proportion has been locally invested, and Congo-Brazzaville has nationalized a few things (Scherk, pp. 124, 125).

19. Cf. Wiles 1962, chapter 14–16; Wiles 1969, chapter 8.

20. But the proportion of gifts to loans is low by capitalist standards, except in the case of China.

21. 'And if you do not want to be my brother I will smash your skull in.'

22. I use this adjective rather than 'Soviet' as it seems more accurate when we speak of the Politburo or Soviet military and diplomatic personnel.

23. In addition to overt capital transfer and the Cuban sugar subsidy, they probably get favourable terms of trade. Cf. Wiles 1969, chapter 14.

24. But only because it went on developing in wartime, while the occupied Ukraine fell back. Cf. Peter J. D. Wiles, *Income Distribution East and West*, Amsterdam 1974, Lecture III.

25. Another surprisingly successful, though not very relevant, case of regional as opposed to racial equalization in USA: over 50 years the states of the union have grown together. This is partly due to the seniority principle in Congress, which gives Southern representatives control over the location of federal expenditures (chapter 18, sec. 5); which too is a willingness to waste money. There has also been unusually complete freedom to migrate. The basic data for this section are from my contribution to *La Distribuzione del Reddito nella Pianificazione Economica*, ISDEE, Trieste 1976.

20

The Convergence of Institutions

20

1. The systems we have described are very different: are they converging? Prophecy is a very dangerous game indeed. I play this game only because others insist on playing it, but crudely, incompletely and emotionally. This treatment is as complete and unemotional as possible, sector by sector and aspect by aspect. But the subject is so enormous and the space so short that it cannot escape crudity. Like all other horoscopes this one represents the author's best efforts with the knowledge available to date. It is surely wrong.

If a new technique arises in another country, including a new technique of management or other social organization, why should we imitate it? First, our government might compel us to do so, owing to some form of *competition*: notably in war or foreign trade. In the latter the decision might of course be taken for us by an independent enterprise.

But secondly the government or other decision centre might simply feel that the technique would be good for our people. This would be *imitation*, justified or not. If it is not, we must speak of international fashion, or keeping-up-with-Jones-land, or 'statistical competition'. This also is imitation, and it is largely due to the revolution in communications. We are simply more intimidated, that is, by foreign examples when we see them on TV or in international statistical year-books. The expansion of higher education is a good example of this.

Now in so far as it is due to sheer imitation, convergence is sheer voluntarism. It would mean (a) that we can choose our social systems, without competitive compulsion, and (b) that we also choose to converge. Indeed there is even a voluntaristic element in international competition: we do not absolutely have to compete.

Thirdly there is *inner necessity*. This can operate in various ways. On the orthodox Marxist level technical progress *imposes* some organizational change upon us, even in an isolated country; and the latter imposes in its turn changes in the 'relations of production' – ownership, managerial organizations, etc. These in turn affect the 'superstructure', i.e. politics, law, etc. If this were true it would only be necessary for someone somewhere to invent a new technique. It would then be imitated by one enterprise in our own country, to make more profit, and this supposition ensures the necessary minimum of cultural and technological diffusion, without which everything would have to be invented over and over again. All other enterprises would be forced to follow suit, and thereafter social superstructures would also converge.

But also without any new technology an organizational change could occur spontaneously, say a new system of management or planning technique, or even a new system of ownership like limited liability or the kolkhoz. Then the changes in the 'superstructure' would follow as before. Indeed, going quite outside Marxism, some social discovery, such as the gross unpopularity of moving belts or the efficiency of peasant farms, may react upon physical technology. We might for instance remove the moving belts or start the serial production of small tractors.

Clearly where there is no internal competition, as in an STE, there is no inner necessity to adopt foreign techniques and methods. Only government decisions count, and these partake of international competition or gratuitous imitation. But once the foreign example has been imported it may impose further changes elsewhere, even in an STE, and these indeed come under 'inner necessity'.

2. 'Inner necessity' smacks of the Hegelian dialectic. 'Economic forces' – that crucial but neglected Marxian concept – are 'released' by some invention, investment or revolution, and 'work themselves out'. In order to accept partially this concept we do not have to be dialecticians: to postulate a self-moving tendency in matter, still less one governed by the logical interplay of essences, or any form of determinism. Nor do we imply that any revolution is necessary. It is enough that once people start thinking about technology or the social sciences they will make 'improvements', and that these have a life, and consequences, of their own. But these consequences, we shall see, are neither easy to know nor strictly determined.

Convergence is a kind of loose *Stufenlehre*: one of those old German doctrines about economic history that arranged it all in a necessary succession of stages, where both development levels and economic organizations went together. It is loose because, obviously, it allows for the simple fact that today there are many organizational forms at one level of development. But it remains a *Stufenlehre* in that it sees a single final stage to which all must inevitably come. However where there is choice between viable alternatives today there may easily be such choice tomorrow. Besides, these large concepts leave so infinitely much untouched: agriculture? R and D? Yugoslavia? It is necessary to test any sweeping vision against *every* gritty little fact.

Convergence is a very unpopular doctrine in at least one country where sweeping visions are very acceptable: USSR. Since this is not the case in Eastern Europe we may posit a psychological reason. People have suffered so enormously in civil war, famine, collectivization, purges and now the cold war to gain their dearly bought 'socialism', they are so conscious of the loss of liberty, that it is morally unacceptable for, say, France to walk into the same 'socialism' by mere convergence. Suffering has always been a virtue in Russian eyes, and it is intolerable that revolution itself should become a path that some countries happened to tread on their way to the common end, but only to hasten their progress. It is true that Marxist ideology also condemns non-revolutionary convergence (though many qualifications made by Engels[1] before he died speak to the contrary). But that is just why all East Europeans are revisionists.

3. I define thus the state to which we are all most likely to converge if at all: *an advanced and rather centralized economy with a lot of sophisticated state planning, a market for detailed matters, little private equity in enterprises, a high social minimum but somewhat unequal earned incomes, considerable worker participation and rough equality of capital holdings.* I shall examine the probability of various systems actually moving in this direction. The theme takes up two chapters. The first is mainly about groups, i.e. management and planning, and the second is mainly about individuals and deeper ideological matters.

Convergence as such is not necessarily good. Mere similarity of economic systems, in particular, does not ensure peace: aggression is more deeply rooted than that, and will find other outlets. Indeed why should not the fact of similarity be itself the outlet? Besides, the posited point of convergence may itself be bad in one way or another, may even denote an inherently imperialistic economic system. So there is nothing tragic if we end prophesying divergence, and our predictions should of course be voided of all moral judgement until they have been worked out.

There will, furthermore, be no convergence in political systems, and that is not the same topic as ours. Not one of the items in our end-state entails freedom or tyranny, many parties or one party, a monarchy, federalism, civil rights, laws against homosexuality or any other thing commonly called political. Power is wielded within any nation state according to its traditions and to historical chance. Imitation of other countries plays a small part, invasion by them a larger one. But the relations between the political and the economic set-up are extremely loose. Such as they are, they are too vast a subject to be properly studied in this book, and we shall make here only the minimal necessary references to them.

The idea that there must, or even will, be political convergence is very common. It has no empirical basis whatsoever, and rests only on an optimism impenetrable by reason; notably on the fallacy that men are good, and willing to make sacrifices for, or to grant, freedom. All this is sufficiently untrue to render such a prophecy ridiculous, though the converse may indeed be true: we shall all go Communist because men are bad and will throw or barter away their freedom. We have, therefore, to deal only with economic trends that are politically neutral, or so strong that politically different régimes have to yield to them.

4. The great fields where convergence from present diversity is most

probable, outside agriculture and crafts, are short-term management and planning. STEs are coming more and more to adopt Western techniques in both arts. In planning, they are becoming less shy of money and prices. They use cost-benefit, input-output, linear programming and a rate of interest (chapter 11, 13). The very people entrusted with these things behave more and more like their Western counterparts: a post-revolutionary bureaucrat and a counter-revolutionary bureaucrat are twins (chapter 21, sec. 9).

Meanwhile ACEs have always both developed and applied modern managerial techniques, but originally they only developed planning techniques for export.[2] This has now changed. The French government surely plans more than the Yugoslav, and only a little less than the Hungarian. In all other ACEs there is now a great deal of more or less co-ordinated state interference. And the objective need for this has risen as the new factors of cost inflation and ecology add weight to all the old ones such as regional inequality, monopoly and unemployment. This is not to say that planners are in fact wise: only that they do on balance improve slightly upon the market, and that their opportunities for so doing are, in theory, unlimited.

But at one point here there is no agreement; STEs other than Hungary (or would it be enough to say 'STEs'?) welcome now more rational prices, but not decentralization. Since the invasion of Czechoslovakia they have even backed away from it. They fear the political consequences of freer enterprise: it would directly weaken central government organs and local Party organs alike. They fear its ideological consequences: it is the opposite of what higher Party organs have been saying since Marxist parties have existed; it is also the opposite of what Marx said.[3] Moreover since their overall economic performance remains good they have no urgent practical reasons to change. So the 'rather centralized economy' in our posited point of convergence is more in doubt than the 'sophisticated state planning'. And this is very proper, since the former is by far the more political of the two issues.

5. In management there has been convergence over a longer period. We have already dealt with the managerial revolution under capitalism. The disappearance of the primitive owner-manager itself constitutes convergence. He has been divided into a nearly fainéant owner, a manager whose word is law in all current matters, and a body of experts. Of these only the first has no counterpart in other systems. On the other side too, convergence is very old. Already in the 1930s the Bolsheviks dropped their exaggerated faith in 'staff' and reverted to 'line and staff' (chapter 11, sec. 11). Meanwhile the managerial type had passed from 'bourgeois expert' to 'proletarian expert' with only a brief interlude of old revolutionary war-horses.[4] The new systems of managerial training are now openly modelled on capitalist ones, and the manager is no longer

obliged to be an engineer:[5] he receives more of a commercial or economic training.

But there are still areas of extreme difference. First, so long as there is a command system, however rational and modernized at the centre, the messages reaching the director's in tray and the reactions they demand, are of a wholly different kind. This fact alone disposes of the frequent allegation that all large-scale economic organizations are the same. It is *not* the same to manipulate demand by advertising and to scrounge for scarce supplies. It is *not* the same to browbeat customers and to lie to command planners. One of the most absurd arguments for convergence is that 'we all now manipulate the market'. Who manipulates it, and how?! Reference here is to a persistent strain in the thinking of J. K. Galbraith,[6] who seems to think that there are no alternatives between perfect competition and the STE; so that if what he sees in ACEs is not the former it must be the latter.

Secondly labour relations remain radically different. The trade union is emasculated and so never crops up as an adversary, only as another part of the administration. But the director pays three penalties for this: his right to fire is severely circumscribed by law (chapter 7), he is often compelled to hire whole categories he does not need (chapter 14), and above all labour relations are the stamping ground of the Party.

The Party too, of course, is converging. Its full-time officials are also post-revolutionary and bureaucratic. It has so far relaxed its claim to omniscience as virtually to exclude the natural sciences from Marxism; to permit rational allocation procedures in central planning offices; to retreat from day-to-day interference in management and to permit sociologists to study labour relations. But there are hardly any independent chairs of sociology, and the whole venture into scientific labour relations is under quite unusually strict Party control.[7] The director has no personnel officer at his command: the trade union secretary is his personnel officer, and on all important matters he goes through the Party. Interference here is as great as ever.[8]

6. The world of self-management and communes is converging too. The original Yugoslav position was that workers' councils should be not merely powerful but also closely in touch with workers; so, implicitly, enterprises had to be small.

Now in fact this early period was one of direct Party dominance in the workers' councils, so the principles came to very little in practice. But in recent years enterprises have expanded, and branch enterprises also abound. Allowing for entry, amalgamation and bankruptcy, the number of industrial enterprises is about constant on a rapidly expanding labour force and output. In the nature of things the (indirectly elected) executive committee of the council became more important,[9] and this put a great distance between the worker and a rather bureaucratic group.

But the executive committee also contained two few technicians to make the important business decisions on technology, production schedules and marketing. These are now informally taken by the fast growing 'business committees': groups of technically competent white-collar employees, summoned for the purpose by the director, and remaining wholly his creatures. Meanwhile the Party has retreated from a direct role.

The workers' council and its executive committee were supposed to manage all the enterprise's affairs. But with increasing complexity this became of course quite unrealistic. It specializes in income distribution and the conditions of labour, because that is what its members know about, and what concerns its electorate most directly. With other matters, however important or unimportant, it deals only formally. All these other aspects, then, are bureaucratized and managerialized automatically. The same fate befalls the council's direct concern only to the extent that the council itself becomes bureaucratized.

Age, so often the joker in any pack of economic factors, also plays its part, when combined with seniority. What appears to be an élitist oligarchy with, say, one worker in seven on a serious committee conceals a gerontocratic male bureaucracy with, say, every other male worker aged 45–64 in such a position. Clearly the young and the women without seniority will have less power – after all, a serious productive Yugoslav enterprise is not a West German university! For similar tendencies among kibbutzim cf. chapter 6.

This form of convergence, then, is irresistible. It is also very simple to explain: as the size of the social unit expands and technology becomes more complex we need more experts and more hierarchs, while specialization and formality increase. But these increasingly similar organizations can still be put to very different uses. Kibbutzim still do maintain equality of consumption. Councils elected by Yugoslav workers still do appropriate too much revenue to personal income and too little to enterprise ploughback. Capitalist dividends still have meaning when there is a take-over bid. Soviet directors are still overwhelmingly more concerned with production than with marketing. It is not obvious why any of these differences should ever disappear.

7. But there is also a contrary trend: *towards* worker-participation. It is safe to say that this will go very far where political power permits it. It is a genuine grass-roots movement everywhere, which owes only a little to the (non-grass-roots) Yugoslav example, much more to the rise in educational levels. Now increasing education is something truly inevitable, arising both from our growing wealth and its status as a consumer good, and from the growing complexity of technology, which makes of at least some education a factor of production. Therefore participation is inevitable, and Yugoslavia has done little more than show the way – a way bestrewn, as we saw, with substantial difficulties.

Wherever there is democracy, then (i.e. a government responsive even to inconvenient popular demands), there will be participation. But how will it be organized? It is much to be feared that participation will only be politically possible if it is union-dominated (chapter 7, sec. 14). It is not possible to imagine a participatory system being imposed from above, still less growing up from below, and least of all surviving, without being captured by the powerful trade unions that dog all non-Communist countries. The main virtue of the Yugoslav system will probably turn out to be that the unions, being Stalinist, were and remain excluded from management, and with them much of the spirit of restriction and monopoly that automatically goes with a union. So participation is inevitable and will be mightily abused, simply because men are bad. Full and direct formal participation in management is the best way to instil responsibility; and this is not the way that will be chosen.

In Yugoslavia itself participation is becoming, as we have just seen, more and more bureaucratized and indirect. So whether or not the trade unions acquire more power, there will be genuine convergence towards a mid-point with ACEs. There will of course be much less participation in STEs, whether formal or informal: for reasons too obvious to mention.

The grass-roots demand for participation, then, comes from educated workers, and Yugoslavia itself was a *lusus naturae*. It follows that UDCs will adopt it slowly, or even abandon it. The great case is Algeria (chapter 7, sec. 10).

8. Will *trade unions* converge? Everything we know about them tells us that they will: see chapter 7 on 'the inevitability of the historic role'. The Soviet-type union, and Yugoslav and Hungarian unions, are picking up strength both locally and centrally. Lenin's 'transmission belt' seems to be about to pick up power from the bottom and deliver it to the top. Cost inflation and restrictive practices, even strikes, are likely to result.

It is far more difficult to forecast the fate of capitalist unions, untrammelled by single parties or by police forces that are above the law. Their behaviour and effect have become so intolerable as to threaten government and even society. It is hard to see any internal movement of reform, for union members do not suffer directly from all this, and militant leadership always defeats socially responsible leadership in the long run. It is also hard to imagine any successful reform by governments, so powerful have these bodies become.

We observed also in chapter 7 substantial differences in union style[10] between one capitalist country and another. The vast improvement in international communications may unify these styles. In many ways British union behaviour has recently become more French, with sit-ins and one-day token strikes; this may be direct imitation, or it may have been absorbed from the new behaviour of British students – which is itself imitative.

The difference between ACEs and UDCs is not obvious here, and this is why I have written 'capitalist countries'. In many ways it is ACEs that are converging on UDCs. It was the latter, notably, that first made cost inflation endemic. It is they too that raise the question, will the unions be totally absorbed into the state-capitalist Establishment? For of course unions play everywhere a role on non-wage issues, in whatever establishment there is. But only in UDCs do they sometimes abandon the arm's-length position characteristic of a mainly one-issue, essentially adversary, body, and become a transmission-belt from (or to) the single party (chapter 7, sec. 8). To judge by current trends this is a transitional phase due to the shortage of politicians and administrators. Rather perhaps, as 'the inevitability of the historic role' imposes itself more and more in UDCs, will more and more unions adopt the arm's-length position, in but not of the Establishment, characteristic of ACEs. Not dissimilar is the breakdown of voluntary pay restraint, negotiated under government auspices at the centre, which used to be the glory of Sweden and the Netherlands.

There is a further prospect of convergence, in the sense that there is an altogether new way of playing the historic role. Under capitalism the *erosion of managerial prerogative* in the 'union-constrained enterprise' (chapter 7, secs. 13, 14) is likely to continue, under the guise of participation. There will be more and more interference in the details of management, but it is not clear that adversary procedures will be abandoned in favour of responsibility. I.e. it is unlikely that unions will truly participate. Now paradoxically the Soviet-type union formally possesses many of these rights to interfere: in the Soviet context, by helping to draw up and execute the plan. So if it gains more genuine independence the Soviet-type enterprise will also be union-constrained. This can already be said of Hungary.

9. Hitherto we have discussed the non-agricultural, non-craft sectors. Agriculture is almost too special to be discussed at all, and the mere mention of it should be enough to sober up the more simple-minded prophets of convergence. Will Texas and Vermont, will Carmarthen and Norfolk converge? Since this seems improbable, why Vyatka and the Dordogne? Even within one type of crop or animal farming across the world it is hard to detect much similarity of organization, or a tendency towards it. The family farm, duly mechanized and helped out by itinerant labour, can do anything in mixed farming that the latifundium or sovkhoz can do: so why should any devotee of either one switch to the other? Specialized farms, however, really do present economies of scale a family cannot grasp, and this might persuade us that at least large areas will tread the road through the latifundium to the sovkhoz. But no: latifundia are extremely unpopular under capitalism and liable to be broken up. Nor will public opinion accept direct sovkhozization as an alternative. The family farm will undoubtedly be preferred, even at some

loss of efficiency, whether alone or in alliance with Danish-type co-operatives. There is also the loose working co-operative of family farms, whose main advantage is to guarantee each farmer a holiday. There has long been a thin trickle of these in Western Europe. The numbers seem now to be increasing.[11]

The question is rather whether Communist latifundia can survive their manifest unpopularity and inefficiency. Agriculture is highly competitive, in the sense of sec. 1, for purposes of both war and foreign trade. The *force des choses* must react upon the sovkhoz and the kolkhoz at least in minor ways. In Hungary the co-ops are very free indeed already, and also internally decentralized to a great extent. Even in USSR there are many signs of the same thing (chapter 6, sec. 9). Probably these trends will continue up to a decent Marxist limit, perhaps round about where Hungary now is. But this will certainly not hinder further *sovkhozizatsia* (chapter 3, sec. 7). For Communists see co-operation, even if only a formality, as backward. They will therefore press on with its abolition, even while the sovkhoz form is itself decentralized, without and within. Not even vertical integration with industry is likely to stem these tendencies, though it has good prospects itself.

Tight working co-operatives (i.e. kolkhozy) are more popular in UDCs as this is written, since their family farms at least are clearly too small. But industrialization and birth control will surely diminish their rural populations. The Mexican experience, and even the Israeli experience (why should we not add Polish and Yugoslav experience?), tell us clearly that the family farm will beat its rivals, and the tight working co-op will break up, unless the government uses force or vast subsidies. I am inclined to dismiss non-Communist interest in kolkhozy as a passing fad. This view is reinforced by the obvious intention of Communists to sovkozize all remaining kolkhozy 'with all deliberate speed'. Such a moribund and unpopular institution is scarcely likely to serve as a beacon for others.

For ownership in Poland and Yugoslavia, see secs. 14 and 15 below.

As to agricultural planning, the main non-command instrument is, as we have seen, the subsidy. This is too expensive for poor countries, but it does not seem that in STEs commands can any longer be a complete substitute for whatever the government can afford to pay (chapter 5, secs. 12, 13). Indeed sovkhozy were always subsidized, and the kolkhoz is now finally entering upon this inheritance too. So we must expect a convergence towards the use of subsidies and taxes. However we have no reason at all to expect that command methods will be actually abandoned in STEs; the present combination must surely continue, simply because agriculture always underfulfils its plans. Poland is here an exception: the new Gierek government has abandoned command methods in relation to its individual peasants. To the extent that China applies methods of command to its small producers' co-operatives, it will surely continue to do so. Broadly, then, sovkhozy and kolkhozy will continue to be commanded, but in a more relaxed way. But there would appear to be no chance whatever of such a thing under capitalism, in STEs or in Yugoslavia. No doubt *negative* restrictions such as cropping quotas (the astounding opposite to Soviet-type commands to grow more) will continue in ACEs with efficient agricultures and strong farmers' unions; but the main element of convergence will be the spread of the agricultural subsidy to UDCs, as economic growth makes it fiscally possible.

10. On crafts it is indeed possible to make a firm, if unexpected, prediction: if we include do-it-yourself and moonlighting there will be a lot more independent skilled craft activity everywhere in the world. This has different reasons everywhere. In UDCs it will simply be a question of development: there will be more of everything, including skilled people working on their own. In Communist countries of all sorts it is a matter of restoring small services that Stalinism abolished, and that command planning, with its petty incoherence and incapacity to repair things, renders more necessary than ever. But Communism also 'subsidizes' moonlighting by the extremely heavy taxes it raises on regular production. It is true that moonlighting income bears a heavy progressive rate of income tax, but it is easy enough not to declare. Indeed it is quite usual to steal the necessary raw materials and tools.

The tax position of the independent craftsman in an ACE is little different. If the indirect taxes levied on other products are smaller the taxes on labour itself are higher. He is in the same advantageous position to evade income tax and steal materials. He has one further selling point: he can undercut union wage-rates. For whereas command planning is simply incapable of rendering small services, advanced capitalism prices them out of the market, and so reduces its citizens to cheating and barter in order to obtain them, just as if they lived in STEs.

One third of urban housing in STEs, all kolkhoz and peasant homes, and all summer cottages are still privately owned, and so also privately built. These are almost always detached one- or two-storey dwellings. Very much of the new urban housing is co-operatively owned, and so built by the state with help from the prospective co-operators. The object is to charge an economic rent, or at least an economic down payment; and so to avoid the state subsidy that afflicts all public housing everywhere. To raise public rents is a very delicate affair even in an STE, and in accordance with Marxism they include no interest charge but are still subsidized. So since co-operators borrow from the state at interest the Treasury profits enormously (individuals put in their own savings). The shrinkage of new public building, then, is a form of rent decontrol. This is a slow process, likely to last long. But co-operative and individual ownership encourage all sorts of private deals, and are definitely a part of the rising 'craft' phenomenon.

Meanwhile in ACEs, subsidized public housing continues to spread, so here again we may speak of a rather paradoxical convergence.

The realities of convergence, we see, the categories of it that are really probable, are far removed from the towering structures of the economic theorists or the philosophers of history. They are positively undignified. It is a cardinal intellectual sin to presume that large trends must be ideologically dignified, or even intellectually interesting.

11. So long as inter-enterprise money is passive in STEs, banking and fiscal systems will only converge in uninteresting ways. For instance STEs will continue to converge onto the capitalist, or strictly the French, structure of thrift sources, as implied by Table 13/I. But they will still have monobanks, and ACEs, including France, will have two-tier banks.

But we discussed in chapter 12, sec. 20 a very striking convergence of the Yugoslav banking system onto the capitalist model: a trend which, good or bad, has surely not yet reached its term. In particular it is clear that Yugoslavia must abandon her Marxist objections to Keynesian fiscal policy. There may well, again, arise a bond and a bill market for banks, enterprises and public bodies, and so some kind of open-market operation. But for all the talk of private equities they are too much to swallow; so there will be no stock exchange.

Banks, however, are technically very flexible institutions, without deep social roots, that societies can rearrange, split up, amalgamate and manipulate. If the banks sometimes dominate the economy it is because the ideology of *laissez-faire* prevents us from asserting ourselves, or because a strong government is using them in a particular way, or because there is a political impasse, and the banks do as they please in the vacuum of power. This is obviously true of Yugoslavia. In a field, then, where there are so few technical limitations, and ideas, often very political, are so important, we should be wise to abstain from any other prophecies. This applies in particular to capitalist banking. Thus we saw in chapter 13 how *Finanzkapital*, never dominant in all ACEs, has yielded again to large corporations as such (USA) or to state capitalism (elsewhere).

12. Our final sector or aspect of an economy is R and D. We saw in chapter 15 how strongly this activity urges on other systems a convergence towards ACEs. Czechoslovak economists before August 1968 were even tempted to believe that an STE could not be a really advanced economy, because of the enormous number of types of article that a rich economy produces, and the brake upon R and D imposed by centralization and arbitrary prices. They were a singularly unempirical generation: they could not answer such ordinary objections as that the very poorest economies produce several million types, or that the Soviet space and

military programmes are successful, or that the DDR is quite generally successful.

But their point is not completely met by these objections. The Soviet space and military effort is very expensive: it evidently uses up more of the nation's total R and D than in comparable ACEs, or the other sectors would not be so demonstrably backward. The DDR is able to borrow, by cultural osmosis and personal intimacy, from the Federal Republic. The complaints of R and D people in STEs are very passionate and quite convincing. The amount of really original work is still very small.

Now this matter remains of the first importance to Communists since 'socialism' must prove its superiority to capitalism above all in this field. For if technology is the 'basis', and the 'basis' determines the 'superstructure' then without a superior technology of which it alone is capable socialism has no *raison d'être* in Marxist theory. Useless to argue that incomes are more equal or that everything has been nationalized: that was all supposed to follow, with the Revolution, upon a prior technical change that capitalism already then could not accommodate. But the Revolution took place in Russia and did not spread (until much later and by force of arms). And it survived for decades without the least pretension to technical superiority. So it is now all the more necessary to develop such superiority *a posteriori*.

Besides, there are overwhelming 'competitive' reasons also, too obvious to mention, why any imperialist state, indeed any nation, should try for technical superiority. So we may count with certainty upon some convergence towards the more efficient capitalist model in the conduct of research. After all personal telephones, foreign travel and free thought in the natural sciences are in no way contrary to Marxism, only to certain Stalinist traditions or to the convenience of the KGB. But the necessary decentralization of development is another matter. It is obvious that this strikes at the root of the command economy (cf. chapter 15, sec. 17–19). It is safest to predict an uneasy compromise. Since the STE is superior in the other aspects of growth it can afford a less efficient system at one point, if ideology stringently requires it.

13. Will all systems tend towards the same income distribution? – one more equal than in ACEs, more unequal, perhaps, than in China, about as equal as in Eastern Europe? We give in chapter 21, sec. 8 good reasons to believe that extreme egalitarianism is always a product of young revolutions, and of simple technologies requiring few specialists. The lapse of time, therefore, will bring China's *policy* back to the East European norm, while her actual statistical *achievement* may not for all we know, be very impressive.[12] We speak, too, of an East European, not a 'Soviet-type', norm because the Soviet Union is still so unequal as we saw. There appears to be no special connexion under socialism between equality and the level or the rate of development. Distribution is political.

It grows more unequal with the lapse of time from the revolution, or from the last left-wing convulsion; less unequal as the death of Stalin recedes, etc.

Capitalism on the other hand has inequality built in. We saw in chapter 16 that no forces within the market, or the family-property-inheritance-system, make for equality, just the reverse; but that technical progress and public education had both in the past been such forces. However in most ACEs inequality has remained about constant since the completion of the welfare state[13] (say about 1950, except for the USA). Automation, having played havoc with blue-collar skills, now threatens also white-collar and even middle-management skills, and for years on end many applicants for jobs at all levels have been formally overqualified. So it is not clear why employers should further equalize or differentiate the skill and pay structure of the jobs they offer. To get at the really poor they should clearly pay less than minimum wages, while particular craftsmen must, it seems, get more and more, but this could hardly affect the total distribution. Besides, in countries where careers have long been open to talent there is little hereditary outstanding talent left to discover. The gene pool is nearly exhausted and with it such minor contribution to equality as this procedure can make.[14]

We referred also in chapter 16 to miscellaneous mysterious accidents, largely connected with war, that have in the past changed macro-factor shares in ACEs. Such an 'accident', this time unconnected with war, is upon us now: cost inflation. It has certainly shifted British macro-factor shares in favour of labour, and squeezed salaries in favour of wages. It looks as if it will continue to do so until trade unions are suppressed; but the whole phenomenon is too recent for us to judge it well.

Broadly, then, hopes of greater equality under capitalism, without revolution or confiscation, must rest upon cost inflation (!) and progressive taxation. The latter has worked tremendous equalizing changes in the past, but it is difficult or impossible to make predictions. There is no reason to suppose that democratic governments, responsive to a taxpaying electorate, will do more than gradually raise the social minimum. This of course international self-respect demands of them (convergence through imitation!). But taxpayers are not egalitarian, and schemes to soak the rich frighten at least half the population. As to undemocratic governments, some of them are certainly capable of heavy taxation. But if they have no egalitarian ideology why should they use this capability? They too, after all, might as well respect the taxpayer.

I conclude this prognosis with a great deal of uncertainty and a little mild optimism. Already Sweden and the UK are as equal as the USSR (Table 16/I): so what surprises are not possible?

Yugoslavia, on the other hand, may well turn her back on the present economic free-for-all (chapter 16, sec. 22), for she has a 'socialist' image to keep up, and a Soviet-type past not altogether forgotten. Having purged the nationalists in Croatia, Marshal Tito turned in November 1972 to purging the liberals in Serbia. In so doing he made many explicit statements about income inequality and the loss of Socialist ideals; and advocated far more direct party interference in the economy. It remains to be seen whether under its aged hero the federal government and party will be strong enough to re-equalize incomes in practice. The Soviet government, it will be remembered, was strong enough; but this is an entirely more doubtful case.

14. We can expect increasing equality in the ownership of capital in ACEs. True, we saw in chapter 16 very strong reasons to believe that the underlying tendency was for large private fortunes to grow more rapidly than small ones. For the rich, including those with capital, save a higher proportion of income than the poor, receive a better yield on their savings, marry each other and bequeath to each other. It needs a strong tax system only to stay in place. It may be doubted whether UDCs will develop, whether under democracies or under non-Communist dictatorships, tax systems strong enough to proceed towards equality. But some ACEs have. Very large fortunes have been split up for all to see, but it is less well known that the bottom has gained, especially since 1969.[15]

In STEs the means of production may not be owned privately, except for the very limited plots and livestock of the collectivized peasantry, and the still smaller holdings in these things by the rest of the population. This leaves for private ownership a surprisingly long list: consumer durables, houses (not more than two), antiques, jewellery, works of art, collectors' items like stamps, cash. The list includes at least three income-yielding assets: savings bank deposits, royalties and spare room that can be rented. Moreover the whole list can still be bequeathed without tax. Though death duties have been advocated from time to time the idea dies hard that what the socialist government allows a man to accumulate is justly accumulated, and needs no fiscal correction.

Obviously it is those with the highest salaries that make the greatest accumulations. They also arrange for their children to be the best educated. Therefore unlimited inequality of capital is a theoretical, very long-run possibility in STEs. It is unbelievable, however, that such egalitarian governments, committed to Full Communism, will permit it. Wealth as such, though perfectly legal, is somewhat suspect. But illegitimate accumulations, e.g. foreign currency and private houses made out of stolen materials, are confiscated with great rigour already. I therefore predict that death duties will be introduced, and that by means of this trivial fiscal convergence indefinite private accumulation will be avoided.

The abolition of the kolkhoz will come as we have seen, one day (chapter 3). This is very certain, and it will be above all a change in the manner of holding property. But it is difficult to classify as 'convergent' or 'divergent' with respect to capitalism, although clearly it will be a divergence from Yugoslav self-management.

It is the Communist market economies that are of greatest interest. Both mixed and private ownership of the means of production are growing in Yugoslavia – just while they are fading away in China and East Germany. For these two countries took the ownership part of their revolution slowly, and the Chinese even retained a market for private and mixed (and, now and again, socialist) enterprises to operate on. But Yugoslavia, starting at the Stalinist extreme and then recreating a market, has allowed first individual peasants, then small private native firms and now large mixed half-foreign firms.

That there are private peasants requires no explanation: collectivization had failed as usual, and the government yielded rather than starve its people and create an unmanageable security problem. Lip-service is still paid to eventual socialization by means of co-operatives, state-provided machinery, etc. (chapter 5, sec. 9). But this is wearing a little thin, and the peasant looks as if he is due to survive and prosper. Since the actual growth of capitalist farmers can hardly be expected, it is difficult to range this phenomenon under convergence or divergence.

The growth of private capitalism in local transport, building and crafts is more remarkable. For it was hardly to be expected, once these things had been abolished, that they should be permitted to revive. It is easy to say that this is 'in the logic of' a market or 'in the logic of' self-management, but what does that really mean? First, then, the market promises release of individual energies hitherto stunted by centralization, spontaneity, adaptability, openness, service to the consumer, attention to detail. But once it becomes evident that the market is not enough, that in some branches public ownership and large firms also stand in the way of these desiderata, these also follow the command economy into oblivion, and the small capitalist is allowed to re-assert himself. Besides, self-management has already blessed *possession by small groups*, and condemned *state ownership*, which is meaningful, in favour of public ownership, which is not (chapter 3). But it is only a step from groups to individuals, and from possession to ownership. So the ideology is loose enough to accommodate innovations that certainly do not seem socialist to the outsider.

Mixed ownership of large enterprises comes in two forms, described in chapter 13, sec. 11. Here we need only say how obviously unsocialist and 'convergent' both of them are.

A really Communist government, on the other hand, like the Hungarian, that has accepted neither self-management nor de-collectivization nor formal changes in ideology, is likely to be able to defend state property in the means of production against the erosion of the market. Thus after the reforms (introduced on 1 January 1968) the collective farms took advantage of the new liberty to found their own small factories, paying higher wages than those of the state (chapter 6, sec. 9). This may easily have been more optimal in the short run, and simultaneously more conducive to growth. But it was a clear threat to the socialist order, and the expansion of these enterprises was stopped in late 1972.

There remains only the rather minor problem that the Hungarian socialist director is rewarded according to the profits of his enterprise. Can he, then, be distinguished from a capitalist manager? He surely can: his income varies *more* directly with enterprise profit![16] And this is, to be sure, an element of convergence. But he has no security of tenure, he owns no equity (there is none on offer), and the government is inhibited by no *ultra vires* rule of any sort. Therefore nothing is likely to develop out of this situation; like so many others it represents a partial convergence, which we should be most unwise to extrapolate.

Neither Yugoslavia nor Hungary has yet introduced proper death duties. But Yugoslavia has been forced to impose a progressive income tax. This is further evidence of the differentiating effects of markets, for as we saw in chapter 16 the STE has no need of such a tax to correct the gross distribution of income that it sets. Hungary happened to be one of those STEs, before 1969, that had succeeded in altogether abolishing the income tax. But complaints about increasing inequality are rife, and in 1975 a new tax was imposed on the larger and more conspicuous consumer durables.

15. Mostly in this book we have defined and answered questions sector by sector rather than country by country. It seems more scientific that way, and economics tries to be a science! But it at least enhances understanding to look at this very general question also by countries, i.e. more historically. I shall confine myself to the countries that have something special about them, and whose probable course of convergence or divergence cannot be easily inferred from what has been said.

France is special because of its planning system. But there is definite convergence between France and other ACEs. The operative parts, as opposed to the rhetoric, of French planning concern more and more the public sector alone. It is increasingly fashionable elsewhere to co-ordinate the public sector and to allow for its effects elsewhere. On the other hand the fiscal agreement, that possibly near-command instrument of planning, is spreading in all capitalist countries (chapter 9, sec. 6). Although French planning has nothing whatever to do with egalitarianism, and has not been used hitherto for redistribution, we may guess that it soon will be.

Of *the STEs* none is very peculiar, not even Poland with her peasants. But this is on condition that *Hungary* be excluded from the category. Our implied prognostication for her was one of stability in her present condition. The government is strong enough, and government and people alike are frightened enough of Soviet invasion, not to go further. Income differentiation will not be allowed to get out of hand, nor will private and collective farm enterprise. Cultural freedom too, which tends to go with economic freedom since it is in part the free exchange of goods and services, will not get out of hand. But the other twin curses of a market, inflation and balance-of-payments crises, threaten her more severely. If she cannot defeat these more serious enemies she must revert to being an STE.

UDCs generally are more malleable and we cannot predict which way they will go. If a UDC is securely anti-Communist its institutions reflect those of ACEs, including French planning. But if it is at all left-wing it is liable to try anything. Tunisia has tried to collectivize agriculture and abandoned it; Algeria has tried self-management and abandoned it; Tanzania has tried villagization and abandoned it . . . the ruler's personal whim is often decisive. It is this organizational instability that justifies, if anything does, the slight treatment UDCs have received at our hands. Communist UDCs share it fully. So we shall not add to the scattered remarks made on *China* by attempting to prophesy her next lurch:

> Canst thou draw out Leviathan with a hook?
> . . . Will he make a covenant with thee?

Indeed institutional change is rare and slow in developed countries. All the great systems we have discussed – 'War' Communism, NEP, the STE, primitive capitalism, self-management, kolkhozy – were introduced into poor or medium-poor countries. ACEs have *slowly developed out of* primitive capitalism. The STEs have *reformed* their pricing and management. Economic development creates vested interests and habits, institutions which are *ex hypothesi* not obviously unsuitable, legions of experts who can defend and adapt the status quo. Convergence, right or wrong, is a doctrine for such circumstances.

16. How may we sum this up? Reverting to the schema of sec. 1, let us take first the 'inner necessity' point of view. Faith in convergence implies, then, (i) a strong belief in the *influence of knowledge on behaviour*: social science, being exact and complete, has only unambiguous messages for humanity, and they will eventually be heeded. This is a form of arrogance, and must be rejected. Social knowledge has often very ambiguous consequences, and there are still vast areas over which there is not even any knowledge. So-called political science is the most important of these; it still slumbers in a never-never-land of bare assertion or purely normative abstraction. So any politician can still believe what he likes, and there is no certainty of political convergence. But political power determines most other things, and since other social sciences deliver only ambiguous messages our political masters can choose also here, *within a range*.[17]

These last three words describe the convergence that there has undeniably been. The range of the permissible has shrunk. *Some* beliefs – except in politics! – have been rendered untenable. The Taylorism that Lenin swallowed whole is all false (chapter 11, sec. 12). Central planning without the right prices is very sub-optimal. Sub-optimality is not crippling. *Laissez-faire* is powerless against externalities and cost inflation. Markets and inheritance generate inequality. Workers' councils refuse to plough back. Peasant farming is quite efficient. Enthusiasm pays off less than skill and persistence.

Even here one has to be cautious. The impermissible is not impossible, and proven knowledge can be rejected. Such is the case with the Communist attitude to peasants, and the capitalist attitude to equality. But still rejected truths seep in, and take their toll.

Or (ii) we might believe in convergence because not social ideas but *institutions have a force of their own*. Thus 'erosion by the market' also bespeaks a form of convergence by inner necessity. It consists of two items: the differential accumulation of private and small co-operative property, and the freer exchange of news and views along with other goods and services. The Yugoslav case shows that there is such a thing. It is this sort of convergence, too, that frightened the Bolsheviks during the NEP, with its stock exchange, convertible ruble, strikes, trade cycle and NEP men. Their fear was evidently not absurd, merely exaggerated. For subsequently Poland has performed the allegedly impossible feat of being an STE with private peasants for about 25 consecutive years; Hungary is remaining adequately Communist under market socialism, and China more so.

With less justification, but still with some, Friedrich Hayek feared the converse: that any derogation from *laissez-faire* would plunge a capitalist country into an STE. This is 'erosion by planning', and it too is a kind of convergence doctrine. We saw in chapter 17 how much credence should be attached also to it. Our answer was essentially the same: human beings, through their governments, are able to resist these 'inner necessities' if they really wish to.

Faith in convergence might imply (iii) a quasi-Marxist belief in the primacy of the technical base over the organizational and ideological superstructure. Marx was wrong, one must say, to predict a proletarian revolution in any advanced country: and all subsequent Communists have been wrong to predict greater technical progress under socialism. But these might have been merely errors in applying the doctrine: the basis does determine the superstructure, and since all technology everywhere will eventually be the same all superstructures must be the same.

This doctrine stumbles against the same objection: technology, too, only limits human choice. No society wishing to survive in a competitive world can do without laboratories, machines, factories, railways and an electric grid. Size and technical complexity, we have seen, do determine a certain style of management and to this extent there has already been a great deal of convergence. The basis does, in this respect, narrowly determine the superstructure.

But it is not obvious how these things should be owned, or what the long-term policy of management should be. There may possibly be one best way, perhaps separate for each of them, but social science does not reveal it. Even in some cases it is not obvious which gadgets are best: cars, lorries and roads *might* be better than railways! Peasant farms are a somewhat similar case, for they too can make progress, in competition with large farms, by using a different but also sophisticated technology. So in the presence of doubt and choice political power does more or less what it likes. All we really know is that technical knowledge is not different under socialism, except by being more backward; and that there is no technology capitalism cannot exploit. Therefore technical progress excludes only some economic systems, and leaves plenty of room for politicians to make, or traditions to impose, different systems.

(iv) So much for inner necessity. But convergence has, as we saw, other sources. *Competition* is a more certain cause. If STEs are to export custom-made goods they must permit the customer direct contact, and weaken the monopoly of the Ministry of Foreign Trade. If they want tourists they must import non-Communist newspapers and make motoring possible.[18] If, above all, any country wants military power it must have better armed forces than its rivals, i.e. of much the same kind. If it wants diplomatic power it must also export capital. But all this means more R and D, and that implies a whole range of social and economic changes, again in STEs (sec. 12). It also means more home-grown food, and that means a more capitalistic agriculture (sec. 9). Competitive convergence is distinctly pro-capitalist, while convergence from inner necessity is rather socialistic on balance.

Lastly (v) *imitative* convergence may operate in almost any direction and is often highly irrational. Planning in non-Communist countries appears to be imitative, either of STEs or of France. There is no factual basis at all for the view that planning in market economies enhances growth or any other good thing; so all such planning must be called keeping-up-with-Jones-land. *Per contra* the Czechoslovak Spring of 1968 took over, just as uncritically, many extreme Chicago doctrines, as if the market had no pathology. On another plane, many patterns of public expenditure are clearly imitative, and without objective necessity.

Notes

1. Conveniently summarized by Karl Popper, *The Open Society and its Enemies*, London 1945, pp. 148–6; R. N. Carew Hunt, *The Theory and Practice of Communism*, London 1957, pp. 76–7.

2. Input-output was invented in USA, but the Eisenhower government

stopped funds for research on its local application. Foreign aid is seldom offered by an ACE to a UDC without a demand for plans more detailed than those customarily prepared by the aid-giving government for its own internal purposes.

3. This is sometimes denied. But cf. Wiles 1962, chapter 18; Wiles in *Economica*, February 1967.

4. Cf. Jeremy Azrael, *Managerial Power and Soviet Politics*, Harvard 1966. The same interlude came to an end in Eastern Europe in the 1960s.

5. STEs were often said to be 'ahead in the number of engineers'. This was true only in a Pickwickian sense: managers went through this inappropriate form of training simply *faute de mieux*. This emphasis on engineering derives from Lenin's Taylorism (chapter 11, sec. 12).

6. Cf., merely for instance, his *New Industrial State* (2nd edn., Boston 1971, pp. 104–8), which however is a much more circumspect formulation than those of his followers.

7. Cf. Leo Labedz in *Survey* (formerly *Soviet Survey*), nos. 26 and 28; Zev Katz in *Problems of Communism*, May–June 1971.

8. Thus in the Shchëkino experiment the director's right to hire and fire, explicitly given him by law in 1965, was for the first time actually allowed to be used in 1969. But each case of firing had to go through the Party. Cf. Jeanne Delamotte, *Shchëkino*, Paris 1973.

9. Each geographically distinct establishment has its own council, but there is only one committee.

10. Style means some way of behaviour chosen from a permissible range, in the absence of a definite or at least of a recognized optimum. Thus there are also styles of economic warfare (Wiles 1969, pp. 494–8) and of profit-seeking (Wiles 1961, pp. 205–6). Style is most often determined by tradition.

11. Cf. OECD, *Group Farming*, Paris 1972.

12. We have no figures for Chinese per capita income distribution. Regional differences in agriculture are presumably very great, and so also those between one agricultural producers' co-operative and another. This probably offsets the greater equality of individual incomes per earner in the state sector. Of the latter we know that money earnings are sharply differentiated, while the social services are quite egalitarian and bulk large in total incomes.

13. Cf. Carlo Zacchia in *La Distribuzione del Reddito nella Pianificazione Economica*, ISDEE, Trieste 1976; Peter J. D. Wiles, *Income Distribution East and West*, Amsterdam 1974, Lecture IV.

14. Let me repeat that I flatly accept important genetical differences in intelligence between rich and poor of the same race. Cf. chapter 16, sec. 10.

15. Wiles, op. cit., 1974, Lecture II/6.

16. But then even under Stalin the Soviet director's bonus was very large, and varied with monthly plan fulfilment (chapter 2, sec. 5). The new Hungarian arrangement could just as well be regarded as the retention of a good feature of Stalinism, under changed circumstances.

17. Cf. Wiles in *History and Theory*, 1/1972.

18. This is 'convergence through foreign trade'. Cf. Wiles 1969, pp. 543–7.

21

The End of Economic Man?

Il Futuro ha un Cuore Antico
Carlo Levi

The world is too much with us; late and soon,
Getting and spending, we lay waste our powers:
Little we see in nature that is ours.
Wordsworth

1. The new visionaries
2. Full Communism, and –
3. the approach to it in advanced STEs and Kibbutzim
4. Chicago, a counter-vision
5. The hippie vision
6. Why there are hippies
7. The proletarization of the bourgeoisie
8. Revolutionaries and premature Full Communism
9. Full Communism and the bourgeois life-style
10. A secular shift in labour supply –
11. is perceptible, but not of a welcome sort
12. A consumption ceiling?
13. Demonetization through social services
14. Social services are not egalitarian, or expanding
15. Primitive moneylessness
16. How to end alienation
17. Convergence or divergence in this field?

21

1. Far beyond the narrow imaginings of the previous chapter, there are great changes of economic behaviour abroad in all developed countries. Voices are heard proclaiming the end of economic scarcity. Many are irrational, counter-factual, ignorant, mystical. The desire to astound, to keep in the swim, to keep in touch with (one per cent of) the young is all too evident. But when he has ploughed through all this cloud-capped rubbish the open-minded pedant (for as such the writer sees himself) is impressed by a solid core of truth and logic. We shall conclude this book by examining the practical medium-term likelihood that scarcity is coming to an end, and the obvious connexions of this with economic institutions and behaviour.

We have again and again condemned the economist's obsession with optimality, and have emphasized that it may be better to be sub-optimal in the short run for the sake of some longer goal that could itself be called optimal only by courtesy. But this is not to deny the fact of economic scarcity, or its central role in human affairs. It is to assert that the optimality problem arises out of scarcity, but is not identical with it. There are very many other 'scarcity problems', and we shall now discuss mainly them.

An economy wholly without scarcity, above all, would necessarily be socialistic. Private property in the means of production, and most of the objects of consumption, would be not only a laughable anomaly but technically indefensible. For there would be no point in either theft or exchange and therefore no law or policy to stop the one or regulate the other. Anybody who wanted anything of mine, except possibly my wife, my antiques and my manuscript, would be welcome to it: I could always get more by going to the warehouse. I might manage a factory, but work is fun and yields no income. So why should I own it, since income from particular bits of capital would be of no more interest to me than income from specific work? But we should still need a sense of obligation to the public good in order to make us work and not grossly waste things. So things would be either no one's property or public property, and everyone would be equal. Therefore, this kind of 'extremely extreme' affluence would bring about convergence – towards a somewhat anarchistic Communism.

Let us descend now from the empyrean to the stratosphere, and examine a few actual Utopias.

2. By far the grandest vision of the end of economics is that of Marx.[1] But it is in one serious respect a very impoverished vision. For he saw

economic scarcity only as class conflict over the distribution of income, not as the necessity of micro-choice between this output and that. The latter concept only overlaps with the former: if there is scarcity while there are classes this *will add an economic element to* class conflict, which will in any case exist and concern political power and social deference. Class conflict over income distribution is perfectly genuine but it is a concept of very small range, that is far from exhausting either economic scarcity or political conflict.

So Marx envisaged a state of society he called Communism or Socialism. Later Marxists extended the transitional phase, which he had spoken of as a brief Dictatorship of the Proletariat, and renamed it Socialism. The final phase of human society is now called by them Communism, by me – in order to avoid confusion – Full Communism.

Full Communism is like a nationwide kibbutz, or an STE that administers also the consumer and the worker. We are all paid, or rather given things to consume, according to our 'needs', as judged by the authorities. This is very nearly but not quite equally: for instance our needs differ physically. Our economic aspirations have been adjusted to this level of consumption. We accept it as natural, and can even be trusted to help ourselves in the 'shops' – which have become mere warehouses. The level of abundance is very great, but not at all so great as would extinguish cupidity and competition in an unreconstructed capitalist psyche: certainly not more than $10,000 per head p.a. in 1972 prices. We work for honour's and conscience's sake; for pleasure; for the material satisfaction of others; for craftsmanship's sake; or for the prosperity of the reified collective – in any case not for our own. We use our specialized skills at tasks agreed with the authorities, in rotation. Most of our consumption, and certainly all major durables, are collectivized. The nuclear family survives as an emotional unit: it provides extra love and companionship and a little personalized upbringing, but has no economic *raison d'être*. There is no money, since all goods and services from labour to consumption are allocated administratively, if they are not superabundant. There is little distinction of life-style between town and country. The 'state', i.e. the organs of political compulsion, ceases to exist. Human organization now exists only in order to administer the economy. This is achieved by persuasion, notably to get us to work at particular unpleasant things. Those who run this organization are a rotating body of non-specialists.

A picture so brief and bald needs qualifications. The biggest concerns the powers of non-economic compulsion. The kibbutz is under an external sovereign state, whose writ runs within it in case of crime, taxation, conscription, etc. The Israeli state has no intention of withering away, and so the problems posed by this part of Marxist doctrine are not raised. No Communist state either shows the smallest sign of withering away, but we may be sure that at least some hypocritical move would be taken in that direction if Full Communism were held to be seriously approaching. For instance a people's militia could be substituted for the KGB, the existing comrades' courts could take over the functions of the regular courts, the Gosplan could become formally a trade-union body. So long as the Communist Party continued to recruit, censor and manipulate, even genuine relaxation of 'state' power should be possible. I hold, however, that men are not perfectible and conflict is inevitable; so that a real withering away of both state and Party would lead to chaos, i.e. to unchecked crime and political disagreement; public opinion, including Party opinion, would not allow such an experiment. It follows that this part of Marxist doctrine is merely absurd, and need not be further discussed in a work of economics. We shall assume a state in what follows.

Secondly, Marx thought specialization would be abandoned as the market died: doubtless because all his thinking on this subject comes from his pre-industrial, or German, period. His words have given Soviet writers great difficulty, but they have eventually plucked up enough courage virtually to contradict him. Only specialization in administration is still banned from their picture: those jobs at any rate must rotate, lest the purely persuasive administration degenerate into a bureaucracy, and so into a state. We shall continue here to assume specialization in both productive and administrative tasks.

Thirdly there is the question of exactly how contumacious non-workers are 'persuaded' to work. The modern Marxist view is that these will be a vanishingly small minority, but 'he who does not work, neither shall he eat'. In other words such people do not receive 'according to their need'. Accordingly there must in any case be enough of a state machine to prevent them from thieving. Note that here too the kibbutz is no good guide, since it has the weapons of expulsion and of calling the police.

We have now set up one of the visions that concern this chapter, though by making it sensible enough to discuss we have seriously denatured it. In the Marxist Utopia individual men are perfect, and Marx would not have entertained his vision had he not been a perfectibilist. It is this vision of human perfection, rather than of the economic details of Full Communism, that sustains both the Trotskyite prisoner and his KGB torturer as they play their separate parts. But since Communism is (for irrelevant reasons) an immoral form of government, its subjects are rather worse individuals even than the rest of us: the perfectibility of man is not an empirical observation one would make in Moscow or Warsaw. Therefore the Communist state is not about to wither away, and the economic details of Full Communism must be separated from the political. And the historical fact is that Marx did have his detailed vision, so Communist governments must realize it. Not only must, but do, hence the real practical value of discussing the subject.

3. Many features of Marx's vision, then, are being introduced into actual

modern STEs, quite apart from premature attempts (sec. 8). The Moscow 'buses were for a brief period recently demonetized; income distribution is quite equal in Eastern Europe and becoming more so in USSR (chapter 16); social services are very large (sec. 14 here).

But above all the problem is tackled directly, by attempts to create the new *homo sovieticus*. Hours have been consistently shortened, at a level of income where workers in ACEs would be demanding overtime so as to buy more goods. Consumers' aspirations are manipulated, though not at all successfully. Logically, then, with productivity for ever increasing against a limited consumption level, the STE is bound for the one-hour day and the Soviet preoccupation with 'free time' (*svobodnoye vremya*) is wise. This is time free from paid labour, and the phrase is preferred to 'leisure' (*dosug*) since the latter has pre-revolutionary connotations of people doing what they like. Free time, on the contrary, is a deadly serious affair arranged by state and Party: one spends it administering things without pay, touring collectively, acquiring culture or even learning new labour skills. Free time, not free opinion, is what Marxists mean by freedom.

'Free time', then, is to be spent as far as possible on what Western economics knows as productive consumption, a set of activities missing from Bentham, though he could easily have included in his scheme of things the use of leisure to upgrade one's saleable skills.[2] This Marxist emphasis on productive consumption is a rather narrow and puritanical version of the abolition of the distinction between work and leisure. For this broader concept cf. sec. 13 below.

The productive use of free time has direct ideological connexions with the labour theory of value itself. For the time budget of a man is central to this, and achieves an almost mystical significance. Then too there is history. The mark of the capitalist Cain was precisely wage-slavery: the long working day, with the product of its surplus hours being expropriated and the hours themselves imposed by the threat of unemployment. To reduce the working day is the greatest triumph of a Communist leader: *vide* Lenin in 1917, Stalin in 1928. Then too the primitive Communist practice still survives in many forms of donating marginal labour-hours. Even in fairly normal times, such as USSR in 1950, unpaid overtime was very common. For the victorious proletariat, that has always lived by labour, is only donating its labour to itself, to defend its own achievements from counter-revolution. Or, in more settled times, its senior administrators, themselves perceiving the threat of bureaucracy, petrifaction and élitism, volunteer for periods of manual labour. Manual labour, it will be remembered, is the great Marxist cure-all for social ills (chapter 8, sec. 8).

This voluntary labour is nearly all hypocrisy. It is forced, by fear of political reprisals. In this the STE is necessarily inferior to the kibbutz, which has the unfair advantage of being able to choose and reject members after a novitiate. Also the society is *smaller*, so that the unanimity of social disapproval can be brought to bear upon non-workers. The Soviet *druzhinniki* (amateur militia) and labour tribunals are a very poor substitute.

Besides the citizen's supply of labour there is his aspiration level as a consumer to manipulate. The main lever here seems, curiously, to be one little recognized by those who manage STEs: the avoidance of new goods. For evidently if there is increasing efficiency but no new goods the law of diminishing marginal utility will one day bring every existing good to zero value, satisfying all aspirations. Thus product innovation is the enemy, and process innovation the friend, of Full Communism. Technical progress must eventually provide us with indefinitely large quantities we want of the things we know, but each new product draws factors away into the satisfaction of a new want, and so renders all factors scarce. For each new product is only 'marginally technically possible' (Wiles 1962, p. 387), and so a large demand for it must exhaust all available inputs.

The managers of STEs do in fact resist new products, but not for long in any given case. They seem not to recognize the full logic of the above argument, but to base their resistance on blind socialist instinct. International competition always beats this instinct. So it has also been in kibbutzim,[3] where however new goods are consciously resisted and the detailed control of aspiration levels has long been an overt aim. Indeed the means of this manipulation lie ready to hand, since the decision on what consumer goods and services to produce is made by one kibbutz committee, and that on what goods and services to 'import' by another. The individual consumer has no money, so no economic pull. He has only indirect 'political' influence, through his vote.

Quite apart from a general reluctance to 'import' or produce new goods, the distribution of all conspicuous goods is rather carefully designed to reduce any envy: either everyone gets a TV or no one does, and it is not normally possible to substitute, say, a car for a TV set and cigarettes. Consumption is not merely equal: it is also uniform. For if some had cars and some had TV sets there would be two demonstration effects instead of one. There might be newer goods than TV sets: the way not to want them is not to see them. There might also, quite irrationally, be mutual envy. This is the basic reason why an equal ration of money is not handed out for everything but only for small goods which are hard to administer.

Different from the issue of uniformity is that of privacy. Private consumers' durables come to be allowed, and snacks are taken in bedrooms out of small private refrigerators. This is another kind of individualism, also in theory compatible with equality and low aspirations. But it leads to differentiated consumption, and so to new goods, and so to envy, as before.

Then in addition to the trivial (and equal) sums of pocket money there are much larger sums for members going on outside errands. These latter must be unequally distributed in any case. Outside income, gifts and inheritances are more easily dealt with: they are confiscated and their fruits are divided up equally. The STE too faces all these envy-creating disturbances.

All in all consumers' sovereignty, even if mediated by a central planner, is contrary to extreme left-wing notions, and rightly so in so far as it makes aspirations very difficult to control. Even so, kibbutzim are dedicated only to equality and a *controlled* rise in aspirations. They have certainly not renounced affluence as such and are guilty of 'group Benthamism'. Indeed while the principles of equality, uniformity and non-privacy still hold, the more elementary one of balancing the budget has in recent years been lost. The committees dealing with consumption are unable to hold down the *general* level, and nearly all kibbutzim are heading for bankruptcy.

4. Capitalist governments have no such grandiose vision. Most of them are democratic, i.e. willing to yield power to a duly elected opposition; and large, dogmatic, published schemes for the far future are hostages to electoral fortune. Some are conservative dictatorships, and conservatism is as bad for futurological visions as dictatorship is good. Dictators and single-party régimes in UDCs do sometimes have visions, but they are not for the far future and so do not concern us.

Visions, then, in capitalist democracies, even in Yugoslavia,[4] are private enterprise. Those who complain of the absence of an official vision should contemplate more closely societies that have one. Only one of these unofficial visions is capitalist: that of the Chicago School.[5] It is of course extremely far from proposing an end to economics – where would economists draw their salaries? It is inserted here simply to show that a capitalist ultimate vision is also possible. In a society of perfect Benthamites and complete information, then, everyone bargains for everything he wants. We are equal before the law, but the law is minimal. For instance heroin is legal, since every schoolchild is perfectly informed about it and suicide is legal; moreover most heroin deaths are due to inadvertent overdoses, and these are wholly due to bad labelling and commercial dishonesty which in turn are due to the illegality of the drug. Education is privately supported and also privately demanded, except that the poor are on the voucher scheme. Instead of social services there is a great deal of private insurance and a negative income tax, which assures the poor of enough money – freely spendable at their own Benthamite discretion – to live. The army, if any, is recruited on the market, and the expense of this system puts a crimp in imperialist designs. Economic equality, a very minor desideratum, is roughly ensured by the market in ways described in chapter 16. Competition is everywhere practically perfect since government is minimal. For spontaneous imperfections of competition, arising from the market, are practically non-existent: it is government, taxes and licensing that create monopoly. As to full employment, it requires only price flexibility – assured by increased competition – and a supply of basic money that expands along with real income. This expansion is one of the irreducible tasks of government. Fiscal policy, and more detailed acts of monetary policy, are renounced. Trade unions and cartels are illegal but no great threat; large amalgamations are innocent unless proved guilty. Mostly they are no threat to competition, since foreign trade is free and the patent system is weakened. Technical progress goes on for ever, but consumers' aspirations rise for ever, and the balance is such as to ensure for ever a scarcity of labour.

This is an ultimate vision indeed. Many day-labourers in the Chicago fields would deny its sway over them, and like Marx's it has never been spelled out. It embodies many more revolutionary changes in institutions and men's minds than its supporters are willing to admit. It has also its fair share of sheer fallacy (neglect of imperfect competition, Keynesian effects and inheritance). But it is certainly not more ridiculous than Full Communism, and it has at least one great advantage: it rests squarely on the fact of human cupidity. For aggression and irrationality, however, it makes scarcely more provision than its great rival. But at least the atmosphere of bogus inevitability, generated by Marx, is wholly absent, and each proposal is frankly and unmystically made as a practical step that this or that government might take.

Nothing is more certain, however, than that most of these steps will not be taken. A basically descriptive book must put probability before desirability, so we turn away to another left-wing vision.

5. It is not obvious that *hippies*[6] should figure in this book at all. Our discussion may well be rendered totally out of date by the time we are in print, and exposed as mere trendiness. I am betting, however, that the hippie and above all the demi-hippie will be permanent and important parts of capitalism; and stating that, since an ounce of fact is worth a ton of theory, this actual first shoot of extreme capitalist affluence merits as much study as all that has been written on Full Communism.

A hippie is a counter-bourgeois. He defines himself by life-style rather than set beliefs, and this life-style is the mirror-image of the bourgeois one in which he was brought up. He is not, then, normally of proletarian origin, or from a UDC, or a member of an oppressed minority; though his way of life does attract a few deviants from such backgrounds, especially in periods of unemployment. His contrasts with the bourgeois are mainly economic, and his vision is a gentle, undogmatic, decentralized Communism. Let us list these contrasts (see overleaf).

The hippie, then, arises out of capitalism's most capitalist class, and is or tries to be its mirror image. He is of course first and foremost a psychological phenomenon: he has rejected his parents. Indeed as this is written

	Modern bourgeois	Hippie
i	insatiability of total wants	drastically lowered economic aspirations, though a fairly sophisticated and knowledgeable consumer
ii	always willing to increase own productivity, adapt self to new techniques, learn more, work hard	obsessed with ancient hand techniques, yet unwilling to master them professionally; very lazy on principle
iii	respects science, technology and education	rejects them utterly
iv	covers own budget, though will use social services if available	unashamed to beg, live off parents, etc.
v	always considers the future; discounts it appropriately, plans ahead, saves	lives only in the present, for immediate gratification
vi	economic individualism, likes private personal property	loose collectivism
vii	little entrepreneurship, no hostility to public enterprise; prefers security	willing to provide petty entrepreneurship; hostile to large enterprises of any kind; despises security
viii	nuclear family; surface monogamy	shifting commune, which performs most functions of the nuclear family; open promiscuity
ix	selfish, works only for nuclear family, but pays taxes and gives alms	surface altruism, but puts himself out for no one, least of all by working
x	easily organized	anarchic, hates organizations and hierarchies
xi	life is a patterned career, chosen from a limited range of models	life is a work of art
xii	rational	irrational, and proud of it
xiii	cool about religion; tends to organized churches with structured theologies	eclectically superstitious, but is serious about it; loves impromptu ceremonies, rejects churches
xiv	clean, hygienic	dirty, contracts avoidable disease
xv	hypocrisy, good manners	surface honesty, 'natural' manners
xvi	prefers drugs that release the tensions created by his life-style (alcohol, nicotine), or that put him to sleep (barbiturates)	prefers contemplative drugs that break down the boundaries of his ego, dampen his aggressions or fill the vacancy in his mind (marijuana, LSD)
xvii	nationalism, tolerance of war	ecumenism, pacifism
xviii	cultural conformism, reverence for culture heroes	stress on the originality and spontaneity of the unskilled; but in practice conformity with other hippies

nearly all hippies are still young, still part of the generation war of the 1960s. Hippiedom certainly began as extended childhood. Hence the impermanency of its institutions. Communes last so short a time and associations between the sexes (we must not say marriages) are so brief, because the people concerned are growing up so rapidly.

However a psychological origin and a youthful composition indicates impermanence only of particular units, not of the movement as such. There have been similar movements in the past, which settled down to a more balanced age-structure, and this one will surely follow suit. For on the one hand hippies breed,[7] and on the other as they age and feel more need for creature comforts, pensions and stability, they do not move completely back into the bourgeoisie, but become demi-hippies. Meanwhile other young people become hippies. Moreover extreme affluence can easily support a minority of such people without provoking legal counter-measures. Indeed there is also a very unexciting, non-psychological explanation for the hippie movement: unemployment among young bourgeois. For if all bourgeois jobs are filled, and your only prospect is perpetual education why *not* be a hippie?

The economic behaviour of the hippie has been described above in defining him. It is of course no less economic, or interesting in itself, for its peculiar origins. Nor could these origins be described as wholly non-economic, since the spiritual rejection that lies at their root is rejection of a certain kind of economic behaviour. Moreover it could not have taken place except on a basis of affluence and security: the hippie's behaviour presupposes a bourgeois, democratic welfare state which will provide social services to non-workers, whose police will (in the intervals of busting him for drugs) protect his life, whose doctors will heal him (see point xiv) and where his parents can earn enough to subsidize him (point iv).

6. There could not be hippies in an STE because they would be arrested for vagrancy or social parasitism. The parental life-style of, say, a Central Committee member is sufficiently bourgeois to generate a very similar spiritual rejection, but the security police, the Party and the state propaganda machine bulk far larger, and rejection focuses on them, so is political.

There are however very many hippie-like groups in non-Communist UDCs, and this makes us doubt whether extreme affluence has done much more than facilitate the phenomenon. It is perceived affluence that counts. The holy beggars and sanyasis of Hinduism, and many young Buddhists who don the saffron robe, show just the same rejection of the bourgeois life-style, which is after all quite plentifully enough represented in their countries. The friars of medieval Europe were at least as similar. If all three examples exhibit a more structured theology and retain some connexion with established religion, this is merely because they live(d) in more theological times and places; by local standards their religion is very antinomian. Indeed the first real hippies of modern Western civilization were the Provos of Amsterdam (*c.* 1962). At that time the Netherlands were about the poorest of the countries we call ACEs. Real income per head was perhaps a quarter of what it is in California today. California, then, is only important because many more people can afford to be hippies.[8] But the governments of poor countries are far less tolerant, and try to exclude the hippie tourist and suppress his native imitator.[9] Such governments, full of development fanaticism, are more hostile than any bourgeois policeman in Los Angeles.

Another reason for the increased numbers of hippies may be LSD and marijuana. If asceticism means pain and effort willingly borne, the hippie is no ascetic: how then do we account for his tolerance of economic deprivation, and the boredom that inevitably follows idleness? The evidence is not in, but it is tempting to think that will-diminishing, imagination-enhancing drugs are *necessary* for such a personality change. Many hippies are high much of the time. Indeed Yablonsky goes further: 'Most hippies that I encountered were under the influence of drugs more often than not' (op. cit., p. 296 and *passim*). Precisely only the Diggers (the Haight-Ashbury hippie group that worked, in order to provide free supply for the others) were very sparing with drugs. This remained true in 1969 of the new rural communes whither people fled from Haight-Ashbury (Houriet op. cit., *passim*). They were stable and economically successful in inverse relation to drug use. It is likely that marijuana lames the will, especially the will to work and consume. It is the anti-economic drug. No wonder it was proscribed in the less affluent 1920s, especially in UDCs like Egypt where it was then most common.

Thus the hippie is a parasite. Even his vision is, however much he may protest, parasitic, since it presupposes a square society that produces a surplus on which he may live. This makes it unlikely that he will reach overwhelming numbers or directly affect the economy.[10] Mass parasitism is not impossible: monastic orders have grown to such a size that governments have had to suppress them largely on economic grounds. But the point is that governments do suppress them. More likely, it seems, is the indefinite infiltration of the capitalist economy by disenchanted demi-hippies. Taking this part or that part of the total syndrome back into bourgeois life, they will be millions strong. Will this have quantifiable effects? Are we, on these or other grounds, slowly moving away from anything recognizable as advanced capitalism?

We deal with the supply of labour in secs. 10 and 11. Let us here consider thrift. The proportion of national income saved is diminishing nowhere in the non-Communist world; even with double-figure cost inflation. Tendencies to immediate self-gratification, such as mark the hippie's sexual behaviour, no doubt spill over into economic life. But they seem not to be serious. Anyway hippies did not invent the new sexual morality, for it ante-dated them. Nor is this matter directly our concern. We must reject the notion that the inculcation of sexual restraint helps to make us thrifty (items v and viii), to a statistically significant degree. We have only Freud's word for this – if we have even so much. The French and Scots should not be the by-words that they are for thrift, nor the Irish such big spenders.

7. But the hippies threaten to replace only the bourgeoisie. What of the proletariat? Their embourgeoisement – a little convergence theory all on its own – has been too often assumed. They are much more skilled and literate than they used to be, but they continue to differ significantly, and in traditional ways. We may sum these up as more immediate gratification in one's ends, more collectivism in one's means. Look back at the list in sec. 5. While in no way at all resembling a hippie, your 'ideal' proletarian still:

(ii) prefers monopoly and restriction to the increase of his individual productivity;
(iii) is indifferent to education;
(vi) is an economic collectivist, but only while at work; he shares the bourgeois love of private personal property;
(xi) does not attempt a patterned career, but reaches his earnings peak early and gets no more promotion. He may however agitate for and receive seniority or tenure, and the absence of a patterned career, though certainly deeply ingrained in his life-style, is not his free choice.

Much indicates in the modern world a proletarization of the bourgeoisie. The mechanization of low- and middle-grade managerial tastes, and the growth of hired as opposed to self-employed professionals, makes them feel proletarian. Inflation causes them to unionize, strike and restrict production. Meanwhile for whatever reason (chapter 16) their incomes are falling in relation to the average. So they have turned more and more to collectivism. In particular they have always, as educated and articulate people, exploited the social services more efficiently than the proletariat. Only perhaps, their patterned career structure and respect for education continue to bespeak a different life-style, and especially a continued rejection of immediate gratification.[11]

Yet a Marxist understanding of this situation seems false. The immiseration of the bourgeoisie is not absolute but relative, and relative to the proletariat! It is in large part due to the success of unionism elsewhere; i.e. the exploitation of capital by manual labour. If middle-rank investment advisers are automated out of existence, while 'bus-drivers continue to climb the social scale, this is not a revolutionary situation, and only Philistine Western market economics has the tools to explain it with – especially in STEs!

Note also the continued presence of an under-class or *Lumpenproletariat*[12] living for immediate gratification but mainly on the social services, and without organizations of collective defence, indeed to some extent without the nuclear family. This is yet another life-style. It is attractive to hippies, who are apt to confuse it with their own. But it arises in fact from incompetence and lack of principle, not idealism and too much principle. There is of course a thinly inhabited borderland between these (and indeed any pair of) life-styles, but that between the *Lumpenproletariat* and the proletariat is quite thickly populated; here is the true continuity.

8. There is also a revolutionary life-style. This differs from all the others in a dozen ways, but it is essentially temporary. Once the revolution is over it must be, and always is, abandoned. Societies must be minimally stable, and victorious revolutionaries are a terrible nuisance. We should therefore hardly need to discuss their life-style were it not for the Chinese attempt to perpetuate the Great Leap Forward syndrome (sec. 15 below, chapter 10, sec. 11), the rather less extreme Albanian version, 'War' Communism and above all Cuba (chapter 2, sec. 11).

The syndrome is a case of 'premature Full Communism'. Before there is anything that a consumer with the lowest aspirations would call abundance, and before the worker has acquired any socialist self-discipline – indeed in most cases any industrial discipline at all – he is expected to behave like a kibbutznik after his novitiate. This is because dedicated revolutionaries are always a tiny minority, drunk with idealism. They never adequately distinguish between themselves and the overwhelming mass of the unregenerate. They suppose not that enthusiasm is artificial and inertia natural, but vice versa; so with a very few external shocks the masses will become dedicated revolutionaries too.

Meanwhile the cadres themselves have a duty: to become 'both red and expert'. This is an ambition of every communist régime, and also of the Society of Jesus. Few Jesuits, in the author's observations, are first-class in their special subjects: they have, after all, so much else to learn and to do. Even the first-class mind is of limited capacity, and there is a temperamental contradiction between the scientist and the priest. This simple human limitation operates with full force on the S.J.'s opposite number, the C.P. Every Communist country has failed, and most have quasi-officially retreated into an acceptance that real experts must be lukewarm Party members, if that. With this acceptance goes a relaxation of the political qualifications for entry into universities, and the ideological content of syllabi.

At the beginning, however, Full Communism, or parts of it, are introduced at once, with two inevitable results: rationing and forced labour. Rationing is of course inevitable under moneylessness until absolute abundance – if that can ever come. As to forced labour, it is not that uneducated people dislike work, but they do dislike different work, and they do need differentiated and very direct incentives to get them to do it. All the same, the degree of force applied under premature Full Communism is fairly small. We do not speak of slavery or imprisonment, but of the direction or, in Trotsky's phrase, militarization of labour. The directed worker is a normal citizen in other respects (chapter 8, sec. 11): indeed the revolutionary expects to be directed himself.

No developed society has ever gone for premature Full Communism. Its very revolutionaries are better educated and more realistic. They opt instead for the long pull, as described above: and themselves settle rapidly into the bureaucratic mould appropriate to it. The attempt failed once in USSR and twice in China, but the nagging question of Cuba remains. By no means wholly underdeveloped or unsophisticated, Cuba has been in a state of virtual 'War' Communism since 1963. It has done her little good except in moral terms, but she survives.

9. Here, then, are the economic aspects of six life-styles. The 'modern bourgeois' life-style is very dominant and easy to slip into, and we can see retrospectively that our definition of institutional convergence means its spread to ruling circles in STEs and Yugoslavia. Also it may well engulf the proletariat and peasantry of all countries. Seen in these global terms, a proletarian is only a feckless, unskilled or honest bourgeois. Peasants are in most ways still closer to this norm.

The 'modern bourgeois' life-style is of course incompatible with the Chicagoan dream. It is a style suiting large corporations and state bureaucracies. Although not many of its elements contradict this dream, enough do to make it impossible (x, xi, above all vii), even if the whole proletariat were *embourgeoisé*.

Where does Full Communism fit in? Its theory, what it recommends, is again rather bourgeois, differing only in items i, iv, vi, ix, xi, xvii. In practice we may discount i, ix and xvii. The Full Communist personality syndrome is not one of our six since it does not occur in nature, but is dreamed up by intellectuals and artificially imposed by education and force. The more successful STEs are, the more there is to consume, the more specialized work becomes – so much the more will the citizenry be autonomous, individualistic, expert: in a word, bourgeois. This simple conflict between Communism and human nature is the root reason why Communism is a totalitarian creed. However such governments are quite efficient enough to impose outward conformity to Full Communism, and some of the institutions appropriate to it. They are moving forward, as we saw, to providing still more, at least in certain countries. I am not willing to predict failure.

The question before us, then, is, are the actual growth of hippiedom and the actual movement in Communist countries towards Full Communism the first swallows of a large new summer, in which certain features of economic man will disappear? Primitive man is not 'economic', though he varies very much from tribe to tribe. So there is nothing impossible about a reversion. Now Full Communism is, as we saw, unnatural: watch any Russian or Pole abroad, and you will see a degree of unblushing private acquisitiveness that is quite unnerving in the relaxed atmosphere of modern capitalism. Hippies on the other hand, while certainly a natural, indeed a persecuted, growth, are few in number and possess no state machine. Their great peak period may well be over, and their dependence on drugs is suspicious. It is not, then, among these that evidence should be sought upon our question, but rather within 'straight' capitalist society.

Specifically, (a) are the aspirations of affluent consumers 'topping off'? – not necessarily those of today's most affluent, but those of the young with good prospects. And (b) are such people more willing to work for the public good at low pay than in the past? Are they more careful of (c) the social effects of the work they do and (d) the way they spend their money, place their savings?

A professor who has been through five student revolutions is bound to be sceptical of the intellectual young. Their idealism is superficial, selective and short-winded, their self-deception verges on hypocrisy, their positive proposals are usually impracticable and indirectly self-interested. But we do not ask here how admirable such people are in general: we ask if they have the four characteristics named, and if they are stable in these respects. And the answer is surely yes in each case. Moreover this group is becoming an ever larger part of the population.

10. Let us take first the supply of labour. It is not at all new that some kinds of labour are an honour and a pleasure to many (chapter 2, sec. 6). We all like to donate our labour, and are constantly doing so for the sake of relations and friends. We donate it also to charitable organizations and to public administration on a massive scale. At least this part of the orthodox Full Communist vision is not absurd. But there is this qualification: we donate our labour to individuals we like or to causes we have adopted, not to enterprises. Whereas under Full Communism precisely the one great national enterprise is supposed to be the 'individual' or 'cause' in question.

The enforced difference between men under various systems could hardly be great.

Under capitalism peasants and shopkeepers do of course donate their labour, since their enterprises are themselves. For the rest only very senior employees ever donate their labour to enterprises – and even this is questionable, since they do not work contractual hours. True, non-unionized secretaries often donate overtime – but is it to an attractive boss or to the enterprise? Under Communism on the other hand we have seen that such donations are compulsory already – the apparent self-contradiction is intended (sec. 3). This particularly applies to Great Leaps Forward and other periods of extremism (sec. 8). Communist unions encourage, instead of forbidding, this kind of donation. Again in capitalist countries unions and their members make no difference between private and public enterprises, and this is the best of the bad evidence we have of the change in the unforced will to work brought about, *ceteris paribus*, by socialization.[13] If there is convergence here, it is in the gradual abandonment of the 'donation' of labour to enterprises. In Eastern Europe, notably, the practice is now quite unusual.

However there is the growing habit of taking paid work among the very rich, despite tremendous taxes on marginal income. This appears to be a genuine quasi-donation, and a genuine change in the attitude towards labour of a social group. But the very rich do also have a strictly selfish reason for the change: their status is far more politically precarious than in the nineteenth century, and they are trying to hide a vast inherited fortune behind a little current effort. In any case the habit of paid work is spreading even to very rich women. Thorstein Veblen's Leisure Class has shrunk into a tiny Jet Set, many of whom work.

It seems – the matter is controversial – to be otherwise with the very poor, who, faced with wages little higher than public support at subsistence level, have always been tempted not to work. Moreover the rules impose a withdrawal of public support in some proportion to the increase in wages; which is effectually a high marginal tax on those wages.[14] The poor aim far more at income than at work, and are reluctant to donate, or nearly donate, their labour for an earned income little in excess of what they can get by not working at all. This is not, so far as one can tell, a new phenomenon at all. But as the public support floor has risen relatively to average wages the 'choosiness' of the very poor has spread to more and more jobs. It becomes more and more difficult to get domestic servants, hospital porters, etc., at real wages that are clearly above subsistence and above what they used to be. To some extent this is also because technology has raised the dignity and pay of other jobs, leaving these behind.

Indeed the whole population has become choosier, so that an ever growing number of vacancies are necessary to accompany any given volume of employment.[15]

11. There is a more complicated and virtuous tendency among the young intelligentsia. These are the 'demi-hippies' of sec. 6. It is evident that low-paid public jobs (e.g. probation officer) and charitable jobs are becoming ever more attractive. No one acquainted with the young intelligentsia can fail to note a drift into more idealistic jobs at lower relative pay. Business recruiters have more and more difficulty: the glamour job is the civil rights lawyer, the slum doctor, the welfare worker. At present we notice little more than a shift in supply curves on

the labour market – and perhaps there will never be anything more dramatic. Indeed the market and capitalism could easily survive a far sharper shift. But in a very real sense economic aspiration levels have fallen. However an alternative explanation must be mentioned: the two classic careers of economic self-sacrifice, the army and the Church, have lost appeal; the percentage of idealists has not changed, and all we see is a diversion. We do not dispose of the statistics that could decide this question.

No doubt, either, this is a response to security and the rise of even low salaries to the level of comfort. But what is the exact nature of this new altruism? – these same people are also abandoning the 'work ethic'! Among them, deliberate unemployment and idleness are no longer a disgrace or a source of personal uneasiness. In sum they are *choosy in an idealistic way* about their jobs, but work as such is not an honour or an obligation. This development in human attitudes is infinitely remote from Full Communism, and indeed would destroy it. It is rather half-way over to hippiedom.

Another kind of shift in the supply of labour is rising crime. For crime is *inter alia* a way of earning one's living, and it takes time and effort, so it is labour. Here again the decline of the work ethic takes us away from, not towards, Full Communism.

We may venture to detect a slow drift, at least within the Western world, from work as something that could only be forced (feudalism, slavery), through the more liberal notion of work as a freely purchasable commodity and therefore not an unmixed evil to its supplier (Benthamism), towards work as pleasure (chapter 2). The change is probably more marked in ideas about work than in the actual conditions of work. There have even been reverse eddies, as when the free craftsman gave way to the machine-minder; and certainly all three sorts of work have always been simultaneously present. But the general drift seems clear: people demand more of their work.

It should not, therefore, surprise us that they are less willing to supply it. On balance we seem to remain as far as ever from the donation of significant quantities of labour on a national scale, and above all from its donation to the appropriate task. All donated labour goes to pleasant or adventurous tasks, and to charitable causes. It does not go to garbage collection. So we may dismiss the substitution of a national dividend for direct wages as something not utterly inconceivable but very distant. Societies of all kinds will continue to break the link between reward and effort only for the very poor, because they wish to enforce a social minimum.

12. On the side of consumption, the idea of Full Communism is much sillier. That we should all go and help ourselves, gratis and unrationed, but moderately, in the shops is 'not on', even in the very richest com-

munities. And we should need no ordinary brainwashing to make it 'on'.

In STEs there is much vague propaganda about such an ultimate state of affairs, and much very direct propaganda against consumerism, greed, Philistinism, etc. But we cannot observe even the beginnings of such restraint among the citizenry. Their talk is all of cars, flats, queues in shops. They pilfer, it would seem, slightly more than in most ACEs and they go far more on to the black market.[16] Their behaviour as tourists abroad is extremely acquisitive. In a field where there are no statistics we can only guess. My guess is that some part of this behaviour is due to the irrationality of prices and outputs, which creates irritating particular shortages vis-à-vis high nominal incomes. Those queuers, pilferers and black marketeers are seeking specific urgently necessary things; so that of two people at bottom equally acquisitive the one living in an STE would expose more of this trait. It is therefore quite impossible to estimate the success of the propaganda, *ceteris* not being *paribus*.

But among the young intelligentsia of ACEs we do note a 'topping off' of consumer aspirations: the small cars consciously preferred, the faded blue jeans, etc. Now in part this could be something permanent and important: they accept that a minimum of physical activity is necessary and might as well be turned to domestic use; they accept that simple pleasures (which are on the whole cheaper) are just as pleasurable as more complicated ones; and they try to 'keep down with the Jones', i.e. they have turned the inverted snobbery characteristic of intellectuals to economic uses. But it is easy to exaggerate. There is little real rejection of consumption *per se*, hardly any refusal to buy goods if financed, say, by a windfall. Mostly it is that leisure is more highly valued, or certain *kinds* of work.

Further to the positive side, the aspirations of this class are as well controlled as their labour supply: they do not, like hippies, fall into beggary by reducing work more than consumption. We receive from all this some slight encouragement to believe that human wants may after all be satiable, even in a free and unrationed society. But the young heroes of our story are only a small class, and exceedingly fashion-prone. In earlier centuries monasticism came in waves. In a century when God is dead and sex is rampant perhaps this is only the best surrogate we can provide for a wave of monasticism. Certainly the consumption of the whole population has not been noticeably affected.

13. STEs are not kibbutzim, and their way is very gradual and partial. Their first approach to Full Communism is through the expansion of social services. For our purposes these are of three kinds: those issued in money, those issued in kind according to state estimate of 'need', and those issued in kind on demand. The latter are still a null class, which further economic growth may or may not begin to fill. In UK, USA and USSR the two former are approximately of these volumes (per cent):[17]

	USSR 1969	USA 1966	UK 1967
Social services in kind, at notional market prices	18·7	8·8	9·8
Social services in money	9·7	7·0	11·2
Other personal outlays in money (i.e. excluding saving)	71·6	84·2	79·0

In Full Communism the social services would be all issued in kind and on demand, and would embrace all consumption. Individuals might or might not be allowed to re-barter the things they had received, so as to get a more appropriate mix. In 'War' Communism, for instance, which is the most complete case of this to date, re-bartering was forbidden but happened anyway (and not all income was in kind). Sub-optimality was, what it normally is not, obvious to the meanest intelligence. How surprising, then, that the very much smaller, but still considerable, social services of ACEs should be so much in kind, and that voucher schemes should be so unpopular.

In other words, we are in the difficult area of *compulsory consumption*. Social services in kind either strongly persuade us or actually compel us to take the particular thing offered. There is strong persuasion when the state as monopolist offers a given object, say a subsidized flat in an inconvenient place, to a poor man who cannot afford the economic price. There is actual compulsion where the truancy officer comes in, or where a man is committed as a lunatic, or in much preventive medicine (fluorine in the water supply). Even monetary hand-outs can be (not very strongly) persuasive: for instance until recently in New York City the welfare officer had a long form enumerating consumer goods, down to lipstick and soap dishes, in respect of which his client was entitled to claim, at specified intervals, money. Since there was, mercifully, no follow-through to discover how the money was spent, it did not matter much.

There lurks, especially among the left wing of the Establishment, the view that the poor are incompetent. This cannot be expressed openly, since the poor are supposed to vote for the left wing of the Establishment, and lack of empathy with them is supposed to characterize the right wing. It is denied, notably, that they cheat the social services: somehow the poor are to be more honest than income-tax payers. But we always oppress those we idealize. The fundamental notion that the poor are 'legal infants' shows through in the weight of compulsory or persuasive consumption, and the resistance to vouchers and straight monetary grants. Moreover the social services are also administered by mildly left-wing people, specially trained for the task by other mildly left-wing people, who all stand to lose their salaries in the event of administrative simplification. Full Communism, then, is seen by many on the moderate left as something suitable for the poor but not, of course, for themselves.

Evidently they confuse the poor with the far smaller category of problem families.

14. Social services need not, of course, be equally distributed (chapter 16, sec. 14). If they provide only a social minimum, for instance, it is logical not actually to distribute this minimum to the rich, but to allow them to pay for the superior private services they can afford. An egalitarian, however, may be dogmatic enough to give them the minimum and let them add to it (which he cannot prevent unless there is a Communist government).[18] This is notably the case in Britain, where all the inconsiderable egalitarian energies of the people are concentrated on this one field. Those who advocate moneyless, direct distribution[19] are highly egalitarian. All attempts to monetize these services, or to charge for them directly, or to graft on to them schemes of individual choice, nay even to rationalize or cut waste – none of which is necessarily inegalitarian – meet with passionate opposition. It is even anathema to suggest that public education or health should in fact provide only a social minimum, and that those who want to learn the violin or to be ill in a separate room should be charged extra. In the short run, many of these reforms would improve performance and painlessly increase revenue. Many, by charging the rich more than the poor, would actually equalize incomes. Behind the technical arguments, not all of them incorrect, upon which this conservatism bases itself is its true animus and dream: a Full Communist Britain, in which the social services are strictly egalitarian, private supplementation is impossible within each sector socialized, and the system has gradually engulfed the whole economy.

In other ACEs there is no such dream or animus. In them, and indeed in practice in Britain too, the rich contrive one way or another to turn state welfare expenditure to their own benefit. There are no rules to describe this process: in general the rich extract more absolutely, but less in relation to their total incomes, than the poor, except for unemployment pay (and, in the special case of Britain, primary and secondary education). To the extent that taxation is generally progressive, they contribute, of course, much more.

In STEs the fundamental philosophy of the social services is, surprisingly, not that they are the royal road to Full Communism, but that they are the *fringe benefits* drawn by the victorious proletariat from its one and only enterprise: the STE (chapter 16, sec. 16). The traditional capitalist view prevails that fringe benefits should be more, but not very much more, egalitarian than take-home pay. The general drift towards equality affects both. The substitution of social services for pay, however, hangs fire in all STEs. It seems, under the influence of Khrushchev and of Chinese ideological competition, to have reached a peak in the 'sixties.[20]

15. Social services, then, are not the same as Full Communism, which

entails a general demonetization. Now of course in Marx that can only happen in an advanced economy. But advanced demonetization is not to be confused with *primitive moneylessness*. All primitive economies are partly moneyless, and often this leaves substantial traces in the economies of UDCs that go Communist. Now the yen for immediate Full Communism is particularly strong in poor Communist countries. Less-well-educated Marxists are leading a less-well-educated population; just as in ordinary UDCs they rely more on charisma, so are more susceptible to personal whim. We described in chapter 10, sec. 11 the economic technicalities of the Great Leap Forward syndrome, and we saw in sec. 8 above that a rush towards premature Full Communism was invariably a part of it. All near approaches to the institutions of Full Communism have historically coincided with Great Leaps Forward: it is only from underdeveloped economies that we know anything empirically about the subject.

Undoubtedly the remaining traces of primitive moneylessness help the enthusiastic new Communist régime to take this position. If rural life generally, and above all the rural guerrilla life through which its leaders have just passed, requires very little money; if in this life there was much equality and many things were rationed, why shouldn't the rest of the population welcome this too? Why not Full Communism here and now? Thus in his original Great Leap Forward (1958) Mao saw the existing rural prevalence of payment in kind as a foundation for his new Communes, and put the countryside in ideological advance over the towns.

To a good Marxist this is a case of voluntarism and the short-circuiting of history. Russians, in particular, are good Marxists, and have never, even under 'War' Communism, tried to base advanced demonetization on primitive moneylessness. In that terrible period they thought they were installing the latest gimmicks of the German war economy in their industry. They permitted private property among peasants, and when they re-introduced money and the market it was precisely for the sake of the peasants.

Yet primitive moneylessness did persist in the Russian village, and was even built into the new system of collective farming (1929). Notably labour-day payments were partly in kind, partly in cash, and ploughing fees to MTS were wholly in kind. But the Russians have never seen in this anything but backwardness, and they have by now almost abolished it.

But the bourgeois philistine may well side, in a snide way, with Mao. What is specially advanced about a commune? Perhaps small communes really are better built on pre-monetary foundations, and are in principle primitive, as the history of the kibbutz shows. For as we saw, development and success have tended to monetize the kibbutz. After all, the mere increase in the variety of inputs and outputs would ensure that. Perhaps then Marxists deceive themselves when they associate any sort of Full Communism with development, since the thing is simply impossible. In this case premature Full Communism is the only kind we shall ever see, even in failure.

Cuba presents here an interesting special case. She does not use her celebrated unpaid voluntary labour in industry, but in certain primitive harvesting operations. The great case is sugar cane. Now sugar used to be a slave crop, and quite especially in Cuba, where liberation came very late (1886). There developed in the twentieth century a skilled and well-paid special force of cane-cutters, like those in Queensland. But technical progress was very slow, and it certainly remained possible to revert to unskilled labour. This is what Castro has done. By the combination of full employment elsewhere with a wage freeze in the cane fields he lost the expert *macheteros*; only he replaced them (with a catastrophic decline in productivity) by volunteers, not slaves! Never was there a more perfect confusion of premature and final Full Communism, of primitive moneylessness and advanced demonetization.[21] But in the writer's opinion the primitive aspect is predominant. One day someone will mechanize the *machete*, and one day Cuba will be less dependent on sugar cane. Then the system of voluntary labour will collapse.

It must not be thought that voluntary labour has proved totally inefficient. The processes on which the Cuban government engages it are, to repeat, simple or simplifiable. Low productivity is acceptable against low pay. The great harvesting failure of 1970, when the 10-million-ton target was not reached after so much fanfare, was due to the refineries not the cutting. But refineries employ highly paid, non-volunteer labour and it may not have been the labour's fault even there.

16. Full Communism is supposed to bring to an end Marxian *alienation*, that Protean concept. Basically this applies to all division of labour in a capitalist market. We are alienated from the product of our labour when, as is necessary under capitalism, we lose ownership of it, and so cannot control it. In particular capital, though basically our product and so our mere creature, acquires an existence of its own and rears itself up against us. In this way the ideal *integration* of man with his social environment is lost; he feels his own creation to be alien to him.

The concept applies to all labour, and is not logically connected with its psychological content. No doubt we think primarily of men on moving belts, but the maintenance men and even the designers are almost equally alienated according to the definition of the young Marx.[22] Frustration and contentment, then, have little to do with it, nor is it connected with incentives, which may or may not be offered. Indeed the need for incentives proves that alienation is present. It is, then, an existential condition, far outstepping the bounds of economics. Yet the concept is in my view much less metaphysical and unconvincing than it seems; on the contrary it is one of Marx's few valid contributions to the social sciences.

We should think particularly, though Marx himself would not have, of the separation of the family from the business, even if it is a family business.[23] This may indeed be *the* notion that has made theoretical economics, technical progress, markets and planning possible. We have invented, above all, the blue- and white-collar employees, for whom by no stretch of imagination can family life be amalgamated with working life. We have created a sphere of production outside the kinship network, and split life into work and leisure. In a word, we are Benthamites in the sense of chapter 2. The whole notion of economic rationality, of there being distinguishable means and ends, of the very existence of a value-free sphere in which human beings are emotionally indifferent to what they do, results from this split.[24] A rational family life might just possibly be conceived of, but who would want to live it? But without this kind of indifference to work methods, technical progress at the workplace could hardly have attained its present massive proportions: it rests precisely on alienation.

True, not all of us have made this split: housewives, heads of state, heads of Oxford and Cambridge colleges, priests, farmers, authors and artists spring to mind as exceptions. They live over the shop, they are still working when they entertain, they resist technical progress, it is difficult to say whether they are lazy or industrious, they do not commute, their tax fiddles are impenetrable. Moreover their manner of life is much admired: the unity of economic and other life is on the whole a source of happiness. Marx however would probably have insisted that this is a technically primitive life-style, and quite alienated because wholly subject to the market. We need not follow him: the market, which he hated so much, is not that important.

This dichotomy continues in full strength under socialism, but not of course in the commune, where family life is subsumed into the life of the enterprise – or vice versa, if you prefer it. Yet primitive peoples know nothing of it. It is not the non-existent primitive commune that we miss in today's advanced societies, nor is it the impersonality of those admirable institutions, perfect markets and central planning, that oppresses us. We are alienated by the rationality and separation from life of the production process, and in just this way primitive man is integrated. When Marx promised us an end of alienation, he should have promised us precisely this re-integration, not central planning, the abolition of markets or the end of the division of labour. Specialized labour, if we are good at it and proud of it and have integrated it into our life-style, is in no way alienating. Some of the most alienated people in the modern world are unskilled labourers, those Jacks of All Trades, who are Masters of None. The specialized smiths, musicians and doctors of primitive man are not alienated at all.

Be that as it may, primitive man's life is not psychologically divided in this way, and this, if anything, is the primitive happiness we have lost.

Alienation is prior to exploitation in the development of Marx's thought.

Exploitation – the diversion to private capital of a part of labour's product – certainly could not happen unless labour were alienated, they do indeed come together under capitalism. However in practice it is, above all, the STE that alienates the producer from his product, even though there is no exploitation in the Marxian sense. There may be no market, and 'social ownership', whatever that means, indeed embraces his product from first to last. But man feels nowhere more helpless, nowhere do capital and society, his creatures, exist more clearly 'over against' him.[25] Alienation is least in units that are both *small* and democratic, like small communes and producers' co-operatives. Yugoslavia, clearly, has the system that has done most to relieve alienation – which has therefore nothing at all to do with efficiency! Hippies, too, are unalienated by each other in their communes, though larger hippie communities, such as the Haight-Ashbury in San Francisco in 1968, engender extreme alienation between their members.

The connexion of size with alienation is so extremely obvious that one wonders how at least Marxists living in free countries cannot grasp it. The answer is their faith in the General Will, their mistrust of formal democratic administration. For Rousseau the community had to be small. His General Will is that of a Swiss mountain village. But for Marx and Marxists the size of a society is irrelevant, since everyone under Full Communism is rational, moral and unanimous. Therefore there is no administrative problem, no conflict, even no need to vote. No one can feel alienated, however large the society is. The size problem has been defined out of existence by the perfection of the individual citizens.

In practice however men are not merely bad but variously bad – or even variously good. Therefore they disagree. Therefore democratic administration concerns them passionately. Therefore they only feel integrated with small societies. Therefore alienation is more a matter of the size of the social unit than of the nature of ownership, the existence of a market, etc. No practical Full Communism, lived in by real human beings, would do much to diminish alienation.

17. So is economics coming to an end? It is not even a long-term prospect. For economists themselves these new things mean simply more to discuss, more specialities within the field. The old things have not stopped. In UDCs they will not stop for a very long time indeed; so why should not rich countries simply render more and more aid, thus prolonging scarcity at home? In any case the 'marginally technically possible' (sec. 3) will ensure scarcity, since there is after all little hope of suppressing technical change in consumption goods. To repeat, if any one thing is scarce, and is a substitute for other things, or uses the same inputs, everything is scarce.

But there *are* new trends, at least in ACEs. Labour supply is shifting towards more altruistic uses. Consumption seems still to lack an upper limit, but consciences are beginning to be sensitive. Keeping up with the Joneses is not automatic any longer. Social services are expanding faster than national income. There is however nothing similar in STEs. Only paid ideologues take these attitudes (in public), everyone else wants a car and a trip to Paris. There never was, then, much divergence in the field of worker-consumer behaviour, and we should have to say that STEs were closing this small gap by converging upon ACEs, were it not for the new trends in the latter.

But in the inter-enterprise sector, money, especially in the form of shadow-prices and cost-benefit, is beginning to bite again in STEs. Meanwhile the full potentialities of these new techniques have not yet been exhausted in ACEs, and are being more rigorously applied in such public sectors as defence and social services. So here is indeed a form of 'managerial' convergence, of the kind discussed in chapter 20. But of fundamental 'ideological' convergence we see no sign.

Notes

1. Wiles 1962, chapters 17, 18, and the sources there mentioned; Erich Goldhagen, Herbert Ritvo and William N. Turpin in *Problems of Communism*, 6/1960; ed. Leonard Schapiro, *The USSR and the Future*, N.Y. 1963; Wiles and Sherman in *Soviet Studies*, July 1970.

2. This concept was however known to the less dogmatic and systematic Adam Smith (John D. Owen, *The Price of Leisure*, Rotterdam 1969, p. 17).

3. I owe this passage to my student Dr. Amir Helman, who is however not responsible for my views. Cf. his London University thesis of 1975, *The Distribution and Allocation of Consumer Goods in the Kibbutz*.

4. In consonance with its general pragmatism, the Yugoslav Establishment has no vision of Full Communism. Cf. Wiles 1962, pp. 342, 352.

5. These people are more careful even than Marx not to state their vision compendiously and directly. I derive this passage, I think honestly and without satire, from much desultory reading and conversation.

6. Lewis Yablonsky, *The Hippie Trip*, N.Y. 1968; *The Observer*, London (magazine section), 14 February 1971; *Transaction* (Washington University, St. Louis, Mo.), December 1967; *The New York Times* (magazine section), 24 September 1967; Robert Houriet, *Getting Back Together*, London 1971; Keith Melville, *Communes in the Counter-Culture*, N.Y. 1972; Frank Musgrove, *Ecstasy and Holiness*, London 1974.

7. What will become of the children of hippies? Hippies make execrable parents (Yablonsky, op. cit., pp. 186–90, 303–5) and I presume that most of their children will turn against them, like other children, and go straight. Note that Sabra (second-generation Israelis) make unenthusiastic kibbutzniks. But there are other sources of recruitment in both cases.

8. Especially since the winters are mild. Warmth and a roof are a very large part of a beggar's income in winter. Very often he simply cannot afford not to work when it is cold.

9. Cf. *New York Times*, 26 July, 20 August, 30 August 1970.

10. Yablonsky estimated ('I would suspect') 200,000 visible and identifiable total hippie drop-outs, and 200,000 visible teeny-boppers and part-time hippies in USA in 1967 (op. cit., p. 36). This is 1·25 per cent of the age-group 16–25, in which hippies are concentrated (p. 343). There are similar numbers in Musgrove, op. cit., pp. 20, 28, 31.

11. On all this compare John H. Goldthorpe *et al.*, *The Affluent Worker*, Cambridge 1968. This deals with the continuance of proletarian traits in an affluent Britain.

12. Cf. Edward C. Banfield, *The Unheavenly City*, Boston 1968, esp. pp. 125–131. Oscar Lewis's celebrated *La Vida*, N.Y. 1968, on the other hand, is about prostitutes and not the *Lumpenproletariat* as a whole.

13. During the Soviet NEP unions were more aggressive against capitalist enterprises. But they were run by Communists, and this was the Party line.

14. In USA a vast experiment was even conducted, with an experimental group and a control group, to determine whether a basic income hand-out to the poor, reduced by say 50¢ for every dollar they earned, would seriously affect their labour supply. This is not the same question as that in chapter 2, sec. 12, which concerns only the effect of a rise in the (net) wage-rate on labour supply. That effect, we saw, is small. So too, it turns out, is this one: cf. Albert Rees in *Human Resources*, 2/1974. But the control group was also in receipt of such substantial social support that some of the experimental group actually switched! So nothing was proved in comparison with a situation of total non-support.

15. I.e. the 'U/V curve' has moved outwards from the origin. Cf. Bowers *et al.* in *National Institute Economic Review*, November 1970 and November 1972.

16. But in China much less. Nor are ACEs on anything like one level of corruption. National characteristics remain extremely important here. For much larger theft cf. chapter 16, sec. 23.

17. All data approximate, workings available on request. Soviet data include, while capitalist data exclude, enterprise fringe benefits (10 per cent of the Soviet figures). All data exclude investment in the social service sector. It has been necessary to inflate the Soviet, but not the other, benefits in kind to allow for the fact that they do not bear the very heavy turnover tax.

18. There is a strong practical argument here: if the rich receive the minimum they will insist on better quality, and so benefit the poor – e.g. appointments instead of queues in doctors' waiting rooms. But one wonders whether this outweighs the financial loss to the state.

19. E.g. any work by the late Richard Titmuss.

20. For workers only: *Narodnoye Khroyaistvo 1973*, p. 586. The peasants are still catching up with this level.

21. It is worth noting that, as always, forced labour accompanies voluntary: soldiers and prisoners also take part. Cf. chapter 2, sec. 3.

22. As opposed to that of Adam Smith, who, not using the word alienation, did concentrate on over-simplified and repetitive labour. Cf. E. G. West in *Oxford Economic Papers*, March 1969, pp. 6, 10–11, 15. On alienation in general cf. Robert Blauner, *Alienation and Freedom*, Chicago 1964; Daniel Bell in *Journal of Philosophy*, November 1959; Robert M. Tucker, *Philosophy and Myth in Karl Marx*, 2nd edn., Cambridge 1972; Paul Craig Roberts, *Alienation and the Soviet Economy*, Albuquerque 1971; Deborah D. Milenkovitch, *Plan and Market in Yugoslav Economic Thought*, New Haven 1971; Richard Schacht, *Alienation*, N.Y. 1970.

23. It appears to be a canard that this separation occurred at the same time as the introduction of double-entry bookkeeping. B. S. Yamey in *Economic History Review*, 1949, p. 109.

24. Note that Max Weber's Idealtypus, the Calvinist businessman improving his every minute and his own lot, by no means divorces work from life. Paradoxical as it may seem, *homo Calvini* is not *homo economicus*. He would above all reject utterly the notion of a separate business ethic. Hence Calvin's support of the usury laws.

25. Cf. Karoly Nagy in *Problems of Communism*, July–August 1966.

Appendix

The Soviet Factor Productivity Residual

I have said little about this in the text, as the FPR rests on bad data and over-sophisticated theory, for which we have little space. But the Soviet results do *seem* to support the claims made in the text.

The making of truly comparable factor productivity residuals began with Abram Bergson[1] and Edward Dennison,[2] and rare are those that rest on other definitions than theirs. Like many, I have great difficulty in accepting Dennison's detailed estimates of the contribution of each element, such as education or the economies of scale, to the residual itself. But I share his implicit rejection of the elasticity of substitution between labour and capital. I would say that the extent of the substitution is uninteresting over short periods, and the method of calculating it hazardous in the extreme – first you must arbitrarily lay down a value for the FPR! Nor is it very different to say: 'the Russians have a low FPR'; and 'the Russians have a high FPR but are forced to substitute capital for labour disadvantageously'.[3] If the elasticity of substitution of capital for labour is low, and we are still making that substitution, then we are inefficient.

The concept governing my choice of definitions is very simple indeed. If some acceptable volume index of outputs increases more (less) rapidly than some acceptable volume index of inputs productivity has risen(fallen). *Both* indices have to be acceptable; neither presents special problems. Both indices present an aggregation problem, for the types of labour and fixed asset are very numerous. In both cases quality change presents a serious problem: the so-called unmeasurability of the volume of capital is identical to the hedonic problem in consumer goods and services (Wiles 1962 ch. 12); nor is the worth of detailed labour-types easier to measure. Again both indices present a substitution problem, for consumer goods are substitutes for each other, and there is a 'consumption function' in the same sense as there is a production function. In both cases adequate allowance is made for substitution by averaging results based on initial-year weights with those based on end-year weights (Fisher's Ideal).[4]

These are only modest stipulations, but the results presented do not live up even to them. All these FPR's are the differences between indices that use Laspeyres, not Fisher's Ideal, for inputs, and surely also – though the matter is not discussed except by Bergson – for outputs. They also aggregate almost all labour-types into one single type measured by the hour, not the money wage, but since they mostly allow for education,[5] age and sex this is not serious. The capital sub-index is of course in all cases built upon local accounting practice, and very shaky. The relative weight of the two sub-indices is by income-shares in capitalist countries, and for Communist countries we simply set out a number of plausible weights (the Soviet weights in Table II are about 75% for labour, 25% for capital).[6]

These appear to be the main qualifications to the use of the 'residual' as a measure of technical progress. Bergson (op. cit. 1960) estimates it as follows (% p.a.):

TABLE I

(a) USSR 1928–40, weights of 1937	0·1–0·5
(b) USSR 1928–40, weights of 1937 for inputs and of each year for outputs	4·9–5·3
(c) USSR 1950–58, either system of weights	2·9–4·3
(d) USA 1869/78–1899/1908, various weights	1·5
(e) USA 1899/1908–1929, various weights	1·8
(f) USA 1929–48, various weights	2·1
(g) USA 1948–57, various weights	1·8

The choice of weights is only really important between (a) and (b). The former uses Paasche for production in the crucial years 1928–37, the second Laspeyres, and the difference is very great (Wiles 1962 chapter 12, sec. 11). It is tempting to try to explain each result separately, but prudent to abstain from comment. The geometric mean of (a) and (b) is 2·5, but this too is a dangerous figure. It is more important for our purposes to observe that the 'residual' is greater in (c) than in (d), (e), (f) or (g). So the Soviet residual in 1928–40 exceeded the American, even in periods technologically comparable for USA, and greater investment alone cannot explain the higher Soviet rate of growth at that time.

We may well wish to deny the name of technical progress to the transfer of the Malthusian surplus in agriculture to any non-agricultural occupation; since evidently the technology of this occupation can be as old as the world and still give rise to some increase in production. But an input index will register equally the useless hours on the farm and the useful hours that take its place. I make no correction at all for this objection, which must be very important for USSR in 1928–40. In any case it is minimal for USSR after 1950.

What other factors than technical progress influence the residual? One is increasing returns to scale. It is very strange indeed that statisticians believe they can take these out of the residual and calculate them separately simply by taking the increase in the whole national product. Returns increase or do not increase at the level of enterprises, not the national product, and if figures are not available for enterprise size this factor must remain in the residual.

But more important in the Communist case are the *diseconomies of Communist reorganization*. In ordinary production functions organizational progress is indeed explicitly left in the residual along with improved productivity. Communism provides many exceptions. Collectivization actually produced a negative residual in Soviet agriculture: minus 1% p.a. in 1928–39 for the whole country,[7] and minus 2% p.a. in 1928–37 for the Ukraine.[8] It was also zero in 1940–55 for the whole country, and zero in 1937–55 for the Ukraine. The Great Purge would surely have had the same effect on industry, if we could calculate those years separately. Some have attributed the fall in the residual in 1958 to Khrushchev's 'hare-brained scheme', the Sovnarkhozy.

Turning now to more modern figures, Table II presents Stanley Cohn's results.[9] The formula is Dennison's:

$\Delta Y = \alpha\Delta L + \beta\Delta K + \gamma\Delta A + \Delta R$ ($\alpha + \beta + \gamma = 1$, A = land, R = residual, Δ = rate of increase)

The fall in the Soviet residual becomes more marked when we add back into it the 'contributions' of age-sex composition and education, as is more normally done: 1950–62, 1·52; 1962–70, 1·6. But more striking is the inferiority to the Japanese and several West European FPRs; i.e. to the residuals of countries as or more advanced than USSR, for whom the 'advantage of technical backwardness' does not count.

Table III presents results for industry only. These are in many ways preferable, since everyone knows that Communist agriculture, services and even construction are inferior. Moreover the service and construction sectors contain in all countries far too much non-marketed product, entered into output at cost, and so incapable of reflecting productivity change. Unless otherwise stated the input weightings are my own. They reflect my profound scepticism of the ability of either theoreticians or statisticians to assign correct weights to labour and capital, even under capitalism. The reader is given this responsibility! He should bear in mind that in more advanced economies the capital weight ought to decrease, whatever the presumed elasticity of substitution, because there is so much less unemployed labour, which clearly raises the elasticity of production of capital. It might be reasonable to judge efficiency by a 0·5 labour weight for Bulgaria and Romania, and for USSR up to 1960, and by a 0·6 weight for all other cases. The Bulgarian residuals seem most improbably low.

Notes

1. *RAND paper P2148*, 29 November 1960.
2. *Why Growth Rates Differ*, Washington 1967.
3. The reference is to Martin L. Weitzmann in *AER* September 1970, where it is implied that the difference is important.

TABLE 2

Comparative Contributions of Factor Inputs and Productivity to Economic Growth (percentage points)

	USSR			Japan	Northwest Europe	USA	France	Germany	Italy	United Kingdom
	1950–62	1962–70	1950–70	1955–68	1950–70					
National Income	6·03	5·37	5·76	10·1	4·76	3·32	4·92	7·26	5·96	2·29
Total Factor Input	4·25	3·70	4·03	4·03	1·69	1·95	1·24	2·78	1·66	1·11
Labour	1·63	1·20	1·45	1·31	0·83	1·12	0·45	1·37	0·96	0·60
Employment	1·09	1·38	1·20	1.03	0·71	0·90	0·08	1·49	0·42	0·50
Hours of work	−0·37	−0·58	−0·45	−0·07	−0·14	−0·17	−0·02	−0·27	0·05	−0·15
Age-sex composition	0·11	0·07	0·04	0·21	0·03	−0·10	0·10	0·04	0·09	−0·04
Education	0·80	0·47	0·66	0·14	0·23	0·49	0·29	0·11	0·40	0·29
Capital	2·61	2·50	2·57	2·72	0·86	0·83	0·79	1·41	0·70	0·51
Non-residential fixed	—	—	1·66	1·62	0·64	0·45	0·56	1·02	0·54	0·43
Housing	—	—	0·31	0·14	0·07	0·25	0·02	0·14	0·07	0·04
Inventories	—	—	0·60	0·96	0·18	0·10	0·19	0·33	0·12	0·09
Land	—	—	0·01	0·00	0·00	0·00	0·00	0·00	0·00	0·00
Output per Unit of Input	1·78	1·67	1·73	6·1	3·07	1·37	3·68	4·48	4·30	1·18

Sources: USSR: Cohn's own work. Japan: Kanamori in *Review of Income and Wealth*, June 1972. Northwest Europe and United States: Dennison op. cit. 1976, p. 192.

Taken from Cohn 1976 pp. 53, 57.

4. It has been shown that Fisher's Ideal coincides well enough with the Tornqvist chain index with perpetually adjusted weights:
$\ln X_1/X_0 = \Sigma\, w_i \ln X_{i1}/X_{i0}$,
where X_i is output of good i and w_i its weight.
Cf. Laurits R. Christensen, Diane Cummings and Dale W. Jorgenson *An International Comparison of Growth in Productivity*, xeroxed, NBER, 1975.

5. Education should be, and is, measured by the cost or time spent, not its quality, in order to keep the latter, or rather the effect of the latter, for the residual. In Tables I and III education is omitted.

6. Deduced from Cohn's Tables 2 and 3. Land is counted as capital.

7. Jerzy Karcz, The Record of Soviet Agriculture at Mid-Century Point, privately circulated, 1966.

8. Andrew G. Frank in *Journal of Political Economy*, Dec. 1958.

9. In *Review of Income and Wealth*, March 1976.

TABLE 3
Industry only

		Industrial Output[b]	Labour Input	Fixed Capital Input	Percentage annual average growth of FPR with a labour weight of				
					0·5	0·6	0·7	0·8	0·9
Bulgaria[c]	1960–72	302·8	153·4	401·0[a]	0·8	1·6	2·4	3·4	4·5
CSR[c]	1960–72	180·3	120·2	175·6	1.7	2·0	2·3	2·7	3·0
DDR[c]	1960–71	175·6	102·0	187·5	1·8	2·3	3·0	3·6	4·3
Hungary[c]	1960–72	225.6	125·0	207·5	2.6	3·0	3·5	4·0	4·5
Poland[c]	1960–72	266·5	146·4	235·0	2·8	3·2	3·6	4·1	4·6
Rumania[c]	1960–72	430·1	180·6	371·6	3·7	4·4	5·0	5·7	6·2
USSR[d]	1951–60	9·9	4·0	11·5	1·3	2·8	3·6	4·4	5·1
(annual %	1961–65	7·2	3·9	11·2	−0·3	0·3	1·1	1·8	2·6
growth)	1966–70	7·0	2·9	8·7	1·2	1·7	2·4	3·0	3·5
U.K[e]	1954–72	2·6	−0·1	3·9	0·7	1·1	1·5	1·9	2·3
FRG[e]	1954–72	6·0	1·9	7·4	1·4	1·9	2·4	3·0	3·5

a. Inc. forestry.
b. Value added.
c. Source: Thad P. Alton in Joint Economic Committee of Congress, *Reorientation and Commercial Relations of the Economies of Eastern Europe*, USGPO August 1974, p. 282.
d. James H. Noren and E. Douglas Whitehouse in *Soviet Economic Prospects for the Seventies*, publisher as in *c*. June 1973, p. 221.
e. Ian Elliott and Alan Hughes in ed. Milivoje Panić, *The UK and West German Manufacturing Industry, 1954–62*, London, NEDO, 1976, pp. 20, 26; Fareeda Marouf, ibid., p. 3. The authors confine themselves to 1963 factor-share weights: 0·62 for UK, 0·65 for FRG.

Index

NOTE

Certain items were too common to be indexed: capitalism, Communism, Communist Party, France, Marx, maximand, monopoly, planning, socialism, UK, USA, USSR, Yugoslavia.